D1521333

THE ANGOLAN REVOLUTION:

EXILE POLITICS AND GUERRILLA WARFARE

(1962–1976)

Map of Angola

Studies in Communism, Revisionism, and Revolution (formerly Studies in International Communism), William E. Griffith, general editor

1. Albania and the Sino-Soviet Rift, William E. Griffith (1963)

2. Communism in North Vietnam, P. J. Honey (1964)

3. The Sino-Soviet Rift, William E. Griffith (1964)

4. Communism in Europe, Vol. 1, William E. Griffith, ed. (1964)

5. Nationalism and Communism in Chile, Ernst Halperin (1965)

6. Communism in Europe, Vol. 2, William E. Griffith, ed. (1966)

7. Viet Cong: The Organization and Techniques of the National Liberation Front of South Vietnam, Douglas Pike (1966)

8. Sino-Soviet Relations, 1964–1965, William E. Griffith (1967)

9. The French Communist Party and the Crisis of International Communism, François Fejtö (1967)

10. The New Rumania: From People's Democracy to Socialist Republic, Stephen Fischer-Galati (1967)

11. Economic Development in Communist Rumania, John Michael Montias (1967)

12. Cuba: Castroism and Communism, 1959–1966, Andrés Suárez (1967)

13. Unity in Diversity: Italian Communism and the Communist World, Donald L. M. Blackmer (1967)

14. Winter in Prague: Documents on Czechoslovak Communism in Crisis, Robin Alison Remington, ed. (1969)

15. The Angolan Revolution, Vol. 1: The Anatomy of an Explosion (1950–1962), John A. Marcum (1969)

16. Radical Politics in West Bengal, Marcus F. Franda (1971)

17. The Warsaw Pact: Case Studies in Communist Conflict Resolution, Robin Alison Remington (1971)

18. The Transformation of Communist Ideology: The Yugoslav Case, 1945–1953, A. Ross Johnson (1972)

19. Radical Politics in South Asia, Paul R. Brass and Marcus F. Franda, eds. (1973)

20. The Canal War: Four-Power Conflict in the Middle East, Lawrence L. Whetten (1974)

21. The World and the Great-Power Triangles, William E. Griffith, ed. (1975)

22. The Angolan Revolution, Vol. 2: Exile Politics and Guerrilla Warfare (1962–1976), John A. Marcum (1978)

THE ANGOLAN REVOLUTION VOLUME II

EXILE POLITICS AND GUERRILLA WARFARE (1962–1976)

John A. Marcum

THE MIT PRESS
Cambridge, Massachusetts, and London, England

Library of Congress Cataloging in Publication Data

Marcum, John A
  The Angolan revolution.

  Bibliographical footnotes.
  CONTENTS:—v. 1. The anatomy of an explosion (1950–1962).—v. 2. Exile politics and guerrilla warfare (1962–1976)
  1. Angola—History—Revolution, 1961–1975—Collected works. I. Title. II. Series.
DT611.75.M37   967′.303   69–11310
ISBN 0–262–13136–6 (v. 2)

2-08-79

FOR EDMUND

CONTENTS

PREFACE

In 1975, Angola exploded upon American consciousness. Superpower collision in a distant and unfamiliar part of southwest Africa threatened to entangle Americans in a new misadventure soon after the time that they had extricated themselves from Vietnam. Uncorked by the Angolan upheaval, the fermenting racial and political issues of all of Southern Africa poured onto the desks of unprepared Washington crisis managers and African affairs became a high priority concern of previously disinterested policymakers.

The hows, whos, and whys of the little-known African insurgency that culminated in civil war, international crisis, and a new phase in American-African relations form the substance of this book. It is based on the study of (fully footnoted) data and interviews collected over many years. The author is responsible for translations, including attributed quotations.

Often, different words and spellings can be used for names of persons, ethnic groups, or places in Angola. In every case, one form, chosen because it is the most common, distinguishable, or simple, is used in this book. References to the Ovimbundu people of central Angola illustrate the point. The singular form, Ochimbundu, is used for individuals. The collective noun, Ovimbundu, is used in place of the adjectival form, Umbundu (which is also the language spoken by the Ovimbundu), so as to avoid confusion with the Kimbundu-speaking Mbundu people to the north. Predominantly Ovimbundu political groups are referred to as southern rather than central because they so perceive themselves relative to more northerly Bakongo and Mbundu groups. The names of Zaire-based Angolan movements are given in French rather than Portuguese in those cases where they have most commonly used the French form themselves.

I wish to thank the Center for International Studies, MIT, for sponsoring this and the preceding volume, the Ford Foundation for an enabling research grant, and the faculty research committee of the University of California, Santa Cruz, for a grant to prepare the final manuscript.

I am enormously grateful to the many African and other informants who made the study possible. The following persons added valuable data or criticism: Gerald J. Bender, Karen Fung, W. David Grenfell, Isebill V. Gruhn, Lawrence W. Henderson, George M. Houser, Bruce D. Larkin, W. Scott Thompson, Patricia K. Tsien, and Stephen R. Weissman. Institutional sources of data included the American Committee on Africa; Hoover Institution and Library, Stanford; United Nations Committee on Decolonization; the G. Mennen Williams Papers, National Archives; the John F. Kennedy Library; the national archives of Zambia; and Dean E. McHenry Library, University of California, Santa Cruz. Finally, special thanks go to my family for enduring me while I grappled at length with the complexities of Angolan politics.

THE ANGOLAN REVOLUTION:

EXILE POLITICS AND GUERRILLA WARFARE

(1962–1976)

PROLOGUE

In early 1961, a sequence of African uprisings shook the foundations of colonial authority in Portuguese Angola, threatening to cut short Portugal's days as a Eurafrican power. Lisbon's perennial oligarch, Dr. António Salazar, responded forcefully and rushed an expeditionary force south of the equator. Using an effective mix of military, police, and psychosocial action (civic projects designed to win African loyalty), he soon managed to contain but not to wipe out the Angolan insurgency. By 1963 and 1964, nationalist movements in Guinea-Bissau and Mozambique had also mounted guerrilla campaigns. Portugal was accordingly fated to spend the next decade stomping down brushfires of insurgency in three far-flung African territories.

Such prolonged colonial conflict was a logical consequence of efforts by a small, underdeveloped European country to cling to the world's last old-style, colonial empire. In the aftermath of World War II, the British, French, and Belgian colonial administrations had, albeit reluctantly and under pressure, permitted African nationalists to organize, politicize, and assume increasing degrees of political power. But the Portuguese had remained contrastingly and consistently intolerant of any expressions of colonial dissent. Arguing that their African "provinces" had been immutably integrated into the mystical body of the Portuguese nation, Portuguese administrators had striven to prevent the development of organized political, or even cultural, movements among Africans. Theirs was an integral colonialism.

Preventive repression was facilitated by centuries of educational neglect. By the 1950s, scarcely 1 percent of the African population was literate in Portuguese (the only legal medium of instruction), and their possibilities for communicating political ideas were thus limited. Those who tried to expand political awareness and to mount political protest action confronted a security apparatus that grew progressively in size and severity. In 1957, the metropolitan *Polícia Internacional de Defesa de Estado* (PIDE) began operating in Angola, quickly built up a complementary network of informers,

1

and by 1959 and 1960 was working effectively in concert with sharply augmented Portuguese military forces.

The same system that barred Africans from participating in the political life of Angola also undercut African prospects for subverting and seizing power by force. Nationalist ideas coming in from the Congo, Ghana, Brazil, and elsewhere did seep through the dikes of censorship. But police surveillance, travel restrictions, illiteracy, and poverty all acted to constrict early expressions of Angolan nationalism to particularist, disconnected, and mostly clandestine political action. When the explosion came, therefore, it represented the released passions of a frustrated, inchoate nationalism that colonial policies had effectively localized and truncated. The upheavals of January–March 1961 were not and simply could not have been a product of broad-scale planning and organization.

"Maria's war," insurrection in Luanda, and rebellion to the north represented uncoordinated, dispersed assaults upon Portuguese power. As a sequential explosion, they served as a series of grim warnings. They jarred the colonial administration into preemptive action that snuffed out incipient revolt in major population centers to the south by making mass arrests in the Bocoio–Balombo region near Lobito.[1]

The 1961 rebellions lacked a single, all-encompassing national focus. Some peasant rebels were motivated by a broad vision of Angolan independence. Others were inspired by parochial religious fervor, for example, Maria's followers and Kimbanguists.[2] Still other rural and urban rebels were propelled toward traditionalist restoration of the Kongo kingdom or Chokwe empire or toward creation of a regional polity, such as a state of South Cuanza.[3] The lack of a common national vision, on the other hand, did not belie the existence of widespread resentment against colonial rule. It attested rather to the effectiveness of Portuguese measures to block the development of politically integrative nationalist movements. If such movements had been permitted a period of legal life, they might have been able to politicize largely illiterate, ethnically and socially diverse peoples in Angola on an inclusive, territory-wide basis.

Large-scale arrests and forced exile decimated the indigenous Angolan leadership after 1957. Some of the several hundred politically aware and badgered Angolan functionaries, students, and intellectuals who fled Angola (or schools in Portugal) regrouped abroad. The locally suppressed *Movimento Popular de Libertação de*

Angola (MPLA) of Luanda-Mbundu origins assumed a new existence in exile—first in Paris, then Conakry, and later Léopoldville. And leaders of northern Angola's Bakongo peasantry moved across the Congo border to join earlier exiles who had already begun to organize among tens of thousands of Angolan Bakongo émigrés in the Lower Congo. The *União das Populações de Angola* (UPA) and *Partido Democrático de Angola* (PDA) first organized (as ethnic movements) in a Congolese sanctuary from where the northern uprising of March 1961 was partially planned and organized. Nonetheless, for both the MPLA and the UPA/PDA, exile logistics—the difficulties of moving and communicating back and forth across frontiers and mobilizing revolutionary forces back inside Angola—proved a formidable handicap to effective action.

Despite all these problems and Portuguese superiority in military manpower, training, and arms, fighting persisted in the north where the insurrection evolved into a small-scale guerrilla war during 1962. Contrary to the expectations of some African nationalists, however, this fighting did not force an early change in Portuguese political attitudes. Lisbon continued to hold firmly to the dogma that Angola, along with Guinea-Bissau and Mozambique, had long ago realized its political destiny as an inalienable part of Portugal. Lisbon continued to reject calls for African self-determination, viewing them as proposals to dismember the Portuguese nation.

The military action of nationalist guerrillas, including, after 1966, soldiers belonging to a third force, the *União Nacional para a Independência Total de Angola* (UNITA), alternately waxed and waned. But insurgency persisted. And though they failed to rout the Portuguese or to induce significant political reform, the nationalists compelled Lisbon's policy makers to accept the burden of a long conflict. To preserve its ascendancy, a heretofore relatively inert colonial administration was obliged to adopt new policies that could only prove expensive, provoke social change, and preclude a return to the comparative stagnancy that had prevailed before 1961.

Coupled with European settlement schemes, Portugal's new development programs were designed to weld the province of Angola more securely to the metropole. If, however, the limited modernization of the 1940s and 1950s had resulted in sufficient group consciousness, economic dislocation, social tension, and political frustration to produce the anticolonial explosion of 1961, the much more ambitious, war-induced efforts to develop and assimilate Angola in the 1960s seemed bound to unleash even stronger forces of self-assertion. In short, it seemed reasonable to expect that Portugal's response to continuing insurgency would hasten the further destruction of social structures, sharpen economic discontinuities, and foster mass aspirations for social betterment and political participation.[4]

The struggle that unfolded during the 1960s brought an end to the old Angola of sequestered colonial stability. Social change became the new reality, even though political control over the purpose, pace, and form of this change remained bitterly at issue. Whether those embattled nationalists whose thought and action are the focus of this book would themselves succeed in gaining or sharing political power seemed highly problematic. It became obvious over time, however, that in the process of seeking power they were forcing the Portuguese to embark upon an abrupt, if belated, socioeconomic transformation of Angolan society. This transformation, accompanied by continuing insurgency and counterinsurgency at heavy economic and military cost to the metropole, in turn generated conflicting political awareness and competing demands for Angolan self-rule on the part of both Africans and Europeans. And it did so on an unprecedented scale. Within this process of fundamental, disjunctive change and open-ended conflict fated to culminate in independence, civil war, and a people's republic, lay the ultimate justification for writing an "Angolan revolution."

The scope of this book extends from late 1962, when the Angolan conflict had assumed the form of an organized guerrilla war, through 1975—more than a decade of nationalist struggle and factional conflict. During these years, the revolution went through two distinct phases. The first was a pan-African phase (1962–1965) during which the promise of collective external African assistance, even intervention, raised hopes for early victory. A period of two-party insurgency, it ended with revolutionary reversals, decline, and fragmentation. The second or tripartite phase (1966–1975) was marked by a rekindling and reorganization of African insurgency, along with stepped-up Portuguese economic and military countermeasures and persisting external involvement. The result was a prolonged attritional conflict. It led ultimately to a military coup (by Portuguese officers frustrated and alienated by three seemingly endless colonial wars) and independence.

Throughout this period a number of persistent, differentiating sociopolitical variables within Angolan nationalism influenced the character and fortunes of the revolution: ethnoregional tripolarity that derived from the original development of Angolan nationalism within the country's three principal ethnocultural communities, Luanda-Mbundu, Bakongo, and Ovimbundu; social cleavage, notably an underlying urban/intellectual versus rural/ peasant class dichotomy; and additional sociopolitical differentiation and commitment based upon factors of race, culture, religion, ideology, leadership, organizational structure, and external alignment.

In addition, over time the exile circumstances of Angolan nationalist leaders emerged as an important, if less-appreciated, variable. The particular perceptual and behavioral problems that beset exiles and tend to impair their capacity for effective political or revolutionary action afflicted Angolan nationalists. Thus the social psychology of exile became an additional key to the understanding of nationalist movements as they surged and stumbled through and beyond the Salazar years toward an uncertain destiny.

As a case study, the Angolan conflict offers evidence for generalizations about the role that such variables may play as catalysts, constraints, or molders in the revolutionary process. It also gives rise to questions about particular aspects of contemporary revolution. How does two- or three-party rivalry among insurgents affect the dynamics of revolution? What is the relative importance of external versus internal support for revolutionary groups? How vital is the role of contiguous states? How significant are transterritorial (or transnational) relations among revolutionary movements? What are the factors that seem most decisive in determining revolutionary success or failure?

PART I

THE PAN-AFRICAN PHASE
(1962–1965)

CHAPTER ONE

THE PATTERN AND PROBLEMS OF TWO-PARTY INSURGENCY

The first months of the Angolan conflict established a salient pattern of two-party, intrarevolutionary rivalry. As it intensified, this rivalry came to divide—almost to dominate—the struggle for independence. This volume, therefore, begins with an analysis of the discordant two-party competition that formed an important background to, as well as dynamic within, the pan-African phase of the revolution.

By late 1962 and early 1963, the MPLA and UPA/PDA—the latter two had joined in March 1962 to form the *Frente Nacional de Libertação de Angola* (FNLA)—had become locked into a two-party contest for revolutionary ascendancy. Each movement sought to eclipse its rival by achieving a decisive advantage in each of three overlapping spheres of intranationalist competition: external relations, internal political functions, and military functions.

EXTERNAL RELATIONS

During the initial stage of the Angolan conflict, nationalist leaders overestimated the impact of external factors on their struggle. They may have been encouraged to do so by the Portuguese government, whose polemical reactions bore out a seasoned truth about revolutions: "in every social upheaval the party attacked claims that the trouble has been stirred up by outside agents and agitators."[1]

The leader of the UPA, Holden Roberto, lobbied from 1959 to 1961 to seek decisive external support at the United Nations (New York) and in Washington, D.C. He optimistically assumed that in the event of a violent Angolan uprising, Portugal would have no external support because its colonial system was widely regarded as "retrograde."[2] Even after Roberto had turned most of his energy toward internal efforts to assert UPA control over the fluid, unstructured rebellion that broke out in the north of Angola in early 1961, the MPLA's president, Mário de Andrade, continued to spend much time traveling in search of external support.[3]

By the time of its First National Conference at Léopoldville in December 1962, however, the MPLA, like the UPA, had recognized the overriding importance of the home front. Henceforth it promised to give priority to internal rather than external action.[4] Nevertheless both movements continued, with reason, to consider it important to win external support, and each purported to view its rival's survival as due more to real or presumed outside financing than to legitimate domestic support. Thus each movement, while energetically professing its own adherence to an independent policy of neutral nonalignment, portrayed its competitor as a tool of foreign interests and cold war politics.

In general, the foreign policies and transterritorial relations of the Angolan nationalists focused on three goals: building *alliances* with nationalists of other Portuguese territories and/or with Portuguese opposition groups within or exiled from metropolitan Portugal; obtaining *external assistance*—that is, material, financial, and political support—from a broad range of third countries; and organizing external *propaganda and diplomatic action* designed to isolate and weaken their common adversary, Portugal.

Alliances

Both the MPLA and FNLA foresaw the advantages that might be gained from coordinating political and military activity with African movements working for the independence of Mozambique and Guinea-Bissau. Yet there was little competition between the Angolan movements at this transterritorial level. Dominant leadership within the principal movements of Mozambique and Guinea-Bissau shared the MPLA leadership's student-intellectual background, Marxist orientation, and multiracial complexion. Given this affinity, the MPLA had an inbuilt advantage. By April 1961, the transterritorial *Conferência das Organizações Nacionalistas das Colónias Portuguesas* (CONCP) had associated the MPLA with the main nationalist movements of the other Portuguese territories.[5] From headquarters in Rabat, Morocco, far from Portuguese Africa but within sailing distance of Portugal's Algarve coast, the CONCP functioned as a publicity center and clearing house for intermovement communication. This high visibility cooperation was not accompanied, however, by coordinated military planning and action—hence its marginal utility. In addition to the MPLA, allied members were the *Partido Africano da Independência da Guiné e Cabo Verde* (PAIGC), with which the MPLA had been associated since 1957;[6] the *Frente de Libertação de Moçambique* (FRELIMO), which in 1962 had inherited CONCP membership from the *União Democrática Nacional de Moçambique* (UDENAMO), one of FRELIMO's founding constituents;[7] and the small *Comitê de Libertação de São Tomé e Principe* (CLSTP), the only organized group of nationalists from the small plantation islands in the Gulf of Guinea.

The sole UPA (pre-FNLA) achievement in intra-Portuguese African cooperation up to and through early 1963 was a paper transterritorial alliance (January 1962) with a minor, faction-ridden Guinea-Bissau group, the *Mouvement de Libération de la Guinée dite Portugaise et des Isles du Cap Vert* (MLGC).[8] (The UPA partially compensated for this isolation by showing more enterprise in terms of other pan-African associations. It was, notably, the only Angolan movement to gain membership in the Pan-African Freedom Movement for East, Central, and Southern Africa [PAFMECSA].)[9]

There was a sharp divergence of attitude concerning the desirability of building alliances with Portuguese opposition groups. Reflecting its own multiracial background, the MPLA favored concerted political action with metropolitan anti-Salazarists. The more uniracial FNLA did not.

As early as December 1961, shortly before he slipped clandestinely into Portugal to help organize an abortive (January 1962) anti-Salazarist coup from the military center of Beja, the Portuguese democrat, General Humberto Delgado, passed through Rabat where he met briefly with CONCP leaders.[10] Although he was particularly impressed with Mário de Andrade, whom he determined to be a man of "culture," Delgado was not then in a position to forge real ties.[11] Later, in mid-1962, however, shortly after Dr. Agostinho Neto's escape from detention in Portugal, an escape made by sea from the Algarve coast to Morocco, Delgado initiated an exchange of letters with the MPLA leader. In response, Neto, soon to take over the MPLA presidency from Andrade, hailed Delgado's earlier (1958) unsuccessful presidential campaign "for democracy" in Portugal and applauded the Portuguese general's apparent readiness to recognize Angola's right to self-determination.[12]

Then in late 1962 a Paris gathering of Portuguese exiles, including the secretary-general of the Portuguese Communist party (PCP), Alvaro Cunhal, established an anti-Salazarist coalition, the *Frente Patriótica de Libertação Nacional* (FPLN). From its inception, this new front, which would later choose General Delgado as its first president, publicly endorsed African self-determination.[13]

Contrastingly other Portuguese opposition forces associated with a former Delgado colleague, Captain Henrique Galvão, did not accept the idea of what they termed African "separatism." Galvão and his strongly anticommunist supporters, grouped within the *Frente Antitotalitária dos Portugueses Livres Exilados* (FAPLE) headquartered in São Paulo, Brazil, rejected any accommodation with African nationalism. To them dictatorship, not colonialism, was the issue. "Cut off the snake's head and you chop off the poison."[14] Overthrow Salazar and you open the way for the creation of a democratic Portuguese Federation of Autonomous States in which European and African differences will dissolve in utopian harmony.[15] Such was their reasoning.

A pro-Galvão group in the United States contacted Mário de Andrade during his visit to New York in 1962. According to a spokesman for the New Jersey-based Committee Pro-Democracy Portugal, however, the encounter confirmed impressions of Andrade's "extremism" and "placed him so radically at the far left, that no exhortation toward moderation appeared to be opportune."[16] Indicative of the attitude with which Galvãoists approached such encounters was their spokesman's further observation that "whatever culture . . . exist[ed] in Portuguese Africa [was] of Portuguese form and expression."[17]

For Angolan nationalists, then, cooperation seemed possible with the formative, Delgado-led FPLN coalition but not with Galvão's supporters.[18] Yet even with the FPLN, concrete linkages were slow to develop. In December 1962, Dr. Neto told a United Nations committee that his movement was prepared to cooperate with Portuguese democrats who accepted Angolan rights to self-determination and independence;[19] and some journalists speculated that General Delgado would develop ties with the CONCP after he moved from Brazil, where he had been leading his own exile *Movimento Nacional Independente* (MNI)[20] to Algeria (where he would assume active leadership of the FPLN.)[21] The fact remained that no firm alliance could be realized during 1963. In May, Agostinho Neto lamented that the Portuguese opposition was still not united on the principle of "total and immediate independence" for Angola;[22] and during the remainder of the year, he concentrated, almost exclusively, upon weathering a series of political crises within his own movement. Consequently, a full seven months later the FPLN found itself vainly suggesting (to the United Nations) that "contacts should be established" and "where appropriate, cooperation and negotiation" should be undertaken between the FPLN and African nationalists.[23] Ironically at year's end it was not Neto's MPLA but Roberto's FNLA, which had displayed little interest in cooperating with the Portuguese opposition,[24] that was being courted in FPLN statements.[25] The FNLA was at that time enjoying a surge of international prestige.

In power terms, the solidity of the Salazar government out-weighed all prospective cooperation between Portuguese demo-crats and African nationalists. Except for some clandestine activity by the small, if well-disciplined, Portuguese Communist party, most internal opposition was either in jail or silenced and moribund. There was as yet little evidence to support an MPLA contention that among the "advantages" Angolan nationalists en-joyed was the fact that they were fighting against a colonial regime "undergoing an internal crisis and reproved by international con-science."[26] A more realistic assessment would have suggested to Af-rican nationalists that, at least in the short run, António Salazar's government had further secured its domestic authority by turning international criticism, along with revulsion against the carnage of the early 1961 uprisings, to its own advantage. Portraying Portugal as a victim of international conspiracy and African barbarism, Salazar relied on deep-seated Portuguese nationalism to galvanize internal support behind his regime.[27] In exhortatory speeches, he invoked the martyrdom of those defending Portuguese sovereignty in Angola and urged defiance of international criticism: "I hope we who are sure that we are right and are convinced that we can prove it shall not allow ourselves to be intimidated."[28]

As for alliances, then, as of 1963 the MPLA enjoyed a loose polit-ical association (CONCP) with nationalists of Mozambique and Guinea-Bissau, an association that helped to publicize the collective African cause against Portuguese colonialism. But neither the MPLA nor the FNLA had as yet developed solid relationships with a fractious Portuguese opposition that had yet to organize itself into a serious political force.

External Assistance

Both the MPLA and FNLA were eager to expand the scope of their other third-party relationships. An MPLA party conference in December 1962 called for "widening" the range of MPLA representation abroad.[29] Translated into subsequent words and action, this meant concerted efforts to gain support from "progressive forces" in the West to add to help already received from Afro-Asian and East European countries.[30] It meant a highly selective quest, inasmuch as Andrade and other MPLA leaders continued to view the United States in general as intent upon replacing Portuguese rule with its own "neocolonial" control.[31] It also meant continuing and expanding the special role of MPLA-oriented students abroad in the creation of local MPLA support committees in Western countries.[32]

A few days after his election as MPLA president at a party conference that stressed the primacy of internal over external affairs, Agostinho Neto left the implementation of party reform to lieutenants in Léopoldville and set out on a long journey in quest of a new balance and efficacy in MPLA external relations. He flew successively to New York, Washington, Rabat, Algiers, Tunis, Bonn, London, and Paris and then added Switzerland and Italy to his itinerary before returning to Léopoldville in early March—after an absence of three months.[33]

Appearing before the Fourth Committee of the General Assembly in New York, Neto hailed the "positive role" of the United Nations and the virtues of cold war nonalignment. "No country or organization," he said, could claim "a monopoly" on aid to the Angolan struggle.[34] He lobbied among diplomatic missions at the United Nations, contacted Angolan students enrolled in American universities, and met with Protestant and other private relief agencies in an effort to line up American assistance for the MPLA's refugee service, the *Corpo Voluntário Angolano de Assistência dos Refugiados* (CVAAR).

Accompanied by Methodist Bishop Ralph E. Dodge, he traveled to Washington, D.C., to put his case before the American government and press.[35] Described as having come to the United States "to remove pro-Communist coloring" from his "movement's image,"[36] Dr. Neto blamed two factors for what he depicted as a distorted American perception of the MPLA: the earlier location of MPLA headquarters in Guinea-Conakry at a time (1960–1961) when that country had close ties with the Soviet Union[37] and charges of communist influence within the MPLA group by Holden Roberto, the first Angolan nationalist to visit the United States. Neto was correct in detecting a negative American predisposition toward his movement. He was not, however, necessarily pinpointing the main reasons for it. Earlier Soviet, French, and Portuguese literature linking the Angolan Communist party (PCA) to the formation of the MPLA (1956) may have had as much or more influence than Roberto on Washington's thinking.[38] In any event, Neto stressed that left "extremists" (Viriato da Cruz and his followers) had been removed from positions of influence by the same MPLA conference that had elected him president, and he argued that the "feeling of distrust" that still separated the MPLA and UPA (FNLA) had nothing to do with communism.[39]

Through the intermediary of Bishop Dodge and others in New York, Neto tried to arrange a personal meeting with Roberto, who was also lobbying at the Seventeenth General Assembly. Roberto refused. Instead, reacting to press reports on Neto's visit to Washington, Roberto wrote to the Baltimore *Sun* in terms scarcely calculated to promote a rapprochement.[40] He dismissed the assertion that he had spread stories of communist influence within the MPLA as "ridiculous" and then denounced the MPLA as composed of privileged "self-styled intellectuals" who "would like nothing better than to have their Portuguese friends come to power so that they could appoint Dr. Neto viceroy of Angola."[41]

Roberto had begun making his annual trips to the United Nations in 1959, and concerned Americans were accustomed to thinking of him as the sole spokesman for Angolan nationalism.[42] The American response to Neto's competing claim to the mantle of revolutionary legitimacy was therefore mixed. The situation differed markedly from that prevailing in Great Britain where Neto was much better known,[43] the MPLA had long been represented, and the unrepresented and less sympathetically viewed UPA was at a clear political disadvantage.[44] Washington sources reportedly remained "wary" of the MPLA's political orientation despite Neto's assurances. According to the Baltimore *Sun*, they pointed to his one-time association with "pro-communist" student groups and to Radio Moscow's preference for the MPLA over the UPA. Given this attitude, "there was some doubt whether Dr. Neto would get much American financial support . . . for the medical clinics [CVAAR] his organization maintains in the Congo as a means of drawing support from Angolan refugees."[45]

But Neto did impress Washington. A July 1963 State Department dispatch to the U.S. embassy in Léopoldville expressed appreciation of and a desire to encourage the UPA's "pro-Western stand." But it also took note of the MPLA's expulsion of Viriato da Cruz and Neto's quest for Western contacts. "U.S. policy," it said, "is not, repeat not, to discourage MPLA (Neto-Andrade faction) move toward West and not to choose between these two movements."[46]

At the end of January, Neto told a Paris press conference that he felt that he had, in fact, "unfrozen" a part of American opinion from its disbelief in the cold war neutrality of the MPLA. A number of American anticolonialist organizations and philanthropic foundations had promised him "important material aid," which constituted an "appreciable" gain in light of the sympathy that the UPA enjoyed inside "government circles in the United States."[47] And back in his Léopoldville headquarters in March, he described his American visit as promising, although he cautioned his followers not to expect immediate results.[48]

During his sojourn in the United States, Dr. Neto appeared particularly anxious to convert presumed private and public support for Roberto's anti-common front stance into political support for or at least neutrality toward the MPLA's proposals for a common front among Angolan nationalist movements. Although he traced MPLA-UPA disunity to dissimilar origins[49] as well as ideological, sectional, and personal differences,[50] Neto clearly felt that American hostility toward the MPLA and assistance to the UPA had helped significantly in the past to perpetuate two-party rivalry.[51]

The presumption of an American roadblock to unity was both reflected in and reinforced by an often-quoted (and misquoted) polemic of February 1962 written by an Angolan (Bazombo) journalist and PDA official, Antoine Matumona. Published shortly before the PDA joined with the UPA to create the FNLA, Matumona's article projected a view that had long circulated within the PDA. According to this view, both the UPA and MPLA had achieved unmerited political advantage over the PDA by cultivating international sources of support. Otherwise unable to understand Roberto's intransigence on the common front issue and imperfectly aware of how their own ethnic particularism (Bazombo) restricted their chances for expanded political influence, Matumona and certain other PDA leaders found in American influence an attractive and plausible explanation for the UPA's relative political success and go-it-alone strategy. Eager to discredit Roberto, whom he held personally responsible for having blocked a rapprochement among contending Angolan movements, Matumona wrote that it was common knowledge that the UPA was receiving almost all of its material and financial support from the American Committee on Africa (ACOA) in New York. "If one believes the numerous bits of gossip in circulation," he added, "this financial aid has been given on the condition that the UPA will not ally itself with the MPLA, which American circles accuse of being pro-communist."[52] Subsequently Portuguese and MPLA publicists repeatedly quoted Matumona's accusation which was denied by the ACOA.[53] And in reproducing it, they consistently omitted the qualifying phrase that labeled it "gossip."[54]

The predilection of many to believe any charges of heavy American assistance to the UPA tied to a reciprocal policy of nonassociation with the MPLA derived in good measure from the centrality of the cold war, anticommunist theme in American foreign policy. And it would ultimately be revealed that Roberto did receive some covert American assistance in the form of money and arms from the Central Intelligence Agency (CIA) from 1962 until about 1969 when he was put on a modest retainer.[55] The CIA reportedly used Tunisia as well as Congo-Léopoldville as a conduit for such clandestine support.[56] But was Roberto's antifront attitude a consequence of American influence? Those who thought so pointed out that widespread African support for the MPLA's common front goal met with implacable resistance on Roberto's part.[57] President Ahmed Ben Bella of newly (July 1962) independent and prestigiously revolutionary Algeria joined Ghana's Kwame Nkrumah and others in backing the MPLA's common front policy. Indeed Ben Bella even sent a special mission to Léopoldville to attempt to reconcile the two Angolan groups.[58] Even though Algerian military training and arms shipments were coveted by Roberto, as well as by Neto, the FNLA leader continued publicly and pointedly to deny that "foreigners" (Algerians) had any right to impose unity on Angolan nationalists.[59]

To what could this attitude be attributed if not to American influence? In part, at least, the answer lay in the idiosyncratic factor, in Roberto's personality—ambitious, cautious, reactive, obdurate. He and most FNLA (especially UPA) leaders lacked self-confidence and feared being overwhelmed by a better-educated, better-organized and better-financed partner. Thus, when as Andrade put it, the MPLA sought the external intervention of African states "to compel the adversaries of unity" to accept a "workable national entente,"[60] or when pro-MPLA outsiders such as the Soviet Union joined in support of common front unity,[61] FNLA apprehensiveness only grew—predictably and proportionately.

Nor did it seem to make a difference if support for unity came channeled through Western-oriented institutions. In April 1963 Agostinho Neto exhorted a seminar of young Angolans organized by the Brussels-based World Assembly of Youth (WAY) to mobilize support for "united action," and the seminar obligingly declared "the unification of Angolan nationalist forces to be an imperative requirement of the armed revolution."[62] The WAY seminar failed to reduce FNLA opposition to a common front just as the prounity recommendations of an international team of WAY observers had failed to make a dent in such opposition earlier.[63]

As of mid-1963, the State Department expressed doubt that even the U.S. government was "in a position to exert much pressure on rival parties to coalesce." The department did not oppose a common front, but it believed the United States should "seek to gain the confidence of both" the UPA and MPLA. It also questioned the "advisability" of "becoming embroiled in a complex African situation which has been a preoccupation of many African leaders without a resolution of the basic split."[64]

While Neto lengthily but inconclusively campaigned in Western countries for political support for MPLA common-front proposals and material support for its refugee service (CVAAR), his movement remained generally suspicious of the intentions of Western politics. Mário de Andrade, the secretary for external affairs, strove to maintain and reinforce non-Western ties. He attended the third Afro-Asian Solidarity Conference (AASC) held at Moshi, Tanganyika, in February 1963 and won a pledge of more Afro-Asian help. He also used that occasion to denounce "NATO powers and financial oligarchies" for supporting the Salazar government. Portuguese settlers in Angola and Mozambique were, he said, really part of a vast "alliance of western economic interests" that dominated both colonies.[65]

On the other hand, speaking at the Brussels headquarters of the World Assembly of Youth in April, Andrade lamented the tendency of Western observers to "insist" upon placing the MPLA on a "cold war chessboard."[66] He argued that the MPLA was truly nonaligned and criticized Western politicians and journalists who continued "to reduce the MPLA's positive neutralism to an alignment with the East, whereas all of its diplomatic action proves that its conception of positive neutralism does not hide a deliberate ideological option and should not be considered as a bargaining tactic."[67] The MPLA's National Conference of December 1962, however, had indeed made explicit a clear preference, if not alignment. It had described Portugal's NATO allies, by virtue of economic investments, as "the true rulers of important sectors in the economy of Angola." Therefore one of the proper aims of MPLA "diplomatic activity," was, it said, to deepen economic "contradictions" inherent in Portugal's relations with "imperialist countries in the western alliance."[68] The MPLA viewed Western economic, military, and religious interests as aligned against it and for similar, self-interested (neocolonial) reasons aligned against prolonged Portuguese rule.

In April 1963, a group of MPLA Protestants in Léopoldville issued an angry statement calling for an end to what they termed "open discrimination" by Western missionaries in favor of the UPA. They charged in particular that MPLA members were being denied equal access to a Protestant-run secondary school for Angolan refugees at Sona Bata in the Lower Congo.[69] Responding to these allegations, Rev. David Grenfell (of BMS, the Baptist Missionary Society), director of an Angolan refugee reception center at Kibentele (near Moerbeke, Lower Congo), visited the MPLA's Léopoldville office and tried to persuade it to submit a list of candidates for the upcoming entrance examinations to the Sona Bata school—but without success.[70] According to Grenfell, when he pointed out that he and others involved in Protestant relief work wished to avoid partisan entanglements and had for several months been trying to promote the formation of an "all party medical committee" to coordinate Angolan refugee assistance, he was told he was "politically naive."[71] Grenfell's close personal associations with Holden Roberto, Eduardo Pinock, and other FNLA officials, however, may have nourished MPLA skepticism about his and other Protestant professions of religious nonalignment in the MPLA-FNLA rift.

During late 1962 and early 1963, the MPLA was more active than the FNLA in lobbying for international support. The FLNA, which presented itself as both a political front and an as-yet-unrecognized government in exile—the *Govêrno Revolucionário de Angola no Exílio* (GRAE)—was bent, however, upon broadening the range of its external associations. Thus in December, while Dr. Neto labored in the United States to win American support, Holden Roberto lobbied among Afro-Asian diplomats in New York against an American proposal to send a United Nations observer to visit Angola and Mozambique.[72] Then in January, Roberto's close personal aide, Johnny Edouard, flew to Belgrade to speak at the Seventh Congress of the People's Youth of Yugoslavia and to seek assistance for GRAE from the Yugoslav government.[73] The Soviet Union and other Eastern European states, however, appeared too heavily committed to the MPLA and its common-front policy to offer promising terrain for GRAE cultivation.[74] For external support, therefore, Roberto continued to rely largely on such African countries as Tunisia, Algeria, Nigeria, and, above all, the Congo-Léopoldville.

Isolating and Weakening Portugal

Because Portugal is a Western nation, Angolan nationalists were obliged to mount propaganda and diplomatic efforts in the West to isolate and weaken the Salazar government. Holden Roberto concentrated on attempting to widen the breach between Washington and Lisbon[75] while the MPLA tried to undermine Portugal's relations with Great Britain and Western Europe.[76]

Neither the FNLA nor MPLA had any chance, however, of seriously weakening Portugal's most crucial external relationship—its ties with Franco Spain. An Atlantic enclave tucked into an otherwise Spanish peninsula, Portugal had traditionally manifested a defensive ambivalence, if not hostility, toward its big neighbor. In 1936, however, the Salazar government offered early and vital support to General Francisco Franco's Nationalists as they set out to overthrow the Spanish republic.[77] Franco's rebels bought arms, took refuge, and relayed communications in Portugal, and some eight thousand men belonging to a twenty-thousand "volunteer" Portuguese Legion de Viriato are said to have given their lives on the battlefield for the Spanish rightists.[78] The debt thus accrued—along with ideological and religious affinities, and formal accords such as the Iberian Pact (1939 and 1943) by which both countries pledged economic, cultural, and military collaboration—assured the external security of Salazar's Estado Novo.[79] American air and naval bases in Spain later added to this security. The special relationship between Madrid and Washington, as well as Lisbon and

Madrid, thus left the Portuguese free to send the bulk of their military forces to Africa.

A visit to Lisbon by Spanish Foreign Minister Fernando Maria Castiella shortly after the outbreak of fighting in Angola in 1961 provided an occasion for the Salazar government to portray the Angolan conflict as part of a "widened international plot against the [whole Iberian] peninsula" and its codefenders of "western civilization and Christian liberties."[80] Shortly thereafter Salazar himself publicly linked Spanish interests to the Portuguese cause in Angola. In that "crisis," he said, Spain "has accompanied us moment by moment with its vivacious temperament and its fervent fraternal affection" because it has "understood" that those who were attacking it were just as likely to attack Spain. Assaults by African "terrorists" against Portugal, he continued, formed part of a broader conspiracy, which included "an intense campaign of international calumny, skillfully directed by communist Russia." Thus forces of black nationalism, which would forcibly "return" distant parts of the Portuguese "Homeland" to "a life of savagery," offered "international communism" a convenient anticolonialist "pretext" for mounting an assault on Portugal—and, by extension, on the Iberian peninsula and the rest of Western Europe. The organizers of this conspiracy knew, Salazar reasoned, that once "this southwestern corner of Europe . . . falls the rest will follow."[81]

By 1963, there were some reports of minor friction between Lisbon and Madrid deriving from Spain's decision to grant political autonomy to its small equatorial African territories of Rio Muni and Fernando Po. GRAE circulated a French press agency story telling of displeasure in some Falangist circles over the inflexibility of Salazar's African policy.[82] And a meeting between Generalissimo Franco and Premier Salazar at Merida, Spain, from May 14 to May 16 failed to produce new support for Portugal's overseas policy.[83] Nevertheless Spain, along with South Africa, remained a loyal defender of Portugal within such international forums as the United Nations General Assembly. Overall Iberian solidarity seemed impregnable to political assault by African nationalists so long as Franco and Salazar ruled.

Portugal's relationship with the rest of Western Europe was more vulnerable. Radio Lisbon daily boomed forth the opening bars of Beethoven's *Fifth Symphony* and announced itself as the "Voice of the West." By tacit mutual agreement, however, Portugal (along with Spain) did not seek and was not invited to join the one association of states that in fact based its membership qualifications upon a devotion to Western values and culture.[84] The founders of the Council of Europe cited the "spiritual and moral values" that formed their "common heritage" as being those that underlay "genuine democracy." The council's statutes (article 3) required that a member state "accept the principles of the rule of law and of the enjoyment by all persons within its jurisdiction of human rights and fundamental freedoms."[85] This the Salazar government was not prepared to do. And thus Portugal was absent from the only Western interstate organization that might have served African nationalists as a logical external arena within which to lobby and mobilize principled political pressure or moral suasion for change in Portuguese colonial policy.

Political principles, however, did not stand in the way of Portugal's participation in Western economic and military associations. Portugal was invited into the postwar Organization for European Economic Cooperation (OEEC) and then (1960) the European Free Trade Association (EFTA). Despite Salazar's conviction that past involvements in European affairs had distracted Portugal from its "overseas tasks,"[86] freer entry through EFTA into British, Swiss, Austrian, and Scandinavian markets was clearly beneficial. Portuguese sales within the EFTA market of a hundred million people rose by over 400 percent between 1959 and 1970.[87] Moreover, the findings of an EFTA study written (1964) by a leading Portuguese economist, V. Xavier Pintado, concluded that "the smallness of Portugal's market in terms of actual and potential demand" rendered its chances for modern industrial development dependent upon such an association with the more highly developed countries of Western Europe. With nine million people, Portugal's average per-capita income ($270 in 1961) was so low that "in terms of total demand it correspond[ed] to less than two and a half million average European consumers, and less than two million average EFTA consumers."[88]

Although EFTA membership thus reinforced Portugal's economic capacity to sustain protracted counterinsurgency operations in Africa, neither the MPLA nor FNLA manifested special awareness of this EFTA linkage. Neither made a concerted effort to arouse public opinion or political groups within EFTA's several neutralist states against economic association with Portugal.[89] Instead it was Portugal's membership in the militarily supportive North Atlantic Treaty Organization (NATO), not EFTA, that drew political fire from African nationalists. Embracing, as it did, all major Western powers, NATO became the symbol of perceived external support for Portugal's military and economic position in Africa. Portuguese membership in an organization whose constitution pledged its members to respect "the principles of democracy, individual liberty and the rule of law" was prima facie illogical. Salazar himself dissociated his country from this "obviously unfortunate" statement of political ideology,[90] and Western scholars described Portugal as the one member of NATO governed under a political system incompatible with democratic and constitutional values shared by the rest of the Atlantic treaty community.[91] The essential purpose of NATO, however, was military. And the importance ascribed to the Azores by Western military strategists was enough to override political reservations concerning Portuguese membership.

It was NATO access to the Azores that mattered. Relatively little value was attached to metropolitan Portugal's participation within the Atlantic organization, and the considerable literature dealing with Atlantic affairs largely failed to discuss Portugal or its role in the defense and diplomacy of the Atlantic community.[92] For example, in his influential reappraisal of the Atlantic Alliance published in 1965 for the Council on Foreign Relations, Henry Kissinger did not once mention Portugal.[93] Having sent most of its armed forces to Africa, the Salazar government, after all, was in no position to make a serious contribution to Atlantic defense.

Noting that American base facilities in Spain reduced whatever initial importance Portugal had for NATO, military analysts such as Alastair Buchan, director of the Institute of Strategic Studies in London, came to question the value of continued Portuguese participation in the organization. Lisbon's colonial policies, Buchan wrote, constitute "an embarrassment to its allies," whose failure to endorse or support these policies is, in turn, viewed as betrayal. "Would either side lose," he asked, "from a severance of the postwar association?"[94]

For Portugal, the answer was "yes." Inclusion within the Atlantic alliance helped to legitimize an otherwise tenuous claim to be of, and to represent, the West (in Africa). The alliance also constituted a framework within which Portugal could effect easy bilateral access to the best of Western military technology, training, and equipment. As Dr. Neto noted, despite assurances the Portuguese government gave to certain NATO countries that NATO arms would not be utilized in Angola, Angolan nationalists were indeed being felled with standard NATO arms.[95]

A serious campaign to mobilize public opinion in favor of expelling Portugal from NATO, however, would have required financial and political resources far greater than those that the Angolan nationalists (even if united) and their anticolonial sympathizers in the West could muster. By means of sizable financial outlays for publicity in the United States, on the other hand, Portugal was in a position to reach a large audience with arguments underscoring its importance to NATO and portraying all African challenges to its continued colonial rule as part of an international communist conspiracy.[96]

Portuguese efforts to influence American policy included periodic threats to quit the alliance.[97] As intended, such threats created anxieties in the American Defense Department and NATO military command, both of which were determined not to lose the Azores. Against such tactics, the modest lobbying efforts of MPLA and FNLA representatives in the United States and other Atlantic countries were ineffectual.

Elsewhere African hopes for bringing pressure on Portugal through Brazil faded in 1962 and 1963 as domestic turmoil preoccupied the shaky regime of Brazilian President João Goulart. During the short term (October 1960–September 1961) of Goulart's predecessor, Jânio Quadros, Brazil had begun to fashion a new, more assertive African policy;[98] and in May 1963, Quadros averred retrospectively that had he remained in office, he would have opened Brazilian universities to "Angolan patriots" and would have sent help to Angolan refugees in the Congo.[99] But he had resigned from office, and his successor faced far more pressing problems. A handful of MPLA students continued to work with a local Brazilian support committee, the *Movimento Afro-Brasileiro pró-Libertação de Angola*, and organized a rally in São Paulo to commemorate the second anniversary of the February 4 uprising in Luanda.[100] The United States continued to encourage Brazil to impress upon Portugal the advisability of securing Portuguese influence in Africa in a "more satisfactory and enduring" manner by accepting the principle of self-determination as the United States had done in Puerto Rico.[101] But Brazil no longer seemed likely to become a major source of material or diplomatic support for Angolan nationalists or of political leverage on Portugal.

It was only at the most inclusive but least critical, or global, level of international relations that Portugal, as of 1963, faced a tangible threat of isolation, isolation from some of the technical and functional services of the international community.[102] Its government was caught in a spillover from the African-led campaign to evict Portugal's ally, the government of South Africa, from a broad spectrum of international organizations.[103] Thus in July 1963, the United Nations Economic and Social Council voted to exclude Portugal as well as South Africa from its Economic Commission for Africa (ECA).[104] In August, the Conference on International Travel and Tourism attended by eighty-seven states in Rome voted (thirty-eight to twenty-five with nine abstentions) to ask both Portugal and South Africa to withdraw because their presence could be deemed "an encouragement to their governments to continue their policy of segregation, repression and colonial domination."[105] And in September, a general meeting of the African Regional Committee of the World Health Organization (WHO) adjourned rather than accept the presence of delegates from Portugal and South Africa.[106]

This emerging campaign might have been parlayed into a systematic eviction of Portugal and South Africa from organizations of central importance, for example, the International Monetary Fund. But so long as the United States and other Western powers consistently and firmly opposed any moves that would inject political issues (such as colonialism and apartheid) into technical international agencies, this could not happen.

In sum, then, for the MPLA and FNLA there was more immediate and tangible competitive advantage to be won from knitting transterritorial alliances (CONCP) and obtaining material assistance abroad than from working to isolate Portugal from its own sources of external material and political support. Relations with contiguous or deeply involved African states such as Congo-Léopoldville and Algeria were especially important to Angolan nationalists. Even so the revolutionary effectiveness and competitive position of both the MPLA and FNLA depended less upon external relationships and activity than upon the quality and demonstrability of their own internal strength. This was implicitly acknowledged in late 1962 by Mário de Andrade, who had directed MPLA external relations for the past two years. "Whatever may be the importance of the help that we may get from friendly countries—and there are many of them—[and] whatever may be the moral and political weight of the United Nations," he said, "nobody will liberate Angola for us."[107]

If the ability of an Angolan or any other revolutionary movement to attract and mesh external support into an internal war depended largely upon the internal quality of that movement's leadership and organization, it remained important to ask, How did the existence of not one but two competing insurgent groups affect the level or efficacy of external aid? Instead of two-dimensional, insurgent-versus-incumbent competition focused on alliances and assistance and on initiatives to deny both of these to an adversary, there was a third dimension of interaction. It involved intranationalist two-party competition at several levels of external community—in the case of Angola at least seven levels. These are listed in Table 1.1 in declining order of inclusiveness. Where competition was high, external support was split (in varying proportions) between the two movements (industrial and African states); where it was low or absent, potential rewards were either slight (United Nations and Portuguese opposition) or they had been preempted by one movement (MPLA re Soviet bloc, AASC, CONCP) or both (Brazil).

Vigorous two-party competition for external support increased the intensity of external lobbying and the propensity of movements to align with external power blocs, for example, East or West in the

TABLE 1.1
TWO-PARTY COMPETITION, LATE 1962 AND EARLY 1963

Level of Community	Competition	Result
United Nations	Low	No advantage
Industrial states	High	Split support
Soviet bloc	Low	MPLA advantage
Western bloc	High	Split with FNLA advantage
Afro-Asia	Low	MPLA advantage (AASC)
Pan-Africa	High	Split support
Transterritorial		
Africa	Low	MPLA advantage (CONCP)
Portuguese		
opposition	Negligible	No advantage
Brazil	Low	MPLA advantage

cold war. This served to increase aggregate benefits, but at the cost of diverting energy and resources into interparty competition, and it locked insurgents into a greater dependency upon external benefactors. In such circumstances, it was in the interests of the targeted incumbent power to play up bifurcating factors such as cold war linkages among its challengers, and, of course, to organize or fund a few movements, or "nonviolent alternatives" of its own, decoys that might both create internal confusion and attract external interest and support away from the insurgents. Unless attenuated by a common front, the bitter intranationalist conflict inherent in a two-party revolution, a situation in which each party denies the legitimacy of the other, must inevitably create conditions particularly favorable to such maneuvers by the incumbent. Also third or fourth movements are more likely to be taken seriously since revolutionary leadership is already contested. Thus with some success, Portuguese diplomacy and public relations promoted the stock of such small collaborationist movements as Nto-Bako, Ngwizako, and the *Mouvement de Défense des Intérêts Angolais* (MDIA).[108]

POLITICAL FUNCTIONS

During 1962–1963, the MPLA and FNLA were both centered in exile within the precarious context of the politically unstable Congo-Léopoldville. There they developed parallel and intensely competitive organizations and programs.

MPLA Leadership, Doctrine, and Structure

The December 1962 conference that elevated Agostinho Neto to the MPLA presidency also confirmed the political defeat of the movement's long-time party secretary Viriato da Cruz.[109] Cryptic autocriticism designed to explain the movement's failure to gain uncontested leadership of the Angolan insurgency attributed difficulties to a hostile environment: Portuguese jails that swallowed its leaders, parochial Bakongo peasants and émigrés who rejected its direction, and Congolese political turbulence that denied it neighborly support. But da Cruz was also blamed personally for faulty work by a secretariat that had been slow, negligent, and averse to planning. Internal security and discipline were said to have deteriorated because he allowed destructive criticism to undermine the prestige and authority of the organization and its leaders. Party "statutes and rules [had been] systematically betrayed" as the secretary-general thwarted the principle of collective leadership and used his control over party machinery to amass political power at the expense of the president (Andrade) and his department of external affairs.[110]

Implicitly the December conference absolved Andrade of responsibility for such past mistakes. And Andrade himself later faulted da Cruz, or "those in charge of the secretariat," asserting that the party's propaganda had overplayed charges of racism and tribalism within the UPA. Such charges, he said, had only antagonized UPA military units and helped to set the stage for *Upista* attacks on MPLA soldiers.[111]

The December conference also linked the MPLA's relative military weakness to what it described as the previous leadership's lack of courage and consequent failure to command intense loyalty. Because they had not recognized "in time" the "necessity" of "risk[ing] their [own] lives at the forefront of the fight," MPLA officials had not been able to demand that their followers put their lives on the line.[112] In short the top leadership had concentrated on lobbying outside, not fighting inside.

To correct this situation, which had "slowly undermined [its] inner power," the MPLA, under Dr. Neto's leadership, set about reordering politico-military priorities.[113] Henceforth action inside Angola was to take priority over action outside, political authority was to prevail over the military, and party leadership was to be made both responsible and collective.[114] Repudiating "sectarianism" and "mimetism"—attributed by implication to the da Cruz faction—the movement set forth a purportedly new "body of political doctrine."[115]

The new political line and action program outlined by the December conference built upon earlier statements.[116] The movement rededicated itself to the goals of political and economic independence under a nonaligned, democratic government, goals to be attained by leading the "popular masses" in a struggle for "total liberation."[117] It recommitted itself to multiracialism and to cooperation with opposition elements within or exiled from Portugal as well as with "progressive Portuguese born in Angola, some of whom . . . try to fight for the same objectives as the Angolan nationalist movements."[118] It took a flexible stance on the desirability of economic independence, having concluded that during the initial postindependence phase the paucity of indigenous capital and skills in Angola would present a need for some foreign investment and technical assistance.[119]

What was new was a strong emphasis on the role of the peasantry, now described as "the most exploited" and "largest social class" in Angola. Bringing representatives of the "peasant masses" into party leadership and military ranks became a matter of top priority.[120] Reviewing the consequences of their earlier neglect of rural issues, MPLA leaders concluded that peasants would probably fight with "more determination" if they felt that they were fighting for their land. Land reform therefore became what was termed the "watch word" of a new effort to win support within the class that was now hailed as having suffered "most directly" from the colonial system.[121] To overcome the "great deficiencies"—"prejudices, myths and tribalist feelings"—of an evidently still to be politically distrusted peasantry thus became "the most urgent task" confronting the movement.[122] Paradoxically in order to spur the political education and military mobilization of the peasantry, MPLA modernists advocated the reinvigoration of "Angolan culture and *traditions*" as one means of fostering a "unitary spirit" among those challenging Portuguese rule.[123] At the same time, the new ten-man MPLA Steering Committee, of whom half were *mestiços*,[124] continued to reflect the movement's Luanda-Mbundu origins. Mbundu areas such as Dr. Neto's Catete were well represented on the committee, but there was no one to speak for the populous Ovimbundu of the central highlands or for the embattled Bakongo of the northern war zone. The limitations of a sectional-elite leadership, therefore, continued to impede the movement's political appeal in spite of its new doctrinal outreach to the peasantry.

MPLA autocriticism focused on structure as well as leadership and doctrine or ideology: the absence of machinery to oversee the implementation of steering committee directives and the absence of a forum within which MPLA militants could vent grievances and "discuss . . . problems in a friendly atmosphere."[125] Without proper grievance mechanisms, the movement's Steering Committee had been left ill informed about internal problems.[126] In addition the secretariat had reportedly failed to provide for the systematic selection and training of new, high-level leadership cadres; and the MPLA army, or *Exército Popular de Libertação de Angola* (EPLA), had been left adrift to operate as an uncoordinated "separate body" beyond political control.[127]

Accordingly under Dr. Neto, the MPLA set out to restructure itself along "simple and comprehensive" lines with "military discipline" generalized at every level of the movement.[128] On paper the December conference transformed itself into the permanent seventy-man National Political Council (figure 1.1).[129] Operational authority was vested in the ten-member Steering Committee, six of whom were to constitute the supreme Political-Military Committee (PMC).[130] As the unique retainer of "the natural secrets of the Movement," this committee of six was given exclusive jurisdiction over military and security matters, including control of the army (EPLA).[131]

The December conference also created a party cadre school under the direction of the MPLA secretary for organization and cadres, Lúcio Lára.[132] Staff needs, including those for a program of rural politicization that the MPLA sought to carry out from Bakongo border areas southward, required trained, sensitive party organizers with a clear sense of purpose and a grasp of social mobilization techniques. On February 28, 1963, Lára inaugurated a new *Escola de Quadros* at Léopoldville and, in the presence of diplomatic representatives from Guinea-Conakry, dedicated it to the pursuit of a wide-sweeping political, economic, and social revolution. Its purpose, he said, was to prepare "political monitors," who, with subsequent experience and additional theoretical training, would become "political commissars" working patiently inside the country developing the political consciousness and revolutionary élan of the peasantry. In order to follow its chosen "democratic path," he added, the MPLA needed to diffuse responsibility among a large number of such commissars and to maximize its contact with the people. The cadre school was also viewed as essential to the development and consolidation of a "severe but freely accepted" revolutionary discipline.[133] Above all the *Escola de Quadros* was to ensure the primacy of political over military considerations—or of "ideological struggle over armed struggle."[134]

While this leadership training program was seen as a means to accelerate the structuring of a "truly national liberation front" through political education,[135] a separate Permanent Pro-Unity Committee was designated as a new instrument with which to work for the goal of a common front. The single responsibility of this (never-to-be-activated) committee was to be that of "promoting" unity, or at least "keeping [the unity issue] alive."[136]

New efforts were also made to develop or invigorate a whole

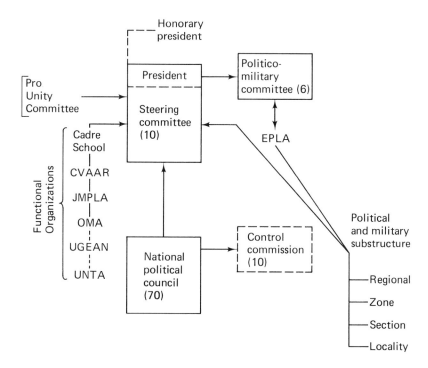

Figure 1.1   Formal structure of MPLA, January 1963

roster of MPLA-related functional organizations: CVAAR-refugee-relief-medical, *Organização das Mulheres de Angola* (OMA) for women, *Juventude do MPLA* (JMPLA) for youth, *União Geral dos Estudantes da Africa Negra sob Dominação Colonial Portuguesa* (UGEAN) for students, and *União Nacional dos Trabalhadores de Angola* (UNTA) for labor. The services and organizational activities of these groups were important to the process of mobilizing political support among thousands of Angolan refugees and émigrés in the Congo.

FNLA/GRAE Leadership, Doctrine, and Structure

Only a few city blocks separated the steel furniture and orderly file cabinets of the MPLA's neat central office on Avenue Tombeur de Tabora from the rickety wood tables and disheveled paper of the UPA's crowded bungalo headquarters straddling a nearby potholed dirt alley. The political distance between the two was of a different order.

The UPA had experienced defections and weathered an internal crisis early in 1962,[137] after which its leadership, doctrine, and structure changed little through the first half of 1963. Throughout this period, it was dominated by Holden Roberto.

Lacking the ideological perspective that linked the MPLA to a worldwide revolutionary left, UPA/FNLA leadership articulated a set of simple nationalist goals: political independence, agrarian reform (meaning redistribution of European land holdings to Africans), economic planning, industrialization, and pan-African (continental) unity.[138] It played down the existence of ideological differences between the two movements. In December 1962, an FNLA statement publicly "assured" MPLA followers that MPLA "integration" within the FNLA "would not mean foregoing the ideals of the [MPLA's] progressive *Programme Majeur*," for that program was, it argued, "not essentially different" from the program of the FNLA. In announcements similar to those of the MPLA's December conference, FNLA publicists concluded that only a "radicalization of the Angolan peasantry during . . . the armed struggle and . . . mobilization [of the peasantry] within the ranks of an [army] resolutely turned toward the future could enable an independent Angola to escape the pitfalls of neo-colonialism."[139] Such ideological pronouncements by the FNLA were rare, however, and did not provide the basis for mounting a concerted program of political education.

33

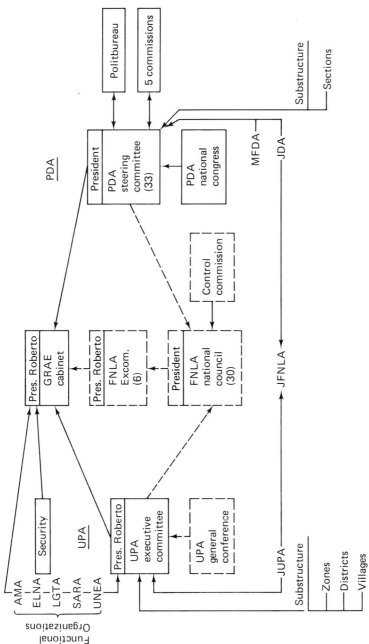

Figure 1.2 Formal structure of the FNLA/GRAE, January 1963. The acronyms are AMA, *Associação das Mulheres de Angola* —UPA women; ELNA, *Exército de Libertação Nacional de Angola* —army; JFNLA, JDA, JUPA, *Jeunesse* —youth; LGTA, *Liga Geral dos Trabalhadores de Angola* —labor; MFDA, *Mouvement des Femmes Democrates de l'Angola* —PDA women; SARA, *Serviço de Assistência aos Refugiados de Angola* —refugee aid; and UNEA, *União Nacional dos Estudantes Angolanos* —student.

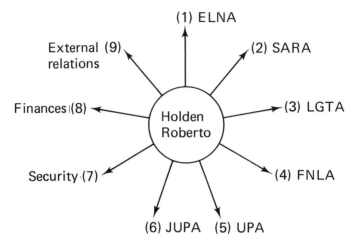

Figure 1.3   Roberto and the FNLA/GRAE

On paper the FNLA/GRAE structure was more diffuse and complicated than that of the MPLA. It was constructed from a loose, two-party alliance. This alliance was institutionalized on two levels: a political front (FNLA) and an exile government (GRAE). Much of this structure (see figure 1.2) existed only on paper (UPA general conference) or soon became partially or totally moribund (all FNLA organs), and what functioned did so under highly personalized (rather than collective) direction. Holden Roberto was president of and dominated the executive bodies of the UPA, JUPA, FNLA, and GRAE, to all of which he was little more than theoretically accountable for his actions. Contrary to the power diffusion suggested by the structural graph in figure 1.2, political authority was personally and idiosyncratically centered (figure 1.3).

Roberto built his power upon a combination of formal and informal arrangements. (1) ELNA: As commander-in-chief, he exercised personal control over the army general staff. (2) SARA: As principal fund raiser (partly American sources) and through personal relations with staff (including both his uncle, Barros Necaca, and expatriate doctors), he maintained considerable, if not total, control over SARA's medical and health services. (3) LGTA: Through a Cuban labor adviser, Carlos Kassel, and through extended family ties with LGTA President Pedro Barreiro Lulendo, he secured the political loyalty of the UPA's trade union affiliate. (4) FNLA: As president, he convened few meetings and obstructed the functional development of the FNLA executive council (within which PDA leaders had expected to wield political influence). (5) UPA: Similarly as UPA president, though he shared a measure of power with a few others (notably party secretary Jonas Savimbi and Vice-President Rosário Neto), he prevented the party executive committee from developing into a collective decision-making body. (6) JUPA: By assuming the presidency of the *Jeunesse* and making its vice-president responsible directly to him, he curtailed youthful political deviance, for example, expression of pro–common front sentiment. (7) Security: As GRAE president, he named a close aide and troubleshooter with no independent political base—José Manuel Peterson—to head a new internal security apparatus, soon to be staffed by a small cadre of sûreté police trained in Israel. (8) Finances: Wearing whichever presidential hat (or hats) he deemed appropriate, he raised funds from external sources and Angolan émigré entrepreneurs in the Congo and doled out money on the basis of personal preference. Neither GRAE ministers nor UPA/

FNLA officials drew fixed, regular salaries, and, while Roberto's subordinates were financially accountable to a UPA/GRAE treasury, he was accountable only to himself. (9) External relations: As GRAE president, he relied heavily upon "summitry" or personal relationships (friendship with Congolese Premier Cyrille Adoula) and diplomacy (lobbying in Tunis, Algiers, New York). And by naming a trusted aide (Johnny Edouard) as secretary of state for foreign affairs, he bypassed his (GRAE) foreign minister and potential rival, Jonas Savimbi. In general Angolans upon whom Roberto relied for an informal extension of his personal power (Lulendo, Necaca, Peterson, Edouard) were all Bakongo and linked to the Matadi and Léopoldville groups that had originally founded the UPA.[140]

The centrality of Roberto's role notwithstanding, two other persons exercised a significant degree of real or potential political influence within the FNLA/GRAE structure: Jonas Savimbi and Emmanuel Kunzika. As UPA secretary-general, GRAE foreign minister, and most importantly, the leading Ochimbundu[141] in the UPA/GRAE, Jonas Savimbi was developing an independent power base. He built his own network of diplomatic contacts (notably with Arab states) and undertook to reorganize and place his supporters within the UPA secretariat. In addition, through the intermediary of other Ovimbundu—including the director of SARA, Dr. José Liahuca, the commander of the Army (ELNA), José Kalundungo, and several student leaders (UNEA) in Europe and the United States, he began to knit together an informal leadership nexus commonly referred to as "southern" though largely from central Angola. This group was joined occasionally by free floaters such as UPA Vice-President Rosário Neto, who developed and guarded his own connections among Mbundu chiefs in the regions of Kasanje (Malange) and Kwango (Congo),[142] and the head of UPA Cabindan operations, Alexandre Taty, who had a following among Cabindan émigrés and refugees in the Congo-Léopoldville.[143]

In pursuit of a common desire to limit Roberto's personal dominance, Savimbi occasionally cooperated with the de facto leader of the PDA, Emmanuel Kunzika.[144] And together Savimbi and Kunzika pressured Roberto to activate the FNLA's collegial machinery.

As the UPA/GRAE depended upon Savimbi's "southern" nexus for its multiethnicity, the FNLA/GRAE depended upon the PDA for its two-party status. Able to draw upon its own limited source of funds—from contractors, merchants, and white-collar employees, a middle-class stratum within the émigré Bazombo community of Léopoldville and the Lower Congo—the PDA neither depended upon nor profited from the external fund raising Roberto carried out in the name of the FNLA/GRAE. Responsible to a functioning, counciliar structure (a PDA steering committee that met regularly), the PDA's top leaders relished the somewhat empty status that came with GRAE "ministerial posts." Kunzika became vice-premier, though initially he had no responsibilities in any specified field; and the PDA secretary-general, Ferdinand Dombele, became minister of social and refugee affairs but with no jurisdiction over SARA, the principal FNLA agency operating in this field.[145]

The FNLA/GRAE: Simulation

The MPLA maintained that the FNLA as a front was a deceptive fiction that simply served Roberto as an excuse for rejecting external (or internal) pressure for the creation of a meaningful common front with the MPLA. "Why," Roberto could ask, "destroy an existing front just to create another?" Failure to activate the FNLA's on-paper structure rendered it at best an uneasy, asymmetrical alliance. Even at the level of its youth wing, the *Jeunesse*-FNLA, created by the JDA and JUPA in early 1963, it remained an empty formality as the two components continued to function independently with little liaison between them.[146] The PDA maintained a separate women's organization (MFDA) and separate ties with Bazombo students in and out of UNEA, as well as links with a *Confédération des Syndicats Libres de l'Angola* (CSLA)[147] and other exile trade union rivals of the UPA-controlled *Liga Geral dos Trabalhadores de Angola* (LGTA).

Unable to force Roberto to develop FNLA structures into a functioning two-party partnership, the PDA was left with only a limited internal veto power, illustrated by the following incident. On February 8, 1963, the LGTA trade union executive sent a letter to the FNLA executive committee formally requesting membership in the front.[148] The request was linked to an ambitious program for expanded LGTA activities designed by the organization's counsellor, Carlos Kassel, and adopted by its executive bureau. During the first three months of 1963, the LGTA planned to establish new branch offices (at Tshikapa, Kasongo-Lunda, and Matadi) and to organize a body of "political commissars" within the army (ELNA) to "spread the ideological principles of the revolution among the soldiers, officers and the civilian population in liberated territory [inside Angola]."[149] Two weeks later, the labor group announced that it had begun training political commissars for ELNA, had by that time enrolled over eight thousand union members, of whom some four thousand had been recruited among the inhabitants of nationalist-held villages inside Angola, and had applied for full FNLA membership.[150] The head of its Cabindan section announced the endorsement of the FNLA membership application by his "1500 member" branch, which was assertedly "consolidating" its position within interior regions of Cabinda under ELNA control.[151]

Roberto supported (or inspired) this bid. It was nevertheless rejected at one of the infrequent meetings (March 1963) of the FNLA executive.[152] The PDA considered the LGTA, with its role in ELNA and its external support from the International Confederation of Free Trade Unions (ICFTU-Brussels),[153] the *Union Générale des Travailleurs Tunisiens* (UGTT), and the American AFL-CIO,[154] to be part of Roberto's private power base and blocked its entry. But the PDA victory was pyrrhic. It reinforced Roberto's view that FNLA's two-party structure constituted a potential constraint on his personal political power that ought not to be encouraged.

Reflective of Roberto's insecurity and aversion to political competition, the UPA/FNLA failed to develop a leadership training program comparable to that of the MPLA's *Escola de Quadros*. Roberto was more concerned with obtaining arms and expanding military operations than with building a strong politico-administrative apparatus. On the other hand, he did wish to convey externally the impression that the FNLA's second dimension, the GRAE, constituted a functioning governmental body.[155] Energy was invested in symbols and simulation. While denying their earlier stated, but unfulfilled, desire for diplomatic recognition,[156] GRAE leaders exulted in ministerial titles and stationery, produced a flood of "governmental" communiqués, sent "official" telegrams to foreign governments and political organizations (for example, condolences to the British Labour party on the death of Hugh Gaitskell),[157] and thrived on protocol and ceremony replete with flag and anthem. Largely fictional, these devices were meant to project a serious governmental image.

Appearances aside, the GRAE represented a self-deluding formula chosen by one of two contenders, the UPA-dominated FNLA, wishing to gain an advantage over an adversary, the MPLA. Except for two-party competition and the consequent desire to get ahead of its rival, the exile government strategy might not have been tried. In effect, the political dynamics of two-party insurgency encouraged the premature creation of a "revolutionary" government. Once embarked upon, the very process of government simulation created its own reality. And while the terms "GRAE" and "FNLA" might reasonably be held to refer to essentially the same thing, a loose two-movement coalition, "ministers" and functionaries within the GRAE came to view themselves as members of a real government.[158] They all confused form with substance, ceremony with function, and in the process convinced themselves and some external observers of their claim to official governmental status.

MILITARY FUNCTIONS

The UPA/GRAE's principal advantage over the MPLA was military. With the nucleus of an officer corps trained in Algeria and a large training and deployment base located at Kinkuzu in the Lower Congo, the *Exército de Libertação Nacional de Angola* (ELNA) developed into an organized force of several thousand men.[159] Expectations of what would happen when its externally trained and equipped units entered the fighting zones of northern Angola accounted for some expansive optimism on the occasion of the second anniversary of the March 15, 1961, uprising. Roberto and his associates foresaw themselves as soon negotiating, like the Algerians before them, with a European government weary of a debilitating colonial war.

In Léopoldville Congolese Premier Cyrille Adoula joined Roberto and Kunzika at March 15 ceremonies in calling for a timely peace settlement of the Angolan conflict to be based upon national independence and future cooperation with Portugal. Roberto warned that it was time for the Portuguese to show more "realism and understanding" in order to assure themselves of a place in Angola: "It is clear, that the future of the Portuguese living in our country rests in their own hands."[160] Then in follow-up ceremonies at the Kinkuzu military base, amid a display of gymnastics, machine gun, and bomb detonating exercises, Roberto, as head of the army, spoke of "his faith and firm hope that March 15, 1964 would be commemorated not in the Congo but in the interior of Angola."[161]

Earlier in January, Roberto had told newsmen in Tunis: "Our

base in the Congo . . . will permit us within the next few months to send [into Angola] some five to six thousand men, well trained and fully equipped, in order to intensify our struggle for liberation."[162] Lending weight to this prediction was an offer by the Algerian government of one hundred tons of arms and ammunition for FNLA units.[163]

In Léopoldville, the GRAE Ministry of Information issued frequent communiqués reporting military encounters, in each of which Angolan insurgents were said to have inflicted from five to ten casualties on the enemy. It announced plans to open a new training base in Katanga; and ELNA forces began to operate across the Kwango River from a new staging base near Kasongo-Lunda, into a small "liberated area" (the Iaca [Bakongo] region) of northeast Angola.

The MPLA had also been building the nucleus of a rival military force of its own for some time. In late January, Dr. Neto announced that a military cadre of three hundred men had completed training in Algeria and Morocco.[164] Under the command of Manuel Lima, a former officer in the Portuguese army, this cadre was reassembled in the Congo-Léopoldville as the core of a People's Liberation army, *Exército Popular de Libertação de Angola* (EPLA).[165] As secretary of war and a member of the MPLA Steering Committee, Lima was responsible for maintaining political control over the army. Henceforth EPLA officers were to be commissioned by the MPLA's six-man Political-Military Committee only after completing a course of military training and after giving evidence of "revolutionary faith." EPLA was expected to disseminate the MPLA's revolutionary program among the people, and whenever a dispute arose between a political and a military officer, the former was to prevail. Operating in commando groups of five or squads of ten men—in turn organized in command units of platoons (thirty men), companies (one hundred), and battalions (five hundred)— EPLA, according to Lima, was "to expand the armed struggle from the northern part of the country, where it [had] hitherto been waged, to the entire country."[166] Much of the EPLA officer cadre was mestiço or Mbundu, a handicap in the competition with Roberto's ELNA for recruits and support within black, and especially Bakongo, rural-exile communities in the Congo.[167]

On January 20, 1963, the MPLA's fledgling army made its combat debut. An EPLA unit attacked the post of Massabi in Cabinda and claimed the lives of nineteen Portuguese soldiers.[168] Luanda reported the raid but acknowledged the death of only one Portuguese soldier and said that the attackers had been routed, leaving behind a "large number of dead."[169] One of the raiders, a talkative young man, Mateus André Suami, defected.

Portuguese officials interrogated Suami and then flew him to Luanda where they presented him to the press. According to his "confession" which followed and which offered some insight into MPLA recruitment and training operations, he came from the northern district of Zaire (Bakongo), where he had attended a Protestant school at Capongo from 1954 to 1959. Though he had allegedly listened to a Canadian Protestant missionary extol the Congo's independence in 1960, he said he had refused to be coerced into working with UPA "bandits" organizing inside Angola. Nevertheless he came to fear that the Portuguese might kill all blacks in retaliation for UPA activity. Therefore, he fled north through the Lower Congo and on to Pointe Noire (Congo-Brazzaville) where he joined and sailed off with a group of 180 Angolans that, he said, had been promised overseas scholarships by the MPLA. Landing at Casablanca, he and his group were driven to an Algerian (FLN) military camp at Dar-Quel-Denib, Morocco. After three months of training there under the supervision of Commander Manuel Lima, they then returned to temporary quarters in Léopoldville where "a mestiço named Viriato da Cruz came twice a week to give [them] political lessons."[170] From there Suami and a contingent of fifty-six men crossed the Congo River to Brazzaville, proceeded to Pointe Noire and then, on January 20, moved into the Massabi area of Cabinda. Portuguese troops quickly surrounded the Cabinda raiders and, Mateus André Suami, in his words "disillusioned with [an involuntary] bandit life"—he had "only wanted to study nursing"—surrendered to Portuguese authorities.[171] Reacting to his well-publicized story, MPLA sources charged that Suami had been betrayed by local Cabindans and then "brain washed" by his Portuguese captors.[172]

Mateus André Suami notwithstanding, the January 20 raid represented an important step in the MPLA's effort to establish its military credentials. Other MPLA incursions from the Congo-Brazzaville into Cabinda followed. Meanwhile Roberto's rival ELNA forces mounted their own raids into the underside of Cabinda from the Tshela district of Congo-Léopoldville. And the Portuguese high command responded by moving several thousand well-armed infantrymen into the thickly forested enclave.

Chetniks and Partisans

Initially Lisbon had attributed the war in northern Angola to Congolese "invaders" and "outside agitators" acting upon a rabble of hemp-smoking *indigenas*.[173] This self-exonerating thesis blamed everything on external factors[174] and proved convincing to some disinterested observers.[175] It led logically to such distorted perception as the "discovery" of Ghanaian troops among the rebels, a finding later acknowledged to be in error.[176]

The initial northern upheaval was partially planned and organized by the UPA, though not all of the insurgents operated under even nominal UPA direction.[177] By 1963, UPA forces, organized as an Angolan Army of National Liberation (ELNA), were operating in three zones: the Lower Congo (Kongo Central Province) approaches to the Angola border; Fuesse-(UPA) administrative region (inside Angola); and Bembe-Nambuangongo military theater. The MPLA contested exclusive ELNA control over frontier access via the Lower Congo and challenged tenuous ELNA links with areas of Mbundu insurgency deep within the interior.

Border Approaches   Holden Roberto relied on his personal relations with central government officials, notably Premier Adoula, and upon the political savvy of veteran Bakongo leaders, such as Eduardo Pinock, to offset longstanding hostility among Abako provincial administrators in the Lower Congo.[178] As GRAE minister of interior, Pinock visited refugee centers along the Angolan border and ensured that SARA relief supplies (food, clothes, medicine) were distributed in such fashion as to maximize UPA/GRAE political influence among strategically located refugees and Congolese (Bakongo) officialdom.[179]

Except at Kinkuzu, ELNA forces did not bear arms inside the Congo. They transported their weapons to the Angola frontier in trucks accompanied by Congolese soldiers. And when they returned from action inside Angola, they had to sequester their arms at depositories along the frontier.[180]

The Portuguese army lacked the manpower or mobility, in the absence of good roads, to seal off the border area.[181] And to avoid complicating border incidents, the Portuguese air force, though it stepped up strafing and bombing to interdict incoming nationalist supplies and reinforcements, kept its planes well back from the Congolese frontier.

Within Congolese territory, the UPA/GRAE relied upon the central government to deny border access to the MPLA. In 1962, two MPLA military units en route to the border were reportedly intercepted, disarmed, and their weapons handed over to the UPA by the Congolese.[182] UPA/ELNA units moving southward from their base at Kinkuzu enjoyed contrastingly privileged and unimpeded entry into the closest zone of operations, a UPA-administered region of northern Angola centered at Fuesse.

Fuesse Administrative Region   In an area extending approximately forty miles along the border (from Luvo on the west to a point to the east of Buela) and some fifty miles south to where the M'Bridge River flows west below Madimba, the UPA established a direct, if rudimentary, administration over a complex of interlinked nationalist villages. A frequently shifting forest headquarters known as Fuesse, located near São Salvador, served as a communications center under the occasional supervision of Holden Roberto's roving troubleshooter and UPA administrative secretary, José Manuel Peterson.[183] Though top GRAE officials such as Roberto seem not to have ventured into the area, the center represented the closest approximation to internal government achieved by GRAE, which had originally been planned not as a government in exile but as a "Provisional Government inside Angola."[184] The Fuesse region also constituted a formidable obstacle course, or barrier, interposed between the MPLA's Léopoldville headquarters and its potential operational base within Mbundu areas to the south.

Bembe-Nambuangongo Military Theater   In late 1961, a young UPA field commander, João Batista, established his military headquarters some fifty miles south of Fuesse-São Salvador near the town of Bembe.[185] There he set about establishing effective control over guerrilla forces operating in the Bembe-Lucunga region and over insurgents ranging over a wide expanse of forested country to the south, from Quimbumbe on the west to Carmona on the east, and areas below the Dange River. In these areas remote from the Congolese border, rebel groups had organized locally, often under the leadership of Africans who had served in the Portuguese army. They had functioned independently or sometimes cooperatively but without overall military-political direction.[186] In 1961 and 1962, Batista began to establish some authority over a number of these disparate rebel bands and to displace freewheeling desperados who had, seemingly in some instances, assumed local leadership in the name of the UPA, even though the UPA exercised no control over them. Batista, for example, reportedly ended the despotism of Antoine Gérard de Ninganessa, an itinerant Kimbanguist said to have terrorized the Lucunga-Bembe area under "UPA orders" to massacre fetishists, assimilados, and mestiços.[187] But Batista's efforts to establish order and discipline over military *senzalas* (villages) and to organize and politicize hundreds, even thousands, of displaced Bakongo and Mbundu peasants who were somehow surviving in remote insurgent areas, were cut short by his death (probably during an attack on the Portuguese fort at Bembe) in February 1962.[188]

The impact of Batista's death, followed by the defection in Léopoldville of ELNA's chief of staff, Marcos Kassanga, was twofold. First, it collapsed Batista's campaign to assert real UPA/ELNA politico-military control over insurgent zones of the interior around and to the south of Bembe. Second, when coupled with the return of a UPA/ELNA military cadre from training in Algeria and its assignment to the new training-deployment base at Kinkuzu in mid-1962, it meant that central military authority (ELNA), like political authority (GRAE) before it, would henceforth be headquartered entirely in exile, not within the country. By mid-1963, armed ELNA patrols from Kinkuzu reportedly began to venture into the Nambuangongo-Dembos region where insurgent forces had been operating for over two years.[189] But there were no reports during 1963 of a post-Batista effort to establish a major interior ELNA command post or to impose an overall command structure and political discipline over guerrilla forces operating in the area.

Some insurgent forces, mostly those south of the Dange River but a few operating to the north, were in fact oriented toward the MPLA, not the UPA. MPLA communications with and supplies to its would-be partisans in these areas had to slip through border controls and cross the Fuesse administrative zone undetected by the Congolese or UPA/ELNA. Consequently MPLA headquarters in Léopoldville achieved only irregular contact with pro-MPLA insurgents, such as those led by Ferraz Bomboko in the Mbundu area of Colua (near Quitexe, north of the Dange).[190] In November 1961, UPA forces apprehended a twenty-man MPLA patrol at the M'Bridge River en route to reinforce Bomboko's beleaguered rebels, force-marched the men to Fuesse, then executed them. Despite such fearsome tactics, however, Roberto failed to establish UPA authority over the Colua area. In late 1962, he had his secretary of state for armaments, Rev. Fernando Gourjel, dispatch a UPA detachment to raid villages still under Bomboko's control.[191] But rather than submit to UPA orders, some of the villages, discouraged, enfeebled, and out of ammunition, gave themselves over to the Portuguese. Others marched more than one hundred kilometers to the west to join up with MPLA-oriented forces near Nambuangongo.[192]

In March 1963, a group of ten Mbundu villages known as Mazumbo de Nambuangongo dispatched a thirty-man mission to Léopoldville in quest of arms, ammunition, medicine, and military reinforcements from the MPLA.[193] Traveling through the Fuesse region bearing possibly forged UPA documents, the mission returned safely after spending two weeks in Léopoldville where its leaders arranged for the expedition of an armed MPLA contingent to their area. On April 28, that contingent, already deep inside Angola and preparing to cross to the south bank of the Loge (or Loje) River, was intercepted by UPA/ELNA forces.

According to MPLA sources, the detachment, fourteen EPLA soldiers and seven partisans from Nambuangongo, fought back for three hours and inflicted heavy casualties on its attackers. But MPLA losses were severe—ten soldiers and three partisans dead.[194] The UPA/FNLA initially dismissed MPLA charges of fratricide as a lie designed to create a false issue and thus compromise Angolan unity.[195] On May 17, however, Anibal de Melo, the MPLA director of information, presented a group of wounded survivors to the Léopoldville press as evidence of a "treacherous attack,"[196] which Roberto denied at the time,[197] but later acknowledged.[198] In an open letter to the UPA Steering Committee, MPLA leaders lamented that such "fratricide" seriously undermined the cause of Angolan nationalism. They called upon "true nationalists" within the UPA to demand that the movement renounce such barbarous tactics.[199]

News of the Loge affair further polarized insurgents in the Nambuangongo-Dembos area into hostile clusters of pro-UPA and pro-MPLA villages. Several Mbundu areas reportedly renounced their tenuous ties with the UPA. And on July 26, the leader of Mazumbo de Nambuangongo, Marcelino Mirando, convened villagers, including representatives from Dembos areas south of the Dange River, and proposed that a delegation of elders be sent to

Léopoldville to press Holden Roberto to work for, not against, nationalist unity. Mirando's project was reportedly delayed, first by opposition from a pro-UPA Mazumbo village (Kifuta), next by the arrival of a contingent of UPA troops from Kinkuzu, and finally by instructions from UPA headquarters in Léopoldville ordering UPA villages (to the north) not to let Mirando's delegation pass.[200] All the while, UPA/GRAE officials continued to deny publicly that MPLA forces existed in "any part of Angola."[201]

How much more effective might Angolan insurgents have been if unified under a single command pursuing a cohesive strategy?[202] At the very least, the energy that the UPA/ELNA expended shutting the MPLA out of the military campaign was energy deflected from the fight for independence. And although, as of January 1963, Roberto could point to a dozen MPLA soldiers trained in Morocco who had defected and joined ELNA in search of military action, his policies effectively constricted the bulk of the MPLA's military cadre to a frustrating barracks life on the outskirts of Léopoldville.[203] That insurgent forces in the interior continued to function at all, carrying out small raids and ambushes, was testimony to the tenacity of anticolonial sentiment rather than evidence of effective nationalist organization (Map 1.1).

TWO-PARTY INSURGENCY

One way of assessing two-party insurgency like that of Angola is to view it as a particular system and to ask some questions. Who are the competing actors? What issues divide them? To what extent are they polarized? What is their organizational interaction, if any? And what is the distribution of resources and capabilities between them?

The Actors

The two movements that dominated Angolan insurgency during 1962 and 1963 were led by competing elites with dissimilar social backgrounds. They reflected vertical and horizontal cleavages inherent in Angolan nationalism, that is, differences grounded in ethnic genesis and cultural, class, and racial stratification.

Vertical Cleavage   Ethnicity was manifest in the composition of movement leadership and the regional locus of movement activity. It was especially strong within the UPA/FNLA. Excluding Savimbi's

Map 1.1   Zones of insurgent activity, 1963

Ovimbundu nexus, the historical referents for UPA/FNLA leadership were to the former Kongo (Bakongo) kingdom centered at São Salvador.[204] MPLA literature focused contrastingly upon Mbundu resistance to Portuguese rule by the seventeenth-century "Queen Jinga" (Nzinga Mbande) of Matamba and later "anonymous warriors of the Dembos tribe."[205] Although each movement sought to transcend its origins, managed to attract some representation from other ethnolinguistic communities, and presented itself as genuinely multiethnic, each received much of its support from a primary ethnic segment, and each perceived its rival as being exclusively and antagonistically ethnocentric.[206]

Religious factors reinforced ethnic cleavage. Proportionately MPLA leadership counted more persons with Catholic backgrounds and occasionally accused the UPA of wishing to impose Protestantism on all Angolans.[207] In general, however, Catholic versus Protestant conflict was more central to Portuguese than African perceptions.[208]

More apparent was an intra-Protestant dichotomy reflecting the coincidence of Protestant territoriality and African ethnicity.[209] MPLA leadership mirrored Methodist presence in the Luanda-Mbundu area, and UPA leadership reflected both the implantation of the Baptist Missionary Society in the Bakongo north and of the United Church of Christ (Congregational) and United Church of Canada in the Ovimbundu central highlands. If such religious differentiation was of little intrinsic political importance, it had some impact on external aid alignment: leaders, students, and refugees of each movement tended to look abroad to "their church" for humanitarian help.

Horizontal Cleavage   Interrelated factors of culture, class, and race also set Angolan nationalists apart. In the process of introducing Portuguese culture, Portuguese Catholic mission schools transplanted the rigidly class-based and -oriented educational system of Portugal into Angola.[210] Elitist this education extended to only a handful of Africans and created a diminutive class (thirty thousand by 1950) of culturally assimilated blacks (assimilados). To become an assimilado, an African was obliged to disassociate himself from his "uncivilized," or indigena, family and past. And he was taught to rank fellow assimilados socially by level of formal education.

The social status of most African assimilados remained inferior to that of a relatively more privileged class or caste of over fifty thousand mestiços. Mestiços were, by and large, considered automatically assimilated by virtue of their racially mixed parentage. The result of a colonial system that, in the absence of white women, had encouraged Portuguese men to exploit African women sexually, mestiços were, in turn, kept in a second-class relationship to the European settlers. Europeans streamed into Angola after World War II, more than doubling the white stratum of Angolan society between 1950 and 1960, by which time they had reached nearly two hundred thousand.

Angolan society thus came to consist of a four-layer culture-class-race pyramid moving up from a broad base of black commoners, to a wafer-thin layer of African assimilados, to mestiços, to whites. Culture, class, and race constituted mutually reinforcing categories or barriers to social mobility. Of these, race was the most visible and irreducible and hence the most convenient basis for social stratification.

Among Angolan nationalists, this social pyramid produced a perceptual duality. Some stressed the centrality of class conflict. Others insisted upon the importance of racial cleavage. The result was a tonal dichotomy: urban/acculturated-intellectual/multiracial versus rural/ethnopopulist/uniracial. And it was this horizontal dichotomy, reinforced by primary ethnolinguistic vertical cleavage, that most importantly set apart the MPLA and FNLA.

The Issues

Each group in perceiving, assessing and asserting its own and, negatively, its rival's identity overdrew these differences. The two quarreled about who they were and what they should be. The FNLA pictured MPLA leadership as consisting uniquely of privileged mestiços and assimilados who, within the Portuguese colonial system, had enjoyed the advantages of "education, exemption from forced labor, access to property and professions, civil rights, [and a higher] standard of living." Given the social and psychological gulf driven between the oppressed indigenato and the civilized strata from which MPLA leaders came, it was understandable, argued an FNLA tract, that the peasant majority would fear and reject domination by this elite after independence. Given that Angola would lack industry and capital at the onset of independence, MPLA leaders could be expected to assume "the class role of *compradores* should they succeed in monopolizing control of the Revolution on grounds of cultural superiority."[211] The argu-

	MPLA	FNLA
Ethnic/ Religious	Mbundu Catholic/Methodist	Bakongo/Baptist Ovimbindu/United Church
Class	Urban	Rural
Culture	Acculturated-intellectual	Ethnopopulist
Race	Multiracial	Uniracial

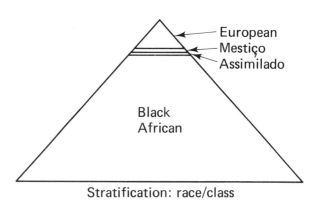

Stratification: race/class

Figure 1.4   Nationalist dichotomy, 1963. The dichotomy was not absolute. For example, the leadership of both movements consisted of educated elites, for the most part literate in Portuguese. But the leadership of one (MPLA) was more deeply impacted by Portuguese culture and more assertively "intellectual." That of the other (FNLA) had fewer social ties with Europeans in Angola or Portugal and was, or perceived itself to be, more firmly rooted in African culture.

ment was premised on an assumption that the MPLA's leadership would not or could not transcend its social background, that is, commit "class suicide."[212]

The MPLA leadership depicted the FNLA as parochial, the victim of an inferiority complex. It saw Roberto's UPA as "traumatized" by the "limits of its knowledge of the [real] Angola, by an intellectual emptiness attributable to its lack of [educated] cadres, and by the fact that its power extended to a mass whose national perspective was constricted to a Bakongo-horizon [vertical segment]." On the basis of this weakness, MPLA reasoning continued, the UPA's largely émigré (culturally alienated) leadership tried defensively and illegitimately to assert a monopoly role for itself as the sole representative of Angolan aspirations. Thus it formed a "government" that excluded and ignored its adversary, the MPLA.[213] This MPLA perspective assumed the inability of the UPA/GRAE leadership to transcend racial prejudice and cultural parochialism.

Inevitably both the polemics and substance of culture-class-race differentiation became a focal point of intranationalist conflict. Perceptual disagreements concerning the nature and relative importance of these three variables fostered and, in turn, were exacerbated by ideological differences. They became the focus of chronic dispute.

The urban/acculturated-intellectual/multiracial character of the MPLA led it to attach greater value than did its adversaries to Portuguese culture as a factor favoring national integration; to minimize the importance of race as against class as an influence on sociopolitical relationships; and to attach much importance to the refinement of and commitment to a political ideology.

Portuguese Culture   On the one hand, Portuguese education was a force for societal integration across segmental ethnic lines. On the other, with its idealization of the poet-philosopher and its low esteem for democratic process or manual labor, it fostered a regard for rule by a small superordinate elite of multihued Portuguese Angolans. One of its major detractors, Emmanuel Kunzika (PDA), argued that Portuguese culture and education divided Angolans into two categories: a Portuguese-educated elite with a "superiority complex" and an uneducated mass with an "inferiority complex."[214] He did not contend that a modern education was unnecessary for contemporary Angolan political leadership. But he maintained that a Portuguese education ought not to be regarded as essential. What about émigré leaders, such as Kunzika, educated in French not Portuguese language schools in the Congo? Were the movements they founded and led (PDA, UPA) any less Angolan than those organized by lusophone nationalists inside or more recently exiled from the country?

The answer might be yes insofar as Angolan political movements founded in the Congo in the 1950s were patterned on Congolese (Belgian) models, were caught up in the fortunes and intrigues of Congolese politics, and had less firsthand experiential knowledge of conditions prevailing in Angola.[215] And the fact that someone like Johnny Edouard (he later used the Portuguese spelling, Eduardo), the son of the São Salvador émigré Eduardo Pinock, did not speak Portuguese (he later learned it), inevitably undermined the credibility of his role as secretary of state for foreign affairs in an Angolan government. Was Johnny Edouard, who spoke French and Kikongo, Angolan?

A similar identity problem faced English-speaking Angolan émigrés within Luvale, Luchazi, and Chokwe communities in Northern Rhodesia (Zambia). Were those who spoke English and their home tongue but not Portuguese really Angolan? Did knowledge of a colonial lingua franca constitute a legitimate test of nationality?

As head of a party (PDA) supported by an upwardly mobile (Bazombo) émigré community, Emmanuel Kunzika met this issue head on. Outside of Angola, he said, "wholly Portuguese educated" Angolans flaunted themselves before "Angolans with a French or other cultural background." They found it "difficult to accept as Angolan" Africans not "wholly conversant with the tongue of Camoëns."[216] They treated long-time Angolan refugees in the Congo as "foreigners" or Congolese whereas they really had no right "to question the citizenship of Angolans" who fled "Portuguese oppression" and had "the privilege of assimilating a culture which is equal if not superior in spiritual content to Portuguese culture." After all, they would have been "entirely deprived of cultural training had they remained in Angola." "Instead of showing contempt," Kunzika argued, "those who have recently left Angola or Portugal should show admiration for their brothers who are refugees of long standing and who even so are not indifferent to the fate of their country." Because of them and the independence of the Congo, it was possible "to organize and coordinate the struggle for the liberation of Angola."[217]

Kunzika and his PDA adopted a legal-rational approach to politics. Where Roberto was parochial and defiant, Kunzika appealed for mutual understanding. Eschewing revolutionary rhetoric, he argued for tolerance and cultural pluralism: ". . . let us appreciate that the Angola of the future will be a land of contrasts, where different cultures will flourish and come together to serve the Angolan nation."[218] Any future role for such émigré nationalists, as well as those still immersed in indigenous ethnic culture, depended upon an expansive and flexible definition of who and what were legitimately Angolan. But as Kunzika himself pointed out in 1963, the very inability of the FNLA and MPLA to discuss such matters, "the absence of a spirit of tolerance," left the issue unresolved and showed that "we carry the root causes of our weakness within ourselves."[219]

The Racial Variable   While the FNLA defended the nationalist legitimacy of Angolans little conversant with Portuguese culture, "expatriates" in the MPLA lexicon,[220] the MPLA defended the leadership credentials of mestiço and assimilado intellectuals and petit bourgeois who spoke Portuguese but no African language. Such acculturated persons were described as "the driving force behind the awakening of political consciousness" in Angola,[221] and their racial origins were depicted as irrelevant. Influenced by Marxist thought, they viewed the Angolan struggle as essentially a class not a racial conflict against colonial and imperialist politico-economic exploitation.[222]

The MPLA undertook to ally itself with "progressive Portuguese born in Angola, some of whom," it said, "[tried] to neutralize the support that [Portuguese] settlers [gave] to the forces of repression and [tried] to fight for the same objectives as [those of] the Angolan nationalist movements."[223] The movement's ability to operate across racial lines was confirmed in April 1963 by a *Le figaro* correspondent, Max Clos. After a wide-ranging tour of the territory, Clos reported that he had met numerous Portuguese liberals hostile to the Salazar government. Almost all of them, he said, had come from metropolitan Portugal in the employ of a large company and had maintained ties with opposition elements in Portugal itself. "Most of them," he added, had contact with Angolan rebels, "almost always with members of the MPLA." Through the intermediary of these white liberals, Clos wrote, he was able to meet local MPLA officials "just about everywhere."[224] Anticipating an MPLA government after the war and hoping to keep Angola closely tied to Portugal, he reasoned, Portuguese democrats were aiding the MPLA.[225] MPLA leaders, in turn, carefully distinguished between the Salazar regime and the Portuguese people.[226] The UPA, by way of contrast, was, in Clos's view, "openly racist" and resentful of mestiços who thought they would run Angola after independence.[227]

A number of MPLA leaders, including Dr. Neto, had married Portuguese women. And in due course (1968), a party conference would determine that white spouses as well as other whites "born or resident in Angola" could become "sympathizer-members" of the movement.[228] The MPLA was an advocate and product of multiracialism.

The more rural/ethnopopulist/uniracial FNLA viewed such matters differently. Rooted in an ethnically conscious, to the Portuguese, "uncivilized" black peasantry, it perceived socioeconomic cleavage in racial categories. It held that, through cultural assimilation and racial miscegenation, the white ruling class had coopted and reinforced its ranks with an assimilado and mestiço additive.[229] But as an extension of European rule, this additive became "Portuguese." Neither numerous nor influential enough to modify the reality of white rule, mestiços and African assimilados, from an FNLA perspective, became for all practical purposes "white." The great mass of the population, by virtue of its unassimilable, irreducible blackness, was contrastingly fated to remain an ascriptively exploited racial caste.

This racial issue is important and complex. The popular thesis that Portuguese colonialism was devoid of racial antagonisms long persisted, despite much counterevidence, including protest literature that decried racial discrimination. A striking example of such literature appeared as early as the turn of the century in an anthology of angry articles published as *Voz D'Angola Clamando No Deserto* (1901).[230] Social discrimination and economic barriers against the advancement of nonwhites grew in the late nineteenth century "as more Europeans came to Angola."[231] By 1912, when Norton de Matos began his first term as governor general of Angola, feelings of "racial superiority" had become very intense.[232] De Matos found that slavery and forced labor were widely approved within a local European population that had been infected by what he called "Germanic" racism; resident whites considered the black man to be inherently inferior.[233] De Matos himself opposed miscegenation.[234] Over time European settlers asserted their own group interests within political movements such as the *Partido Pró-Angola* (founded in 1924 and resuscitated after World War II), which favored autonomy from a Lisbon seen as tending to be too solicitous of African interests.

It was commonly asserted that "of all the European groups in Africa," the Portuguese "maintained the friendliest and least race-conscious relations with black Africans."[235] Projecting from this contention, contemporary historians blamed the UPA and its partisans for unleashing racism in Angola (in March 1961). Failure to situate what they termed the "bestial" massacre of Europeans in early 1961 within the historical context of a colonial system that had inculcated deep and abiding racial antagonism prompted Eurocentric writers to saddle African nationalists with near total responsibility for the deepened racial cleavage that did indeed follow the reciprocal slaughter in 1961.[236] But African racial attitudes were not simply a creation of the UPA. In late 1963, Lloyd Garrison of the *New York Times* wrote that "after interviewing scores of Africans in Portuguese-held Angola as well as in the rebel north," he had a "single overwhelming impression that black and white in Angola are separated by a gulf so wide and deep it may never be bridged."[237] Other observers pointed to racial bitterness deriving from a long tradition of sexual exploitation of African women by European men and credited it with providing at least a partial explanation of "the way in which Portuguese women suffered [from African attacks in 1961] in isolated *fazendas* in the North of Angola."[238]

In the uniracialist view of the FNLA, white interests differed collectively from those of Africans. It thus followed that political alliances with white groups could only do harm to the African cause. Because he feared competition from skilled and educated Africans, the petit-blanc or "European proletarian" might support a communist party as he did in Algeria, yet "with only a few heroic exceptions" would remain allied (as in Algeria) with the "colonial bourgeoisie" (the white's own oppressor) in opposition to African nationalism. Even the most disadvantaged among the "civilized," according to uniracialists, enjoyed a privileged position worth defending against the black masses. The only alternative open to white settlers was a return to the hopeless poverty of Portugal.

The sociopolitical role of the mestiço, as well as that of the white, was an issue that sharply divided Angolan nationalists. The MPLA maintained that antimestiço racism had prompted UPA insurgents to exterminate mestiços during the 1961 uprising.[239] The UPA countered that it had always distinguished between "sincere" Angolan patriots and those (not all) mestiços whom the Portuguese had armed and used to combat black Africans.[240] Denying that it would "absurdly" judge Angolans by "the color of their skin," the UPA/FNLA argued that its relationships with mestiços—as individuals and groups—were determined by the extent to which the mestiços concerned were "integrated into colonial society" and consequently alienated from African society. The UPA/FNLA barred any political role for *fils de colons* (mestiços recognized by their Portuguese fathers and coopted into colonial society). Such mestiços rejected the culture of their African mothers, accepted that of paternal (European) oppressors, and generally joined forces with marginal whites in opposing African nationalists who threatened their color-based, socioeconomic privilege. The UPA/FNLA attributed segregationist and negrophobia sentiments to most mestiços and maintained that mestiços as a group sought to monopolize access to higher and technical education.[241]

Finally the fact that the MPLA's leaders came from "civilized" Angolans and that its ranks included "numerous" members of colon parentage was seen by the FNLA as being responsible for much of the MPLA's hostility toward the FNLA. While it perceived the multiracial MPLA as compromised by its involvement with the "liberal fringe" of Angola's white bourgeoisie, the FNLA saw itself as fighting for the total destruction of colonial culture and racism—the champion of an indigenous national culture based upon "Negro-African civilization."[242]

Ideology   Another issue of dispute within Angolan nationalism centered on ideology. Differences concerned contrasting degrees of ideological commitment and refinement and the extent to which ideology took on a general or international, as distinct from purely national, revolutionary perspective.

The statements outlining the political goals and priorities of the UPA/FNLA were comparatively simple, even rudimentary.[243] They included pronouncements in favor of such general goals as national independence, democratic government, agrarian reform (suggesting an acreage limit on all holdings), economic development, and pan-African unity.[244]

Of the UPA's initial platform of 1960,[245] Mário de Andrade wrote (in 1964) that he found nothing in it that was fundamentally incompatible with "essential points" of the MPLA's more detailed Maximum Program.[246] However, the UPA's failure further to define and refine its ideological position, he said, constituted an impediment to two-party entente. In his view, the MPLA confer- ence in December 1962 had elaborated a "genuine ideology in the philosophical sense of the word," whereas the UPA still lacked a coherent program.[247] And indeed, while Holden Roberto would long maintain that ideological considerations should be put off until after independence,[248] his stance represented an implicit re- jection of the intellectual Marxism articulated in the MPLA's world view.[249]

MPLA concern for ideological discourse implied a clear subordi- nation of other considerations, such as race. An exiled Portuguese writer, António de Figueiredo, comparing Angola's nationalist movements, noted that many MPLA leaders were "the husbands of Portuguese women" and that their political conceptions were formatively influenced by the Portuguese opposition. He thus foresaw a "socialist" Angola under MPLA rule, an Angola wherein "Africans would not be unduly disturbed by the continued pres- ence of white Portuguese socialists in their sparsely populated country." Having enjoyed the support of European "democrats" in Angola, a victorious MPLA, he concluded, might reciprocate by al- lowing Angola to serve as the springboard for a war for democracy in Portugal itself."[250] Such speculation about the transcendance of ideological over racial affinity nourished interparty disagreement and distrust.

A second level of ideological dispute concerned the extent of ideological commitment to an international revolutionary outlook or weltanschauung. It pitted what was generally seen as the UPA's "strictly nationalist and pro-western orientation" against the MPLA's *"progressiste"* and prosocialist leanings.[251] Despite his occa- sional denials of international ideological alignment,[252] Mário de Andrade contrasted what he saw as the UPA's constricted national perspective with a broader MPLA world view.[253] Seen from An- drade's angle, the Angolan war constituted part of a worldwide struggle by "progressive forces" against international (Western) imperialism.[254] FNLA-MPLA rivalry was caught up in the rigidify- ing cold war rhetoric, maneuvers, and hostilities of global politics.

As a corollary to its ideological outreach, the MPLA attached par- ticular importance to external factors in the Angolan conflict. An underlying motive in its drive for an Angolan common front, or "politico-military alliance," was its expectation that the achievement of such a front would set into motion an external chain reaction. Once unity was achieved, the reasoning went, "nothing could prevent the mobilization of all African countries behind the Angolan people's struggle." External support would then "set into motion" factors inside Portugal (as distinct from Angola) "that would precipitate the fall of the Salazar regime" and thus assure the triumph of Angolan nationalists.[255] FNLA thinking was contrastingly limited to a more ad hoc, short-range focus on matters of proximate political and military expediency.

Polarization

Military collisions sharply polarized Angola's two-party insurgency. The FNLA ambush of MPLA soldiers at the Loge River in April 1963, coming on the heels of a conciliatory statement by Mário de Andrade to the effect that "fratricidal" conflict between "Angolan brothers" had ended, widened the gulf between the two movements.[256] Such encounters built psychological barriers of bitterness, guilt, and fear. Nationalist competition became a zero-sum game between two mortally hostile protagonists. An advantage for one meant an equal disadvantage for the other.

Conflict polarity projected out from military collision (EPLA versus ELNA) to such relatively uncritical levels as relief work (CVAAR versus SARA). Its intensity served to divert dissent within a movement—for instance, resentment against Roberto's personalist control of the UPA/GRAE system—away from its proper target. Thus political hostility within was converted into a unifying reaction against a common (MPLA) threat from without.

The MPLA continued to press for the creation of a common nationalist front, at the same time that the FNLA strove to reinforce polarity. Since neither movement was able to absorb, eliminate, or eclipse its rival, intense polarization enhanced Portuguese capacity to manipulate African insurgents, promote internecine conflict, and minimize metropolitan losses.

Organizational Interaction in the System

The absence of any formal or informal organizational structure linking or relating the FNLA and MPLA mirrored the absence of a minimal degree of mutual intermovement confidence or respect at top leadership levels. There was some cross-party contact among individual, lower-echelon militants, within religious and cultural associations,[257] among students, or at occasional conferences such as the Angolan Youth Seminar organized at Léopoldville by the World Assembly of Youth in April 1963. But such contacts were fragile, suspect, and without appreciable political influence. The fact that Dr. José Liahuca, head of the UPA's medical service (SARA), maintained social contacts with former medical school colleagues now serving with the MPLA's rival CVAAR, for instance, aroused chronic suspicion about his loyalty and diminished his political influence with the UPA/GRAE.[258] A militant, negative posture toward the members of the other movement became essential to a nationalist's political influence and credibility within his own movement.

In March 1963, the MPLA and then the FNLA each announced that it was adding football to its roster of organized activities.[259] Their teams, however, never played across party lines. The list of parallel but separate FNLA/MPLA structures and activities grew, but even at the level of organized sports—which might have offered an opportunity for harmless, cathartic competition—contact remained negligible. Both movements extolled the principle of unity in the fight against Portugal. But both disagreed on the procedures for achieving it and the substantive form that it should take.

FNLA leaders argued that it was up to the MPLA to submit a formal application for FNLA membership. The MPLA bid would then be processed by a special committee as provided for in the FNLA's constitution.[260] MPLA leaders countered that they should not be expected to apply for membership in a front whose constitution they had had no part in formulating.[261] The FNLA argued that the existing front represented a considerable achievement, which should not be dismantled.[262] The MPLA contended that it could not associate with others unless first permitted to participate in the elaboration of a minimal common program. The procedural deadlock was complete. Neither Holden Roberto nor Dr. Neto seems to have sought through direct or indirect private contact to break the impasse so they might together hammer out a procedural compromise. Logic suggested a formula permitting simultaneous discussions concerning both MPLA membership and adjustments in the FNLA program. The FNLA after all had publicly offered to "modify its constitution if that should be necessary in order to facilitate the adhesion of a new member."[263]

Although both the PDA and Savimbi's faction within the UPA were predisposed to favor an association with the MPLA if this could curtail Roberto's power without leading to MPLA hegemony, the MPLA made no apparent efforts to contact and gain the confidence of these two prospective allies. Instead the MPLA relied upon public prounity pressure by independent African states[264] and public petitions by Angolans calling for the creation of a new national front.[265] So long as FNLA defiance of prounity advice did not mean the loss to it of really important external or internal support, this open pressure only decreased the likelihood of FNLA concessions because it nourished suspicion and increased the loss of face that concessions would entail.

In addition to procedural deadlock, there were also differences concerning what the structure of a common front ought to be. The GRAE called for full "integration" under the "collective direction" of a front (the FNLA).[266] The MPLA argued for a loose arrangement that would preserve the autonomy of constituent units.[267] The "cartel" or alliance system proposed by the MPLA was to be known as the *Frente de Libertação de Angola* (FLA). It was criticized by opponents as a plan designed by the MPLA to gain access to and freedom of military and political action within the Congo and northern regions of Angola at the price of minimal organizational or ideological concessions to the authority of a common front.[268]

In the absence of a serious dialogue, it was unclear whether differing concepts of what a united front should be constituted a major impediment to union. Despite their public advocacy of a relatively centralized front, after all, FNLA leaders had not achieved functional integration within their own PDA/UPA front and seemed eager to discredit the MPLA's (FLA) formula without having to discuss it with MPLA leaders. Rhetoric and technical points aside, the overriding factor remained Holden Roberto's hostility to any association with the MPLA.

There was no coordination of nationalist strategy against the colonial incumbent. This rendered a maximal military challenge impossible. Lisbon was left to respond to separate, competitive thrusts of African military and diplomatic action. It could portray African adversaries as fratricidal terrorists, scarcely qualified to offer a credible political alternative to the status quo. And by hammering on nationalist differences, by reducing the MPLA to "Soviet dominated" and "communist" and the FNLA to "American/Protestant financed" and "tribalist," Portuguese publicists were able both to capitalize on and nourish these differences. So long as an MPLA gain entailed a roughly equivalent FNLA loss, or vice versa, and neither movement achieved a dominant, organizing role within the insurgency, the Portuguese had a much better chance of holding on.

Resource and Capability Distribution

By early 1963, neither the FNLA nor the MPLA enjoyed a decisive advantage in terms of available resources or organizational capacity. In geopolitical and military terms, the FNLA had the edge; it had a strong émigré-refugee base in the Congo and unobstructed access to contiguous areas of ethnopolitical support within Angola. In administrative-organizational terms, the MPLA was the more impressive with its educated cadres and developing structure and political programs.

During 1963, however, external pan-African factors would strongly affect the comparative resource and capability standing of the two movements. And for some months the Angolan conflict would command serious international attention.

CHAPTER TWO

PAN-AFRICAN TAKEOFF

The pan-African phase of the Angolan war followed closely upon the overthrow of French colonial authority in Algeria and the defeat of Belgian-linked secession in Katanga. It began in a climate of optimism over prospects for the liberation of all white-ruled Southern Africa.

Algerian independence (July 1, 1962), hailed throughout Africa and elsewhere as a triumph of revolutionary will, inspired confidence in the practicality of revolutionary action. And it promised to thrust Algerian manpower and materiel into a campaign to internationalize black Africa's first modern war for independence.

Algerians had been training Angolan guerrilla forces since mid-1961.[1] At that time, Holden Roberto had sent a group of twenty to twenty-five men to Tunisia to be trained under Algerian forces commanded by Colonel Houari Boumedienne. MPLA militants were subsequently sent to Morocco to train there under Algerian units, which later played a role in Ahmed Ben Bella's successful bid for political power. In the first exuberant flush of independence, Algeria under Ben Bella reached out to appropriate the Angolan conflict as an outward extension of its own revolutionary mission.

NORTH AFRICAN INTRUSION

Eager to capitalize on longstanding[2] Algerian interest in the Angolan cause, Mário de Andrade and Lúcio Lára visited Algiers in early November 1962. President Ben Bella seized the occasion to announce that he had already "warned" President John F. Kennedy that "if in 1963 the United Nations did not live up to its responsibilities to stop [the Angolan] war" and see to it that the Angolan people exercised their right to self-determination and independence, "then Algeria would take it upon itself to assist [Angolan] liberation movements in their armed struggle." If need be,

PAN-AFRICAN TAKEOFF   63

he said, "we shall send volunteers and technicians and finance this war." In so doing, Algeria would be defending its "own sacred liberation," for the construction of a new Algeria would not be possible unless the whole African continent marched with it "toward the same political objectives, the same political choices."[3]

That Ben Bella was serious and might indeed intervene in the Angolan conflict seemed increasingly possible to outside observers. Mário de Andrade announced that an office to recruit Algerian volunteers for the Angolan war would soon be opened in Algiers;[4] and the MPLA made clear its readiness to welcome the North Africans.[5]

Holden Roberto made his own bid for Algerian support. A close association with the late philosopher-ambassador of the Algerian revolution, Frantz Fanon, had linked him to the Algerian cause as early as 1958.[6] And this relationship helped to account for Roberto's emulation of Algerian political precedents, for example, his creation of a government in exile[7] and his call in January 1963 for an all-African foreign ministers' conference on Angola to be patterned on the 1959 conference on Algeria at Monrovia, Liberia.[8]

Eager to inherit arms stocks left over from the Algerian war, Roberto visited Algiers en route to Léopoldville from lobbying at the Seventeenth General Assembly of the United Nations in New York. On January 17, 1963, he addressed the first congress of the *Union Générale des Travailleurs Algériens* (UGTA) and averred that his movement was following in the footsteps of the Algerian revolution. To Roberto's embarrassment, an attending MPLA representative, Dr. Eduardo dos Santos, demanded the right to reply and proclaimed that the MPLA was the "only authentic Angolan movement."[9] UGTA delegates chanting "unity" obliged Ben Bella to intervene. In an impromptu speech, he repeated earlier appeals[10] for the disputants to settle their differences and unite within a single liberation front.[11] At the same time, he revealed that forty-eight hours after he had received a request for arms from Holden Roberto, a shipment had been placed at the latter's disposal.[12] This action was viewed by some as an erratic shift from previous pro-MPLA policy, a shift that could only exacerbate FNLA-MPLA competition and division.[13]

On January 19, Roberto dined with Ben Bella and his adviser on Angolan affairs, Commander Slimane (Kaid Ahmed),[14] at the presidential villa. At a press conference afterward, the Algerian president said that he and Roberto had been studying ways to reinforce

Angolan insurgency and repeated his promise of "all aid needed" to ensure the liberation of the Angolan people.[15] Roberto reviewed his relations with Algerian nationalists—beginning with the All African People's Conference of Accra (1958)[16]—praised the spirit and goals of the Algerian revolution, and announced that Ben Bella had agreed to permit the FNLA to open an office in Algiers. Hoping to placate Algerian displeasure over Angolan disunity, Roberto also said that he was aware of the need for unity among the Angolan liberation movements. But he held firm to the procedural condition that unity should be achieved by others joining *his* movement: "[Unity] is our major concern and thus it is that we have created an FLN which has left its door open to all those who speak the language of the legitimate violence of African Nationalism."[17]

Ben Bella indicated that he would not insist upon unity as a precondition to further aid, but he would use aid to both parties as a means to press for such unity. He also announced the imminent departure of a special mission to Léopoldville for the purpose of promoting a rapprochement between Angola's two nationalist organizations.[18] While Holden Roberto flew on to Tunisia for talks with officials of the Bourguiba government, a staunch backer of the UPA/GRAE,[19] Commander Slimane and Brahimi Lakdar, of the Algerian Ministry of Foreign Affairs, enplaned for the Congo.[20]

The Algerians met with Congolese officials as well as, separately, with members of the FNLA and MPLA. Because they were supportive of the MPLA's quest for a common front, the mission's proposals received a mixed reception. *Vitória ou Morte* (MPLA) published an interview with Commander Slimane in which he cited the example of Algeria's two nationalist parties who had put aside their debilitating differences and joined forces for the essential objective, overthrow of the colonial system. Together they had launched an armed struggle on November 1, 1954, as a united National Liberation Front (FLN). Now that Algeria was independent, "Angola and its people had taken its place at the head of the African struggle against colonialism." Given the transcendent importance of the Angolan war, Slimane said, it was the "overriding duty" of independent African states to mobilize all their genius and resources in the fight to crush Portuguese colonialism. For such assistance to be effective, however, Angolan nationalists would have to unite around specific objectives. It was up to Angolans to work out an appropriate formula for unity based on a search for "reciprocal understanding." Slimane also said that Algeria had a pan-African right ("duty") to intervene and help to facilitate a rapprochement that was "close to the heart of [the Algerian] people." "Algeria had been torn by divisions and had a horror of them."[21]

The Slimane mission was not well timed. Agostinho Neto was in Europe, and Holden Roberto was in Tunisia. The only occasion on which the Algerian team managed to get the two movements together was a "cordial" three-hour farewell dinner (January 28) at the Léopoldville city hall.[22] Mário de Andrade later attributed the failure of the Slimane mission to Roberto's absence,[23] but there is no reason to believe that Roberto could have been pressured into agreeing to a resumption of the direct two-party conversations that had collapsed after one session the year previous.[24] Rather than await Roberto's return, the Slimane mission departed from Léopoldville on January 30.[25] According to one report, Slimane and Lakdar "fell over each other in their haste to get out of the Congo to give as adverse a report as they could concoct of what they had seen and learned."[26] Nevertheless they repeated assurances of Algerian aid to both parties.[27]

Meanwhile Agostinho Neto flew to Algiers on his own quest for Algerian support. On February 4, the second anniversary of nationalist upheaval in Luanda, he joined MPLA representative Dr. Eduardo dos Santos at ceremonies opening a local MPLA office.[28] Present for the occasion were President Ben Bella, other top Algerian officials, and several members of the diplomatic corps, including the Chinese, Czechoslovak, and Bulgarian ambassadors.[29] Jacques Vergès, editor and ideologue of the influential weekly *Révolution africaine* spoke, hailing the MPLA's assault upon the "gigantic imperialist octopus" that dominated all of Southern Africa,[30] and Algerian television and radio gave the occasion extensive coverage. Dr. Neto and Dr. dos Santos also had "excellent" private discussions with Ben Bella. Then Neto proceeded on to Rabat, Morocco, where he attended a second North African ceremony commemorating February 4, 1961.[31]

By assuming the role of mediator between and supporter of both Angolan movements, Algeria became increasingly involved in the internal politics of Angolan nationalism. It made arms and training available to both FNLA and MPLA forces, although Algeria favored the MPLA, which welcomed (whereas Roberto and the FNLA avoided) Algerian offers of "good offices" (for unity) and military volunteers.[32] The prospect of Algerian volunteers gave rise to a host of questions in Léopoldville, among them that they might be drawn into internecine quarrels and military encounters between rival Angolans. Pressure increased on both the Angolans and their Congolese hosts to work for a common Angolan political front and a common military high command. On the other hand, Algiers apparently did not analyze the logistics and expense of transporting and supplying Algerian volunteer units.[33] And it seems unlikely that it could have obtained the necessary approval and cooperation of a Congolese government that was inevitably concerned about the potentially disruptive implications of such an influx. Whatever the offer's degree of seriousness or feasibility, however, repeated mention of it in the Algerian press sustained the notion that the Angolan conflict might be "internationalized" by Algerian intervention.[34]

HOST-STATE STAKES: CONGO-LÉOPOLDVILLE

If the MPLA enjoyed an advantage over the FNLA in relations with Algeria, the opposite held for Congolese relations. In March 1963, shortly after his arrival back in the Congolese capital from lobbying abroad, Agostinho Neto sent open letters to President Joseph Kasavubu and Premier Cyrille Adoula complaining of discrimination against his movement. The central government, he wrote, had arrested and seized the arms of MPLA soldiers but granted freedom of movement and even a training base to those of the FNLA.[35] In March, two MPLA units crossing Congolese territory en route to the border of Angola's eastern Lunda district were arrested, disarmed, and jailed in Luluabourg, Kasai.[36] Neto detailed MPLA grievances in a letter to the Congolese Parliament: despite démarches by Morocco and Algeria, the Congolese government refused to authorize the MPLA to receive North African arms and munitions.[37]

Past MPLA association with "leftist" Congolese opposition elements, such as Christophe Gbenye[38] and Antoine Gizenga, contrasted with Roberto's close personal ties to Premier Adoula[39] and other government leaders. As Mário de Andrade noted, several UPA leaders had participated in the development of the Congo's nationalist movement. In return, they quite naturally received "personal support" and "easier access to certain ministers." Contrastingly MPLA leaders had only Angolan, no Congolese, roots—and could not rewrite history. Nevertheless in late April 1963, Andrade indicated that the Congo, increasingly torn by internal divisions and unclear about its policy on the issue of Angolan unity, was to "a certain degree" aiding "everyone." When discriminated against, the MPLA protested and, he said, "generally obtain[ed] satisfaction."[40]

The MPLA cultivated ties with Abako officials in the Lower Congo, a number of whom had long harbored antipathy toward the UPA. In return for a right to function in Lower Congo areas, the MPLA arranged for the refugee-medical services and relief supplies of its CVAAR to be available to the local (Abakist) Congolese community.[41]

At the outset of 1963, Congo-Léopoldville offered exiled Angolan nationalists their only access route to the interior of Angola. Of the Congo's 1,327-mile border with Angola, only the northwest frontier, which sliced through Bakongo country, was open to the nationalists. Because of the length and related hazards of communication lines from Léopoldville southward to the border, it was difficult to transport arms and extend insurgency operations deep into the Angolan interior.

The importance of the Congo as a contiguous-host state grew considerably on January 14, 1963, when the leader of the breakaway province of Katanga, Moïse Tshombe, capitulated to United Nations troops and announced that he and his ministers "were prepared to declare" their secession "terminated."[42] As a polyglot U.N. expeditionary force occupied Katanga's major urban centers, both the MPLA and FNLA announced their intention to establish operational bases in that strategic province, which had escaped Léopoldville's jurisdiction during two and a half years of de facto independence.[43]

Until the end of Tshombe's regime, the Portuguese government gave open encouragement and clandestine aid to the Katanga secessionists. Shortly before the final collapse of Katangese resistance, Adrian Porter of the Associated Press reported the arrival in Kolwezi, Katanga, of a train from Lobito loaded with arms, ammunition, and gasoline.[44]

With the defeat of Tshombe's forces, Katangese gendarmes and mercenaries fled to Angola where, Premier Adoula soon charged, they began regrouping and preparing for a new military venture against the Congo.[45] As of March approximately eighteen thousand other gendarmes were still roaming at large in the Katangese bush.[46] Thus it was with understandable caution that Adoula considered Angolan requests for an operational base in

Katanga. He did not wish to provide provocation or pretext for a Portuguese-backed incursion into the recuperated province before his government had consolidated its authority.

In a maneuver typical of his political style, however, Roberto did obtain Adoula's permission to send a personal representative to Katanga to begin building a political apparatus there among Angolan refugees and émigrés. For the assignment, he chose his trusted Bakongo aide and past itinerant administrator over the Fuesse-São Salvador zone of northern Angola, José Manuel Peterson. Peterson arrived in Elizabethville in February 1963. Though accredited as a representative of the GRAE, he set about creating a more narrowly conceived local committee of the UPA.[47]

While the MPLA waited in vain for permission to operate in Katanga, Roberto, acting through Peterson, began organizing a UPA apparatus directly responsible to himself. He short-circuited his PDA partners, who had seen in Katanga a possibility for expanding their ethnic base beyond the limits of the Bazombo community of the north. The PDA had circulated political tracts in Katanga in an effort to establish a presence of its own and tried to persuade Roberto to allow it as well as the UPA to organize in the province. Alternatively it proposed that Angolans in Katanga be recruited directly into an integrated FNLA.[48] Perhaps partly in retaliation for the PDA veto of his plan to elevate the UPA labor affiliate (LGTA) into full FNLA membership status, Roberto vetoed any PDA role in Katanga, thereby destroying its chance to recruit within a non-Bakongo community.[49]

Roberto found it more difficult to prevent Jonas Savimbi from building an independent political base in Katanga. Savimbi had not been consulted on the choice of or on the political instructions given to Peterson. And he was determined to use his position as UPA secretary-general, to build an organization loyal to himself among (Ovimbundu, Chokwe, and other) Angolans residing in Katanga.[50]

Much of the UPA's regional strength in Léopoldville and the Lower Congo derived from the perceived ethnic legitimacy of its senior Bakongo leadership, notably such figures as Eduardo Pinock and Borralho Lulendo. In Katanga, however, by bypassing Savimbi and his Ovimbundu supporters and relying instead upon a Bakongo "outsider" to build a political organization, Roberto defied communal reality in trying to extend his personal power.

Within a short time, José Peterson was at odds with the local committee that he had selected. Resentful of what they considered to be Peterson's autocratic behavior and privileged access to party funds (which he allegedly squandered on a local Bakwanga brewery venture), two of its most prominent members resigned. The head of the UPA committee, Jorge Jonatão, an Ochimbundu from Nova Sintra (Bié district) and a colleague, David Afonso, who had served in the Portuguese army, left and joined up with two of Roberto's bitterest political enemies to form a new Angolan movement, the *União Nacional Angolana* (UNA).[51]

The collapse of Katanga's secession had found ELNA's original chief of staff, Marcos Kassanga, and the LGTA's ex-secretary-general, André Kassinda, in West Africa lobbying against Roberto and the UPA with whom they had broken in March 1962.[52] Since August of that year, they had been traveling about Africa, speaking in the name of a paper *Comité Préparatoire du Congrès Populaire Angolais* (CPCP) and seeking external support for the idea of a broadly inclusive congress of Angolan nationalists that would create a "single National Liberation Front."[53] Then in February 1963, seeing Katanga's reintegration into the Congo as an opportunity for them to establish a new political base within reach of Angola's eastern-central boundaries, Kassanga and Kassinda dropped their CPCP junketing and hastened to Elizabethville.

They quickly exploited Roberto's failure to follow the political formula that had assured his UPA of a solid northern power base—his failure to rely upon indigenous, ethnic leadership to mobilize popular support and build a local party structure. With energetic salesmanship and acceptable ethnic credentials, Kassinda (a Sele who spoke some Umbundu) and Kassanga (a Ganguela) worked with Jorge Jonatão and David Afonso to attract support away from the UPA. By late May, when he sent a high-level UPA investigatory mission to Elizabethville and simultaneously appointed an Ochimbundu to be the official UPA representative, Roberto's Katanga operation was a shambles. The UPA mission, headed by Vice-President Rosário Neto (Mbundu) and Reverend Fernando Gourjel (mestiço), compounded local resentment to the extent that it was taken as another example of dictation from Léopoldville.[54]

João Chisseva, an Ochimbundu and former leader of the *Juventude Cristã de Angola* (JCA) inside Angola, who had fled to the Congo and joined the UPA in mid-1962, took over as UPA representative in Elizabethville at the end of May.[55] But Peterson re-

mained, as "GRAE representative," and as such continued to control funds and access to Roberto. When Chisseva arrived in
Elizabethville, he "found the Party almost without members."[56]
Kassanga and Kassinda had astutely played upon anti-Bakongo
sentiment that derived from 1961 reports that UPA-Bakongo insurgents massacred Ovimbundu and other non-Bakongo *con-
tratados* (contract laborers) in Angola's northern coffee country.[57]
They had also cultivated good relations with local officials, establishing symbiotic ties with the ethnic *Association des Tshokwe du Congo
de l'Angola et de la Rhodésie* (ATCAR) led by Ambroise Muhunga.[58]
Fancying himself the future ruler, or Mwachisenge, of a modern-
day Chokwe state,[59] Muhunga hoped to gain control of the local
provincial government of Lualaba as a step toward that goal. The
westernmost of three new provinces then being carved out of
Katanga, Lualaba extended west and north from Kolwezi along the
Angolan border. In return for a UNA pledge not to compete with
ATCAR for Chokwe membership, Muhunga undertook both to
encourage other (non-Chokwe) Angolans to join the anti-Roberto
UNA and also to harass the UPA in the Kolwezi area.[60]

The UNA held an organizational conference at Elizabethville,
July 5–7, 1963, elected Kassinda president, and adopted an elaborate constitution and hortatory program.[61] While UPA representatives flew back and forth between Léopoldville and Katanga on
Congolese military planes, Kassinda maneuvered nimbly in the
local thicket of Katanga politics. He fashioned a new exile movement within the central-southern stream of Angolan nationalism.

Holden Roberto concentrated less on Katanga than upon nurtur-
ing his political ties at the center of Congolese politics—
Léopoldville. And in May, when Premier Adoula flew off to Addis
Ababa to attend the founding conference of the Organization of
African Unity (OAU), Roberto was on Adoula's plane.

PAN-AFRICAN CONTEXT

Algeria and Congo-Léopoldville played leading roles within the
opposing blocs into which African states had been organized since
1961. Algeria was associated with Ghana, Guinea, Mali, Morocco, and
United Arab Republic (UAR) in the Casablanca group, which was
the more assertive in supporting the goals of pan-African unity and
political/racial liberation in Southern Africa.[62] Congo-Léopoldville
belonged to the larger, twenty-state Monrovia group, which was

generally more conservative in its approach to the issues of unity and liberation. A proposed charter for continental association drawn up by a meeting of Monrovia powers at Lagos, Nigeria, in January 1962 elaborated goals and structures for interstate cooperation, opposed "any intervention, directly or indirectly, for any reason whatever, in the internal affairs of any member," and made no mention of the colonial and racial issues of Southern Africa.[63] When the Monrovia and Casablanca groups finally came together in Addis Ababa (May 22–25, 1963) to form the OAU, they adopted a charter similar to what had been proposed at Lagos—including a nonintervention clause and machinery for the peaceful settlement of disputes among members.[64] But in a concession to the Casablancans, they also agreed to make one of the OAU's purposes "to eradicate all forms of colonialism from the continent of Africa."[65] In line with the precedent established by the Pan-African Freedom Movement for East, Central and Southern Africa (PAFMECSA)'s modest Freedom Fund for liberation movements,[66] they armed the OAU with a special fund for the purpose of aiding national liberation movements.

In the weeks preceding the Addis Ababa conference, the MPLA worked closely with Algeria's Ben Bella who by then had assumed the role of leading international spokesman for the Angolan cause. Mário de Andrade held strategy discussions with the Algerian premier in Algiers,[67] while two teams of Algerian diplomats visited West and East African countries to lay the groundwork for what one of them described as "something solid" on Angola at the Addis Ababa meeting.[68]

As "an intellectual on loan to the revolution," Andrade told the Algiers press that he and the MPLA had fully agreed to what Ben Bella planned to propose at the forthcoming summit. He predicted that Portugal and its NATO allies would be forced to reckon with concerted African diplomacy. Not even a Portuguese alliance with South Africa, he reasoned, could long withstand the pressures of a solid all-African alliance. Andrade envisaged pan-African initiatives producing an international economic boycott of Portugal and leading to its expulsion from the United Nations. Anticipating that the Addis Ababa meeting would demand unity in Angolan ranks in return for material assistance, he exuded optimism. He affirmed publicly that the MPLA's army had grown to a force of ten thousand men headed by an elite cadre of 250 officers trained in guerrilla tactics.[69] He cited Algeria, Morocco, Ghana, and the UAR as sources of financial and material support. And he called for a study of the possibility of introducing "African volunteers" into the Angolan struggle.[70]

For his part, Holden Roberto, working with the Congolese government, proposed the creation of an "inter-African body to aid those who are fighting" and "coordination of the activities of liberation movements in Southern Africa." In an FNLA memorandum, which made no mention of African volunteers or of an Angolan common front, Roberto declared that assistance should not be tied to ideological options (a form of "interference"), and he generally stressed nationalist autonomy. "Rational" inter-African assistance would enable Angolans to elaborate long-term plans, accelerate the armed struggle, assist refugees, and train political-administrative cadres. As for coordinating regional liberation strategy, the FNLA indicated that it planned to convene in Léopoldville a meeting of "all the liberation movements of Southern Africa that [were] determined to wage an armed struggle in order to liberate their countries."[71] Speaking to a group of Southern African students in New York the previous December, Roberto had pledged that once Angola won its independence, it would not hesitate to give "moral and material support to all those African brothers whose liberation [might] require an armed combat."[72]

Ben Bella "set the temper" for the debates at the long-awaited summit gathering in Ethiopia.[73] Urging his African brothers "to die a little, even completely, so that the peoples still under colonial domination [might] be freed and African unity [might] not be a vain word," Ben Bella announced that ten thousand Algerian volunteers stood ready to join the fight in Angola.[74] Caught up in the rhetoric of the occasion, Uganda's Prime Minister Milton Obote offered his country as a "training ground" for freedom fighters,[75] and President Sékou Touré of Guinea proposed that every independent African state should contribute 1 percent of its national budget to the OAU's liberation fund.[76] The conference voted to establish a coordinating committee, better known as the African Liberation Committee (ALC), with responsibility for managing a special fund raised by voluntary contributions of unspecified amounts and for harmonizing collective assistance to liberation movements.

ALC membership was carefully distributed. It included three former Casablanca states—Algeria, Guinea, and the UAR—and Uganda (a backer of Kwame Nkrumah's proposals for a pan-African government). Balancing these were four former Monrovia states—Congo-Léopoldville, Ethiopia, Nigeria, and Senegal. The ninth, pivotal member, Tanganyika, provided the ALC with its headquarters (the ex-PAFMECSA office in Dar es Salaam), its chairman (Foreign Minister Oscar Kambona), and its staff (headed by Sebastian Chale). Conspicuously missing from the committee was Ghana.

President Nkrumah had antagonized many of his colleagues by pushing unflaggingly for acceptance of his own, more ambitious, formula for African unity. With considerable fanfare at Addis Ababa, he presented each head of state with a copy of a new manifesto, *Africa Must Unite*, which spelled out his formula for a confederal African union.[77] Nkrumah pressed his case well after it was hopeless, and in doing so, he isolated himself—a rejected prophet. Among those who criticized the Ghanaian leader was Holden Roberto. He said of Nkrumah: "He talks big but does little. He does not want to help, he wants to give orders." Citing Algeria, Tunisia, Congo-Léopoldville, and Nigeria as the countries that had really helped, Roberto went on: "Ghana makes a big shout about the nothing it gives us. Nigeria gave us 25,000 pounds sterling and said nothing . . . We know now who our friends are."[78] A strong advocate of common-front unity, of course, the Nkrumah government had long ceased to support Roberto.[79]

The May summit did agree with Ghana and Algeria, however, on the issue of liberation group unity. It "earnestly invite[d] all national liberation movements to coordinate their efforts by establishing common action fronts wherever necessary so as to strengthen the effectiveness of their struggle and the rational use of the concerted assistance given them."[80]

THE CONGO ALLIANCE

On the fringes of the summit meeting, Holden Roberto held discussions with leaders of other liberation groups. He then proposed to Adoula to invite not "all" (as proposed in his FNLA memorandum) but rather a select group of movements—one per territory—to establish politico-military headquarters in Congo-Léopoldville.[81]

With Katanga's secession behind him, Adoula was ready to assume a new pan-African role. Doing so could help to establish the legitimacy of his government in the eyes of ex-Casablanca states (Algeria, Guinea, UAR) who had earlier supported a dissident "Lumumbist" regime led by Antoine Gizenga in Stanleyville. From the Congolese point of view, however, it did seem prudent to restrict the invitation to a list of compatible, noncompetitive movements. Internal conflict, confusion, and political maneuvering occasioned by FNLA and MPLA rivalry probably weighed heavily in Adoula's decision to accept Roberto's nominees for participation in a Congo Alliance of congruous liberation movements.

Adoula invited to fly with him from Addis Ababa to Léopoldville in his private plane the leaders of groups with which Roberto and the UPA had a natural affinity on at least two counts. Their movements were uniracial and skeptical of intellectuals and multiracialism and nationalist and wary of ideological issues. The leaders were Paulo Gumane, president of the *União Democrática Nacional de Moçambique* (UDENAMO); Nana Mahomo, London representative of the Pan-Africanist Congress (PAC) of South Africa; Sam Nujoma, president of the South West Africa Peoples' Organization (SWAPO); and Reverend Ndbaningi Sithole, national chairman of the Zimbabwe African People's Union (ZAPU).

Carefully guarding his privileged access to Aboula and other Congolese ministers, Roberto acted as an unofficial extension of the Congolese government in organizing the new alliance. And just as the MPLA had played a preeminent role in 1961 in the creation of the CONCP interterritorial alliance, the UPA/GRAE now took the lead in building a counteralliance. Membership in the multiracialist CONCP automatically disqualified a movement for participation in the Congo grouping. Roberto had a seasoned (if somewhat ambivalent) acquaintanceship with Eduardo Mondlane, whom he had only recently recognized publicly as the principal spokesman for Mozambique nationalism.[82] But Mondlane's *Frente de Libertação de Moçambique* (FRELIMO) was allied with the MPLA in the CONCP. Though Mondlane was no less angry for the reasoning, Roberto established formal relations with UDENAMO.

The scope of the CONCP was limited to Portuguese Africa; but collectively and individually, its members related to other Southern African movements who shared similar racial and ideological perspectives. As early as mid-1962, CONCP secretary Marcelino dos Santos (FRELIMO) held discussions with the African National Congress (ANC) of South Africa and announced that the CONCP and ANC would "pursue their cooperation" and undertake "to tighten their links."[83] Thus although the CONCP was intensively Luso-African (including Guinea-Bissau and São Tomé) and the Congo Alliance was more a regional (Southern Africa) grouping, the two were inherently competitive.[84] So while Casablanca and Monrovia states were coming together, African liberation movements were polarizing into antagonistic leagues.

The Adoula government extended interim financial assistance to the five movements of the new alliance to tide them over until the OAU liberation fund became operational. It also promised expanded facilities to house the Angolan Government in Exile and a *Maison des nationalistes* to provide office space for the other movements.[85] The Angolans offered to share facilities of the Kin-

TABLE 2.1

LIBERATION ALLIANCE SYSTEM

		CONCP	Congo Alliance	
Portuguese territories	São Tomé	CLSTP		
	Guinea-Bissau	PAIGC		
	Mozambique	FRELIMO	UDENAMO	
	Angola	MPLA	FNLA	
	South Africa	ANC	PAC	Southern region
	South West Africa		SWAPO[a]	
	Rhodesia		ZANU [b]	

[a]UPA/GRAE interest in contiguous South West Africa outstripped its concern for distant Guinea-Bissau. This was indicative of the regional focus in its alliance system. Already in mid-1962, Roberto had reached an accord with Jacob Kuhangua, national secretary of SWAPO, for collaboration between their respective movements. John Marcum, *The Angolan Revolution: Anatomy of an Explosion (1950–1962)* (Cambridge: The MIT Press, 1969), 1: 310–311. According to Kuhangua: "One of the main purposes of signing an agreement was to signal to the world community our desire to form in the future a Federation of the Independent States of Angola, Bechuanaland [Botswana] and South West Africa governed by a Central Government which will eventually become part of the Federal States of Africa. . . . The present boundaries existing between our countries were created by the imperialist colonizers. . . . And it is our desire to destroy these lines." "Angola and South West Africa Sign an Agreement," in UPA Information Service, New York, *Free Angola* (Sept. 1962): 5.

[b]Reverend Sithole and his supporters broke with ZAPU president Joshua Nkomo in July 1963 and formed a new movement, the *Zimbabwe African National Union* (ZANU). Sithole prevailed upon Roberto to recognize ZANU as the rightful heir to membership in the Congo Alliance. This role was contested by ZAPU representatives until the time the alliance collapsed in mid-1964.

kuzu training base with their allies, who, in turn, hoped to see their forces move southward with the advance of the Angolan revolution.

A CONGOLESE COUP

Parallel to FNLA-MPLA rivalry, Congolese-Algerian competition for influence in Angolan affairs intensified during May and June, 1963. According to Dr. Eduardo dos Santos, in Algiers, Algerian volunteers were flocking to the local MPLA office—though dos Santos seemed to manifest more interest in obtaining material and financial help and military training.[86] Contending for Algerian aid, Roberto sent Johnny Edouard to Algiers to open a GRAE office.[87] Edouard arrived in time to meet Ben Bella just before the Algerian leader left for the May Addis Ababa conference and declared on the Algiers radio that ELNA's Algerian-trained officers were now training eight thousand Angolan soldiers in the Congo for guerrilla warfare in Angola. He added that Algerian military assistance to GRAE included bazookas, mortars, cannons, and heavy machine guns.[88] Johnny Edouard's Algiers mission was soon complicated, however, when *Time* magazine quoted Roberto in Addis Ababa as having "snapped" the following response to Ben Bella's offer of ten thousand volunteers: "We will kill them if they show up. We are nobody's puppets."[89] In Algiers Edouard disavowed the "alleged statement" as a "complete fantasy,"[90] and Roberto cabled Ben Bella repudiating *Time*'s "erroneous interpretation" of his position and "regretting that opponents have profited from this unhappy event in an attempt to destroy the cordial atmosphere of our relations."[91] He did not, however, invite volunteers.

Meanwhile Ben Bella continued to assert his role as champion of the Angolan cause. He warned the United States that it would do itself "much harm in Africa" if it placed Azores bases "ahead of independence for Angola."[92] And on June 14, the Algerian Foreign Ministry announced that Ben Bella would tour Africa in September seeking financial and military support for Angolan nationalists.[93]

The fact remained that all external aid, including possible volunteer units, would have to pass through the Congo. This was publicly acknowledged in Algiers by the MPLA and the FLN journal, *Révolution africaine*, both of which criticized the Léopoldville government for favoring the UPA/ELNA with military facilities to the exclusion of the MPLA.[94]

Some observers, such as Aquino Bragança, a Goan journalist who had worked earlier with the CONCP secretariat in Rabat, saw hope for the MPLA with the appointment in April of a "young leftwing sociologist," Augustin Mabika-Kalanda, as Congolese foreign minister. Replacing Justin Bomboko, a close friend of Roberto, Mabika-Kalanda, a recent graduate of the Ford Foundation–funded *Ecole Nationale de Droit et d'Administration*, told Bragança that he favored the unification of Angola's conflicted nationalist movements. Concerning the ELNA base at Kinkuzu, Mabika-Kalanda commented: "The one military base that the Congo has put at the disposition of nationalist forces should be for the use of all nationalist forces, with no exclusions." This view, concluded *Révolution africaine*, augered well for a new, more neutral policy on the part of the Congolese government.[95]

It was not the young, intellectual Mabika-Kalanda, however, but political veterans Adoula and Bomboko (then minister of justice) who fashioned Congolese policy on Angolan matters. On June 11, Premier Adoula met aboard a Congo River boat with President Fulbert Youlou of neighboring Congo-Brazzaville. In a joint communiqué issued after four hours of talks, the two leaders announced that as a follow-up to the Addis Ababa OAU meeting, they would refuse to accept any Portuguese invitations for diplomatic discussions until Lisbon had begun to decolonize Angola.[96] Adoula also reportedly reached a verbal understanding with Youlou, an erstwhile ally of secessionist Moïse Tshombe,[97] concerning relations with Angolan nationalists. Though Youlou promptly reneged on this accord (possibly under French pressure),[98] Adoula proceeded with unilateral action. On June 29, 1963, his government extended de jure recognition to the GRAE. The Congolese foreign ministry announced:

Considering the right of peoples to determine their own fate,

Anxious to make its contribution to hasten the decolonization of the African continent,

Desirous of putting the recommendations of the Addis Ababa Conference into effect,

Conscious of the responsibility incumbent upon it in this regard given its geographic location,

Estimating that the valiant Angolan people have, in two years of fighting, demonstrated their determination to win their independence,

Considering the persistence of the *Portuguese Government* in pursuing a policy condemned by reason of history, world opinion and international organizations,

Noting that the recent appeal made to that Government to reconsider its attitude has had no result,

The Republic of the Congo-Léopoldville grants *de jure* recognition to the Revolutionary Government of Angola from this day forward and will provide it with all aid and assistance with a view toward the realization of the patriotic and legitimate aspirations of its people.[99]

By this move, which Roberto greeted "with profound satisfaction,"[100] Adoula asserted Congolese paramountcy within a mounting pan-African involvement in Angolan affairs. It represented a logical extension of his earlier decision to limit the Congo Alliance to one liberation movement per country and, short of curtailing MPLA activities, enhanced the prestige of the GRAE. His action was denounced as unwarranted and unwise by such pro-MPLA states as Morocco and Ghana.[101] More ominously, it brought forth angry reactions in the Portuguese press[102] and risked provoking reprisals by the Portuguese government.

Lisbon recalled its chargé d'affaires from Léopoldville after the latter had delivered a strong protest to the Adoula government and announced that it would be "forced to make a general revision of [its] attitude on problems of interest" to itself and Léopoldville.[103] By so limiting its response, however, the Portuguese government avoided the full diplomatic break that would have cost it a valuable low-key presence in Léopoldville.[104] That presence served the interests of some five thousand Portuguese entrepreneurs and traders in the Congo-Léopoldville,[105] assured Lisbon of a constant flow of intelligence data gathered by African informants, and safeguarded a useful manipulative role in the intrigues of Angolan exile politics. As for the Congolese government, it depended heavily upon the Benguela Railroad for the export of Katangan copper and cobalt and was not eager to proceed to the total break in relations that its formal recognition of Angolan insurgents made logical—logical at least under international law. Neither party showed much interest in pressing the legal issue.[106]

Clearly stunned by the Congo's action, the MPLA Steering Committee rushed out a statement calling upon MPLA militants to remain calm and at their posts pending a full explanation of what had happened. MPLA leaders, it noted, had recently had cordial talks with Adoula and Mabika-Kalanda concerning the problem of Angolan unity.[107]

Given fulsome American financial and material support for both the United Nations campaign in Katanga and the Adoula government in Léopoldville, there were those who saw an American hand in Adoula's sudden recognition of the GRAE. Indicative of just how prepared some were to see American mischief in such matters, even Ben Bella's earlier offer of arms to the FNLA had been interpreted in the French press as a nod by Algiers to Washington.[108] To Premier Salazar, given the "very special relations" existing between the United States and the Congo, it came as "no surprise" when the Adoula government "recognized *de jure* a kind of terrorist association set up at Léopoldville for the purpose of operating in Angola and avowedly supported by funds from Americans."[109]

Specifically the fact that Assistant Secretary of State G. Mennen Williams visited Léopoldville and met with Adoula a few days before the announcement of recognition struck some as circumstantial evidence of U.S. involvement in the decision. Lúcio Lára interpreted "the sudden [revolutionary] solidarity" manifested by a Congolese government "inspired by American imperialists" as part of an overall American plan to prevent the development of a truly revolutionary war in Southern Africa where Americans hoped to protect important economic interests.[110] To others, the Congo's action simply suggested that, given American sympathy for Roberto's movement, Adoula could recognize it without fear of incurring serious American displeasure.

Did the evidence bear out such interpretations? On May 21, 1963, President Kennedy named Admiral George Anderson as ambassador to Lisbon.[111] By dispatching the admiral from the Pentagon, where he was a center of intramural controversy, to Lisbon, Kennedy reinforced the weight of the military in the formulation of American policy toward Portugal and its colonies. The appointment increased Washington's sensitivity to Portuguese demands for continued evidence of fidelity as a NATO ally in return for continued use of the Azores bases.

If the Department of Defense was bent on placating Lisbon for Atlantic reasons, the Department of State and the White House were anxious that the successful conclusion to long, costly, and complicated U.N. operations in Katanga not be jeopardized by action that might provoke the Portuguese into permitting, even helping, Tshombe's exiled forces mount a new secessionist campaign from bases in Angola. Moreover, although Roberto enjoyed some sympathy (by no means unanimous) within the State Department's Bureau of African Affairs and was generally considered as a reasonably friendly nationalist, American officials did not hold his "government" to be worthy of diplomatic recognition. GRAE had yet to prove itself as either broadly representative of the Angolan

people or capable of extending its authority over and of command-
ing support within more than a small northern sector of the country.[112]

During his June conversations with G. Mennen Williams, Adoula
did raise the question of Angola and his intentions concerning the
GRAE. According to what Adoula later told Roberto about this discussion, however, Williams attempted to dissuade the Congolese
leader from carrying out his plan to recognize the Angolan exile
regime. Adoula held firm against American counsel that recognition would be premature and imprudent. Embittered by what he
saw as an effort by a Kennedy administration that he had once so
admired to undercut him politically, Roberto denounced "American hypocrisy." Americans, he said, pay "lip service to self-
determination" but supply Portugal "with the arms that are used to
kill us."[113] Looking back upon his talks with Adoula, Williams subsequently confirmed that he did undertake to convince Adoula that
"his [proposed] act of recognition" would constitute a "mistake."[114]
U.S. embassy officials joined Williams in trying to "dissuade" the
Congolese. The principal American concern was that recognition
would "obviously impair" the possibility of "meaningful discussions" between the Portuguese and Africans, discussions "which
in our view will inevitably lead" to the topic of self-determination.
Moreover, recognition seemed to go against the "strong desire of
Africans for a unified nationalist movement behind which they can
rally." When Adoula persisted in his decision, the State Department then instructed American embassies in Africa and Europe to
dispel any notion that the United States "engineered" it and to
"stress our hope that constructive dialogue between Portugal and
Africans can [still] be initiated." In Washington's view, Congolese
motives were "based on pursuit of leadership in Africa and sparked
by a desire to avoid large-scale Algerian involvement in Angolan
nationalist activity in the Congo."[115]

YOULOU'S RESPONSE AND A SECOND FRONT

The day following the GRAE's recognition, a smartly uniformed,
well-drilled contingent of ELNA soldiers paraded down Léopoldville's broad avenues and past President Kasavubu's reviewing
stand as participants in Congolese independence day celebrations.
Ten days later, Rosário Neto, GRAE minister of information, announced a new series of twice-weekly Radio Léopoldville broad-

casts, the Voice of Free Angola, to be beamed southward in French, Portuguese, Kikongo, Kimbundu, Chokwe, and Umbundu.[116]

Not to be outdone, President Youlou of Brazzaville proceeded with an Angolan plan of his own. Two days after Léopoldville's coup de théâtre, he convened a roundtable meeting of six Angolan movements on his side of the river. Present were delegations from the FNLA (led by Holden Roberto and Emmanuel Kunzika), MPLA (headed by Vice-President Domingos da Silva),[117] and four Bakongo groups, the *Mouvement de Défense des Intérêts de l'Angola* (MDIA), the *Movimento Nacional Angolano* (MNA), the *União Nacional dos Trabalhadores de Angola* (UNTA, informally linked to the MPLA) and the *Mouvement pour la Libération de l'Enclave de Cabinda* (MLEC). In his opening remarks, Youlou implicitly rejected Léopoldville's diplomatic recognition of the GRAE and enjoined the assembled movements "not to leave this hall" before having first realized "unity of movement and action."[118] The FNLA restated its standard contention that it already represented a united front to which others might adhere.[119] But the other five groups, aware of the political advantage gained by the FNLA/GRAE as a result of Léopoldville's nod and encouraged by the Youlou government, began serious discussions. Abbé Youlou had something special in mind for Cabinda, so MLEC dropped out.[120] However, another Bakongo group not initially involved, the *Ngwizani a Kongo* (Ngwizako), joined in the conversations underway.

A few days later, the MPLA revealed that the five groups had reached a preliminary agreement to form a nationalist "cartel" under a joint coordinating committee, which would in turn study the possibility of creating a "true" nationalist front.[121] Then on July 10, in a press conference at the Léopoldville Zoo Restaurant, Dr. Neto announced that the Brazzaville roundtable discussions had culminated in the formation of a new *Frente Democrática de Libertação de Angola* (FDLA).[122]

Neto apparently reasoned that by creating an MPLA-Bakongo alliance, or a front of his own, he would be in a stronger position from which to negotiate for entry into the GRAE. Congolese recognition, he declared, "seems to indicate that in the wake of the historic Addis Ababa Conference, the government of this brother country has determined to place at the disposal of Angolan nationalism a useful instrument for accelerating decolonisation in Africa." "This Government in Exile," he continued, "will be able to contribute to a more rapid solution of current problems facing our struggle." Thus it was "desirable" that the GRAE become sufficiently representative to gain the recognition of all the states of Africa and, above all, "to command respect for itself in the eyes of all Angolans."[123]

Thus, in a dramatic about-face, Dr. Neto sought to join what he had previously dismissed as a meritless marionette: "We wish to say that the integration of representatives of the FDLA into the existing GRAE is necessary. We also wish to say that the Democratic Front is ready to participate in this Government."[124]

After thanking President Youlou for his efforts "to conciliate and unify Angolans," Neto declared that the movements that formed the Democratic Front had agreed upon a platform demanding immediate independence. And while desirous of a negotiated settlement with Portugal, consistent with earlier MPLA statements on the subject,[125] they rejected "any solution of a reformist character" that might perpetuate foreign domination under a new form.[126] For several FDLA members, this represented a considerable radicalization of previous positions and led to both internal upheavals and timely, revolutionary conversions.

UNTA

Long a supporter of the MPLA and its revolutionary and common front policy, UNTA (along with its recently created youth wing) was the most logical candidate for membership in the new front.[127] As the MPLA's unofficial labor affiliate,[128] UNTA had forged useful international contacts (for example, a UNTA delegation had attended 1963 May Day celebrations in China).[129] Like the MPLA's newer FDLA allies, its leadership and membership came from (Angolan) Bakongo émigré and refugee communities in the Congo.

MNA

The three other FDLA adherents were linked to three Bakongo ethnic subgroups. Of these movements, the smallest was an obscure association of the Sorongo, a people who inhabit the north coastal area of Angola between the Congo estuary and Ambriz.[130] The *Movimento Nacional Angolano* (MNA) had recently been reorganized under a new president, Francisco Mayembe (or Maiembe), one of those who had resigned from the UPA in December 1961 in opposition to Roberto's demand for more militant tactics.[131] Previously committed to nonviolence, the MNA had also been "pro-unity"—and was for a time associated with Kassinda and Kassanga's *Comité Préparatoire du Congrès Populaire Angolais* (CPCP). More recently it had established close relations with UNTA.[132]

Ngwizako

The oldest of the three Bakongo parties to join the FDLA was the faction-ridden, predominantly Catholic, Bakongo royalist Ngwizako—or more correctly, a faction of it. Long frustrated in its attempts to negotiate with Lisbon for the restoration of an autonomous Kongo kingdom centered at São Salvador,[133] Ngwizako had suffered from the fragmentation that often accompanies political failure. The *Aliança* faction that joined the FDLA represented a breakaway group that despaired of achieving political concessions by appealing to or collaborating with the Portuguese.[134]

What remained the non-FDLA hard-core *Associação* faction of Ngwizako held a congress at Léopoldville from June 29 to July 1, announced the reconciliation of three estranged "grand councillors,"[135] and declared its intention to send a delegation to São Salvador to enthrone a successor to the late Kongolese king, Dom Pedro VIII. To this end, negotiations were to be resumed with the Portuguese embassies in Léopoldville and Brazzaville. With recent OAU and Congolese initiatives in mind, Ngwizako's unreconstructed royalists complained that African countries were "endeavoring to sabotage" the historic Kongo kingdom. And on July 8, they denounced those who, by joining the FDLA, had implicitly recognized the GRAE.[136] In sum, there were now two Ngwizakos. The smaller of the two was prepared to forsake the dream of a new Muchikongo monarchy. It joined forces with old enemies, those whom the Kongo royalists had long considered to be the favorites of "the Apostles of the Protestant Missions,"[137] (the partisans of Angolan nationalism).

MDIA

The third group of Bakongo activists to join the FDLA consisted mainly of Bazombo émigrés. Its members were defectors from a movement that the MPLA had only recently denounced for trying to mislead Angolans and outsiders into believing in the possibility of political reform within Angola.[138] The MPLA had reacted to a March 24 statement by the president of the MDIA, Jean Pierre

M'Bala, who, returned from discussions in Lisbon, had allowed his imagination to soar and predicted that before the end of the year Portugal would organize general elections based upon universal suffrage for a territorial legislature that would then form an African-led government.[139] M'Bala had been traveling to Luanda and Lisbon and holding exuberant press conferences in Léopoldville for over two years.[140] But his political tourism had earned him little more than a few financial handouts. In 1962, the United Nations Special Committee on Territories under Portuguese Administration commented: "During its visit to Léopoldville, the Committee heard the representative of the MDIA and from his statement in reply to questions is convinced that the MDIA is being used by the Portuguese government solely for the purpose of being able to claim that it has the cooperation of some Angolan group."[141]

Sensing that M'Bala's "pacifist policy"[142] was not bearing results, a faction of the MDIA executive committee led by Augustin Kaziluki and Simon Diallo Mingiedi (both of whom had quit the UPA in December 1961 in opposition to armed struggle) broke with M'Bala (who had also left the UPA) in July and jumped aboard the revolutionary bandwagon. While a loyalist faction remained with M'Bala, who flew from Brazzaville to Luanda on July 5 at the invitation of the Angolan governor-general,[143] the others joined the FDLA and publicized their new revolutionary calling. To the press, they announced the creation of a new MDIA "war department" and solicited volunteers for military training abroad.[144]

Nto-Bako Angola

One would-be participant, Nto-Bako, was not included in the FDLA Bakongo lineup. Having served the Portuguese earlier as an instrument through which to harass UPA/ELNA forces and to persuade Bakongo refugees to return to Angola,[145] Nto-Bako had since lost its usefulness, and thus Portuguese favor, and had split into rival factions. On June 10, the leader of one faction dispatched a letter of discouragement to the United Nations. On the basis of a 1961 agreement with Portuguese officials, he reported that Nto-Bako had sent its vice-president, Francisco Thomaz, to Luanda to begin establishing Nto-Bako branches inside the country. According to the letter, however, Francisco Thomaz and his associates had been "incarcerated in various prisons in Angola, where they [were] subject daily to inhuman torture and social injustices."[146]

Like the MDIA's M'Bala, Nto-Bako president Angelino Alberto had been a frequent visitor to Luanda and Lisbon since 1961. His trips had similarly failed to reap significant rewards for his party,[147] and, as a derided symbol of unsuccessful collaboration with Portugal, Alberto was not invited to participate in the Brazzaville roundtable discussions.

It was not long, however, before the Nto-Bako secretary-general, François Lélé, whom Alberto had expelled some months earlier "for failing to obey his instructions,"[148] was declaring his readiness to negotiate an Nto-Bako entry into the FDLA.[149] On July 10, Lélé denounced Alberto, who was then in Luanda, as a PIDE agent and expelled him from the party.[150] And on August 1, *Le progrès* in Léopoldville carried what proved to be a false report that Lélé's faction of Nto-Bako had joined the FDLA. The same edition had a story datelined Luanda based on an interview with Alberto as he boarded a plane en route back to Brazzaville. Alberto asserted that he would now undertake "to rally elements of the MPLA and FDLA to his own party." Agostinho Neto labeled Alberto a "traitor" and decried his efforts "to spread confusion."[151] Confusion there was, and though neither Lélé's nor Alberto's Nto-Bako was in fact ever admitted into the Democratic Front, the FDLA's image suffered from their hopeful embrace.[152]

The MPLA constituted the core of the FDLA. It assumed three key executive posts—president, foreign affairs, war. And together with its long-time ally, UNTA, it controlled five executive posts against four for the Bakongo parties on the FDLA's nine-man executive committee. The committee was expected to carry out "general policy" set by a larger (six delegates per movement) National Council and to "arbitrate" any disputes that might arise between or among member organizations.[153] At the same time, because the new front represented an alliance, not a merger, the MPLA was left autonomous, free to pursue its own interests and policies should its new Bakongo associates prove, after all, reticent revolutionaries.

SCHISM IN THE MPLA

The price that the MPLA would pay for creating a front of its own proved exorbitant, internally and externally. Dr. Neto's willingness to join forces with Bakongo groups widely assumed to have been infiltrated and financed by the Portuguese brought to a head a crisis that had been building within his movement ever since

TABLE 2.2
FDLA: PROJECTED STRUCTURE AND LEADERSHIP

	President	Agostinho Neto	MPLA
	1st Vice-Pres.	Emmanuel Loureiro	Ngwizako
	2d Vice-Pres.	Pascal Luvualu	UNTA
Executive	Foreign Affairs	Mário de Andrade	MPLA
committee	War	Armindo Freitas	MPLA
(9 officers)	Finance	Augustin Kaziluki	MDIA
	Information	José Tito	MNA
	Social Affairs	Bernard Dombele	UNTA
	Interior	Augusto Monteiro	Ngwizako

Policy Committee of National Council

National	President	Francisco Mayembe	MNA
council	1st Vice-Pres.	Daniel Chipenda	MPLA
(6 delegates	2d Vice-Pres.	Pierre Milton M'Vulu	Ngwizako
per movement;	3d Vice-Pres.	Emile M'Bidi Dongala	UNTA
total, 30)			

Source: Based upon FDLA, "Convention du Front Démocratique pour la Libération de l'Angola" (Léopoldville, July 8, 1963, mimeo.) and *Courrrier d'Afrique* (July 16, 1963).

he had assumed its leadership in December 1962. At that time, Neto had been able to defeat what he termed "extremist" elements led by the former secretary-general, Viriato da Cruz. He had simultaneously launched upon a major overhaul of the movement's policies and structures. But he had continued to face internal dissidence.

Matias Miguéis, a veteran nationalist from Novo Redondo and former editor of the MPLA organ *Unidade Angolano*,[154] resigned only a few days after being named first vice-president by the December conference.[155] And in March, the MPLA Steering Committee, referring to "factional, anarchist and anti-revolutionary" activity that preceded[156] and to a "decreasing extent" followed the December conference, announced a crackdown on troublesome militants who exploited "internal democracy" and "freedom to criticize" in order to sabotage the movement. An "anti-revolutionary" faction allegedly even called for a new "national conference" near the Angolan frontier, a meeting expected to "dismiss" the organization's executive leadership. Invoking "military discipline," the Steering Committee cited verbal and physical attacks against party leaders and militants and suspended four persons, including a former Steering Committee member, José Miguel.[157]

Dissidence boiled up again in early July following Congolese recognition of the GRAE and the Brazzaville talks that led to the formation of the FDLA. The challenge to Neto's leadership was once again organized by Viriato da Cruz, who had recently returned from the Chinese-sponsored Asian-African Journalists' Conference at Djakarta, Indonesia (April 20–24).[158] On July 5, da Cruz along with Matias Miguéis convened about fifty of the MPLA's disaffected members in a "Sovereign General Assembly" that "dismissed" the MPLA Steering Committee, elected a provisional "supreme executive" to take its place, hailed Congolese recognition of the GRAE ("an important contribution to the decolonization of the Continent"), and declared a readiness to join the FNLA and the GRAE. It called for an MPLA congress to be held within three months to elect a permanent executive. In the meantime, leadership was to be assumed by a provisional committee of six: Matias Miguéis, José Bernardo Domingos, Viriato da Cruz, Georges Manteya Freitas, José Miguel, and António Alexandre (the last was the only one who had not previously been a steering committee member). Another former steering committeeman, Graça da Silva Tavares, helped to organize and participated in the July 5 meeting. To encourage additional high-level defections, the provisional committee was authorized to coopt four additional members into its ranks.[159]

On July 7, the dissidents broke into a meeting of the loyalist (pro-Neto) Steering Committee at its headquarters. They touched off a bitter chair-throwing battle for control of the MPLA offices. Miguéis and another rebel militant received knife wounds before Congolese police intervened, broke up the melee and arrested forty-three of the dissident intruders.[160] Elsewhere fifty to sixty EPLA soldiers defected to the rebel committee and took over their own living quarters just outside Léopoldville in defiance of MPLA officers (preponderantly mestiços) who remained loyal to Dr. Neto.

In a statement to the press, Miguéis explained that he and his colleagues had acted under pressure from the MPLA rank and file. By "removing" an ineffectual executive committee, he argued, they would restore the internal unity that constituted a necessary prerequisite to proper MPLA participation within a "common front."

TABLE 2.3

MID-1963 ORGANIZATIONAL DIVISIONS AND REALIGNMENTS

	Bakongo	
MPLA	*Ngwizako (Aliança)*	*MDIA*

FDLA		
President	**President**	**President**
Agostinho Neto	Emmanuel Loureiro	Augustin Kaziluki
Vice-President	Antoine Menga	(ex-UPA)
Rev. Domingos da	Albert Matundu	
Silva	(ex-UPA, ex-MDIA)	**Vice-President**
Lúcio Lára	Pierre Milton	Simon Diallo
Anibal de Melo	M'vulu	Mingiedi
Déolinda Rodrigues	Augusto Monteiro	(ex-UPA)
de Almeida	Casimiro E. Milokwa	
Desidério da Graça		**Secretary-General**
Henrique Carreira		Ferdinand Pembele
		José Toto
		Martin Sumbu
		Alphonse Masseko

MPLA	*Ngwizako (Associação)*	*MDIA*

Unaffiliated		
Provisional		
Executive	**President**	**President**
Viriato da Cruz	José dos Santos	Jean P. M'Bala
Matias Miguéis	Kasakanga	(ex-UPA)
José Bernardo	José Milton	
Domingos	Putuilu	**Secretary-General**
Georges Manteya	Garcia Faustino	Pierre Tecka
Freitas	Malheiros	Michel Lusueki
José Miguel	André Monteiro	Philippe Bosso
António Alexandre	Kiangala	Léon Matondo
	Manuel Baptista	Alberto Zôao
(Graçia de Tavares)	N'Dimba	

Bakongo (cont.)

MNA	UNTA	Nto-Bako[a]
President Francisco Mayembe (ex-UPA, ex-MDIA)	**Secretary-General** Pascal Luvualu	**President** François Lélé
Vice-President José Tito	**Ass't. Secretary-General** Bernard Dombele	**Secretary-General** Daniel Dongala [Garcia]
Secretary-General Edouard Tshimpi Albert Gomez João Lenge Daniel Nolo	Emile M'bidi Dongala Miguel Luzolo Henri Kunfunda Simon Luyindula	**Political Director** José Feruado
		Nto-Bako
		President Angelino Alberto
		National Chairman Francisco Thomaz
		Jean Domingiele Jacob-Jacques Zimeni

[a]Applied for membership but not accepted into FDLA.

He alleged that the MPLA's "dismissed" leadership had had "suspicious relations" with a predominantly European group of Angolan exiles, the *Frente de Unidade Angolana* (FUA).[161] He also charged that a "Portuguese businessman" with "considerable investments in Angola" had made contact with MPLA leaders during a recent visit to Léopoldville[162] (apparently a reference to Manuel Vinhas, a wealthy and liberal Portuguese industrialist who favored political reform for Angola).[163]

Such allegations underscored the fact that the da Cruz-Miguéis faction was to a considerable extent a reflection of populist/black versus intellectual/mestiço stratification. In a July 12 press statement, the MPLA rebels criticized the "superiority complex" of those who, having already been "removed" from office, had nonetheless presumed to join the MPLA in a front with MDIA collaborators and thereby raised new impediments to the unification of Angola's authentic *"forces combattantes."* It was not enough to accept "armed struggle" (to which the MDIA was an unconvincing convert). Those who would create a proper Angolan nationalist front, the dissidents argued, would refrain from understandings (*"intelligences"*) with the European oppressor. The tone of the dissidents' July 12 statement[164] thus contrasted sharply with standard MPLA multiracialism.[165]

In a subsequent analysis of these events, Viriato da Cruz asserted that the only really organized opposition in Portugal, the small Portuguese Communist party (PCP), had been a disappointment to Angolan nationalists. Its help had been "practically nil." Unable to pull disparate "anti-fascist groups and individuals" into a broad and cohesive opposition[166] and unprepared to assume the leadership of the newly created exile Patriotic Front (FPLN),[167] the PCP had provided no (European) leadership for the Angolan struggle. Given this failure and the fact that the white settler community "virtually monopolized class domination and exploitation," it was logical, he concluded, that "in the consciousness of the peasant masses, the [colonial] conflict between Africans and settlers" would be viewed as a racial as distinct from a class struggle.[168] For Marxist da Cruz, the quintessence of history remained class struggle. He was simply arguing that MPLA leaders had not sufficiently taken into account "the objective impossibility [for] peasants [by themselves] to become aware of the economic basis of their struggles." Because "the capitalist process of exploitation only spared a microscopic African bourgeoisie"—that is, a few assimilados without political influence—"privileged conditions [class] and race were, one and the same."

There was an intellectual and student stratum within the MPLA, da Cruz continued, that had been influenced by Portuguese propaganda presenting the nationalist uprising as "basically racist." Unfamiliar with the history and conditions of peasant life, this elite was incapable of understanding Marx's observation that "the tradition of all the dead generations weighs like a nightmare on the brain of the living. And just when [the living] seem engaged in revolutionizing themselves and things, in creating something entirely new, precisely in such epochs of revolutionary crisis they anxiously conjure up the spirits of the past to their service and borrow from them names, battle slogans and costumes in order to present the new scene of world history in this time-honoured disguise and this borrowed language."[169] Because of an inability to understand this, the MPLA's intellectual-student stratum overreacted to what it termed "racist excesses" among peasant combatants (UPA forces). It came to consider its own leadership, validated by diplomas and self-esteem, as "indispensable"—if the revolution was to follow a "decent" path. Captives of "the deficiencies and prejudices of their [own] colonial education" and divorced from the peasant masses, such persons saw the "salvation" of the revolution in a "union of the 'spirit' " (the educated and assimilados) with the " 'mass without spirit' " ("the ignorant peasantry and proletariat"). "This," concluded da Cruz, "was the old arrogant and reactionary duality."[170] Having built up a "myth" around the personality of Dr. Neto during two years of "exaggerated propaganda," the intellectual-student stratum was able to parlay his mid-1962 escape from Portugal into a campaign that propelled him and them into control of the movement.

For military access to Angola, da Cruz argued, it was essential that the MPLA achieve an understanding with the FNLA. By taking over the Steering Committee at the national conference in December 1962 and thereby aggravating a "profound" internal division already extant and "well known" in Léopoldville; by renewing personal relationships with "revisionist" elements of "a certain Portuguese 'Left' "; by confronting FNLA competition with overblown propaganda about military action; and by trying to persuade Western (American) sources to cut off assistance to the FNLA and help the MPLA instead, the MPLA killed any incentive that the FNLA might have had for reaching an accord. "The situation thus created," wrote da Cruz, "obliged scores of well-trained soldiers of the MPLA to enlist within the ranks of the FNLA, where they taught the use of arms to thousands of Angolan peasants."[171]

So on July 12, the MPLA/Viriato, as it was to become known, saluted Congolese recognition of the GRAE as "an important and irreversible contribution" to Angolan liberation. Declaring as an "evident" fact that it was the GRAE's "historic task . . . to direct and control the resistance of the Angolan People and the armed liberation struggle," the dissidents, like the loyalists two days before, proclaimed that it was their historic responsibility to infuse the GRAE with a legitimacy it yet lacked. Given that the recognition was "irreversible," it was for the MPLA/Viriato to see that the GRAE developed "more and more as the authentic depository and faithful protector of the people's interests."[172]

The MPLA/Viriato July 12 statement did not mention Roberto or refer to the program, or lack of program, of the FNLA. Indeed, da Cruz considered that the "real motives" that lay behind the Roberto/FNLA practice of denying that the MPLA had any military forces in Angola were lamentable. Such denials provided a pretext for avoiding a common front and stemmed from "an attachment to certain aims, values and alliances incompatible with those of other Angolan parties." Nonetheless it was only by working from inside the FNLA, which controlled access to Angola's "fighting front," that true revolutionaries could unite Angolan insurgents, transform the peasants into politically conscious fighters, develop a politically and ideologically "solid" organization, spread the armed struggle throughout the country, and "bring to the benefit of the people of Angola the support of a sincere revolutionary internationalism."[173] Such then were the assumptions that lay behind the MPLA/Viriato decision to dispatch a formal letter to the FNLA expressing a desire to negotiate entry into the front.[174]

Predictably the MPLA/Neto denounced and expelled its challengers as divisive opportunists[175] and denied having any suspicious relations with FUA or with Portuguese businessmen.[176] On the evening of July 10, five days after the creation of the MPLA/Viriato, three after the fight at MPLA headquarters, and a few hours after the press conference announcing formation of the Democratic Front, Dr. Neto led an FDLA delegation, including Vice-President Emmanuel Loureiro (Ngwizako) and José Tito (MNA), to the Léopoldville airport to greet a special OAU commission that had come to meet with and conciliate Angolan nationalists.[177]

THE OAU AS ARBITER

The OAU's Liberation Committee (ALC) met in Dar es Salaam from June 25 to July 4 and decided to focus its attention on Africa's one ongoing anticolonial insurgency. It received conflicting advice. The MPLA sought support for its long-proposed common *Frente de Libertação de Angola* (FLA) and denounced UPA fratricide and Congolese partiality.[178] The FNLA restated its claim to be the only movement "actively in combat," invited the ALC to visit its *maquis*, and denied the right of its competitors ("windbags" who pretended to lead the struggle) to any share of the forthcoming OAU assistance.[179] Confronted with this internecine conflict, the ALC decided that its first order of business should be one of reconciliation. Accordingly the ALC chairman (and foreign minister of Tanganyika), Oscar Kambona, announced the dispatch of a special goodwill mission to Léopoldville to include the heads of five (out of nine) ALC delegations: Algeria, Congo-Léopoldville, Guinea, Nigeria, and Uganda.[180] At the last minute, Senegal was added as a sixth member.

The makeup of the goodwill mission and its terms of reference appeared to be congenial to the MPLA. Four of the six members—Algeria, Guinea, Senegal, and Uganda—were considered to be pro-common front. And all six were bound by terms of reference that stated that "as a condition of assistance the [ALC] should insist on the creation of one Common Action Front in each territory."[181]

Algeria was expected to be especially forceful in its support of unity. Commenting upon the Congo government's diplomatic recognition of the GRAE, Premier Ben Bella had warned that it would be "dangerous" to channel all aid "to one movement alone."[182] According to Peter Braestrup of the *New York Times*, "Luis d'Almeida, the young intellectual" then heading the MPLA's Algiers Office, "clearly [had] the private sympathies of Algerian officials" because his movement espoused "neutralism and 'revolutionary socialism' close to Algerian notions."[183] New statements by Holden Roberto rejecting the need for Algerian volunteers[1] ("we have enough men"),[184] moreover, seemed likely to reinforce Algerian preference for the MPLA. Roberto detailed his objections to the "generous and fraternal offer" of Algerian volunteers in a memorandum to the ALC. Outside volunteers, he wrote, "would not speak the same language as our freedom fighters," could not "communicate with the local populations whose cooperation is indispensable," and would require months "to get used to operations over a new terrain"—which meant they would hinder "the conduct of the Revolution."[185]

Roberto was nominally positive on the unity issue. In a press interview just after Congolese recognition, he repeated his frequent assertion that "the doors of the FNLA [were] wide open to all those prepared to use the same language as ourselves, namely that of legitimate violence, so long as Portuguese authorities persist in their stubborn ways." Thus, he said, the FNLA sought unity, but unity that grew out of what Frantz Fanon had called the "unifying force" of shared hopes and dangers experienced within the armed struggle.[186] Now that the MPLA was knocking on those FNLA/ GRAE doors would they prove to be open? Writing in the *New York Times*, J. Anthony Lukas was dubious. Observers in Léopoldville, he reported, felt that Roberto would be "reluctant" to accept the MPLA into a front (FNLA) even of his own making because he was believed "to fear" that this action would lead to efforts "to overthrow him from within." Nonetheless, Lukas predicted, Roberto would come under strong pressure from the OAU's goodwill mission to accept Neto's bid for unity.[187]

As the goodwill mission assembled in Léopoldville, the quickening drama that had opened with Congolese recognition of the GRAE, and continued with the Brazzaville roundtable, the creation of an FDLA counterfront, and the MPLA schism moved into a surprise final act. The mission began its work on the morning of July 14 when it elected its ranking diplomatic personality, Foreign Minister Jaja Wachuku of Nigeria, as chairman. Wachuku was a forceful parliamentarian and a close personal friend of Roberto.

The FNLA delegation, headed by Roberto, was carefully chosen to suggest organizational unity and ethnic diversity. It did not include common-front advocates such as Dr. José Liahuca but did include Jonas Savimbi (Ochimbundu), Rosário Neto (Mbundu), and Reverend Fernando Gourjel (mestiço) for ethnic-racial balance.

The MPLA delegation, led by Agostinho Neto, was weakened by the absence of Mário de Andrade, rumored to have prolonged a mission to Cairo in protest against the creation of the FDLA.[188] When Neto attempted to testify in the name of the FDLA (rather than the MPLA), Wachuku ruled on a point of order that the OAU mission could not "listen to him in this capacity as its mandate clearly stated that it was to help reconcile the two known Angolan Nationalist Organizations which gave evidence [in June] at Dar es

Salaam." And when Neto sought to testify in Portuguese (since escaping from Portugal, he had had little time in which to perfect his French or English), the chair ruled that because of the absence of adequate translation facilities, he would have to speak in French. A person of reserved and introspective manner, Neto was thrown off balance. The next day when he presented a written request for an opportunity to present the MPLA's (not the FDLA's) case more amply, Wachuku ruled that it was too late.[189] Most important of all, the mission acted favorably on a written petition from Viriato da Cruz to the chairman requesting an opportunity to testify in the name of the "Provisional Executive Committee" of the MPLA. This led to a bruising in camera confrontation between da Cruz and Neto.

In its own presentation to the closed hearings, the FNLA stressed military accomplishments, stated that nearly four thousand men had been trained at Kinkuzu, and invited the mission to visit both Kinkuzu and FNLA-controlled areas inside Angola where, it asserted, some three thousand Kinkuzu-trained soldiers were now fighting: "We have invited you to visit our maquis and we defy any other movement to do likewise."[190] The FNLA capitalized on the confusion and controversy surrounding the FDLA, warning against infiltration by "collaborators and secessionists" who would argue for unity or reconciliation in order to enter and sabotage the revolution from within. It quoted from a July 8 statement by Ngwizako denouncing the GRAE (without identifying that statement as coming from the Ngwizako faction that had not joined the FDLA). Then referring to requests for GRAE membership made by both the FDLA and MPLA/Viriato, the FNLA asked rhetorically, "When there are two committees each for the MPLA and Ngwizako, how is one to know who represents what?"[191]

Dr. Neto was upstaged by da Cruz who explained the reasons behind his defection, assailed the FDLA, and told the mission that of a total of 250 EPLA soldiers in the Congo, up to fifty had by now joined the FNLA-ELNA and the remainder were split between the two contending MPLA factions.[192] Andrade was not present to defend or explain his earlier press statements claiming an EPLA force of ten thousand (presumably a reference to Mbundu insurgents in the forests of Dembos and Nambuangongo) inside Angola led by an elite cadre of 250 (which had been denied access to the interior). Under questioning, according to Algeria's *Révolution africaine*, the MPLA's military commander, Manuel Lima, who had been less

sanguine than Andrade in earlier press comments,[193] acknowledged that he no longer exercised authority over a military force.
And in a telling, self-inflicted coup de grâce, Neto reportedly conceded that the MPLA did not have an organizational structure inside Angola and that the Angolan-Congolese frontier was entirely
under FNLA control.[194]

When Neto pointed to the Congolese government as being responsible for the MPLA's military weakness (no training base, no
border access), he again found himself undercut by other
testimony—this time by Congolese Foreign Minister Mabika-
Kalanda. Subordinating his personal preference for the MPLA, the
young minister said that in the past his government had helped
both of the Angolan movements but that because of its desire to
help those who were actually fighting, the government had now
recognized the GRAE in hopes of uniting Angolans around it.[195]

The testimony of the senior Congolese spokesman, Minister of Justice Justin Bomboko, was even more telling. A close political ally of
Roberto's, he had remained influential on Angolan affairs after
leaving the Foreign Ministry in April. That he vigorously supported the GRAE and scorned the MPLA was of particular moment given the special role that the ALC ascribed to contiguous
states in all national liberation struggles. The ALC had adopted
work guidelines based on four principles: (1) that "the relation,
concern and interest" of geographical neighbors should be
weighed when considering aid to any given colonial or dependent
territory; (2) that contiguous states by virtue of "their local knowledge and proximity, should play a vital role in the advancement
and progress" of any struggle; (3) that the "host country" should be
given "the right of supervision" over a liberation movement operating within its borders; and (4) that care should be taken "to evolve a
policy of action" that would not impair "the sovereignty and independence" or prejudice the "security" of the host state.[196]

The result of the Léopoldville meeting was an unanticipated but,
under the circumstances, explicable political triumph for the
FNLA/GRAE and rout for the MPLA/FDLA. On July 18, the
goodwill mission presented its findings and recommendations in an
open session. Because the FNLA's "fighting force" was "far larger
than any other," it controlled "the only real fighting front in Angola," and the "continued existence of another [and] minor front"
such as that of the MPLA (presumably a reference to Cabinda)
would be detrimental to the rapid achievement of independence,

the mission concluded that it was "necessary for the FNLA to continue the leadership that has so far proved effective." Without visiting Kinkuzu or FNLA-held areas within Angola, the mission recommended by unanimous vote: that all African or external aid to the Angolans be channeled through the Congolese government and earmarked for the FNLA exclusively; that all "units and persons" having had military training, including the "fighting force of the MPLA," seek admission into the FNLA; that African governments "be requested not to entertain or offer help to other organizations in their territory who claim to be working for the liberation of Angola"; and, finally, that the OAU Council of Ministers at its next meeting recommend to all independent African states that they accord diplomatic recognition to the GRAE.[197]

Dr. Neto and those who remained with him decried the Léopoldville hearings as unfair and put together a new case to present to the OAU foreign ministers scheduled to meet at Dakar on August 2.[198] In an eighteen-page memorandum presented in the name of the MPLA (not FDLA) at Dakar, Neto argued that FNLA military strength in the Congo had no necessary relationship to the struggle inside Angola where MPLA units were fighting in the Nambuangongo-Dembos regions. He also tried to discredit the FNLA by resurrecting the (Antoine Matumona) allegation that American aid to the UPA had been used to block the way to a united front.[199]

But his protests proved ineffective. Jaja Wachuku presented the goodwill mission's recommendations to the OAU foreign ministers, stressing the special role accorded to contiguous independent states. Because of the "exaggerated claims" often made by liberation movements, it was necessary, he argued, to rely heavily upon the local "knowledge and experience" of contiguous states—in this instance, the Congo-Léopoldville. The head of the MPLA, he said, had never crossed the Angolan-Congolese frontier into the fighting zone (the same could have been said about the head of the UPA/GRAE), and a number of the MPLA's Algerian- and Moroccan-trained officers had "retreated" from the border "in fright." Wachuku said the goodwill mission had "proof" that the FNLA controlled "at least 4,000 well-trained men operating to a depth of over 150 kilometers inside the country." Instead of heeding reasoned advice to achieve unity by joining the FNLA, he concluded, the MPLA had formed a new political front with collaborators whose function it was to spy for the Portuguese. Therefore the

OAU mission to Léopoldville recommended that "the head of the FNLA alone should have the right to judge" all membership applications so that it might not be destroyed from within. The OAU foreign ministers adopted the goodwill mission's recommendations without dissent.[200]

The Léopoldville hearings had followed an easy course, concentrating upon the evident disarray of one movement without making a serious effort to plummet the real strengths and weaknesses of its opponent. Subsequent analyses of the MPLA's political-diplomatic disaster attributed it to different variables: the creation of the FDLA,[201] the related defection of the MPLA/Viriato,[202] propaganda oversell that boomeranged,[203] intellectual arrogance or insensitivity to peasant perceptions on the part of a racial-class elite,[204] Congolese recognition of the GRAE (with presumed American connivance),[205] and (MPLA) time wasted (Neto's three-month journey) on cultivating support in Western countries while neglecting internal priorities (structure and strategy).[206]

The forceful but publicity-shy MPLA organizing secretary, Lúcio Lára, ascribed the movement's plight to debilitating obstruction by the Adoula government. A special core of fifty well-trained (Ghana and North Africa), ethnically diverse militants, he argued, had stood ready to set up politico-military bases at selected locales inside Angola. The one unresolved issue had been how to supply these bases with arms that were at the movement's disposal. Adoula posed difficult conditions. He insisted that all arms be brought into the Congo by easily monitored air transport. And when the MPLA found a way to do this, Adoula posed new conditions. According to Lára, the MPLA's evident military disadvantage was attributable not to organizational weakness but to partisan, host state interposition.[207]

Dr. Neto attributed the MPLA's setback to external factors—the influence of "American imperialism" and "its agents" combined with African "concessions to reaction." Together, he maintained, these factors led to OAU recognition of the GRAE and forced a "tactical retreat" and reorganization of his movement.[208]

To one seasoned observer of Angolan affairs, author Basil Davidson, the most damaging allegation against the MPLA had been that of collusion with white settler elements within Angola—which to him explained the alliance with FDLA collaborators. Previously sympathetic to the MPLA, in late 1963 Davidson wrote that "Neto's claim to leadership" had "ended" and that his movement "fractured, split, and reduced . . . to a nullity" had "ceased to count." "A bitter story of anger and frustration," he wrote, lay behind the OAU action, especially true with regard to Algeria, which "had lately done a great deal for the MPLA"[209] but which had concurred in the OAU decision.[210] The Algerians "were by no means alone in feeling that leaders of the MPLA had deliberately led them up the garden [path]" by misrepresenting the facts. Testimony had revealed MPLA forces to be few, out of control, and on the Congo side of the border. "Neto himself was brought to agree, to cap it all, that the MPLA no longer had any political structure inside Angola. So instead of trying to reconcile the two movements the good will mission sensibly recommended that the MPLA should forthwith be ignored."[211]

Davidson closed his analysis, however, by presciently pointing toward what was to be the ultimate test of the decisions and events of June–July 1963. Angola, he wrote, "has at last the hope of achieving a unified nationalist movement," and what Angolan insurgents required for success was "an exile movement capable of unifying all strands and segments of nationalist opinion." This, he concluded, might "prove no mean achievement."[212] FNLA/GRAE leadership had won an opportunity to build a strong organization. The moment was ripe for Holden Roberto to reach out, draw new and broader participation into his movement's top- and middle-level leadership ranks, recruit and mobilize new membership inside Angola, and expand the scope and intensity of all operations. The period immediately ahead promised to be an acid test of Roberto's political skill and vision.[213]

CHAPTER THREE

PAN-AFRICAN TRAJECTORY

Angola ranked first on the OAU's liberation agenda. The Dakar decision to grant exclusive pan-African support to the FNLA was expected to preclude further diversionary two-party competition. New advances in the nationalist campaign against Portugal seemed assured. And yet the year that followed the Dakar decision proved to be a year of breakdown, not breakthrough.

RESPONSE TO RECOGNITION: GRAE ORGANIZATION

To consolidate its gains and advance to higher levels of capability, the FNLA/GRAE needed to reorganize. In August 1963, from his new office in Algiers (where the Algerian government had promptly joined its Tunisian and Moroccan neighbors in recognizing the GRAE), Johnny Edouard announced that the FNLA was preparing to convene its first congress. The FNLA National Council would submit a new program to a broad nationalist congress that would include military, labor, peasant, women, youth, and student representatives. While continuing to rely heavily for its membership upon the poorest and "most combative" social class, Angola's peasants and farm laborers, it was time, Edouard said, to expand the revolution to the country's mines, industries, and cities. It was time to open new combat fronts, to broaden the outreach of GRAE diplomacy (to include eastern countries), and to implant a solid organization within Angola's "liberated zones."[1]

Five months later, Edouard repeated his announcement that preparations were under way for an FNLA congress, which, he said would be held shortly in Léopoldville.[2] Although the FNLA's rarely convened National Council did meet in a general review session in December, the anticipated congress at which FNLA program, structure, and leadership were to be submitted for popular discussion, revision, and approval, did not. Edouard's announcements may have represented more prod than plan. Months passed. There was no congress, no political reorganization. UPA/GRAE operations remained constricted by Roberto's tight hold on decision making. Expectations of a rational devolution of functional authority to the GRAE ministers slowly dissolved. By the third anniversary (1964) of the March 15 uprising, internal disenchantment with Roberto's leadership was rife. The GRAE vice-premier, Emmanuel Kunzika, and foreign secretary, Jonas Savimbi, with their supporters, boycotted the annual commemoration ceremonies.

There were some efforts, which fell short of needed structural reform and personnel changes, to improve the efficiency of GRAE operations. For example, an Italian journalist, Antonio Acone of the Rome newspaper *Messaggero*, flew to Léopoldville to review and recommend improvements in the GRAE information-propaganda service. Without a regular ministerial income, however, functionaries such as Information Minister Rosário Neto depended upon moonlighting ventures such as trade in elephant tusks to supplement irregular handouts from Roberto. They thus gave less than full attention to their GRAE responsibilities. This was evident in the performance of the information service, which remained no less perfunctory and ineffectual for having received Acone's technical advice. The plight of the GRAE office in New York further illustrated the organizational dysfunction. Meant to keep U.N. delegations and American press and political organizations abreast of GRAE activities, it received only infrequent communications from Léopoldville. It was not unusual for the New York representative, Carlos Gonçalves Kambandu, to seek information from those he was meant to inform. This drew attention to GRAE inefficiency and turned the New York office into an expensive liability rather than an asset by souring U.N. diplomats and prospective sources of American support.[3]

Roberto repeatedly raised, then dashed, expectations of organizational reform. In November 1963, he announced that the GRAE would create a cadre school to train political commissioners and prepare for the day of self-governance.[4] For the organization of an *Ecole de cadres angolais*, he turned to a young Swiss journalist, Walter Artho. Earlier in response to appeals from Jonas Savimbi (while the latter was a student at the University of Lausanne), Artho and other Swiss sympathizers had formed the Swiss Friends of Angola, which raised funds for more than thirty Angolans to study in Switzerland. Artho had also conceived of and planned for an autonomous secondary and technical school for Angolan refugee students in the Congo. Following Congolese and OAU recognition of the exile government, his project was placed under GRAE jurisdiction. Plans called for a two-year curriculum in social sciences and public administration to be taught by expatriate faculty—excluding Americans, in deference to Roberto's sensitivity to accusations that he was under U.S. influence.[5] Negotiations with the Congolese government for a construction site then awaited Roberto's initiative. Otherwise preoccupied, Roberto refused to delegate the matter. The prolonged delay stalled the project. As political discord developed within the FNLA/GRAE, the project and its Swiss director designate were caught in a crossfire of internecine political conflict. The undertaking aborted.

The FNLA/GRAE was left with no leadership-administrative cadre training program whatsoever. The failure to create one contrasted sharply with the MPLA's earlier *Escola de Quadros*. It also contrasted with personal efforts by Emmanuel Kunzika, GRAE's vice-premier newly charged with educational affairs, to launch educational programs for Angolan refugees. Kunzika first worked with Artho and the cadre school project. When that aborted, he acted on his own. With funds raised independently of the GRAE among his PDA (Bazombo) supporters, Kunzika had already organized a primary school. By mid-1963, his school was serving some three hundred Angolan children in Léopoldville, and Kunzika was elaborating plans for its expansion into a secondary school. Rhetoric aside, Roberto seemed little concerned about educating new leadership. He was concentrating instead on matters of short-term political and military gain.

In addition to a need for structural reorganization and a program to prepare administrative, middle-level cadres, the FNLA/GRAE needed a greater degree of popular participation in its ranks if it was to meet new expectations and gather new strength. Instead of adopting a confident, expansive strategy of magnanimity in victory, however, Roberto made no timely moves to rally remnants of his political competition. He welcomed only individual MPLA military defectors into the FNLA/GRAE fold. Though he was in a strong position to negotiate for MPLA/Neto (as distinct from a more dubious FDLA) entry on terms that would safeguard (at least short run) UPA preeminence, Roberto responded with a silent, non recevoir to Dr. Neto's public request for entry into the GRAE. Believing that he could safely disregard Neto and his supporters, Roberto began protracted discussions with the smaller, breakaway MPLA/Viriato.[6] Jonas Savimbi and his Ovimbundu supporters feared a maneuver to reduce their influence within the FNLA/GRAE and bitterly opposed these discussions. They rejected da Cruz as a "radical, pro-Chinese mestiço."[7] Roberto persisted. In April 1964, choosing a moment when Savimbi was traveling in Europe, Roberto pushed a resolution through the FNLA National Council accepting the da Cruz group as a third member of the FNLA.[8] After taking nearly a year to process the MPLA/Viriato application for FNLA membership, however, Roberto still held back from bringing the da Cruz group into the machinery of the exile government.[9] Viriato da Cruz and Matias Miguéis were reportedly eager to acquire authority in military and educational fields, hoping to create new politico-military structures within liberated zones of Angola. But they were forced to shelve such plans while waiting for Roberto to give practical meaning to their FNLA membership—and waiting for him to proceed with the FNLA-GRAE's long-delayed reorganization.[10]

Emmanuel Kunzika's PDA was a minor beneficiary of the OAU recognition. Convinced that they had bet on the wrong party, MDIA leaders who had joined Agostinho Neto's FDLA in July changed their minds in November.[11] Making their third political switch in as many years, Augustin Kaziluki, Simon Diallo Mingiedi, and other one-time UPA leaders palavered with Kunzika, broke with the FDLA (November 23), and, citing OAU recommendations, entered the FNLA—by joining fellow Bazombo in the PDA.[12] Denounced for this "illegal" act by the MDIA's continuing pro-Portuguese faction led by Jean Pierre M'Bala and Pierre Tecka,[13] these Bazombo politicians completed a full circle of political peregrinations from Aliazo (PDA), to UPA, to MDIA, to MDIA-FDLA, to PDA. Rather than constituting a net gain for the FNLA, however, the entry of Roberto's old Bazombo adversaries into the ranks of his FNLA partner added new strain to PDA-UPA relations and provided Roberto with a new reason for not convening an FNLA congress. The ex-MDIA group could be counted upon to support any challenge to Roberto's leadership that might develop at such a gathering.

The PDA brought other new faces into its leadership.[14] These infusions did not alter the PDA's ethnic character, although they did serve to broaden its (northern) regional leadership. Second-echelon leaders who had been displaced to make room for the newcomers were resentful. But in a party election on December 13, 1964, Kunzika sought and won a mandate as PDA president.[15]

Functional organizations affiliated with the UPA/GRAE were only modestly affected by the OAU recognition of August 1963, although they did benefit from a certain spillover of political optimism. Previously uncommitted Angolan students in exile rallied to the pro-GRAE National Union of Angolan Students (UNEA). UNEA president Jorge Alicerces Valentim [16] in Léopoldville at the time of the OAU goodwill mission's visit, produced a stream of pro-GRAE UNEA communiqués.[17] And indicative of how seriously GRAE now took its "governmental" status, shortly after winning OAU recognition it announced that it intended to bestow its own recognition on UNEA as the only organization qualified to speak for Angolan students.[18] In Vienna, the *Angolan Student*, a previously unaffiliated "organ for promotion of understanding" among Angolan students abroad, declared itself pro-GRAE: "If we wish to see independence by 15 March 1964, we must all give unstinting support to the GRAE!"[19] The paper denounced the (pro-MPLA) *União Geral dos Estudantes da Africa Negra sob Dominação Colonial Portuguesa* (UGEAN) and published GRAE's anticipated statement recognizing UNEA as "the only national student organization of Angola."[20]

The UPA/GRAE's women's association, the *Associação das Mulheres de Angola* (AMA), headed by Maria de Conceição Neto (wife of Rosário Neto), assumed new visibility.[21] Seeking international support for AMA educational and relief projects among refugee women and children, Maria Neto traveled to Algeria and issued a series of appeals and communiqués.[22]

Despite the failure of its bid for official FNLA membership earlier in the year, the *Liga Geral dos Trabalhadores de Angola* (LGTA) also realized a modest expansion of its activities during 1963. It organized a women's section (FLGTA),[23] augmented educational programs associated with its youth section (JLGTA),[24] continued to recruit members among insurgents and villagers within nationalist-held areas of Angola,[25] participated in a seminar on trade unionism organized locally for Congolese labor movements by the ICFTU,[26] and sent two of its officials to international labor seminars in Europe.[27] In November 1963, LGTA secretary-general Pedro Barreiro Lulendo flew to the United States where he attended the annual AFL-CIO conference and met with George Meany and other AFL-CIO leaders, seeking to arouse interest in and support for Angolan nationalism and the LGTA.[28] Lulendo also conferred in New York with the general secretary of the ICFTU, Omer Becu, and subsequently visited the Brussels headquarters of the ICFTU, which was providing the LGTA, its official Angolan affiliate, with an annual subsidy.[29]

In December the LGTA executive sent an organizing mission headed by a veteran internal recruiter, Manuel Lino, into Angola with instructions to establish LGTA branches in the region of Quicabo just north of Luanda.[30] And though financial limitations forced the postponement of some projects, such as the publication of a regular union bulletin, the LGTA laid plans for creating new sections among Angolan workers in Katanga and Northern Rhodesia. In general LGTA leadership shared the prevailing optimism that 1964 would be a decisive year in the struggle for Angolan independence.[31]

The medical and relief work of the *Serviço de Assistência dos Refugiados de Angola* (SARA), under Dr. José Liahuca, expanded only modestly during 1963. Dependent upon support from international Protestant and Catholic relief organizations and American groups (including the American Committee on Africa, the International Rescue Committee, and the Africa Service Institute), SARA instituted a program for training medical technicians and nurses. Directed by a Canadian physician, Dr. Ian Gilchrist, and a Haitian surgeon, Dr. Marc A. Woolley, this ongoing training program was separate from but complementary to training received by a group of UPA/ELNA medics in Israel. Unable to serve but a small fraction of the dispersed Angolan refugee population in the Congo and fewer still of the insurgent forces and villages inside Angola, the SARA staff of three doctors and a handful of technicians waited with increasing impatience for OAU funds to provide it with personnel, equipment, and supplies to match the dimensions of its task. Along with the leadership of other UPA/GRAE functional organizations, Dr. Liahuca and his Angolan staff also waited for the promised call to participate in a national congress to reorganize the FNLA.

RESPONSE TO RECOGNITION: GRAE GEOETHNIC OUTREACH

Roberto's privileged relationship with Adoula gave the UPA/GRAE an opportunity to extend its operations to the east and south—into the Angolan border areas of Kwango, Kasai, and Katanga. Moreover, with Northern Rhodesia entering the last phase of self-government prior to independence slated for October 1964, opportunity beckoned Angolan nationalists on a yet more distant horizon. The ability of the UPA/GRAE to broaden its ethnic and geographic base and more fully accommodate within it the "southern," or Ovimbundu-Chokwe-Ganguela stream of Angolan nationalism, was to be a crucial test of its ability to measure up to the mission with which the OAU had charged it.

Katanga

In early July 1963, UPA Katanga representative João Chisseva flew to Léopoldville and reported that the UPA had made a disastrous start under José Peterson. Alarmed by evidence that Kassanga and Kassinda's UNA was making inroads into the UPA's and his potential Katanga constituency, Jonas Savimbi, accompanied by student protégé Jorge Valentim (UNEA), hastened to Elizabethville. Savimbi spent two weeks with Angolan émigrés and refugees in Elizabethville, Jadotville, and Kolwezi. As UPA secretary-general, he responded to local grievances against Léopoldville on "Bakongo dictation." He agreed to the election of a regional UPA committee for Katanga that would negotiate its relationship with Léopoldville, a relationship that he said should combine a measure of local autonomy with a voice in decision making at the national level. Savimbi attacked the UNA for making concessions to Chokwe separatism and made preliminary arrangements for the recruitment of a contingent of 150 Ovimbundu and Chokwe guerrilla (ELNA) volunteers. These men were to fly on Congolese military planes to Léopoldville and then proceed by road to Kinkuzu.

At Savimbi's insistence, Jorge Valentim, after journeying with Holden Roberto on a late August fund-raising mission to Nigeria, assumed overall direction of UPA/GRAE operations in Katanga. Continued competition from the UNA, which had warned the OAU foreign ministers in August against recognizing a "tribalist, racist, extremist" GRAE, had given Savimbi the leverage to insist upon José Peterson's removal from Elizabethville.[32] Once on the spot, Valentim acted swiftly. He persuaded Congolese authorities to arrest the UNA president, André Kassinda.[33] Other UNA leaders, including Marcos Kassanga and John Victor,[34] escaped south to Northern Rhodesia, where UNA representatives had already (July 1963) established contact with Kenneth Kaunda and officials

of his United National Independence Party (UNIP). With the reported approval of UNIP's ranking Lozi official, Munukayumbwa
Sipalo, the UNA had, it seems, begun organizing among Angolan
workers at Chingola in the Copperbelt.[35] And for some months
after the UNA ceased to function in Katanga, its Northern Rhodesian (Zambian) branch continued to operate as a separate, if minor,
nationalist group led by John Victor (secretary-general) and Paul
Kassongo.[36] As for Marcos Kassanga, he journeyed through East
Africa, ending up in Bujumbura, Burundi, where during the
spring of 1964, he safely waited out the last three months of the
Adoula government.[37]

With the UNA out of the way, Valentim implemented Savimbi's
plans for sending military recruits to Kinkuzu. After a Kinkuzu
training period of three months, these recruits were to return to
Katanga. It was expected that once back (U.N. troops having been
replaced by the Congolese army in the interim), they would quietly
establish a new ELNA training and operational base preparatory to
opening a military front in the eastern Lunda and Moxico districts
of Angola. While putting this plan in motion, Valentim publicly accused the Portuguese of regrouping twenty-five hundred Katangese gendarmes on their side of the border in preparation for attacks on Katanga.[38] Portuguese colonialists, he warned, were
threatening reprisals against the Congo because of its support of
Angolan nationalists.[39]

After an initial period during which he issued ebullient communiqués about local UPA organizational activities,[40] Valentim's
relations with an unresponsive FNLA/Léopoldville turned sour.
On January 25, 1964, he cabled Roberto: "Please send money via
Prime Minister Adoula for local operations in absence of which
office will close." But Roberto's attention was riveted on persons
and problems close at hand, and he ignored Valentim's appeals for
funds. This may have been in part a calculated reaction to youthful
impatience and indiscretion. Radio Katanga and the Congolese
press widely publicized Valentim's announcement that GRAE had
decided to create an operational base at Dilolo, a Congo-Angola
border town on the Benguela rail line.[41] This had embarrassed
Roberto and irritated Congolese officials, who had counseled
against offering the Portuguese any pretext for supporting a
second Katanga secession. The Congolese central government was
still consolidating its authority in the breakaway province.

By March, Valentim's public statements featured praise for his political mentor and fellow Ochimbundu, Savimbi, and made no mention of Roberto.[42] Then in mid-April, Valentim left Katanga for Europe where, as UNEA president, he began organizing student opposition to Roberto's GRAE leadership. And in late May, after a clandestine journey to Léopoldville (via Brazzaville), Valentim circulated among student organizations throughout the world a critical memorandum in which he demanded that the long "imminent" FNLA congress to reorganize the FNLA be convened without further delay.[43] Meanwhile, left leaderless, the UPA/GRAE Katanga office closed.

Northern Rhodesia

Holden Roberto and Kenneth Kaunda enjoyed a friendship that dated back to the first All African Peoples' Conference at Accra in December 1958. Thus, when José Peterson visited Lusaka in May 1963 to explore possibilities for extending GRAE operations into Northern Rhodesia, Kaunda received him cordially,[44] a courtesy repeated for Jorge Valentim the following January.[45] Already in June 1962, Smart Chata, the president of an Angolan Chokwe association in Northern Rhodesia, the *Ukwashi Wa Chokwe*, had established contact with the UPA in Léopoldville.[46] And in January 1963, Chata reportedly organized a meeting of over a hundred Angolans in Chingola to hear a newly arrived Ovimbundu refugee, (Ramalho) Domingos Gil, report on conditions inside Angola. The gathering decided to organize Northern Rhodesia's first UPA committee. The initiative aborted, however, when the fledgling committee dissolved in a leadership dispute.[47]

Communal competition among the three principal Angolan ethnic associations of Northern Rhodesia—*Ukwashi Wa Chokwe, Vilanga Va Kambungo* (Luchazi), and *Chijilochalimbo* (Lwena, or Luvale)—led to protracted maneuvering for local UPA leadership. A second UPA committee formed at Kitwe in February 1963 and headed by Smart Chata apparently aroused fears of Chokwe dominance.[48] In late 1963, a third, rival committee organized by a Lwena, Nelson Chicoma, was formed in Lusaka with the cooperation of the Ovimbundu refugee, Domingos Gil, who, during a visit to Léopoldville earlier in the year, had been authorized by Roberto (as well as by Valentim in Elizabethville) to organize an officially sanctioned UPA committee in Northern Rhodesia.[49] After some final dickering over offices, rival factions got together, substituted the word *Angola* for *Mozambique* in a constitution borrowed from the local office of UDENAMO, and, on March 13, 1964, opened a registered UPA section in Northern Rhodesia headed by Domingos Gil.[50] The new committee cabled news of its founding to Roberto—who responded by sending funds via a mission lead by José Peterson. Distance saved the Northern Rhodesian office from becoming immediately embroiled in the internal dissension then (early 1964) welling up within the UPA/GRAE in Léopoldville. And the concurrent collapse of the UPA Katanga office added protective space. With substantial independence, the Lusaka group set about opening branch offices and recruiting new members— activity that it freely pursued throughout 1964.

Kasai

In July 1963, Roberto sent a UPA/GRAE representative to open an office in Tshikapa, Kasai, about one hundred miles north of the Angolan diamond center at Dundo. Although his emissary was to organize among Angolan Chokwe residing in the area, Roberto, given his penchant for direct personal control, bypassed local Tshikapa leadership. He failed to consult such local leaders as José Paulo Chiringueno (originally from Dundo, Angola), whom Smart Chata had introduced to UPA circles in Léopoldville in mid-1962. As organizer he chose a young Bakongo protégé (vice-president of the local Léopoldville branch of UNEA), Simão Andrade Freitas. Just as in Katanga, his failure to introduce the UPA/GRAE through someone with appropriate ethnolinguistic and regional credentials proved costly.

Roberto's strategy incited Chiringueno to found his own movement. Thus on November 25, 1963, Chiringueno and a group of Tshikapa Chokwe, some of whom had belonged to the MPLA and UPA since 1961, renounced those movements ("whose policies had become tribalistic") and set about organizing a Chokwe-oriented *Partido Nacional Africano* (PNA), which undercut UPA/GRAE efforts to organize in the Kasai region.[51]

Kwango

As the UPA/GRAE's ranking Mbundu, Rosário Neto aspired to a leadership role within Angolan refugee-émigré communities located along the Congolese border east of the Kwango River. There he maintained contact with traditional chiefs[52] and others who passed in and out of Malange.[53] (According to his critics, he engaged in ivory trade with some of them.) Cultivating relations with Kwango provincial officials and politicians in Léopoldville, Rosário Neto made occasional political tours of their region, including visits to a new base at Kasongo-Lunda from which armed ELNA patrols raided across the river boundary.[54] His visits to Kwango were, however, infrequent. A man of slack habits, the former Catholic journalist from Malange did not apply himself determinedly to the goal of converting a potential political following into a solid Kwango-based political organization. Nor did Roberto encourage him to do so. The Kwango opening was left languishing.

Lobito-Central Angola

Throughout 1963, Roberto maintained tenuous links with an underground movement centered in the busy central coast port of Lobito. Formed in May 1961 by young nationalists who had escaped the raids and roundups of vigilantes and police that had come in the wake of the northern uprising of the previous March, the Lobito *Comitê Secreto Revolucionário do Sul de Angola* (CSRSA) enjoyed the cooperation of a few anti-Salazarist Europeans, notably persons previously associated with the *Frente de Unidade Angolana* (FUA).[55] It apparently spun a web of informants stretching from São Salvador in the north to CSRSA groups in Nova Lisboa, Sá da Bandeira, and Moçâmedes. Periodically a sailor courier carried CSRSA data concerning Portuguese troop movements and military supplies as well as political developments within the country to the UPA/GRAE office in Matadi. In return the CSRSA received UPA/GRAE communications—some assertedly as coded messages tucked into the twice weekly "Free Angola" broadcasts beamed southward by Radio Léopoldville.[56]

In May 1963, the CSRSA assumed the status of a clandestine political party, the *União Nacional dos Africanos do Sul de Angola* (UNASA). Following OAU recognition of the GRAE in August, its leadership sent a congratulatory message to Roberto. Calling for the "annihilation of reactionary and tribal [Angolan] organizations" in the Congo, it commended Roberto for refusing to cooperate with what it termed mestiço-dominated organizations that were quite properly viewed as "non-African." It rejected the MPLA, an organization devoid of "patriots," for allegedly launching the

Luanda uprising of February 1961 in haste and without strategy and for then "abandoning" the struggle. UNASA's leaders pledged to continue providing the "Government of the Republic" with data concerning the locale, numbers, and weaponry of Portuguese troops, and expressed their "deepest gratitude" to African states that had recognized GRAE as Angola's "legal Government."[57]

UNASA's information-gathering *Serviços Secretos* traced the group's origins back to 1961 and to political action centered in Bocoio (about forty miles from Lobito) led by Julio Cacunda—"a dynamic nationalist who was killed by the colonialists after having been exposed by a *mestiço* traitor."[58] The severity of Portuguese security measures over a wide area—including Bocoio, Balombo, Lobito, Canjala, Novo Redondo, and Gabela—had forced a temporary pause in nationalist activity.[59] Reenergized, the survivors of the catastrophe of 1961 later turned to small-scale underground organizational work designed to prepare the African population psychologically for the struggle ahead. Made up of "genuine blacks" who felt no need for "formal statutes," UNASA expressed "entire confidence" in the GRAE as the "legal representative" of the "Angolan Republic." And in doing so, it requested that the exile government consider the formation of a "single party" to maximize nationalist strength and convey to independent African states the need to commit themselves to concerted and consistent rather than uncoordinated and "sporadic" supportive action.[60]

The long-distance UNASA-GRAE linkage was in all ways fragile. According to UNASA sources, Holden Roberto wrote several times urging UNASA to sabotage the Benguela Railroad (Roberto had smuggled some grenades to the Lobito underground to do so). With the experience of Luanda (February 1961) in mind, however, the Lobito group held that it could not responsibly carry out local sabotage until the GRAE was also prepared to send in well-trained guerrilla soldiers to back up and exploit sabotage as part of an overall insurgent strategy. Otherwise, it argued, they could not justify the price that would be swiftly and brutally exacted in innocent lives.[61] To discuss this and other issues of political and military strategy, in November 1963, UNASA sent its secretary-general, Adão Kapilango, on a mission to GRAE headquarters in Léopoldville.[62]

Government authorities, meanwhile, had heard rumors of nationalist sentiment and activity in the Lobito region. Their initial response was to break up the local branch of an officially sanctioned social organization, the *Liga Nacional Africana* (LNA).

In January 1964, pursuant to talks with Kapilango in Léopoldville, Roberto requested a secret meeting at the Katanga border town of Dilolo to discuss with a UNASA representative possibilities for initiating military action in central Angola. The Lobito group sent a representative to Dilolo, but he apparently arrived too late to meet Roberto's emissary. Then before a meeting could be rescheduled, a letter from Kapilango in Léopoldville to the group in Lobito fell into the hands of the Portuguese police (PIDE). A security crackdown by Lobito port authorities had barred African sailors from going ashore, and UNASA's regular sailor-courier had chosen to pass Kapilango's letter on through a third party. A preliminary police inquiry (after the letter had been delivered) tipped UNASA leader Osseia Oliveira Chinyama to the fact that PIDE had cracked the group's communications system and that arrests were imminent. Chinyama alerted other members of the group. Then he and two close associates, Jeremias Cussia Chinhundo and Luciano Kassoma,[63] fled (four UNASA leaders were arrested).

Slipping past the Portuguese soldiers posted at entry points into the city, the three UNASA leaders made their way to a nearby sugar plantation where—with tickets purchased for them by a cooperative passerby—they boarded a train to Caala (Vila Robert Williams). From there they hiked into Nova Lisboa where they bribed a sympathetic Portuguese official and obtained false travel documents. After a brief visit to the home of a Canadian missionary, who gave them some *escudos*, the three traveled for four days by train. At a small station (Kamishito) a few miles from the Katanga border, they contrived to dismount by helping an old woman unload her baggage, and so doing, eluded soldiers on the train who had become interested in their destination.

Setting out on foot for the Congolese border, the UNASA threesome passed the fresh graves of three less fortunate Vila Luso students. One of the graves bore a crudely printed epitaph: "Let This Be a Lesson to Those Who Would Steal Off to Join the Rebels." Twice they ran afoul of army patrols, and twice they escaped capture, the first time because of a rain squall and the second by the chance appearance of a lion.[64] In April 1964, after a roundabout trek through the wooded, sparsely populated eastern Angolan bush, they crossed into Katanga. It was in such fashion that the lucky among the fugitive African nationalists managed to escape Angola and rejoin the struggle outside.

When the three Lobitans and other UNASA militants who soon followed them into Katanga sought out the moribund UPA/GRAE office in Elizabethville, they were quickly disillusioned with what they found.[65] They refused to join forces with the "Government of the Republic" that they had so admired from afar. Their reasons, as outlined subsequently by Luciano Kassoma, constituted a broad political indictment of Holden Roberto, whom they accused of allowing undisciplined ELNA soldiers to commit atrocities and thus alienate both whites and blacks in Angola; refusing to work inclusively with all Angolans out of ethnic-regional bias in favor of northerners; refusing to accept the help of Portuguese army deserters and civilians, persons such as António Ferronha, who, during the summer of 1963, had offered to help the GRAE establish a secondary school in the Congo;[66] refusing to work with "educated Angolans" for fear they might compete for leadership; failing to work with or listen to the uneducated "masses"; and misusing, and thereby alienating potential sources of, external assistance.[67]

This indictment by nationalists predisposed to accept Roberto's leadership helps to explain why the UPA/GRAE did not realize its potential for ethnogeographic expansion. With the temporary exception of organizational work by a locally created and autonomous UPA committee in distant Northern Rhodesia, GRAE geoethnic outreach was condemned to early collapse. Whether by the inaction or heavy hand of shortsighted leadership, one opportunity after another was lost, one potential source of support after another was alienated.

RESPONSE TO RECOGNITION: GRAE MILITARY ACTION

At the OAU foreign ministers' conference in Dakar, Holden Roberto announced that beginning in September, his forces would "seriously intensify" their military operations.[68] During the second half of 1963, ELNA communiqués reported an accelerating incidence of guerrilla encounters with Portuguese forces and sometimes listed names and service numbers of felled Portuguese soldiers.[69] In late August, a team of Egyptian diplomats visited Kinkuzu, where ELNA trainees performed a series of demonstration exercises using bazookas, heavy machine guns, and mines, part of a shipment of seventy tons of arms from Algeria and Tunisia that had arrived earlier that month aboard a Yugoslav ship.[70] Contrary to prevalent rumors, however, no North Africans or other non-Angolans were instructing ELNA recruits in the use of this equipment. Fear of external political influence led Roberto to forego the help of foreign military expertise.

Expectations of intensified military action were fanned by press reports that money was flowing into the ALC liberation fund. By early August, Nigeria was said to have contributed £110,000, Algeria £70,000, Tanganyika £30,000, Ethiopia £21,430, and Uganda £10,000, the total reaching over £240,000 (or $672,000).[71] In its report to the Dakar foreign ministers' meeting, the ALC called upon African states to give almost £1.5 million to a broad roster of liberation movements. The report, leaked to the press, set forth detailed proposals for training and equipping militants of these movements for more effective political action, sabotage, and guerrilla warfare.[72] As a top priority, Angola, meaning the FNLA/GRAE, was allocated an initial sum of £60,000—nearly $170,000—money desperately needed for trucks and staples with which to sustain the hundreds of ELNA recruits training at Kinkuzu.[73]

Over forty thousand Portuguese troops braced for an autumn offensive by nationalist forces estimated to number somewhere between four thousand and seventy-five hundred.[74] With the coming of the rainy season in October, cloud cover and laterite mud would curtail Portuguese air and motorized assaults on rebel strongholds in the hills and forests of such regions as Nambuangongo and Bessa Monteiro. During September and October, an estimated twenty-two hundred freshly trained guerrillas equipped with plastic explosives, dynamite, mortars, rifles, and a few heavy machine guns moved inside Angola.[75] At year's end, Lloyd Garrison of the *New York Times* visited an ELNA redoubt in the Serra de Canda mountains about sixty-five miles south of the Congo border. There he found a force of a thousand guerrillas mining roads, laying ambushes, singing *horas* learned from Israeli-trained guerrilla medics, and living on a subsistence diet alongside several thousand ragged civilians who had fled (1961 and after) into the forests in search of shelter from Portuguese bombing. In Garrison's words: "In northern Angola there are regions the size of Massachusetts with no roads at all. There are vast wilderness areas with jungle-sheathed mountains and high plateaus. The buffalo, antelope and elephant roam without fear. So does the rebel army."[76] The Portuguese controlled the towns and valley roads. The rebels dominated the high ground. Garrison, who had earlier toured with Portuguese forces, placed the southern territorial limits of the fighting zone—reduced

to perhaps half its original (March–May 1961) size—at the heavily
patrolled Dange (or Dande) River, south of which open grasslands
rise slowly to Angola's central highlands.

In the Serra de Canda, Garrison encountered a group of young
men in tatters making their way on bare, bleeding feet to
Léopoldville in quest of arms. They came from the forests of Nambuangongo where, reportedly, people were in desperate need of
food and clothing.[77] Conditions in nationalist areas where sickly,
undernourished peasants tried to grow manioc and beans in un-
suitable wooded shade were so bad that most of the estimated
270,000 who had originally taken refuge in the rain forests had returned to Portuguese-held areas by early 1964. Responding to the
dictates of their situation and to the Portuguese army's psychosocial
campaign, many resettled in government-built villages, each with
its own school, church, and medical dispensary. In the Carmona
area south of the Serra de Canda, returnees were given land, coffee
seedlings, fertilizer, and technical advice. And local administrators
were charged with seeing that Africans were not paid dis-
criminatorily low prices for their coffee and other cash crops—thus
acting to eliminate one of the abuses that underlay the 1961 uprising. It remained questionable, however, whether this program
would ensure the future loyalty of Africans so long as the Portuguese denied them an active political role and treated them with
racial paternalism. Garrison found that "most Portuguese continue[d] to address Africans in the familiar 'tu' form, which Africans consider[ed] patronizing" and continued to view most Africans as children who needed to be "looked after, occasionally
spoiled, and above all, reared with a firm hand." In return, Africans privately expressed doubts that the new order with its aboli-
tion of legal distinctions between civilized and indigenato would in
fact benefit them. In the words of a Luanda dock worker: "How
can I be Portuguese when I am black? Making me a Portuguese
citizen changes nothing except I can be tried in a white man's
court."[78]

In the short run, the psychosocial campaign had the effect of re-
trieving all but perhaps thirty thousand of northern Angola's
internal refugees. It thus deprived nationalist forces of the contex-
tual support of a large, destitute civilian population.[79] And for reasons having more to do with nationalist political incapacity than
with Portuguese military strength, it left these forces to fend for
themselves in contained isolation. Because GRAE/ELNA strategy

concentrated on military action narrowly construed (rather than political recruitment, indoctrination, organization, and guerrilla action), it failed to use the reversed (internal refugee) population flow to infiltrate the resettlement villages. Most importantly, GRAE/ELNA forces made no systematic effort to penetrate or organize within African population centers under Portuguese administration. If GRAE leadership was consciously seeking to emulate Algerian experience, it displayed little understanding of how crucial the support of an extensive political underground had been to that experience.

The guerrillas did press ahead with a relatively small-scale war of ambush and foray, though they were now fish in a shallow and isolated pond. And the 250,000 to 300,000 refugees who had moved across the border into the Congo continued to provide a compensatory external manpower and material resource base for rebel forces.[80] At the same time, the conflict took on a pattern of decreasing physical contact. African raiders dynamited bridges and mined roads; Portuguese patrols mined trails and water holes; and Portuguese aircraft bombed, strafed, and dropped napalm on nationalist sanctuaries.[81] By official count, as of August 1963 after two years of fighting, Portuguese forces had suffered some 1,200 casualties (300 killed, 940 wounded).[82] African losses, while assuredly much higher, could only be speculated about.

Roberto's belief in the centrality of military, as opposed to political, action was further underscored in autumn 1963 when young men from Mozambique (UDENAMO), South West Africa (SWAPO),[83] and South Africa (PAC) began arriving at Kinkuzu for basic, guerrilla training.[84] These Southern African volunteers expected to receive advanced military instruction in combat alongside Angolans. And it was anticipated that once trained, at least some of them would, within the framework of the Congo Alliance, be attached to ELNA units inside Angola.

Among the several hundred new arrivals, only a small core of South African guerrilla officers came with acquired organizational and military skills. The commander of this core, Nga Mamba Machema, was a former Langa township organizer and veteran of the PAC's 1960 mass march on the Cape Town parliament. He had subsequently undergone instruction in unconventional warfare in Egypt and Yugoslavia. In November, Machema arrived at Kinkuzu with an advance group of PAC militants. Starting from Dar es Salaam, they had argued, bribed, and driven their way by Land

Rover past armed road blocks and on across the vast, politically chaotic Congo to the grassy hills of Kinkuzu. There they were joined by compatriots airlifted to the Congo from Bechuanaland (Botswana), where PAC militants congregated at the end of an "underground railroad" out of the republic.

For the Angolans, this apparent promise of PAC input in military skills and dedication proved illusory. Along with more numerous but wholly unofficered raw recruits from Mozambique and South West Africa, the South Africans almost immediately became a diversionary headache for Roberto and ELNA. Of the advance PAC group of fourteen men from Dar es Salaam, nine deserted shortly after arrival. By February (1964), the PAC military nucleus at Kinkuzu numbered no more than fifty men—far from the 357 of which the GRAE office in Algiers boasted in a communiqué that imprudently informed Pretoria of what the PAC liked to perceive as secret military activities.[85]

By April, the PAC project, known as Operation Tape Recorder, had collapsed. Following the lead of earlier deserters, two of whom had received enticing scholarships from the American embassy, would-be PAC guerrillas broke camp and descended upon Léopoldville. Men who had expected to fashion a military force that could ultimately challenge white rule in South Africa became wards of local Catholic and Protestant relief agencies and the representatives of the United Nations High Commissioner for Refugees (UNHCR). Their despairing commander, when confronted with impending mutiny, flew off to East Africa to seek deliverance in the protracted political unity talks under way there among ranking PAC leaders. The debilitating quarrels of exile, however, had left distracted PAC leaders with neither the time nor the resolve to direct, develop, or sustain, let alone salvage, an operation such as that undertaken in the Congo. The demoralized "sons of apartheid" so recently assembled as the nucleus of an army were left to roam, debauch, and panhandle in the streets of Léopoldville. As leaderless Mozambican and South West African recruits also abandoned their Kinkuzu *barracas* (huts) to wander aimlessly about the Lower Congo countryside, the transnational Congo Alliance of liberation movements disintegrated. In May, remnants of PAC's army boarded a Congolese riverboat and began a long, slow journey back across the continent to regroup in the enervating idleness of exile compounds and Freedom Fighter camps in Zambia and Tanzania (formerly Tanganyika).

Their experience pointed up a range of problems susceptible of affecting efforts by any political movement to build a strong military force in exile. The inability of PAC militants to adapt to the harsh, rural environment of Kinkuzu illustrated the difficulty that displaced persons may have in adjusting to circumstances that contrast sharply with those of their own sociopsychological, cultural, and physical conditioning. Most PAC partisans were gregarious township dwellers unused to rustic, rural isolation. Unable to speak the languages of their new environment, unwilling to accept an Angolan (ELNA) diet of manioc, rice, and dried fish (they wanted cornmeal), lacking medical attendants and medicine yet as vulnerable as Europeans to malaria and other tropical diseases, they felt oppressed by Kinkuzu's hot, muggy climate and crude barracas.

The PAC experience demonstrated how the low frustration tolerance to be anticipated among distressed and insecure exiles can foster aggressive and regressive behavior and thus undermine organizational discipline and self-reliance.[86] The discomforts and frustrations of a remote and lonely base some fifteen hundred miles from home conduced PAC militants to mutinous impatience over such things as delay in the arrival of promised uniforms and equipment. Exile stress activated latent social cleavage, pitting Cape Province Xhosa (which, as it happened, included most of the officers) against (lower-ranked) Johannesburg urbanites. It fanned in-group separatist sentiment among Natal Zulu. It nourished camp resentment against project leaders who were headquartered in Léopoldville and seen less as links to outside sources of supply than as self-indulgent men enjoying an enviable social life centered around the city's diplomatic parties and dance halls. Above all, PAC's army-in-exile was quick to experience a collective and debilitating sense of abandonment by a distant, fractious party leadership that was unable to provide either a unifying sense of purpose or a timely response to material needs.

This South African misadventure also served to point up serious organizational deficiencies and exile dependencies afflicting the PAC's Angolan hosts. Leaders of PAC, as well as UDENAMO and SWAPO, had counted upon Angolan support to tide them over while they organized self-reliant operations of their own. But instead the Angolans offered a demoralizing example of politicomilitary improvidence and indiscipline.

The Kinkuzu base was located in open countryside suitable for farming. Thousands of nearby peasant refugees (in addition to

Kinkuzu recruits) assured it a readily available work force. Yet GRAE/ELNA leadership had made no effort to grow local produce to feed its several thousand trainees. Rather than cultivate manioc or raise chickens, the GRAE seemed content to rely on a combination of handouts from international relief agencies and food purchases made with scarce funds that might better have been used for military supplies. Gifts and purchases of foodstuffs had to be trucked in from Léopoldville. And since GRAE lacked the funds with which to purchase a reliable truck, Kinkuzu lived in precarious dependence on irregular deliveries by rented, unreliable vehicles. Kinkuzu soldiers ate irregularly—six days out of ten according to the base commander.[87] Chronic food shortages at the base led in due course to anxiety, discontent, and, finally, to rioting and mutiny.

Aggravating this malaise, in early 1964 Roberto accepted the gift of a black Mercedes from an anonymous (rumored German) benefactor. Defying the role model need to identify publicly with the hardships, as well as the aspirations, of real and potential supporters, Roberto took to driving about the Congolese capital in his shiny new status symbol.[88] One could only wonder whether he considered the political and military advantage that might accrue from publicly acknowledging the gift, then trading it in on a supply vehicle for Kinkuzu.

GRAE/ELNA leadership generally proved insensitive to the need to build revolutionary authority upon a solid reputation for self-discipline, courage, and integrity. ELNA officers at Kinkuzu indulged in conspicuous privilege—frequent trips to Léopoldville, special base quarters for wives, and arbitrary, aggrandizing behavior toward those under their command. Dysfunctional class antagonism cleaved the officers from the trainees.

Another ELNA weakness surfaced during March–April 1964. Ovimbundu and other "southerners" had been recruited to form the core of a force that would push into eastern Angola from Katanga. After completing their training, however, these Katanga recruits had been obliged to mark time at Kinkuzu. Their requests to be returned to Katanga became strident as time passed. But the Congolese government was in no hurry to complicate a still insecure situation in Katanga. It feared to introduce an Angolan variable that might escape its control.

In March, the United Nations received reports that some six hundred former Katangese gendarmes (secessionists) had left jobs in Kolwezi and Jadotville to cross the border into Angola. There they became part of a force of an estimated eighteen hundred former gendarmes (led by twenty newly recruited European mercenaries) that was presumably preparing to strike out in support of a second Katanga secession.[89] The Portuguese government decried such reports as unfounded. But the Adoula government was anxious that Angolan nationalists not provide Lisbon with a pretext for unleashing such a Katangese force or for closing the Benguela Railroad outlet to Katanga copper.

If Roberto's hands were tied, he was unable to convince GRAE/ELNA Ovimbundu leadership of the situation. His personal relationship with Jonas Savimbi had already deteriorated, poisoned by the mutual distrust and intrigue of competing ambitions. And the (Ovimbundu) commander at Kinkuzu, José Kalundungo, grew bitter as, he later reported, Roberto twice called upon the Congolese army to intervene at the ELNA base. Adoula's troops forced the return to camp of some 325 "southerners" who, according to Kalundungo, tried to desert in protest against the "slowdown of the war imposed by Roberto." Another sixty-five Ovimbundu deserters from Kinkuzu managed to descend upon Léopoldville where they angrily confronted Roberto, who responded by having Congolese forces throw them into Ndolo prison.[90]

Military analysts commonly view an army that has been ridden with insubordination and desertions as hopeless unless rebuilt from the bottom up. By late spring 1964 ELNA needed such a drastic overhaul, but the political will to carry it out was lacking.

External factors compounded GRAE's military disarray. OAU funds were slow in coming and less than anticipated. As late as April 1964, little if anything had been received from the OAU.[91] More serious, beginning in January Congolese rebels led by Pierre Mulele launched a rural insurgency against government forces in the Congo's Kwilu Province. "Lumumbist" opposition to the Adoula government, dissidents who had organized within the Brazzaville-based *Conseil National de Libération* (CNL), then joined in with a campaign of urban terrorism in Léopoldville. Within weeks the Lumumbists had mounted a major insurrection that soon overran most of Orientale, Kivu, and North Katanga. By September, the eastern half of the Congo had fallen under the sway of a fractious revolutionary government headed by Christophe Gbenye.[92] As the authority of the Adoula government disintegrated along with its feckless army, the self-confidence, security, and

morale of Angolan and other Southern African exiles who depended upon Adoula's support also sagged. Lingering hope that
Roberto might in fact allow Viriato da Cruz and Matias Miguéis
(MPLA/viriato) to carry out a reorganization of FNLA/GRAE
political and military structure was quashed by the rebellion. The
Congolese government's suspicions of da Cruz's reputed Chinese
(and conjectured Mulelist or CNL) associations rendered him per-
sona non grata in Léopoldville.

A year after OAU recognition of the GRAE, then, the dual
promise of escalated insurgency and massive pan-African support
remained unfulfilled. In June 1964, the Algerian ambassador to
Léopoldville was still expressing public confidence in the potential
development of the Angolan army and promising that OAU aid
would soon be forthcoming.[93] But journalists sympathetic to the
GRAE reported military stalemate rather than new insurgent
momentum within northern Angola.[94] And by mid-1964, Portuguese counterinsurgency forces were moving into areas along the
Congolese frontier, planting mines and burning the cover off a
wide swath of border land in an effort to cut ELNA infiltration
routes into the country.[95]

REJECTION BUT SURVIVAL: MPLA/FDLA

The MPLA managed to continue functioning in Congo-
Léopoldville for several months after the OAU determined that its
continued existence would be detrimental to the cause of early independence for Angola.[96] But in early November 1963, the Congolese government ordered Dr. Neto's movement to close its
Léopoldville office and discontinue the medical/relief operations of
some twenty-seven CVAAR dispensaries in the Kwango and
Kongo Central districts.[97] The extent to which CVAAR services
had been winning local support for the MPLA (and away from the
GRAE) was reflected in concerted, but vain, efforts by Kwango authorities to dissuade the central government from this decision.[98]
And as late as October 31, 1963, the anti-GRAE government of
Kongo Central (Lower Congo) authorized the MPLA to transport
fifteen tons of arms and ammunition from Brazzaville across its
territory into Angola.[99] The head of the Kongo Central government, [Vital Moanda, and other Abako authorities of Kongo
Central protested against alleged mutiny, kidnapping, and murder
perpetrated by undisciplined UPA soldiers said to be terrorizing

local residents, both Congolese and Angolan.[100] But the central government in Léopoldville, invoking the Dakar decision of August 1963, insisted on evicting the MPLA, which had already shifted its main headquarters across the river to Brazzaville. MPLA militants who tried to continue operating in Congo-Léopoldville found themselves harassed at every turn. Two senior MPLA officials were arrested and confined to Ndolo prison for two months;[101] and the top leaders of the pro-MPLA labor union, *União Nacional dos Trabalhadores de Angola* (UNTA), were arrested briefly after publicly proclaiming that an "absence of united action and capable leadership" was leading the Angolan "revolution" toward "bitter defeat."[102] Though formally linked to the MPLA within the Democratic Front (FDLA), UNTA was not, curiously, obliged to shut down its Congo-Léopoldville operations.

Having proved a liability rather than an asset during the OAU deliberations of July and August 1963, the FDLA ceased to figure prominently in MPLA strategy from then on—though along with the MPLA, it formally regrouped in Brazzaville.[103] Nearly a year later, the MPLA foreign affairs secretary, Mário de Andrade, confirmed reports[104] that his failure to show up at the (1963) OAU hearings in Léopoldville and Dakar had indeed represented a rejection of the Democratic Front on whose executive he had been asked to serve. Andrade broke silence in June 1964. Writing in Algeria's *Révolution africaine*, he depicted the FDLA as a compromising expediency. He blamed President Fulbert Youlou who, he said, intended the FDLA to become a vehicle for negotiating a settlement with Portuguese authorities based on limited autonomy for Angola.[105] The MPLA military commander, Manuel Lima, also reportedly resigned in opposition to the FDLA;[106] and the creation of the front gave rise to divisive debate among MPLA students in Europe and Africa.[107]

But the MPLA survived. On August 13, 1963, a timely general strike and army intervention in Brazzaville brought down the Youlou government. Despite overtures by Holden Roberto, the new, left-oriented regime headed by Alphonse Massamba-Debat decided that Brazzaville should continue to host the MPLA, with which it was ideologically compatible.[108] The Massamba-Debat government also agreed to host Lumumbist (CNL) enemies of the Adoula government, who were natural MPLA allies.[109]

From January 3 to 10, 1964, some fifty MPLA loyalists,[110] including students attending schools in Europe,[111] gathered in Braz-

zaville for a *Conferência dos Quadros*. Reminiscent of the party's December 1962 conference, the meeting criticized the movement's
leadership for inadequate training, discipline, and coordination of
MPLA political and military units and deplored in particular its
failure to establish a military base inside Cabinda.[112] It produced a
new, if little altered, party program, which reemphasized the
MPLA's revolutionary commitment to independence, agrarian reform, free cultural (ethnic) expression, and democratic government;[113] it called upon Léopoldville to cease its repression of the
MPLA;[114] and it began the process of rebuilding the movement as a
serious revolutionary force.

BRAZZAVILLE'S RESPONSE TO RECOGNITION: OPERATION CABINDA

A year after the OAU recommended that all African states grant
formal diplomatic recognition to the Angolan government in exile,
eighteen had done so.[115] They were joined by one non-African
state, Iraq.[116] Following precedent set with the Adoula government's action of June 29, 1963, however, diplomatic recognition
generally seemed rhetorical, casual, and symbolic and not meant to
entail legal consequences. The Congolese and Portuguese governments, after all, had found it possible to continue dealing with one
another as if nothing much had happened. And, indeed, in most
instances of recognition of the GRAE, little happened beyond an
exchange of formal letters and issuance of a press release.[117] GRAE
fantasies about embarking upon "active cooperation" and "normal
diplomatic relations" with other countries,[118] and gala diplomatic
receptions thrown in its honor by governments such as (previously
pro-MPLA) Mali,[119] added to the aura of unreality. Over time this
simulated recognition of a simulated government that did not govern came to project a less than serious image of African diplomacy.
Certain African and international responses to GRAE's rise to sudden prominence were more significant, however, especially the
machinations of neighboring Congo-Brazzaville.

Rather than go along with Cyrille Adoula's decision to give exclusive backing to Holden Roberto's FNLA/GRAE, Brazzaville's Fulbert Youlou countered with initiatives of his own. Not only did he
promote the creation of a rival Angolan Democratic Front (FDLA),
but he undertook to negotiate unilaterally with the Portuguese. In
early June 1963, Foreign Minister Alberto Franco Nogueira pro-

posed "frank and practical conversations" with Portugal's African neighbors, offering collaboration in such fields as communications, transport, and commerce.[120] Youlou decided to take up the offer. After discussing the Angolan situation with President Charles de Gaulle, he met in mid-July with the Portuguese ambassador to Paris.[121] The ambassador apparently persuaded him that Lisbon would grant local autonomy to Angola and Cabinda and that as a step in that direction it would organize territorial elections before the end of 1963.[122] In an August 7 press conference, Youlou announced that he would work for a negotiated settlement of the Angolan conflict on the basis of a letter written to him by Portugal's António Salazar.[123] By offering his good offices, he said, he hoped to promote a "realistic" solution that could lead to independence by stages.[124] A week later Youlou was overthrown.

That Fulbert Youlou had some Angola-related ambitions of his own was made obvious by a series of initiatives concerning Cabinda. He clearly saw the valuable hardwood forests of the Cabinda enclave as falling within Brazzaville's proper sphere of interest. Already in December 1962, Youlou's representative at the United Nations, Jean Biyoudi, had stressed his country's special concern for that diminutive territory, which he described as a contiguous region that "we know particularly well."[125] Representatives of the separatist *Movement pour la Libération de l'Enclave de Cabinda* (MLEC) attended Youlou's Angolan roundtable discussions of July 1, discussions that led to the creation of the FDLA. But while he assured Angolan nationalists of a desire to work in concert with them, MLEC president Luis Ranque Franque indicated that his movement's overriding interest was to bring unity to the ranks of Cabindans.[126]

On August 2, President Youlou opened a Cabindan unity conference at Pointe Noire, a few miles north of the enclave border. It brought together representatives of MLEC, the *Comité d'Action d'Union Nationale des Cabindais* (CAUNC),[127] and the recently organized *Alliance de Mayumbe* (Alliama), which spoke for the interests of the Mayumbe ethnic minority in the Cabinda interior. Among some two hundred persons in attendance were members of the Cabindan émigré community of the Pointe Noire area who had been invited to participate as observers (non-congressistes).[128] The theme of the proceedings was set by CAUNC leader Henriques Tiago N'zita who declaimed on the separateness of Cabinda and Angola. The conferees affirmed Cabinda's right to self-determination and independence and proclaimed their willingness to engage in "constructive dialogue with Portuguese authorities" in order to arrange an orderly transfer of power. They called for the election of a Cabindan legislature with full participation in it to be accorded Cabindans then resident in Congo-Brazzaville.[129]

The Pointe Noire conference succeeded in merging its three participating movements into a single *Front pour la Libération de l'Enclave de Cabinda* (FLEC).[130] Headed by MLEC's Luis Ranque Franque, the new movement immediately appealed for recognition by independent African states.[131] Seen by the leadership of the FNLA/GRAE as a counterrevolutionary, separatist movement created and funded by Fulbert Youlou,[132] FLEC nonetheless persisted as an active organization under the Massamba-Debat regime, continuing to demand independence for the 2,895-square mile territory.[133] In September, it sent a letter to U.N. Secretary-General U Thant alleging that both "Angolan [GRAE] and Portuguese Imperialists" were murdering, terrorizing, and arresting people within the enclave.[134] And in the years that followed FLEC would prove a considerable nuisance to the MPLA.

PORTUGAL HOLDS FAST

World reactions to GRAE's summer leap to newsworthiness varied widely. Roberto's African and Western supporters were euphoric. Pro-MPLA stalwarts such as Nkrumah's Ghana and the Soviet Union were silent. Lisbon was outraged.

In an August 12 address to the nation, Premier Salazar reaffirmed his government's commitment to imperial mission. He spoke just a few days after the U.N. Security Council had voted eight to zero (United States, Britain, France abstaining)[135] requesting that Lisbon recognize the right of its African territories to self-determination and independence; cease "all acts of repression" and withdraw "all military and other forces" so engaged; grant "unconditional political amnesty" and establish conditions permitting "the free functioning of political parties"; negotiate with representatives of political parties within and without for a "transfer of power" to freely elected political institutions; and grant independence immediately.[136] Portugal's Atlantic allies failed to vote against this resolution, which also called upon all third parties to refrain from supplying arms or otherwise assisting Portugal in Africa. Ambassador Adlai Stevenson expressed verbal approval of the "essential substance" which he saw as an endorsement of "the principle of self-determination."[137] And Portugal's lusophone offspring, Brazil, voted for the resolution despite the fact that the resolution "deprecat[ed] the attitude of the Portuguese Government," which had repeatedly violated "the principles of the United Nations Charter" and which continued to refuse to implement United Nations resolutions. Not only continued refusal but total defiance marked Salazar's August 12 response to mounting anticolonial pressure from African nationalism and international diplomacy.

He had no doubts. To keep faith with its "sacred heritage" and to defend the West's true interests, Portugal had to maintain its overseas territories as "integral parts of the Portuguese nation." It was Portugal's duty to fight to the limit of its human and material resources to keep them so. Salazar approved of administrative decentralization. Nevertheless, despite the "loud cries" raised abroad in favor of Angolan independence, Angola was "a Portuguese creation." It could "not exist without Portugal." Its "national conscience" was "Portuguese," and its inhabitants were "Portuguese of Angola" (not Angolans).[138] The *New York Times* concluded from Salazar's policy statement, substantial excerpts from which it published,[139] that the aging strongman was "incapable of understanding that Africans want to be Africans" and not Portuguese "in the sense of being like the people of Portugal."[140] Such a judgment, however, illustrated exactly what Salazar had in mind when he assailed the United States for pursuing an anticolonial policy that allegedly favored communist (Chinese and Soviet) expansion at the expense of an Atlantic ally. Nor was the United States simply a misguided but innocent dupe. Americans were motivated by economic ambitions. The "big capitalist syndicates" of the West, as well as the "strong State economies" of the East, he maintained, sought "to capture and control markets." The consequence of such big power competition for Africa was likely to be "an era of neocolonialism."[141] (See appendix 1.)

In a tart retort that failed to suggest limiting or controlling the role of "private" American corporate power in Portuguese Africa, Secretary of State Dean Rusk said that Washington could not "be expected to like" the allegation that it wished to "extend some sort of [American] sphere of influence." It was "well known," Rusk said, that Americans "really do attach importance to the simple notion that governments derive their just powers from the consent of the governed, and that what the people of a particular territory think about their circumstances or situation is an important question." Portugal's presence in Africa could be properly sustained only if given "the demonstrated consent" of Africans.[142]

As if to have the last word, on August 28 Premier Salazar spoke to a rally of some 250,000 persons massed in Lisbon's Palace Square. Organized to dramatize support for his newly reaffirmed overseas policy, the throng cheered as the seventy-four-year-old premier extolled the virtue of sacrifice for country and proclaimed the "right" of "Overseas Lands [to] belong to the Nation." His four-minute address whipped the flames of Portuguese nationalism. "One word only occurs to me, one reality alone can attain the level of this act of patriotic communion: that word is Portugal."[143]

U.S. Assistant Secretary for African Affairs G. Mennen Williams offered Lisbon verbal assurance that the United States had no intention of substituting its own influence for that of Portugal in Angola and Mozambique.[144] Nevertheless the Kennedy administration was caught in an intensifying crossfire between Portuguese allegations that it was betraying the West and African charges that it was supporting colonial repression.[145]

In late August, President John Kennedy dispatched Undersecretary of State George W. Ball to Lisbon where he and Premier Salazar talked for three days. Ball was convinced that "the loss of Angola and Mozambique would be catastrophic for Portugal." If African insurgency were to succeed, half a million overseas Portuguese "would debouch" into an overcrowded, economically underdeveloped metropole. Unable to persuade Salazar to accept the principle of self-determination, Kennedy's Eurocentric emissary was himself persuaded of the need for a "Eurafrican" solution to Portugal's colonial problems.[146] Unimpressed by African insurgents who came from "unpopular" tribal "minorities" and of independent African states who lacked "the military resources to do anything effective," he concluded that a grant of independence to Angola and Mozambique would only lead to civil war. Drawing upon experience in the Congo, he foresaw a danger of another "long-term intervention" by a United Nations "peacekeeping force," with the United States again paying most of the bill. The Congo undertaking had cost the American government over $400 million.[147]

To enable Portugal's "extensive and strategically important territories" to "mature in a friendly atmosphere," George Ball advised, would require a two-step Eurafrican strategy. First, Portugal would have to be brought by stages into the European Economic Community. Its community partners could then provide it "with the capital required to raise the standard of living in the metropole to the point where the overseas territories were no longer needed as dumping grounds for her landless peasants or as a happy hunting grounds for her commercial interests." Second, Angola and Mozambique would have to be brought into the community's "preferential trading system," following which "measures toward self-determination could be taken in a calm atmosphere quite unlike the frantic concern" that had so far surrounded the question.[148]

Despite Ball's sympathy for the Portuguese position, his discussions with Salazar "resulted in no meeting of the minds between [the] two governments."[149] When the Portuguese chief of state, President Américo Thomaz, arrived in Luanda for a twenty-three day visit to Angola in September, he was greeted by a cheering crowd of fifty thousand and placards denouncing the United States: "America, You Are Playing with a Two-Faced Coin—Your Self-Seeking Is Known!"[150] And in the corridors of United Nations headquarters in New York, Foreign Minister Franco Nogueira alleged that the United States was secretly financing Holden Roberto's GRAE as part of a self-serving strategy to replace Portuguese interests in Angola.[151]

If Washington's efforts to persuade Portugal to accept the principle of self-determination only confirmed Lisbon's suspicions of American neocolonial designs, so its parallel efforts to persuade African states to accept the idea of sending U.N. rapporteurs on fact-finding missions to Angola and Mozambique only provoked African scorn. Its U.N. fact-finding proposal was seen as a dilatory half-measure designed to cover up Washington's continued military aid to Portugal.[152] Their rejection of the American scheme, however, did not prevent African states from engaging in their own U.N. dialogue with Portugal over the central issue of self-determination.

The previously discussed Security Council resolution of July 1963 had called upon the secretary-general to do what he could to "ensure the implementation" of its provisions. Accordingly that September U Thant sent a special representative, Godfrey Amachree, to Lisbon. The way was opened for talks between Portuguese and African diplomats under the auspices of the secretary-general. The discussions began in mid-October against a tense background of charges by Congolese Premier Adoula that Portugal was threatening to block the Congo River estuary,[153] was allowing Katangese secessionists to regroup in Angola, and was permitting its soldiers to violate Congolese territory repeatedly.[154] Covering the second fortnight of October, the talks focused squarely on the issue of self-determination. The nine African states participating found Portugal's foreign minister quite prepared to accept self-determination as a relevant principle.[155] But he defined the concept differently from the others. To Franco Nogueira self-determination did not necessarily mean the right to choose freely one's political status, including independence. It could, he said, just as well mean "participation" at "all levels" of "administration and political life" within a previously accepted (and thus previously given) "political structure, type of State and administrative organization." And since the populations of Portugal's overseas territories were participating in decision making and the electoral process at all levels, from rural areas to the National Assembly, Portugal had not denied the principle of self-determination to Angola or any other territory.[156]

Portuguese-African discussions ended in a predictable impasse. Although Secretary-General U Thant considered "encouraging" the fact that they could take place at all,[157] his subsequent efforts to relaunch them met with bitter opposition from Holden Roberto[158] and disinterest on the part of the discussants.[159] Both parties had quite fully and firmly stated their positions.

At the end of 1963, Foreign Minister Franco Nogueira tried another route to dialogue. In an appearance before the Security Council, he invited the secretary-general to "visit Angola and Mozambique at his discretion and convenience" with a promise that the Portuguese government would "accord him all facilities required."[160] Rather than authorize such a visit, however, the Security Council expressed regret that agreement had not been reached "on the United Nations interpretation of self-determination" and criticized Portugal's continuing failure to recognize the right of Angolans and Mozambicans to that kind of self-determination.[161] Symbolic of how far Lisbon was from opening up diplomatic dialogue, the year ended with the newly independent government of Kenya ordering the closure of Portugal's consulates in Nairobi and Mombasa.[162]

CHAPTER FOUR

PAN-AFRICAN CRASH: THE END OF AN ILLUSION

Basking in the warmth of OAU recognition, Holden Roberto called a press conference in early September 1963 and laid down the conditions under which he would accept a cease-fire. He proposed that Portugal recognize Angola's right to independence, grant a general political amnesty, withdraw all its "pacification" forces, and agree to negotiate a transfer of power in accordance with United Nations recommendations.[1] Portugal was not about to agree. But Roberto's international stature seemed sufficiently secured by OAU recognition for a senior French diplomat to venture onto the Léopoldville reviewing stand during the FNLA's next (third) anniversary celebrations commemorating the March 1961 uprising.[2] And well on into the second half of 1964, Roberto's government in exile continued to garner diplomatic recognition. The increasing external stature of the FNLA was, however, unconnected to internal reality. Roberto's political standing began to decline within a few months of his summer triumph of 1963. And, paradoxically, that very triumph contributed to his political downfall.

OAU recognition encouraged the FNLA's tendencies as an exile organization to avoid reality. Its expectations of benevolent external intervention drew its attention away from the central importance of building internal strength and self-reliance. His mind focused on international role playing and global strategies, Roberto allowed the FNLA/GRAE to collapse from within. The presence of a French diplomat at March 15 anniversary celebrations in 1964 in no way compensated for the boycott of those celebrations by GRAE's own foreign minister and vice-president—Jonas Savimbi and Emmanuel Kunzika—and their supporters.

EXTERNAL DEPENDENCY

The failure of anticipated OAU and other external support to materialize in the months after GRAE won pan-African endorsement frustrated GRAE leadership. Finally in January 1964, Roberto concluded publicly that despite "undoubted" goodwill, African states could not meet his growing need for material assistance. "With our present support we could go on fighting for another twenty years." "In the end," he complained, "there would be no one left to liberate." Pointing out that African states were purchasers and not producers of arms, he asserted that it would be "a betrayal of the suffering of the Angolan people" not to turn to those who produced and thus could provide modern weapons.[3]

With considerable bitterness, Roberto also concluded that though Western countries could, they would not provide such assistance. He was especially frustrated by American unresponsiveness. As the leader of a movement that had long seen the United States as a prospective champion of Angolan independence,[4] he for some time had viewed President John F. Kennedy as the personification of his hope for American support.[5] But the Kennedy administration muted its anticolonialism in order to assuage Portugal and assure continued American use of air transport and antisubmarine bases in the Azores.[6]

Roberto sent a letter to President Kennedy on November 27, 1962, writing of the "growing indignation" of "the Angolan people" over an increasing compatibility between American and Portuguese policies. A month later, following an American vote against a U.N. General Assembly resolution highly critical of Portugal,[7] Roberto wrote a second letter to the president. Invoking "the warmth" of the meeting that the two had had when Kennedy was still a senator, Roberto recalled: "You had already adopted a courageous position with regard to Algeria and you were concerned with the welfare of the people of Angola." But now in 1963, he complained, Portuguese officials were stating that they had "official assurances" that even American "humanitarian" aid to Angolan refugees and students would be "cut off." Roberto appealed for a hearing: "I would certainly welcome an opportunity to talk with you again in person, but I am under no illusions as to the difficulties such a meeting could create. I do, however, request that you make possible a meeting with a White House representative to whom I could outline my views and who could discuss with me in detail what can be done to assist the people of Angola in this moment of their great sacrifice and struggle to which you must certainly still subscribe."[8]

As of November 22, 1963, the day of President Kennedy's assassination, Holden Roberto had received no reply to or acknowledgment of his letters? Unlike the American-educated Mozambican leader, Eduardo Mondlane, who had friends of long standing in Washington and whose movement had not yet begun hostilities against the Portuguese, Roberto was consistently denied access to White House or Department of State officials. Yet Roberto did not blame the president. In New York at the time of Kennedy's death, Roberto (along with numerous other Africans at the United Nations) saw the assassination as part of a deep-seated conspiracy against the president's liberal racial and anticolonial policies.[10] With his lingering hopes for either an American arms embargo against Portugal or for substantial American material assistance crushed, Roberto took stock. He had visited the United States at least once a year since 1959. He made the 1963 visit, from which he returned to Léopoldville "broken hearted," his last.[11]

Convinced that major external assistance constituted a sine qua non for success, Roberto turned to the one potential aid source that he had not previously importuned: major communist states. He met in Nairobi with Chinese Foreign Minister Chen Yi during Kenya's independence celebrations (December 12, 1963) and with Soviet and Cuban representatives at the United Nations and then announced that he had been assured of "whatever we need in arms and money." Lashing out at the "hypocrisy" of Westerners who paid lip-service to self-determination but supplied Portugal with arms, Roberto described his turn to the East as a "radical change" from a policy that had heretofore kept GRAE "out of the cold war and within the framework of African politics."[12]

Roberto's moves seemed more convincing as a reaction against old associates who had failed him than as an embrace of new bene-factors.[13] His announcement that he expected to dispatch a mission to Peking within a month and to follow it with another to the Soviet Union flew in the face of existing Congolese (host state) foreign policy. Just that November, Premier Adoula had expelled staff members of the Soviet embassy, accusing them of aiding anti-government Lumumbist insurgents. And Léopoldville maintained diplomatic relations with Taipei, not Peking. Roberto's response to this apparent policy conflict, however, was to assert that Adoula would, of course, "understand that we need help" and that, in any case, "the Congolese should not interfere in our internal affairs." Roberto seemed to be signaling the Congolese government that it was hosting an impulsive state-within-a-state.

Léopoldville reacted sharply. Warning that Angolans could not "behave in the Congo as in conquered territory," Acting Foreign Minister Marcel Lengema announced that the Congo had attached a condition to its recognition of GRAE: "All material assistance" had to be "channeled through the Congolese Government," and Angolans were not authorized to accept aid "directly from abroad." And while the Congolese government most likely would permit the entry of Chinese arms, the entry of Chinese personnel was "an entirely different matter."[14]

There were, however, some contrastingly enthusiastic reactions to GRAE's proposed international realignment.[15] Noting that Roberto had become increasingly critical of Western "hypocrisy,"[16] Soviet observers concluded that realism was "forcing" him "to re-examine his position." The Soviet view remained censorious of Roberto's refusal to cooperate with the MPLA. But it "evaluat[ed] positively" his changed "attitude" toward "socialist countries."[17] Despite periodic communiqués heralding an imminent departure,[18] however, GRAE's promised missions to China and Eastern Europe were delayed until, with the sudden fall of the Adoula government and the improbable rise of Katanga secessionist Moïse Tshombe to power in July 1964, they became politically unfeasible.

Confronted with a growing Lumumbist insurgency in the eastern Congo that had already toppled Adoula and had at least nominal Sino-Soviet backing, Tshombe was not about to allow Angolan nationalists to establish ties with China and the Soviet Union.[19] He was not about to allow the Angolans to receive military aid from other external sources either. His symbiotic relationship with the Portuguese was well known. So was his dislike for Roberto, whom he had been denouncing earlier from exile in Madrid as an ambitious fraud who knew nothing of Angola.[20]

Sealed off by Tshombe from external aid previously funneled through Congolese channels and upon which it had become so dependent, GRAE had to fall back upon its own resources. And therein lay disaster. By the time that Moïse Tshombe assumed power in Léopoldville, GRAE was, beneath its "governmental" pose, an organizational fiasco.

MALAISE TO SCHISM: GRAE

Having failed to capitalize on its postrecognition opportunity to rethink, recruit, restructure, and reach out, GRAE proved especially vulnerable to external constraints and disappointments. External factors helped to dash hopes for an early insurgent victory and hastened a decline in morale and rise in dissension within Angolan ranks. But the malaise within GRAE was attributable primarily to internal causes—something that few outside observers understood.

There were some exceptions. As early as January 1964, the Swiss press was commenting on north-south ethnic (Bakongo-Ovimbundu) cleavage within GRAE, centered around a growing rift between Roberto and Savimbi.[21] And by March, a respected British periodical was pointing to an internal crisis within the Angolan movement and venturing that it "would not be surprising if Savimbi were to displace Roberto."[22]

Beginning in late 1963, Savimbi had begun organizing his "southern" followers into a sub rosa force capable of challenging Roberto's leadership. Factional suspicion and hostility mounted steadily. By April, the two men were conspiring against one another. For example, Roberto precipitated the admission of Viriato da Cruz into the FNLA during Savimbi's absence, and Savimbi undertook a secret journey to Moscow, Prague, Budapest, and East Berlin in quest of personal support.[23] "Unfortunately," Savimbi would later comment, the Soviets and East Europeans "were only interested in recruiting new members for [the] MPLA."[24] Savimbi had also been cultivating relations with Arab states, notably the UAR and Iraq, where he carefully dissociated himself from Roberto's policy of accepting aid from Israel.

Nominally Jonas Savimbi remained GRAE foreign minister. But by April or May, he and Roberto were no longer speaking to one another. Roberto assumed full responsibility for external affairs, relying on the assistance of an inexperienced student who had recently volunteered his services.[25] And Savimbi, cut off from any participation in UPA/GRAE affairs, was left with little to do but conspire. He sent emissaries to the MPLA to discuss possible terms for cooperation.[26] At the same time, among his close supporters he broached the idea of creating a breakaway movement, the *Partido de Acção Revolucionária Angolana* (PARA).[27]

In Europe, a former GRAE Katanga representative, Jorge Valentim, sought to mobilize student opinion for Savimbi and against Roberto. He persuaded a group of some sixteen participants at an "extraordinary assembly" of the National Union of Angolan Students (UNEA) held at Wisen, Switzerland (May 2–3, 1964), to query the admission of Viriato da Cruz into the FNLA. Savimbi and his student associates saw da Cruz as a rival would-be successor to Roberto and deplored his entry into the FNLA as contributing to "nationalist disunity."[28]

In organizing his own shadow movement preparatory to a final break, Savimbi estimated that he could count on the support of 350 soldiers at Kinkuzu in addition to the sixty-five ELNA recruits from Katanga that Roberto had had imprisoned at Ndolo.[29] He further calculated that he had some eighty-five supporters (mainly Ovim-bundu, Chokwe, Ganguela and Ovambo) within and about GRAE's Léopoldville offices.[30] And as disillusionment with Roberto's iron sway spread, Savimbi found sympathy among some of GRAE's northern leaders, including the (Cabindan) minister of armaments, Alexandre Taty.

A parallel surge of anti-Roberto sentiment developed within the PDA leadership. It reached such intensity by March 1964 that Emmanuel Kunzika wrote a letter to Agostinho Neto suggesting that they put their quarrels behind them and seek an accommoda-tion.[31] However, Roberto managed to salve PDA sensitivities tem-porarily by means of short-term gestures, such as including the PDA secretary-general, Ferdinand Dombele, on the GRAE delega-tion to an OAU Liberation Committee meeting (April 1964) in Dar es Salaam. He was thus able to enlist PDA support for the admis-sion of Viriato da Cruz into the FNLA and to ensure against coales-cence of a Savimbi/PDA anti-Roberto alliance that might have commanded a clear majority in the National Council of the FNLA. Adept at playing his challengers off, one against the other, Roberto seemed relatively unconcerned about long-term prospects for what the PDA certainly had in mind when it supported da Cruz—a da Cruz/PDA alliance to counter his personal ascendancy.

All the while, Roberto made certain that the PDA's role was kept to that of a tolerated and useful but junior partner. Alleging that Roberto ran GRAE's military base as though it were his own private property, Commander José Kalundungo later commented: "The PDA, which was not an active participant [at Kinkuzu], never counted for more than thirty soldiers out of a thousand."[32]

A year after participating in the humiliation of the MPLA, Jonas Savimbi and his Ovimbundu-Chokwe, or southern, nexus had adopted as their own most of the arguments that the MPLA had used in trying to stave off pan-African endorsement of GRAE. Now they too accused Roberto of tribalism (Bakongo favoritism), racism (antimestiço, antiwhite), and corruption (diverting movement funds to his own foreign bank accounts).[33] But above all, they denounced him for resisting their demands that GRAE military operations be extended to the Katanga-Angola frontier, and they reviled him for arresting and jailing soldiers who had tried to hold him to his promise that they could set up a logistics base in Katanga. In late May 1964, Jorge Valentim complained in a widely circulated UNEA statement that Roberto opposed a Katanga military front, reorganization of the FNLA and the army, and acceleration of the struggle. It was at the request of GRAE, Valentim asserted, that Congolese security officials were preventing "Angolan patriots" who did favor such actions from leaving the confines of Léopold-ville.[34] To hold his movement together, Roberto was desperately resorting to internal (UPA) and outside (Congolese host state) coercion. By July 1964, when African heads of state convened in Cairo for the first anniversary summit meeting of the Organization of African Unity, GRAE had all but split asunder.

THE CAIRO CONFERENCE

Having failed to gain quick acceptance of himself as the Congo's new premier—he was invited not to attend the OAU meeting—Moïse Tshombe did not object to Holden Roberto's participation at the Cairo Conference of Heads of State and Government. He probably hoped thereby to suggest to African governments that he was not about to suppress Angolan nationalists in deference to his Portuguese connections. Unlike the days when he needed an Angolan base for his secessionist forces, he could now afford to disappoint the Portuguese more than he could afford to add confrontation with the OAU and Roberto's military forces to the already serious challenge of a Lumumbist insurgency.[35]

Rather than reassurance and improved stature and bargaining power, however, Cairo brought Roberto new problems. His troubles began when Jonas Savimbi, ostensibly returned to his university studies at Lausanne since May, showed up at the preliminary session of African foreign ministers only to find his place taken by Roberto's confidant and Algiers representative, Johnny Edouard. Savimbi sought out Roberto at his personal Cairo quarters. Roberto refused to see him. Rebuffed and frustrated, Savimbi struck back. On the eve of the summit meeting, he called a press conference and resigned from GRAE.[36] Reversing the optimism with which he had portrayed Angolan insurgency for Radio Moscow just that

April,[37] he decried disunity and confusion with the movement and charged that GRAE, "far from intensifying military action and regrouping the popular masses—the only way to hasten the liberation of Angola—had limit[ed] itself to empty speeches." He called upon African states to reopen the questions of Angolan unity and GRAE recognition and to convene a congress of all active Angolan nationalists.[38]

Savimbi's action set off a bitter battle of words in which the protagonists persistently tried to affix a pro-American, antiunity, and tribalist label on each other. Amplifying his Cairo allegations, Savimbi hurled charges of collusion with "American imperialism." Most startling was his assertion (echoed by Ghana's Kwame Nkrumah, among others) that an American veteran of Vietnam service had assumed command of the Angolan army (ELNA).[39] In question was a young Afro-American, Bernard Manhertz, who had served as a noncommissioned officer in South Vietnam. He had been deeply alienated by American racism. Identifying with the cause of black African insurgency in Angola, he had volunteered his services through the GRAE office in New York. Hoping to impart skills that he had learned in the American army, Manhertz flew to Léopoldville in spring 1964. After much delay, Roberto permitted him to visit Kinkuzu. Though black, Manhertz was no less American. He spoke neither Portuguese nor French. He was unable to communicate with ELNA officers, unable to get them to listen to, let alone to understand, him. After a few weeks of trying, he returned to Léopoldville suffering from an acute tropical fever. Physically and psychologically depleted, he flew to New York, disillusioned by his experience. The idea that Manhertz had assumed a key military role in GRAE was simply an ironic example of the paranoia that intruded into the perceptions and verbal vendettas that followed Savimbi's resignation.[40]

GRAE spokesmen countered with allegations that Savimbi, a beneficiary of American Protestant scholarships, was himself an "anticommunist." They portrayed him as someone who sought Western advice, resisted ties with socialist countries (they did not mention his trip to Eastern Europe), and opposed Roberto's projected trip to China because it might displease the United States.[41]

Savimbi blamed Roberto for perpetuating Angolan disunity because he resisted an entente with the MPLA (Neto), and Roberto blamed Savimbi for perpetuating Angolan disunity because he opposed an entente with the MPLA (da Cruz). As for "tribalism,"

Savimbi accused Roberto of favoring fellow Bakongo with a near monopoly of political posts in GRAE, and Roberto accused Savimbi of promoting mutiny among Ovimbundu soldiers at Kinkuzu.[42]

Savimbi's Cairo broadside against Roberto served to arouse or to reinforce doubts among African leaders concerning the wisdom of their Angolan option of the year before. President Nkrumah seized upon evidence of a faltering and conflicted Angolan insurgency as ammunition for his argument that the OAU's first year had been one of retrogression. Along with border clashes (Algeria versus Morocco, Somalia versus Kenya and Ethiopia), army mutinies (Kenya, Tanganyika, Uganda), and civil war in the Congo, the failure of the OAU's Liberation Committee (ALC) to work effectively for the liberation of Southern Africa, he said, proved the inadequacy of a "step-by-step" course toward unity. Only the Nkrumah formula for continent-wide Union Government could save Africa from being sacrificed "on the altar of neo-colonialism."[43]

Already the previous August, *Spark,* the organ of Accra's Bureau of African Affairs, had begun attacking the ALC (from which Ghana had been excluded). The Liberation Committee, said *Spark,* had handed primary responsibility for helping liberation movements to contiguous countries such as the Congo and exceeded its authority in deciding for recognition of Roberto's GRAE. It was thus serving imperialist designs.[44]

Speaking at the Cairo conference on July 19, Nkrumah threw his prestige behind *Spark*'s criticism. He alleged that the ALC had inexcusably rejected the counsel of military specialists "on ideological grounds" and argued: "If the Liberation Committee had made effective use of the military experience of Egypt and Algeria, where neo-colonialist interference and espionage had been frustrated and held at bay, we would have given freedom fighters the necessary help in their liberation struggle." Instead the ALC had supported the idea of training forces in the Congo (the GRAE's Congo Alliance) where they were exposed to "espionage, intrigues, frustrations and disappointments."

The Tanganyika-based ALC, Nkrumah averred, had failed to provide security, arms, food, clothing, or medicine to guerrilla trainees. It had "let down the freedom fighters." Ghana would never contribute financially to such a committee. "By raising a threat at Addis Ababa and not being able to take effective action against apartheid and colonialism," Nkrumah concluded, "we have worsened the plight of our kinsmen in Angola, Mozambique,

Southern Rhodesia and South Africa." The OAU simply "frightened the imperialists sufficiently to strengthen their defences and repression in southern Africa."[45]

"The fat was in the fire":[46] Tanganyika's Julius Nyerere tore up his prepared speech and retorted that Ghana had refused to contribute to the ALC liberation fund for the "extremely petty" reason that it had not been included on the committee and that Dar es Salaam, not Accra, had been chosen as committee headquarters. Accusing "the Great Osagefo" of mounting "strenuous efforts" to block regional unity in East Africa while carrying out "incessant" propaganda for his own impractical scheme for continental unity "in one act," Nyerere called upon the Ghanaian leader to "at least refrain from undermining the effectiveness of the Liberation Movement, including the Committee of Nine [ALC]."[47]

Not to be deterred, the day after Nyerere's address Nkrumah reopened the issue of the OAU's recognition of GRAE.[48] Referring to the fact that the MPLA had embarked upon military action in Cabinda, Nkrumah told the conference: "It is not fair of us to recognize one side and leave the other because both of them are engaged in war. If you recognize one, it discourages the other." Military not political priorities should prevail during an armed struggle, and therefore the proper task of the OAU was to bring the two Angolan groups together in a common front against Portugal. This is what Ghana had been trying to accomplish for several years. "My point is—let's look very carefully and see how we can get those people together."[49]

In remarks preceding those of Nkrumah, Roberto "deplored" the fact that "certain brother countries take advantage of the weakness of some of us to spread doubt." "Paradoxical as it may seem," he added, "those who meddle in our affairs are precisely those who do not help us." Reiterating GRAE appeals made at OAU meetings earlier in the year,[50] he pleaded for OAU assistance commensurate with the scope and nature of GRAE insurgency.[51] According to the Franco-Tunisian weekly, *Jeune Afrique*, GRAE had finally received about $154,000 during the first year of the OAU Liberation Fund, less than it had been receiving previously through bilateral aid now replaced by collective assistance.[52]

Following Nkrumah's intervention, Roberto angrily accused the Ghanaian leader of systematic opposition to his movement. He "had not wanted to speak up," Roberto said, but Nkrumah's remarks had "forced" him to do so: "If we are in difficulty, Ghana is responsible for it." Like Nyerere the day before, Roberto defied Nkrumah. "We cannot tolerate that while our brothers are falling, we should be confronted with false problems. The Committee of Nine is aware of the situation, Mr. [Sebastian] Chale [ALC administrative secretary] who came to Léopoldville saw and [studied] the situation. If you do not trust the Committee of Nine, then I retire." In anger he blurted: "We started our struggle before the birth of the OAU. If you are going to raise new problems for us, I am sorry to inform you that we shall retire from the OAU but the struggle will go on."[53]

The Cairo conference did raise new problems for GRAE. But Roberto did not retire, and Nkrumah did not succeed in persuading his peers to rescind its recognition of GRAE. The problems were posed sharply by Brazzaville's President Massamba-Debat. Declaring himself a seasoned advocate of Angolan unity, he criticized Roberto for refusing to accept others, meaning the MPLA, except on a piecemeal, individual basis. As a consequence of this negativism, he said, the MPLA had regrouped in Congo-Brazzaville, assembling an armed force of at least fifteen hundred, of whom six hundred had received military training. Respecting OAU Dakar recommendations that African states help only GRAE, the Brazzaville government had had no "official contact with the MPLA." Moreover it had declined to deliver arms shipments meant for the MPLA but seized and still held by the Brazzaville security service.[54] Asserting his neutrality between the two Angolan movements (an assertion Roberto challenged),[55] the Brazzaville leader told the summit that the MPLA had quite independently organized "raids all along the Cabinda border, which we cannot even watch as we do not have a substantial security service." In pursuit, Portuguese forces were entering Brazzaville's territory and killing "poor peasants in the fields."[56]

Did the OAU expect his government to shut down the activities of these "real fighters"? And, raising the specter of Tshombe that hovered over the whole discussion on Angola, he asked, what if GRAE were forced to flee to Brazzaville (like the MPLA before it) while the two movements were still at odds? Massamba-Debat gave the impression of being prepared to pay the costs of the first (MPLA raids) but not the second (two-party friction). His questions prompted Kenneth Kaunda of Zambia to "venture to suggest that we continue to support what has been recognized as the majority organization in Angola" but "at the same time appoint a Committee" to seek once again a "reconciliation" between the two Angolan movements.[57] Kaunda's proposal won general support[58] and then formalization by Algeria's Ben Bella into a concrete proposal. Citing the experience of the Algerian revolution and the triumph of his own movement over an unassimilable rival,[59] Ben Bella cautioned against trying to impose a unity on the Angolans. In words reminiscent of Frantz Fanon, he counseled: "It is the struggle, the development of that struggle, the contradictions, the obstacles, that ultimately determine the leading team, the group that will shoulder the responsibilities of the Revolution."[60] Accordingly the OAU should "continue seriously helping the Government we have recognized and . . . request that those who [have not yet recognized it] do so at once" and appoint a conciliation committee to attempt once again to mediate differences and promote voluntary unity among the Angolans.[61] His proposal was adopted.

The chairman of the session, President Sékou Touré of Guinea, named Congo-Brazzaville, Ghana, and the United Arab Republic, three countries sympathetic to the MPLA, to constitute the conciliation committee. And in response to Massamba-Debat's questions, Touré ruled that pending the results of the new committee's efforts, Congo-Brazzaville was obliged to hold the MPLA-destined arms that it had seized, yet at the same time allow the MPLA (and even the Cabindan separatists) to continue to operate in its territory.[62]

Thus the OAU unanimously reaffirmed its recognition of Holden Roberto but simultaneously named a committee of governments hostile to GRAE to reconcile it with an adversary that the OAU had itself rejected the previous year as unworthy of continued existence. GRAE's period of exclusive pan-African legitimacy had lasted just one year. As if in response to this setback, in October 1964, Johnny Edouard produced one of his by then familiar communiqués from Algiers announcing an impending reorganization of FNLA/GRAE structure and leadership.[63]

THE TSHOMBE SQUEEZE

GRAE fortunes continued to plummet after the OAU's Cairo summit. Within weeks the Léopoldville press was reporting mutiny, allegedly the fifth, at the Kinkuzu base.[64] And by November 1965, the end of Moïse Tshombe's ascendancy in Léopoldville, Angolan insurgency had come to a near standstill. Tshombe pursued a policy of gradual suffocation, encouraging the natural process of splintering and crumbling that often accompanies deceleration in revolutionary action. His tough Katangan associate and minister of interior, Godefroid Munongo, who described Portugal as "one of our best friends," equated "subversion" in Angola with that of Lumumbist rebels in the Congo and blamed Arab "slavedrivers" Ben Bella and Gamal Abdel Nasser for "sustaining" insurgency in both countries.[65] Munongo clearly favored a crackdown on GRAE, but Tshombe held out against outright suppression. He was undoubtedly influenced by a desire not to complicate efforts to gain support from "moderate" African governments and intercession on Holden Roberto's behalf from his fellow Bakongo, President Joseph Kasavubu, as well as a concern for the potential cost of a military showdown with ELNA forces based on Congolese territory. Acting with customary guile, Tshombe cut off external and internal supplies of arms and ammunition (some of which he feared might end up in Congolese rebel hands), encouraged the provincial government of Kongo Central to harass Roberto's supporters, and fostered a political climate that facilitated Portuguese efforts to infiltrate nationalist groups and enflame dissensions. He hoped thereby to hasten the decomposition of the Angolan government in exile while publicly asserting his belief in Angolan nationalism.

The 1964–1965 period of Tshombe's rule demonstrated how a loss of momentum, whatever its cause, will reduce cohesion in a revolutionary movement and encourage retreat back to primordial goals and loyalties. Slowdown and discouragement led to a resurgence of ethnic and subethnic conflict. Groups and individuals that had jumped on the revolutionary bandwagon in mid-1963 began to drop off. By April 1965, some of the disenchanted had rejoined the depleted ranks of Angolan separatists and collaborationists and had clustered within two counterrevolutionary fronts.

Bakongo Separatism

Four groups of Bakongo separatists (émigrés, exiles, and refugees) linked up on April 20, 1965 to form the avowedly pacifist *Front Patriotique pour l'Indépendance du Kongo Dit Portugais* (FPIKP). The principal organizers were leaders of a small Bazombo youth movement, *Ajeunal*,[66] which in November 1963 had transformed itself into a political party, the *Parti Progressiste Angolais* (PPA).[67] Sometime supporters of an Angolan common front,[68] the PPA's Alphonse Proença Matondo and Edouard Makumbi[69] turned away from the multiethnic notion of Angolan nationalism, opportunely echoed Tshombe's denunciation of Arab influence in the OAU,[70] and channeled their ambition into a revival of Bakongo separatism—independence for the "Portuguese Kongo."[71] They found conditions propitious for assembling a flimsy collection of Bakongo nationalists and presenting it as a newsworthy anti-GRAE alliance.[72] Included along with the PPA were a faction of the Ngwizako royalists that had not joined the MPLA-sponsored Democratic Front (FDLA);[73] the small, traditionalist *Rassemblement des Chefs Coutumiers du Kongo Portugais* (RCCKP); and some elements, or remnants, of the collaborationist Nto-Bako.

As its main thrust, the Bakongo Front reasserted the case for a historical and juridical separation of the Kongo Kingdom from Angola. Curiously it credited the Portuguese (Angolan) segment of the former kingdom with a population of four and a half million (600,000 was closer to reality) and argued that "Angola" was simply a "scientific" name given to the Kongo by Portugal.[74] Did this mean that the FPIKP dreamed of Bakongo hegemony over all the people and territory of contemporary Angola? Whatever the scope of its ambitions, the FPIKP took a clear stand against violent action and asked the United Nations "to designate without delay a selected group of political figures who could accompany [FPIKP leaders] to Portugal for the purpose of opening talks on self-determination for our country."[75]

In August 1965, the Bakongo Front garnered another affiliate. War-weary Sosso (Bakongo subgroup) refugees from the northern region of 31 de Janeiro formed a new exile movement and joined it with the FPIKP. Their creation, the *União Progressista de Nsosso em Angola* (UPRONA), reflected a growing loss of faith in the efficacy of revolutionary action. Some UPRONA members were defectors from the MPLA.[76] At the outset, the Sosso group presented itself as a regional ethnic movement (open to "inhabitants of Nsosso Mbianda Ngunga").[77] Though it later changed its name to *União Progressista Nacional de Angola*, it remained a communal organization.

After five years of a war that to him promised no "solution," UPRONA's president and prime mover, Carlos Pinto Nunes Vunzi,[78] sought through "non-violence" and public appeals aimed at Portuguese officials, the United Nations, and random personalities abroad, the independence that had eluded Angolan insurgents.[79] UPRONA petitioned Salazar[80] and invoked the Bible, the Universal Declaration of Human Rights, and the honor of Portugal in support of its cause. These tactics had been used without success by northern groups prior to and just after the outbreak of fighting in 1961,[81] and they continued to prove futile.

Locked into a compulsive repetition of demonstrably fruitless political action, the FPIKP-UPRONA organizers of resurgent Bakongo separatism seemed determined to take no notice of past experience. In particular, they refused to reckon with the fact that as of that time (1964–1965) Nto-Bako and the *Mouvement de Défense des Intérêts de l'Angola* (MDIA), whose members had previously served as collaborators and exponents of nonviolence, were being decimated and their leadership imprisoned within Angola because they had lost their counterrevolutionary usefulness.[82] Repeated appeals to the Portuguese government and United Nations by the François Lélé–led faction of Nto-Bako on behalf of party organizers imprisoned in Angola bore no results.[83] Nto-Bako clamor was ignored. And in 1966, even an unrelentingly pro-Portuguese faction of Nto-Bako led by Angelino Alberto reported to the United Nations its concern for the fate of its collaborator-leader. He had not been heard from since leaving for Angola in late 1963. "If you like," they urged the U.N., "you can ask the Portuguese Government where he is."[84]

In October 1965, the MDIA sent the following cable to U.N. Secretary-General U Thant:

Committees and several families members Mouvement Défense Intérêts Angola have been interior Angola since 19 August 1965 purpose struggling peacefully gradual independence. We have learned that they have been deported unknown destinations. We request United Nations commission inquiry. Thank you highest consideration.[85]

In April 1968, Nto-Bako sent its own four-man investigative team into Angola in search of Alberto and others. After a quest of nearly two years, they located members of the Nto-Bako (Alberto) executive committee among some 185 political prisoners held at a camp on the small island of São Nicolau north of Moçâmedes.[86] Held along with these Nto-Bakists were Jean Pierre M'Bala and Pierre Tecka, top leaders of the MDIA, who had last been reported in 1965 as working with the Portuguese to promote the return of refugees in the Congo to Angola.[87] As for the disappeared

Angelino Alberto, however, São Nicolau detainees reported in 1970 that he had been sent to far-off Lisbon.[88] Needing to believe in Portuguese goodwill, however, FPIKP-UPRONA organizers took no heed of what was befalling those who preceded them on the pacifist-separatist path.

An Anti-GRAE Countergovernment

In addition to nourishing Bakongo separatism, Tshombe's rise to power conduced the emergence of a new multiethnic exile coalition bent upon displacing Holden Roberto and GRAE. Roberto's resilient political foes, André Kassinda and Marcos Kassanga, saw a new opportunity to topple him. Since escaping from a Léopoldville jail in November 1963, Kassinda had been marking time. Operating out of Brazzaville, he had continued to speak in the name of the *União Nacional Angolana* (UNA) that he and Kassanga had organized in Katanga in 1963.[89] In a UNA memorandum to the July 1964 OAU summit in Cairo, he attacked Cyrille Adoula for having supported Roberto's "imaginary" government. He did so on behalf of the dubious reality of UNA "shock troops" backed up by over "385,000 [UNA] members" and "950,000 sympathizers."[90]

Marcos Kassanga had been marking time at Bujumbura on the Congo's eastern border. Shortly after becoming premier, Tshombe flew into the Bujumbura airport en route to rebel-beseiged Bukavu. Kassanga wrangled an interview with and a visa from him,[91] and shortly thereafter teamed up again with Kassinda.[92] "The Government of M. Tshombe having shown great understanding with regard to the Angolan problem and having agreed to permit the UNA to resume its activities in the Democratic Republic of the Congo," Kassanga later recounted, "the headquarters of the organization established itself once again in Léopoldville."[93]

Using palaver and leaflets, Kassanga and Kassinda threw themselves into the intrigue of exile politics in Kinshasa.[94] By April 1965, they had assembled a disparate coalition of anti-GRAE groups. With fanfare they announced at a public rally a new multiparty *Conselho do Povo Angolano* (CPA), or Council of the Angolan People. In delegating to itself the responsibility for "cleansing" the "Angolan Liberation Movement" of "destructive elements and saboteurs" and replacing bankrupt leadership with "true and sincere Angolans," their new coalition used the language of nationalist revolution.[95] But speaking with local journalists, André Kassinda communicated a different message. The advent of Tshombe's Government of Public Safety offered Angolans an opportunity to express their discontent with and to withdraw their recognition from Holden Roberto's leadership. With Roberto thrust aside, the way would be open for a negotiated settlement with Portugal. Therefore "armed struggle against Portugal" should not even be "considered" until after a coalition of all Angolan forces had made "an effort to persuade Portugal to negotiate."[96] The CPA proposed to shut down Kinkuzu and still all continuing insurgency inside Angola as a prelude to striking a deal with Lisbon.

In addition to their own remnant UNA, Kassanga and Kassinda lined up a mix of real and fictive groups to form the CPA alliance. Small but real were the *Comitê Unidade Nacional Angolana* (CUNA), created in July 1963[97] by Bakongo refugees from the Bembe-Carmona region of northern Angola;[98] the *Movimento Nacional Angolano* (MNA) of Sorongo (Bakongo subgroup), which had joined the MPLA's ill-fated Democratic Front (FDLA) in 1963;[99] and the *Partido Nacional Africano* (PNA), the Tshikapa-based Chokwe movement formed in November 1963 by defectors from what PNA described as the "tribalized" MPLA and UPA.[100] So small as to be fictive were the *Union Générale des Travailleurs de l'Angola* (UGTA), a paper labor organization created by Kassinda when he broke with the UPA-linked exile labor movement in 1962[101] and the *Liga Geral dos Trabalhadores de Angola* (LGTA), composed of a few defectors from the LGTA labor organization proper, which remained tied to Roberto's GRAE.[102]

On April 30, 1965, representatives of the CPA's six "authentically revolutionary" movements signed a convention creating "one great compulsive and impulsive Revolutionary Force" with which to pursue the struggle for national independence.[103] It was followed by a press campaign to discredit Roberto. Given that he had secretly contacted the Portuguese on at least three occasions, only to be rebuffed because his true nationality and integrity were in doubt, Roberto clearly lacked the moral stature with which "to force" the Portuguese to negotiate. He ran GRAE as a business for his personal enrichment, and his leadership meant "endless war." Roberto had to be overthrown and replaced with "authentic" Angolan leadership.[104]

Working to that end, Kassinda and Kassanga were well enough financed to devote full time to political intrigue.[105] They conspired to displace and destroy Roberto and GRAE in a relentless series of plots. In so doing, they enjoyed the benevolent neutrality of Moïse

Tshombe and the active complicity of Vital Moanda's provincial government in the Lower Congo. While Tshombe reassured both Roberto and suspicious African governments that he intended to continue Adoula's policy of support for Angolan nationalism,[106] he quietly nourished the frustration, dissension, and pessimism that threatened to engulf GRAE. Congolese officials confiscated arms destined for Kinkuzu and harassed GRAE soldiers and functionaries. Twice they stopped Roberto from boarding a plane to Lusaka and meeting with Zambian President Kenneth Kaunda.[107] And Portuguese authorities reported, despite his denials, that Tshombe visited Lisbon on June 8, confirming his continued contact with the Salazar government.[108] While some Tshombe lieutenants accused Roberto of having joined his guerrillas with those of Lumumbist rebels,[109] leaders of the Lumumbist *Conseil National de Libération* (CNL) simultaneously accused him of sending his forces to fight with Tshombe against insurgents led by Pierre Mulele in Kwilu.[110] Speaking on Radio Zanzibar in January 1965, an exiled leader of the then fading CNL insurgency in the eastern Congo described Roberto as "the second biggest enemy in the African world"—next to Tshombe.[111]

Clinging to his Congolese base, Roberto refused to be provoked into an open break with Tshombe. In Algiers, however, his spokesman, Johnny Edouard, churned out communiqués and interviews that dissociated GRAE from the Katangan.[112] In June, Roberto wrote Tshombe lamenting "acts of sabotage" against GRAE that had created "an atmosphere of tension, hate and despair." He requested the return of GRAE arms and ammunition confiscated by provincial authorities at Matadi, Songololo, and Tshela and said that unless the central government intervened to correct these matters, he would speak out publicly. Angolan soldiers were being felled for lack of arms. Failure to respond to the resentment of his army (ELNA) or to inquiries from the African and world press would only invite charges of GRAE complicity with the Portuguese.[113]

Moïse Tshombe, however, had decreasing reason to be concerned about Roberto. By mid-1965, with the aid of several hundred European mercenaries and a Belgo-American airborne intervention at Stanleyville (November 1964), he broke the Lumumbist insurgency. He was still loathe to arrest Roberto and close the Kinkuzu base in return for Portuguese financial aid, but he was prepared to foster internecine conflict among Angolans at levels that would provide him with an excuse to intervene in the name of national security.[114] Just such intensified conflict was receiving a crescendo coverage in the Congolese press by May–June 1965.

For Roberto the headlines were grim. On May 11, the director of GRAE military training, Armindo Freitas, defected to the CPA, alleging that Roberto had put his underfed, mutiny-ridden army (ELNA) under the command of illiterate relatives.[115] On June 6, dissidents within the GRAE labor affiliate, the *Liga Geral dos Trabalhadores de Angola* (LGTA), announced that they had deposed the union's pro-Roberto leadership, formed a rival executive headed by Francisco Manuel Bento—and declared themselves for a nonviolent solution to the colonial issue in Angola.[116] And on June 20, GRAE's minister of armaments, Alexandre Taty, announced that he and an unidentified "military junta" had replaced Roberto as head of GRAE.[117] At first Taty's coup d'état seemed to represent little more than an empty, one-man *pronunciamento*. Then two days later, Kongo Central police directed by the provincial security chief, Joseph Matuba, intercepted a GRAE military supply truck and handed it over to Taty.[118] It soon developed that Taty's putsch enjoyed support as well from the Portuguese secret police (PIDE).[119] Earlier that June (1965), Taty, accompanied by a Cabindan collaborator and a PIDE agent attached to a Portuguese commercial firm in Léopoldville, had traveled to Luanda to confer with PIDE officials.[120] What was needed to parlay Taty's plotting into concerted action, however, was the frenetic energy of two ambitious allies: the CPA's André Kassinda and the would-be (Swiss) director of a GRAE cadre school, Walter Artho.[121] Kassinda charmed and cajoled while Artho organized and financed what became a concerted operation to depose Roberto. There were dissidents from GRAE medical,[122] labor, and army groups, a rebellious PDA youth wing,[123] and an assortment of CPA (notably UNA-CUNA) supporters. The lot was cheered on by Bakongo separatists and collaborators and by the Tshombe press.[124]

Assembled from among these dissidents and led by Armindo Freitas, a group of over a hundred attacked and occupied GRAE's Léopoldville compound at 4:30 A.M. on June 25.[125] While Taty, Kassinda, Artho, Campos (PIDE), and Matuba (provincial police) looked on, assailants emptied GRAE offices of Roberto's safe, political and military papers, archives, typewriters, and furniture, loaded it all into the GRAE truck that had been hijacked for Taty three days earlier, and drove off toward the Angolan border.[126] During the brief battle for control of the compound (one attacker was killed and many on both sides wounded), no one thought to storm or seal off Holden Roberto's personal residence located a few city blocks away. Quickly informed of what was happening, Roberto circumvented Tshombe (who had apparently promised no interference) by appealing for help from Congolese circles still friendly to him. By 7:30 A.M. he managed to reoccupy GRAE headquarters with the aid of a contingent of Congolese gendarmes. Kassinda, Freitas, and other leaders were arrested (though released three days later on Tshombe's orders); another fifty or so ended up in GRAE custody; Artho fled to Switzerland;[127] and Roberto clung to the barren offices and diminished authority of his presidency in exile.

Denying any responsibility for the coup manqué, Tshombe called a special meeting of African ambassadors at which he professed neutrality vis-à-vis Angolan partisan conflict.[128] The Kongo Central's Vital Moanda was more candid. To Roberto's charges of complicity in the plots against GRAE, the provincial governor riposted: "Holden's troops are undisciplined and constitute a public danger."[129]

In the midst of the June fracas, Roberto's uncle and political mentor, Barros Necaca,[130] broke a long public silence. He charged that his nephew's "incompetent meddling" had blocked the reorganization of GRAE's malfunctioning medical/relief service (SARA) and accused his one-time protégé of countenancing corruption by political friends.[131] A few weeks later in Algiers, Johnny Edouard once again heralded an "impending announcement" from Léopoldville, concerning "important decisions" being taken "to reorganize and restructure the Revolution."[132] But once again there was no follow-through.

THE MOBUTU REPRIEVE

During autumn 1965, Congolese politics took a new turn. President Kasavubu fired Premier Tshombe; then, after several weeks of political confusion, the head of the army, Lieutenant General Joseph-Désiré Mobutu, overthrew Kasavubu. Mobutu's military coup on November 24 placed a personal friend and political ally of Holden Roberto at the head of the Congolese government once again.

For Roberto the coup came none too soon. He had barely survived the Tshombe interlude by adopting a policy of low-risk, scaled-down activity characterized by heavy reliance upon primary ethnic and familial ties. Indicative of this contraction, by the time Mobutu took power Roberto's movement had returned (for the first time since March 1962) to publishing a UPA (party) instead of an FNLA/GRAE (front-government) news bulletin.[133]

The political climate in Léopoldville, or Kinshasa as it was renamed by General Mobutu, became steadily more congenial. Logistical problems cleared up when the new government, intent on breaking up provincial fiefdoms, sent Vital Moanda to Kisangani (Stanleyville) and replaced him as governor of Kongo Central with a nonpolitical administrator.

Separatists and collaborationist groups that flourished under Tshombe adjusted so as to appear in tune with Mobutu's policy of support for Angolan nationalism and insurgency. The Bakongo independence front (FPIKP) joined in pushing a proposal made by a new Good Offices Committee—*Comité des Bons Offices Angolais* (CBOA)—for a unity congress of all Angolan nationalists.[134] Created by a Bakongo businessman, Emmanuel Norman Lamvu,[135] the CBOA sought in vain to persuade the Mobutu government to sponsor and finance such a congress.[136]

André Kassinda, undaunted by the failure of the June 1965 putsch and driven by indefatigable ambition, abandoned his advocacy of nonviolence. In October, he flew to Accra to seek OAU support for a merger of the MPLA, GRAE, and CPA[137] and in December to New York in quest of American money and U.N. exposure.[138] Finally in April 1966, after months of "intense revolutionary work" during which the CPA assertedly organized a public health service[139] and a "disciplined army" of two thousand men,[140] Kassinda called an assembly of the CPA to elect a new executive committee.[141] Dubbed the *Comissão Nacional Executivo* (CNE), this new committee included Kassinda's old partner, Marcos Kassanga, then a student in the United States, as secretary for foreign relations,[142] and got considerable publicity in the Congolese and foreign press as a "third force" or "new Angolan Government in Exile."[143] Striking a revolutionary posture, Kassinda denounced such former associates as Alexandre Taty, who had by now moved what he called his *Junta Militar Angolano no Exílio* (JMAE) across the border into Cabinda to work openly with the Portuguese.[144] Kassinda and the CPA, however, were not able to convince the Mobutu government, let alone Holden Roberto, of their revolutionary credentials.[145] Exasperated by their clamorous theatrics and pressed by Holden Roberto to move against them, General Mobutu finally authorized a midyear crackdown on the FPIKP, CPA, and CBOA. Their anti-GRAE activities proved costly.

On July 15, 1966, his letters to Roberto not having been answered, E. N. Lamvu of the CBOA ventured into GRAE's Kinshasa compound to request an audience. Roberto immediately arrested and transported him to Kinkuzu. There Lamvu was incarcerated along with what soon became approximately sixty political prisoners, including a former MPLA commander and national committeeman, João Benedito.[146] One week later, on July 27, Congolese police arrested André Kassinda and turned him over to the head of Roberto's sûreté, José Manuel Peterson.[147] Kassinda, too, ended up at Kinkuzu—until November 26 when he was reportedly "transferred"; in all likelihood, he was shot.[148] In March 1967, after seven months of "brutalized," underfed imprisonment at Kinkuzu, Lamvu and two MPLA partisans managed to cut a hole in their prison hut and escape across the Congo River. But few others were so lucky as to escape from what Lamvu likened to an African Buchenwald.[149]

Reversing the situation under Tshombe, the GRAE now enjoyed the benevolent neutrality of the Congolese as it employed fair means and foul to eliminate its rivals. By allowing Roberto to arrest political adversaries, Mobutu encouraged the GRAE leader to withdraw even further into a parochial shell. Pressure to confront and resolve serious problems that beset GRAE by means of inclusive, constituency-building activity decreased as Roberto forcibly silenced his political opposition. This new capacity for coercion reinforced the GRAE pattern of survival/no win politics.

Events preceding and following the July 1966 arrest of another of Roberto's political enemies, Simon Diallo Mingiedi, events marked by turmoil in the PDA, serve to show how little the Mobutu reprieve did to help a negatively led GRAE overcome internal blocks to political effectiveness. Mingiedi belonged to a group of politically aware Bazombo that had joined the PDA in November 1963 following OAU recognition of Roberto's government in exile.[150] As GRAE fortunes declined during 1964–1965, this group, along with the PDA youth (JDA) movement, became increasingly restive. And as Roberto postponed the reorganization of the FNLA/GRAE and retreated into dependency upon a smaller and smaller coterie of UPA loyalists, the PDA president, Emmanuel Kunzika, faced mounting criticism from Mingiedi and other PDA politicians. As GRAE vice-premier, Kunzika was expected to exert an influence upon (and to bear responsibility for) GRAE policy and action. But his influence had always been modest, and in mid-1965 his position further weakened.

An insatiable student who enrolled in one "continuing education" program after another,[151] Kunzika was able to analyze, if not correct, the cause of his and GRAE's political difficulties. In the wake of the attempted coup by Taty, Kassinda, and the others, he offered the following appraisal. The Portuguese were encouraging talk of, yet making no concessions to, the principle of negotiated independence. In so doing they pursued two aims. First, they sought to deprive Angolan nationalists of a sizable refugee support base. To that end they subsidized a variety of fringe political organizations (Nto-Bako, MDIA, and so forth) whose function was to persuade Angolan refugees to return home. Second, they fostered communal (ethnic and regional) conflict among and within Angolan movements so as to destroy nationalist coherence. They were abetted in this double pursuit by African states who, in President Kasavubu's words, "dishonored their promises" to assist Angolan nationalists through the OAU. But nationalist setbacks could not all be attributed to external causes. "Lack of cohesion" within the FNLA/GRAE derived largely from the fact that its constituents worked at a counterpurpose. The only way to resolve this problem, Kunzika argued, was to bring the three FNLA parties (UPA, PDA, MPLA-Viriato) and their youth, student, and labor affiliates together at a national conference to concert views, close ranks, and prepare the way for an even more inclusive national congress.[152]

The predicament of Kunzika and his PDA confirmed the internal character of FNLA/GRAE weakness. The previous December, Kunzika had written a report to Roberto deploring the defection of Jonas Savimbi and others and warning that unless Roberto personally stepped out to mobilize popular support, he would leave the way open for a "demagogue" to turn the people against GRAE. He also warned that unless Roberto assured top GRAE collaborators of regular stipends (they competed for handouts from Roberto), their work and morale would suffer and at least some would seek questionable external support—which portended more decay and defection. Caught in the middle, Kunzika pleaded with Roberto to reach out and work with others and thereby void the cause of increasing bitterness and restiveness within the PDA.[153]

For a time Roberto seemed to respond. The FNLA National

Council took on signs of new life. At Roberto's initiative, it met near the Angola-Congo frontier from April 5 to 9, 1965, for a special session attended by ELNA commanders from inside Angola.[154] And on April 28, it met again and scheduled meetings to hear long-deferred reports from two special committees: the first commissioned to fashion proposals for constitutional revision and to devise a set of internal (FNLA) rules and procedures (chaired by PDA Secretary-General Ferdinand Dombele);[155] the second commissioned to lay plans for an FNLA congress (chaired by Kunzika). What happened next is best conveyed in an August 2, 1965, letter to Roberto drafted by Kunzika and signed by the thirty MPLA/ Viriato and PDA members of the FNLA National Council.[156]

Mr. President:

We the signatories of this letter and members of the National Council, the supreme organ of the National Front for the Liberation of Angola and members of the Democratic Party of Angola (PDA) and People's Movement for the Liberation of Angola (MPLA) led by Messrs. Viriato da Cruz and Matias Miguéis, deeply regret that the National Council is no longer able to meet given the refusal of members of your party [UPA] to participate at scheduled meetings.

You will recall that at the meeting of April 28, 1965 the following committees were renewed, namely:

1) Committee mandated to devise a new constitution and internal statutes for the FNLA, taking into account the admission of the MPLA and the experience of four years of struggle;
2) Committee for an FNLA Congress formed back in 1964;

and it was decided that these committees would present their reports respectively on June 28 and July 28, 1965.

Pursuant to this decision the National Council [chaired by André Massaki] was convoked successively for June 28, July 3, and July 31, but could not hold a valid meeting because your [UPA] members were each time absent. In a letter of July 2 you requested that the July 3 meeting be postponed because of an important meeting scheduled for your own party.

Then in another letter of July 21, you argued that conditions were not then suitable for a meeting of the council on July 31 and that furthermore earlier decisions had been taken in the absence of a quorum. You added that out of concern for democracy you wished for five officers [from Kinkuzu] to participate in the discussions but that communication with the base being impossible, circumstances prevented you from obtaining such participation.

Precisely because it cannot meet during difficult times, we must conclude that for your party the National Council has lost its *raison d'être*.

As for us, we believe that such a Front uniting three parties should:
— reinforce and orient the Revolution, concerting all our energies into an *organized revolution* instead of an *anarchic revolt*,
— define war aims and political views and outline a national policy to

put before all the Angolan people near and far, and unite them around the ideal of the Revolution by means of common action and propaganda,
— define the prerogatives and specific duties of our institutions so that they may function effectively in an orderly context—disorder paralyzes and kills.

Setting aside objectives which cannot be realized without full discussion and confrontation of opinions, you prefer to retreat to the notion of party where, it seems to you, there will be no divergence of views or opinions. For you the Front is not a means for advancing the struggle but for encumbering it with discussion.

If this is in fact how you view matters, in the interest of the Revolution you should cease maintaining the illusion of a real union and pronounce the dissolution of a Front that you find so prejudicial that it can no longer function. Rest assured, as for us, that we will in no way resist such action, as for others you will no doubt know. We have come to the conclusion that it is better to let the Revolution move forward than to smother it in quarrelsome discussion.

It is up to you and your party, your hands are free—which should prove our desire not to stand in the way of the Revolution.

Counting on a just reply, we remain fraternally yours.[157]

Roberto did not acknowledge the letter, although he made an occasional gesture in Kunzika's direction. On September 29, he sent a note saying that he was leaving for Tunis and Algiers to discuss arrangements for arms shipments and would talk with Kunzika on his return. But he returned, went off again to attend an OAU summit meeting in Accra (October 21–25)[158] and returned again without contacting him. Roberto's habit of protecting his authority by hoarding information and holding himself inaccessible except to a fluctuating core of noncompetitive loyalists frustrated all of Kunzika's efforts to bring him around to a different leadership style. Shut out politically and financially, the PDA leader sent a letter to the OAU Liberation Committee asking why it had seemingly cut off assistance to the GRAE after a brief period (March–August) in 1964;[159] wrote a long report (for 1965) to Roberto in which he added to his grievances the charge that Roberto was purposely undercutting the authority of senior associates by favoring and manipulating certain of their subordinates and by encouraging the Congolese (and/or UPA) sûreté to harass PDA officials;[160] and wrote to General Mobutu urging that he eschew favoritism and aid all genuine Angolan nationalists.[161] Still unable to evoke any response from Roberto, Kunzika accepted that he had no room for maneuver. Given the " eloquent silence" of Mobutu, he later wrote: "I understood that the PDA could not force the situation and ac-

cordingly advised PDA members to adhere to concerted and considered action, not campaigns based on hate and passion."[162] The
role of the contiguous state as political arbiter in exile politics was
clear. For Roberto, Mobutu represented not only a reprieve but,
within the Angolan exile community, an exclusive license.

Still eager as minister of education to develop an Angolan
secondary school and to continue organizing primary schools for
hundreds of Angolan schoolchildren in Kinshasa, Kongo Central,
and remote rebel-held areas of northern Angola, Kunzika set out
in January 1966 on a two-month personal fund-raising journey. He
traveled to the United States, Canada, Belgium, France, and Switzerland with an architect's drawings for an *Institut d'Enseignement
Secondaire Angolais* (IESA) and a list of needs in books, materials,
and teacher support for the some twelve hundred students already
being schooled.[163] But during his absence from Kinshasa, what
Kunzika most feared came to pass: the PDA began to disintegrate.
Under an acting president, António Josias, party funds flowed to
the dissident "Casablanca group" of ex-MDIA leaders and other
restive, anti-Roberto partisans who demanded a national congress
to reorganize the FNLA/GRAE.[164] The Casablancans were joined
by the party youth movement (JDA) whose impatience and youthful ambitions had earned it earlier party censure.[165] Together their
anti-GRAE polemics soon splashed onto the pages of Kinshasa's
influential Catholic daily, the *Courrier d'Afrique*.[166] In April, the
paper carried a long and bitter article by Simon Diallo Mingiedi.
Asserting that guerrilla activity inside Angola had ground to a halt,
Mingiedi charged that as a political organization, the FNLA was
moribund. The National Council of the Front had not met for a
full year. Publicly airing grievances that Kunzika had argued in
private letters to Roberto, Mingiedi said that the PDA and UPA
were linked only by occasional contact through a few PDA
apologists for Roberto, specifically Kunzika.[167]

Upon his return to Kinshasa, Kunzika tendered his resignation
but was reconfirmed as PDA president at a party conference from
May 28 to 30.[168] Political infighting continued. Mingiedi intensified
his press attacks on Roberto and Kunzika,[169] finally forcing Kunzika to purge him from the party.[170] This in turn led to the resignation of the PDA vice-president, Josias.[171] Then, after Roberto had
made a seemingly conciliatory gesture by speaking at Kunzika's
refugee school July 1966 promotion exercises,[172] Kunzika suffered
new political humiliation at Roberto's hands. The JDA, acting with

a feisty sense of generational autonomy common to political youth movements,[173] forged an opportunistic alliance with Roberto. Together they and Roberto organized the arrest of the purged PDA leader Simon Diallo Mingiedi[174]—leaving Kunzika to be blamed.[175] Mingiedi ended up a prisoner at Kinkuzu.[176] Kunzika disbanded the executive committee of the JDA,[177] after announcing that contrary to some press reports,[178] the PDA itself had not been dissolved.[179] The price for continued PDA political existence under Roberto, whether in Tshombe's or Mobutu's Congo, seemed to be political inefficacy.

Roberto's moves to pump life back into his movement following Mobutu's rise to power in late 1965 were made exclusively within the UPA/FNLA. He recalled Johnny Edouard from Algiers to reorganize the FNLA and prepare for an FNLA conference in 1966, but then he refused to let him carry through with either.[180] He integrated two young (Bakongo) graduates of the University of Redlands, California, into his UPA/GRAE office,[181] but continued to rely on the coercive hand of José Peterson and the UPA sûreté.[182] He issued a new FNLA platform policy statement that called for a new society to be built upon the "traditional collective and cooperative" patterns of Angolan peasant communities and state control over major natural resources and industrial ventures, but he also called for postrevolutionary treason trials for those who had collaborated with the Portuguese.[183] A poisonous, fratricidal climate pervaded Angolan exile politics in the Congo.[184]

DEMISE OF THE THIRD PARTY: MPLA/VIRIATO

The MPLA/Viriato's formal entry into the FNLA, though it could not really be implemented because of Congolese government hostility and Holden Roberto's ambivalence, enraged the followers of Agostinho Neto.[185] They viewed collaboration with Roberto as treasonous. Externally, the participation of da Cruz and Matias Miguéis, alongside Roberto on the GRAE delegation to the Conference of Non-Aligned States at Cairo in October 1964[186] and da Cruz's close association with the GRAE office in Algiers (where he resided), reinforced Roberto's credentials in the wake of Savimbi's exit. Potentially the MPLA breakaway group represented a compelling intellectual and ideological injection into the FNLA/GRAE.

An opportunity for lethal revenge presented itself to Dr. Neto's MPLA on November 12, 1965, when two of the da Cruz group's principal leaders sought to travel through Brazzaville on their return to Kinshasa from an international conference in Indonesia. The MPLA foreign secretary, Luis de Azevedo, Jr., apprehended Miguéis and José Miguel as they were boarding a motor launch to cross the Congo River. At Azevedo's request, the Congo-Brazzaville police delivered the two travelers to local MPLA headquarters. MPLA/Neto officials then transported Miguéis and Miguel to the movement's guerrilla camp near Dolisie, where they were tried and executed.[187]

MPLA/Viriato youth threatened to retaliate in a blood feud,[188] but it was soon apparent that the FNLA's third party had been delivered a mortal blow. It took several years for the MPLA/Viriato to fade away completely, but its publications were henceforth limited to commemorations of the deaths at Dolisie.[189] Viriato da Cruz, who viewed himself more as a poet than as a revolutionary but who had stuck to the struggle in deference to such colleagues as Miguéis, was personally demoralized.[190] And though there were rumors that da Cruz would respond by forming a new movement of dissidents from both GRAE and the MPLA, he did not do so.[191] Instead he flew to Peking where he devoted himself to a literary life. He worked for the Afro-Asian Writers' Bureau and Afro-Asian Journalists' Association based in the Chinese capital. And according to his MPLA/Neto adversaries, he also worked to poison their relations with China by portraying them as pro-Soviet.[192] He was heard from occasionally through the Hsinhua news agency, which published his speeches and statements dealing with the "immortal and invincible thought" of Mao Tse-tung, the evils of Soviet revisionism and American imperialism, and the moral imperative of mounting a "people's war" to liberate Angola.[193] On June 13, 1973, da Cruz died in a Peking hospital after a long illness and years of political obscurity.[194]

SPLINTERING ON THE MARGINS: LABOR

In part a projection of exile politics, in part an escape into pure exile "make believe," Angolan labor movements mirrored the disabling factionalism that characterized Angolan nationalism during the 1964–1966 period. Labor groups organized and functioned as a benign subsystem within the Angolan Bakongo émigré-refugee community and provided an avenue by which ambitious, underemployed young Angolans could acquire real or fancied leadership roles. Functionally these groups served a useful purpose as mechanisms through which to develop organization and impart trade skills and to distribute refugee relief aid.

From 1964 to 1966, dissident groups split off from the larger, politically oriented unions, leading to a spectrum of seven labor movements (not counting youth wings) in varying degrees of competition and alliance. (Figure 4.1 represents a graphic overview of the movements.)

LGTA

Dissidents who broke with the LGTA's pro-Roberto leadership in June 1965 were joined by a prominent defector from the UNTA's pro-Neto leadership and, in November of that year, created the ephemeral *Union des Syndicats Révolutionnaires de l'Angola* (USRA).[195] The LGTA's privileged position vis-à-vis the International Confederation of Free Trade Unions (ICFTU) and American AFL-CIO remained intact, however, despite adverse publicity and efforts by LGTA dissidents to obtain support for their cause.[196] And the LGTA, which claimed eleven thousand members as of June 1964, attempted to secure its lead position by introducing new adult vocational education programs—sewing, auto mechanics, and building trades.[197]

UNTA

UNTA was the only MPLA/FDLA affiliate permitted to continue legal activity in Léopoldville after the MPLA's party office closed in November 1963. Its operations were apparently not considered important enough to warrant a clampdown, though its leaders were subject to police harassment.[198] UNTA bulletins continued to carry statements by the MPLA,[199] and UNTA members continued to travel on missions to such revolution-support centers as Algiers and Peking.[200] But the pro–common-front affiliate of the MPLA[201] also suffered from the factional conflict. In mid-1964, a disgruntled segment (largely Bazombo) broke away and formed the *Fédération Nationale des Travailleurs de l'Angola* (FNTA),[202] which promptly joined the ranks of Angolan labor groups vying for external financial subsidies.[203] Then a year later, UNTA's long-time second-ranking official, Foreign Secretary Bernard Dombele, denounced the movement for "political deviation" and joined LGTA dissidents in setting up the USRA splinter group.[204] In June 1964, UNTA

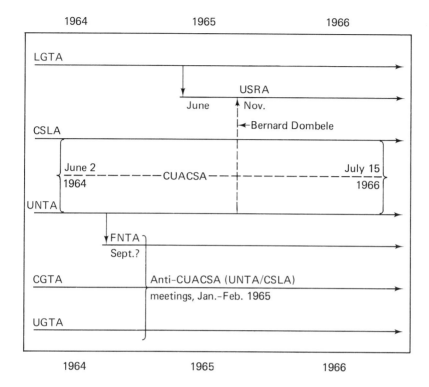

Figure 4.1   Exile Angolan labor movements. The acronyms are CGTA, *Confédération Générale des Travailleurs de l'Angola;* CSLA, *Confédération des Syndicats Libres Angolais;* CUACSA, *Comité de Unidade de Acção e de Coordenação Sindical de l'Angola;* FNTA, *Fédération Nationale des Travailleurs de l'Angola;* LGTA, *Liga Geral dos Trabalhadores Angolanos;* UGTA, *Union Générale des Travailleurs de l'Angola;* UNTA, *Uniãco Nacional dos Trabalhadores de Angola;* and USRA, *Union des Syndicats Révolutionnaires de l'Angola.*

signed a paper alliance with another group, the *Confédération des Syndicats Libres Angolais* (CSLA), a small but strident partisan of "nonviolence";[205] but in July 1966, its CSLA partner denounced and ended the alliance, known as the *Comitê de Unidade de Acção e de Coordenação Sindical de Angola* (CUACSA),[206] which, anyway, had never really functioned.[207] Perhaps the alliance's most noteworthy action was to take a public sideswipe at other movements,[208] causing three of them—the FNTA, the Catholic-oriented *Confédération Générale des Travailleurs de l'Angola* (CGTA), and Kassinda's shadowy *Union Générale des Travailleurs de l'Angola* (UGTA)—to meet and level a collective broadside at UNTA ("not Angolan"—meaning really Congolese) and the CSLA (an "imaginary body").[209]

CGTA

In reality, the CGTA was the only labor movement other than the LGTA and UNTA that could be considered a substantial, functioning organization.[210] Aided by the international and Congolese Catholic trade union movement, the CGTA, which underwent a leadership change in early 1964,[211] maintained its independence from all political parties[212] and concentrated on obtaining training for its officials[213] and organizing educational and rural development programs for its members (which it estimated at five thousand).[214] Whether the work of the CGTA, or any of the exile Angolan labor movements, would later contribute to the socioeconomic development of Angola (as distinct from the Congo) seemed doubtful. But they were improving the lives of hundreds, perhaps thousands, of émigrés and refugees, as well as adding on the margins to the complexity of Angolan exile politics.

RISE OF A THIRD FORCE: UNITA

After leaving the GRAE in July 1964, Savimbi remained for a short while in Cairo where he befriended another visitor to Egypt, Malcolm X, and then flew to Algiers.[215] In Algiers Premier Ben Bella helped him arrange for a "long trip to the Far-East." Savimbi traveled to China where he met Chairman Mao Tse-tung and Premier Chou En-lai. The Chinese told him "frankly that they could not trust" him—after all, only a few months earlier he had been arguing Viriato da Cruz's pro-Chinese stance as a reason for opposing his entry into the FNLA. But they did propose "to train some of [his] men and to give them support" to help him launch a genuine people's war inside Angola.[216] He also visited North Korea and North Vietnam, where he conferred with General Vo Nguyen Giap. Returning to Algiers by way of Eastern Europe, Savimbi consulted in the Algerian capital with yet another expert in guerrilla warfare, Che Guevara. Then, after following through with arrangements to send a group of his followers to take up promised military scholarships in China, he returned to complete his studies at the University of Lausanne.[217]

He interrupted his work that autumn to fly to Brazzaville for talks with Agostinho Neto, Daniel Chipenda, and other MPLA officials, who invited him to join their movement. Relishing his autonomy and ambition, Savimbi stalled.[218] In February (1965), he reconnoitered the political scene in newly independent (October 1964) Zambia. Then, after completing a *licence* in political and legal sciences at Lausanne that July, he decided the time was right to reenter the political arena. He returned to Zambia (via Tanzania) in the fall and began organizing a new political movement near Angola's back door. In doing so he was able to draw upon the ready loyalty of three distinct constituencies.

Ex-GRAE

First, there were the scattered ranks of supporters who had preceded or followed Savimbi out of GRAE in 1964. These included a nucleus of experienced military and political leaders. Among the more notable was the ELNA chief of staff, José Kalundungo, who had fled to Brazzaville, denounced Roberto, and publicly detailed ELNA weaknesses including the traumas of Kinkuzu—mutinies, Congolese intervention, arrests.[219] It was for Kalundungo and a small contingent of ex-ELNA officers that Savimbi, pursuant to his secret 1964 talks in Peking, arranged guerrilla training in China.

Among other UPA/GRAE defectors who congregated in Brazzaville was the head of SARA, Dr. José Liahuca, along with several medical aides.[220] And in December 1964, twenty-four predominantly Ovimbundu, pro-Savimbi nationalists, speaking as the *Amigos do Manifesto Angolano* (Amangola), issued a Brazzaville manifesto in which they called upon exiled Angolans to move back inside their country and mobilize the masses for guerrilla warfare.[221]

Initially Amangola partisans cooperated with the MPLA in Brazzaville. Dr. Neto's followers had, in fact, helped Savimbi's people escape across the river and had welcomed them to Brazzaville with financial help. But Savimbi's February (1965) scouting in Lusaka showed that he intended to organize a movement of his own in Zambia; and the MPLA was intent upon organizing there itself. Relations deteriorated. In July, Amangola militants acknowledged: "We used to cooperate with the MPLA without being members of that party. We no longer do because the MPLA complained that we did not fully cooperate, especially not in Zambia where our brother Jonas Savimbi demobilized some [MPLA] members. Since the MPLA demanded that we take a clear stand on cooperation, i.e., sign MPLA party cards, we . . . ceased to cooperate."[222] Head-on competition led the MPLA to break all relations with the Savimbi group,[223] a break that was accompanied by some verbal and physical violence in Brazzaville.[224] It was then that Savimbi returned to Africa proclaiming what was to be his central political theme: the need to carry the struggle from the futile, conflicted realm of exile politics back inside to the exploited peasants and laborers who awaited mobilization within Angola.[225]

Students

The second pro-Savimbi constituency ready to rally consisted of a core of politically active students grouped within the *União Nacional dos Estudantes Angolanos* (UNEA). These students were led by GRAE's ex-Katanga representative, Jorge Valentim. Valentim had been elected assistant secretary for African affairs of the Western-oriented International Student Conference (COSEC, Leiden, Netherlands) at its annual meeting (Christchurch, New Zealand) in July 1964. In October 1964, Valentim sought and obtained a Léopoldville meeting with Roberto to whom he put the case for a national conference to reunite and restructure the FNLA/GRAE.[226] Roberto was unmoved. Frustrated and responding to rising student disillusionment with exile politicians,[227] Valentim decided to use COSEC travel funds and his position as UNEA president in a campaign to detach UNEA from GRAE (while averting UNEA ties with the MPLA). He began publishing a series of anti-GRAE student bulletins and pamphlets.[228] And in December 1964, he journeyed to Zambia where he lobbied against GRAE and circulated a memorandum that excoriated Roberto as an agent of American imperialism and praised Jonas Savimbi and Agostinho Neto as true "patriots."[229]

When he returned to Europe, Valentim supported moves to

break off unity talks underway between UNEA and the pro-MPLA *União Geral dos Estudantes da Africa Negra sob Dominação Colonial Portuguesa* (UGEAN), [230] a sharp critic of COSEC.[231] He took the lead in organizing a "special" UNEA assembly at Utrecht (August 31– September 3, 1965), an assembly that voted for a new UNEA constitution, a policy of political nonalignment, and a new executive committee headed by an apolitical exponent of student unity, José Belo Chipenda. The key post of vice-president for external affairs went to a Savimbi supporter and Valentim protégé, Jorge Isaac Sangumba.[232] And although there was some resistance from Bakongo students in the United States and elsewhere, Valentim achieved his goal.[233] UNEA ceased to be part of GRAE.

In late 1965, eager to undercut both GRAE and the MPLA, Valentim embraced Kassinda's CPA as a possible third force and published the CPA's manifesto alongside that of Amangola in one of his Leiden pamphlets.[234] His flirtation with the CPA, however, brought a sharp remonstrance from Savimbi, who had refused to cooperate with Kassinda since first being asked in 1964. On the verge of creating a third force of his own, Savimbi warned Valentim against the intrigues of exile politics and noted that "not everyone who opposed Holden or the MPLA was necessarily a revolutionary." Savimbi emphasized the need for a new party with a coherent revolutionary policy to mobilize the "exploited masses" inside Angola.[235] In January 1966, as a first step toward meeting that need, Savimbi formed the *Comitê Preparatório da Acção Directa* (CPAD) in Lusaka.[236]

Ex-UPA Lusaka

The preparatory committee included several sometime *Upistas*[237] from what Savimbi could count as his third ready-made constituency. Crucial at the outset of his work in Zambia, this group consisted of local leaders of former Chokwe, Lwena, and Luchazi self-help associations and Angolan refugees more recently arrived in Zambia and Katanga, who, together in 1964–1965, staffed the UPA/GRAE Lusaka office.

Distance and travel restrictions had limited Roberto's personal contact with the Lusaka office during Tshombe's premiership. He visited only once, in October 1964, when he led a GRAE delegation to attend Zambian independence celebrations.[238] That was the only occasion on which he met with his regional Lusaka organizers. On his return to Léopoldville, he boasted publicly that the Zambian government, responsive to GRAE's "popularity" and to OAU recommendations (August 1963), would not authorize any other Angolan political movement to operate in Lusaka.[239]

As in all other cases of UPA/GRAE attempts at geoethnic outreach, however, the local committee in Zambia found itself persistently at loggerheads with Roberto and his Léopoldville associates. Independent and resourceful, the Lusaka office opened branches and organized among Angolan workers in the Copperbelt, set about building a solid regional party structure, and gained favorable attention—even modest financial help—from a prestigious visitor to Zambia, Tanzania's President Julius Nyerere.[240] Roberto viewed these achievements with more concern than satisfaction. Aware of Savimbi's latent political appeal among Angolans from central and southern areas, he defensively ignored all correspondence from the Lusaka group but dispatched his Bakongo troubleshooter, José M. Peterson, to keep it in line. This action only hastened impending estrangement.

The total collapse of UPA/GRAE operations came shortly after Jorge Valentim's December 1964 visit to Lusaka. It was signaled by a desperate appeal from the Lusaka group to the OAU's Liberation Committee. Echoing a familiar theme, the group urged the OAU to call a conference of Angolan nationalists for the purpose of reorganizing the Angolan government in exile. In its January 1965 appeal, the UPA-Zambia office expounded on the frustrations of working for Roberto. The UPA president had not once replied to their letters seeking "instructions" on "what we should do" and "how we should direct people." He had blocked a three-man Lusaka office delegation (that reached Elizabethville) from proceeding on to Léopoldville in quest of such instructions. Neither Roberto (during his October visit) nor his emissaries had provided an explanation for the 1964 defection of Savimbi and "many" ELNA soldiers, nor had they produced a (revised) list of GRAE cabinet officers. It seemed that there was no GRAE cabinet—indeed that there was no GRAE in any organized sense. After nearly a year of operations in Zambia, "not a single man" had been sent off for military training or for advanced education. On its own initiative, the Lusaka office had sent militants on organizing missions inside Angola.[241] But without funds it was unable to continue such work. Anticipating by nearly a year what was to be a similar inquiry to the OAU from Kunzika,[242] the Lusaka group wrote: "We have never received any financial assistance from Léopoldville so that our work would be made easier. Now we wonder whether the African Liberation Committee does at all give any financial assistance to GRAE for the liberation of Angola?"[243] The Lusaka memorandum would hardly encourage the OAU to do so.

Declaring its readiness "to go and live in the hills, forests and villages of Angola" to do "whatever" the OAU expected it "to do for the paralysis of the Portuguese regime,"[244] the UPA Lusaka leadership concluded that its real problem was the paralysis of its own government in exile. In the absence of any sign that the OAU would in fact convene a conference of Angolan nationalists to restructure the GRAE, the Lusaka organization quietly disintegrated. Officially a moribund UPA/GRAE office continued to exist for a while longer. Roberto named Adão Kapilango, a former member of the Lobito underground,[245] to head it. And when the United Nations Committee on Decolonization visited Lusaka in May 1965, Kapilango testified in the name of the UPA.[246] Shortly thereafter, however, Kapilango accepted a scholarship and flew to the United States, leaving the UPA/GRAE unrepresented in Zambia.

Leaders of the defunct UPA/GRAE organization presented themselves to the United Nations that May (1965) as unaffiliated spokesmen for "Angolan refugees in Zambia."[247] Eight months later, in January 1966, they regrouped as the nucleus of Savimbi's *Comitê Preparatório da Acção Directa* (CPAD). Along with the Brazzaville (Amangola) and student (UNEA) constituencies, and a number of refugees from central and southern Angola gathered in Katanga (all at odds with Roberto's Katanga representatives),[248] they formed the constituent elements of a significant new force in Angolan nationalist politics.

While marking time in Dar es Salaam during the summer of 1965 waiting for permission to proceed to Zambia, Savimbi refined his rationale for creating a new political movement. In a September 1965 letter to former missionaries of the United Church of Christ, he set forth the gist of this political thinking. The liberation of Angola would not come from outside. Only Angolans within Angola could free the country from foreign domination. And it was vital that Angolans of all "tribes, clans and classes" participate in the liberation struggle. Moreover the participation of different groups ought to be in proportion to their numbers within Angolan society. The MPLA was essentially Mbundu, the GRAE essentially Bakongo. This left "outside the political struggle more than half the population." The MPLA was "pro-Communist" and under Moscow's influence, and GRAE was "supported by western forces." What was needed, then, was a new political movement to represent the interests of the majority inside (Ovimbundu, Chokwe, Ovambo, Ganguela, and so forth) and to work for the total independence of all Angolans vis-à-vis political forces outside.[249]

Savimbi argued prophetically for the need to avoid "a direct or indirect confrontation of the great powers" in Angola. He warned against an "ideological struggle" and advocated a purposively inclusive approach to political mobilization.[250] The choice before Angolan nationalists abroad, he said, was between a "return to the Father-Mother Land or [an] exile which is bitter, dishonorable and prolonged." George Washington could not have freed the British colonies of America by fighting "from a base of exile [against] an army superior in numbers and equipment."[251] Revolutionary effectiveness depended upon transcending exile, upon returning home to fight.

When he reached Zambia in October 1965, Savimbi persuaded Kenneth Kaunda to invite Holden Roberto and Agostinho Neto to Lusaka for discussions about creating a united front of Angolan nationalists.[252] But they declined, and Savimbi continued with preparations to form his own movement.

In March 1966, Savimbi hiked into Angola. He and some sixty-seven others assembled near Muangai in the lightly populated savanna of Moxico district about 250 miles from the Zambian border. Climaxing months of preparatory work by exiles in Zambia and Katanga and by itinerant organizers who trekked into eastern Angola, the Muangai Conference (March 5–25) created Savimbi's third force, the *União Nacional para a Independência Total de Angola* (UNITA).[253] The gathering adopted a constitution that called upon UNITA to educate "all Angolans living outside the country [to] the idea that real independence for Angola will only be achieved through an armed struggle waged against the Portuguese Colonial Power inside the country."[254] It elected a provisional central committee[255] and gave it a threefold charge: to organize a "popular armed struggle" based on "Anti-Colonialism and Anti-Imperialism"; to "exhaust" all possibilities for creating a "United Front of all Angolan anti-colonial forces"; and to prepare a general assembly to elect a permanent national central committee.[256] By the time the Muangai conference was held, UNITA partisans had reportedly derailed a Portuguese train near Teixeira de Sousa, set fire to several gasoline stations, and destroyed a host of small river bridges.[257] UNITA leadership had already approached the FNLA, suggesting that the two groups launch "discussions to find a platform of cooperation" in their "common struggle." Roberto responded by publicly deriding the overture.[258] On September 18, 1966, a followup congress of forty-seven UNITA delegates convened in Lusaka and elected a permanent Central Committee led by Jonas Savimbi (president) and by Smart Chata, Kaniumbu Muliata, and Solomon K. Njolomba (vice-presidents).[259] To head UNITA's military forces, the Lusaka meeting chose Chinese-trained Kapesi Fundanga (chief of staff) and José Kalundungo (head of military operations).[260]

Because of economic and geographic vulnerability, Zambia's official policy disallowed use of its territory as a base for guerrilla operations against neighboring states.[261] UNITA's stress on activity inside Angola thus seemed particularly appropriate. In keeping with its theme of self-reliance, it organized strictly on its own a rural political and military thrust into Angola.

Political Education

Concluding that the struggle for independence would be long, bitter, and cruel, UNITA's leaders emphasized the need to organize and act from the base of a politically educated peasantry.[262] Requiring patience and discipline, they noted, the political mobilization of an illiterate, widely dispersed peasantry was inevitably a difficult task avoided by those (MPLA and GRAE) who preferred the easy and self-deceiving payoff of an external propaganda campaign. To overcome peasant suspicion of newcomers and new ideas, revolutionary organizers had to share the adversities of peasant life. "A revolutionary who [took] with him a camp-bed and tinned foods [was] incapable [of winning] the peasants' confidence and . . . cooperation."[263] In Savimbi's view, the UPA-led insurgency in northern Angola had failed because Roberto had not understood the importance of political education. Roberto's policy of handing out weapons and urging people to fight without first imparting a clear sense of sociopolitical purpose had been and continued to be self-defeating.[264] UNITA organizers were instructed to relate to the peasantry through local sociocultural values and economic grievances. Within pastoral communities of eastern Angola, UNITA assumed the role of protector of African women and African cattle against ravage and theft by colonial forces. By identifying the abstract concept of anti-imperialism with well-understood and concrete local issues, it sought to mobilize support among the politically least sophisticated but economically most abused. It urged peasants to refuse to pay taxes. It eulogized the exploits of women militants who lured Portuguese soldiers "blinded" by "satanic instincts" into ambush or who denounced a husband as a PIDE informer.[265] It launched what it hoped to develop into a long, massively supported political campaign of civil disobedience that would erode colonial authority while it soldered African unity.[266]

Military Actions

UNITA's military thrust took the form of small-scale, geographically dispersed ambushes and hit-and-run attacks by guerrilla units. Simultaneously UNITA began organizing and training peasant militias whose revolutionary tasks ranged from food production and village self-defense to intelligence gathering and military sabotage. Consistent with its claim that it could function self-reliantly, independent of external recognition or assistance, UNITA stressed to both mobile guerrillas and stationary militias the importance of capturing arms from Portuguese soldiers and civilians.[267] Its military impact in a previously somnolent area of Angola soon earned favorable attention in the Zambian press. And Savimbi's tactic of holding to relatively modest claims about UNITA's military action—he pretended to a force of no more than six hundred men—added measurably to his political stature and credibility.[268] Insurgent activity in eastern Angola also prompted a violent Portuguese response. While gunboats patroled the Zambezi, planes bombed suspected nationalist villages, troops evacuated and mined areas along the border, and some two thousand Angolan refugees crossed into Zambia—the inevitable consequence of expanding war.[269]

UNITA was not alone in activating Angola's eastern front. Indeed it was engaged in a regional race for nationalist ascendancy with a bitter rival, the MPLA. Savimbi reported having witnessed over 170 MPLA recruits from Zambia transit Dar es Salaam en route for training in the Soviet Union during the summer of 1965.[270] The MPLA was preparing cadres for politico-military penetration of Chokwe, Lwena, Luchazi, Bunda, and Ovimbundu communities. And once in Zambia, Savimbi found himself under some pressure from Zambian authorities to join forces with the MPLA, which had outpaced him in establishing a local organization. Savimbi and his supporters, however, would have no part of what they considered an interloping movement of assimilados and mestiços. The stage was set for years of interparty conflict like that which had pitted GRAE against the MPLA in the north. In its first issue (April 1966), UNITA's official bulletin, *Kwacha-Angola*, charged that "MPLA/Neto" had "once more" created an "atmosphere of fratricide" by sending some fifty-five of its soldiers into "a region already under [UNITA] control."

RESURGENCE AND REVERSES: THE MPLA

The decline of the UPA/GRAE during 1964–1966 was matched by a striking MPLA recovery. Dr. Neto's self-inflicted embarrassment, the *Frente Democrática de Libertação de Angola* (FDLA), lingered for some time as an obstacle to such recovery. Vaunting its survival despite "violent attacks" and "repression" by the OAU and "certain African states," the FDLA announced in May 1964 that it remained a "true force" in Angolan nationalism prepared to reach an understanding with "the other existing front" (FNLA).[271] Although its promoters promised a major reorganization to improve FDLA effectiveness, change was limited to a shuffle in the lineup of its Bakongo movements—the MDIA left, CUNA joined.[272] An occasional FDLA communiqué provided GRAE publicists with an opportunity to slam the MPLA's "procolonialist" albatross.[273] But by early 1965, GRAE's Johnny Edouard was asking, "Since when has the FDLA ceased to exist?"[274] No exact answer was possible. The FDLA faded away in 1965, and MPLA publications subsequently expunged it from history.[275]

As the FDLA disappeared, the MPLA's former poet-president, Mário de Andrade, reappeared. Andrade flew to Brazzaville in August 1964 for discussions with the MPLA Steering Committee, discussions that dissipated past "misunderstandings" and led to his "complete reintegration into the ranks of the Organization."[276] Andrade was reinstated as an ordinary rank-and-file member, however, and assumed a leadership role only as an Algiers-based political-cultural coordinator in the interterritorial *Conferência das Organizações Nacionalistas das Colónias Portuguesas* (CONCP).[277] But his return, along with those of lesser errant sons, gave a boost to

MPLA morale. It came as a response to a conscious party policy of outreach and reconciliation by Neto loyalists desirous of rebuilding their movement and eclipsing the "antirevolutionary" UPA.[278]

The MPLA's rebound was most spectacular where it had suffered the greatest setback—in the OAU. It ceaselessly challenged the OAU's decision to grant exclusive recognition to GRAE. In February 1964, Neto complained to the OAU Liberation Committee that since the Dakar decision of August 1963, "no financial or material aid has been received by the MPLA, either from the Liberation Committee or from sister countries which formerly assisted [it] and which now contribute to the [OAU's] Liberation Fund."[279] Fighting back against a campaign to "smother and destroy" his movement, the MPLA leader urged the OAU Council of Ministers to grant "freedom of action" and a portion of OAU liberation funds to the MPLA.[280] In May the MPLA foreign secretary, Luis de Azevedo, Jr., invited the OAU Liberation Committee to accompany MPLA guerrillas into Cabinda,[281] and the party Steering Committee again called for "freedom of action" for the MPLA and urged the OAU to convene a unity "Congress of All Angolan Nationalist Organizations."[282] In June, the MPLA repeated these invitations and requests in a long memorandum to the Liberation Committee replete with detailed accounts of dissidence and violence inside GRAE.[283] And in July, at the OAU summit conference in Cairo, the MPLA again set forth its arguments in a petition, which, quantifying the movement's recovery, claimed a membership growth to seventy thousand, including ten thousand underground organizers and activists.[284] The Cairo conference decision to create a three-state Conciliation Committee to reconcile the FNLA/GRAE and MPLA and reexamine OAU policy of exclusive support for GRAE constituted a major MPLA victory, a victory facilitated by Jonas Savimbi's dramatic Cairo resignation.[285]

In a climate of growing skepticism about the wisdom of the OAU's recognition of GRAE,[286] the Conciliation Committee held its first deliberations in Cairo that October. Roberto boycotted the committee, considering it hopelessly hostile. After a visit to Brazzaville and an MPLA guerrilla base near the Cabinda border (like the 1963 goodwill committee, it declined invitations to go to "liberated territory"), the committee met next in November at Dar es Salaam where it reported its findings to the OAU's Liberation Committee. The Conciliation Committee concluded that the MPLA was a "serious, active and capable movement able to lead an efficient fight" and recommended that the Liberation Committee extend to it both technical (training) and material assistance.[287] The Liberation Committee "accepted the conclusions of the report," agreed to submit them "for the approval" of the OAU Council of Ministers, and decided meanwhile to begin aiding "the fighting front opened by the MPLA in the enclave of Cabinda and in Angola."[288] GRAE professed to be astonished at the Liberation Committee's action.[289] And when the report was presented to the OAU Council of Ministers (Nairobi, February 26–March 9, 1965) Holden Roberto argued in person against its adoption.[290]

No longer satisfied with "freedom of action" and a portion of OAU aid, the MPLA escalated its demands. It urged approval of the tripartite report and "sufficient and exclusive" assistance for itself as the "only Angolan nationalist movement" actually fighting Portuguese colonialism.[291] After indecisive debate, the council simply "took note" of the three-power Conciliation Committee report.[292] But the Liberation Committee would feel free henceforth to give an ever larger proportion of its Angolan assistance to the MPLA.

In 1965, the OAU's annual summer summit scheduled for Accra, Ghana, was delayed until October and met just after the downfall of Moïse Tshombe. Exuding new post-Tshombe optimism, Holden Roberto accompanied President Joseph Kasavubu to the conference but was unable to regain his diplomatic initiative.[293] By this time, the Liberation Committee was reportedly allocating a third of its Angolan assistance to the MPLA.[294] The Conciliation Committee continued to press for a reconciliation of the two movements, while GRAE posed procedural preconditions to its participation in unity discussions,[295] and the MPLA pushed for an outright, formal derecognition of GRAE.[296]

The upturn in MPLA fortunes was also striking at the global, extra-African level. In 1964, after having paused following Neto's OAU debacle, the Soviet Union resumed active and exclusive support of the MPLA.[297] It also reverted to the practice of heaping criticism on the UPA/GRAE. The Russians accused Roberto of collaborating with Tshombe and slowing down the Angolan insurgency in response to American pressure.[298] They sent reporters to Congo-Brazzaville to visit and write enthusiastically of MPLA operations on the Cabinda front.[299] In March–April 1966, *Pravda* carried a series of articles by T. Kolesnichenko, who, after spending a week with MPLA guerrillas, commended them for their spirit, discipline, and political awareness.[300] Kolesnichenko reported that UPA guerrillas, disillusioned by Roberto's ties with Western imperialism, were defecting to the MPLA.[301] And while Roberto countered with attacks on the Soviets as "reactionary revisionists," who, during four years of fighting had never extended any aid to his movement,[302] MPLA leaders thanked the Soviet Union for having discredited Roberto as an "American puppet" and declared that when independence was won, "our first words of gratitude will be addressed to our most loyal friends, the people and government of the USSR."[303] Relaying Agostinho Neto's appreciation for "tremendous help" extended by the Soviet Union,[304] *Pravda*'s Kolesnichenko concluded that by rendering "all-around assistance," the Soviet Union and "other socialist countries" were playing "an important part in spreading the ideas of socialism and revolutionary anticolonialist ideology without which the participation of vast masses in the liberation fight is impossible." "Armed with these ideas," he wrote, the MPLA had become a real "fighting force."[305]

The MPLA's stock was similarly ascendant among "other [pro-Soviet] socialist countries" and European communist parties.[306] And despite involvement with China on the part of Savimbi, da Cruz, and Roberto,[307] the MPLA also maintained contact with the Chinese and Chinese-oriented countries through 1964–1966.[308] But the Chinese carefully limited their support.[309] Cuba, on the other hand, came forth as a new source of assistance for the MPLA only. During a 1965 visit to Brazzaville, Cuba's celebrated revolutionary, Che Guevara, looked in on the MPLA and conferred with Agostinho Neto.[310] And when Cubans, perhaps a thousand, came to train the Congo-Brazzaville militia, some became involved in training Angolan guerrillas as well.[311]

The MPLA was largely successful in reasserting itself as the sole Angolan movement worthy of "non-aligned" Afro-Asian support. Roberto's participation in the Second Conference of Non-Aligned States at Cairo (October 5–10, 1964) was one of GRAE's last appearances at a major Third World conference.[312] MPLA lobbying was effective in having GRAE barred from the Fourth Afro-Asian People's Solidarity Conference held in May 1965 at Winneba, Ghana.[313] And the MPLA became the exclusive representative of Angola at the well-publicized Third World "Tricontinental Conference" at Havana, Cuba, in January 1966.[314]

Recouped international status was reinforced by reports of MPLA political activity inside Angola, notably within urban centers such as Luanda, Nova Lisboa, Malange, Benguela, and Cubal. Arrests of MPLA underground leaders in Angola and Lisbon dramatized MPLA resilience.[315] By mid-1966, academic observers such as University of California Professor Ronald Chilcote concluded that the MPLA, led by an "intelligentsia" that was "known throughout the country," was "emerging as Angola's most important nationalist group."[316]

Serious setbacks and intractable problems continued nonetheless to plague and slow the MPLA's political comeback. Like GRAE, the MPLA fell prey to an epidemic of desertions. These included the flight of its military chief of staff, José Ferreira, to Luanda;[317] the exodus of veteran steering committeeman Dr. Eduardo dos Santos;[318] the self-publicized escape of a dissident military officer, Costa Sozinho da Fonseca, from political imprisonment and possible execution in Brazzaville;[319] and the defection of six graduates of MPLA's military *Centro de Instrucção Revolucionária* (CIR) at Dolisie, Congo-Brazzaville. After giving themselves over to Portuguese authorities, the group obliged their hosts with a press conference at Luanda in June 1966.[320]

Congo-Léopoldville persistently constricted MPLA efforts to regain political and military momentum. The MPLA appealed to the Tshombe government to grant it "freedom of action."[321] But Tshombe was hardly more interested in Neto's variety of revolution than Roberto's and held a number of MPLA militants (one of whom reportedly died of maltreatment) in Congolese prisons.[322] After Mobutu's rise to power in November, the MPLA petitioned him to allow its militants in Congo-Kinshasa to cross the river to Brazzaville. But even this request was denied.[323]

Contrastingly on the Brazzaville side of the river, the Massamba-Debat government extended wide political-military latitude to the MPLA; it even connived in the arrest and execution of MPLA dissidents Matias Miguéis and José Miguel.[324] Curiously, however, Brazzaville authorities also permitted Cabinda separatists, whose *Front pour la Libération de l'Enclave de Cabinda* (FLEC) had been founded under the aegis of the ousted regime of Fulbert Youlou, to continue political operations. Opposed to union with Angola, FLEC championed full independence for the enclave. As nuisance competition, FLEC drew fire from the MPLA, which urged African foreign ministers not to be distracted by FLEC's claims[325] and asserted that people within the enclave really supported the military action that had brought the MPLA into control

of a large part of the territory.[326] MPLA supporters argued that
FLEC was simply a "tribal and regional" group whose real role was
to "sabotage the activities" of the Angolan movement.[327] And in
March 1965, the MPLA Steering Committee announced that it had
uncovered espionage activities by FLEC members who had been
furnishing the Portuguese with information on MPLA military activity and carrying out "counterrevolutionary" action against the
Congo-Brazzaville.[328] FLEC nevertheless continued to operate as a
legal competition to the MPLA in the Brazzaville republic.

During 1964, 1965, and much of 1966, Cabinda was the only territory to which the MPLA had direct access from a contiguous operational base. UPA/ELNA military incursions across the enclave
border from the Luali-Tshela area of Congo-Léopoldville had
waned.[329] Indeed they had been largely superseded by the counterrevolutionary activity of African collaborators led by the former
GRAE minister of armaments, Alexandre Taty. Working with Portuguese authorities, Taty and his *Junta Militar Angolano no Exílio*
(JMAE) campaigned in person and by leaflet urging Cabindan refugees to return home[330] and offered regular pay, food, and clothes
to both UPA and MPLA defectors.[331] Taty notwithstanding, MPLA
guerrillas trained at Dolisie (CIR),[332] repeatedly raided the enclave,
blew up bridges, and ambushed Portuguese soldiers. And if partisan accounts exaggerated MPLA exploits—Algeria's *Révolution
africaine* had the MPLA fighting a fifteen-thousand man Portuguese army in an enclave of two hundred thousand people[333]—
Cabinda at least became for the MPLA a kind of "laboratory of revolutionary warfare."[334] By mid-1966, the MPLA was claiming that
its forces controlled a fourth of the territory and had killed over
fifteen hundred Portuguese soldiers there during the last ten
months of 1965.[335]

In fact MPLA operations were modest in scope. And although
MPLA organizers were now obliged to take a preparatory *curso de
monitores politicos*,[336] they largely failed in efforts to mobilize political support among Cabindans. Cabinda's rural Mayumbe[337] (Bakongo) inhabiting interior regions along the border of the Brazzaville republic were most resistant to MPLA penetration, preferring either to work with the Portuguese or to seek refuge in one of
the Congos. Interviewing MPLA guerrillas, Basil Davidson determined that the Mayumbe region was "hard to cross," but "beyond
it, in [the more coastal] Bailongo and Cabinda districts, where the
consequences of colonization were more intensive, the people

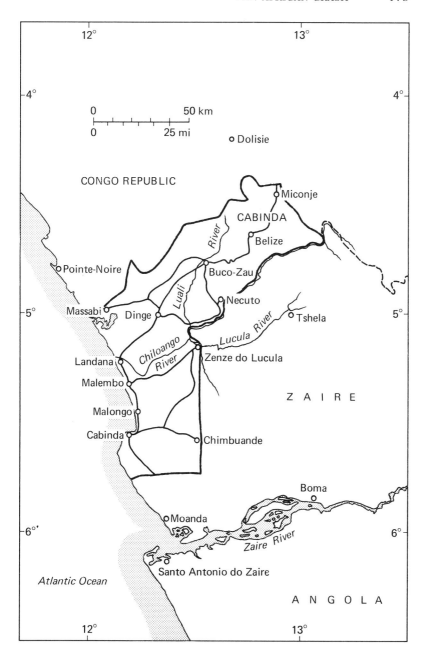

Map 4.1   Cabinda

proved far more welcoming and ready to participate."[338] But the MPLA lacked the military manpower with which to mount a sustained military campaign deep within the enclave.[339] And skeptics in Léopoldville took to writing of assimilados who frequented the bistros, restaurants, and fashionable shops of Brazzaville and "invented" Cabindan war stories. "One hears on the radio about a portion of Cabinda having been liberated, whereas it is a public scandal that [MPLA] guerrillas scarcely dare to cross the Congo-Cabindan frontier."[340] Adding to MPLA problems, the resistance of Cabindan refugees to MPLA proselytizers in Congo-Brazzaville provoked a harsh, sometimes violent, MPLA response which, in turn, led to friction with Brazzaville authorities and some (wishful) reports that Neto's movement might be expelled.[341]

Shut out of Congo-Léopoldville, the MPLA remained cut off from and unable to reinforce or supply its partisans in the Dembos-Nambuangongo area of northern Angola.[342] Those of its supporters in the area who marched north through Backongo country in quest of outside help risked ambush at the hands of UPA/ELNA patrols.[343] And MPLA units that attempted to filter southward through Congolese and UPA territory to resupply and augment isolated MPLA redoubts ran a similar risk. In May 1966, for instance, thirty-two MPLA militants heading for Nambuangongo were reportedly killed by UPA forces.[344]

In September 1966, however, a group of seventy-two heavily armed guerrillas let by Jacob Caetano (survivor of a 1963 UPA ambush on the Loge River),[345] known as the Cienfuegos Column (after the Cuban revolutionary, Camilo Cienfuegos), did manage to make it all the way south to MPLA territory.[346] Once they arrived in Dembos-Nambuangongo, they altered the local balance of power between MPLA and UPA supporters, prompted the immediate release of MPLA partisans held captive by UPA forces,[347] and recruited an initial contingent of 180 volunteers to return north for military training at Dolisie. That November (1966), they managed to convoke a general meeting of nationalists from some forty different centers in the Dembos-Mazumbo de Nambuangongo region.[348] Working with the local MPLA military commander, Amadeu João Paulo, and the head of the local MPLA "action committee," Almeida João Pereira, the Cienfuegos group mounted an ambitious program of military and political education for men, women, and children of the area. Its goal was to build a solid revolutionary base in the rolling forest country of Dembos-

Nambuangongo. Its work was modestly reinforced in early 1967 with the arrival of the nineteen members of a follow-up 158-man Cami Column who managed to survive a gauntlet of UPA and Portuguese ambushes.[349]

The import of the Cienfuegos breakthrough was reduced by the persistence of debilitating regional ethnic cleavage, however. A local MPLA leader noted the MPLA senzalas remained exclusively Mbundu, whereas UPA senzalas were predominantly Bakongo.[350] And to the detriment of their common goal of independence, the two movements continued to squander their energies and resources in ethnically related Chetnik-versus-Partisan conflict.

Taking advantage of this nationalist disarray, the Portuguese air-dropped thousands of red-and-green leaflets over presumed guerrilla strongholds. Written in Portuguese, Kikongo, and Kimbundu they read on one side, "Present this paper to the soldiers and you will receive good treatment," and on the other: "Bring guns and ammunition and receive money."[351] Hundreds of discouraged nationalists took up the offer.

By mid-1966, the MPLA had become embroiled in intense two-party competition on yet another front—the new front in eastern Angola. On May 18, two months after Jonas Savimbi's UNITA had held its founding conference at Muangai in the Moxico district, the MPLA began military operations in the Cazombo area of the Angolan panhandle that juts into Zambia above Balovale.

The MPLA had begun the groundwork for this third front in 1964. After first getting approval from Tanzania's Julius Nyerere to establish an office in Dar es Salaam (where it could count on the political support of its CONCP ally, the Mozambique Liberation Front [FRELIMO]), it sent two organizers to Lusaka. There, on September 14, 1964, Daniel Chipenda and Ciel da Conceição, who carried pistols, cash, and Chinese and Soviet literature in their luggage, were promptly arrested. The two Angolans argued that they had no subversive intent and were simply hoping to set up a refugee relief center. But a Lusaka court sentenced them to four months at hard labor.[352]

With the coming of Zambian independence in October 1964 and the collapse of the UPA/GRAE Lusaka office in early 1965, however, the situation changed. Veteran MPLA official Anibal de Melo obtained permission to open an MPLA office in Lusaka.[353] By mid-year, Angolan refugees and émigrés were passing through Dar es Salaam under MPLA auspices en route to military training in Eastern Europe.[354] Others were sent into the Moxico and Cuando Cubango districts bordering on Zambia to begin building a "minimal network of political cooperation"[355] within the vast, lightly populated expanses of eastern Angola. At the same time, in Dar es Salaam Agostinho Neto organized a small flow of military supplies southward to Zambia, preparatory to beginning military action within eastern Angola in May 1966.

As soon as fighting began, the MPLA produced a flow of effusive communiqués—one alleging that seventy-five Portuguese soldiers had been killed in just one ambush along the Zambezi. Although grossly exaggerated, these communiqués cited MPLA forces along the Upper Zambezi and Lungué-Bungo Rivers, especially between Lumbala and Cazombo, where they did in fact ambush Portuguese forces and sabotage bridges, roads and river barges.[356] In September, the Portuguese defense minister, General Gomes de Araujo, returned to Lisbon from an inspection tour in Angola and confirmed that a new front had been opened in the east by MPLA (no mention of UNITA) units infiltrating from Zambia.[357]

With the opening of the eastern front, nationalist insurgency within Angola (like exile action outside) came to reflect the underlying tripolarity of Angolan politics. Henceforth the Angolan conflict would be fought on three fronts (Cabinda and northern and eastern Angola) as a three-party (FNLA, UNITA, MPLA) insurgency within the context of a three-territory (Angola, Guinea-Bissau, Mozambique) anticolonial war of attrition against a gradually wearying colonial power.

THE TRIPARTITE PHASE

(1966–1976)

INTRODUCTION TO PART II

The liberation movements of Portuguese Africa lacked the skills, discipline, and weaponry of Vietnamese or Palestinian insurgents. But they refused to give up. Over time they developed into potent catalysts of social, economic, and, finally, political change. By 1968, when the more modern though still ultraconservative government of Marcello Caetano succeeded that of Lisbon's oligarch, António Salazar, African insurgents were draining the energies of Europe's last colonial power.

During the 1960s, Portugal's armed forces more than doubled in size[1] as did its defense expenditures, which by 1971 consumed 45 to 50 percent of the government budget.[2] Despite the growing strains of war, however, Portugal, severely policed and politically anesthetized, was slow to produce an internal antiwar movement. Government control of the press ensured against a François Mauriac or *L'Express* mobilizing public opinion as had happened in France during the Algerian war. A persecuted, largely clandestine, opposition, notably the Communist party (PCP), managed to sur-

179

vive, but open protest against the African wars could be voiced only in exile.

Exile and the Portuguese Opposition

It was from far-off Algiers that some forty militants of the *Frente Patriótica de Libertação Nacional* (FPLN) led by General Humberto Delgado attempted to organize a political campaign against the Salazar regime. But in July 1964, the same month that Jonas Savimbi and Holden Roberto parted ways at Cairo, Delgado broke with cautious Communist (PCP) leadership inside the FPLN. A partisan of early, aggressive action in Portugal, Delgado with his supporters proposed to infiltrate the Portuguese military and government through an internal underground, or *Junta Revolucionária Portuguesa*. He dismissed external propaganda as "paper bullets";[3] refused to support demands by the pro-Soviet PCP that representatives of a small, pro-Chinese *Frente de Acção Popular* (FAP) be expelled from Algiers;[4] boycotted an October 1964 congress of the FPLN, which adopted the conservative PCP strategy calling for a long struggle leading toward a mass "popular uprising";[5] and convened instead his own meeting of impatient Portuguese democrats along the Spanish-Portuguese border.[6]

In the political maneuvering that followed, the Delgado supporters, who changed the "P" in their FPLN from *Patriótica* to *Portuguesa*, came out second best. Delgado warned in December 1964 that Algerians might become impatient with the internecine conflict of exiles. He cited recent history. In 1934, the Spanish republic had welcomed and assisted Portuguese opposition leaders in Madrid. But Spaniards soon fatigued of incessant "personal quarrels" that pitted Portuguese exiles against one another. Then suddenly, without warning, Spanish officials cut off all assistance.[7] The same thing could happen in Algeria, Delgado predicted.

Three months later the Algerian government ejected Delgado from his FPLN office.[8] And within weeks the slain body of the former air force general was discovered in Spain, near the Portuguese border,[9] leaving the Communist party in secure control of the FPLN, the most prominent group of anti-Salazarist exiles.[10] During the years that followed, the FPLN produced a steady flow of publications[11] and radio rhetoric from Algiers. But it played only a peripheral role in the drama that finally led to the overthrow of the Salazarists by military coup. The FPLN was handicapped, as the Delgado episode illustrates, by the chronic vicissitudes of exile politics.

Exile and the Angolan Nationalists

Among Angolans the dysfunctional impact of exile was also evident—strikingly so during the period of Tshombe's rule in the Congo (1964–1965). Lisbon took advantage of Tshombe's rise to power to infiltrate factions, enflame dissensions, and nourish (Bakongo and Chokwe) secessionists and collaborators within Angolan exile-émigré ranks.

Title and status then seemed within reach of anyone with imagination enough to invent a new Angolan organization. One enterprising youth printed calling cards that identified him as the Reverend Pastor Dr. John Bunga. Masquerading as president of the Angolan Red Cross, he presented himself to the Protestant Relief Center of Kinshasa in quest of support and issued anti-FNLA political statements that were published in the local press.[12]

Exile continued to be an important political factor even after Tshombe, though much of Angola's nationalist leadership and most political analysts seemed little aware of the impact that the exile condition had upon political perceptions and behavior. Four types of problems, as identified in clinical research on frustration[13] and examined in studies distributed by the United Nations High Commissioner for Refugees (UNHCR),[14] were predictable. These related to tendencies toward (1) aggression—physical violence or antisocial outbursts that release personal tension but undermine organization discipline, morale, and unity; (2) regression—retreat from unpleasant reality and "adaptional levels of self-reliance," which leads to immature dependency, refusal to accept responsibility for one's fate, and escapist fantasies of external deliverance; (3) apathy—loss of hope, prudence, and drive after a protracted period of goal frustration; and (4) compulsive repetition—persistence in demonstrably unproductive or self-defeating activities and attitudes that give the illusion of being functional.[15]

Most salient among Angolans at times of declining fortune or increasing frustration, such tendencies were evident in factional quarrels and defections, distractive and excessive diplomatic traveling, lax security, dependence on external assistance, hyperbolic communiqués, and military claims so exaggerated as to defy credence. An example of the last was the MPLA's claim in 1969, at a time of military reverses, that a third of Angola's population, or approximately 1.5 million people, was then living in "liberated areas," an assertion at such variance with all reportorial evidence as to invite ridicule.[16] Insecurity and perceptual distortion caused by duress encouraged a propensity to attribute all quarrels and divisiveness to an external "imperialist" conspiracy that manipulated the personal avarice of particular leaders. Angolan exiles were vulnerable to external dependency relationships and manipulation; but to blame all intranationalist conflict on external conspiracy alone was to deny Angolan nationalism of its own independent qualities, its own discrete reality.

Scholars generally avoided dealing with the exile dimension of Angolan and other Southern African liberation movements. The intensely partisan and polemical nature of such politics discouraged research and threatened hostile response from those whose very condition reduced tolerance for critical analysis.[17] As one writer who did plunge into the subject put it, "To report . . . feuds and squabbles is sometimes held as inimical to the cause of African freedom, as though silence would alter the unpleasant reality. All too often, in any case, important developments within the liberation movements go unreported, even by the few veteran observers of the scene who indeed know what is happening."[18]

Speaking to a university audience in Dar es Salaam, shortly before the Portuguese coup in 1974, Agostinho Neto acknowledged that Angolan nationalists had been weakened by the need to work outside where they could be sidetracked into the pursuit of inappropriate deals and models. He concurred with an "intelligent friend" who said that the "worst thing the Portuguese did to us was to oblige us to wage a liberation struggle from abroad."[19] As the war progressed, there was an increasing awareness among Angolan nationalists of the basic truth that political exiles must organize and effect a return, by guerrilla and/or underground action, to the political life of their home country if they were to prevent political exile from becoming a voluntary or involuntary escape into political irrelevance.

Jonas Savimbi was the first Angolan leader to return from exile to lead his movement from inside. In conformity with UNITA doctrine, which criticized overreliance on outside help and stressed the need to mobilize for a people's war inside,[20] Savimbi proselytized and organized among villagers of eastern Angola from late 1966 until the 1974 coup (except for an exile interlude in 1967–1968).

Like the respected on-the-spot revolutionary leader of Guinea-Bissau, Amilcar Cabral, Savimbi won praise from the press for his courage[21]—but unlike Cabral, he received little material help. In 1968, Agostinho Neto announced that the MPLA was shifting its headquarters inside Angola, a statement of intent to be only partially realized. Neto and other top MPLA officials did make occasional treks into the country but were more often outside than in.[22] In Kinshasa, Zaire—the new name that President Mobutu Sésé Séko gave to the former (Belgian) Congo—FNLA leadership contrastingly made no move to return from exile to Angola. It enjoyed the advantages of an external base superior to that of either of its rivals. And its reliance on that base, its dependency on exile-émigré manpower, and its immersion in the Zairian political system clearly conditioned its failure to develop a program of political education and mobilization within Angola. Its top leadership did not go into the country; Holden Roberto never ventured across the Zaire-Angola border.

CHAPTER FIVE

THE PATTERN AND PROBLEMS OF THREE-PARTY INSURGENCY (1966–1974)

Exile was only one factor influencing the bitter competition that hobbled Angola's three-party insurgency from 1966 to 1974. Other factors—ethnicity, culture, class, and race—had already established the basic character of the three movements. But the discrete political development, military action and external relations of the three movements produced a complex pattern of constantly changing fortunes and interrelationships. The history and reality of fierce competition and persistent tripolarity remained imperfectly known or understood among Angolans, let alone by others. Then suddenly, with the collapse of the Portuguese colonial order in 1974 and 1975, Angola plunged to the center of the world stage. Understanding little of the forces that threatened to tear Angola into three or more antagonistic ethnolinguistic states, a host of external powers, great and small, near and far, dashed in to steal the last improvised act of the Angolan revolution.

POLITICAL LEADERSHIP, DOCTRINE, AND STRUCTURE

The FNLA

Holden Roberto ran the FNLA with a seasoned iron hand. He personally hoarded or doled out all funds and information. He systematically eliminated potential rivals from leadership roles. He undercut the authority of top associates by forging direct ties with their subordinates. (Thus, for example, when the PDA fired its vice-president, Pedro Gadimpovi, in 1969, Roberto kept Gadimpovi on as a foreign affairs official in his exile government over protests from the PDA's president, Emmanuel Kunzika.)[1] Roberto was reluctant to delegate and quick to withdraw authority. When in

185

his view Savimbi's short-termed successor as secretary-general of the UPA, Manuel André Miranda,[2] exceeded instructions by signing a December 1966 peace accord with the MPLA,[3] Roberto disowned the agreement[4] and shunted Miranda off to the FNLA office in Lubumbashi.

Roberto relied most heavily on personal aides who, because they had no political following or base of their own, were totally dependent upon him. Thus he continued to rely on his Bakongo security chief, José Manuel Peterson, for the ruthless dispatch of political adversaries despite widespread reports that Peterson was dangerously corrupt.[5] Only after Peterson and a Zairian official had profitably arranged the escape of seven Portuguese soldiers being held as prisoners-of-war by the FNLA did Roberto belatedly fire him.[6] As his *directeur du cabinet,* Roberto chose a fellow Bakongo émigré who had grown up in Brazzaville, Paul Touba. Touba had earned a university degree in the United States where he manned GRAE's New York office until 1969 when he flew to Kinshasa and assumed a leadership role in the FNLA as Paulo Tuba.[7]

The one senior FNLA official of importance who was neither Bakongo nor a member of Roberto's extended family was the UPA vice-president, Rosário Neto. In late 1965 and early 1966, Neto spent eight months organizing among Mbundu and Chokwe refugees and émigrés in the Kwango district[8] where he established personal ties with local Congolese officials.[9] After enjoying a period of enhanced prominence, however, he lost favor, began drinking heavily, and became increasingly critical of Roberto.[10] Roberto, in turn, distrusted Neto for building an independent political base. In March 1969, Neto wrote to supporters in Kwango accusing Roberto of tribalism and nepotism. His letters fell into the hands of the GRAE secretary of war, Fernando Gourjel, to whom Neto had complained about the harsh conditions under which a number of MPLA militants were being held prisoner by the FNLA.[11] Like Savimbi in early 1964, Neto then found himself ostracized. In November, when he tried to resign as GRAE minister of information, he was arrested, charged with being treasonously pro-MPLA, and incarcerated in a hut on the FNLA's Kinshasa compound.[12]

Roberto maintained a distrustful eye over all FNLA affairs from behind the defensive barricade of ever-present dark glasses. The movement's collective organs, never strong, withered. At the time of the tenth anniversary of the war in March 1971, it was reported that there had been no meetings of the FNLA National Council since 1967 or of the GRAE Council of Ministers since 1968.[13]

Political discontent surfaced in July and August 1966 when regional PDA and UPA officials gathered at Luvaka in the Lower Congo (now Bas Zaire) to discuss what had become "widespread dissatisfaction" with the way FNLA/GRAE affairs were being run.[14] FNLA soldiers complained to the assemblage about the low quality and paucity of manioc and other food being contributed to Kinkuzu by the Angolan émigré community; FNLA officials responded with allegations that some leaders were diverting local food donations to Kinshasa markets. The Luvaka gathering sent a mildly worded statement to Kinshasa urging that regional FNLA officials be regularly informed, visited, and provided with authorization necessary for them to function. The PDA leadership replied promptly and positively. The UPA did not reply. This provoked a "snorter" of a letter to Roberto from the unhappy *Upistas*.[15] At that point Roberto did indeed respond. He dispatched to Luvaka a truck of Congolese soldiers who rounded up, beat up, and transported the dissidents to Kinshasa. There Roberto dressed them down. Characteristically, he acted coercively, then dropped the matter to fly abroad in quest of external support, whereas Emmanuel Kunzika and Ferdinand Dombele of the PDA followed through with an informational, fence-mending tour of the Bas Zaire area.[16] The combined response restored FNLA authority. But the Luvaka episode further soured relations between Roberto and the PDA. And the FNLA floundered as Roberto continued to resist basic structural and procedural reform. In June 1971, the Organization of African Unity (OAU) formally withdrew the recognition that it had extended to his exile government in 1963. Commenting on the action, OAU Assistant Secretary-General Mohamed Sahnoun said that "far from strengthening the liberation struggle, the recognition of the GRAE had been detrimental to it."[17]

Simmering discontent finally boiled over in early 1972. The previous November some twenty-two out of thirty-three officers at the Kinkuzu military base had sent a letter to Roberto complaining of inadequate food, clothing, arms, and facilities. Roberto invited them to send a delegation to Kinshasa to discuss their grievances. They refused. He finally went to the base to confront them personally. After a tense and inconclusive meeting, Kinkuzu remained in a state of incipient rebellion. A January mediation effort by President Mobutu failed. Another visit to Kinkuzu hazarded by Roberto met defiance, and he managed to leave the base only after staring down a guard allegedly instructed by the leading dissident officer

to shoot him.[18] Increasing violence in which some twenty-five Kinkuzu soldiers died threatened to spill over into the large Angolan
refugee and émigré community, a danger bound to worry Mobutu.
On March 17, he dispatched two battalions of Zairian troops to
subdue and occupy the Angolan military center.[19] There was no resistance. Thirteen[20] of the Angolan officers who had challenged
Roberto's leadership were executed.[21] Others were imprisoned.

Responding to what but for Mobutu's intervention would probably have been a successful move to oust him from leadership of the
FNLA, Roberto moved swiftly against political associates implicated
in the Kinkuzu affair.[22] Purged from the ranks of FNLA/GRAE
leadership were such "deviationists" and "adventurers" as Fernando Gourjel, whose son was one of those executed at Kinkuzu;
Barros Necaca, evicted from the SARA medical service; Manuel
Miranda, reportedly under arrest (but later "rehabilitated"); and
the team of Emmanuel Kunzika and Ferdinand Dombele who had
been dominant PDA figures for over a decade.[23] For a time the
PDA continued to exist as a separate but docile entity under new
leadership acceptable to Holden Roberto.[24] Kunzika, who, in his
capacity as GRAE minister of education, had devoted much of his
energies to developing an Angolan secondary school in Kinshasa,[25]
disappeared from public view.[26] And in early 1973, so did the
movement that he had led, as Roberto dissolved the PDA and UPA
and merged them into the single framework of the FNLA.[27]

Pressed by Mobutu and the need to rebuild a shattered movement, Roberto finally plunged into a long overdue reorganization
of the FNLA. He began by convoking a general political gathering
(April 30–May 1, 1972) in order to explain Kinkuzu and mobilize
support for his leadership.[28] By mid-May he had formed what was
the first functioning GRAE Council of Ministers since 1964. Ap-
propriating for himself the title of Head of the Nation and Leader
of the Revolution, Roberto elevated three new personalities into
leadership roles. He gave a multilingual Luandan, Ngola Kabangu,
who had studied electronics in Yugoslavia (1963–1969), the key organizing post of Minister of Interior;[29] he appointed another
Luandan, Mateus João Neto, who had studied at the College of Agriculture in Vienna and the School of Economics at Stockholm
University, Minister of Information, Plan and Economics;[30] and he
named a mission-educated Methodist from Malange, Dr. Samuel
Francisco da Costa Abrigada, who had studied theology in England
and medicine in West Germany, to be Minister of Health.[31] The

other departments were allocated to veteran Roberto loyalists, among them, Johnny Eduardo (Pinock), foreign affairs,[32] and Carlos Kambandu, finance,[33] and from the PDA, Pedro Gadimpovi who took over education (including management of the IESA secondary school) from Kunzika, and Sébastien Lubaki Ntemo, who became Minister of Social Affairs.[34]

Roberto announced a three-year plan to develop health, education, social, and agriculture projects within "liberated areas" of Angola and to mobilize Angolans in exile in support of what he termed the "new phase of the Revolution."[35] There followed a flurry of activity: regular council meetings and publications,[36] efforts to rebuild UPA committees in Bas Zaire and Shaba (formerly Katanga),[37] new moves to launch a cadre training program and convene a national conference of the FNLA,[38] a campaign to oblige all Angolans in Zaire to buy GRAE identity cards (at about $1.40 each) and pay a "voluntary" war tax,[39] and new initiatives in military, external, and intermovement affairs. But politically the FNLA remained an exile movement dependent on the goodwill of its Zairian hosts and dominated by a reclusive émigré who by this time lived with a new, Zairian wife in a fashionable Kinshasa (Binza) villa guarded by Zairian troops.

There was little change in FNLA doctrine following the Kinkuzu affair. It continued to be narrowly nationalist,[40] non-Marxist,[41] and peasant oriented.[42] Through its uniracial prisms, it continued to see the MPLA as controlled by a privileged class of mestiços.[43] And it was encouraged in these views by Zairian officials who declared that they would support only those whose "African authenticity" protected them from a "prejudicial acceptance" of "communist or capitalist ideology," protected them from becoming satellites.[44]

No longer preoccupied with keeping up the pretense of leading a government—GRAE as distinct from the FNLA was recognized only by Zaire after June 1971—from 1972 on Roberto concentrated on what had long seemed most important to him: building a strong military force. However secondary in this scheme of things, FNLA-associated groups, such as the women's association (AMA),[45] student movement (UNEA),[46] refugee school system (primary schools and IESA),[47] and medical service (SARA),[48] did continue to function. And as of 1967 the LGTA labor union, semiautonomous by virtue of its own sources of external financial support, claimed twenty-seven thousand members[49] and a program that continued to focus on its sewing center, literacy classes, and vocational training. The LGTA sent a few members to seminars and short training programs in West Germany, Israel, and Dahomey (the Pan African Cooperative Training Center in what is now Benin).[50]

After surveying the field of exile Angolan labor groups in Kinshasa (reduced since Tshombe days),[51] the New York–based African-American Labor Center (AALC) joined with the *Union Nationale des Travailleurs Congolais* (UNTC—later UNTZa [Zairois]) to offer leadership training seminars and then open joint AALC-UNTZa courses in such subjects as labor history, organizing, administration, and rural cooperatives to members of the LGTA and the (Catholic-oriented) CGTA.[52] In 1973, the LGTA, with help from an Italian union, established a training center of its own.[53] And in November of that year, LGTA-CGTA cooperation climaxed in a merger of the two groups, who formed the *Centrale Syndicale Angolaise* (CSA), of which GRAE's secretary of state for education, João Baptista Nguvulu, became secretary-general.[54]

Just as the number of Angolan exile labor groups declined, so did the number and organized activity of the FNLA's Bakongo competitors in Kinshasa who had espoused nonviolence and "negotiations" with Portugal. Though they no longer constituted a serious problem or distraction for Roberto and the FNLA, some did manage occasional sorties into public view. For example, after escaping from Roberto's prison at Kinkuzu in March 1967, Emmanuel Lamvu resumed his public campaign for a congress of all Angolan nationalists to be organized by his *Comité des Bons Offices Angolais* (CBOA). He did so, however, from the relative security of Brazzaville.[55] Lamvu's campaign was echoed in 1968 by a new but short-lived Kinshasa coalition of Bakongo for nonviolence, the *Cartel des Nationalistes Angolais* (CNA).[56] That same year yet another group, the *União Progressista Nacional de Angola* (UPRONA), sent letters petitioning the Portuguese government to agree to independence negotiations. And having "learned with indescribable joy that the problem of decolonizing the entire world absorb[ed] a great deal of . . . attention in the Security Council and the General Assembly of the United Nations," UPRONA forwarded copies of its appeals to New York.[57]

But little was heard of these groups after 1968. Roberto's most enduring Bakongo adversaries, the royalists of Ngwizako,[58] were still trying to persuade Portugal to restore the Kongo kingdom.[59] But they were unable to obtain Portuguese visas so they could return and lobby inside Angola (to which end they vainly sought the good offices of the Spanish ambassador in Kinshasa).[60] And from 1966 on, Ngwizako was subjected to what it termed "savage" repression by the FNLA, including the arrest and imprisonment of several of its activists at Kinkuzu.[61] In the view of Ngwizako leaders, this was all part of a "religious war" of extermination that Roberto's Protestant UPA was waging against the Catholics of the (Portuguese) Kongo.[62] More to the point, this was in fact part of a concerted Roberto-Mobutu policy of making certain that efforts to build up the FNLA were not challenged by local competition.

UNITA

For UNITA, political competition within the confines of its external support base, Zambia, was of a different order of magnitude. The MPLA bent every effort to eliminate what it viewed as an "interloper" from the scene. Jonas Savimbi sought out the MPLA's Lusaka representative, Anibal de Melo, in July and again in August 1966. But MPLA headquarters in Brazzaville was in no mood to authorize what Savimbi proposed, a new round of discussions with UNITA.[63]

Savimbi wanted an entente, a united front, not a merger. But a formula that would leave him and his associates with a "free hand to work for ourselves" was not acceptable to the MPLA—or the FNLA.[64] In September, Zambian President Kenneth Kaunda brought Holden Roberto together with Savimbi for unity talks at Lusaka's State House. Roberto agreed to a reconciliation but on his own terms. Savimbi should write a letter apologizing for his 1964 walkout, dissolve UNITA and then, with his colleagues, join the FNLA as individuals.[65] Roberto apparently believed that Savimbi might be persuaded to accept these terms by Kaunda, who threatened to close down Savimbi's "divisive" third-party operations.[66] And Roberto was under pressure not to concede more from those whose status within the FNLA would be threatened by Savimbi's return, notably Johnny Eduardo, who had replaced Savimbi at the head of GRAE foreign affairs, and José Domingos Sikunda, GRAE representative at the time in Elizabethville (Lubumbashi).[67]

The Lusaka talks were inconclusive, but it was agreed that Roberto would return for a second round after consulting in Kinshasa.[68] When, however, after two months, nothing further had been heard from Roberto, Savimbi left Lusaka for Angola where he organized a Christmas day attack by several hundred UNITA partisans on the border railroad town of Teixeira de Sousa.[69] UNITA casualties were high—nearly three hundred dead among a poorly armed, little-trained force of mostly Chokwe attackers.[70] But the Benguela Railroad had been cut, and Zambian copper shipments were held up for a week. UNITA had forced the world to take notice of its entry into the Angolan war.[71]

Savimbi returned to Lusaka in February 1967 where he held a press conference, asserting that UNITA had organized an Angolan guerrilla force of a thousand equipped entirely with arms captured from the Portuguese.[72] He was hailed in the Zambian press as an example of realism and courage to those "freedom fighters" in Lusaka who did "little else than produce dozens of pamphlets condemning the regimes of Portugal, South Africa, or Rhodesia." To them he said: "Go into your country and see for yourself what is happening. Then fight. Others will follow. You can only work from inside."[73] Savimbi then flew off to Cairo to attend a meeting of leaders of "progressive" African governments called by Egyptian President Gamal Abdel Nasser[74] and to seek through them to persuade Agostinho Neto to discuss an MPLA-UNITA front. But Neto declined to talk,[75] leaving Savimbi to conclude ruefully that he had been right when he told his followers inside that their "brothers outside" were interested not in cooperation but in "liquidating UNITA."[76]

When in March, during Savimbi's absence UNITA units twice derailed trains and the Benguela line was closed to Zambian copper traffic for several weeks, both the Zambian and Zairian governments had a foretaste of what the consequences would be if the Portuguese shut down the railroad for an extended period. The Portuguese threatened to do just that unless such attacks ceased. Zambian authorities had already warned Savimbi that the railroad should not be cut. But if Savimbi sent orders inside proscribing such a cut, as he subsequently said he had, they arrived too late.[77] The MPLA and FNLA were quick to dissociate themselves from the rail disruptions.[78] When Savimbi belatedly returned to Lusaka in June 1967, he was arrested, held in the Kabwata-Lusaka prison for six days, and then expelled from the country.[79]

Gloom pervaded the "bare, badly lit" UNITA office "halfway down a dirty back alley" in central Lusaka.[80] Pressure from the Portuguese, Tanganyika Concessions (who owned the railroad),[81] the MPLA,[82] and Zambians (Savimbi had made friends and enemies)[83] along with Savimbi's reputation for being something of a playboy,[84] had combined to snap Kaunda's patience and leave UNITA bereft of leadership. "UNITA's Lost Without Dr. Savimbi," the *Zambia News* headlined.[85] Just three years after his dramatic break with Roberto at Cairo in July 1964, Savimbi found himself back in the Egyptian capital, three thousand miles from Angola. In response to press predictions that UNITA would "slowly fold,"[86] UNITA Vice-President Smart Chata acknowledged a temporary setback but insisted that UNITA was not "dead."[87]

A year later, via the organizational channel of the South West Africa People's Organization (SWAPO),[88] Savimbi slipped back through Zambia into Angola. From that time, June 1968, until the Lisbon coup of April 1974, he remained underground. Though he tried many times to persuade Zambia to lift its banishment order, his efforts failed. He apologized in taped and written messages for past mistakes.[89] Then he warned that he might not be able to constrain UNITA guerrillas from attacking the Benguela line so long as the Portuguese army used it and Zambia refused to open an external supply line to UNITA.[90] But his pleas went unheeded. In 1972, Savimbi complained to a Zambian journalist that although UNITA had "complied" with Zambia's strictures against disruption of the railroad, recognition was still being denied. "So what can we do?" he asked.[91]

What he did was make a virtue of necessity. He extolled self-reliance and argued that the proper way to speed the liberation of Angola was for the MPLA and FNLA leaders also to abandon "exile life" and join him "inside."[92]

Savimbi portrayed UNITA and the FNLA as polar opposites on the exile issue.[93] The background characteristics of UNITA leadership, however, were rural/ethnopopulist/uniracial and therefore more like those of the FNLA than of the MPLA. This was evident from UNITA literature. Because the "peasantry of the south" was the last to lay down arms against the Portuguese (1919–1920) and possessed "revolutionary qualities" that Lisbon could not ignore, a Savimbi associate from Ovambo country wrote in 1971, UNITA chose "to implant itself" in the supportive "anti-colonial milieu" of the rural southeast.[94] And resentment of the leadership aspirations of mestiços was strong enough to be an obstacle to collaboration between a uniracial UNITA and a multiracial MPLA. This resentment stood forth as well in party publications: "UNITA has waged a very fierce revolution against the Portuguese Colonial puppets

Regime and their stupid MULLATOS [*sic*] who cannot see beyond their noses."[95] In 1967, UNITA circulated a letter attributed to an MPLA militant who wrote that he was resigning from his movement because, among other things, it could not "lead the black masses of Angola" and was "full of nothing but white dictators."[96]

Although MPLA sources cast doubts on his credentials as a "returned-from-exile" leader,[97] Savimbi was several times interviewed and photographed beside railroad markers or in villages deep within the country.[98] He undertook to build an internal leadership cadre grounded within the various ethnic communities of east, central, and southern Angola. This meant a reduced role for UNITA's veteran Angolan nationalist organizers in Zambia and for pro-UNITA students in Europe and the United States.

Underscoring the national as against regional aspirations of his movement, Savimbi selected as principal organizer for the UNITA underground a young, Tunisian-trained agronomist from an aristocratic family in the northern enclave of Cabinda. A personable political strategist, Miguel N'Zau Puna returned to Angola with Savimbi in 1968. He was appointed at an internal Conference of Cadres (August 31–September 5) in 1968 and confirmed at UNITA's second congress in 1969 as both secretary-general of the movement and "general political commissar" of its guerrilla forces.[99]

In August 1969, eighty UNITA partisans met at a secret encampment in eastern Angola to elect a new slate of party leaders and listen to the political oratory of Savimbi, Puna, and the then chief of military operations, Moises Kayombo. By acclamation this second UNITA congress elected a twenty-five member Central Committee, the first twelve members of which formed a top-level Political Bureau.[100] Several among them would play central roles during the next five years, including two Ovimbundu military commanders, José Samuel Chiwale,[101] an ex-schoolteacher who received his military training from the Chinese, and Samuel Chitunda,[102] who had served in the Portuguese army, and UNITA's principal external spokesman, Jorge Isaac Sangumba,[103] who had earned a university degree in the United States. Sangumba operated from an office in London.[104]

In the early 1970s, a return flow of students from higher education abroad began injecting new skills and breadth into this leadership.[105] One of the more noteworthy was Luciano Kassoma[106] who undertook to apply American training in agriculture and soil sciences to the development of cooperative farming within UNITA-administered zones of eastern Angola.[107]

Capitalizing on his rhetorical skills and the mystery surrounding his movements, Savimbi remained the dominant personality of UNITA, though no longer "a one man band" without able lieutenants.[108] It was he who stated and restated UNITA doctrine in letters to former Protestant missionaries, speeches, interviews, and special messages.[109]

The themes were consistent and persistent. UNITA was nationalist and anti-imperialist—including anti-Soviet "social imperialism."[110] It placed constant emphasis on self-reliance and cited the wisdom of "the brilliant Thinker of oppressed people," China's Mao Tse-tung.[111] It called for a socialist state that would accommodate an African cultural heritage but create a new "liberated man."[112] It called for an economy based on cooperative instead of exploitative systems of production and for majority rule in which Europeans might assume responsibilities but not leadership.[113] And it held that the means to these political ends were absolutely crucial. To achieve these goals would require a long, sacrificial struggle.[114] There was no easy route.[115] Indispensable to the task was a strong revolutionary party to educate and mobilize the peasants (95 percent of the population). UNITA's emphasis was on political not military action.

Everything depended on how the struggle developed. If led "correctly" from within Angola's oppressed peasant and shantytown communities and aided by "intellectual revolutionaries," it would culminate in a new society based on "scientific socialism" adapted to Angolan needs and realities. UNITA distinguished sharply between this "practical ideology" grounded in local experience and that which derived from "the luxury of ideological exercises from the comfort and security" of hotels in Europe and Africa.[116]

By 1970, UNITA began focusing on the importance of infiltrating major population centers and moving in from the peripheral areas of guerrilla action to organize the rural and urban "masses."[117] This meant pushing westward through Bié into the Ovimbundu heartland of the central plateau. But UNITA efforts were impeded on the one hand by a pervasive and widespread fear of the Portuguese police (PIDE) and attraction to the psychosocial campaigns of the Portuguese army[118] and on the other by MPLA attacks from the east, which "time and time again" forced UNITA to turn around from its "advance westward" to defend its "people in the rear."[119]

Though UNITA avowedly eschewed exile hyperbola, Jonas Savimbi made some exaggerated claims for his movement: twenty-nine hundred party branches and sixty-six military detachments as of 1967;[120] control over some one million Angolans by 1970.[121] However, UNITA did build a pyramidal structure of elected councils from the village level up within the confines of its limited zone of operations.[122] And after visiting UNITA territory in 1971, Austrian journalist Fritz Sitte reported that the area was "well-organized and well-run," the "administrative process worked," and discipline was the best of the many guerrilla and underground movements he had seen.[123]

A third-party congress held in August 1973 reorganized UNITA structures, grouping villages into aggregates of sixteen, each of which was to form a "people's assembly." Central organs (the Politbureau and Central Committee) were slightly reduced in size so as to be more flexible and efficient. The congress, attended by 221 delegates and a number of foreign observers, including black Americans representing the African Liberation Support Committee (ALSC) in the United States,[124] listened to Jonas Savimbi on the virtues of self-reliance and adopted resolutions calling for an intensification of the struggle in all domains from growing crops to mobilizing women.[125]

Its London office aside, UNITA maintained little external structure. It continued to draw support from students in Europe and the United States, attracting a number of Bakongo students from the FNLA.[126] And in January 1971, Jorge Sangumba convened a meeting of UNITA militants and sympathizers at Zöfingen, Switzerland, to consider how to mobilize external support and publicity for the movement, a domain in which the MPLA enjoyed an overwhelming advantage.[127] But UNITA had no labor union or other functional affiliates in exile. Its schools, including two for political-military cadres, were all inside the country.[128] If it therefore suffered a comparative disadvantage in external visibility, it was left relatively unbothered by activities of minor exile movements such as the Bakongo and Cabindan groups that plagued the FNLA and MPLA. Following UNITA's costly Chokwe-led Christmas Day 1966 attack on Teixeira de Sousa, a group of Chokwe separatists denounced UNITA's "blood letting" and called for peaceful negotiations with Portugal to establish an independent (Chokwe) Republic of Moxico. Their broadside, addressed to Premier Salazar and signed by José Paulo Chiringueno (ex-PNA-CPA),[129] was the only detectable, albeit ineffectual, challenge of a separatist or collaborationist nature to confront UNITA.[130]

The MPLA

There was a remarkable continuity of leadership at the apex of Angola's liberation movements. Like Roberto (1961) and Savimbi (1966), Agostinho Neto, from the time (1962) that he first assumed his movement's presidency, held that post without interruption until the end of the war for independence. Twice, however, Neto's leadership was a focal point of controversy within a crippling, internal power struggle. Thus ten years after political schisms that nearly destroyed it in 1963–1964, the movement underwent a new internal crisis that left it almost fatally fragmented on the eve of the Lisbon coup of April 1974.

The characteristics and problems of MPLA leadership (1966–1974) represented logical projections in time. Ethnocentrism as a motivating force persisted more significantly within the rural-based FNLA and UNITA than within the more urban MPLA, which had been heavily impacted by the integrative imposition of Portuguese language and culture.

The shift of major MPLA politico-military activity to the eastern front after 1966, however, placed a premium on developing new leadership from within the Bunda, Luchazi, Chokwe, and other communities of that vast region. And a 1970 visit to the area by Basil Davidson led him to conclude that the movement was capitalizing on its opportunity to break out of the "old ethnic narrowness of the late 1950s and 1960s," when "it was based effectively" upon the Mbundu in and around Luanda.[131] Remote from the schools and towns of the coast and highlands, however, Angola's thinly dispersed eastern population was mostly illiterate and politically uneducated. Although the MPLA plunged in to train local military and political cadres,[132] the preeminence of Luandans at higher levels of authority continued. The legendary Mbundu warrior–queen Nzinga Mbande (1582–1663) remained the most prominent ethnohistorical referent.[133] And conflict over the leadership role of largely Luandan mestiços remained a cause of chronic tension.[134] On the other hand, some of the MPLA's most able Luandan leaders gave their lives to the struggle—struck down by one or the other of two enemies, the Portuguese and the FNLA.

Whenever an opportunity arose to physically eliminate MPLA leadership, a chronically insecure and increasingly calloused Holden Roberto seized it. In March 1967, his forces apprehended a group of twenty MPLA militants returning to Zaire from northern Angola. Among them were five women, including Déolinda Rodrigues (de Almeida), a leading member of the MPLA executive committee.[135] Roberto imprisoned her at Kinkuzu, where she wrote defiant poetry. Committed to life, she struggled on

Between lurking suicide
And this mad vortex
Until morning comes
To come out of the death camp alive
And be able to be useful
In freedom of choice
Of responsibility
And freedom of action
To fulfill it.

"Under the murderers' flag and in the cell" she and her companions "flung" their voices out to join the revolution. Rather than submit to her captors, she asked the MPLA in smuggled messages for poison. In the end she was executed.[136]

Arrested in Kinshasa in 1966 along with nine other militants, MPLA executive committee member Commander João Gonçalves Benedito was also imprisoned at Kinkuzu.[137] In January 1968, Agostinho Neto alleged that Benedito, one of the nearly one hundred MPLA prisoners at Kinkuzu, was being kept in a nearly lightless cell and was losing his sight.[138] Benedito was never to see or be seen again.[139]

The MPLA lost two other top leaders to Portuguese arms in 1968. Its chief military commander, Major Hoji Ia Henda, fell during an assault on a Portuguese outpost at Karipande near the Zambian border.[140] The head of its *Serviço de Assistência Médica do MPLA* (SAM), Dr. Américo Boavida,[141] was killed during a Portuguese helicopter attack on an MPLA camp, Hanoi II, in Moxico, where he was training medical technicians to work with MPLA guerrillas.[142]

MPLA leadership also suffered from second-level defections, which were exploited by the Portuguese press,[143] and from arrests of underground leaders in Luanda.[144] On the other hand, there were also reports of defections of African soldiers from the Portuguese army to the MPLA,[145] and the 1969 arrests in Luanda confirmed that the MPLA was continuing, despite police harassment, to organize in urban areas.[146]

The effectiveness of MPLA leadership was also undercut by the wide dispersion of MPLA operations directed from offices in Brazzaville, Dar es Salaam, and Lusaka into Cabinda, Dembos-Nambuangongo, and eastern Angola. This dispersion rendered politico-military coordination difficult. Steering Committee members could not be convened for "regular or frequent meetings."[147] In April 1970, therefore, the consolidated, five-man Political and Military Coordinating Committee (CCPM) assumed authority over the movement's sprawling organizational structure.[148] Representing an effort to assert functional central control, the committee was composed of President Agostinho Neto; Henrique Teles "Iko" Carreira, who headed up Cabindan, and later eastern, operations;[149] Daniel Júlio Chipenda, the movement's ranking Ochimbundu and overall organizer of the eastern front;[150] Lúcio Lára, long-time administrative secretary and head of the MPLA Brazzaville office;[151] and "Spartacus" Floribert Monimambu, a Bakongo officer in command of MPLA forces in the Eastern region.[152]

The new committee, however, was soon torn by conflict. The discord was not over doctrine.[153] The MPLA remained an eclectic front, and plans discussed at a February 1968 conference at Dolisie, Congo-Brazzaville,[154] to convert it into a "revolutionary party" were deferred until such time as internal study groups could produce a solid nucleus of ideologically prepared cadres.[155] The movement's conversion into a "vanguard party" was to come at "the correct stage" in the development of the struggle.[156] Meanwhile, Monimambu, among others, declared his personal commitment to "scientific socialism,"[157] and a close observer of the MPLA, Basil Davidson, depicted the movement's ideology as revolutionary and Marxist but not communist.[158] Agostinho Neto expounded upon familiar multiracial, egalitarian, and anti-imperialist themes,[159] while new stress was placed on the principle of self-reliance.[160]

Discord derived, instead, from faulty communication, military reverses, and competing ambitions. In a 1970 New Year's Day message, Agostinho Neto acknowledged that MPLA "combat fronts" sometimes waited passively "for months and months" for instructions from outside. He exhorted local units to take more initiative, capture arms and other necessities from the Portuguese, attack the enemy, grow crops, and organize schools without waiting for "outside assistance" to "resolve all of our material problems."[161] To encourage such initiative and eliminate the gap between exile leadership and the internal organization, the MPLA (like UNITA) began preaching the virtues of return from exile.[162] Already in June 1967, Neto had presided over a meeting of the MPLA's regional committee within Moxico with the aim of spurring internal initiative through the organizing of local militias, cadre training, dispensaries, food production, and "people's stores" to distribute essential staples within MPLA-held areas.[163] In January 1968, he announced that the MPLA was moving its headquarters inside Angola.[164] And in August, he participated in a regional assembly attended by some eighty delegates near Ninda about thirty miles from the Zambian border.[165]

The leadership assertedly succeeded in speeding up the communication system between department heads "at the rear or outside" and military commanders "far away at the front." And the presence of top leaders inside the country was now recognized as important to "the confidence and morale" of MPLA guerrillas.[166] But Agostinho Neto and his chief lieutenants were still more often outside than in. A July 1972 visit to the MPLA's outside headquarters in Dar es Salaam and Lusaka by a mission from the radical Liberation Support Movement (LSM) of North America revealed "signs" of "disorganization." According to the LSM, communication had become "increasingly irregular and undependable" with an MPLA that seemed unable to follow up on "support projects." The LSM had, for example, sent a printing press, but the MPLA had "failed to provide a shop and cadre to be trained."[167] Reminiscent of an old, never-to-be-consummated quest in FNLA experience, calls for and promises of a national congress to resolve MPLA leadership and structural problems began appearing in 1971.[168] Meeting inside Angola in mid-1971, the MPLA Steering Committee decided to enlarge itself and the Political-Military Coordination Committee (CCPM) and to organize a full national congress.[169] Increasingly the movement seemed disoriented by internal conflict, at least some of which was traceable to military reverses.

In the summer of 1968, the Portuguese, using helicopters, light bombers, and commando forces, mounted a dry season "search and destroy" offensive that razed MPLA encampments and lowered MPLA morale. As Commander "Iko" Carreira noted later, the nationalists had become "too confident" and "allowed the development of large concentrations at fixed points." Hanoi II, where Dr. Boavida was slain, was a case in point. Not enough emphasis had been placed on mobility and local food supplies.[170] Although staggered, the MPLA survived. It altered tactics and gradually extended the range of its guerrilla action, only to be set back once more by new Portuguese offensives in 1972 and 1973.[171] In February 1972, the Portuguese launched Operation Attila in the East. Raining napalm and defoliants in a "scorched earth" assault on nationalist villages, they inflicted serious defeats on MPLA forces.[172] By May 1973 the Lisbon press carried articles confidently describing the decline in insurgent activity.[173]

Military reverses were bound to exacerbate conflicts between political and military authority. Such conflict had been acknowledged by Agostinho Neto in 1970 when he cited the "militarist" tendency of soldiers to set themselves aside from political leadership. His was a "common African dilemma," wrote Basil Davidson: "how to get or keep power with soldiers, but how then to prevent the soldiers from taking it for themselves."[174] Just as some initial (1966–1967) Bunda and Luchazi supporters of UNITA had turned against that movement when its (largely Ovimbundu) leadership was unable to make good on promises of arms and had turned to the Soviet-supplied (albeit modestly) MPLA,[175] so in 1972 and 1973 MPLA guerrilla commanders blamed the political leaders of their movement for their declining military fortunes. The eastern front commanders who came from the MPLA's traditional Luanda/Mbundu constituencies to the north themselves became targets of local, adversity-induced resentment and disaffection.

Because of the MPLA's growing disarray, the Soviet Union reportedly withdrew support from Agostinho Neto during 1972 and 1973. According to British journalist Colin Legum, the Russians had found Neto difficult to deal with, "an introverted, secretive, touchy, cold and proud man, who tended to keep his counsels very much to himself."[176] After a period of support for Neto's volatile rival for power, Daniel Chipenda, however, the Russians apparently abandoned Chipenda and invited Neto to Moscow in early 1973 to inform him that their intelligence sources in Lusaka had learned that Chipenda supporters were planning to assassinate him.[177] When he returned to Zambia, Neto moved against his adversaries and on June 3, 1973, delivered the following note to the Zambian government:[178]

As in the cases of FRELIMO [Mozambique Liberation Front] and PAIGC [Independence Party of Guinea-Bissau and Cape Verde Islands],[179] the Portuguese secret police (PIDE) infiltrated [a] large number of agents into our Movement, with the aim of collecting information, demoralizing the militants and organising plots. This subversive action, together with large military offensives, the use of defoliants to destroy crops in liberated areas, and intense propaganda, led to a considerable retreat of our forces inside the country.

The enemy pressure found support within our Movement among tribalist elements who agitated the masses against the Movement. Above all, as soon as there were concrete possibilities of an agreement with MPLA [FNLA?], these tribalists became even more active;[180] so during the past year the tribalists of Umbundu [Ovimbundu] origin organised a plot to destroy MPLA and obstruct unity with FNLA; [they were] completely tribally motivated and [acted] to avoid alleged domination of [the] "South" by the "North."

The Umbundu tribe occupies the central part of Angola. It is this tribe which has provided most of the leaders of UNITA, amongst them Savimbi. Daniel Chipenda, [a] member of the Executive of our Movement also comes from this tribe and it was precisely he who was the head of the plot.

Daniel Chipenda is motivated by strong personal ambition, aspiring to become the head of our Movement.

In April this year a plot was discovered and subversive elements began to be detained. At present the following counter-revolutionaries are prisoners in [the] Kalombo [western Zambia] camp: Paganini,[181] Roquete, Wandundu, Luabis and Kassoma. They have all confessed that overall, Daniel Júlio Chipenda was head, that the objective was to physically eliminate the President of MPLA, and that Chipenda should be President of the Organisation. They further said that one of the chief leaders of this plot was an individual by the name of Isaac Welema, expelled from the Movement five months ago and at present in Lusaka.

This plot has longstanding antecedents. For some years now, Daniel Chipenda whilst head of Logistics, provided arms for UNITA for tribal reasons, thus closely aligning himself with the counter-revolution.[182] The tribalists unleashed a great underground campaign to demoralize the militants, trying to bring discredit on the leadership, which had the result of diverting the attention of some organs of leadership from their main work, so blocking the development of the struggle. Chipenda himself is implicated in several shady cases, such as the attempted assassination of our comrade Jessé Matos with a grenade and a lengthy campaign to discredit our comrade [Spartacus] Monimambu, then leader of the Southern Sub-Region, as well as the diverting of the organisation's money by a militant called Mivuva. The plotters tried to carry the tribes from Eastern Angola against the Movement but on the [one] hand . . . their own tribalism, and on the other, the political action of our Organisation did not allow this merger to take place. So . . . the plot remained almost entirely within the limits of the Umbundu tribe.

Two attempts were made to kill the leaders of the Movement, one in October 1972 and another in January 1973. Both failed because of dissension amongst the plotters. If the plot had succeeded, the consequences would have been catastrophic: the complete destruction of the Movement, anarchy, chaos; because apart from ambition the counter-revolutionaries were not guided by any political perspective.

The collaborationist character of UNITA is unquestionable. Its few and weak detachments inside the country are maintained by their effective collaboration with the Portuguese colonialists, who see them as [a] political counterweight to the MPLA. Even in the midst of [the MPLA] there were PIDE agents, as shown by the desertion to the Portuguese of Manuel Muti (alias "Angola Livre")[183] immediately after the first detentions.

Because of [all] this, MPLA requests the following of the Zambian Government:

That there should be better cooperation with UNIP [ruling United National Independence party] and [such] organisations as [the] police, CID [intelligence], and local authorities.

That the Zambian authorities at all levels take more into account the information given by the leaders of the Movement.

That the Zambian authorities should not interfere in the question of the prisoners in Kalombo camp.

That [Jacob] Khamalata should not continue to be considered as Representative of the Movement in Lusaka, and that he should not be allowed any contact with Chipenda.

That Daniel Chipenda should not be authorized to leave Zambia before MPLA has taken a decision on this question. We also inform the Zambian Government that he has already been suspended from his activities in the leadership of the Movement.

That the Zambian authorities intensify their struggle against UNITA, and [in this regard] always . . . take into account that it is SWAPO which is the large-scale supplier of arms to UNITA and which provides Zambian travel documents for it, under the completely false pretext that UNITA should control South East Angola, which is a vital passage to Namibia.

That Isaac Welema, who is in Lusaka, should not escape Zambian authorities. Jacob Khamalata and the mechanic Nunes resident in Lilanda township know well with whom and where is living Welema.

Denying his involvement in any assassination plans, Chipenda counterattacked by denouncing what he described as the common use (from 1967 on) of "executions without trial" to eliminate dissent within the MPLA. In 1969, he said, a group of several hundred militants, demoralized by military defeat, marched from eastern Angola to the MPLA's operational staging base at Sikongo, Zambia. There they demanded that MPLA military commanders move inside Angola, that easterners be promoted to positions of military command and political leadership, and that future trials of militants be held in public. According to Chipenda, Agostinho Neto was traveling abroad and failed to respond to these popular grievances. Consequently "From 1971 onwards, the regional and tribal problem spread like wildfire amongst the militants." In March 1972, Commander Monimambu was expelled from Sikongo. And from that time on, "all" politico-military leadership was "outside the country" and "most" of the eastern guerrillas were congregated in Zambia.[184]

Chipenda and Neto agreed on one point—that African deserters from the Portuguese army had infiltrated MPLA ranks on behalf of the Portuguese in order to sharpen internal conflict.[185] But Chipenda maintained that Neto's broadscoped criticism of "Umbundu tribalists" only encouraged easterners to suspect that 1972 unity negotiations with the FNLA were aimed at gaining access through Zaire to the northern, Mbundu front and at preparing the way for an abandonment of the eastern front. At meetings with eastern cadres at Sikongo and Lusaka in January 1973, just after signing a common front accord with Holden Roberto,[186] Neto allegedly revealed his intention to transfer "cadres, finance, war material and transport" to the north where, he said, there are people "who want to fight."[187] Maintaining that he was being made a scapegoat, Chipenda held on to a regional following and Zambian protection and thus secured a factional stalemate. The MPLA bogged down in the east. Zaire passage failed to open in the north. And though Agostinho Neto appealed to leaders of the movement to "avoid falling into a psychological state of excessive fear and distrust,"[188] by early 1974 many had done just that. Foreshadowing yet another division, in February 1974, a group of MPLA intellectuals led by such former leaders as Mário de Andrade transmitted criticisms of Neto's leadership, as well as dismay over "regression" in the guerrilla struggle, to African states that had been supporting the MPLA.[189]

The educational, public health, agricultural, and other work of MPLA functional units inside Angola was also considerably curtailed. The *União Nacional dos Trabalhadores Angolanos* (UNTA), which had paralleled the MPLA with a January 1968 announcement that it was moving inside Angola[190] and had then taken on responsibility for the development of agricultural cooperatives and production in MPLA-held territory,[191] became once again largely an exile labor organization. Despite its open linkage with the MPLA, UNTA was still able to maintain offices and to publish pro-MPLA literature in Kinshasa, thus providing the MPLA with a door into a house otherwise closed to it.[192]

One other MPLA group, the *União dos Estudantes Angolanos* (UEA), was strictly an external organization.[193] It provided an umbrella under which MPLA students in Europe and elsewhere could organize political orientation meetings such as that which assembled Angolans studying in the Soviet Union at Kiev in February 1969.[194] The MPLA's principal political and adult education *Centro de Instrucção Revolucionária* (CIR) continued to function externally at Dolisie in Congo-Brazzaville.[195]

The Brazzaville government gave fulsome support to the MPLA; but it also continued, despite MPLA displeasure, to allow Cabindan separatists to organize on its territory.[196] The MPLA concentrated its military thrust on the eastern front after 1966. And though MPLA patrols still stabbed across the Cabinda border (notably around Miconje) and forced the Portuguese to maintain several thousand troops in the enclave, Cabinda became a secondary MPLA target. But Cabindan independence remained the undiminished passion of Cabindan nationalists.[197]

Emulating the MPLA and FNLA, the Cabindan Liberation Front (FLEC) undertook to establish "revolutionary" and "governmental" credentials. In January 1967, it set up the *Comité Révolutionnaire Cabindais* (CRC) in the Congolese port of Pointe Noire just north of the enclave.[198] The MPLA immediately denounced FLEC's new arm as a tribalist tool of colonialism calculated to undermine MPLA military action and prepare the way for the "balkanization" of Angola.[199] The head of the new committee, veteran Cabindan nationalist, Henriques Tiago Nzita, however, said that the aim of the committee was to advance the cause of Cabindan self-determination under which eighty thousand Cabindans could freely choose between independence and federation with Congo-Brazzaville, Zaire, or Angola.[200]

FLEC also created a government in exile. On January 10, 1967, it sent a letter to the United Nations announcing that the "Fiot peoples" of Cabinda, desirous of "complete, immediate and unconditional independence," had formed a *Gouvernement Provisoire des Révolutionnaires Fiotes en Exil* (GPRFE).[201] Reflecting a two-way tug on the Cabindans, FLEC's "revolutionary" committee (CRC) functioned in Congo-Brazzaville, while the exile government (GPRFE), headed by Prime Minister Pedro Simba Macosso, was headquartered in the border town of Tshela in Zaire.[202]

Beginning in the late 1960s, the Gulf Oil Corporation's exploitation of petroleum deposits prompted refugees to return to participate in the oil boom and provided a new, economic rationale for Cabindan separatism. The MPLA met increased resistance from the local populace. Fighting receded.[203] And with the coup that felled the Caetano government in 1974, Cabindan national sentiment surged.

TRIPOLARITY AND THE QUEST FOR UNITY

Viewed systemically, Angolan nationalist actors remained sharply polarized by a host of ethnoregional, racial, ideological, and idiosyncratic issues.[204] They interacted only negatively, and no one of them was able to amass resources and capabilities sufficient to eclipse its rivals and emerge as a dominant, successful nationalist force. The FNLA enjoyed a fleeting ascendancy in 1963 and 1964, the MPLA in 1970 and 1971. But neither achieved lasting preeminence before the collapse of Portuguese rule.

All unity proposals, negotiations, and compacts, beginning with a 1960 pledge of cooperation between Roberto and the MPLA, aborted.[205] In general, a movement actively sought unity with one or both rivals when it was comparatively weak and in danger of eclipse or when it felt confident of turning an alliance to its own advantage. It purposely shunned unity when it perceived itself as strong enough to achieve ascendancy alone or was fearful of being subordinated or absorbed within an alliance. Accordingly UNITA persistently sought an alliance with the FNLA in the face of MPLA efforts to destroy it; the MPLA intermittently sought a common front with the FNLA, which was politically weaker than UNITA, although the MPLA manifested less interest in linking up with the FNLA at times of mounting MPLA fortune, and the FNLA consistently avoided the risk of testing its political strength in an alliance with either the MPLA or UNITA.

Competition in a three-party insurgency is not that of a simple zero sum game in which a loss for one is necessarily a comparable gain for the other. In tripartite interaction, two parties may gain and a third lose, or vice versa. Any two could combine to eliminate a weak rival. A two-party alliance to eliminate a third, however, is likely only if both of the allies believe that they will be the principal beneficiary. Since either an MPLA/UNITA or MPLS/FNLA alliance quite clearly entailed a risk of placing the relatively stronger MPLA in a dominant position, it did not appeal much to either of the MPLA's competitors. A two-party alliance with the more limited goal of heading off a leading or strong third party—for example, FNLA-UNITA cooperation to contain the MPLA—risked less and was more appealing.

There were, of course, other factors that tended to array the FNLA and UNITA against the MPLA: the tonal dichotomy of rural/ethnopopulist/uniracial versus urban/acculturated–intellectual/multiracial affinities and external assistance alignments. But the tripartite system of competition itself induced checkmate and tended to self-perpetuate.

The system invited exploitation by the colonial incumbent. Portuguese newspapers doted on internecine conflict,[206] and Portuguese political and military authorities undertook to preserve, manipulate, and fuel it.[207] Contrastingly African states acting through the Organization of African Unity pressed regularly for the creation of a common Angolan nationalist front. They were concerned that three-party insurgency should not mean three lose, none win. The OAU secretary-general, Diallo Telli, confronted Holden Roberto with direct public demands that he promote unity, while the OAU Liberation Committee (ALC) withheld financial and material support for the FNLA until he did. But the FNLA's recalcitrant loner responded by blaming disunity on the OAU and its member states for failing to respect the 1963 decision to grant exclusive recognition to the FNLA and for extending it only "insignificant" material aid.[208]

In 1967, the OAU created a new five member Conciliation Committee (Congo-Brazzaville, Congo-Kinshasa, Ghana, Egypt, and Zambia) to press for unity.[209] The committee promptly recommended withdrawal of OAU recognition of Roberto's GRAE;[210] and the OAU Liberation Committee increased its support for the MPLA.[211] But an organization-wide consensus to withdraw recognition was slow to develop,[212] and Roberto continued to defy OAU/ALC common-front counsel. For the duration of the anticolonial insurgency, highly polarized Angolan disunity proved stubbornly resistant to all forms of external, common-front pressure.

Fearful of becoming the victim of a two-against-one alliance, UNITA was a tireless advocate of tripartite unity and an active suitor of the FNLA. Initial failure to persuade Holden Roberto through Kenneth Kaunda of Zambia to link (not merge) the FNLA and UNITA within a two-party front did not deter Jonas Savimbi from pursuing this goal by other routes. In 1969, he wrote contritely to Foreign Minister Bomboko of Congo-Kinshasa:[213]

You will recall our meeting in Lusaka in 1966. At that time I indicated my profound wish to unite with the forces under the direction of brother Holden Roberto. Despite the failure of those contacts, it is essential that the unity dialogue now reopen in order that we unite our dispersed forces for the good of our beloved country. It is certain that our unity will hasten the hour of deliverance for our suffering people.

I have already written to his Excellency, the President of the Republic, General Joseph Désiré Mobutu. I am now asking that you use your influence with brother Roberto to facilitate a reconciliation.

It is my duty as an African nationalist to acknowledge the errors that I have committed in your regard [Savimbi had earlier supported Congolese rebel forces led by Gaston Soumialot][214] and in relations with my Angolan brothers with whom I was associated for over three years. All that was due to a lack of experience which allowed many false African brothers to lead me into error simply to serve their own interests.

I would also like to draw your attention to certain maneuvers being undertaken by some members of the OAU Liberation Committee. The MPLA is destined to disappear from the Angolan political scene because it represents nothing and is very unpopular here in the interior of the country. However, before it will disappear these maneuvers must be headed off. Seeing itself cornered by the truth of our struggle, the MPLA has recently intensified its massacres of ordinary, unarmed citizens, using for this purpose arms furnished to it by the Liberation Committee.

A so-called [OAU] military commission led by an Algerian has just spent some time on the Angolan frontier with Zambia. It goes without saying that this commission did not even try to appear to be impartial and enter zones controlled by UNITA. Its report will be aimed simply at saving the MPLA from its own fantasies and legendary lies.

You are called upon to play a central role in the liberation of the rest of the Continent. I assure you that your firmness vis-à-vis these maneuvers will be our only guarantee of liberty in Southern Africa, and our union with brother Roberto can deliver a final blow to the illusions of those who wish to recolonize us once we have been liberated from Portuguese colonialism.

Savimbi received no response to his appeal, so, in 1970, he turned to Brazzaville. He wrote to its vice-president, Alfred Raoul—with identical results.[215] He seized every opportunity to proclaim UNITA's pro-unity stance.[216] But because of his movement's relative military weakness, the only response he could provoke was a sneer from the MPLA representative in Zambia who said that UNITA was "finished" and that Savimbi was hiding in Lusaka.[217]

The MPLA pursued an intermittent quest for unity with the UPA/FNLA even after ambush, arrest, and execution had locked those two movements into a blood feud. Given past experience, Agostinho Neto retained a surprising capacity for optimism,[218] and for a brief period in late 1966, his optimism seemed justified. That October[219] the OAU Conciliation Committee[220] on Angola, sparked by Egyptian Foreign Minister Mohamed Fayek, managed to get FNLA and MPLA delegates to sit down at the same table and negotiate. An accord was signed on October 13 that called for an immediate halt to all forms of hostile propaganda, the release of all militants detained by one or the other of the two movements, creation of a new OAU military commission of inquiry to reevaluate assistance needs, and formation of a mixed FNLA/MPLA committee under OAU auspices "to study methods of cooperation between the two movements, in the military and political fields."[221] Widely hailed as marking an end to fratricidal conflict,[222] the accord was promptly repudiated by Roberto.[223] MPLA leaders could only deplore the abortion.[224]

At times of rising self-confidence and/or frustration with FNLA negativism, the MPLA pulled back from common front advocacy. In an interview at Conakry in November 1965, for instance, Agostinho Neto argued that the FNLA was disintegrating and that to persist in a quest for unity with it was to serve the cause of "imperialism."[225] After the 1966 Cairo debacle, it was not until 1972 that conditions became propitious for another major common front effort.

The same June 1971 annual meeting of OAU heads of government that withdrew OAU recognition from Roberto's government in exile (but not the FNLA) mandated four presidents—Kaunda, Mobutu, Nyerere, and Marien Ngouabi (Congo-Brazzaville)—to try to reconcile the FNLA and MPLA.[226] The OAU did not recognize UNITA. In May and June 1972, Ngouabi and Mobutu convoked representatives of the FNLA and MPLA for a series of meetings in Brazzaville.[227] By that time, the MPLA, facing new Portuguese offensives in eastern Angola, anxious to gain access to its northern home front (Dembos) through Zaire, and persuaded that the Kinkuzu mutiny and political dissent of early 1972 had weakened the FNLA and its ability to obstruct unity in the face of strong OAU resolve,[228] was disposed to negotiate. The FNLA, confident in its political reorganization and of Zairian support but needful of arms and eager, as was Mobutu, to appear cooperative and thus worthy of OAU and other external support, was also ready to talk. The initial discussions led to a dramatic, though reserved, June 8 reconciliation by Agostinho Neto and Holden Roberto and a pledge to work for unity.[229]

Endorsed by the ninth OAU summit in Rabat,[230] the Neto-Roberto pledge was followed in November by a week of hard bargaining by representatives of each movement in Kinshasa.[231] The result was a formal agreement signed in the Zairian capital on

December 13, 1972.[232] It called for the two movements to end all hostile acts toward each other and for the creation of the *Conselho Supremo da Libertação de Angola* (CSLA) to coordinate a unified military command and a political council. Membership on all three bodies was to be based on absolute parity. The FNLA would chair the Supreme Council (CSLA), a status coup for Roberto, but without a tie-breaking vote unless this was agreed to by the head of both the military (MPLA) and political (FNLA) committees. Representatives of the four OAU sponsoring presidents were to form an arbitration committee to oversee the carrying out of the agreement and to arbitrate disputes.[233]

Once again the news of an FNLA-MPLA accord drew pan-African applause: "The last obstacles to a unified struggle have been removed."[234] But beginning in February 1973, follow-up meetings to implement the agreement proved inconclusive.[235] In June, Dr. Neto insisted under questioning that ideological and other differences were not such that they should block realization of the unity agreement.[236] As of early 1974, MPLA officials still hoped that the accord would be implemented.[237] Some observers on the left, however, had all along considered the 1972 conciliation efforts an imperialist plot to infiltrate or destroy the MPLA.[238] Had the pact with an old and despised enemy brought the MPLA the principal result it sought—the opening of Zaire territory to MPLA military units—it might easily have been accepted. But MPLA guerrillas were still not permitted to transit, and MPLA militants were still subject to arrest within, Zaire.[239] A hollow agreement that consumed energy and aroused false hopes, however, was destined to exacerbate internal dissatisfaction with Neto's political leadership.

UNITA, which decried its exclusion from the CSLA agreement,[240] took solace in delays that suggested that Roberto had not changed his devious ways. UNITA again urged its competitors to unite with it and thus increase their "political and military capacity inside Angola."[241] But as of April 1974, when the captains of Portugal's Armed Forces Movement mounted their Lisbon coup, Angola's three nationalist movements were still locked in a relentless, draining competition for power.

THE GUERRILLAS: MINES AND HELICOPTERS

Nothing intensified or raised the costs of tripartite division as much as competitive military action. "Infighting," wrote Gilbert

Comte, became "a substitute for struggle against the common enemy" and obviated a "properly coordinated" nationalist military campaign.[242]

The FNLA blocked attempts by the MPLA to supply or reinforce its northern, Mbundu, home front. As a result, the MPLA, whose northern headquarters base of Brno fell to the Portuguese in 1968,[243] made two desperate and disastrous efforts to infiltrate relief columns hundreds of miles overland from Zambia and the eastern fighting zone on through to Dembos in the northwest. Both the Bomboko (1968) and Benedito (1970) columns were intercepted and destroyed by Portuguese forces.[244] Within the Dembos-Nambuangongo sector, FNLA soldiers pressed the MPLA into a small area south of the Dange River where it sought to survive the attacks of those for whom it entertained a "mortal hatred." There was no need to be concerned about the MPLA in that area, wrote one Portuguese journalist, for the FNLA would "eliminate" it.[245] Cut off by the FNLA from outside supplies and reinforcements, MPLA soldiers were hard put to survive despite their superior training and discipline. According to Portuguese officers, hatred between the two forces was such that MPLA informers "often" disclosed FNLA positions and let the Portuguese wipe out an FNLA unit.[246] In the east, the MPLA undertook to "pursue" and "liquidate" the FNLA wherever it appeared.[247] When combined with the MPLA's military setbacks in the east (1968, 1972), however, this debilitating no-win fratricide understandably conditioned Agostinho Neto to grasp for a possible political breakthrough via a common front with the FNLA; hence the ill-fated two-party agreement of December 1972.

UNITA repeatedly denounced the MPLA for ambushing, shooting, and launching a veritable "civil war" against its militants.[248] In 1972, an MPLA deserter alleged that his unit had, in fact, done most of its fighting against UNITA.[249] With superior Soviet weaponry, the MPLA drove ill-equipped UNITA forces out of the southeastern district of Cuando Cubango—and a number of discouraged UNITA units defected to the Portuguese.[250] According to the MPLA, UNITA then took to collaborating with the Portuguese against it;[251] and there were reports by neutral observers that the Portuguese were deliberately holding back from a knockout blow against a UNITA that was still fighting the MPLA.[252]

Between the FNLA and UNITA, however, there seems to have been a tacit agreement to avoid military clashes. A January 1970 chance encounter between FNLA and UNITA patrols north of Nova Chaves in Lunda district evoked the following comment from UNITA: "As the UPA soldiers did not manifest any aggressive intentions no military clash was registered."[253]

Exército Popular de Libertação de Angola (EPLA-MPLA)

At the outset of its eastern campaign, the MPLA issued a torrent of military communiqués claiming uniformly lopsided victories over Portuguese forces deep within the remote, empty vastnesses of Moxico, Lunda, and Cuando Cubango districts. In May 1967, British journalist John de St. Jorre, explaining his unwillingness to file stories based on nationalist claims, pulled some mimeographed sheets from a pile on his Lusaka desk and read of five engagements in which a total of 280 Portuguese were said to have been killed at a cost of just one wounded MPLA guerrilla and one lost gun.[254] Credibility is essential to effective propaganda, and it was not fostered by easily refuted claims such as the assertion that MPLA guerrillas had destroyed the port of Benguela.[255] Exaggeration notwithstanding, however, by mid-1968 the MPLA had parlayed its eastern action into a serious military challenge.

EPLA patrols ambushed Portuguese convoys and blew up bridges, roads, and river barges along the upper Zambezi, Lungué-Bungo, and other rivers lacing the eastern savanna. South African journalists described ambushes by "efficiently trained" and "well armed" guerrillas: "They hide in the rank undergrowth or dig in behind grass patches in the open, mere yards from the road but nigh invisible in Chinese camouflage uniforms, their Simonov automatic rifles and Kalashnikov submachine guns aimed." Their initial target was likely to be an armored car (Unimog) at which they leveled a minute of "shattering" fire power. Then they threw grenades to pin down their quarry and disappeared.[256]

There were an estimated five hundred such guerrillas operating in the east at this time. The Portuguese pulled back into small, armed, island-like outposts linked by rutted dirt roads and began resettling the sparse local population in fixed, armed villages.[257] The costs of counterinsurgency in both manpower and materiel soared. Sympathetic observers concluded that the only way Portugal could end the war was to smash MPLA logistical and supply bases inside Zambia—which, of course, would risk igniting a conflagration in all Southern Africa.[258] But there was one weapon that offered the Portuguese the possibility of a temporary reprieve—the helicopter. "With ten helicopters or even five," argued a senior Portuguese officer at the lonely eastern command center of Gago Coutinho "we could clear the MPLA out of Eastern Angola in no time."[259]

The Portuguese bought helicopters—Alouette IIIs and Pumas—from the French and used them with devastating effect.[260] Helicopter-borne commandos disrupted MPLA supply routes and raided behind MPLA lines along the Zambian border.[261] The MPLA had reaggregated eastern villagers within bush encampments where the scanty forest cover of the east left them exposed and vulnerable to air assault. When the helicopters swooped in, many of those whom the MPLA had sometimes coercively assembled fled to the relative safety of Portuguese "protected villages" (*dandandas*). Illiterate and not yet exposed to in-depth political indoctrination, they switched political loyalties easily.

EPLA then reorganized into a more mobile force, which made increased use of a minimal contact, hit-and-run weapon—the land mine. Mines, booby traps, and ambushes killed, maimed, and demoralized Portuguese soldiers. MPLA guerrillas pursued the slow, unspectacular strategy of attritional warfare. Moving with the guerrillas in June–July 1970, Basil Davidson found them to be "extremely well organized" though not so well armed as he had anticipated.[262] They obtained much of their food from sympathizers in woodland villages (*kimbos*) who shared manioc and maize—but whose garden plots then became targets of airborne herbicide attacks. Portuguese aircraft sprayed herbicides and defoliants on African crops, damaging livestock, fish, and wildlife, as well as the human population, which developed pulmonary constriction, digestive disorders, and birth defects. According to MPLA reports, these "criminal" attacks left "thousands of Angolans in the liberated areas" in "an alarming state of hunger," and none of the MPLA's countermeasures offered prospects of "any immediate effect."[263]

When MPLA detachments attacked Portuguese outposts, they faced counterattacks from the air. This, for example, happened in 1970 when the detachment with which Basil Davidson was hiking approached the eastern town of Muié. MPLA soldiers had attacked Muié shortly before. In response, the Portuguese began "bombing wildly in the area" and brought in helicopters—from which, an MPLA guide later recounted, they could land "heli-troops to attack villages or our detachments." The MPLA thus decided to return Davidson to Zambia. On the return march, the detachment "listened as MPLA mines exploded on a bridge along the Gago Coutinho/Lumbala road, destroying several Portuguese trucks." This, in turn, was followed by "a lot of wild bombing."[264] That year, 1970, mines reportedly accounted for half the casualties suffered by Portugal's Angolan forces (355 dead, 2,655 missing, 1,242 wounded).[265]

According to the MPLA's "Iko" Carreira, in 1971, "after two years of marking time," the MPLA regained its "forward motion."[266] The Portuguese, using M-16 rifles and armored cars, launched new offensives the following year,[267] however, and internal political dissension severely undercut MPLA military effectiveness. The MPLA, which reportedly had carried out some 59 percent of nationalist actions against the Portuguese in 1970,[268] including the hijacking of an airplane,[269] declined as a military force from 1972 on. An important ("Ho Chi Minh") base in the east surrendered.[270] A prominent military commander, "Angola Livre" (Manuel Muti) defected—an intelligence coup for the Portuguese.[271] And Agostinho Neto reportedly transferred some eight hundred guerrillas loyal to him (and opposed to Daniel Chipenda) from Zambia to Congo-Brazzaville. By early 1974, MPLA eastern operations were largely limited to "sporadic mine and ambush incidents" in the vicinity of the Zambian border.[272]

Forças Armadas de Libertação de Angola (FALA-UNITA)

Chokwe troops formed the core of UNITA's initial military force. They bore the brunt of the Christmas 1966 attack on Teixeira de Sousa. Their commander, Samuel Chyala (Tshilualu), or "MwanaNgola," had earlier trained at the FNLA base of Kinkuzu, then defected along with Jonas Savimbi in 1964. He was one of those whom Savimbi subsequently sent to China for special guerrilla training. But over time, MwanaNgola and his followers became disillusioned as Savimbi proved unable to acquire arms for them.

In mid-1968, Holden Roberto sent some well-equipped FNLA units across the border from Zaire into the Angolan bush north and west of Teixeira de Sousa. He ordered them to avoid altercations with UNITA soldiers and used them successfully to attract MwanaNgola back to the FNLA. In November 1968, the Chokwe

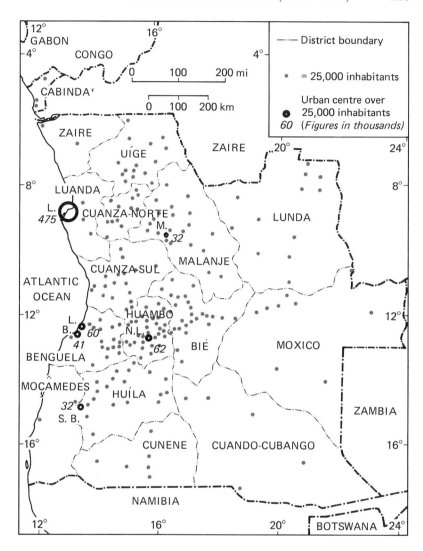

Map 5.1   Population of Angola, 1970 (provisional data). Based on United Nations map no. 2663, January 1974.

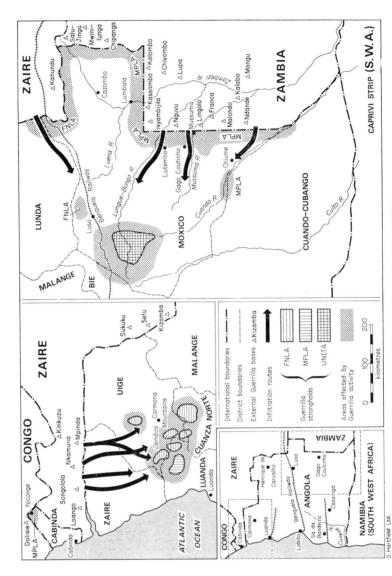

G. Hartfield Ltd.

Map 5.2   Angola, April 1974 (*Survival*, September–October 1974)

leader and his followers presented themselves to FNLA officials in Dilolo.[273] UNITA was left with only a small military force operating principally in the Cangumbe/Mucanda/Lungué-Bungo River region west and south of Luso.[274] In 1972, it claimed that its guerrilla force (FALA) consisted of four thousand trained men,[275] though the Portuguese estimate of April 1974 went as low as three hundred, and a report published by the International Institute for Strategic Studies in London credited UNITA with "probably over 1000."[276] UNITA guerrillas proved their existence by hosting occasional visiting journalists.[277] But UNITA reportedly accounted for as little as 4 percent of the action against the Portuguese in 1970.[278] The popular head of its military training program, David Chingunji, or "Samuimbila," died in combat in July 1970;[279] and although its guerrilla force did benefit from cooperation with elements of the South West Africa People's Organization (SWAPO) who infiltrated through southeast Angola to the border with Ovamboland,[280] UNITA relied largely on a little-combat, low-profile strategy focused on constructing a self-reliant political underground.

It was deemed crucial to build a political base and survive.[281] As early as 1967, Savimbi was said to be calculating that the Portuguese would eventually withdraw from costly military confrontation in Angola's economically unimportant (except for the Benguela Railroad) eastern regions. When that happened, he hoped, UNITA would emerge as an interlocuteur valable with demonstrable political, if not military, strength.[282] And in 1972, after years of trying had failed to pry recognition or significant material support from the OAU and non-African states—with the largely rhetorical exception of China[283]—a UNITA spokesman gave the following explanation of overall strategy. UNITA had no need of arms from outside. "Our army is not an instrument of power. It must above all protect our educational work and agricultural cooperatives. To liberate territory is of no interest to us, we want to liberate consciousness." The Portuguese military could occupy UNITA villages but it could not control liberated minds. UNITA, however, needed to study and emulate Portuguese pacification techniques, which had some success in winning local support. It needed to see to it that UNITA soldiers used arms for civil construction, not oppression. "The army and the armed struggle are in a way secondary, for one does not conduct a nationalist war in the absence of national consciousness."[284]

After the Lisbon coup, letters purportedly exchanged between Jonas Savimbi and Portuguese officers in 1972 were published in Europe as evidence that the survival motive had led UNITA into direct collaboration with colonial authorities against the "common enemy," the MPLA.[285] This, however, ran counter to the thrust of comments attributed to the Portuguese military commander in Luanda in July 1974 to the effect that of the three movements, UNITA, recently, had confronted Portugal with the "liveliest resistance."[286] And a Portuguese eastern zone commander told a British observer in April 1974 that government policy was to avoid large-scale military operations to crush UNITA, operations that would alienate civilians under UNITA's control. With only some three thousand troops to cover the whole eastern zone, the Portuguese had chosen to weaken UNITA by encouraging defections. However, UNITA possibly owed its survival to its being perceived by some Portuguese as a useful counterbalance to the MPLA and "possibly . . . the most likely organization with which they could ultimately negotiate."[287]

Exército de Libertação Nacional de Angola (ELNA-FNLA)

The main theater of FNLA military activity continued to be the Bakongo north—especially the "rotten triangle" of rolling wooded country stretching from Bessa Monteiro and Bembe some ninety miles south to the neighborhood of Caxito.[288] ELNA guerrillas made sporadic sorties from remote encampments in the thickly forested Dembos and Serra de Canda mountains to ambush, raid, and lay mines.[289] From time to time they captured a Portuguese soldier or two—which then became an occasion for a Kinshasa press conference with the captive(s) on display to prove that the war continued.[290] ELNA patrols also made hit-and-run raids from across the Zaire border.

The flight of some four hundred thousand Bakongo from bombs and bullets had effectively relocated much of the FNLA's political constituency in Zaire. ELNA guerrillas were fish in a drained pond. Food, medicine, and clothing were scarce in their widely dispersed forest hideouts. ELNA's principal Operational Command in Angola (COA) was located south of the Loge River "under a large cliff" equipped with three typewriters and a radio transmitter, which, for want of batteries, was often inoperable.[291] Napalm, bombs, and herbicides formed a part of daily existence, as the Portuguese employed unchallenged air power to prevent FNLA rebels from "consolidating their administration" and mounting local offenses.[292] There were reports that the Portuguese resorted to mass arrests and executions of villagers suspected of cooperation with the guerrillas.[293] In November 1969, the Portuguese raided the Zairian border village of Mpinda, which was being used as a rest camp and staging base for ELNA troops. Zaire authorities then shut down three such border camps and pulled all ELNA soldiers back to Kinkuzu from where incursions into Angola were more difficult to launch.[294] By 1970, fighting had declined in the north—and the Zaire frontier had reopened to local trade.[295]

In 1968, the FNLA opened its own eastern front to the north of UNITA-MPLA operational zones. ELNA patrols moved from a staging base, Nzilo III near Kolwezi, across the Kasai River and on through the swamps and open grasslands of eastern Lunda district toward the hills to the west. Once again it was mines versus helicopters. Illustrative is the account of an ELNA detachment that entered Angola near Teixeira de Sousa in mid-1970. The Portuguese, having learned of its entry, sent out a search party, which ran into ELNA mines. "The next contact [was] three days later when they attacked our camp in Chinyemba with helicopters." There was no further effort to reach the guerrillas overland. Instead the Portuguese "continued bombing the forest around us not particularly caring whether the bombs were hitting any targets." The incident was representative of what ELNA depicted as a Portuguese strategy of containment, stalemate, and minimum physical contact.[296]

Portuguese lack of enthusiasm for the battlefield was further evidenced by the increasing recruitment and use of African troops. "All reported patrols sighted by our reconnaissance and our networks," wrote an ELNA commander, "are composed either one hundred percent of African militia and/or JE's [*Junta Exército* commandos] or in some cases twenty to thirty Africans accompanied by one or two Portuguese soldiers." And "if the Portuguese ever go out on a patrol they put the African population in front of them with wooden sticks to detect the mines. This they do irrespective of age and sex. Women and children must do this dreadful thing."[297]

To insulate them from the nationalists, the Portuguese herded Africans into consolidated, "protected" villages (dandandas), headed by *sobas* (chiefs) of colonial choice. The soba, often of traditional chiefly lineage, was responsible for collecting a yearly tax of 250 escudos for each male over fifteen. (Age was determined by

looking under a young man's armpit; if he had hair, he was fifteen.)
The soba was also responsible for recruiting a militia and keeping
the administration informed of any nationalist activity. But most
dandandas lacked schools, medical facilities, even weapons with
which to protect themselves from roving bands of armed bandits
(that is, ex-guerrillas). Being in a dandanda was no guarantee
against being bombed when the Portuguese sought revenge for
losses sustained in the same area. "*Dandandas* became, therefore,
nothing more than hostages." Collective suffering and Portuguese
brutality led to rising bitterness. And where sobas came to sym-
pathize with the guerrillas, the dandandas became centers of
nationalist support.[298]

The FNLA chose the hills and gorges of its farthest penetration
around Cangumbe and Alto Chicapa as best suited for a base of
guerrilla operations. However, even there the forest cover was not
thick, and food was scarce. The FNLA's eastern effort failed to develop into a major military front. From their vantage point north of
the Benguela Railroad, however, FNLA patrols felt relatively well
off as they watched their UNITA-MPLA competitors to the south
tear at each other in "pitched battles"—sometimes inside the dandandas where the cost was heavy in civilian casualties.[299] Overall
the revolutionary thrust in the east faded. The Portuguese and
guerrilla forces settled down to a routine conflict of mines and
helicopters that no one seemed able to win or lose.[300]

This low-intensity stalemate contributed to the internal malaise
that climaxed in the FNLA's Kinkuzu mutiny of early 1972. Zairian
intervention rescued Holden Roberto from almost certain overthrow. It also placed the FNLA under closer Zairian tutelage. As
President Mobutu moved to assert himself as a new pan-African
leader,[301] Zaire's army took an active role in reorganizing, retrain-
ing, and equipping FNLA forces, and the Mobutu government authorized large-scale recruitment (virtual conscription) of new soldiers from within the Angolan refugee-émigré population in
Zaire.[302] Zairian officials took a tougher stance toward Portugal
and proclaimed the cause of the FNLA to be identical with that of
Zaire's governing *Mouvement Populaire de la Révolution* (MPR).[303] By
early 1974, the FNLA could parade impressive contingents of
smartly uniformed troops before diplomatic representatives of
twenty-two states flown to Kinkuzu in Zairian helicopters;[304] escort
visitors about a reorganized Kinkuzu replete with manioc fields,
flour mill, bakery, school, and hospital;[305] announce the arrival of

sixteen tons of arms from General Idi Amin of Uganda;[306] and vaunt promises of major new military support from China and Rumania.[307] Just as the Lisbon government of Marcello Caetano fell, the "external variable" strongly favored the FNLA. Outside aid was infusing the FNLA with radically enhanced military capacity. Contrastingly in early 1974, after an investigative visit to Portugal and Angola by Soviet "journalist" Victor Louis, the Soviet Union suspended its assistance to the MPLA, which was at that juncture politically fractured and militarily moribund.[308]

THE EXTERNAL VARIABLE: ALLIANCES, ASSISTANCE, AND THE ADVERSARY

External moral and material support can prove crucial, even decisive, to the fortunes of an insurgent and/or exile movement. It can represent the margin of advantage leading to the eclipse of a rival or the collapse of incumbent authority. It can also be dysfunctional. It sometimes encourages escapism—diverting energy into the self-delusion of exile governments, diplomatic travel, and international conferences; divisiveness—superimposing external cleavages (for example, Sino-Soviet, Soviet-American, and Arab-Israeli) that foster, reinforce, or manipulate internecine rivalries; and dependency—substituting charity and patron-client relationships for self-reliance, realism, and independence. Ultimately revolutionary fulfillment derives from internal strength. External help can facilitate, enable. But it can divert, deform, or dominate if it is allowed to substitute for the internal generation of revolutionary purpose, structure, and action.[309]

The experience of UNITA illustrates how the absence of appreciable external support can limit insurgent capacity. Deprived of a contiguous staging base (Zambia) and unable to obtain substantial material assistance from outside, UNITA's ill-armed guerrillas were unable to capitalize on the fact that their movement had its ethnopolitical roots in east and central Angola. UNITA lost military momentum and its comparative regional advantage when it was confronted with the modern weaponry of colonial and rival nationalist forces. It made a virtue of the necessity of capturing arms from its enemies,[310] but it also tried to buy arms with funds it could collect inside and out. In such transactions, it was at the mercy of freelance arms dealers. Jonas Savimbi later commented, "Many persons who promised us weapons disappeared immediately after receiving the money."[311]

The experience of the MPLA demonstrates, however, that the advantage of substantial material assistance can be nullified by the refusal of a contiguous state (Zaire) to accord a movement access to its basic political constituency (Mbundu). And the experience of the FNLA shows that arms deliveries and contiguous territorial access together may not prove enough to overcome the handicap of basic political ineptitude.

Ultimately a seasoned alliance (CONCP-FPLN) and a long-term, though inconstant, assistance relationship (Soviet Union) did prove decisive in determining the outcome of tripartite competition for political power in Angola. The relative capabilities of the three movements at the outset of the final phase of competition in 1974 were indeed in part factors of their external relations during the previous eight years.

Transnational Alliances

Angolan nationalists to varying degrees perceived of themselves as part of a larger struggle against Portuguese colonialism and global imperialism. Accordingly they allied themselves with similar revolutionary movements of the other Portuguese territories, white-ruled southern Africa, Third World nations in general, and Portugal.[312]

Other Portuguese Territories   The *Conferência das Organizações Nacionalistas das Colónias Portugesas* (CONCP) brought together its four allied movements in a (second) conference at Dar es Salaam in September 1965.[313] For several years, two of its three major movements, the Independence party of Guinea-Bissau (PAIGC) and the Mozambique Liberation Movement (FRELIMO),[314] had enjoyed exclusive recognition and support from the Organization of African Unity. In turn, the prestige and intercession of these movements helped the third, the MPLA, to win OAU support at the expense of the previously favored FNLA.[315] All the CONCP movements received significant support from the Soviet Union (two observers from the USSR's Afro-Asian Solidarity Committee attended the Dar es Salaam meeting) and considered their revolutions part of a global struggle against imperialist forces led by the United States. The guest of honor at the Dar es Salaam conference was a representative of the South Vietnam National Liberation Front, Nguyen Van Tien.

Much of the importance of the CONCP conference necessarily resided in secret discussions involving a "careful comparison of [guerrilla] techniques and tactics." Its ultimate significance depended less upon published rhetoric than upon follow-up measures to achieve "effective" political and military coordination, because, in the words of the *Standard* of Dar es Salaam: "It is only commonsense that Portugal cannot possibly afford to fight an escalating war on three fronts and the result of a joint action is bound to lead to a speedier liberation for all."[316]

As reorganized in 1965, the CONCP was placed under a Council of Directors consisting of the heads of the four member movements with a collegiate secretariat—there was no secretary-general.[317] It provided a framework for bilateral consultation, exchanges of information and study missions at the military level, and joint representation and lobbying at international meetings.[318] The council decided to establish a cultural center at Dakar[319] and an information office in Algiers.[320] But given the preoccupying need to adapt insurgent activity to the discrete realities of geographically widely separated territories, the CONCP allies did not achieve a high degree of synchronization in military and diplomatic strategy. Political affinities guaranteed continued cooperation. But the CONCP as a formal structure faded in the late 1960s.

Both the FNLA and UNITA maintained cordial bilateral relations with the small, anti-FRELIMO *Comité Revolucionário de Moçambique* (COREMO) headquartered in Lusaka.[321] Benjamin Pinto-Bull, the leader of the anti-PAIGC, Dakar-based *Frente para a Libertação e Independência da Guiné Portugesa* (FLING), asserted in 1968 that he had the accord de principe of Holden Roberto for the creation of a new, anti-CONCP alliance grouping GRAE, COREMO, FLING, and an unnamed São Tomé movement.[322] But a formal anti-CONCP alliance was never realized.

The CONCP-linked PAIGC and FRELIMO mounted and sustained increasingly effective guerrilla wars in Guinea-Bissau and Mozambique. With skill and dedication, PAIGC leadership indoctrinated, trained, and mobilized a mass-based swamp and forest guerrilla army that ground up Portuguese will.[323] After some initial setbacks, FRELIMO forces slipped southward into Tete, blowing up railroads, lying in ambush along roads, mobilizing villagers, and wearing down Portuguese resolve.[324] Thus steady and, over time, escalating military pressure from the MPLA's two CONCP allies more than made up for the relative decline in Angolan insurgency.

When the PAIGC and FRELIMO, as the clear embodiments of "revolutionary legitimacy," assumed power in their own countries upon the collapse of Portuguese rule, they acted as staunch advocates of the MPLA's cause in Angola.

Southern Africa   The Luso-African CONCP tied into a regional alliance of southern African liberation movements partly through political affinity, partly through Soviet initiative. Longstanding CONCP cooperation with the African National Congress (ANC) of South Africa[325] was extended to include the ANC's ally, the Zimbabwe African People's Union (ZAPU) and, to a lesser extent, the South West Africa People's Organization (SWAPO).[326]

In January 1969, Soviet initiative brought these six movements together into formal association. In keeping with Soviet prescriptions for three-way alliance among socialist countries, liberation movements, and "revolutionary and progressive movements" in capitalist countries, the Soviet-oriented World Peace Council and Afro-Asian People's Solidarity Organization (AAPSO) jointly convened the International Conference in Support of the Peoples of the Portuguese Colonies and Southern Africa at Khartoum.[327] The conference was attended by some two hundred delegates from fifty countries, though representatives from African states were notable by what the *African Communist* termed their "inexplicable absence,"[328] and the Chinese were excluded.[329] The conference set up an ad hoc Mobilization Committee in Cairo to coordinate international assistance to the Khartoum six.[330] The MPLA expressed hope that the conference would prove to be "the starting point for a vast and irreversible process that will channel dynamic support and the largest possible volume of international aid" to Africa's liberation struggles.[331] Henceforth the MPLA and its five Khartoum allies often lobbied as a bloc at international conferences and meetings of international organizations.

Occasionally, albeit in an informal fashion, an anti-Khartoum counterleague manifested itself. Shades of the old Congo Alliance, leaders of the PAC, COREMO, and ZANU attended 1967 Kinshasa celebrations marking the sixth anniversary of the March 1961 uprising by the UPA (FNLA).[332] A few weeks earlier, representatives of the PAC, COREMO, and SWAPO had attended Jonas Savimbi's press conference in Lusaka marking his return from an initial stint inside Angola.[333] Given the enduring attraction of uniracial, ethnopopulist affinities, pressure from the MPLA, the Soviets, and the South African ANC failed to prevent SWAPO from persisting in pragmatic cooperation with UNITA.[334] SWAPO was joined by the PAC and ZANU in what a UNITA publication described as "limited scale" collaboration "to coordinate the struggle in southern Africa."[335]

Neither UNITA nor the FNLA, however, undertook to organize a formal transterritorial league of Southern African liberation movements. The most visible anti-Khartoum action came in the form of "joint-statements" catalyzed by the Chinese in which African movements praised Maoist thought and condemned Soviet-sponsored activities.[336]

Third-World Revolutionaries   The MPLA was over time a consistent participant in activities of the Afro-Asian People's Solidarity Organization (AAPSO).[337] It assumed an active role in the Tricontinental (OSPAAAL) formed at Havana in 1966. Representing the CONCP alliance, Paulo Jorge of the MPLA became a member of the OSPAAAL executive. Membership in this worldwide association of revolutionaries, he noted, served movements like the MPLA in two ways: it provided an "effective means for publicizing" the liberation struggle and a framework within which to promote cooperation among those fighting imperialism.[338] Perceiving Holden Roberto as an American pawn,[339] the government of Fidel Castro, host of the Tricontinental organization, provided military and technical training for MPLA militants in Cuba, and the Cuban press eulogized the MPLA's military struggle inside Angola.[340] As early as October 1966, a group of ninety MPLA recruits flew to Cuba for seven months of military training.[341]

In the view of the MPLA's competitors, the Tricontinental gave the MPLA a platform from which to "fabricate and distort facts." Arguing that it, UNITA, also understood that "the struggle against U.S.-led imperialism" was a "vital key" to the whole Southern African problem and that UNITA alone among the Angolan movements had followed the Cuban example of fighting the revolution from inside not from exile, Jorge Sangumba criticized OSPAAAL for encouraging movements "whose main preoccupation is diplomatic paddling in the tidal waters of the sea of peaceful coexistence."[342] But UNITA remained a revolutionary outsider. The Chinese failed to sponsor a competing, anti-Soviet alliance of Third World revolutionary movements in which UNITA and/or the FNLA could find a niche. Indicative of the MPLA's superior stature as a

Third World revolutionary force, in September 1970 Agostinho Neto was chosen to speak on behalf of the six Khartoum movements plus Somali and Comores nationalists at the Third Conference of Non-Aligned States held at Lusaka, Zambia.[343] In addition, it received ongoing support from Europe's honorary Third World power, Yugoslavia.[344] Contrastingly, the military government of Brazil, once a Third World center of support for the MPLA, stood staunchly behind Lisbon. In May 1973, Brazilian President Emilio G. Médici made a state visit to Portugal.[345]

Portugal Though they perceived the "diversity of ideologies" within the oppositional *Frente Patriótica de Libertação Nacional* (FPLN) as preventing it from defining "clear, contradiction free" policies or mounting effective political action, the CONCP movements nonetheless formally allied themselves with FPLN, of which the Portuguese Communist party (PCP) formed "the backbone."[346] The CONCP decision to enter into "fraternal collaboration" with the FPLN came at a meeting of its Council of Directors in August 1966. In addition to information exchange and joint diplomatic initiatives, it led to what would ultimately prove to be significant cooperation in the propaganda field. The CONCP movements collaborated with the FPLN in distributing antiwar publications (for example, *Passa Palavra*) to Portuguese soldiers in Angola, Guinea-Bissau, and Mozambique.[347] Collaboration extended to welcoming Portuguese deserters.[348] CONCP leaders regularly appealed for support from Portuguese civilians and military in broadcasts over the FPLN's "Voice of Liberty" (Algiers). By furthering the growing awareness of and sympathy toward their cause within the Portuguese military, the CONCP-FPLN alliance helped prepare the way for the April 1974 Lisbon coup.[349]

Here again the MPLA enjoyed an advantage over its rivals. The FNLA through its Algiers office voiced occasional praise of the Maoist *Frente de Acção Popular* (FAP)[350] and then entered into cooperation with the *Frente Portugal Livre* (FPL), a liberal exile movement anchored in the large Portuguese community in France. By associating with the FPL, Roberto's FNLA established useful contacts with Portuguese democrats and demonstrated that it was capable of some cooperation across racial lines.[351] In 1972, an FNLA delegation participated with Portuguese socialists, among others, in a mass meeting in Paris to protest the decision of the French government to expel the FPL's leader, Manuel Rio, from France.[352]

The FNLA-FPL relationship, however, unlike that of the CONCP-FPLN, was limited to rhetorical solidarity.[353] And UNITA, with only a single-office presence outside Angola, developed no relations with Portuguese opposition movements.

African Assistance

Although nominally it continued to recognize and support both the FNLA and MPLA, the Organization of African Unity extended preferential aid to the MPLA from 1966 to 1972. Secretary-General Diallo Telli and other OAU officials held Holden Roberto responsible for continuing Angolan disunity,[354] and the bulk of the arms and funds funneled through the OAU Liberation Committee for the Angolan war went to the MPLA.[355] Roberto repeatedly described OAU assistance to his movement as "insignificant";[356] it had received only one arms shipment (1967) as of late 1972.[357] Having cut off all assistance to the FNLA from 1968 on,[358] the OAU officially derecognized Roberto's government in exile (GRAE) in June 1971.[359]

Then in 1972 and 1973, as the FNLA reorganized under Zairian tutelage and the MPLA fragmented after military reverses, the OAU did an about-face. During its lean years, the FNLA had received some modest military and financial assistance from some African states, including Tunisia, Morocco, and the Ivory Coast. But under Mobutu's aegis, Roberto launched a diplomatic drive to regain lost pan-African support. He began his campaign with a July 1972 flight to Algeria (which had provided the MPLA with some $300,000 worth of weapons in 1968)[360] to participate in festivities marking that country's tenth anniversary of independence. It escalated in November when President Mobutu took fellow Presidents Kaunda, Ngouabi, and Nyerere, who with him formed the OAU committee mandated to unify Angolan nationalists, on a helicopter visit to Roberto's military base at Kinkuzu.

In 1973, Roberto twice visited Dar es Salaam, long a locus of both MPLA and FRELIMO headquarters. In May, he accompanied President Nyerere from the OAU annual summit meeting in Addis Ababa to Dar es Salaam and then on to a meeting with Kaunda, Mobutu, and Nyerere in Kitwe, Zambia. In July, after participating in another meeting with the same three presidents of the Zaire-Zambia-Tanzania "tripartite"[361] at Lubumbashi,[362] Roberto made a four-day visit to Dar es Salaam at the special invitation of Nye-

rere.[363] This soldering of new ties with Tanzania and its widely respected African opinion leader, Julius Nyerere, led to the opening
of an FNLA office in Dar es Salaam—and a new phase in FNLA
external relations. It was immediately followed by August talks between Roberto and the OAU administrative secretary-general, Nzo
Ekangaki, in Kinshasa, as well as a weeks's visit by two top officials
of the OAU Liberation Committee to Kinkuzu.[364] The resumption
of OAU assistance was dwarfed in importance, however, by
another dramatic FNLA breakthrough. Through the good offices
of Nyerere, who had lost confidence in the politically fragmented
MPLA, the door to China opened to the FNLA. In December,
1973, following upon Mobutu Sésé Séko's journey to Peking the
previous January, Holden Roberto led an FNLA delegation to
China—finally making that aborted visit of ten years before.

Another indicator of changed fortunes—after a decade of being
locked out of Congo-Brazzaville—was that Roberto received and
accepted an invitation to attend Brazzaville's August 1973 celebra-
tion of the tenth anniversary of the Congolese revolution (overthrow of Fulbert Youlou).[365] The MPLA continued to maintain
functioning though demoralized offices in Brazzaville and Dar es
Salaam. But in Zambia, where the MPLA had ingratiated itself in
October 1967 by capturing and turning over the rebellious religious fanatic, Alice Lenshina, and fifty followers to Zambian authorities,[366] the MPLA's position disintegrated as Daniel Chipenda's partisans continued their opposition to the leadership of Agostinho Neto. MPLA supporters could take solace only in the fact that
their eastern rival, UNITA, remained unrecognized and unaided.
During the entire period of 1966 to 1974, Jonas Savimbi later asserted, UNITA received help from only one country—Egypt.[367]

Meanwhile at the initiative of the African states that had come to
constitute its largest voting bloc, the United Nations and its
Specialized Agencies began extending aid to Southern African liberation movements, including the two Angolan groups recognized
by the OAU—the MPLA and FNLA. While researchers in the U.N.
secretariat provided valuable background data and analysis on
conditions in the Portuguese territories,[368] the Specialized Agencies mounted a variety of assistance programs. The Food and Agriculture Organization, World Health Organization, International
Labor Organization, and UNESCO began providing technical,
educational, medical, and other material assistance of a humanitarian nature. In April 1973, the United Nations, in cooperation with

the Organization of African Unity, convened the Conference on Southern Africa in Oslo, Norway, to assess needs and catalyze assistance to liberation movements. Agostinho Neto was elected vice-president of the conference.[369]

Soviet Union

Quantitatively the most important source of external support for Angolan nationalists was the Soviet Union. In 1971, Basil Davidson estimated that 70 to 80 percent of the MPLA's arms came from the Soviets and such "satellite countries" as Czechoslovakia.[370] American State Department sources later evaluated Soviet assistance to the MPLA up to the time of the April 1974 Portuguese coup at approximately $63 million.[371] In addition, hundreds of MPLA students and military personnel received training in the Soviet Union.[372]

In his speeches and interviews during frequent travels to the Soviet Union and associated states, Dr. Neto expressed appropriate gratitude for the assistance of "socialist countries."[373] Through the agency of the World Peace Council, the Soviets helped to organize the International Conference of Support to the Peoples of the Portuguese Colonies in Rome (June 27–29, 1970)[374] designed to mobilize support for the CONCP movements among "progressive" governments and organizations in Western Europe and beyond.[375] To the distress of Lisbon, an on-the-spot payoff of the Rome conference was a papal audience for Neto and his CONCP associates, Marcelino dos Santos and Amilcar Cabral.[376] And MPLA-Soviet relations appeared solid.

Soviet aid began to wane in 1972, however, and ceased entirely by early 1974.[377] Looking for an explanation outside the MPLA's own organizational disarray, Agostinho Neto reportedly had visions of a secret (1973) American-Soviet agreement that placed Angola within an American and Mozambique within a Soviet sphere of influence.[378] In his mistrust of the big powers, he turned to Scandinavia for help.

China

In keeping with the principle that where two or more liberation movements compete for political power and one accepts aid and close association with the Soviet Union, China will cultivate the other(s),[379] Peking extended modest assistance to UNITA into the early 1970s. Just how modest is indicated by M. J. Marshment who reported in 1970 after an interview with Savimbi inside Angola that Chinese support up to that time totaled £5,000.[380] Peking singled out UNITA for exclusive mention in press coverage of the Angolan war,[381] and UNITA reciprocated with praise for Maoist achievements extending from the Chinese Cultural Revolution to the exploits of Albanian women.[382] As late as August 1973, UNITA's Third Congress extended its "gratitude to the People's Republic of China for her continuous support of our struggle for national liberation" and saluted her entry into the United Nations as a "resounding victory" for "oppressed people of the world."[383]

By early 1971, however, the MPLA also began reappearing in Chinese news releases.[384] Peking, moving toward a more even-handed policy in its relations with Angolan nationalists, began funneling assistance through the OAU Liberation Committee.[385] In July 1971, Agostinho Neto flew with a five-man MPLA delegation to North Vietnam, North Korea, and China, where he had a "friendly conversation" with Premier Chou En-lai and Chief of General Staff General Huang Yung-sheng.[386] Although relations were now nominally cordial,[387] the MPLA seems not to have convinced the Chinese of its independence of the Soviet Union, a factor still central to Peking's attitudes.

In December 1973, at the invitation of the Chinese People's Association for Friendship in Foreign Countries, Holden Roberto led an FNLA delegation[388] on an eighteen-day "working trip" to China. The journey included visits to military, agricultural, and industrial centers in and about Peking, Canton, and Shanghai, where Roberto had a shoulder cyst removed in an acupuncture operation.[389] Most importantly Roberto had "cordial and friendly conversations" with Vice-Minister of Foreign Affairs Ho Ying and then with Vice-Premier Teng Hsiao-ping. He returned to Kinshasa with a promise of substantial Chinese aid.[390]

Two weeks after his successful trip to China, Roberto flew to Bucharest for talks with President Nicolae Ceausescu of Rumania. In a joint declaration of "cooperation and friendship" between the Rumanian Communist party and the FNLA signed on January 21, 1974, the Rumanians followed the Chinese lead in promising assistance to what had hitherto been considered an anticommunist movement.[391] Back in Zaire, on March 17 at ceremonies marking the thirteenth anniversary of the uprising in northern Angola, Roberto hailed the joint promise of "very special aid" from China and Rumania, aid destined to give the Angolan struggle a "new thrust."[392]

India

China's nonaligned southern neighbor was a source of contrastingly unheralded but long-term assistance to the FNLA. In February 1967, the Indian ambassador in Kinshasa presented Holden Roberto with a shipment of pharmaceutical supplies for use by the FNLA's medical-refugee service (SARA).[393] That same year, after having completed an English-language course in the former Portuguese colony of Goa, seven FNLA trainees entered the Indian Military Academy at Dehra Dun. Upon finishing two years of officer training, they were scheduled to become military instructors at Kinkuzu and other FNLA military centers.[394] Three other FNLA militants entered the Police Training College at Phillaur, Punjab.[395]

Many (perhaps most) of those trained in India were among the leaders of the Kinkuzu rebellion of March 1972. They died in the fighting or were subsequently executed.[396] Nonetheless, as part of the diplomatic offensive that followed upon the reorganization of the FNLA, in September 1972 the GRAE minister of interior, Ngola Kabangu, flew to India. Speaking at the Menezes Braganza Institute in Panjim, Goa, he thanked the Indian government for its past help in the form of clothing, medicine, and training, and for the recent acceptance of a second group of Angolan students in Goa.[397]

Western Europe

Efforts by African nationalists to prevail upon Western powers to refrain from selling arms, granting loans, exporting capital, buying goods, sending tourists, and otherwise supporting Portugal failed. In return for a tracking station (Azores) and air base facilities (Beja), France and West Germany, in particular, provided standard NATO weaponry on favorable terms. African guerrilla forces had to pursue their wars of attrition against Portuguese forces whose counterinsurgency capacity, albeit limited, was built upon the availability of western European arms—airplanes, helicopters, corvettes.[398]

Great Britain held firm to its traditional ties to Portugal, and in 1973 Premier Caetano made an official visit to London. Only in

Scandinavia was there governmental sympathy and support for the cause of Africans fighting for independence from Portugal. In 1970, Agostinho Neto made a tour of the Scandinavian countries at the invitation of the region's Social Democratic parties.[399] Sweden's socialist premier, Olaf Palme, led the way in mounting assistance at the governmental level. During the 1972-1973 fiscal year, the Swedish government allocated some $3 million in assistance for "civilian activities" of the MPLA, FRELIMO, and PAIGC.[400] And in 1973 the government of Norway appropriated $2 million and that of Denmark $1.3 million for "victims of apartheid and colonialism."[401] A variety of Scandinavian nongovernmental organizations (such as church, student, and youth groups), raised funds for medical, educational, and other assistance. The MPLA was the almost exclusive Angolan beneficiary; Swedish governmental aid to Dr. Neto's movement in 1972-1973 totaled approximately $433,000.[402]

In November 1972, Holden Roberto made a late entry into the Scandinavian arena, leading an FNLA delegation to attend a congress of the Swedish Liberal party at Göteborg.[403] UNITA, which distributed occasional Swedish versions of its organ, *Kwacha-Angola*, through a local student representative, Stella Makunga, made an unsuccessful bid for Swedish assistance,[404] but the MPLA maintained its initial advantage.

The MPLA was also the principal Angolan beneficiary of the activities of a number of anticolonial support groups in Western Europe. The most visible and resourceful was the *Angola Comité* founded in Amsterdam in 1961.[405] In addition to raising funds and collecting blankets for the CONCP movements, the *Angola Comité* published a series of booklets and periodicals.[406] It also organized a successful boycott of Angolan coffee in the Netherlands, which reduced the Angolan percentage of Dutch coffee imports from about 30 down to 2.[407] While generally critical of Western countries for investing in Angolan mining, increasing Angolan imports, and exporting the "criminal weapons of herbicides and arboricides," in 1973 Agostinho Neto hailed the contrasting record of the Netherlands, which had by then stopped its imports of Angolan petroleum as well as coffee.[408]

The MPLA and the cause of Angolan independence received support as well from the Committee for Freedom in Mozambique, Angola and Guiné (London),[409] *Afrika Kommittee* (West Berlin), *Comité National de Soutien aux Luttes de Libération dans les Colonies Por-*

tugaises (Paris), and *Movimento Liberazione e Sviluppo* (Milan). Among Angolans the MPLA alone enjoyed revolutionary legitimacy in the eyes of these groups. In a 1971 call for a conference of liberation support committees from all over Western Europe, the *Angola Comité* urged those invited to "bring with you your information on GRAE and UNITA, so that a common attack on those movements can be made."[410]

The FNLA and UNITA also had some support in Western Europe. Beginning in 1962, a Geneva schoolteacher and part-time journalist, Sylvain Goujon, and two associates undertook to organize support and publicity for the FNLA. They were of the "non-traditionalist" left that had aided the National Liberation Front (FLN) of Algeria—and squarely anti-MPLA.[411] Goujon described himself as "a revolutionary Marxist" and a member of the Association of the Friends of Cuba. His ideas were "in harmony with those of Frantz Fanon, the Fourth International and even the People's Republic of China," which meant not with those of the Soviet Union.[412] The Roberto-Savimbi split of 1964 complicated the Goujon group's task, and Goujon ended up doing most of the work alone: disseminating FNLA material as a *Service de Presse Européen du FNLA*; making occasional visits to Kinshasa to help organize the FNLA information office; and distributing FNLA material, arranging trips to Kinshasa-Angola for journalists, and writing articles for the European press.[413]

Another Geneva-based source of assistance to Angolan nationalists emerged in 1970 in the form of the World Council of Churches' Special Program to Combat Racism. That year, it allocated $20,000 each to the FNLA and MPLA and $10,000 to UNITA. In 1971, however, the program's allocations were altered to $25,000 dollars for the MPLA and $7,500 each for the FNLA and UNITA. The FNLA rejected its reduced grant out of embarrassment and anger, and Sylvain Goujon organized a barrage of FNLA criticism against the World Council's "political partiality."[414] UNITA, with whose followers in Europe Goujon kept in contact, criticized the council's "bias" but accepted the funds.[415] In 1972, the World Council of Churches readjusted its grants, giving MPLA and FNLA each $10,000 and UNITA $6,000.[416]

From his office in London, the UNITA foreign secretary, Jorge Sangumba, tried to break through what he described as a "conspiracy of silence" against his movement.[417] There was an occasional success, such as Fritz Sitte's report on his journey with UNITA in the *Observer* of London.[418] But by and large, UNITA did well to get a few stories and interviews into regional papers[419] and relied mostly on its own mimeograph machine to get word out about itself.

The United States

Angolan liberation movements received little help from the United States. Confronted with a continuing choice between incumbent and insurgent, by the mid-1960s Washington leaned increasingly toward the incumbent. In Washington Assistant Secretary of State G. Mennen Williams concluded that the nationalist strategy of violent revolution had proved ineffective.[420] From Lisbon U.S. Ambassador George Anderson invoked the primacy of North Atlantic defense needs and argued that a "more sympathetic attitude" toward Portugal's African policies would probably produce a "very remarkable change in Portuguese views on NATO."[421] Concern about Portuguese views grew in 1966 as President Charles de Gaulle pulled France out of integrated NATO military operations, and NATO naval command facilities (IBERLANT) were moved from Brest to Lisbon. It was feared that Salazar might emulate de Gaulle.[422] In 1967, when Scandinavian disapproval of Portuguese colonial policy threatened a confrontation on the issue among NATO ministers, Anderson's successor as ambassador, William T. Bennett, advised against joining in the criticism: "If there is to be a Donnybrook, let us leave it to the Danes."[423]

Pentagon officials influential in the White House argued that, even if united, Angolan insurgents could not win so long as Portugal moved ahead with economic development and multiracial education. They were impressed with the quality of Portuguese military leadership and looked upon its younger ranks as reformist.[424] Security affairs analysts reasoned that Portugal's "strategic assets," notably the Azores, had to be a "constraining factor on diplomatic policy" concerning Portuguese Africa.[425] Sensing that the United States was now ready to respond positively, in November 1968, during the last days of the Vietnam-ensnarled Johnson administration, Portuguese Foreign Minister Franco Nogueira notified Washington that Portugal planned to make some specific proposals relating to future American use of bases in the Azores.[426]

Concomitantly Henry Kissinger, tagged to head the National Security Council under president-elect Richard Nixon, was selecting his senior staff assistant for Africa, Roger Morris. By April 1969, Morris was at work contributing to and coordinating a major review of American policy toward all of Southern Africa.[427] The result of that review by the Interdepartmental Group for Africa was the formulation and adoption of what became known as the "tar baby" option, calling for increased American communication rather than confrontation with white regimes in the area.[428] The study perceived those white regimes as "tough, determined and increasingly self-confident" and queried "the depth and permanence of black resolve," concluding that "military realities rule out a black victory at any stage."[429] At no point did its authors, high-level military, intelligence, and foreign policy specialists, question the durability of Portuguese resolve. As in the case of Vietnam, American policy makers failed to reckon with the basic verity that for rebels to "win," it is necessary only for incumbents to "lose."

African nationalists embittered by continuing American military and economic relations with Portugal had sought and found help in the Soviet Union, Cuba, and China, and they had committed themselves to work for postindependence structural change along socialist lines. It followed that the tilt toward incumbents evident in American policy after 1969 was premised both on an assumption that black nationalists could not win and, on the part of at least some, a conviction that they ought not to win. Germane were Dr. Kissinger's own ideas. In a 1965 review of the NATO alliance, he warned: "A national Communist regime in Eastern Europe is an improvement over the previous condition of absolute Soviet control. A similar regime in Latin America or Africa would inevitably become a center of anti-Western policy."[430] And Washington tended to consider any professedly Marxist government to be "communist."

A relaxation of relations with Portugal, accompanied by disingenuous official insistence that there had been no change in the American policy of support for the principle of self-determination in Portuguese Africa,[431] reinforced Lisbon's resolve to continue its African wars. Specifically it produced a December 1971 Azores accord that extended American base rights through 1973 in return for an aid package that included $30 million in agricultural commodities under the PL 480 program to generate funds for economic development, $5 million or more in drawing rights on U.S. Defense Department stocks of excess nonmilitary equipment (for example, road-building machinery), and eligibility for up to $400 million in Export-Import Bank financing for a variety of infrastructure and other development projects.[432] Premier Caetano described the agreement reached after "long and difficult negotiations" as rendering the United States and Portugal allies once again;[433] and he gave fair warning that he anticipated getting yet more favorable terms at renewal time two years hence.[434] Space satellites and the increased range of aircraft had reduced the importance of the Azores as a NATO-related staging, refueling, and submarine tracking base.[435] But in October 1973, during the Yom Kippur war, Portugal allowed the United States to use the Azores to resupply Israel, which was beyond nonstop range of American air-cargo craft. It thereby won Washington's goodwill. Other West European allies had declined to let their airfields be so used. When Kissinger visited Lisbon that December, he expressed American gratitude and discussed renewal of the Azores accord—for which Portugal now sought American arms for use in Africa. Kissinger publicly acknowledged "a large area of agreement" with respect to "problems of concern" to both countries[436] and, according to some sources, privately agreed to meet Portugal's request for arms.[437] But the April coup obviated such a direct American involvement in Portugal's African wars.

Portugal received indirect, circumspect American military assistance for its colonial wars: Portuguese jet fighter pilots trained in West Germany using U.S. Air Force facilities; a group of Portuguese officers reportedly underwent counterinsurgency training at the U.S. Army's Jungle Warfare School at Fort Gulick, Panama Canal Zone;[438] and an estimated one hundred Portuguese officers were experiencing specialized training at such American centers as the Naval Postgraduate School of Monterey, California, at any given time.[439] In early 1971, the Nixon administration authorized the sale of Boeing 707s directly to the Portuguese government, which wanted them to ferry troops to and between its African territories.[440] And while the American government professed continuing adherence to an embargo on arms for use in Portuguese Africa,[441] it excluded heavy duty trucks and jeeps (stripped of guns) from the embargo list, permitted the sale of helicopters for "civilian" use in Mozambique, and stood by passively as U.S. herbicides and defoliants were used to destroy insurgents' food crops.[442] When questioned about herbicide sales, the assistant secretary for African affairs, David D. Newsom, explained that herbicide exports in general were not licensed or monitored and that there was therefore no way to determine whether any had been going to Portuguese Africa.[443]

Even before the pronounced post-1969 government tilt toward the colonial incumbent, the American private sector had become a major support factor in Portugal's war efforts. The costs of counterinsurgency and related efforts to secure African loyalty with belated educational and economic development projects forced the Salazar government to subordinate its fear of neocolonial penetration by private corporations with huge budgets and surpassing expertise[444] to the need for external capital. In 1964 and 1965, therefore, the Portuguese government altered investment laws so as to broaden guarantees and simplify procedures leading to what the *New York Times* correctly predicted would be a "surge of investments" from abroad.[445]

In 1966, the Gulf Oil Corporation discovered oil in Cabinda, and by 1972 it was pumping over $60 million a year into the Portuguese-Angolan treasury.[446] In the absence of a constraining public policy, by 1973 American private sector contributions to the Portuguese economy—including tourism ($80 million), Azores base operations ($13 million), Angolan coffee imports ($100 million), and Mozambican cashew imports ($9 million)—totaled nearly $400 million a year, at a time when Portugal's military-security budget was just over $400 million a year.[447] With the rise in oil prices stemming from the Arab-Israeli war of 1973, Cabindan oil revenues alone soared to over $400 million a year.[448] And American capital poured into new extractive, capital-intensive projects to exploit Angolan petroleum, diamonds, and phosphates.[449]

American involvement was not, however, entirely on the side of the incumbent. Washington funneled covert assistance to Holden Roberto as a fallback option in case of a Portuguese defeat. From 1962 until 1969, the U.S. Central Intelligence Agency (CIA), using Congolese and other channels, provided Roberto with what was probably a modest supply of money and arms. Then with the advent of the Nixon administration and the "tar baby" option, the CIA "deactivated" Roberto, though it left him on a $10,000 annual retainer for "intelligence collection."[450] Roberto's well-known anticommunism notwithstanding, the Nixon administration placed all its bets on Portugal. It was persuaded by the counsel of such pro-colonial advisers as the former ambassador to Lisbon and member of the president's Foreign Intelligence Advisory Board, George Anderson. Rather than an "overemphasis" on "political progress" for people who were not "ready," Anderson said, the United States ought to help Portugal end the guerrilla warfare that drained resources away from the development of Angola and the other Afri-

can territories.[451] Concomitantly Lisbon's public relations activities
in the United States focused increasingly upon investment and
trade opportunities in its African territories,[452] and the giant business firm, *Companhia União Fabril* (CUF), commissioned the Hudson Institute to carry out and disseminate a study of development
prospects in Angola.[453]

Initially most American private sector support for Angolan
nationalists took the form of food, medicine, seeds, and educational assistance for refugees in the Congo (Zaire). Some of this
help was funneled through the FNLA-associated medical-relief organization (SARA). But the help was modest in scope.[454] The potentially important black American constituency limited its support
largely to pro-African rhetoric and resolutions at meetings of the
short-lived (1962–1967) American Negro Leadership Conference
on Africa (ANLCA).[455]

By the early 1970s, however, the war in Vietnam had fostered,
especially among young Americans, a new awareness of and sympathy for liberation struggles in the Third World at large. While
assistance from old (ACOA) and new (Liberation Support Movement) sources now flowed principally to the MPLA, overtly political
support groups raised funds and publicized the cause of all three of
the Angolan movements.

At the University of Iowa in 1966, a handful of antiwar students
formed the nucleus of what would become a U.S.-Canadian organization of young radicals devoted to the cause of Marxist revolution and "socialist internationalism."[456] Under its chairman, an
American social anthropologist, Don Barnett, who subsequently
joined the faculty of Simon Fraser University in British Columbia,
the Liberation Support Movement (LSM) established "fraternal relations" with the MPLA. Barnett and a colleague, Roy Harvey,
hiked inside Angola to attend the MPLA's eastern regional conference in August 1968.[457] "Thus began six years of collaboration" in
which the diminutive but dedicated LSM sent medical supplies,
tents, and food, provided "research on means to counter chemical
defoliants," published and distributed MPLA literature, sent "vital
components and information dealing with radio transmission," arranged a North American tour by MPLA Commander Toka
(1970), and produced albums of MPLA "revolutionary music."[458]
However, ideological schisms within the LSM (1968–1970) followed by MPLA political-military reverses (1972–1974) brought
strain to the LSM-MPLA relationship. At the time of the April 1974

coup, Agostinho Neto was beginning a tour of Canada, but not under the auspices of the avowedly Marxist-Leninist, Canadian-based, LSM. Don Barnett decried the "tactical abandonment of principled behavior" that led Neto to seek support from "liberal/ religious organizations" and to travel under the sponsorship of an "imperialist tool," the Canadian University Students Overseas (CUSO).[459] But after a hiatus for critical analysis, the LSM resumed its support for the MPLA, still the "only progressive and revolutionary force in Angola."[460]

As the multiracial-socialist orientation of the MPLA appealed to white radicals of the LSM and kindred groups,[461] so the uniracial-populist bent of UNITA appealed to black power activists. UNITA won support among black students at such diverse institutions as Atlanta University and Harvard-Radcliffe[462] and from black organizations such as the Inter-religious Foundation for Community Organizing (IFCO) and Africa Information Service.[463] The organizer of mass demonstrations in Washington, D.C., San Francisco, Toronto, and other cities in favor of African political emancipation, the black African Liberation Support Committee (ALSC), founded in 1972, made UNITA a beneficiary of a pro-liberation United African Appeal.[464] In August 1973, Kwando Akpan, a member of the ALSC Central Committee, attended UNITA's third congress in a forest-covered amphitheater deep inside Angola and announced a grant of about $7,000 to UNITA, which in 1970 had named one of its military units the "Black Panthers."[465] The congress responded: "UNITA reiterates its militant and active solidarity with the African brothers and sisters in the Americas who are heroically fighting against imperialist oppression."[466]

While the theme of black self-reliance was winning an increasing audience for UNITA, the FNLA faded as a contender for private American support. In 1969, an FNLA support group organized with the dual aim of keeping the FNLA Angola office in New York open and of mobilizing refugee and educational assistance. The American Friends of the Angolan Revolution (AFAR) published a newsletter, distributed an FNLA film by photographer Charles Dorkins, and undertook to organize public opposition to the United States' Azores-before-Africa foreign policy.[467] Both AFAR and the Angola office closed after mid-1970, however, leaving Holden Roberto, the first Angolan nationalist to visit and lobby for support in the United States, virtually without organized private American support.

MPLA multiracialism offered white liberals and radicals an opportunity for support roles not possible with black-power movements. UNITA uniracialism offered black activists an opportunity to associate with a movement that shared an aversion to manipulation or control by whites (or mestiços), whether liberal or radical. And FNLA anticommunism presented global or cold war "realists" in the U.S. government with what they saw as a marginally acceptable alternative to continued Portuguese rule. At both the public and private level, Americans intervened in support of (or in opposition to) one set of nationalist contenders against the others. In the process they invoked conflicting world views formulated in terms of anti-imperialism, racial emancipation, or antitotalitarianism. They did so at the inevitable risk of arrogating to themselves the right to prescribe among nationalist alternatives in a distant African country.

The fact remained that the preponderant thrust of American involvement, economic and military, was to support the colonial status quo. In general, most Americans deluded themselves into accepting the Gulf Oil Corporation's Cabindan quest for oil for the "free world" as a "politically neutral" act and U.S.-Portuguese military cooperation within the NATO framework as irrelevant to the wars in Africa. In this light, those who became partisans of one or another of the Angolan nationalist alternatives might be said to have embarked upon compensatory counterintervention.

The failure to generate and implement a comprehensive, consistent, and principled public policy to govern or guide the totality of the American involvement was at the very least as shortsighted as it was expedient. Glaring inconsistencies between statement and action, between public and private intrusion, raised questions about both the credibility and consequences of American policy similar to those raised by America's tragic misadventure in Vietnam.

CHAPTER SIX

COUP TO CIVIL WAR TO PEOPLE'S REPUBLIC

On April 25, 1974, an Armed Forces Movement (AFM) of disillusioned captains, majors, and colonels overthrew the Portuguese government and exiled its discredited leadership to Madeira and then Brazil. The coup proved as popular as it was bloodless. Euphoric chaos in the Lisbon streets contrasted with startled consternation among military and political officials in Washington. Blinded by their Eurocentric assumptions, American officials had failed to read the obvious signs of impending, war-induced political collapse.

Portugal's African wars had been draining the country's spirit and resources. Emigration soared to 170,000 in 1971,[1] including a major outflow of draft-age men.[2] An estimated 100,000 draft resisters left the country; there were fewer than one hundred cadets attending Portugal's four-hundred place military academy; and during the last call up before the coup, some 50 percent refused to report.[3] The toll in Portuguese military casualties in Africa reached 11,000 dead and 30,000 wounded or disabled. Roughly 1.5 million Portuguese sought livelihoods abroad, leaving behind an internal work force of just 3.5 million and a total population reduced to 8.6 million.[4] The country ran a $400 million a year trade deficit,[5] suffered Europe's highest rate of inflation (23 percent),[6] and confronted mounting sabotage by antiwar underground movements unprecedentedly disciplined and effective.[7] Obliged to proclaim a "state of subversion,"[8] the government warned that because of the discovery and arrest of subversive elements within the armed forces, the universities, and labor organizations, the political police (DGS) would henceforth use its power to detain without charges anyone suspected of activities against the security of the state.[9] Under pressure from the rigid right, Premier Caetano retreated from advocacy of cautious reform and declared the real enemy to be "anti-Portuguese [antiwar] collaborators" at home.[10]

Although a special trade treaty of July 1972 did link Portugal to the European Economic Community,[11] hardline Africa-first ultras[12] prevailed over pro-Caetano technocrats, businessmen, and economists who saw the future more in terms of Europe. Efforts were made to rescue Portugal's "African mission" by shifting more of the financial burden of counterinsurgency to provincial budgets in Angola and Mozambique[13] and by replacing metropolitan troops with local African recruits.[14] By way of compensation for this shift in burden and as a response to demands for more autonomy by European economic associations in Angola (1969), Lisbon began to devolve administrative (as distinct from substantive political) authority on the Angolan and other territorial governments.[15] But all these policies were designed to hold on to what could no longer be held.

Policies that on one hand gave separatist-prone white settlers more economic latitude and budgetary responsibility and on the other resorted to recruiting and training thousands of African soldiers while denying Africans participation in the political and economic institutions of their own countries were patently contradictory. Moreover they were too late. Even when combined with a financial boost from Cabindan oil revenue, they could not delay, let alone arrest, the disintegration of imperial Portugal.

What had earlier become apparent to perceptive outside observers—that for Portugal to pursue its African wars was for it to impoverish itself—became apparent to some of Portugal's top-level military leaders by 1973 and 1974.[16] On February 22, 1974, General António de Spínola, the former governor and commander in Guinea-Bissau and a national war hero, published a myth-shattering book, *Portugal and the Future*, in which he declared flatly that Portugal could not win its colonial wars.[17] Fed by the contagious ideas of African revolutionaries, festering discontent was already welling up within the military.[18] In the turmoil that followed the publication of Spínola's instant best-seller, the wave crested.

This sorry but logical process of disintegration had escaped the Vietnam-riveted, global strategists of Dr. Kissinger's foreign policy apparatus in Washington. And long after the resultant coup, American officials persisted in cloudy thinking about its relationship to the African wars. In January 1976, Secretary of State Kissinger, smarting over how the Soviet Union had capitalized on its early and longstanding support of Angolan nationalists, commented before Senator Dick Clark's African Subcommittee of the Senate Foreign Relations Committee: "the overthrow of the Portuguese government in April 1974 and the growing strength of the Portuguese Communist party apparently convinced Moscow that a 'revolutionary situation' was developing in Angola."[19] That a (causal) "revolutionary situation" had long since developed in Angola, Mozambique, and Guinea-Bissau still seemed to elude him.

POST-COUP POLITICS

During the months immediately following the coup, it was unclear whether the federationist sentiments of the provisional president, General Spínola, or the proindependence views of younger officers who organized the coup would prevail. The new Junta of National Salvation initially planned to hold a referendum in Angola to determine the nature of future ties with Portugal.

Long accustomed to Lisbon's centralist, authoritarian rule, the approximately 335,000 whites in Angola,[20] unlike their Rhodesian counterparts, lacked the political experience, audacity, and organization with which to assert a unilateral independence. However, as the government released political prisoners and authorized Angolans to organize, assemble, and speak freely for the first time ever, a plethora of white, black, and multiracial political parties burst upon the scene; more than thirty appeared by the end of May 1974. Some were new; others could trace their origins back to European and regional/ethnic movements of the late 1950s and early 1960s.

Angola's three liberation movements rejected the notion of a referendum and, projecting ahead on the basis of distinct histories, character, and strategies, reconnoitered and girded for what looked increasingly like a wide-open race for political power.[21] The FNLA speeded up its externally backed bid for military ascendancy. UNITA abandoned its revolutionary rhetoric and moved to mobilize support on the political battlefield that it had long preferred. The MPLA, after surviving an intensified internal struggle for political control, strove to anchor itself within its finally accessible Luanda/Mbundu bailiwick.

Profiting from the confusion and the interest of outsiders in their oil, Cabindan nationalists stepped up their efforts to carve out a separate enclave state. And in general, intermovement competition intensified steadily as 1974 progressed.

The Response of White Angolans

In May 1974, Lisbon's military government began releasing hundreds of political prisoners—twelve hundred from Angola's

São Nicolau camp alone. The regime took a sharp turn to the left in June when radical Vasco Gonçalves became premier. White anxiety in Angola mounted. In July, worried Luandan "ultras" exploded into frustrated riot, pillage, and massacre of African slum dwellers. Then as the army restored an uneasy order to the Angolan capital, General Spínola officially proclaimed the right of all the African territories to independence.[22]

From that time on, Lisbon's authority slipped steadily away. In August, it announced that it intended to form a provisional Angolan government that would include representatives of liberation movements and ethnic groups, "including the white population," and would prepare the way for free elections in about two years.[23] The FNLA and MPLA rejected both the proposed political role for "tribal" or racial groups and the election timetable,[24] and whites in Luanda responded to Spínola's announcement with renewed rioting and violent attacks on Africans.

In September–October, growing white opposition to Lisbon's decolonization initiatives climaxed in right-wing plotting to seize power. The Luanda military junta under Rear Admiral Rosa Coutinho arrested a number of implicated military and business figures, notably leaders of the conservative, white separatist (though nominally multiracial) *Partido Cristão Democrático de Angola* (PCDA),[25] with which several pliant African groups had recently merged.[26] The crackdown on the Christian Democrats and associated would-be perpetuators of white ascendancy was effective.

Why had Angolan whites failed to mount a putsch before it was too late? For one thing, the liberation movements had not carried the war into the urban centers where most whites lived. This failure had left the Europeans soft, content, and unprepared. Dazed by the suddenness of the Lisbon coup, they were susceptible of being lulled by General Spínola's initial federalist reassurances.[27] They hesitated and lost.

Only one European movement was able to make a serious bid for authorized inclusion in the new political process, the reincarnated *Frente de Unidade Angolana* (FUA). A liberal politician and initial founder (January 1961), Fernando Falcão,[28] revived FUA in the Benguela-Lobito region in May 1974[29] and launched it, with support from white business interests, as a national movement in mid-September.[30] Appointed as one of three senior secretaries in Admiral Coutinho's Luanda junta, Falcão contacted the leadership of Angola's three liberation movements and worked to get FUA accepted by them and Lisbon as a fourth interlocuteur valable.[31]

Minor Movements

Released after surviving years of often brutal confinement in prisons, labor camps,[32] or island exile, a number of former Bakongo émigrés and ill-fated collaborators promptly plunged into Angola's political void. Now fluent in Portuguese and "legitimated" by their ordeals at the hands of the political police, they created new and resurrected old political movements. Many of their names were familiar. Angelino Alberto, (Daniel) Garcia Dongala, and Francisco Lélé, all ex–Nto-Bako, formed new and rival movements.[33] João Pedro (formerly Jean Pierre) M'Bala and Pedro Teca (formerly Pierre Tecka) led one faction of the old *Movimento de Defesa dos Interesses de Angola* (MDIA).[34] John Bunga, self proclaimed head of a fictitious "Angolan Red Cross" in exile, now became president-general of a paper *Movimento Popular Africano de Angola*.[35] Holden Roberto's long-time adversary, now calling himself Kalamba Mwene Lilunga (Marcos) Kassanga, surfaced in Luanda as head of both a labor and a political movement.[36] Mauricio Luvualu, an exile labor organizer whom Holden Roberto had persuaded Zaire to hand over to the Portuguese in 1971, reassembled old (UGTA) colleagues, rented a Luanda office, bought some typewriters, and formed a labor movement, the *Confederação Nacional dos Trabalhadores Angolanos* (CNTA).[37] In June, when Luandan dockworkers struck, the military government turned to Luvualu who addressed the strikers, negotiated a settlement with port authorities, and became a fleetingly popular figure.[38] The legendary religious protest leader, Simão Toco, returned from exile in the Azores, paid a visit on Holden Roberto in Kinshasa, and relaunched his old socioreligious Red Star (*Estrela Vermelha*) movement.[39]

Some of these groups merged with the Christian Democratic party (PCDA) by late 1974. But in January 1975 the increasingly radicalized Lisbon government decided to recognize only the three African liberation movements. It forced the whole mushrooming lot of postcoup Angolan political organizations to disband or fuse with the FNLA, MPLA, or UNITA.[40]

The FNLA: From the Barrel of a Gun

The FNLA responded to the April coup with an urgent pursuit of its established martial strategy. In June, an advance party of what would soon be a team of some 120 Chinese military instructors arrived at Kinkuzu. There they joined one hundred Zairian paratroopers to train a projected Angolan army of fifteen thousand. According to press reports, under the terms of this joint project, China and Zaire were to share responsibility for equipping a remodeled army, China providing two-thirds, Zaire one-third.[41]

The remainder of Peking's promised team of military instructors arrived in early August, along with 450 tons of armaments (including AK47 rifles, machine guns, rocket-propelled grenades, and light mortars).[42] Making good on their January pledge to Roberto, the Rumanians supplemented this Chinese aid with what the FNLA described as a "very important shipment of military material and diverse equipment."[43] And pursuant to a five-day visit by Roberto to oil-rich Libya, the FNLA announced in August that the government of Colonel Muammar el-Qaddafi too had agreed to provide "substantial, diversified aid."[44]

By the end of July, UNITA and the MPLA both reached tacit cease-fire arrangements with the Portuguese; but during July and August, the FNLA moved military units from Zaire into northern Angola, stepped up action against Portuguese forces,[45] and by late September established an occupied zone in the district of Uige extending southward to regions around the towns of Songo and Carmona.[46] There, in October, FNLA Commander Vuna Vioka denounced the abusive contract system under which thousands of underpaid Bailundu workers tended the area's flourishing coffee plantations. Urging these workers, who as Ovimbundu sympathized with UNITA, to join the FNLA or go home to "rest," Vioka helped precipitate an exodus of some sixty thousand Ovimbundu south to hastily established refugee centers in Huambo.[47] Coffee production came to a standstill as the FNLA consolidated its military control over much of the rural Bakongo north.[48] FNLA emissaries went from village to village recruiting men for military training in Zaire.[49] The MPLA and UNITA managed to retain an organized northern presence only in such urban centers as Carmona.[50] Then on October 12, having ensconced itself militarily in the north, the FNLA signed a cease-fire with a Portuguese mission in Kinshasa. At the end of October, Roberto sent a 94-man delegation headed by Pedro Vaal Hendrick Neto to open a legal office in the capital, Luanda. There the FNLA could count on initial support within a local Bakongo community of 5 to 10 percent of the capital's African population (about 400-500,000).

UNITA: Political Dexterity

Though it had not required the protracted "people's war" that UNITA had sometimes predicted[51] to produce it, the April coup presented exactly the political opening for which Jonas Savimbi and his colleagues had long hoped. Dropping all trace of Maoist rhetoric, they moved quickly to exploit the advantage that came from being poised physically on the edge of their natural political stronghold, the central highlands, with its more than two million Ovimbundu. A month after the coup, UNITA's Central Committee met near Luso with a Catholic priest. Through Father António de Aranjo Oliveira, released UNITA political prisoners had already reestablished contact with Savimbi's movement.[52] Next Oliveira arranged for a meeting between UNITA and local Portuguese military authorities. This resulted in a suspension of hostilities on June 14.[53]

Savimbi proposed a period of political education to prepare Angolans for free elections prior to independence.[54] In quest of white political and financial support, he initiated contact with businessmen in central Angola.[55] Though his movement's annual conference meeting in July boasted that UNITA had faced the Portuguese alone in the past when other nationalists had resorted to "strategic retreat" into contiguous states,[56] Savimbi left the pursuit of any further military action to the FNLA and MPLA and sought to win politically what the lack of external support had made impossible militarily. A spellbinding orator who knew how to tailor his remarks to his audience, he drew large crowds and appealed to nervous whites with assurances that he considered all those who had settled, let alone been born, in Angola to be bonafide Angolans.[57] Gilbert Comte saw in Savimbi, an "able political prestidigitator," who had "sometimes collaborated" with the Portuguese against the MPLA and presented an alternative to the "militarism" of the FNLA and the "militantism" of the MPLA: "Intelligent, intuitive, and gifted with great personal charm, [Savimbi offered] the anxious multitudes the reassuring words they so [wanted] to hear."[58] At the same time, UNITA's foreign affairs spokesmen assured growing numbers of Afro-American sympathizers across the Atlantic of a continuing dedication to black rule and pan-African solidarity. Angola is "so large" and there is "so much to do," said Jorge Sangumba, "any Black man that is willing to settle in Angola" and help develop it into a "progressive" country will be "welcome."[59]

That UNITA was expediently distancing itself from its revolutionary origins became even clearer when statements reassuring whites that they would be welcome to stay expanded to include an implied renunciation of UNITA's long-standing alliance with the South West Africa People's Organization (SWAPO). In November, UNITA's representative in Luanda declared that just as Angolans themselves had fought for their own independence, Namibians should be expected to do the same. Future relations between Angola and South Africa, he added, should be based upon mutual "respect and noninterference."[60]

Although the FNLA denounced Savimbi as a "vile creature of colonialism" whose early move to suspend hostilities constituted "high treason,"[61] and the MPLA circulated what purported to be copies of (1972) letters detailing UNITA-Portuguese military collusion[62] and denied that UNITA was a "valid" organization,[63] UNITA persuaded each of its rivals separately to enter into formal reconciliation agreements with it.[64] The OAU African Liberation Committee (ALC) elevated a May decision to begin assisting UNITA into a November recommendation that UNITA be accorded full OAU recognition.[65] A special October party conference enlarged UNITA's top-level committees to accommodate an expanding leadership.[66] And hundreds of recruits from as far away as Luanda went to UNITA territory in the east for military training so they could provide a military backup to UNITA's political strategy.[67]

The MPLA: Securing a Place

The April coup caught the MPLA unprepared. Agostinho Neto was traveling in Canada,[68] and the movement was beset with crippling internal dissension. Three factions were contending for power.

On May 11, a group of Brazzaville-based exiles calling itself the *Revolta Activa* issued a manifesto in which it attributed MPLA military and political reverses to fear and cynicism caused by insensitive, secretive leadership. Posturing on the left, it accused Agostinho Neto of arbitrary, undemocratic "presidentialism." Consisting mainly of mestiço intellectuals, the group was led by prominent but estranged MPLA figures such as Mário de Andrade, Gentil Viana, and Floribert Monimambu.[69] Their principal demand was for a party congress to resolve the leadership issue.[70]

In early June, the MPLA's "honorary president," Father Joaquim Pinto de Andrade, who had been released after fourteen years of political persecution that had shifted him back and forth between prison and house arrest,[71] met in Brazzaville with both the *Revolta Activa* and Agostinho Neto. All concurred on the need to convene an MPLA congress.[72]

Then on June 8, at Lusaka in the presence of Congolese Premier Henri Lopes and Zambian Prime Minister Mainza Chona, the MPLA's three factions, including what had become known as the *Revolta do Leste* (Eastern Revolt) led by Daniel Chipenda, hammered out an agreement on procedures by which to restore MPLA cohesion. It called for a composite tripartite delegation to represent the MPLA at the OAU's eleventh annual summit at Mogadishu (June 12–15) and a tripartite committee to prepare and convene an MPLA congress on June 21 in Lusaka. Membership on the congress preparatory committee was to be based on parity for the three factions, and Congolese, Zambian, and OAU officials were to monitor the committee's work.[73]

An earlier move by President Mobutu and Holden Roberto, joined by UNITA, to deal with the Chipenda faction as the MPLA had been blocked in late May by Julius Nyerere who insisted that Agostinho Neto and his supporters be part of any agreements linking the MPLA and the other Angolan liberation movements.[74] In the view of Tanzania's president, any arrangement that failed to encompass an FNLA-MPLA/Neto entente could lead only to civil war.[75] Thus in July, at a Bukavu meeting of the four presidents who had been mandated by the OAU to reconcile the FNLA and MPLA (Kaunda, Mobutu, Ngouabi, and Nyerere), Nyerere insisted that the FNLA and all three MPLA factions[76] agree to form a common front immediately following the MPLA congress,[77] which had been delayed by factional bickering.

The supporters of Agostinho Neto had been trying to get the venue of the congress shifted to a place inside Angola held by their forces. But finally, on August 12, amid reports and denials that Neto had announced his intent to resign and set up private medical practice in Dar es Salaam,[78] four hundred delegates assembled at a military camp outside Lusaka for the MPLA's first national conference in twelve years. There were 165 for the "present leadership," 165 for the *Revolta do Leste*, and 70 for the *Revolta Activa*.[79] After eleven days of bitter, close-quarter wrangling, Neto and his followers walked out. They rejected demands for what their adversaries termed a "routine report" on MPLA activities and finances since 1971,[80] repudiated the congress as dominated by factions whose comportment represented a "total and systematic negation of the spirit of unity," and announced plans to hold their own congress inside Angola.[81]

Most of the *Revolta Activa*, with which Pinto de Andrade now associated himself, departed as well, leaving the *Revolta do Leste* in control of a rump congress. Blaming Neto supporters for obstructing all efforts to "democratize" and "restructure" the movement, it proceeded to elect Daniel Chipenda president of a recast MPLA executive.[82]

Distressed by this Lusaka debacle, the four African presidents promptly summoned the leaders of the three warring factions to Brazzaville where the ninth Conference of Heads of State of East and Central Africa was scheduled to begin on August 31. There, on the margins of the conference and under great pressure, Chipenda agreed to relinquish his claim to the MPLA presidency. On September 3, the rival factions signed a pact officially reunifying their movement. They explained publicly that after eighteen years as "the standard bearer of Angolan patriots," the MPLA had fallen prey to an internal crisis. This "tragic" situation had left the masses "without leadership" at a time when it was essential for Angolan nationalists to unite for negotiations leading to a "transfer of power." Therefore, under the "sponsorship" of Presidents Ngouabi, Nyerere, Kaunda, and Mobutu, the contending groups had agreed on a new "provisional leadership" to guide the movement until the next congress to be held after independence. The presidency reverted to Agostinho Neto. Daniel Chipenda and Joaquim Pinto de Andrade became vice-presidents. Representation on the central committee was fixed at "present leadership," or *Ala Presidencialista*, sixteen; *Revolta do Leste*, thirteen; *Revolta Activa*, ten. And each faction was to have three representatives on a nine-member Political Bureau chosen from among members of the Central Committee.[83]

The toasts were scarcely over when the Brazzaville compromise began to fall apart. Daniel Chipenda promptly crossed the river to Kinshasa. President Mobutu then championed Chipenda's cause in mid-September discussions with Portugal's provisional president on the Cape Verde island of Sal. With Roberto and Savimbi in tow, the Zairian leader apparently convinced conservative General Spínola, who calculated that the Chinese-backed FNLA constituted the most serious military threat, that Agostinho Neto and his MPLA could and should be eliminated from the Angolan nationalist spectrum.[84] Spínola, reportedly unhappy with the course of events in Mozambique where FRELIMO was being given a free hand to install a Marxist government, assumed the principal role in setting the political course for Angola. The course he had in mind was reportedly a provisional government with twelve ministers: two each from the FNLA, UNITA, and MPLA and six from various ethnic and white movements. The MPLA ministers were to be Daniel Chipenda and Joaquim Pinto de Andrade.[85]

Out of step with and frustrated by the younger military officers who had placed him in office, however, Spínola resigned at the end of September. General Francisco da Costa Gomes replaced him, and the Lisbon government lurched another notch to the left. Though this shift was bound to help Agostinho Neto, who had longstanding ties with the Portuguese left, Chipenda refused to accept reintegration within a Neto-run movement. He repudiated the Brazzaville compromise[86] and reassembled his supporters, including former central committeeman Luis de Azevedo, Jr., and Lusaka representative Jacob Khamalata, in Kinshasa. Enjoying a popular following centered within the small Bunda population that straddled the eastern border with Zambia,[87] Chipenda retained the loyalty of from two thousand to three thousand eastern (largely Chokwe) MPLA guerrillas. His political statements reflected the fact that his backing came from outlying peasant communities in the east. "Great emphasis," he declaimed, "must be given to the depressed and undeveloped areas of the country." He spoke of schools, skills, and social services and proposed to "rely heavily" on the "wisdom and guidance" of "traditional rulers of the land" and "on the churches." He also renounced any idea of discriminating against whites.[88]

Chipenda railed against the Portuguese when they signed a cease-fire accord with, and thus recognized, Agostinho Neto's MPLA on October 21. He vowed that his forces (newly bolstered with Chinese arms) would continue fighting so long as the Portuguese persisted in such "divisive" maneuvering.[89] But in early December, albeit with an assist from FNLA security guards, he peacefully opened his own headquarters in Luanda.[90] A few days later the MPLA (Neto) officially expelled him from their ranks, and several hundred of Chipenda's eastern followers at Serpa Pinto reportedly negotiated with and then returned to the Neto movement.[91]

Agostinho Neto's fortunes began improving with the Brazzaville compromise. True, Neto got off to a humiliating start when President Kenneth Kaunda refused to allow him to return on his plane from Brazzaville to Lusaka.[92] But Neto understood that power would not now be secured in exile. He flew to Dar es Salaam, where he laid claim to the £115,000 allotted to the MPLA by the OAU's Liberation Committee for June–October 1974 (the same amount was allocated to the FNLA),[93] then moved via Lusaka into eastern Angola.

There on August 1, a group of eighty-three pro-Neto guerrilla officers had already reorganized and rebaptized the MPLA military, known henceforth as the *Forças Armadas Popular para Libertação de Angola* (FAPLA).[94] From September 12 to 21, Agostinho Neto presided over the Inter-Regional Conference of MPLA Militants convened in the Moxico bush and attended by some 250 supporters, including the FAPLA organizers. The Moxico conference adopted a political strategy for the transitional phase ahead and elected a new thirty-five-member Central Committee headed by a ten-member Political Bureau. Membership on the Political Bureau was ranked: (1) Agostinho Neto, president; (2) Lopo do Nascimento, a veteran MPLA underground leader who had left Luanda in 1974 to work with Neto;[95] (3) Lúcio Lára ("Tchiweka"); (4) Carlos Rocha ("Dilolwa"), an organizer of and instructor in cadre training since 1965;[96] (5) José Eduardo (dos Santos), head of the MPLA's Brazzaville office;[97] (6) Joaquim Kapango; (7) Rodrigues João Lopes ("Ludi"); (8) Pedro Maria Tonha ("Pédalé"); (9) Jacob Caetano João ("Monstro Imortal"); and (10) Henrique Teles Carreira ("Iko").[98] As in the past, the leadership was preponderantly mestiço/assimilado/Mbundu.

The new leadership moved swiftly to mount an organizational campaign. With the signing of the MPLA-Portuguese cease-fire on October 21, the political climate favored their efforts. The head of the Angolan junta, Admiral Rosa Coutinho, openly sympathized with Neto's MPLA as a "left leaning" movement of "progressive ideas."[99] On November 6, an estimated fifty thousand persons greeted Lúcio Lára when he arrived in Luanda to open an MPLA office. And about this time, the Soviet Union, realizing that it had miscalculated, reversed itself after a hiatus of some six months and began once again to help Agostinho Neto. With independence promised and the Chinese in league with the FNLA, which had American connections as well, the Soviet Union faced the prospect of being shut out politically after years of diplomatic and material investment in the Angolan cause. Interpreted in Washington at the time as a move to strengthen the MPLA "so it could compete militarily with the then much stronger FNLA,"[100] Soviet assistance apparently resumed in August via the OAU Liberation Committee.[101] Then in October and November, the Soviets began to send military supplies through Congo-Brazzaville. Also, according to American government sources, in December, the MPLA sent 250 men to the Soviet Union for military training. The MPLA's new Luanda office, it seemed, "suffered no lack of funds to propagandize and organize." By January 1975, Neto's movement reportedly had received enough arms "to equip a 5000–7000 man MPLA force (up from perhaps 1500 in August 1974, exclusive of Chipenda's units)." In addition, the MPLA distributed "thousands of AK-47s" to *poder popular* (people's power) groups in the Luanda *musseques*, where they proved useful in skirmishes between MPLA and FNLA partisans beginning in November 1974.[102]

Cabindan Separatists: The Oil Stakes

The fact that Cabindan oil produced government revenue at the rate of $450 million a year by 1974 was central to the calculations of all who contemplated governing Angola. That that same revenue, if reserved for Cabindans alone, could mean an average and rising per-capita income of over $5,600 for 70,000 to 80,000 Cabindans was just as central to the thinking of Cabindan separatists.

Personal, family,[103] and ethnic ambitions, ignited by the April coup and fueled by oil, led to a rivalrous flurry of Cabindan political activity. At a "unity congress" in Pointe Noire on June 30, several separatist factions, including one led by Auguste Tchioufou (until 1971 a Congolese [Brazzaville] civil servant), grouped together under the banner of the Cabindan Liberation Front (FLEC).[104] Tchioufou[105] took over, relegated FLEC veteran Luis Ranque Franque to "honorary president," and made Alexandre Taty (the UPA defector) his defense secretary, thereby acquiring Taty's counterinsurgency unit of several hundred, known as the *Flechas* (Arrows). But Tchioufou was soon at loggerheads with Franque, Taty, and others. And another veteran politician Henriques Tiago Nzita set up his own version of FLEC inside the enclave.[106]

The Cabindan claim to a right to self-determination impressed some Portuguese as reasonable. Socialist leader Mário Soares said that he thought Cabindans should be given the right to vote on the future political status of their territory.[107] FLEC enthusiasts won the sympathy of the local governor, Brigadier General Temudo Barata, who allowed them to organize freely. In early November, by which time it was assured of support from Admiral Coutinho (who had been elevated to high commissioner), and from junior Portuguese officers, however, the MPLA seized the occasion of rioting between FLEC and MPLA partisans in Cabinda city to mount a coup de force. Hundreds of FAPLA soldiers led by Commander Pédalé (Pedro Tonha) streamed out of forest hideouts near the Congolese border. Joined by the Portuguese garrison at Belize, they occupied Cabinda city as other Portuguese troops looked on passively. Some FLEC militants retreated north along the coast to the border town of Massabi. There they held out with the help of a French-Lebanese mercenary, Jean Kay, and Alexandre Taty, until evicted on November 16 by Portuguese troops under a new, pro-MPLA governor, Colonel Lopes Alves.[108]

Despite evident local popularity and covetous, if inconsistent, backing from neighboring states, fledgling FLEC forces fled when confronted with well-trained and armed MPLA guerrillas. Cabindans had little stomach for war.[109] Nevertheless Zaire allowed Ranque Franque to broadcast the Voice of Cabinda over Kinshasa's radio, refused to allow Roberto to move his forces into the territory, and persuaded Daniel Chipenda to endorse Cabindan self-determination.[110]

The Brazzaville government declined to "fault Cabinda" for wanting separate independence[111] and presumably was responsible for persuading the Brazzaville-based *Revolta Activa* (MPLA) to accept the principle of Cabindan autonomy.[112] In addition the president of Gabon, Omar Bongo, expressed his—and it was widely assumed, French—support for the proposition that oil-rich Cabinda constituted a "separate entity."[113]

In January 1975, with Brazzaville's approval, FLEC partisans assembled at the Kouilou Chamber of Commerce of Pointe Noire. Their congress disavowed Auguste Tchioufou (held to be compromised by his connections with the ELF-Congo oil company) and elected a new FLEC central council and an executive body headed by a former Brazzaville premier, Alfred Raoul.[114] Breaking his public silence, Agostinho Neto angrily criticized the Congolese for supporting Cabindan separatism.[115]

COALITION AND TRANSITION: THE ROAD TO CIVIL WAR

In August 1974, U.N. Secretary-General Kurt Waldheim flew to Lisbon where the new Portuguese government pledged "full cooperation to the United Nations" in carrying out a now-acknowledged obligation to transfer power to the people of its colonies. Promising to "oppose any secessionist" moves to dismember Angola, the Portuguese promised also "to make early contacts with liberation movements" to begin formal negotiations.[116] The United States would later decry unilateral third-party intervention in Angola. Neither it nor any other state, however, followed up and capitalized upon the Waldheim visit by acting through the multilateral agency of the United Nations to help Portugal implement this pledge as its authority withered in late 1974 and early 1975.

Under pressure from the OAU and President Jomo Kenyatta in the chair, Neto, Roberto, and Savimbi met in Mombasa, Kenya, from January 3 to 5 and signed a trilateral accord pledging to cooperate peacefully, to safeguard Angolan "territorial integrity," and to facilitate "national reconstruction."[117] The three Angolans then declared themselves ready for formal negotiations with Portugal to establish the procedures and calendar for the country's accession to independence.

Those talks began on January 10 at Alvor in the Portuguese Algarve. They proved difficult. Distrust among the Angolan participants had been only partially muted. But the four parties hammered out and signed the January 15 Alvor agreement,[118] which secured the three liberation movements' status as "the sole legitimate representatives of the people of Angola."[119] It proclaimed Cabinda to be "an unalienable component part of Angola," and it set November 11, 1975, as the date for independence. It allotted ministries in a coalition government, and it mandated that government to draft a provisional constitution and conduct legislative elections during the eleven-month transition to independence. The agreement also provided for the three Angolan movements by phases to pool 8,000 men each into a common national army that would include a 24,000-man Portuguese force to be withdrawn only gradually between October 1, 1975, and February 29, 1976.[120]

The Portuguese hoped by the terms of the agreement to place a premium on political process, on coalition building, and on trans-ethnic alliances. Since only the three liberation movements would participate in the legislative elections, the many white, Bakongo,

Cabindan, and other organized or nascent political groups would have to aggregate within or about one of the three. By creating the need for those three to reach out, mobilize popular electoral support, and organize on a national scale, Lisbon hoped to encourage the construction of a single polity. Placing Angolan government ministries under a tripartite team of nationalists (a minister and two secretaries of state), moreover, provided an opportunity for political rivals to gain positive interpersonal and intergroup experience and to work, compromise and, hopefully, coalesce across partisan lines.

The following transitional government took office on January 31:[121]

High Commissioner: Brigadier General Silva Cardoso

Presidential Council (rotating chair): Lopo do Nascimento (MPLA); Johnny Eduardo Pinock (FNLA); José N'Dele (UNITA)[122]

Ministers:

Information: Manuel Rui Monteiro	
Economic Planning and Finance: Saydi Mingas	MPLA[123]
Justice: Diógenes Boavida	
Interior: Ngola Kabangu	
Health and Social Affairs: Samuel Abrigada	FNLA[124]
Agriculture: Mateus Neto	
Labor and Social Security: António Dembo	
Education and Culture: Jeronimo Elavoco Wanga	UNITA[125]
Natural Resources: Jeremias K. Chitunda	
Economic Affairs: Vasco Vieira de Almeida	
Public Works and Town Planning: Manuel Resende de Oliveira	Portugal
Transport and Communications: Joaquim Antunes da Cunha	

At this juncture, the American government, for the first time since the coup, began to grapple seriously with the issue of what stance and action it should take on Angola. Despite Alvor, the Angolan movements were still deeply divided. A four-way partition (Cabinda, Bakongo, Mbundu, Ovimbundu) seemed possible. There was conjecture about a possible FNLA-UNITA alliance to shut out the MPLA, an alliance that would exclude a central stream of Angolan nationalism (Luanda/Mbundu) and pose the likelihood of chronic violence from an MPLA gone underground. The moment was opportune for public and private support for Portuguese-OAU initiatives seeking a political solution in Angola. It was the crucial time for the United States to employ preventive diplomacy, muster collective support (OAU, U.N., Western) for the cause of a unified Angola, and thus minimize the danger of large-scale external intervention. Given the handicap of a long, discrediting association with the ancien régime and a general desire as a status quo power to encourage global situations of stability resistant to political radicalism, Washington might logically have sought to avoid an open-ended contest for dominant influence. Instead of preventive diplomacy to reinforce a compromise African solution, however, the United States chose unilateral intervention to support a victory by anticommunist forces.[126]

In late January, the National Security Council's "40 Committee" authorized a covert grant of $300,000 to the FNLA, the movement most committed to a military strategy. Apparently moved by past connections and habit to think in terms of "our team" and "theirs," the council rejected a proposal to give $100,000 to UNITA, preferring to bet on one movement only.[127] According to Portuguese military sources, the FNLA military advantage at that time was considerable. An AFM spokesman put troop levels at 21,750 FNLA, 5,500 MPLA, 2,750 MPLA/Chipenda, and 3,000 UNITA,[128] a basic ratio that was confirmed in subsequent analysis by an American researcher who put the January totals of trained and in-training guerrillas at 21,000 FNLA, 8,000 MPLA, 2,000 MPLA/Chipenda, and 8,000 UNITA.[129] On the basis of "best estimates," which credited the FNLA with a force only half so large,[130] the American government expanded an "existing" client relationship that it was confident its "adversaries knew about,"[131] without either undertaking to persuade the FNLA not to seek a zero-sum victory by force of arms or signaling to Moscow a readiness to accept a coalition that would include the MPLA. The Soviet Union was left to draw its own conclusions.

Almost at once, rumors of "heavy continuing CIA support for the FNLA" became prevalent in Luanda, although they were denied by American officials.[132] The FNLA, in a rash of conspicuous spending, took over a Luanda television station and the city's leading daily, *A Província de Angola,* to which it restored its conservative, pre-coup editor, António Carreia de Freitas.[133] The American consulate, unaware of covert U.S. assistance to Roberto, launched an inquiry to discover the source of FNLA funding and reported back to the State Department that it probably came from Portuguese coffee plantation owners in northern Angola.[134] But the Soviet Union had long suspected that the United States would try to assert influence over Angola when Portugal was finally forced out.[135] While the January "40 Committee" decision reassured Mobutu and emboldened Roberto, it also presumably alarmed the Soviets, alerted by their intelligence network.[136]

Next Daniel Chipenda, who continued to head up what he claimed was the real MPLA, joined his forces with those of the FNLA. By setting up offices in the MPLA/Neto stronghold of Luanda, he had provoked a predictably violent reaction. On February 13, MPLA/Neto forces attacked and killed fifteen to twenty Chipenda supporters. They drove his group, which had no legal status under the Alvor agreement, from the city.[137] With his forces eroding,[138] Chipenda then announced on February 22 that he was merging them with the FNLA, which thereby gained perhaps two thousand soldiers and a political outreach into eastern Angola.[139]

That same month, a visiting Swedish journalist, Per Wästberg, described the "organization and discipline" of the MPLA and the frightening "superficial militarism and lavish spending" of the FNLA, whose Luanda propaganda offered free bus rides, hotel rooms, and meals.[140] The transitional government began functioning during February, but in a climate of mistrust and violence. Political leaders carried revolvers for self-defense.[141]

On March 23, FNLA forces attacked MPLA installations, hurling hand grenades through the windows of the MPLA's (Luanda) Vila Alice headquarters where Lopo do Nascimento was working at the time.[142] A few days later at Caxito, thirty miles to the northeast, FNLA troops reportedly attacked an MPLA training camp and killed over fifty recruits.[143] Jane Bergerol wrote in the *Financial Times* (London): "beyond reasonable doubt" what "has occurred is a first terrifying attempt by Kinshasa-based Holden Roberto's FNLA to kill substantial numbers of MPLA soldiers and supporters and instill a climate of fear in the country such as it did in 1961 on the Zaire border."[144] A motorized contingent of five hundred FNLA soldiers arrived in Luanda on March 30 from Zaire, and fighting raged on for days in the Luanda *musseques*.[145]

Dramatizing the MPLA's primacy in Luanda, a throng of 300,000 to 400,000 greeted Agostinho Neto on his symbolically timed return to the capital on February 4. During the years of his exile, the colonial government had never totally eliminated MPLA underground structures, which survived in Luanda's poor, working-class districts. As confrontation with the FNLA intensified, the MPLA distributed guns indiscriminately among its supporters—including teenage boys[146]—in those districts, thereby provoking criticism from an increasingly helpless Portuguese high· commissioner.[147]

In March, Soviet arms deliveries began to increase. They went by air to Brazzaville, by truck to Cabinda, by rail to Pointe Noire, and by small craft down the Angolan coast. In April, chartered aircraft flew perhaps a hundred tons of arms into southern Angola,[148] and large shipments, including heavy mortars and armored vehicles, [149] began to come in on Yugoslav,[150] Greek, and, finally, Soviet ships.[151]

In late April, a new round of fighting broke out as the "FNLA launched a coordinated series of assaults" against MPLA offices in nearly all Luanda's *musseques* and against the headquarters of the UNTA labor union; casualties were put at seven hundred dead, over a thousand wounded.[152] Violence soon spilled into towns to the north and south, from São Salvador to Teixeira de Sousa, with the MPLA increasingly taking the initiative. By this time the MPLA had recruited the 3,500- to 6,000-man anti-Zairian, Katangese gendarmerie who had previously served the Portuguese in fighting Angolan nationalists. Kept intact after the coup as a security against Zairian designs, this well-trained, ex-Tshombe force added significantly to the MPLA's military capability.[153] But it also incensed President Mobutu, and as of mid-May, twelve hundred Zairian soldiers were reported to have moved across the Angola border to operate alongside the FNLA's then in-place army of ten thousand.[154] As the MPLA entered what one of its militant young commanders, Nito Alves, termed a "phase of active defense,"[155] Holden Roberto flew off to the Middle East—Iran, Kuwait, Abu Dhabi—in quest of funds.[156]

The Portuguese army shrank to a demoralized, combat-shy force of less than twenty-four thousand. Thousands of white Angolans made preparations to emigrate. Kenneth Kaunda, in a mid-April visit to Washington, warned the American government that the situation in Angola was deteriorating. Fighting threatened to expand, he said, and with it the danger of large-scale Soviet intervention.[157] Preoccupied with the approaching collapse of the government of South Vietnam, however, the Ford administration dallied. It saw no need for an urgent diplomatic effort to save the fleeting chance that an election rather than a war could determine who governed Angola. It made no move to work through the OAU and U.N. or bilaterally with the Soviet Union to end the growing arms race; to the contrary, it would soon give that race another shove forward. There was no response to a suggestion by the MPLA's Lúcio Lára that the essential first step toward securing peaceful process would be an embargo on arms and personnel coming into Angola by air, sea, and land[158]—that is, across a Zaire border that the Portuguese no longer even pretended to be able to monitor.[159] There was no real effort to create a disinterested "third party" to carry out what the Portuguese had set out to do.

Long an advocate of nonviolence, Kenneth Kaunda's preferences now lay with UNITA.[160] As late as early May, Jonas Savimbi was still predicting that there would be no civil war.[161] Aspiring to the role of reasonable conciliator-aggregator,[162] Savimbi had succeeded in attracting heterogeneous support among whites and Africans alike.[163] UNITA was generally credited with the best prospect for emerging successfully should the October elections take place.[164] But as FNLA-MPLA encounters multiplied, UNITA's efforts to prevent what it termed "anti-election maneuvers" fell victim to its continuing military weakness.[165] As Savimbi traveled to London, Paris, and elsewhere to muster backing for both UNITA and the Alvor agreement,[166] UNITA tried to remain aloof from the fighting. By June, however, it found itself caught in a crossfire of mounting warfare. Perhaps Luandan "radicals" associated with Nito Alves had decided independently to force UNITA's hand. In any case, MPLA soldiers attacked and killed a group of young UNITA recruits scheduled to go south for military training.[167] The war was thus spiraling out of control when African diplomacy provided a last reprieve.

African states prevailed upon Neto and Roberto to meet together with Savimbi at Nakuru, Kenya. There from June 16 to 21, again under Jomo Kenyatta's chairmanship, they negotiated a new, more detailed accord renouncing the use of force and delineating responsibilities for the remainder of the transition.[168] During a respite extending through the first week in July, the transitional government came forth with a draft constitution, and the first company of an Angolan national army was formed in Cabinda. But on July 9, heavy fighting broke out and spread swiftly throughout the country. Within a week, the MPLA had forced the FNLA out of Luanda.[169] The FNLA, now joined by a number of right-wing Portuguese (ex-PIDE agents and army officers), eliminated all remaining MPLA presence in the northern towns of the Uige and Zaire districts. The transitional government collapsed.

On July 20, the FNLA accused the Portuguese of siding with the MPLA and declared that it was planning to march on Luanda and would attack any Portuguese troops that tried to stop it. The next day Holden Roberto emerged from nearly life-long exile in Zaire to take command of the FNLA march on the capital. Cease-fires arranged in a chaotic series of meetings by the Portuguese were immediately violated. On July 24, FNLA troops, led by a former Portuguese counterinsurgency officer, Lieutenant Colonel Gilberto Santos e Castro, took Caxito.[170] The day after, Daniel Chipenda, since April 15 an FNLA official, announced that the FNLA hoped to enter Luanda within "the next few days." He added: "We do not think that new negotiations are possible any longer; we are going to Luanda, not to negotiate, but to lead." Nito Alves of the MPLA responded in kind: "We are one hundred percent enemies and can never come to any agreement. Our fight must go on until FNLA is defeated as the American imperialists were in Vietnam."[171]

Consolidating their control over Mbundu territory, MPLA forces moved inland beyond Malange to take the strategic Lunda city of Henrique de Carvalho (Saurimo). Its troops also enjoyed de facto control in the enclave of Cabinda where, in May, they were described as "mercilessly" tracking down and eliminating FLEC militants.[172] Despite self-interested political support from Brazzaville[173] and Kinshasa,[174] the Cabindans were no match for the MPLA military. A FLEC army of sorts tried. It was an ill-trained assemblage of probably fewer than the four thousand to six thousand men credited to it by Lisbon's usually well-informed weekly, *Expresso*. Led by a mysterious Commander Jean da Costa with French connections,[175] it mostly watched from exile in June as the MPLA secured control over the territory and positioned itself to inherit huge oil revenues.

Believing that the growing conflict in Angola proper might yet open the way for them, Cabinda's divided nationalists postured expectantly outside. On July 24, one group led by Henriques Tiago Nzita announced from Paris that it was setting up a provisional Cabindan government. In Kinshasa on August 1, Luis Ranque Franque proclaimed Cabindan independence and announced formation of a rival government headed by a former FNLA official, FLEC secretary-general, and now "premier," Francisco Lubota.[176]

A few days later President Ngouabi declared that Brazzaville could not accept that the MPLA had any right to impose itself by force in Cabinda.[177] But it so imposed. And aside from a quickly routed incursion by Zaire-backed FLEC forces in early November, frustrated Cabindan nationalists were sidelined for the rest of the Angolan war.

Meeting at Kampala in late July, the annual OAU heads-of-state summit deplored the Angolan fighting, appealed to the three movements "to lay down their arms," and "earnestly requested Portugal to assume, without delay and in an impartial manner, its responsibilities in Angola." They created an OAU Commission of Enquiry and asked it to consider the organization and dispatch of an OAU peace force for Angola.[178] But Portugal no longer had the capability to assume its "responsibilities"—and some of its army units were reportedly aiding the MPLA. It was time for action, not inquiry. African states had undermined confidence in the OAU as a mediating agency by allowing Uganda's erratic and controversial General Idi Amin to become its chairman.[179] Failure to act decisively at this juncture could only encourage extra-African powers to expand their intervention.

A ten-member Commission of Enquiry[180] spent ten days in Angola and reported back that UNITA had the largest popular support, followed in order by the FNLA and MPLA.[181] Follow-up proposals for the expedition of an OAU peace-keeping force, however, met with resolute opposition from the militarily increasingly ascendant MPLA. Through the fall the OAU palavered away its opportunity to influence the course of events.[182]

"By mid-July the military situation radically favored the MPLA. As the military position of the FNLA and UNITA deteriorated the governments of Zaire and Zambia grew more and more concerned about the implications for their own security. Those two countries turned to the United States for assistance."[183] Thus did Secretary Kissinger describe in retrospect the circumstances leading up to a July 17 decision of the National Security Council's "40 Committee" to provide covert assistance to both the FNLA and UNITA.[184]

Kenneth Kaunda's unheeded April warning now rang in Dr. Kissinger's ears. Furthermore Kissinger was sensitive to importuning from Zaire, where some $800 million in American investment was threatened by latent internal instability related to a drastic fall in world copper prices, failure to develop agricultural production above preindependence levels, and the conspicuous affluence of an aggrandizing government elite. Moreover in June, President

Mobutu chose to charge the United States with complicity in an attempted military coup and evicted the American ambassador from Kinshasa. Helping the FNLA, therefore, might be one way of helping to restore U.S.-Zaire relations.

If the military situation in mid-July "radically favored the MPLA," as Secretary Kissinger alleged, why was it so? In Angola, the July observations of a correspondent of the sober London *Times* showed that the "major advantage" of the MPLA, which "did not possess any significant weapon superiority" over its rivals, was a "manifestly superior organizational and infrastructural capability."[185] Under such circumstances, to pour in American money and arms was unlikely to alter the situation. (Washington seemed not to have learned much from the calamitous misadventure in Vietnam.)

Assistant Secretary Nathaniel Davis and his State Department Bureau of African Affairs recommended against becoming more deeply involved. To do so, they argued, would likely leave the United States tied to the losing side, jeopardize the governments of Zaire and Zambia, link the United States with South Africa, and lead to increased Soviet involvement.[186] The only public discussion of American policy toward Angola took place in hearings before the Clark committee in the Senate, where three academics—Gerald J. Bender, Douglas L. Wheeler, and this author—urged against American intervention.[187]

Beginning with $6 million, used partly to replace arms that could be provided quickly by Zaire and Zambia, American aid was successively increased during the summer and fall.[188] After adjusting for what appeared to be a consistent undervaluation of materiel sent, real American assistance appeared to be about twice the figure of $32 million eventually acknowledged.[189] After factoring in aid provided by China, France, Great Britain, West Germany, South Africa, and others, it is reasonable to conclude that the FNLA and UNITA received roughly the same amount that the CIA estimated the MPLA received from the Soviet Union—about $80 million through October 1975.[190] Although it might never be possible to pinpoint who gave how much to whom and when, it is possible to declare that there was no significant difference in the amount of outside assistance to the two sides (MPLA versus FNLA/UNITA) between July and October.[191]

THE SECOND WAR OF NATIONAL LIBERATION: MPLA TO PRA

By September, Angola's liberation movements were dug into their respective ethnic bastions. Additionally the MPLA had pocketed Cabinda and captured a number of ports and inland towns to the south. It enjoyed a local following in southern urban centers of relatively high political consciousness and sizable mestiço communities, for example, Moçâmedes and Sá da Bandeira. Partition seemed a real possibility as tens of thousands of Africans shifted from multiethnic towns and plantation regions back to areas of their ethnic origin, a retreat to the past that accelerated with the collapse of the transitional government and the withdrawal of Portuguese troops. Prolonged ethnic warfare seemed likely unless outside assistance combined with superior internal skill and organization to tip the balance one way or another. During August and September, massive departures of panic stricken white Angolans by airlift, fishing boat, and overland caravan added to the disjunctive chaos—and deprived UNITA of a vital political constituency.

The external variable—alliances old and new—assumed great importance. In journalists' reports and in the perceptions of the Angolan protagonists themselves, outside intervention came to overshadow internal factors such as comparative qualities of leadership, constituency, ideology, organization, and military skill. In reality, however, the underlying internal strengths and weaknesses of the three movements remained basic determinants of what some observers have portrayed as an African equivalent of the Spanish Civil War.[192] Nevertheless superimposed Soviet-American global jockeying and a veritable international free-for-all in Angola did constitute high political drama and did impact crucially on the civil war within the Angolan revolution.

China and Rumania

Motivated by a consuming rivalry with the Soviet Union and eager to parlay excellent relations in East Africa and Zaire into an Angolan shutout of the Russians, the Chinese committed arms, skills, and prestige to the FNLA. Displaying a risky independence, China's ally, but Soviet neighbor, Rumania, joined in backing a nonsocialist movement whose victory could be expected to humble Leonid Brezhnev and secure a special role for Peking and Bucharest in West-Central Africa (Angola/Cabinda/Zaire).

At the same time, however, China and Rumania maintained an official stance of neutrality that conformed to the position that the OAU adopted in 1975. Presumably sensitive to what critics described as an "unholy alliance" with "American imperialism,"[193] the

Chinese left the welcome mat out for all three Angolan movements. Samuel Chiwale headed a UNITA delegation to Peking in March;[194] Lúcio Lára followed for the MPLA in June;[195] and Pedro Vaal Hendrik Neto of the FNLA met there with Teng Hsiao-ping in July.[196] Despite a pessimistic public prognosis by Savimbi that the Chinese would not help,[197] UNITA, properly anti-Soviet and exhibiting demonstrable political strength, won a promise of Chinese arms. Lára reportedly obtained assurances that China favored tripartite unity, not FNLA hegemony, though the Chinese were not yet prepared to withdraw their military instructors.[198] The FNLA found the Chinese, whose military association with the FNLA had taught them something of FNLA leadership and organizational deficiencies,[199] somewhat less forthcoming than before. Though Roberto had told the Paris press in June that all his troops were Chinese trained, subsequent desultory performance by those troops proved no great credit to the Chinese. Shared antipathy for the Soviet Union—China ceaselessly berated the Soviets for "stirring up the civil war" by choosing sides and shipping arms[200]—was not enough, and Peking realized that both distance and resource capabilities would preclude it from matching the Soviets in an Angolan arms race.

Peking reportedly did authorize Zaire to release additional Chinese arms to the FNLA,[201] and a shipment of ninety-three tons of Chinese arms destined for UNITA did arrive in Dar es Salaam. Influenced by Samora Machel of FRELIMO, the MPLA's victorious CONCP ally,[202] and put off by UNITA reluctance to enter upon a two-party MPLA-UNITA alliance against the FNLA,[203] however, Julius Nyerere refused to allow the arms to proceed on via Zambia to Angola.[204]

In September, Chinese Foreign Minister Chiao Kuan-hua stated that his government had ceased sending arms once a date for independence had been set.[205] On October 27, China's military instructors quit the FNLA. In departure ceremonies at the Kinshasa airport, the leader of the military mission, Li Lung, announced that his mission's task had been accomplished and assured the FNLA, Holden Roberto, and the Angolan people of China's "eternal friendship."[206]

Rumania, too, pulled back. It had continued to aid the MPLA even after joining the Chinese venture with the FNLA.[207] And though President Ceausescu promised "cooperation and solidarity" to Jonas Savimbi during an April visit to Bucharest by the UNITA

leader,[208] the Rumanians shied away from a head-on Angolan collision with the Soviets. In October, when Ceausescu made a four-day
visit to Lisbon, Portuguese officials sought to enlist his support in a
last-gasp mediation effort.[209] But by then the MPLA looked as if it
would be the military victor (or South Africa's victim), and Rumania
declined to get caught up in a costly political gesture.

South Africa

Close cooperation among the military and intelligence services of
Portugal, South Africa, and Rhodesia was one of the factors that
had earlier convinced Washington that African guerrillas could not
win. Regularly a council of senior intelligence officers of the three
countries exchanged information, including that gathered by some
two thousand full-time South African agents and by Portuguese
infiltrators within the top ranks of the Angolan and Mozambican
nationalist movements.[210] South Africa assigned intelligence
officers to its consulates general in Luanda and Lourenço Marques
with instructions to work with the Portuguese military.

Starting in 1966 when the Angolan insurgency spread to the east,
South Africa conducted helicopter patrols over southern border
regions of Angola. Later, by the terms of a 1968 agreement, South
Africa was allowed to operate an air unit composed of Alouette
III helicopters and Cessna 185s within eastern Angola. A joint
Portuguese-South African command center was established at
Cuito Cuanavale inside the southeast operational sector assigned to
South Africa (see map 6.1). From it the South Africans carried out
visual and photo reconnaissance and even transported assault
troops in actions against both Angolan nationalists and Namibian
(SWAPO) guerrillas.[211] This military role coincided with a growing
infusion of South African capital and sale of South African
machinery and manufactures in Angola.[212]

With the collapse of Portuguese rule, South Africa adopted an
adaptive policy of détente. It quickly accommodated to the rise of a
radical FRELIMO government to power in Mozambique. As late as
April 1975, its officials were declaring publicly that their military
forces would not intervene in Angola under "any circumstances."[213] But the government of Prime Minister John Vorster
had no intention of making unnecessary concessions to black African nationalism. If there should arise what looked like a low-risk
opportunity to eliminate a "radical" in favor of a more congenial

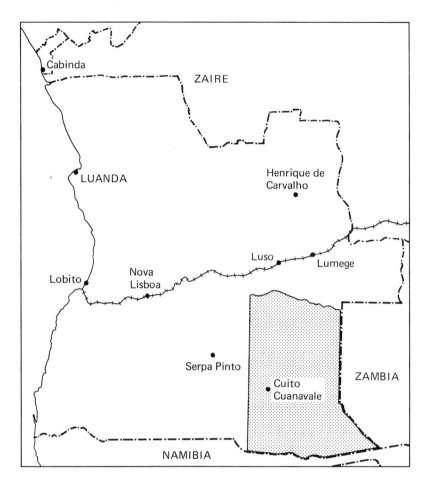

Map 6.1   South African operational sector

"moderate" alternative by means of military intervention, nothing in South Africa's détente strategy suggested that the opportunity should be spurned. At some point in mid-1975, Pretoria did indeed decide that the chaos in Angola provided it with a low-risk opportunity to smash both the MPLA and SWAPO and secure the future for "moderate" alternatives in Angola and Namibia.[214]

In June, South African troops reportedly took up positions at the Ruacana Falls on the Cunene River just inside Angola.[215] From there on August 9, they moved a few miles north to occupy the site of the South African–financed Cunene River hydroelectric project, which was scheduled to provide power for uranium mining and industry in Namibia and water for irrigation in Ovamboland.[216] In early September, South African troops backed by helicopters swept some thirty-five miles north through the Ongiva (Pereira de Eça) and Roçadas region, a move allegedly prompted by a September 1 attack by SWAPO guerrillas with "Russian made rockets" on a South African army camp.[217] South African units made deeper sorties against SWAPO camps, and the MPLA expressed misgivings about South African intentions.[218]

They had reason. At the end of May, the *Windhoek Advertiser* had headlined: "Black Guerrilla Leader in Windhoek."[219] It was Daniel Chipenda. He had flown in with an FNLA "political commissar," Mário Moutinho, and Portuguese bodyguards for what was referred to as "medical treatment." Earlier that month, Jonas Savimbi, who had already met with South African officials, had cited Prime Minister Vorster as "a responsible leader" and a man of "realism" and pronounced against the need for armed struggle in Namibia and Rhodesia.[220] A few weeks later the press quoted Savimbi as saying that Angola's own problems would prevent it from helping SWAPO.[221] These were but the external signs of what was being prepared in Namibia.

Some would later argue that if UNITA had been well armed by August when it was reluctantly pushed into the war[222] with relatively few arms,[223] the MPLA would have come to terms with it and UNITA would not have entered upon a fatal alliance with South Africa. As it was American arms began arriving only in late August, and the arms shipped from China never did arrive. Meanwhile though Savimbi had hastily mustered an army roughly estimated at some twenty thousand men, it was handicapped as much by a lack of training, organizational coherence, combat experience, infrastructural backup, and discipline as by a shortage of weapons.[224]

Savimbi, Chipenda, and Roberto[225] all turned to South Africa. Savimbi apparently acted on three assumptions: that South Africa was "the greatest military power" on the continent; that it was solidly linked to NATO powers that would "not let the Russians take control of Angola";[226] and that South Africa's détente policy toward such states as Zambia, Zaire, and even Mozambique had reduced the liabilities of association with it. In late August, the South Africans agreed to set up a training camp for UNITA at Calombo south of Silva Porto and another for the FNLA/Chipenda at Mapupa in southern Angola. On September 21, a South African commandant and eighteen instructors arrived in Silva Porto; and on October 6 they helped a company of UNITA troops halt MPLA forces advancing on Nova Lisboa.[227] Zaire provided several armored cars and perhaps 120 soldiers—adding to the twelve hundred to thirteen hundred Zaire regulars already fighting alongside the FNLA in the north.[228] Further reinforced by a South African squadron of twenty-two armored cars, UNITA was able to secure its position generally within the Ovimbundu-central highland region.[229]

Then on October 14, the South Africans mounted Operation Zulu from a staging base at Runtu, Namibia. A motorized force of Bushmen (some of whom had fought earlier for the Portuguese) together with a group of Portuguese officers and about one thousand followers of Daniel Chipenda crossed into Angola at Cuangar. Led by a South African commander nicknamed "Rommel" and a handful of South African officers and technicians, the column swiftly dislodged MPLA forces from Pereira de Eça. Moving on to Roçadas, it was joined by South African units (twenty armored cars and a platoon of 81mm mortars) and by a band of forty-seven rightwing Portuguese.[230] Air supplied and accompanied by helicopter gunships, the column moved on through Sá da Bandeira (Lubango) and up the coast from Moçâmedes to Benguela/Lobito to Novo Redondo, where it arrived on November 14. The column had traveled nearly five hundred miles north of its entry point on the Namibian border. FNLA and UNITA units moved in from the rear.[231]

Meanwhile in the north, FNLA and MPLA troops fought seesaw battles on the northern outskirts of Luanda, and American arms poured in on C130s from Zaire to the FNLA's staging centers at Ambriz and the former Portuguese airbase of Negage. In the north, the South Africans helped the FNLA—with 130mm howitzers.[232]

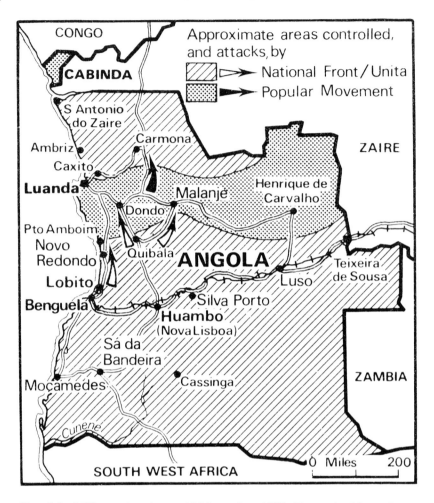

Map 6.2   Military situation, mid-November 1975 (*Economist*, November 22, 1975)

The MPLA, besieged in its capital, held only a swath of Mbundu country that flared on out to the east of Malange to include the diamond mines of Dundo and the railroad-border town of Teixeira de Sousa.

As a quid pro quo for South African help, according to American intelligence sources, Jonas Savimbi provided information on the location of SWAPO guerrilla bases.[233] And while the Ford administration sought in vain to persuade Congress to grant roughly $60 million to another intervening power, Zaire,[234] the State Department issued carefully constructed statements seeking to convey the impression that the United States was in no way implicated in the South African intervention.[235] However, suspicion that the faulty intelligence upon which the United States based its own intervention derived partially from the CIA's "close liaison with the South African security service"[236] was reinforced by official acknowledgment that South Africa and the United States did regularly exchange intelligence data.[237] Although Secretary Kissinger denied any "collusion" with them,[238] Pretoria officials insisted that South Africa's intervention was based upon an understanding with American officials that the United States would match any weaponry made available to the MPLA.[239] To the question of whether Washington had "solicited" South African involvement, Prime Minister Vorster subsequently responded that he would not call anyone who said that it had a "liar."[240]

By the time of the South African incursion, Portugal had withdrawn the bulk of its army. Divided and irresolute, the Lisbon government had made a feeble effort in July to restore its authority in Angola to the extent of sending in troop reinforcements. Confronted with the hostility of hopelessly divided liberation movements, however, it soon faltered. In late August, it formally annulled the Alvor agreement and dissolved the defunct transitional government, but it proved unable to muster the political and military will to intervene decisively to impose an orderly transfer of power. All its efforts to promote a new cease-fire or coalition having failed, Lisbon held firm to one thing—its determination to leave. Independence remained fixed for November 11.

High Commissioner Commodore Leonel Cardoso and his remnant entourage folded the Portuguese flag and, in a pathetic end to centuries of colonial rule, stole out of besieged Luanda a day early, leaving the Angolans to fight it out. The MPLA immediately proclaimed an independent People's Republic of Angola (PRA).[241]

Having activated support from its CONCP allies at a special meeting in Lourenço Marques (November 9),[242] having convinced the conservative Brazilian government that his was the winning movement, and having obtained a prior commitment for prompt diplomatic recognition from the Soviet Union, Yugoslavia, North Vietnam, and other communist states, Agostinho Neto launched his People's Republic. He was clearly relying on the MPLA's "internationalist" (rather than pan-African) orientation and alliances.[243] As president he announced the PRA's first government. It was predictably multiracial, predominantly mestiço/assimilado/ Mbundu;[244] Lopo do Nascimento, premier; Henrique "Iko" Carreira, defense; David Aires Machado, labor;[245] José Eduardo dos Santos, foreign affairs; João Felipe Martins, information; Nito Alves, interior;[246] Diógenes Boavida, justice; Carlos Rocha, planning and finance. At first most African states withheld recognition, however; they instead held to the general OAU stance in favor of a cease-fire, transitional coalition, and free election to choose the government of the new state.[247]

Then as South Africa's intervention became evident, despite denials[248] and efforts to screen it from journalists, African attitudes shifted. On November 27, the Nigerian government, which just two weeks before had denounced Soviet intervention on the side of the MPLA,[249] announced its recognition of the PRA, citing South African intervention as the reason.[250] Quickly followed by Tanzania,[251] Ghana, Sudan, and several other African states, the Nigerians assailed what they saw as an American–South African plot to destroy a "sister African country."[252] Demonstrators stoned the American embassy in Lagos, and the Nigerian government gave the MPLA $20 million.[253]

Cuba and the Soviet Union

A month after setting out on its dash north, the South African commando column stalled on the Queve River about 120 miles south of Luanda. There in the second half of November, the logistically extended South Africans confronted a regrouped and dug-in MPLA force that had been reinforced by elements of a Cuban expeditionary force numbering by that time about three thousand.[254]

It had been only natural for the MPLA to turn to Cuba for military instructors to help rebuild its military (FAPLA) after the 1974 leadership crisis and defection of Chipenda's *Revolta do Leste*. When by March 1975 FNLA-MPLA fighting and feverish efforts by all three movements to build up separate armies portended a military race to power, the MPLA sought Cuban counterparts to the Chinese who were training FNLA forces. By late spring 1975, some 230 Cuban military advisers had reportedly set up and staffed four FAPLA training camps.[255] As fighting escalated in June and July, the MPLA appealed for increased help.[256] In August, after clearing with pro-MPLA leadership within the Lisbon junta and ascertaining that the Soviets would not themselves send troops for fear of triggering an American response, the MPLA reportedly welcomed another two hundred Cuban infantry instructors in Luanda. Then, encouraged by the MPLA's African supporters (Algeria, Congo, Guinea-Bissau, Guinea-Conakry, Mozambique) and assured that the Soviets would finance the effort, Havana moved its support up another notch. By late September and early October, Cuban ships carrying heavy arms and hundreds of soldiers began arriving at Pointe Noire (Congo) and then such Angolan ports as Porto Amboim and Novo Redondo.[257] In Washington at about this same time, the head of the CIA's Angolan task force was warning that Zaire's intervention in northern Angola would be answered by an intrusion of "large numbers of Cuban troops, 10–15,000."[258] By mid-October, when the South Africans sped north from their southern Angola base, probably eleven hundred to fifteen hundred Cuban soldiers were bolstering the MPLA.[259]

South Africa's bold, clumsily covert offensive injected a new sense of urgency into Cuba's mission. Underestimating the convulsive potential of its own spectacularly successful intervention, Pretoria simultaneously created the visible need for and legitimized Cuban help. Needing to believe, if only for reasons of self-respect, that economic and military power far outweigh the racial variable in setting the terms of its relations with black Africa, South Africa badly miscalculated. At the same time that it destroyed the external credibility of those (UNITA and FNLA) that it sought to help, it destroyed the basis for collective African (OAU) support for a compromise, political solution in Angola.

Invoking a specter of conquest by white supremacists, Cuba and the Soviet Union moved with impunity to exploit their advantage. Beginning on November 7, Cuba began airlifting combat troops from Havana to Luanda in a major escalation that became known as Operation Carlota. (This operation was named after a black woman who led an 1843 slave uprising in Cuba.)[260] The Russians flew huge Antonov-22 transport planes containing arms directly to Luanda and Henrique de Carvalho and helped fly in thousands of Cuban combat troops to instruct MPLA recruits in the use of, and finally to man, sophisticated Soviet weaponry that included T54 and T34 tanks. Most tellingly, Cubans operated mobile 122mm rocket launchers (Stalin's Organs) that screeched, terrified, and blasted holes in the FNLA military front that had been pressing in on Luanda from the north. (South Africa later claimed that only earlier American appeals for it to desist had deterred it from taking the Angolan capital from the south.)[261]

The tide of battle took a final turn. With the approach of independence, in late October the FNLA had prepared what was meant to be a knockout blow. Shortly before, the MPLA, with Cuban organizational help, had pushed it back from Quifangondo, just twelve miles to the north of Luanda.[262] And Roberto wanted to be in the capital on November 11. From out of Zaire in early November, FLEC forces launched a diversionary attack on Cabinda while the FNLA prepared for its drive on Luanda. But FLEC's soldiers fled back into Zaire[263] before November 10 when Roberto, disregarding the counsel of Portuguese, South African, and American military advisers, sent a single column of several thousand troops down the road from Caxito toward the capital. Roberto had been saved from previous military disaster only because, "happily," when he "played general," his orders "were not always followed."[264] But this time his orders were followed. Roberto failed to mount standard diversionary forays and flanking moves. His compact single-assault column crumbled and ran under a hail of 122mm rockets and artillery fire. The FNLA army, weak in discipline and without political indoctrination, never recovered from what became known as the Battle of Death Road. "To the bitter end, the 122mm rocket, a noisy but relatively ineffectual weapon, sowed utter panic in the ranks of [Roberto's] troops who never became accustomed to conventional warfare."[265] Chinese (and rumored North Korean)[266] guerrilla training had been either inappropriate or insufficient.

Using heavy weaponry, encircling tactics, and the full concentration of a Cuban army that reached some seven thousand by late 1975 (and ten thousand to twelve thousand by early 1976), the MPLA eliminated the FNLA as a fighting force by early January. As it collapsed, the FNLA army received no help from the twelve hundred to fifteen hundred Zairian troops, whose role was to provide artillery and armored vehicle support. The Zairians looted, hoarded, then panicked and ran ahead of the Angolans—and together they left behind quantities of unused American and other Western arms.[267]

Cuba's intervention marked a decisive turning point in the civil war, but it followed upon substantial intervention by others, including Zaire and South Africa. Though Premier Fidel Castro's statement that "the first material aid and the first Cuban instructors reached Angola at the beginning of October" when it "was being insolently invaded by foreign forces" surely postdates Cuba's involvement, it seems likely that Castro is correct in saying that Cuba had not earlier expected "to participate directly in the fight." According to him, it was on November 5, at the urgent request of the MPLA (the Soviet Union "never requested" it), that Cuba decided to send "a battalion of regular troops with antitank weapons." When the first Cuban unit of Operation Carlota arrived, 140mm artillery (FNLA) was bombarding the suburbs of Luanda, and South African troops had "penetrated more than 700 kilometers" north from Namibia, "while Cabinda was heroically defended by MPLA fighters and a handful of Cuban instructors." Once in and legitimized by the South Africans, "Cuba sent the men and weapons necessary to win."[268] There can be quarrels over time sequences, but there is no question that Cuba's intervention was partly an improvised response to South Africa's. And in Africa it was widely, though not universally, seen as the action of a small Third World David humbling the Goliath of Western imperialism. Such a perception might logically have been anticipated in Pretoria and Washington.

For the first time, albeit as an unexpectedly successful improvisation in response to unanticipated opportunity, Soviet military power projected through an ally to determine the outcome of an African conflict. In the process, Soviet audacity increased Soviet influence throughout racially torn Southern Africa.

CONTINUITIES AND VERITIES

As the Angolan conflict proceeded on to a convincing MPLA military victory and beyond, the continuities of Angola's revolution remained remarkably strong. The FNLA's disintegration came in a context of continuing ethnic parochialism—the FNLA's ranking Mbundu, Mateos Neto, defected in July;[269] racial dogmatism—unable to trust its own white supporters, the FNLA remained motivated by an obsessive hostility toward mestiço leadership (and thus the MPLA);[270] structural incoherence—Roberto's lieutenants (for example, Ngola Kabangu and Johnny Eduardo Pinock) squabbled for position,[271] while Roberto continued to run the movement as a one-man show devoid of regular process or cohesive organization; negative doctrine—FNLA leadership continued to rely on visceral anticommunism and a faith in the power of physical weaponry.[272] Association with China and Rumania did nothing to encourage it to develop and inculcate a political philosophy or program. The FNLA proved consistent in its inability to transcend constrictive social origins with a geoethnic outreach to create a larger, integrated political community. The adhesion of Daniel Chipenda's *Revolta do Leste* to the FNLA, for example, never became more than a loose expediency, an alliance that enabled Chipenda to freewheel with South Africans and Portuguese in what was really a fourth, south-eastern-based movement.

With independence on November 11, the FNLA and UNITA patched together a formal government to counter that of the PRA. Their compromise took two weeks of discordant bargaining in Kinshasa. Their Democratic People's Republic of Angola (DPRA) reflected continuing communal and organizational cleavage, dramatized by the inability of the DPRA partners, even in extremis, to create a functioning alternative to the Luanda government. While Roberto operated from a northern "capital" at Ambriz (and Kinshasa), the DPRA set up offices in Huambo-Savimbi country. But the premiership was to rotate monthly between the two movements whose three armies remained unintegrated (ELNA/Roberto, ELNA/Chipenda, FALA).[273] The DPRA never got itself organized or recognized.

Then, as MPLA/Cuban forces turned south after routing Roberto's army, the uneasy FNLA/Chipenda-UNITA alliance fell apart. Overall Chipenda's freebooters probably "spent more time looting, robbing banks, raping," and jousting for positions against UNITA than they did in fighting the MPLA.[274] In any case, a Christmas Eve shootout in Huambo escalated into an FNLA-UNITA war within a war that led to the defeat and disintegration of Chipenda's army by early January.[275] (UNITA forces were not allowed to operate in Roberto's northern stronghold.)

The continuities within UNITA were also striking. It maintained a strong ethnoregional appeal among Ovimbundu, Chokwe, Lwena, and Ovambo; shared (if less intensively) FNLA hostility toward mestiço leadership;[276] and continued to rely on an Afrocentric populism that was at the same time aggressive and demogogic. Savimbi still carried political flexibility to the point of gross inconsistency, if not transparent deceit, in desperate efforts to survive. His bargaining with South Africa transformed Namibian nationalists of SWAPO from adversaries of the MPLA [277] to adversaries of UNITA.[278] And although UNITA would later charge that the MPLA was guilty of cooperating with South Africa,[279] on November 10 and again on December 20, 1975, Savimbi reportedly flew to Pretoria to meet with Prime Minister Vorster and South African military officials and persuade them to delay their withdrawal[280]—further undercutting what remaining sympathy he enjoyed in the OAU. On January 22, after a long delayed meeting of the OAU (January 10-12) had failed to produce majority support for a tripartite political solution or a condemnation of Cuban/Soviet intervention, South Africa withdrew the bulk of what had grown to a two-thousand man expeditionary force.[281] Faced by chronic disadvantage in external aid, UNITA had long oscillated between resourceful political self-reliance and desperate expediencies (for example, its arrangements with the Portuguese, Roberto, the South Africans). Of the three movements, only its army had not benefited from a heavy input of outside training. A 1975 program employing mercenaries to train a large UNITA army came too late.[282] In January and February, bitter, ill-disciplined UNITA forces retreated in disarray before better-equipped and -led MPLA/Cuban forces. Flailing out in a penultimate spasm of death in a civil war that had taken thousands of lives more than the fight against Portugal, UNITA units pulling out of Huambo reportedly massacred local MPLA officials and supporters.[283]

By mid-1976, Roberto had resumed a shadowy, reclusive role in the exile from which President Mobutu had shoved him in July 1975, and FNLA forces were once again active in forest retreats of the Bakongo north. Savimbi had returned to his Guevarist, against-the-odds role as head of an army in the bush. Joined by cadres of young, educated Ovimbundu, UNITA's roster of still intact, ethnically diverse leadership[284] organized a new, or renewed, rural insurgency against what Savimbi now called "Soviet/Cuban occupation."[285] Savimbi, with continuing assistance from South Africans who helped train his troops at Grootfontein, Namibia, was still following an odd-man-out, common-front strategy of trying to prove the essentiality of UNITA participation to any government that hoped to rule Angola.

But one thing had changed: the MPLA was the government. The MPLA capitalized on its continuities, notably its ethnocultural assets, including a relatively large cadre of educated followers and a political constituency strategically centered in the capital. It drew strength from its longstanding commitment to ideologically grounded political education and mobilization. And it benefited from a well-tested system of alliances ranging from the Portuguese left to CONCP to Cuba to the Soviet Union—all of which helped at crucial junctures. It was precisely the ideological radicalism and the Soviet-Cuban linkages that worried Washington's eleventh-hour policy makers. Mesmerized by global strategies, they had discounted the importance of discrete, informal realities. Choosing not to tell Moscow of American concerns and intentions until it had built up a stock of "bargaining chips," Washington responded to Soviet arms shipments by escalating its own military involvement. It was only in late October 1975, when Soviet prestige was on the line and its side was winning that the American secretary of state suggested to Moscow a readiness "to use our influence to bring about a cessation of foreign military assistance and to encourage an African solution if they would do the same."[286] The U.S. administration had failed to respond to Senegal's (July) and Portugal's (September-October) appeals for initiatives through the forum of the United Nations.[287] It had not called in OAU ambassadors, contacted key African leaders, or offered American support for collective African initiatives. And its disregard for internal political realities had extended to its own political milieu.

Soviet leadership seemed able to understand what Secretary Kissinger was unable to accept: that neither the American public nor Congress, chastened and disillusioned by a lost war in Vietnam, would tolerate military involvement in another distant, unfathomable, civil conflict. As the nature and extent of American intervention leaked out, the media sounded the alarm,[288] and in mid-December the Senate voted fifty-four to twenty-two to cut off further covert aid.[289] Unprepared to stand "alone" for the "free world,"[290] the other major miscalculator, South Africa, pulled out too. And on February 11, African states accredited the MPLA/PRA victory by according the Luanda government membership in the OAU.

But did subsequent events not vindicate Dr. Kissinger's pessimistic view that an MPLA victory would mean a Soviet/Cuban satellite? Washington estimated, after all, that the Soviet Union had invested approximately $300 million in the MPLA during the year ending with the February military success and would expect dividends. It seems less than evident that the Soviet Union gained more than transient advantage. While President Agostinho Neto signed in

Moscow a treaty of friendship and cooperation, which included a mutual defense clause,[291] the PRA constitution expressly prohibited "the installation of foreign military bases" (art. 16), and the Soviet navy has yet to appear in Lobito. Although Lúcio Lára confirmed plans to convert the MPLA into a "vanguard" Marxist-Leninist party to lead Angola to "scientific socialism,"[292] PRA economic policy focused on reconstruction and trade with the West (who would buy Angolan coffee, diamonds, iron, oil) under a constitution that "recognizes, protects and guarantees private property" (art. 10).

More evident than satellization were continuities in the established character of the MPLA. The top levels of MPLA/PRA leadership were held by skilled, educated, and dedicated men— many of them mestiço, a few white. When the black, reputedly pro-Soviet minister of interior, Nito Alves, challenged mestiço power, he lost his job. Under the tough, low-key, resilient leadership of its president of fourteen years, Agostinho Neto, the MPLA held firm to its advocacy and practice of multiracialism.[293] African names remained scarce in a government that marked the ascendancy of the urban/acculturated-intellectual/multiracialists. Ideology remained a focus of attention and commitment. The MPLA mobilized people's power (*poder popular*) in the *musseques* but confronted continuing opposition from *Revolta Activa* supporters of Joaquim Pinto de Andrade and a Maoist *Organização dos Comunistas de Angola* (OCA). Assessing that their natural base resided in an as yet very small urban working class, MPLA leaders saw their task as one of both improving economic conditions throughout the country and overcoming the "tribal prejudices" of the large rural population.[294]

One inevitable legacy of centuries of colonial denigration of cultural values among Angola's diverse peoples is continuing, mutual ignorance and suspicion among ethnic groups. Any hope for building an integrated Angolan nation through consensual rather than coercive process must depend upon conscious, sensitive, and informed efforts to reduce communal tension by promoting interethnic and interracial understanding and respect. To bind the wounds of war and construct a unified socialist state, the MPLA will need more than the weapons and men of the Soviet Union and Cuba. It will need to surmount the limits of its own social origins and reach out to those who continue to see it as an instrument of alien (Portuguese/Cuban) rule. The alternative is rule by force with continued rural violence.

The punitive policy of nonrecognition Henry Kissinger followed in the year after the MPLA victory only increased Angola's dependency on Cuba and antipathy toward the United States. It did nothing to encourage the Luanda government to accept a policy of generosity toward the ethnic communities of those whom it had defeated. It did not (and could not) prevent the PRA from acting out of " revolutionary solidarity" in support of SWAPO in a mounting confrontation with South Africa in Namibia.

A central lesson of the Angolan revolution stands forth: external powers that continue to deny or defy the discrete, informal realities of political conflict in countries like Angola and regions like Southern Africa will continue to pay the price of miscalculation. Only an understanding of an Angola's own particular history, culture, social structure, and material circumstances, only an appreciation of the special dynamics of, for example, its political tripolarity, viewed systematically, systemically, and in its regional as well as global setting, can provide the external policy maker with a basis for a reasonable, constructive relationship.

In a world characterized by resurgent ethnic nationalism (from Wales, Catalonia, and Quebec to Eritrea) and declining interstate cohesion and organization, there is a likelihood that an Angola, a territory that is economically and strategically enticing but politically weak or splintered, will lure outsiders into a secretive, coercive competition for special influence and gain. Unconstrained by the inhibiting impact of vigorous multilateral diplomacy, external interveners risk getting caught up in an escalating chain of action and reaction from which they find it increasingly difficult to disengage. They put their prestige on the line. A victory or defeat for a foreign client or ally that earlier would have been considered of marginal concern becomes a test of national will or honor. Thus, those—be they Portuguese, American, South African, Zairian, Cuban, or Russian—who try by force to "shape events" (a favorite Kissinger phrase) may bring upon themselves and those whom they would shape the long agony of a Vietnam or the briefer humiliation of an Angola.

That Angolan independence came amid violence and chaos is directly traceable to the divide-and-rule policies of a particularly repressive and tenacious colonialism. But foreign domination left most African societies politically disunited, economically underdeveloped, and vulnerable to continued domestic strife and external manipulation. Internal cleavages and external dependencies do not dissolve with independence. And those who govern Africa's new states face enormous problems, beginning with the need to weld their countries into cohesive polities.

Only detailed knowledge of the colonial crucible and the history and character of those who have broken out of it can permit us to understand what follows independence. In the case of Angola, for example, only such knowledge enables us to understand why black African leaders (Nito Alves and Jacob Caetano) who spent perilous years in the MPLA maquis fighting for independence would try to overthrow a (multiracial) MPLA government just a year and a half after independence;[295] why UNITA but not the FNLA might be both determined and able to sustain anti-MPLA insurgency in the bush;[296] why the Gulf Oil Corporation would be allowed transitionally to operate in the Cabinda enclave while local separatists continue to agitate from exile;[297] or why a host of external powers, Zaire, South Africa, Cuba, the Soviet Union, China, and the United States, would continue to involve themselves deeply in Angolan issues. Clearly the same sort of knowledge necessary for an understanding of Angola will be necessary for predictive or retrospective insight into the looming crises of Rhodesia, Namibia, and South Africa or the past or present traumas of such places as Nigeria, Zaire, and the Horn of Africa.

PORTUGAL'S COLONIAL MINDSET

An understanding of the political movements that assumed power in Angola, Guinea-Bissau, and Mozambique requires an understanding of the colonial order that produced and fought them. Perhaps the surest way to gain this understanding is to look at the thoughts of those who led Portugal's ancien regime.

The stern steward of Portugal's *Estado Novo*, Premier António Salazar, never left Europe to visit a colonial empire that he insisted should take economic and political precedence over a Europe for whose values he nonetheless purported to speak. In the context of a persistent challenge from African insurgents, Salazar defended his country's sacred mission. He did so most notably in an August 1963 radio address made shortly after the recognition of the Angolan government in exile (GRAE) by the Organization of African Unity (OAU) and a 1965 policy statement to the executive committee of his ruling National Union party.

Salazar's successor, Marcello Caetano, a more modern though conservative man, was expected to devise a more rational colonial policy. Specifically it was thought that he might jettison the small, economically uninteresting and militarily costly colony of Guinea-Bissau and grant political autonomy to pliant European-mestiço-assimilado governments in Luanda and Lourenço Marques so as to hold on to what really counted. Whether by personal conviction, pressure from ultra nationalist and military circles, or both, Caetano did not do so. He proved an ardent defender of the empire, which he did visit. His reasoning was set forth in, among other pronouncements, a speech to the National Assembly (November 1968) and a policy statement made in Luanda (1969).

283

António Salazar, Declaration on Overseas Policy, August 12, 1963[1]

I

. . . The concept of Nation is inseparable, in the Portuguese case, from the idea of civilizing mission, far beyond and very different from the introduction of new techniques and of the exploitation of the natural wealth of the territories found. In the case of a collection of peoples of different races, languages and religions and of unequal economic levels, nationalizing action cannot cut itself off from the effort which moulded the populations, turned to good account the useful elements in the cultures found along the way, sobered down tribal rivalries and divisive tendencies, made all take part in common work and finally awakened a conscience of the *national*, that is, created a fatherland and raised the populations to the level of a higher civilisation. Those who disbelieve this smile disdainfully at us; but this is our way of being in the world, as others have already observed.

It makes no difference to the clarification of the present problem that our big empire of the XVI century was lost in the vicissitudes of history, because, although it was in part taken over and exploited by others, they too have lost it already. But it is worth stressing that wherever the Portuguese were given time by their competitors to instal themselves, cling to the land, live together and mix with the populations and guide them after the Portuguese manner; where and when this was possible, the Portuguese either left an indelible mark of their Lusitanism or purely and simply extended Portugal. And thus it is that we are also, besides other things and with a better title than others, an African nation.

One hears it said outside, loud cries are raised claiming independence for Angola: but Angola is a Portuguese creation and does not exist without Portugal. The only national conscience rooted in the Province is not Angolan, it is Portuguese; even as there are no Angolans but Portuguese of Angola. If Portugal be excluded, there is the NGWIZAKO asking for the reconstitution of the Kingdom of the Congo as a modern State; there are the ethnic groups of the districts of Moxico and Lunda asking us to create a Republic of Mushiko, independent of the rest. If there is no Angola, the Congo will have to break up; the outlet to the sea will have to be closed to Leopoldville and the ex-Belgian Congo will have to be turned into an inland State; there will have to be slicing in the South of the Province or more wisely in Southeast Africa in order to reconstruct the empire of the Cuanhamas which had its capital among us at Ngiva, today Vila Pereira de Eça. . . .

The leaders of today bear the tremendous responsibility of a crisis in the African continent, which will not improve, much less heal, in two or three centuries, given the many wars which will be fought there, the pretended geographical or racial readjustments, the annexations, the divisions of some States, regrouping of others, the instability of public authority, the lack of means of progress. . . .

1. From António de Oliveira Salazar, *Declaration on Overseas Policy* (Lisbon: Secretariado Nacional da Informação, 1963).

As for us, the African crisis touched us at a moment when it is still possible to witness revivals of past stages of evolution which have not been fully erased by our nationalizing effort. These revivals, arising naturally in times of convulsion, are being incited by foreign interests but they are not by themselves vigorous enough to counter the unity which has been acquired. Is the language which we teach those peoples superior to their dialects or not? Does the religion preached constitute a nation of civilized expression and world projection by the missionaries surpass fetichism or not? Is it not better to constitute a nation of civilized expression and world projection than to shut up in narrow regionalism without incentives to development, without means of defence and without supports for progress? If our reply to these questions is affirmative, we cannot but conclude that the state of national conscience created by the Portuguese among such divers peoples has been a benefit to all, a benefit which would be wholly lost if we agreed to retrogress.

The existence of the nationalizing element in the inspiration of this political conception has resulted in all everywhere being Portuguese; variation in geographical conditions and in climates as also the preponderance of certain ethnic backgrounds make some Europeans, others Africans, others Asiatics. And these differences project themselves in the political and administrative norms by which we are governed and in the way the populations live together. National unity does not require that a distinction should be made between metropolitan and other territories, which distinction may even be regarded as aberrant dualism, but it requires a capital, a government, a policy; the variety of populations calls for juridical equality of all ethnic groups, that is to say, multiracialism in laws and in life. The diversity of territories, of their size and their natural conditions leads to a certain differentiation in the constitution and in the powers of the organs charged with local administration and in the relations of these with the central organs.

In the measure in which territories achieve economic and social progress and local élites become more numerous and capable, centrifugal forces may make their appearance aspiring to the plenitude of power and to the monopoly of situations, and this involves a risk to the unity of the Nation. In the Portuguese case, however, the avenues of access to the highest posts are open and are made increasingly easier—Adrian, born in Spain, could become emperor in Rome; on the other hand, though the populations are almost balanced, there is still a great imbalance in the possibilities available in the European and overseas parts of Portugal and, therefore, if those centrifugal forces exist, they represent the selfish interests of minorities which act against themselves as well as against the collectivity and the general interest. In this direction or tendency, they must be opposed, but at the same time utilised to the maximum and channeled into working for the common welfare.

The multiracialism, which today begins to be mentioned and admitted by those who had practically never accepted it before, may be said to be a Portuguese creation. It derives, on the one hand, from our character and, on the other, from the moral principles of which we were the bearers. Were it not for the fact that conspicuous examples of such mixed—luso-tropical—

societies can be shown today, perhaps it would even be denied that we contributed to their historical existence. The black racism which the newly independent African States proclaim and which they declare that they wish to see implanted in that continent is, on this point, a negation of our conceptions, yet it will not be maintained unless those same conceptions are adopted. It is beginning to be seen that the only probability of success for those new States lies in following those same principles of nondiscrimination or of racial equality which we proclaim and have always practised. The big difficulty lies in the fact that a multiracial society is not a juridical construction or a conventional regime of minorities, but above all a way of life and a state of mind which can be maintained in equilibrium and peace only with the support of a long tradition. In this context, it is not we who have to change our course; it is the others who have to take it in their own interest. And those centrifugal minorities to whom I referred above, whatever the ethnic group they belong to, would do well to ponder that they have no future if they ignore these fundamental truths.

National unity, once its essential elements are respected—one capital, one Government, one policy—is perfectly compatible with a maximum of administrative decentralization, in the constitution of local organs and in the definition of their powers. Evidently, the administration has to move within the larger circle that is the national policy and will have to abide by its directives. In order to be coherent, therefore, we ought not to forget, while amplifying administrative decentralization, the part which the various territories play in the constitution and functioning of the higher organs of the Nation and also the need to follow the line of national policy. The development of the territories results in a multiplication of local problems requiring organs to deal with them directly: there has never been any difficulty in recognizing this fact. The difficulty lies in knowing how to harmonize a fully autonomous administration with governmental unity at the national level; in defining the co-ordination of national services with similar provincial services, in organizing the Overseas Ministry both in the sphere of its exclusive competence and as an intermediary between the local organs and the Government. Now all this involves so many and such delicate problems that we cannot be sure that these have always been solved in the best way. . . .

II

During an official visit to Brazzaville, at the beginning of June, the President of the Republic of Guinea, referring to the peoples of Africa who in his opinion are still colonial, declared: "If those peoples do not desire independence, we who are conscious and free are in duty bound to liberate the whole of Africa." It is from this mental position so clearly expressed by one of the African leaders that stem the attitudes taken by the independent States of Africa towards Portugal. These attitudes are based on two postulates: a definition of colonial territory adopted for their own use; the claim of a right to proceed to the "liberation" of "oppressed" peoples, even though the latter, like the Portuguese peoples, have long been free and thus decline being now liberated by others.

Secure in their notion of colonialism and invested with a providential mission, various African countries are engaged in a campaign which has helped them obtain undeniable triumphs in the United Nations and culminated not long ago in the conference of the 32 African heads of State and of Government—almost the totality—in Addis-Ababa. It was decided there to pool efforts together in a very special manner against our territories in Africa and principles and resolutions were voted which have already begun to be applied by some: breaking off diplomatic and consular relations; embargo on trade and on navigation by sea and air; refusal of co-operation to Portugal in the international technical bodies.

As already explained, the rupture of diplomatic relations effected by the few African countries with which we had established such relations, at times at their request, does not in general have anything more than a spectacular character without positive results. Evidently, where we have colonies of Portuguese people, refusal of consular representation, if also included, may indirectly affect the defence of the legitimate interests which those colonies seek and represent. But as the consequences may indeed by harmful to the very parties that have taken the initiative to break off relations, it may well be that the Addis-Ababa decisions will in some cases come to be weighed against the ill-effects of their implementation.

As for trade with the African continent, excepting that part which is Portugal there as well, such trade is limited enough so that no serious losses will be caused by its suspension. In regard to air navigation, the local agreements are few and restricted in scope; as for the rights to use the air space recognized by international conventions, I think they ought to be respected, at least until they are denounced by the interested countries, but then it will be to the detriment of world traffic.

The fight against the presence of Portugal in international technical organs, where we are by full right, is a fact which does not stand in favour of the Africans and reflects no credit on the Westerners. It was easy for us to avoid the affronts by not appearing at the meetings or by not insisting integrally on our rights. The position which has seemed preferable to us is, however, to force our adversaries by our presence to take openly the path of illegality, and it is in illegality, that is, in clear contempt of the statutory norms of those organs that our adversaries are indeed acting. Our attitude may yield one of these two consequences: either a generalized awareness of the misconduct, leading to a reversal or a recognition that, under such conditions, there can be no functioning of the organs whose greatest benefits, it can be boldly said, go to the countries of recent independence.

Let us make it clear that the African countries would not be strong enough to impose on us their excommunications, had they not been supported by the vote of the communist governments seeking to destroy the West and by the attitude of some countries of the West which should be regarded as a desertion if it did not mean a desire to win the sympathy of the Africans with a view to furthering what they consider to be their interests. Thus Africa is being used as the field where two worlds are at loggerheads: we are only an occasion and a pretext. . . .

The countries represented at Addis-Ababa certainly thought that those resolutions were not sufficient—although, as sanctions to be applied against

Portugal, they are contrary to the Charter of the United Nations—and accordingly they permitted themselves to go to greater extremes. These, already in execution here and there, are as follows: concession of training camps to revolutionary elements; offer of volunteers or mercenaries; subscription of funds to defray the expenses of terrorist campaigns; supply of arms and technicians for subversive warfare. In this regard, there is an open departure from the norms which until recently governed the international community. As matters stood very few years ago, this would mean that all these countries, to the extent to which they carried out such decisions, should be regarded as being in a state of war with Portugal. Today, however, it is not so; and this not only by virtue of the facts of the recent past which were passed over in silence or left without a reply but also because the "sacred ambitions" which certain persons and peoples embody in certain instances prevail over all duties and all rights. Those persons and peoples would even be lacking legitimacy to defend themselves.

Within the logic of this position, it does not matter that our territories are relatively more advanced and for that very reason many African States insist obstinately in not having that advancement checked; nor is any importance attached to the real will of the populations which live in peace, enjoying full juridical equality with all others; nor to the bases of their political organization and of their administration; nor to the fact that those territories are integral parts of an independent State and have been so since long before most African States became independent. . . .

When matters are taken to these extremes of passion and deviation from human reason, there is no possibility of discussion or of mutual understanding. Either the more responsible powers put in an efficacious word calling for a return to good sense or nothing remains for each one but to use his natural right to defend himself and his people. Thus wars begin. . . .

In present day Africa one witnesses a double phenomenon: whenever possible, a revolutionary movement is hitched to the process of the independence of the territories. This movement is more pronounced in the countries of the Mediterranean coast but it extends already to the other countries which those seek to dominate or to lead with their extremism fanned as it is to spread to Africa south of the Sahara, under their leadership, new ideas of political and social revolution, not to mention the dreamed of unification of the continent. Currently, one hears suspicious words: neutralism; socialist state; total economic independence; inadaptability of monarchies to new conditions; formation of new social and political structures, regardless whether they are viable in the prevailing sociological conditions. For example, the interest in Angola of Algeria and of UAR—a country that is half African and today half Asiatic—cannot be religious or racial or humanitarian or economic or that of a liberator from any oppression. On the part of those States and of others which are deep in the fight against us, while trying to disguise the hostility between Arabs and Africans, there can be only one interest—the revolutionary interest; and this interest is far from being shared by all, even because they fear it. But the target has been well chosen, because it is known that we represent, in that sense and in the modesty of our resources, a barrier to be crossed. We only raise a corner of this problem, because we believe that they are labouring under an illusion who think that, through their dubious patronage, they will later lead the newly independent African countries, like meek flocks, into their folds.

But may there not be a mistake also in regard to the very phenomenon of decolonization both on the part of the decolonized as of the colonisers?

In resolution 1541 (XV) of the General Assembly of the United Nations (15th December, 1960), there was a search for a definition of colonial territories and mention is made of territories which are geographically separated and ethnically or culturally distinct from the administering country. It was, however, prudently added that there are other elements to be taken into account—of administrative, political, juridical, economic or historical nature—which seemed fully to cover the Portuguese Overseas Provinces, the more so as in another resolution (1514 (XV) of 14th December 1960), it is stated: "Any attempt aimed at the partial or total disruption of the national unity and the territorial integrity of a country is incompatible with the purposes and principles of the Charter of the United Nations." The Portuguese case clearly fits in here, but the passion which prevails in these matters has not permitted justice to be done to us in accordance with the texts.

In international campaigns and forums demands are made constantly for decolonization: this is said to be the greatest need of the century and the highest work which mankind in our days could undertake. As no care has been taken to define the term, we do not yet have an idea of the precise content of such a complex phenomenon. When, however, one looks carefully on the intimate connection established every now and again between de-colonization and independence, it is seen that the essence of the de-colonization is to be found in the exclusive possession of power or in the transfer of power from the white man, wherever he holds it, to the negro who claims it and is said to have the right to it only because of his numerical superiority. In these circumstances, one should not avoid at least a primary condition—that of the populations being capable of choosing their government and of the élites being sufficiently prepared to make the structures of administration function. But it has already been solemnly proclaimed and voted in the same United Nations that lack of preparation in the political, economic and social domains or in that of instruction should never serve as a pretext to delay the granting of independence (Resolution 1514 (XV)). Independence must be given immediately, whatever happens thereafter.

Even though this is not a matter which concerns us, it is difficult to admit this thesis which considers the independence of peoples as containing in itself all the virtualities so that no account need be taken either of the size of the territories or of the number and value of the populations or of the resources at the disposal of the rulers to achieve the common good. The truth is that the territories to which we refer are—and they admit it themselves—underdeveloped, demographically, economically and culturally. It is to no purpose to follow the path of complicated theories which might disclose the causes: we know that many of those theories have been formulated and developed so as to find arguments to blame the coloniser, as the basis of his responsibilities towards the colonised. But it is essential to remember that the progress considered necessary requires technicians, capital and labour, the latter, at least in part, to be recruited locally, the other factors from outside. Now, however much we may try to shape the interventions of more advanced and richer countries, we shall always find a minimum of conditions attached to such technique and to such capital. They are so to say organic and natural requirements, whether the local economy takes the path of socialism or accepts a greater or lesser degree of economic freedom and of private enterprise. The peoples who, fearing some such external influence, do not choose this course, will have to fall back on others—that of progress going so slow that it cannot be regarded as such or that of a return to lower standards of life.

In this connection we have seen some of the boldest theories being set forth. There are countries which thought they had sufficient means to raise the African continent in their arms and to make it as progressive in a few decades as Europe became after centuries. Soon, however, they realized that the task was excessively heavy and they are now trying to make others share the burden in the form of humanitarian grants, technical co-operation and incentive for the opening and conquest of markets. We have seen other countries bent on speeding up the preparation of leaders, technicians and skilled labour as a means to rapidly filling the local vacuum: *formation of cadres* continues to be an obsession in Africa. To satisfy this obsession, the milieu in which the populations develop, their psychic climate, is left out of account and candidates are hurried to every corner of the world, whence the countries collect back technicians and politicians of the most varied formations. In this task revealing much flurried haste and naïveté, there seems to be a confusion between civilization and material progress, progress and industrialization, detribalization and freedom, freedom and expulsion of white man, and this after seeing how useful is co-operation in the organization of enterprises and in the orientation of labour. And thus, in none of these domains have the aspirations been found to correspond to the realities.

We also find, with regard to self-determination and independence, the same confusion of concepts as in the case of de-colonization. Article 73 of the Charter of the United Nations contains no allusion to independence of the territories to which it refers but only to the possibility of self-government, which seems to mean autonomous administration conducted by the local people and compatible with many forms of inclusion in the framework of a State. But when self-determination is linked with independence, as has been done in the various votes taken in respect of Portugal, it is ignored that self-determination means the possibility of divers options and that to indicate or impose independence as its goal is tantamount to restricting it to a single objective, thus partially denying it.

We have another doubt as well and we have found no reply to it either. It is this: if self-determination aims fundamentally at verifying the assent given to the form of State or of Government under which populations live, it is not understood how there can be a single method of achieving this purpose or of determining that assent, the single method being a plebiscite following the illegitimate demands of the United Nations. The entire past, all the interventions in political life and in the organization of public authority would not then have the slightest value, in despite of reason and of history.

These two serious confusions—self-determination equal to independence; self-determination equal to a plebiscite—begin to be noticed and the United States itself seems to have evolved in the last two years in the direction of good sense. The fact is that such anomalous constructions of the United Nations, made *ad odium* and for certain purposes, end by giving people the impression of independence imposed from outside taking the place of a healthy natural evolution.

From the foregoing I deduce that the hard lessons of experience are going to make the African peoples less ambitious. These lessons are going to ensure that this excitement is followed by states or greater calm in which the living together of races and the co-operation of nations will prevail over the unbridled idealisms of today. . . .

From what I have said and is to be understood from the foregoing, I deduce the following propositions for our conduct vis-à-vis the African peoples:

— the closest and most friendly co-operation, if they find it useful;
— the greatest propriety, if our collaboration is dispensed with;
— defence of the territories which constitute Portugal to the limit of our human and other resources, if they see fit to turn their threats into acts of war and to bring war into our territories.

III

We have now to examine the position vis-à-vis the United Nations or rather vis-à-vis the universal government into which some are seeking to transform the United Nations with a view to furthering the objectives of their national policy.

When that body was set up and for many years thereafter, we abstained from seeking admission, as we were not convinced of the advantages which would derive therefrom. We did so later, at the request of Great Britain and of the United States, who saw in our admission a means of strengthening the position of the West in the United Nations; but as Russia, whose vote was indispensable, had precisely the same view of the matter, it became necessary to wait until a wider arrangement had been made. Thus, Portugal had plenty of time to examine the negative aspect of the question—that is, if she might not reap disadvantages from her admission in the United Nations.

We thought we should remain tranquil in view of Article 2 (7) of the Charter which prescribes: "Nothing contained in the present Charter shall authorize the United Nations to intervene in matters which are essentially within the domestic jurisdiction of any State or shall require the Members to submit such matters to settlement under the present Charter." But there was Chapter XI—Articles 73 and 74—regarding non-self-governing territories and it was prudent to see how the United Nations understood and applied it. Now, when we were admitted in the Organization, it had been peacefully settled that it was the States responsible for any territories that were competent to declare them and to consider themselves subject or not to the obligation of supplying to the Secretary General statistical or other technical information on the economic, social and educational conditions in the territories for which they were responsible.

The trouble however did not lie in giving information; it lay in the fact that, by giving information under Article 73, one necessarily accepted the orientation defined in the United Nations for certain political solutions which collided or could collide with our constitutional doctrine. These were the only points and reservations: no one could doubt our good faith nor could we doubt the good faith of the other powers, since our interpretation of the Charter was based on its letter and spirit, on the doctrine of commentators, and on the jurisprudence and practice of the Organization.

It happened, however, that two movements arose subsequently; the first tending to affirm the universality of the Organization, which may be held to be in conformity with the Charter; the other, tending to increase the powers of the General Assembly. Members of the Security Council, tired of the Russian veto, were inclined to entrust to the Assembly consideration of problems of the utmost gravity in international life; and, in the supposition that they would continue to hold the majority, entrusted those problems to it under conditions of greatly reduced guarantee. Thus it has come about that the Assembly has not only arrogated to itself a kind of generic capacity to deal with every problem in the world but has begun to regard itself as the exclusive source of its own competence.

The Charter contains provisions for its revision and amendment; but the process prescribed in Articles 108 and 109 has never been utilized. Since the massive entry of the Afro-Asian members in the organization and once these discovered the weight which they had acquired as a result of the support of the communist countries and even of others of Western formation, the United Nations has come to function as a machine whose connections with the Charter are of the slenderest and just for that very reason to constitute a menace to peace and to the orderly life of Nations. Once the principle is accepted that the doctrine of the Charter is that which the majority chooses to define in each General Assembly and that the United Nations has the competence which is attributed to it on each occasion, the functioning of the institution has become a serious risk to the nations which, not being members of any partisan blocs, belong to the inorganic minorities, do not negotiate solutions, do not trade their votes, do not join in lobby arrangements. The situation has to be studied, if the institution is to be saved, the more so as the big powers deal with their most important problems and discuss their differences outside the Organization and, in case of convenience or necessity, do not even comply with its decisions, as they have themselves declared, without running any risk thereby.

More recently, the United Nations have had as their main and most burning topic the discussion of our overseas policy and the fact that we hold that our overseas territories are and ought to continue to be integral parts of the Portuguese Nation. These campaigns should not cause surprise, given the deification of the institution and the contempt with which the majority formed around the subject regard some of the fundamental principles of the Charter. But it may perhaps be surprising that such a doctrine is adopted by the very nations which had undertaken to defend our overseas territories or declared in the past that it is necessary for the defence of the West that they should be in Portuguese hands. I recall the so-called Declaration of Windsor of 14th October, 1899, and the words which President

Roosevelt addressed me in his letter of 8th July, 1941: "In the opinion of the Government of the United States, the continued exercise of unimpaired and sovereign jurisdiction by the Government of Portugal (over all the overseas territories) offers complete assurance of security to the Western Hemisphere insofar as regions mentioned are concerned . . . . It is, consequently, the consistent desire of the United States that there be no infringement of Portuguese sovereign control over those territories." Since geography has not changed, it is difficult to admit that ideas can have changed. . . .

Communist thinking in relation to Africa is a matter of public knowledge: Lenin divided the process into three phases—anticolonialism, nationalism, communism; and though the Leninist position was revised in 1960, the general line has been maintained, and it can be said that the first phase, that is, decolonization, has been almost entirely achieved. It would be puerile to think that the most colonialist regime of our time, which imposed its domination on many free States and reduced to colonies territories which ought to have been liberated, it would be puerile to think that in this vast political operation there is a minimum of purpose to liberate African peoples. The fact is that, as Africa constitutes communities of various types together with West European countries, a disintegration of the system would by itself provoke a decline in the respective economic and political potential. The satisfaction with which we are told in some quarters that no communist societies are seen in Africa—this is said to be a proof of Moscow's incapacity to establish itself there—that satisfaction makes us smile, because what Moscow wished to do is being done by the West, while the rest of the programme will be carried out in its own good time. In any case, it is known that Russia is behind all the movements of pseudo-emancipation, sets herself up discreetly everywhere and maintains the necessary economic, political and cultural contacts with the leaders with a view to marking her presence and action without alarm. These contracts will yield fruits which will be gathered but only when they are ripe.

On the other hand, the United States makes no secret of its Africa policy: great significance attaches to the official statements and to the facts of American administration designed to work for and help with all its power set up independent States all over Africa, corresponding to the former colonies or territories integrated in European nations. From this point of view, American and Russian policies may be looked upon as parallel and the fact that the United States aids the so-called emancipation of Africa to keep it free from Russia or communist influence makes little difference to the essence of things. It matters little that one power starts from the purpose, widely invoked as a national imperative, of giving freedom to all men and peoples, while the other starts from its concept of a world revolution which is supposed to make for the full happiness of Man—the two Nations pursue the same policy, though for apparently different ends.

Beyond this, however, there is a substantial difference: while Russian policy is coherent and logical, American policy involves a serious principle of contradiction. And it is this: while the fundamental principle of the policy of the United States is to help the defence of Europe, for which it has already made sacrifices in two great wars, it begins by provoking a reduction in the potential of its European allies in favour of the potential of its enemy which is communism. The contradiction is so evident and the American position so open to doubts that the African Nations permitted themselves, at the recent Security Council, to throw out a challenge to the United States to make a choice, knowing that it was impossible for the United States to make it without sacrificing beyond repair the defence of Europe and of the West. Even if most of the African States had been inclined to fall in line with the European and pro-American policy, there would be replacement of values of a like kind. But I have already said enough to enable the inference that such is not the situation. And it may indeed be doubted if, in a given moment, Europe would accept to fight for interests which would not then be hers.

Apart from the interests of European defence badly shaken as they are by the Africa policy of the United States, one factor stands out in clear evidence: the African Continent is the big space in which the two most powerful Nations compete—the United States and Russia—or three, for Communist China has also put in her appearance there. The fact that this is known, that it is evident, has offered the African Nations great possibilities of manoeuvring in all the negotiations and claims which they advance. The political attitudes of those new States being neutralized for the time being— to put it in the most favourable light—the competition will have to go on in economic and technical domains. This phenomenon involves the risk of reaching very close to the goals which have been indicated: to the East, by the strong State economies; to the West, by the big capitalist syndicates— both aiming to capture and control markets. We cannot find it surprising if, as a result, the African Continent begins to witness—and soon enough—the era of neo-colonialism which is so much feared there.

This competition taking place in African space may well lead to an entente such as was formerly designated by definition of zones of influence but may now take another name. To avoid this, it has been suggested that the United Nations may be entrusted with the task of concerting aids, collecting and distributing financial resources and supervising their use in various coun- tries. This is a formula, but not a solution of the problem, because, in addition to keeping out all private enterprise, the lack of agreement among the sources of financial and technical aid and the origin and constitution of the majority set up in the General Assembly do not make for smooth functioning of the system. Nor has it been shown that dependence on a collective body is easier and more unassailable than that which it seeks to replace, particularly when that body is intoxicated with political and racial hatred and is convinced that it has found in the political freedom of some countries the key to all problems.

The very special relations between the Congo and the United States are well known. Consequently, no surprise was caused when the Congolese Government recognized *de jure* a kind of terrorist association set up at Leopoldville for the purpose of operating in Angola and avowedly sup- ported by funds from Americans (Statement made in Leopoldville on 28th July). On the other coast and outside the national territory, a professor of a United States university appears likewise as the leader of the liberation of Mozambique, but we do not know if he will continue to be paid by that university. These are perhaps simple coincidences, but they are nonetheless unfortunate coincidences which those in responsible positions have by no means tried to clarify; and the misfortune will be even greater when it becomes generally known that Russia also has placed at the disposal of the terrorist association referred to resources to fight for the "liberation" of Angola. This may mean that some countries do not merely defend theoretically the liberation of colonised peoples but also place some favourable pawns in position for possible games in the Portuguese Provinces.

After analysing these problems and entirely discounting the chances of a political collaboration favourable to Europe I am led to this conclusion: we should implore Providence to work the miracle of granting to the African countries, until recently led by France, England, Belgium or Italy, the possibility of finding a formula of close cooperation with those Nations such as would be capable of solving the problems which independence has created for them. That would be the best way of resisting being used as playthings in world competitions which, no matter under which flag they show up, will end by subjecting African States to unpleasant servitudes for the benefit of interests which are foreign to Africa.

This struggle against Portugal in Africa which has the United Nations for its stage and the African countries for its direct agents is merely a repetition of that which, under various pretexts, we have had to face in the past and particularly in the four decades between 1898 and 1938: now the pretext is openly political—the independence of all the Overseas Provinces; previously, certain agreements arrived at and certain uncompleted negotiations between Powers who were our friends and allies were based on our bad administration and the paucity of our resources for the suitable development of our territories. There were those, it seems, who were ready to provide such resources with liberality and Portugal was too poor and small for her to be spread over such vast areas. And now, with similar objectives, we find the argument once again in circulation.

However, since the agreements I have mentioned were never implemented, one would have thought that Portugal's overseas territories could not but have become a shameful stain of backwardness in the evolution of the African Continent. It is known that this is not so and that those territories stand comparison with the others, in Africa, and, from many points of view, have reached a higher level of development. There are three reasons for this: historically speaking, Portugal has not lived on but for the Overseas Provinces; the development of a territory in which the population is settled is operated in a way that differs from that of territories subject to purely colonial exploitation in which the "colon," once his work has finished, withdraws taking with him all that he brought and all that he has earned. Finally, since the Portuguese Overseas Provinces are not closed to foreign capital investments, these have floated great enterprises there, because private capital is attracted above all by the stability and honesty of the administration, as reflected, in practice, in security for investments. And we do not speak of the fact that the Development Plans which we have financed or guaranteed have fertilized the territories as would not, in the past, have been thought possible. It is obvious that the result would be greater and more outstanding if the criticisms addressed to us were substituted by the financial aid which we see widely distributed without the guarantees that we give and, in other cases, with very doubtful guarantees.

It is gratifying, although at the same time a little strange, to see the surprise of many of those who visit us in Africa, because, not knowing how the action of the Portuguese among the coloured peoples is processed, they find there a true multiracial society and at the same time a form of civilized and progressive life, of Western type. It is chiefly the loss of this, in the confusion in which these problems are dealt with, that should be feared. And let us hope that at least the more responsible Powers in the UN, recognizing at last our honest and productive effort, will let us continue to work in peace.

IV

. . . Some of us are particularly concerned with the expenses we are called on to bear; others with all the clamour which appears to be universal and which is raised at the United Nations against the Portuguese nation. The expenses have, up to now, been met by our surplus ordinary revenue, which is almost a miracle of our administration, and no one would or will be surprised if for the future things have to be otherwise. The pity of it is that such vast sums should not be devoted to providing material and cultural benefits for the populations instead of their being solely given over to protecting the security and the peace which were theirs and of which circumstances are now endeavouring to deprive them.

I confess that a little courage is needed to listen unperturbed to the clamour that is being raised against Portugal and to the strange judgements of men, some of them eminent and with a heavy load of responsibilities in governing peoples. If, however, we place principles on one side and, on the other, the interests and passions which are all-pervading, we shall find it possible to follow such speeches without feeling that the reasons which support our case have been shaken or considering that our right has been undermined.

There are in the world two erroneous ideas concerning our cause. Some there are who hold that outbursts of anti-Portuguese nationalism spring from the policy of oppression, which is said to be ours in Africa, as it is here, as it was in Goa, now "liberated" and unhappy in her liberation. We know by heart this theme by which it is sought either to bring about the downfall of the internal framework by throwing away the Portuguese existence of the Overseas Provinces, or to solve the overseas problems expeditiously through recourse to the subversion of the national policy. But no one seems to be able to explain how it is that this policy only yields fruits of terrorism, and even then scant and withered, when the ferment of alien interests is injected into the mass so as to leaven it.

Others believe that Portugal lives mainly on her Overseas Provinces and that their eventual loss will spell total ruin for her. The Norwegian Ambassador at the latest Security Council meeting to be devoted to us went so far as to suggest that the rich countries should contribute towards compensating us for our losses and helping us to place our life on a different basis. When it becomes possible to publish certain papers which I possess, it will be seen that the idea is not original and that this generous compensation has already been offered us in the past. The simple truth, however, is that Portugal overseas may be the victim of attack but is not for sale.

These problems in which the Nation's very existence and identity are at stake are the gravest that can face any government, since the positions taken or to be taken at each moment are decisive for all and final for the future. Some people claim that these positions are by now clear enough for firm opinions to be held about them: it has been precisely my wish to contribute to this end with the assistance which the Government can and ought to give by means of facts within its knowledge. Not that I have any doubts as to the feelings of the Portuguese people, both here and overseas, concerning the defence of the Nation's integrity: the people who work and fight will not need long discussions in order to decide the course they must take. But I can only see advantage in their pronouncing themselves in a solemn and public act on what they think of the overseas policy which the Government has been following.

The way in which the country has responded to the demands we have made on it is a lesson for us all: without hesitation, without grumbling, naturally as one who lives life, men march to inhospitable climates and distant lands doing their duty in obedience to the dictates of their heart and of the torch of faith and patriotism which lights their path. In the presence of this lesson I feel that we should not mourn the dead. Rather: we will have to mourn the dead if the living are unworthy of them.

António Salazar, Errors and Failures in the Politics of our Time, February 18, 1965[2]

In spite of the efforts of the Organization for African Unity, the divisions and incompatibilities which set the African countries against one another are becoming increasingly evident. Several countries south of the Equator have revealed their lack of trust in the disinterestedness of the Arabs who seek to assume their leadership. On the other hand, the latter and some others seek to lead the African revolution, now not merely towards the independence of colonial territories, but towards a policy that is supported, ideologically and economically, by the communist bloc. The Zanzibar revolution and the union with Tanganyika have made a breach that will be difficult to fill up. Through this area particularly but also by the west coast, there enter the ideas, the men and the weapons aimed at the heart of Africa and designed to achieve its domination by the communists.

As at the present moment no African country enjoys a sufficient state of economic and social development to enable the implantation of communism, the support given by the communist bloc will mean chiefly a substitution of western positions, those held by Europe, and a peril for African independence, as far as Africa itself is concerned. The so-called African socialism can be no more in our time than the expropriation and in

2. From Salazar, *Errors and Failures in the Politics of Our Time* (Lisbon, Secretariado Nacional da Informaçào, 1965), pp. 11–15.

many cases the seizure of property, means of production and undertakings that the Europeans set up there. Black racism insofar as it is intolerant of the presence of the white man, may be regarded as the outburst of racial incompatibility, a seeking after redress or a retaliation, but for many agitators it is no less an economic operation, though a poorly reproductive one owing to the difficulty in organizing labour and maintaining the level of production with local elements.

Those European Nations that gave up their political positions but believed that nevertheless they would be able to go on guiding the independent African peoples with their superior technical skill, the force of their capital either lent or freely given and the brilliance of their culture, have now to contend with difficult competitors foreign to the continent of Africa and who, quite apart from the political and economic implications, jeopardize the work undertaken there.

Some weeks ago subversive elements coming from Tanganyika, either directly or through Malawi, broke into Mozambique to carry out acts of sabotage and to murder black Portuguese citizens, as had been announced. They are trying to repeat there the events of Guinea and Angola with the aid and collaboration of Tanganyika, although so far much less intensely than in the other cases, since they found us prepared and alert. Tanganyika is a member State of the British Commonwealth and we are thus led to believe that Great Britain, not to mention the obligations of alliances, considers itself unable to say a word of moderation to a member of the Commonwealth that is behaving so contrary to the juridical and political good conduct due to neighbour States. To make up for this, retaliation for attacks which are protected in the countries whence they proceed is beginning to be accepted by States as normal, perfectly justified behaviour.

This is the way of the present-day world; it is within this framework that we are called upon to defend our territories. It is a pity that the three and a half billion escudos spent yearly on this defence, besides many other hundreds of thousands spent for the same purpose by the bigger provinces, cannot be applied here and there to roads, ports, schools, hospitals, the improvement of the land, the setting up of industries or the working of mines. With such amounts one could increase the happiness of many people instead of disturbing and sacrificing their lives just to feed the vanity of ideologues or of adventurers who dreamt one day of empires that have proved after all to be outside the grasp of their ambitions.

Are not these sums spent on the overseas provinces perhaps ill spent? The question cannot be posed in these terms, but only in the light of the imperative of political duty and in relation to our national resources. Duty done does not have to be an entry in a book keeping ledger; our resources are those produced by our efforts which, if necessity demands that they be even more toilsome and prolonged, will be so without hesitation.

I know that into weaker minds the enemy pours a subtle poison by stating that such problems can only be solved politically, never militarily, and that any prolongation of the struggle is ruinous for the exchequer and useless for the Nation. My answer is this: the terrorism we are obliged to combat is not an outburst of feeling of peoples who, not being part of a nation, consciously aspire to independence. It is only the work of subversive elements, the majority of them alien to the territories concerned, paid by foreign powers for their own political ends. As elements alien to the national community, they will wither away the moment they are warned off the territory where they are organized and trained and are refused political support and the aid they received in weapons and money. Thus the "political solution," if not envisaging national disintegration (which all pretend to repel), lies not in us but in those neighbour countries whom we may, by such means as we have at our disposal, gradually make to understand their obligations as responsible States with a duty to us and to the poor people who are being stupidly sacrificed to serve the interests of third parties. But, in this context, military defence is the only means of reaching a political solution that, at bottom, is to ensure order in the territories and the peaceful progress of the populations, as we had been doing.

The struggle has been going on for almost four years: has anything been gained with the money of the common folk, the blood of our soldiers and their mothers' tears? I dare to answer "yes." On the international plane, at the outset, the Portuguese position was roundly condemned; then some doubt was expressed about the validity of the reasons against it; many of the most responsible men finally recognized that after all Portugal is fighting not only to confirm a right but to defend principles and interests that are common to the entire West. On the African plane, four years of sacrifices have given time for a better clarification of the problem of the Portuguese Overseas Provinces, the diversity of the situations created in Africa in the course of centuries and the profit or loss, at any rate the difficulties which the independence so ambitiously sought by a few has brought to everyone else and which the leaders are still unable to solve. Thus several African peoples seem to us to understand better the realities of the situation and to have assumed a more moderate attitude. This is the positive gain from a battle in which we, the Portuguese of Europe and of Africa, are fighting quietly, without allies, proudly alone.

Marcello Caetano, Address on Overseas Provinces, November 28, 1968.[3]

We are all aware of the basic significance of the Overseas Provinces in Portuguese public affairs at the present time. Up to 1961 the civilizing of the peoples, and enhancement of the land, in the overseas provinces were gradually occupying an increasingly significant and outstanding part in the concern of Portuguese leaders. In that year a very violent outbreak of terrorism in Angola led to the massacre of thousands of people, at times whole families being butchered, and to the devastation of vast areas where only ruin and desolation came to reign.

The swift, forceful reaction of the people of Angola themselves, aided by the small military and police forces then available in the province, dominated events and would very quickly have overcome the insurrection but for

3. From Marcello Caetano, *Portugal's Reasons for Remaining in the Overseas Provinces* (Lisbon: Secretária de Estado da Informação e Turismo, 1970).

the material aid the insurgents received from neighbouring territories and, to say the least, the moral support of other countries which thought they might have something to gain from the destruction of Portuguese authority.

In spite of this raging storm Portugal has calmly maintained her position. Some people in various countries thought this persistence was simply born of Dr. Salazar's obstinacy in the matter. But the fact is that Portugal's attitude could not have been other.

Hundreds of thousands of white people live, work and fulfil their destiny in Angola. Many were born there, and some belong to the third, fourth or even fifth generation of families settled in the province. They are Africans. Side by side with them are millions of negroes who for centuries were only familiar with the tribal organization, its groupings and its rivalries, but who have found within the Portuguese Nation a common homeland, a basis for social intercourse and the basic conditions thanks to which, by development, they could gradually acquire the possibility of facing their problems and making use of those resources proper to the present day.

Portugal is responsible for the security of the population and the preservation of all they have created and all that forms the basis of their way of life.

Portugal cannot abandon her people, of all colours and all races, living in the overseas provinces to the caprices of violence, to furious resentment, to the hatred of clans or the tightrope manoeuvres of international politics; nor can she gamble away the values that, in the shade of her flag, have turned barbarous lands into promising territories on the high road to civilization.

Could the Portuguese watch in total calm the savage destruction of a civilized way of life?

Could the Portuguese allow racial hostility to grow and widen a gulf between two races, when the progress of southern Africa depends on their close association and collaboration?

Could the Portuguese watch the destruction of an achievement which, while incomplete like all human enterprises, is a positive expression of the institution of multiracial societies dear to, and accepted by, blacks and whites alike, in an example of understanding and collaboration that has, unluckily, few imitators in other regions?

We have declared war on nobody. We are at war with nobody. Subversion bears no name and its attacks are ordered by unidentifiable persons. We merely defend ourselves. We defend lives and property. We defend, not one civilization, but all civilization. Against the tragic improvisations that have held up the progress of the peoples of Africa and endangered world peace, we defend the steady, secure development which will lead territories to the maturing of full economic and cultural development, so as to permit the progressive participation of the natives in the work of administration and government.

In short, we are defending the real interests of the peoples who form part of the Portuguese Nation, inside which they can steadily proceed towards their goal, against catastrophic fictions which serve to hide irresponsible, detestable manifestations of neo-colonialism.

Can anyone doubt that behind the groups which make themselves out to be the defenders of the rights of the native population there are imperialist designs which struggle for world supremacy? We have constant proof of this, but nowhere so clearly as in Guinea.

The great majority of the population of Guinea are fighting with the regular forces against the terrorists. But in this province the terrorist movement appears to be far more extensively and effectively supported by the socialist powers, especially the U. S. S. R., than in other provinces. The impression is that a persevering, urgent effort is being made there, with no restriction on supplies of weapons and other aids. The reason for this special interest is not hard to find. Those responsible do not hide the fact that Guinea is a necessary basis for an attack on Cape Verde, the islands which occupy a key position on the lines of communication between the northern and southern halves of the Atlantic, and also between the two shores—east and west—of that ocean.

At a time when the Russian fleet in the Mediterranean is daily growing and when Russia is seeking to set up military bases, and cement alliances, in the Middle East and North Africa, no one can be blind to the importance of Cape Verde if it were in the power of those friendly to Russia. Europe is being surrounded.

Nowadays the security of countries cannot be defended on their frontiers. Nations are integrated into vast blocs, whose common fate they share. The liberty and independence of the countries of Western Europe is at stake both in Europe itself and in Africa. This is why we must defend Guinea: in its own interest, of course, but also on behalf of the West of Europe and even the Americas.

We Portuguese are sincere peace-lovers. I myself am one, nor can I understand how any balanced individual can desire, applaud or provoke the solution of disputes by bringing about massacre and the extensive destruction of property, with all the consequent but unforeseeable damage and extension of the strife. But this fact itself makes it the duty of those who wish to preserve the peace to discourage aggressors, as it is their duty to mete out punishment to those who disturb the peace and to restrain their activities.

In Africa we are defending the peace. We should like it only too well if fighting could stop, if the terrorists ceased to enjoy the support thanks to which they penetrate into our territories and worry and disturb their inhabitants. But until that happens the work of the authorities and the troops is increasingly directed towards winning people over rather than taking lives, to bringing forth the harvest instead of laying waste the land. But we cannot let up our efforts when faced with an adversary who would reveal himself to be true to the African tradition in being intolerant and implacable, who would unearth all old racial hates, would not hesitate to sacrifice lives and property, and would entrench at points vital to the future of southern Africa positions manned by the enemies of Portugal and of the West.

Marcello Caetano, Statement on Angola, Luanda, April 15, 1969.[4]

In our Homeland there is room for all who were born under the guiding shadow of our flag, regardless of the colour of their skin, their social customs, their religious beliefs. The Homeland is, as it were, a cauldron in which all differences melt away and all divergences mingle. In the heart of that Homeland an open society is developing, providing a communion of races and classes, as a further step towards a real community of life and culture. This lovable Homeland is the synthesis of the natural qualities of a hard-working, affable, long-suffering people, capable of all forms of generosity and ready to make any sacrifice.

Angola is part of that wide Homeland, great Angola where, over five centuries, the characteristics of the Portuguese mentality have taken deep root, and which, in its turn, has made so great a contribution to the universal features of the Portuguese-speaking world, in Europe, Brazil and the African Provinces.

To provide Angola as quickly as possible with the future which belongs to it by right, all forms of loyal collaboration are desirable. We are open to the entrance of capital, to try out new forms of enterprise, to apply new techniques. We only seek to prevent any loss of the concern to enhance the land and people of Angola above all. We find the concept of an economy of exploitation repellent.

The contemporary economy must be imbued with a deeply humanist sense. We are only interested in wealth when it really serves man. Man is God's creature, from whom the light of the mind shines forth, and he cannot be only in theory the king of Nature. All men must be given an actual share in the benefits that human ingenuity manages to wrest from the world about us. We want Angola to be rich and prosperous, but we do not want the children of Angola to be strangers to the wealth and prosperity of their homeland.

Let us boldly face the difficulties! Let us not be cast down by the temptations of discouragement, much less let ourselves be poisoned by the virus of disbelief in the virtue of our own efforts! Angola has set before the world admirable examples of constancy, firmness, energy, perseverance and victory. In combat it is the most obstinate that win the battle. The secret of triumph lies in the strength of one's will to conquer.

Angola is quite firmly determined to remain Portuguese!

Angola, Portuguese Angola or Angolan Portugal, has a brilliant future before it, clearly visible, a future that all we Portuguese together shall gain, to show the world, to the good of Africa, to the greater glory and enhancement of Portugal!

4. From Caetano, *Portugal's Reasons* . . . .

THE ROLE OF CONTIGUOUS STATES

The hospitality of a contiguous state can be decisive for political exiles from or insurgents within a territory such as Angola. For the host state, it can mean an opportunity to influence events in a fashion congenial to its own interests; but it can also mean risking that revolutionary guests with their own political agendas will prove difficult to control.

These two sides of the contiguous state coin are illustrated by the two documents below. The first is the report of the OAU mission recommending collective and exclusive recognition of the GRAE, a client movement of the Democratic Republic of the Congo (Zaire). Noting that the OAU mission had a "difficult task," the losing contender, in this instance the MPLA, later lamented the powerful influence that contiguous states can have: "At the garden party given upon the Mission's arrival [in Léopoldville], Mr. Adoula [the Congolese premier] warned its members against any attempt to make him revise his decision. For him there is nothing but FNLA/ GRAE."[1]

The second document reflects an effort by Zambia, which bordered on four territories facing active or latent nationalist insurgency, to regulate exile activities and assure its own political authority. The Zambian government had already issued regulations severely restricting the operations of liberation movements. Each was permitted one office in Lusaka with no more than six officeholders. None was to campaign for funds in Zambia. And all activity outside Lusaka required special permission.[2] Faced with a danger of reprisals from target states (Angola, Mozambique,

1. MPLA, "Reminder on the Angolan Question for the OAU Conference of Foreign Ministers" (Lagos, Feb. 24, 1964, mimeo.).

2. Regulations established in January 1965. *Africa Research Bulletin* (PSC series) 2, no. 1 (Jan. 1965): 228.

Rhodesia and South Africa), the Zambian government followed up with the additional constraints of its November 1965 directive.

General Report of the Goodwill Mission of the Coordinating Committee for the Liberation of Africa to the Angolan Nationalists, Léopoldville, July 13–18, 1963.

The Coordinating Committee for the Liberation of Africa at its meeting in Dar es Salaam on July 1, 1963, at the express wish of the two main Angolan Nationalist Movements (FNLA and MPLA) and following the recognition by the Government of Congo (Léopoldville) of the Revolutionary Government of Angola in Exile (GRAE) decided to send a Goodwill Mission consisting of the Heads of Delegations of Algeria, Congo (Léopoldville), Guinea, Nigeria, and Uganda, members of the aforementioned committee—to Léopoldville in order to help reconcile the various Angolan Nationalist Movements.[3]

The Goodwill Mission in the discharge of its functions of reconciliation, was to bear in mind the following principles laid down by the Coordinating Committee as the basis of the future activity of the Committee in extending assistance, financial or otherwise, to the Nationalist Movements of non-independent Africa:

(a)   In considering aid to any given colonial or dependent territory, the relation, concern and interest of the immediate neighboring independent African countries with contiguous boundaries must be taken into consideration as well.

(b)   Independent countries geographically contiguous to a given non-independent territory because of their local knowledge and proximity, should play a vital role in the advancement and progress of that territory to the goal of liberation and independence.

(c)   As a condition of assistance the Committee should insist on the creation of one Common Action Front in each territory.

(d)   In case of failure to get a Common Action Front the Committee should reserve the right of selection and recognition of the movement entitled to assistance.

(e)   The Committee should insist that Movements themselves be broad based internally and have effective following or popular support within the territory.

(f)   The Common Front must submit a statement of account at regular intervals to the Committee.

(g)   In the case of a Liberation Movement operating in an independent country, the host country should be given the right of supervision.

(h)   Where an independent State is used as a base for the purpose of liberation of a colonial territory, care must be taken to evolve such a

3. Already scheduled to participate in similar hearings on Guinea-Bissau, Senegal was added at the last minute as a member of the mission.

policy of action as would not lead to the destruction of the sovereignty and independence of that State or prejudicing its security.

Sittings

The Goodwill Mission assembled in Léopoldville on Saturday, 13 July, 1963 in an informal meeting and suggested a provisional agenda.

The Goodwill Mission then adjourned to meet again next day, Sunday, 14 July, 1963, at 10 A.M. when it elected the leader of the Nigerian Delegation, Hon. Jaja Wachaku, the Minister of Foreign Affairs and Commonwealth Relations of the Federation of Nigeria to its chairman and agreed on the following agenda:

1. Election of Chairman.
2. Chairman's explanation of the purpose of the Goodwill Mission to the Angolan Nationalists.
3. Hearing of statements by Angolan Nationalists—
   (a) FNLA
   (b) MPLA
4. Receiving views of the Congolese Government.
5. Conclusions and Recommendations.

At this meeting the Goodwill Mission also agreed to coopt Senegal as a member considering that Senegal is a member of the Standing Committee on General Policy.

On Monday, 15 July, the meeting of the Goodwill Mission was opened with the Chairman's speech in which he explained the purpose of the mission to the Angolan Nationalists. This portion of the meeting was open to the public. The text of the Chairman's speech is hereby attached.

After the Chairman's opening remark, the meeting adjourned for a short period to enable the public to withdraw. After the withdrawal of the press and members of the public, the mission resumed sitting in private session and took up the third item on its agenda. The Goodwill Mission spent the whole of Monday on this item. When it resumed on Tuesday, 16 July, it continued with the same item and later took up item four of the agenda and heard the views of the representatives of the Government of the Republic of Congo (Léopoldville).

On Wednesday, 17 July, the Goodwill Mission considered the evidence it heard and agreed on the basic conclusions and recommendations. After deciding on the form in which its report and findings should be presented, the Committee adjourned in order to allow time for the drafting of the findings and conclusions.

The Goodwill Mission resumed on Thursday, 18 July, and after approving its report and findings, invited the representatives of the Angolan Nationalist Movements to their closing session. The press was once more admitted when the findings and the recommendations of the Goodwill Mission were read to the Angolan Nationalists.

Hearings

Invitations were issued to the following organizations to give evidence before the Committee:

(a)   FNLA, led by Mr. Holden Roberto;

(b)   MPLA, led by Dr. Agostinho Neto.

In giving his evidence, Mr. Holden Roberto was supported by a number of persons who represented the organization in Dar es Salaam, as well as leaders from different parts of Angola. Dr. Agostinho Neto declined to give evidence on behalf of the MPLA on the grounds that a new front, the FDLA, of which he was the President, had been formed. The Committee was not, however, prepared to listen to him in this capacity as its mandate clearly stated that it was to help reconcile the two known Angolan Nationalist Organizations which gave evidence at Dar es Salaam.

During its meeting the Goodwill Mission received a letter from a Mr. da Cruz seeking an opportunity to speak on behalf of the "Provisional Steering Committee of the MPLA."

This request was considered and the views expressed were heard in the presence of other Angolan nationalists. Dr. Agostinho Neto, who was present was invited to comment on the points made by Mr. da Cruz, and answered the questions from members of the Committee in connection with the MPLA and the strength of its political and military following.

The views of the Government of the Republic of Congo on the liberation of Angola were expressed by the Minister of Justice, His Excellency Mr. Justin Bomboko and the Minister of Foreign Affairs, His Excellency Mr. Mabika-Kalanda.

Summary of Evidence

The Goodwill Mission heard evidence of the FNLA from the time it was formed by the two political parties, UPA and PDA. The developments that followed the revolution in Angola were explained as well as the formation of the Revolutionary Government of Angola in exile which was recently recognized by the Government of the Republic of Congo (Léopoldville). The Committee heard evidence of the scope of activity and the extent of the following of the FNLA. Information about the organization's fighting strength was given as well as the territory of Angola it had under its control. The Goodwill Mission was informed of the efforts that the FNLA was making to give more Angolans military and other training.

The Goodwill Mission was informed that there had been a split in the MPLA, that a good number of the few people who have received military training under the auspices of that organization had either gone over to the FNLA, left the MPLA, or those still with the MPLA are not involved in any military action. There was evidence of the strength and following of the MPLA and compared with that of the FNLA, the MPLA's support and following seemed rather small.

The Congolese Government gave the Goodwill Mission the reason which led it to recognize the Revolutionary Government of Angola in exile and also informed the Mission of the support it was giving to the Angolan Nationalist Organizations towards the liberation of their country.

Conclusion

The Goodwill Mission, after considering all the facts available to it, came to the following conclusions:

(1) that the Fighting Force of the FNLA for the liberation of Angola is by

far larger than any other, is the most effective, and indeed the only real fighting front in Angola.

(2) that the best channel for extending aid to the fighters for Angolan Liberation is through the Government of the Republic of Congo (Léopoldville).

(3) that the continued separate existence of another minor front such as the MPLA is detrimental to the rapid achievement of independence by the Angolan peoples.

(4) that it is necessary for the FNLA to continue the leadership that has so far proved effective.

Recommendations

The Goodwill Mission agreed to the following recommendations:

(1) that all aid from Africa and/or foreign countries to the Angolan Nationalist Front should be channeled through the Government of the Republic of Congo (Léopoldville) in cooperation, of course, with the Coordinating Committee for the Liberation of Africa.

(2) that the FNLA should be the only fighting front for the Liberation of Angola.

(3) that the organization of other fronts in Angola should be discouraged and the present fighting force of the MPLA should join the FNLA.

(4) that units and persons who have received military training for the liberation of Angola should be requested to seek admission into the FNLA Fighting Front.

(5) that all African Governments be requested not to entertain or offer help to other organizations in their territory who claim to be working for the liberation of Angola.

(6) that the Goodwill Mission requests the Council of Ministers of OAU at its next meeting in Dakar to recommend to all independent African States to accord recognition to the Revolutionary Government of Angola in Exile as this is a very effective and positive action against Portugal, and for the speedy liberation of Angola.

Zambian Instructions to Angolan Nationalist Organizations, November 4, 1965.

Ref: S/OP/119/06

OFFICE OF THE PRESIDENT,
P.O. Box 208,
Lusaka.
4th November, 1965.

The Chief Representative,
The Union of Populations of Angola,
P.O. Box 2358,
Lusaka

     Certain activities by some Alien Nationalist Organisations have been brought to the attention of His Excellency the President who has directed that clear instructions explaining the policy of the Government should be issued to cover the points concerned in order to ensure that there is no room for misunderstanding in the future.

Firstly, there is the question of citizens of Zambia. It must be understood clearly by all Nationalist Organisations that the recruitment of Zambians by such organisations for military training or for any activity associated with such organisations will not be countenanced by the Government.

Secondly, there is the question of alien nationals who are ordinarily resident in Zambia. Although such people are not Zambians it is clear that they have chosen to reside in Zambia and, therefore, their interests must be protected. In the event of any foreign nationalist organisation wishing to recruit for military training a foreign national who is ordinarily resident in Zambia, application must be made to the Office of the President setting out the name and address of the individual concerned, the type of training for which he is being recruited and the country in which it is proposed the training should take place. No actual recruitment of such persons should be commenced until authority has been obtained from the Office of the President.

Thirdly, there is the question of the movement through Zambia of foreign nationals who have been recruited from their countries of origin for training in other African States or overseas countries. It is the policy of this Government to assist foreign nationalist organisations in their respective struggles for independence. Nevertheless the Immigration laws of Zambia must be complied with and before any foreign nationals are brought into Zambia prior authority must be obtained from the Ministry of Home Affairs. This will not be given unless the persons concerned are documented and until the Government of the country to which the persons concerned are proceeding has confirmed that it will accept them. In the event of foreign nationals entering Zambia of their own accord it is the view of the Government that the Headquarter Organisations in Lusaka must be responsible for such individuals and must report their arrival and intentions to the Ministry of Home Affairs.

The opportunity is also taken of reminding officials of Alien Nationalist Parties that the Government of the Republic of Zambia will not agree to the Territory of Zambia being used as a military base for operations by followers of such parties who have received military training elsewhere.

The Ministry of Home Affairs is issuing separate instructions regarding compliance with the Immigration Laws of Zambia.

The above instructions are to be complied with strictly and if it comes to the notice of the Government that any foreign nationalist organisation is not complying strictly with them the Government will take whatever action it considers necessary. This may result in the withdrawal of recognition from the organisation concerned.

D.C. Mulaisho
Permanent Secretary

Office of the President

THE LIBERATION STRUGGLE
IN A WORLD CONTEXT

On February 7, 1974, a few weeks before the Lisbon coup, Agostinho Neto set forth his political weltanschauung in a lecture at the University of Dar es Salaam. Entitled "Who is the Enemy? What is Our Objective?" and written for an audience of intellectual peers, it offers insight into the thinking of the man who would in less than two years time become the first president of independent Angola.

He introduced his address by stating that it would reflect both his personal experience and the "common desire of men in the world to regard themselves as free." He continued:

In my opinion, the national liberation struggle in Africa cannot be dissociated from the present context in which it is taking place; it cannot be isolated from the world. A workers' strike in England, the imposition of fascism on the Chilean people or an atomic explosion in the Pacific are all phenomena of this same life that we are living and in which we are seeking ways to a happy existence for man in this world. This universal fact is however rendered particular in Africa through current political, economic and cultural concepts.

The historical bonds between our peoples and other peoples in the world are becoming ever closer, since there can be no other trend on earth. Isolation is impossible and is contrary to the idea of technical, cultural and political progress.

The problem facing us Africans now is how to transform unjust relations with other countries and peoples in the world, generally relations of political and economic subordination, without this transformation taking place to the detriment of the social progress which must of necessity be injected into action to win freedom, and without which one's behavior would be that of a man coming out of one form of discrimination only to fall into another as negative as the first; as a simple inversion of the intervening factors. And within this same African society, the national liberation movement also seeks to ensure that the internal socio-economic forces, that is, those that evolve within each country, are restructured in the direction of progress.

In Africa we are making every effort to put a final end to paleo-colonialism, which barely exists today in the territories dominated by Portugal, contrary to the general belief, since they are in fact dominated by a vast imperialist partnership which is unjustly protecting the selfish interests of men, economic organizations, and groups of countries.

The so-called white minority racist regimes are merely a consequence and a special form of paleo-colonialism in which links with the metropoles have become slack and less distinct in favor of a white minority dictatorship. This visible, clear and open form of colonialism does not prevent the existence on our continent of another more subtle form of domination which goes by the name of neo-colonialism, in which he who exploits is no longer identified by the name coloniser, but acts in the same way at various levels.

However, internal forms of subjugation caused by fragmentation into small ethnic or linguistic groupings, by the development of privileged classes endowed with their own dynamism, are also forms of oppression linked with the visible forms known as colonialism, old or new, and racism. They easily ally themselves with imperialism and facilitate its penetration and influence.

These phenomena are universal and they are found or have been found in all societies in the world, but at the present time they are acute and very tangible in Africa, and it is here that they most concern us Africans, as well as other nations with which we have relations either of subjugation or cooperation.

Colonial and racist domination and oppression are exercised in different ways and at different levels. They do not take place in a uniform way on our continent, they do not always use the same agents, and they do not always act on the same social stratum or on the same type of political or economic organization. For this reason, everyone, whether colonizer or colonized, feels in a different way this phenomenon which is today anachronistic and which it is desired to replace by other kinds of relations (and we Africans are not yet very clear or very much in agreement on these new kinds of relations).

Whereas for some people colonialism meant and still means forced labor, to others it is a racial discrimination, while for still others it is economic segregation and the impossibility of political advancement. But the plunder of African lands by the colonizers, the enslavement of the worker, corporal punishment and the intensive exploitation of the wealth that belongs to us are forms of the same colonialism; and the capacity of each person to apply himself to the dynamics of solving the colonial problem, with greater or lesser intelligence and clarity, depends on a broad understanding of all these factors.

And, as previously stated, action against colonialism is closely linked with and part of something else of an apparently internal nature, but which is in fact as universal as the first, which is the need for social transformations, so that humanity may be truly free in every country and every continent in the world. The way in which this aspect of the problem is tackled is also very important to the stand taken and the line to be followed in the liberation process. These two crucial problems of our continent and of our era are therefore closely interconnected with relations with foreign peoples, on the one hand, and with the relations among the ready forces within each country.

The correctness of attitude and the emotional intensity with which we embark upon action for liberation depend on how we see the world, how we foresee our country's future and the extent to which we feel in our skin the action of the foreign forces. The national liberation struggle in our era is therefore influenced not only by the historical factors determining colonialism, neo-colonialism or racist regimes, but also by its own prospects, its objectives and the way each person sees the world and life. Reaction to foreign domination, whether individual, collective or organized, must of necessity be influenced by the two factors mentioned, which have to do with both past and future history.

This is why the importance of the national liberation movements is much greater than is generally admitted, because through their activity they are transforming themselves into accelerators of history, of the development of the society within which they are acting and also outside it, imparting fresh dynamism to social processes to transcend the present stage, even that in politically independent countries.

The different types of colonization in Africa have endowed us Africans with different ways of seeing the problem of liberation, and it is natural that it should be thus, since our consciousness cannot draw upon material to form itself except from the field of lived experience and from our possibilities of knowing the world. Sometimes we differ in our concepts and, hence, in the practical implementation of combat programs, and the line taken in action for liberation does not always fulfill the twofold need to concentrate both on transforming the relations between peoples and intrinsically transforming the life of the nation. Hence the need to see the problem clearly and to provide clear answers to the following specific questions:

(1) *Who is the enemy and what is the enemy?*
(2) *What is our objective?*

The answers to these questions do not depend simply on the desire to be free; they also depend on knowledge and on a concept of the world and life, on lived experience. This means that they cannot be dissociated from acquired political ideas, from ideological positions which generally result from the origins of each and every one of us. Without wishing to go into an analysis of the Angolan problem in its specific aspects, I should nevertheless like to clarify the ideas I have just put forward and shall put forward later, basing myself on my own experience.

Angola is a vast country which today has a very low population density and which has been colonized by the Portuguese since 1482. This is the generally accepted idea. However, as far as colonization is concerned, Portugal did not succeed in dominating all of our territory on its first contact. It took centuries before it was able to impose its political and economic rule over the whole of our people. And I wish again to emphasize that neither is it true that Angola is dominated only by Portugal. The world is sufficiently enlightened on this point to know that the political and economic interests of several world powers are involved in Angola. Portugal's administration has not prevented the presence of its partners, a presence which has been there for centuries. For example, Great Britain, the country with the largest volume of capital investments in Angola, and the United States of America, with growing economic interests and longing to control our country's strategic position, as well as other countries of Europe, America, and Asia, are competing for the domination of our people and the exploitation of the wealth that belongs to us.

Small and backward Portugal is not the chief factor of colonization. Without the capital of other countries, without growing investments and technical cooperation, without complicity at various levels, radical transformations would already have taken place many years ago.

Therefore, if we can say that Portugal is the manager of a series of politico-economic deals, we will see that it is not our principal enemy but merely our direct enemy. At the same time, it is the weakest link in the whole chain established for the domination of peoples. If we look at Portugal itself, at the internal picture it presents, we see a society which is still striving to transcend an obsolete form of oligarchic government, incapable of abandoning the use of violence against its people for the benefit of just a few families, with a peasant class struggling in the most dire poverty in Europe, and where every citizen feels himself a prisoner in his own country. The Portuguese themselves are right when they say that their country is today one of the greatest disgraces of Europe and the world.

The enemy of Africa is often confused with the white man. Skin color is still a factor used by many to determine the enemy. There are historical and social reasons and lived facts which consolidate this idea on our continent. It is absolutely understandable that a worker in the South African mines who is segregated and coerced, and whose last drop of sweat is wrung from him should feel that the white man he sees before him, for whom he produces wealth, is the principal enemy. It is for him that he builds cities and well-paved roads and maintains hygienic and salubrious conditions which he himself does not have. Consciousness, as I have said, is formed chiefly from one's experience of life. The experience of South Africa could lead to this immediate conclusion, which is to a certain extent logical and emotionally valid.

All the more so in that the society created by the colonialists, to come back to the case of Angola, created various racial defense mechanisms which were made to serve colonialism. The same poor, wretched and oppressed peasant who is exploited in his own country is the object of special attention when he establishes himself in one of "its" colonies. He is not only imbued with a lot of jingoism, but he also starts to enjoy economic and social privileges which he could never have before. Thus he becomes a part of the system. He starts to get a taste for colonialism and becomes a watchdog of the interests of the fascist oligarchy.

However, deep in their hearts both the watchdog and the exploiter nonetheless feel themselves slaves of the system as a whole. We can therefore say today that the phenomenon of colonial or neo-colonial oppression in our continent cannot be seen in terms of the color of individuals.

The same system as oppresses and exploits the peasant in Portugal also oppresses and exploits the Angolan citizen, using different motivation, different techniques, but always with the same goal—to exploit. And the establishment of just relations is possible between Portuguese people and Angolan, Mozambican and Guinean people, that is, the establishment of relations which prevent the exploitation of one people by another. The racial factor will play only a secondary role, and for a little time more, once relations between master and slave are ended.

An ideological understanding of this problem also makes it easier to solve it once the objectives of the liberation struggle are defined. In special conditions there are already cases where the racial problem is overcome. This is what happens in the war. There are conscious Portuguese who desert to join the nationalist ranks in one way or another. Our experience of clandestine struggle showed that there can be such racial cooperation in the struggle against the system.

In terms of what we basically want, I do not think that the national liberation struggle is directed towards inverting systems of oppression in such a way that the master of today will be the slave of tomorrow. To think in this way is to go against the current of history. Attitudes of social revenge can never be what we want, which is the freedom of humanity.

And I should like again to emphasize that the liberation struggles are not aimed solely at violently correcting the relations between peoples and especially the production relations *within the country*—they are an important factor for the positive transformation of our entire continent and the whole world. The national liberation struggle is also a means of overthrowing a whole unjust system of oppression existing in the world. Let us look at the question pragmatically: We do not find a single country in Africa which does not maintain preferential relations with its former metropole, even through the absorption of the inevitable cultural values of a regime of a colonial type. What is more, the forms of exploitation do not end and neither, consequently, do the forms of racial discrimination, accentuated to a greater or lesser degree. In such cases, liberation is not yet complete.

Under independence in which there is not merely apparent political independence, but also economic and cultural independence, where respect for true national values exists, so as to make it possible to abolish exploitation, I believe that the human society would find true freedom.

To answer our question, we would say that the enemy is colonialism, the colonial system, and also imperialism, which sustains the former, to the point of being the principal enemy. These enemies use on their own behalf all the contradictions they can find in the dominated society: racial, tribal, class and other factors. On them they build their foundation for exploitation and maintain it, changing its appearance when it can no longer be maintained.

Thus, in Africa formal political domination can no longer prevail, but no one is yet free from economic domination. It is present there, and it is for this very reason that I am very pleased by the formula adopted by some political parties in power in Africa when they say that they too are national liberation movements. This expresses the full significance of the phenomenon of liberation. This broader concept of national liberation has vitally important consequences as regards the necessary cooperation between the oppressed of the world. I shall therefore go on to say that national liberation must be a stage for the achievement of a vaster form of liberation, which is the liberation of humanity. If one loses sight of this idea, dynamism disappears and the essential contradictions in a country remain..

The Angolan experience has already shown that pure anti-racism cannot permit the full development of the liberation struggle. For centuries our society has had within it white people who came as occupiers, as conquerors, but who had time to establish roots, to multiply, and to live for generations and generations on our territory. This white population dominates the urban centers, giving rise to the fact of people who are racially mixed, making our society interlinked in its racial components. If the liberation struggle overlooks the realities of the country, and if formulations are taken up which are pleasing to nationalists who are sincere but not over-concerned about the aspect of the people's socio-historical development, it weakens itself and cannot attain its political and human objectives. Everyone in a country who wants to participate in whatever way in the liberation struggle should be able to do so.

The preoccupation in Africa of making the liberation struggle a racial struggle of blacks against whites is not only superficial, but we can say that it is reactionary and that this view has no future at the very time when we see more contact between blacks and whites on the continent than in the era of colonialism. The expanded relations with socialist countries and with countries which are against colonialism (in its old form), and the so-called relations of cooperation with the former metropoles have brought to Africa a noteworthy number of Europeans, Americans and Asians, more than there have ever been in any era of Africa's history. Therefore, to pose the problem as one of black against white is to falsify the question and deflect us from our objective.

What we want is an independent life as a nation, a life in which economic relations are just both between countries and within the country, a revival of cultural values which are still valid for our era.

The literary concept of negritude, born of philosophico-literary trends which have had their day, like existentialism and surrealism, posed with discernment the problem of arousing the cultural consciousness of the black man in the world, irrespective of the geographical area to which he had been dispersed. Like the idea of Pan-Africanism, the concept of negritude started at a certain point to falsify the black problem. It is and was correct to heighten the essence of cultural values which black people took to all the continents, and predominantly to the American continent. Our culture must be defended and developed, which does not mean that it must remain stagnant. Basically, and as various thinkers have asserted, the national liberation struggle is a struggle for culture. But I do not believe that cultural links in any way prevent political compartmentalisation. This has been an equivocal point in many alleged demonstrations of national liberation.

I cannot fail to express my full political identification with the struggle of the black peoples of America where they are, and to admire the vitality of descendents of Africans who today are still oppressed and segregated in American society, especially in the United States. I say *especially* in the United States, because I do not very much believe in the full freedom of blacks or the national equality in Brazil of which they talk so much and are trying to convince us. The social advancement of the black American has been noteworthy, to the extent that today the black American distinguishes himself in Africa not only by his comportment but also by his intellectual and technical level.

Only rarely do the physical characteristics of black Americans allow any doubt as to their country of origin. Thus, the phenomenon of miscegenation has produced a new kind of person. The type that the ordinary person in Angola calls a white person or a mulatto is a black person in the United States. There is therefore no physical identity and there are strong cultural differences, as there could not fail to be. Therefore, without confusing origins with political compartments, America is America and Africa is Africa.

Today we are all linked in solidarity in a liberation struggle against oppressors who have the same color, but tomorrow there will certainly be different social personalities to be preserved. And the evolutionary process of mankind through which differences are obliterated cannot but bring about an even greater mingling of the now antagonistic ethnic groups in the United States. America has its own life, just as Angola and Mozambique have their own life. Although we have to identify with each other as black men in defending our values, I cannot conceal my sometimes illfounded concern at the way some of our brothers from the other side of the Atlantic have a messianic desire to find a Moses for a return to Africa. For many this theory is certainly out of date.

But I should like to return to the question of knowing who is our enemy. As stated previously, according to my understanding the first reactions against a system of oppression stem from the way one lives, from the way one feels this oppression. I cited the case of South Africa.

I do not wish to ignore at this moment the pressure that is exerted on the liberation movements to maintain so-called *black purity*. The case of America, where the racial struggle is the most apparent to the blacks, is often cited. What I am saying should not be taken as criticism of our brave black American brothers, who know better than anyone how to orient their struggle, how to envisage the transformation of American society so that man will be free there. But allow me also to reject any idea on the transformation of the national liberation struggle in Angola into a racial struggle.

I would say that in Angola the struggle *also* assumes racial aspects since discrimination is a fact. The black man is exploited there. But it is fundamentally a struggle against the colonial system and its chief ally, imperialism. I also reject the idea of black liberation, since the unity of Africa is one of the principles universally accepted by the OAU, and knowing that in Africa there are Arab peoples, that there are some areas which are not black. The problem cannot be purely racial. So long as there is imperialism, it will be possible to continue colonialism. And as I have said, for us they are the enemies.

What we want is to establish a new society where black and white can live together. Naturally, and so as not to be misinterpreted, I must add that the democratic process must be exercised in such a way that the most exploited masses (who are black) have control of political power, since they can go furthest in establishing proper rights for all. A people's struggle for political power, for economic independence, for the restoration of cultural life, to end alienation, for relations with all peoples on a basis of equality and fraternity—these are the objectives of our struggle.

These objectives are set by defining who is the enemy, by defining who are the people and what is the character of our struggle, which is a revolutionary struggle affecting not only the foundations of the colonial system but also the foundations of our own society as a nation and as a people. But can such liberation take place at this stage?

We are in a period in which the imperialist forces are deploying themselves on the African scene with dynamism and tenacity. Together with the Portuguese colonialists, with the racist regimes in Southern Africa, imperialism is present on our continent. Its influence can be felt. Its activity is causing alarm in the life of Africa. Neo-colonialism is a fact. Everywhere in Africa there is still the need to struggle for independence, whether political in some areas, economic in others, or cultural almost everywhere. Imperialism is doing everything it can to maintain sources of raw materials and cheap labor. This is a phenomenon which is being debated not only in Africa but in the whole of the so-called Third World.

In a world divided into blocs, among which it was customary to distinguish between the socialist bloc and the capitalist block, non-alignment has arisen to try to seek a balance and to defend the less developed. And within this division, it is the socialists who hold high the banner of internationalism and in fact give the most support to the liberation movements. But today the socialist camp is divided, weakened by irreconcilable ideological concepts, and the relations of solidarity which made these countries an impenetrable iron fortress have broken down and are taking a long time to be restored. The relations of solidarity have changed and conflicts of greater or lesser importance have marred the avowed ideal of socialism.

Thus, in the same way as a number of African countries have on their markets products from countries dominated by the enemy, from South Africa, Portugal and Rhodesia, we see with great concern the increase by some socialist countries of commercial and cultural relations with especially Portugal. So, let us be realistic, the national liberation struggle in Africa does not have very sound bases in the international arena, and it is not political or ideological affinities that count, nor even the objectives themselves, for in most cases other interests dominate relations between the liberation forces and the world. We are in another era. The world is changing and we have to take note of this fact.

Thus, there are many cracks through which the enemy can penetrate. However, an essential factor we must recognize is that the national liberation struggle is today a cause which few people fail to support, with greater or lesser sincerity. Political independence for the African majority is an attainment of our time. And since various political currents and ideological trends are involved, with sometimes antagonistic interests, the liberation movements find themselves at grips with the problem of their political and ideological independence, the problem of preserving their personality, which must reflect the social image of the country.

To preserve independence is not easy, and sometimes the struggle is affected by our own contradictions. And contradictions can stem from different concepts from which our definition of who is the enemy and of our objectives derives. Some would like to see the liberation movement take the direction of a class struggle, as in Europe. Others would like to see it tribalized, federalized, according to their idea of a country which they do not know. Others, idealists, would like to see us heading along the path to political compromise with the enemy.

These efforts to transform the liberation movements into satellites of parties in power, subject to unacceptable paternalism, and caused by the fact that most of the liberation movements conducting an armed struggle have to do so from outside their countries.

Exile has its effects: "The worst thing the Portuguese did to us," said one of my most intelligent friends, "was to oblige us to wage a liberation struggle from abroad." I agree.

The Organization of African Unity, which has done something, especially politically, to promote the national liberation movements, will still have to help them enough for them to be independent, respecting the conventions and the programmatic involvement of different organizations, in accordance with the realities of the country. The dialogue between independent Africa and dependent Africa is still not satisfactory, and for this very reason the political battles are not taking place with the required force.

... We could, for example, cooperate on economic matters so as to wage the battle in this field too. With regard to Portugal, its plunder of our resources, like oil, coffee, diamonds, iron, etc., products which are marketed by international bodies in which Africans participate, could be prevented or at least decreased.

And what harm would there be in involving the liberation movements in discussions on the crucial problems of our times which will certainly affect the development of our continent, like for example the broader association of Africa with the Common Market, or problems of European security? And the problem of Southern Africa? . . .

A PARTIAL LIST OF ANGOLAN NATIONALIST MOVEMENTS—1962–1976

I. *MPLA-Related*

CVAAR	Corpo Voluntário Angolano de Assistência dos Refugiados
EPLA	Exército Popular de Libertação de Angola
FAPLA	Forças Armadas Popular para Libertação de Angola
FDLA	Frente Democrática de Libertação de Angola
JMPLA	Juventude do MPLA
MPLA	Movimento Popular de Libertação de Angola
OMA	Organização das Mulheres de Angola
———	Revolta Activa (MPLA dissidents)
———	Revolta do Leste (MPLA dissidents)
SAM	Serviço de Assistência Médica do MPLA
UEA	União dos Estudantes Angolanos

II. *FNLA-Related*

AMA	Associação das Mulheres de Angola
ELNA	Exército de Libertação Nacional de Angola
FNLA	Frente Nacional de Libertação de Angola
GRAE	Govêrno Revolucionário de Angola no Exílio
JDA	Jeunesse Democrate de l'Angola
JFNLA	Jeunesse-FNLA
JUPA	Juventude-UPA
MFDA	Mouvement de Femmes Democrates de l'Angola
PDA	Partido Democrático de Angola
SARA	Serviço de Assistência aos Refugiados de Angola
UNEA	Uniao Nacional dos Estudantes Angolanos
UPA	União das Populações de Angola

III. *UNITA-Related*

AMANGOLA	Amigos do Manifesto Angolano
CPAD	Comitê Preparatório da Acção Directa
FALA	Forças Armadas de Libertação de Angola (UNITA)
PARA	Partido de Acção Revolucionária Angolana

| UNEA | União Nacional dos Estudantes Angolanos |
| UNITA | União Nacional para a Independência Total de Angola |

IV. *CPA-Related*

CASA	Centro de Assistência Sócio-Sanitária
CNE	Comissão Nacional Executivo
CPA	Conselho do Povo Angolano
CPCP	Gomité Préparatoire du Congrès Populaire Angolais
CUNA	Comitê Unidade Nacional Angolana
FALA	Forças Armadas de Libertação de Angola (CPA)
JUNA	Movimento de Juventude Nacional Angolana
PNA	Partido Nacional Africano
UNA	União Nacional Angolana

V. *Ethnic/Regional: Bakongo*

AJEUNAL	Alliance des Jeunes Angolais pour la Liberté
CBOA	Comité des Bons Offices Angolais
CNA	Cartel des Nationalistes Angolais (Tulenga)
CUNA	Comitê Unidade Nacional Angolana
FPIKP	Front Patriotique pour l'Indépendance du Kongo Dit Portugais
MDIA	Movimento de Defesa dos Interesses de Angola
MNA	Movimento Nacional Angolano
MPAA	Movimento Popular Africano de Angola
NGWIZAKO	Ngwizani a Kongo also, Aliança, or Associação, dos Conguenses de Expressão Portuguesa
NTOBAKO	Nto-Bako Angola
PPA	Parti Progressiste Angolais
PRPA	Partido de Reunificação do Povo Angolano
RCCKP	Rassemblement des Chefs Coutumiers du Congo Portugais
UNA	União Nacionalista Angolano
UPRONA	União Progressista de Nsosso em Angola União Progressista Nacional de Angola

VI. *Ethnic/Regional: Central Angola*

ATCAR	Association des Tshokwe du Congo de l'Angola et de la Rhodésie
CAK	Comité des Angolais au Katanga
CSRSA	Comitê Secreto Revolucionário do Sul de Angola
PNA	Partido Nacional Africano
UNA	União Nacional Angolano
UNASA	União Nacional dos Africanos do Sul de Angola

VII. *Cabinda*

ALLIAMA	Alliance de Mayumbe
CAUNC	Comité d'Action d'Union Nationale des Cabindais
CRC	Comité Révolutionnaire Cabindais
FLEC	Frente para Libertação do Enclave de Cabinda
GPRFE	Gouvernement Provisoire des Révolutionnaires Fiotes en Exil
JMAE	Junta Militar Angolano no Exílio
MLEC	Mouvement pour la Libération de l'Enclave de Cabinda

VIII. *Labor Movements*

CGTA	Confédération Générale des Travailleurs de l'Angola
CNTA	Confederação Nacional dos Trabalhadores Angolanos
CSA	Centrale Syndicale Angolaise
CSLA	Confédération des Syndicats Libres de l'Angola
CUACSA	Comitê de Unidade de Acção e de Coordenação Sindical de l'Angola
FNTA	Fédération Nationale des Travailleurs de l'Angola
LGTA	Liga Geral dos Trabalhadores Angolanos
MJOA	Mouvement de la Jeunesse Ouvrière Angolaise
UGTA	Union Générale des Travailleurs de l'Angola
UNTA	União Nacional dos Trabalhadores de Angola
USRA	Union des Syndicats Révolutionnaires de l'Angola

IX. *Common Fronts*

CSLA	Conselho Supremo da Libertação de Angola
FLA	Frente de Libertaçao de Angola

X. *Angolan Whites*

FUA	Frente de Unidade Angolana
PCDA	Partido Cristão Democrático de Angola

XI. *Interterritorial*

CONCP	Conferência das Organizações Nacionalistas das Colónias Portuguesas
UGEAN	União Geral dos Estudantes da Africa Negra sob Dominação Colonial Portuguesa

XII. *Related-Portuguese*

FAP	Frente de Acçâo Popular
FPL	Frente Portugal Livre
FPLN	Frente Patriótica de Libertação Nacional
FPLN	Frente Portuguesa de Libertação Nacional (Delgado)

NOTES

Notes to Prologue

1. See John Marcum, *The Angolan Revolution: The Anatomy of an Explosion.* (1950–1962) (Cambridge: The MIT Press, 1969), 1:154–155.

2. Ibid., pp. 124–126. For reports of local Kimbanguist leadership in the northern rebellion, see Robert Davezies, *La Guerre d'Angola* (Bordeaux: Ducros, 1968), pp. 22–23.

3. The Portuguese police were easily able to break up isolated ventures like the reported establishment of a "government" of South Cuanza at Novo Redondo, and journalists were barred from inquiry into the human consequences of these initiatives, said, in this case to have been thirty deaths and thirty-three arrests. *New York Times,* Apr. 21, 1961.

4. For an analysis of the disruption and violence commonly associated with such a "modernization" process, see Samuel P. Huntington, *Political Order in Changing Societies* (New Haven, Conn.: Yale University Press, 1968).

Notes to Chapter 1

1. Lyford P. Edwards, *The Natural History of Revolution* (Chicago: University of Chicago Press, 1927), p. 24; see also John Marcum, *The Angolan Revolution: The Anatomy of an Explosion (1950–1962)* (Cambridge: The MIT Press, 1969), 1:130–135, 147–148, 185–186.

2. See Marcum, *Angolan Revolution,* esp. 1:69, 221–222.

3. For example, Andrade attended a meeting of the Afro-Asian Solidarity Council (AASC) in Indonesia during the height of the northern uprising in April 1961. For the text of Andrade's appeal for Afro-Asian support, see Conseil de Solidarité Afro-Asiatique, "Intervention de M. Mário de Andrade, président du Mouvement Populaire de Libération de l'Angola" (Bandung, Apr. 10–15, 1961, mimeo.).

4. MPLA, *First National Conference of the People's Movement for the Liberation of Angola* (Dec. 1962), p. 21.

5. Marcum, *Angolan Revolution,* 1:160–161.

6. First within the *Movimento Anti-Colonialista* (MAC, 1957–1960), then within the *Frente Revolucionária Africana para Independência Nacional* (FRAIN, 1960–1961). See ibid., p. 41.

7. See ibid., pp. 283–284.

8. The ephemeral UPA-MLGC alliance known as the *Front Africain contre*

le Colonialisme Portugais (FACCP); see ibid., pp. 309–310. A UPA-linked labor union, the *Liga Geral dos Trabalhadores Angolanos* (LGTA), proposed but failed to organize with Mozambican and Guinean counterparts a triterritorial African Federation of Workers from Portuguese Colonies. *Courrier d'Afrique*, Sept. 4, 1962.

9. Marcum, *Angolan Revolution*, pp. 311–312.

10. In an interview published in *Maroc informations* (Rabat), Nov. 28, 1961, Delgado expressed support for "the principle of self-determination," leaving open the possibility either of "strong decentralization" or independence.

11. General Delgado to Ronald H. Chilcote, June 6, 1963.

12. Delgado wrote from Rio de Janeiro to Neto in Morocco, Sept. 25, 1962; Neto replied from Léopoldville on Nov. 27, 1962. See also *Jornal do Brasil* (Rio de Janeiro), Feb. 17, 1963.

13. The three movements that formed the FPLN, Dec. 19–20, 1962, were the *Movimento Acção Revolucionário, Movimento de Resistência Republicana e Socialista*, and *Partido Comunista Português*. See *Christian Science Monitor*, Mar. 4, 1963; see also FPLN statement, "The Anti Colonialist Policy of the Portuguese Democrats and the Colonial Policy of the Salazar Government," Dec. 20, 1963, reproduced as United Nations, Committee on Decolonization, A/AC/109/Pet. 239, Apr. 28, 1964. See also FPLN statement supporting African independence in *Révolution africaine* (Algiers), June 15, 1963, p. 8.

14. Quoted from Abilio de Oliveira Aguas of the pro-Galvão Committee Pro-Democracy Portugal, Newark, N.J., to George Houser, Apr. 26, 1963.

15. See Henrique Galvão, *Colonialismo, Anticolonialismo, Autodeterminação* (Rio de Janeiro: Livraria Editora Germinal, 1961). See also the English translation of a report by Galvão distributed by the Committee Pro-Democracy Portugal, "The Political Situation in Portugal," May 10, 1963, and the Galvãoist journal, *Tribuna de Portugal* (São Paulo).

16. Abilio Aguas to Ronald H. Chilcote, Jan. 2, 1963. Mário de Andrade met with the group's legal adviser, Aristides Andrade.

17. Ibid.

18. Some leaders in the FNLA remained totally negative. Jonas Savimbi professed to see no difference between the Galvão and Delgado groups, neither of which, in his estimation, unequivocally recognized Angola's right to independence. GRAE, *Uhuru-Angola* (Lausanne ?), no. 4 (July 1963). In a written interview of July 15, 1963, Henrique Galvão professed a readiness to cooperate with select, "non-Communist, non-barbarous," African nationalists in a program to overthrow the Salazar dictatorship and replace it with a democratic regime. This he said could open the way for self-determination as "humanly and progressively understood." Galvão, "Colonialism, Nationalism and Independence," in Ronald H. Chilcote, *Emerging Nationalism in Portuguese Africa* (Stanford: Hoover Institution Press, 1972), pp. 34–39

19. United Nations, General Assembly, Fourth Committee, "Déclaration faite par M. Agostinho Neto, Président du Mouvement Populaire de Libération de l'Angola (MPLA)," 1427 sess. (New York, Dec. 17, 1962, mimeo.).

20. See *The Memoirs of General Delgado* (London: Cassell, 1964), pp. 143–184.

21. *Christian Science Monitor*, Mar. 4, 1963.

22. *African Revolution* (Algiers) 1, no. 1 (May 1963): 25.

23. FPLN, "Anti Colonialist Policy."

24. In October 1963, British journalist Colin Legum reported that General Delgado had both received an emissary from Holden Roberto (Dr. Jorge de Goyenola) and assured Roberto of support for his insurgent cause. *Observer* (London), Oct. 20, 1963.

25. FPLN, "Anti Colonialist Policy." In Paris, FPLN leader Pedro Soares commented: "We are at the disposition of Messrs. Holden Roberto, [Eduardo] Mondlane and other African nationalists." *Le monde*, Feb. 1, 1964.

26. MPLA, *First National Conference*, p. 3.

27. For helpful, if uncritical, insight into Salazar's thinking and strategy, see Hugh Kay, *Salazar and Modern Portugal* (New York: Hawthorn Books, 1970), pp. 293, 389, and passim. See also *Guardian* (Manchester), Aug. 17, 1961.

28. Speech by Premier Salazar to the National Assembly, June 30, 1961. *The Portuguese Overseas Territories and the United Nations Organization* (Lisbon: Secretariado Nacional de Informação, 1961), p. 14.

29. MPLA, *First National Conference*, p. 26.

30. The MPLA's "minimum program" set forth in 1961 had called for an alliance with "progressive forces of the world," phraseology that encompassed both the "socialist camp" and certain left/anticolonial movements within Western countries. MPLA, *Angola, exploitation esclavagiste, résistance nationale* (Dakar: A. Diop, 1961), p. 63.

31. In April 1961, a full year before Holden Roberto and the FNLA formed an exile government (Govêrno Revolucionário de Angola no Exílio-GRAE) at Léopoldville, Andrade cautioned against "imperialist" intervention "under the cover of a benevolent technical assistance aimed at bringing about the creation of puppet governments." Such intervention, he said, could well confront Angola with the fate of the Congo: "neocolonial domination." Conseil de Solidarité Afro-Asiatique, "Intervention de M. Mário de Andrade." For a similar MPLA appraisal of American intentions, see Agostinho Neto's interview in *Revolución* (Havana), Aug. 17, 1962, and Marcum, *Angolan Revolution*, 1:200–201, 276–277.

32. Witness the part played by law student Fernando Van Dunem in the establishment of an active and influential committee in the Netherlands. In due course, Dutch sympathizers grouped within an Amsterdam-based *Angola Comité* mounted an internationally significant research and publicity campaign for the MPLA and other CONCP movements. *Vitória ou Morte* (Léopoldville) (French ed.), Feb. 4, 1963. As of Dec. 1962, MPLA support committees also existed in France, West Germany, Belgium, Italy, Sweden, Brazil, and India. MPLA, *First National Conference*, p. 13. See also Marcum, *Angolan Revolution*, 1: 200–202.

33. *Courrier d'Afrique* (Léopoldville), Mar. 14, 1963, and MPLA, *Vitória ou Morte*, Mar. 12, 1963, p. 18.

34. "Déclaration faite par M. Agostinho Neto."

35. For background on Bishop Dodge's association with Neto, see Marcum, *Angolan Revolution*, 1: 37, 330–332. See also statement by Dodge in U.S., Senate, *Hearings before the Subcommittee on African Affairs, Committee on Foreign Relations*, 94th Cong., 2d sess.. 1976, pp. 202–210.

36. *Sun* (Baltimore), Dec. 21, 1962.

37. Andrade had made this same point during his visit to the United States the previous year. *Christian Science Monitor*, Jan. 8, 1962.

38. See Marcum, *Angolan Revolution*, 1: 28.

39. *Sun*, Dec. 21, 1962.

40. See Marcum, *Angolan Revolution*, 1: 265. In an interview with the author on Dec. 21, 1962, Dr. Neto suggested that the MPLA had been guilty of some propaganda excesses and other "errors" in the past and said that his own letter of Aug. 8, 1962, to Roberto (following which the FNLA broke off unity talks) had contained some unfortunate wording that had escaped his notice at the time he signed it. Roberto had subsequently held out for (an unlikely) public retraction of charges of tribalism and fratricide contained in Neto's letter as a prerequisite to reopening these talks. Not prepared to concede, Neto ascribed Roberto's continued refusal to meet and discuss differences to personal ambition. After all, he reasoned, the eviction of "extremists" from the MPLA's leadership guaranteed its strict nonalignment and meant that there was now no conceivable justification for continued MPLA-UPA division.

41. "I have had many news conferences in this country, spoken on numerous public platforms, written hundreds of letters. . . . Dr. Neto cannot produce one quotation, from speech or letter, where I have made such charges [of communist influence], or even intimated them." Roberto to *Sun*, Dec. 27, 1962, in *Sun,* Jan. 6, 1963.

42. Portuguese observers projected the not inconsiderable sympathy that Roberto had built up in American church, labor, and liberal political circles from 1959 on into a vision of massive American support for Roberto's UPA. Indeed some Portuguese sources pictured the UPA as virtually "a North American movement." Such a perception of massive American support served to provide an external, conspiratorial explanation for the persistence of the Angolan insurrection. Included in this conspiracy thesis was a specific Portuguese contention that the American press was willfully keeping racist and tribalist crimes of the UPA from the American public, while American government officials manifested more or less open sympathy for Roberto. Eduardo dos Santos, *Maza: Elementos de etno-história para a interpretação do terrorismo no noroeste de Angola* (Lisbon: Edição do Autor, 1965), pp. 354–355, and João Baptista Nunes Pereiro Neto, "Movimentos Subversivos de Angola: Tentativa de esboço socío-político," in *Angola, curso de extensão universitária, ano lectivo de 1963–64* (Lisbon: Instituto Superior de Ciência Sociais e Política Ultramarina [1964], pp. 371–372.

43. For earlier activity on Dr. Neto's behalf by anticolonial groups in the United Kingdom see Marcum, *Angolan Revolution*, 1: 202–203. According to Mário de Andrade, "the English played an important part" in the July 1962 escape of Dr. Neto from Portugal to Morocco. *Spearhead* (Dar es Salaam) 11, no. 1 (Jan. 1963): 27.

44. See Basil Davidson, "Phase Two in Angola," *West Africa* (London), Jan. 26, 1963, p. 87; *Africa 1963* (London), Feb. 1, 1963.

45. *Sun*, Dec. 21, 1962.

46. Department of State, Circular 92, telegram to embassies in Africa, July 16, 1963.

47. *Le monde*, Feb. 1, 1963; *La tribune socialiste* (Paris), Feb. 9, 1963.

48. Reporting on his three-month journey to a meeting of MPLA militants in Léopoldville on March 17, Neto said that during his sojourn in the United States, he had encountered a defamatory campaign "conducted by enemies of the Angolan people, according to whom the MPLA was a movement of whites that could not adequately defend the interests of the popular masses, the interests of the true Angolan people." Now, he said, "clarifications and the collaboration of Angolan students in the United States, have condemned this campaign of rumors to disbelief and disappearance. Thus, many philanthropic organizations which did not recognize the political merit of the MPLA have become sympathetic to it and are prepared to aid it. Be it added, however, that we cannot count on immediate results from this journey." MPLA, *Vitória ou Morte*, Mar. 27, 1963, p. 4.

49. Neto stressed to American journalists that whereas the MPLA had grown out of student resistance groups in Angola and Portugal, the UPA had been formed primarily by Angolan expatriates in the Congo. *Sun*, Dec. 21, 1962.

50. At a Paris news conference, Neto cited Roberto's personal "intransigence" and Congolese interference as principal causes of division among Angolan nationalists. *Le monde*, Feb. 1, 1963.

51. The MPLA saw this rivalry as between itself and the UPA, the dominant partner within the FNLA (UPA/PDA). It did not recognize or ever mention the FNLA by name.

52. *Courrier d'Afrique*, Feb. 5, 1962.

53. The executive director of the ACOA, George M. Houser, denied that he or the committee ever advised or expressed opinions to Roberto or to other Angolan leaders on the common front issue.

54. For example, Eduardo dos Santos in *Maza* (p. 355) paraphrased Matumona without attribution in writing that "it appeared" that a condition of ACOA assistance to the UPA was the latter's commitment not to join in a front with the MPLA. Beginning in 1962, MPLA literature quoting Matumona simply deleted the qualifying phrase "*si l'on croit les multiples potins en cours*" and replaced it with the three silent dots of an ellipsis. MPLA, Comité Directeur, "Memorandum aux gouvernements africains sur la formation d'un prétendu Gouvernement Provisoire de la République de l'Angola" (Léopoldville, Apr. 15, 1962, mimeo.), and subsequently *L'Angola* (Algiers: Information CONCP, 1969), p. 98n, and "MPLA informations" (Algiers, Mar. 1969, mimeo.), part 2, p. 3.

55. *New York Times*, Sept. 25, 1975. Roberto continued to receive a $10,000 annual retainer, or "look in money," for intelligence data after other aid to him was cut in 1969, ibid., Feb. 19, 1977. Roberto's guerrillas were nonetheless ill equipped and his exile government poorly housed, suggesting that the CIA input was modest (or Roberto's bank accounts large).

56. Colin Legum, "A Letter on Angola to American Liberals," *New Republic*, Jan. 31, 1976, p. 17.

57. For example, in September 1962 at Libreville, Gabon, Mário de Andrade succeeded in firing up enthusiasm for the common-front idea at a meeting of the conservative, twelve-state francophone *Union Africaine et Malgache* (UAM). The influential chairman of the Libreville conference,

President Félix Houphouet-Boigny of the Ivory Coast, personally called upon Angolan leaders to unite without delay so that prospective UAM assistance could be put to more effective use. See Andrade, "Angola, propositions de paix," *Jeune Afrique*, Nov. 26–Dec. 2, 1962, p. 16; see also *Spearhead* 11, no. 1 (Jan. 1963): 24. This Ivory Coast advice had little impact, however, and the UAM gave no assistance. See Albert Tevoedjre, *Pan-Africanism in Action: An Account of the UAM*, Harvard University Center for International Affairs, Occasional Papers in International Affairs, no. 11 (1965), p. 19.

58. See chap. 2.

59. *Courrier d'Afrique*, Apr. 20, 1963.

60. Andrade, "L'Angola et le problème de l'unité" (Algiers, [May?] 1963, mimeo.).

61. *Pravda* (Moscow), Mar. 19, 1962.

62. See *Toward Angolan Independence* (Brussels: World Assembly of Youth, 1964), pp. 12, 31. The seminar was held Apr. 13–20, 1963, at Léopoldville.

63. See WAY, "Report of the WAY Mission on Angola," doc. no. 1984 (Brussels, June 1962, mimeo.), pp. 47, 93. The UPA's youth wing (JUPA) refused to join in setting up a multiparty youth *comité de coordination* as proposed by the JMPLA at the WAY seminar. JMPLA, "Communiqué," doc. no. 8/64 (Brazzaville, Feb. 2, 1964, mimeo.). On the other hand the JUPA's *Juventude Revolucionária* (Léopoldiville) Apr. 30, 1963, reflecting latent prounity sentiment within the UPA's younger ranks, hailed the WAY seminar for having "laid the foundations for understanding, conciliation, and fraternity which, we hope, will soon bear their fruit."

64. Department of State, Circular 92, telegram to embassies in Africa, July 16, 1963.

65. For Andrade's speech at the conference (Feb. 4–11, 1963), see *Vitória ou Morte* (French ed.), May 20, 1963, pp. 12–13. The conference named Angola (MPLA) to its fourteen-state Permanent Secretariat (along with China, the USSR, Algeria, and Guinea) and passed resolutions that endorsed the CONCP Alliance, promised CONCP aid through a Conference Solidarity Fund, urged that all Afro-Asian governments and mass organizations aid the MPLA's guerrilla army, and recommended that the fourth of February be observed henceforth as "Angola Day." Ibid., ibid (Portuguese ed.), Mar. 12, 1963.

66. MPLA, Délegation Permanente en Algérie, "Déclaration" by Mário de Andrade, Brussels, Apr. 27, 1963 (Algiers, Apr. 1963, mimeo.).

67. Andrade, "L'Angola et le problème de l'unité." For a similar statement by Andrade made a year earlier, see MPLA, "Rapport presenté devant le comité spécial des Nations Unies sur les territoires sous administration portugaises" by Mário de Andrade (Léopoldville, May 24, 1962, mimeo.).

68. MPLA, *First National Conference*, pp. 13–14.

69. "Crentes e sympatizantes evangelicos" (Léopoldville, Apr. 1963, mimeo.), said to have been signed by over five hundred persons and sent to the Baptist Missionary Society (BMS, London), Methodist Board of Missions (New York), United Church of Canada (Toronto), Congolese Protestant Council (CPC), World Council of Churches (Geneva), and Bishop Ralph Dodge (Salisbury, Southern Rhodesia).

70. Grenfell concluded that the MPLA's failure to respond positively to this and earlier invitations to submit candidates for the Sona Bata school reflected an inability to come up with a creditable list. He estimated that in the past, about half of the successful candidates (most of whom were perforce Bakongo) belonged to the UPA, although no inquiries were made nor records kept concerning the party affiliations of Sona Bata students. David Grenfell, "Memorandum re Complaints from MPLA Protestant Party Members" (Léopoldville, June 13, 1963, unpublished typescript).

71. Ibid.

72. Simon Malley, "Angola. Holden ouvre la porte," *Jeune Afrique*, Jan. 28–Feb. 3, 1963, p. 11; and FNLA, *Angola: Bulletin d'information* (Léopoldville) 1 (Feb. 1963): 7; and Marcum, *Angolan Revolution*, 1:269–270.

73. See the text of Edouard's speech to the Yugoslav youth conference, in JUPA, *Juventude Revolucionária*, Mar. 15, 1963, p. 11.

74. See Marcum, *Angolan Revolution*, 1: 200, 253.

75. Ibid., pp. 182–183, 186, 221–222.

76. Ibid., pp. 45, 200–203.

77. Pro-Salazar writers attribute Portuguese intervention to a belief that Spanish Republicans wished to "subjugate Spain," and possibly Portugal as well, to "Communism." For a detailed exposition of this thesis see Kay, *Salazar and Modern Portugal*, pp. 86–120.

78. According to historian Hugh Thomas, some of the twenty thousand were "unwilling conscripts." Thomas, *The Spanish Civil War* (New York: Harper and Bros., 1961), pp. 231, 635. These facts and figures are challenged by Kay, *Salazar and Modern Portugal*, p. 92.

79. Some sources asserted that the Iberian Pact pledged Spanish assistance to Salazar in case of an "internal upheaval" as well as of an external attack. *Hispanic American Report* (Stanford) 15, no. 11 (Nov. 1962): 1079. John Davis Lodge, former American ambassador to Spain (1955–1961), wrote in 1962 that the Iberian Pact not only remained in "full vigor" at that time but constituted a "cornerstone" of both Portuguese and Spanish foreign policy. See his "The Iberian Peninsula and Western Europe," *Journal of International Affairs* 16, no. 1 (1962): 83.

80. Portugal, National Office of Information, "Hispano Portuguese Understanding and the International Situation," *Portugal, An Informative Review* 5, no. 2 (Mar.–Apr. 1961): 99–100.

81. *Portuguese Overseas Territories*, pp. 14–15.

82. GRAE, Ministère de l'Information, *Revue de presse*, no. 20 (Aug. 19, 1963).

83. *Hispanic American Report* 16, no. 5 (July 1963): 424.

84. See Ben T. Moore, *NATO and the Future of Europe* (New York: Harper and Bros., 1958), p. 139.

85. See statutes in A. H. Robertson, *The Council of Europe: Its Structures, Functions and Achievements* (New York: Frederick Praeger, 1961), pp. 257–258.

86. *Diário de Notícias* (Lisbon), July 27, 1949.

87. *EFTA Bulletin* (Geneva) 11 (Apr. 1970): 4.

88. V. Xavier Pintado, *Structure and Growth of the Portuguese Economy* (Geneva: EFTA, 1964), pp. 12–13.

89. EFTA neutralists included Sweden, Switzerland, and Austria.

90. *Diário de Notícias*, July 28, 1949.

91. Karl W. Deutsch et al., *Political Community and the North Atlantic Area: International Organization in the Light of Historical Experience* (Princeton: Princeton University Press, 1957), pp. 124, 127.

92. One observer put it this way: "So far as Lisbon and Washington are concerned, the less notice taken by public opinion of the collaboration between these two politically incompatible governments, the better." Olive Holmes, "Portugal: Atlantic Pact Ally," *American Perspective* 4, no. 1 (Winter 1950): 45.

93. Henry A. Kissinger, *The Troubled Partnership: A Re-Appraisal of the Atlantic Alliance* (New York: McGraw-Hill, 1965). In *Integration and Disintegration in NATO* (Columbus: Ohio State University Press, 1969), Francis A. Beer mentioned Portugal only cursorily (as of peripheral importance) and did not once allude to Portuguese military and political involvement in Africa.

94. Alastair Buchan, "The Future of NATO," *International Conciliation* (New York), no. 565 (Nov. 1967): 34.

95. "Déclaration faite par M. Agostinho Neto."

96. See Marcum, *Angolan Revolution*, 1: 130–135, 185–186, 190.

97. See Alvin J. Cottrell and James E. Dougherty, *The Politics of the Atlantic Alliance* (New York: Praeger, 1964), p. 230.

98. Marcum, *Angolan Revolution*, 1: 189.

99. Expressing a hope that he would soon be meeting Mário de Andrade in Brazil, he called for "unity" of all forces fighting against the "Portuguese dictatorship." MNI, "Declaration of Dr. Jânio Quadros, ex-president of the Brazilian Republic to the Newspaper *'Portugal Democrático'* " (São Paulo, Brazil, Mar. 20, 1963, mimeo.). See also *Portugal Democrático* 8, no. 70 (Apr. 1963): 1.

100. *Vitória ou Morte*, Apr. 4, 1963, pp. 9–10.

101. Memorandum of conversation, Secretary Dean Rusk and Foreign Minister Francisco Dantas (Brazil), Apr. 3, 1962.

102. Combined Afro-Asian/East European majorities in the United Nations General Assembly (Resolution 1819, XVII, Dec. 18, 1962) and Security Council (doc. S/5380, July 31, 1963) continued to condemn Portuguese colonial policy. This had no visible impact upon the Lisbon government, which continued to refuse to allow the Committee on the Implementation of the Declaration on the Granting of Independence to Colonial Countries and Peoples (better known as Committee on Decolonization or "Committee of 24") to visit Lisbon or Luanda. See United Nations Doc. A/AC. 109/36, Apr. 1, 1963.

103. During 1963, South Africa withdrew under fire from both the Food and Agriculture Organization and the International Labor Organization. *Yearbook of the United Nations, 1963* (New York: Columbia University Press, 1965), p. 19.

104. Ibid., pp. 271–273, 718.

105. Ibid., p. 401.

106. Ibid., p. 615.

107. MPLA, *First National Conference*, p. 6.

108. See Marcum, *Angolan Revolution*, 1: 285–286, 289–290.

109. da Cruz had already lost the post of party secretary-general in a confrontation with then acting president Mário de Andrade in May 1962. See ibid., p. 254.

110. MPLA, *First National Conference*, pp. 19–20.

111. Andrade, "La crise du nationalisme angolais," *Révolution africaine* (Algiers), June 27, 1964, p. 13.

112. MPLA, *First National Conference*, p. 19.

113. Ibid., p. 20.

114. Approaching the end of the second year of its war, the Algerian *Front de Libération Nationale* had held its Congress of Soummam (Cairo, Aug. 1956) and, settling disagreements over strategy, had similarly opted for the interior over exterior, political over military, and collegiate over personalized decision making. For a discussion, see William B. Quandt, *Revolution and Political Leadership: Algeria, 1954–1968* (Cambridge, Mass.: The MIT Press, 1969), p. 100.

115. "It is . . . to be acknowledged that the Movement suffered from a lack of a stated political line for action" at the time that the liberation struggle began. MPLA, *First National Conference*, p. 9.

116. See MPLA, *Angola, exploitation esclavagiste*.

117. MPLA, *First National Conference*, p. 14.

118. Ibid., p. 16.

119. Ibid., p. 15.

120. Ibid., p. 14.

121. Consonant with its rural origins, the rival UPA already stressed land reform in its program. See Marcum, *Angolan Revolution*, 1: 223.

122. MPLA, *First National Conference*, p. 21.

123. Italics added. Ibid., p. 14.

124. Mário de Andrade, Henrique Carreira, Lúcio Lára, Manuel Lima, Anibal de Melo.

125. Andrade cited "structural rigidity" and the slow pace of MPLA organizational development as important causes of internal dissension. Andrade, "La crise du nationalisme angolais."

126. MPLA, *First National Conference*, p. 20.

127. Ibid., p. 19.

128. Ibid., p. 27. For a sympathetic analysis of the MPLA (December 1962) Conference re political and military structure, see Newton do Espirito Santo, "Os Movimentos Nacionalistas Angolanos," *Revista Brasileira de Política Internacional* (Rio de Janeiro) 6, no. 23 (Sept. 1963): 457–478.

129. It was never to meet again, however, and its projected ten-man "control commission" was apparently never activated. See Viriato da Cruz, "What Kind of Independence for Angola?" *Révolution* (Paris) 1, no. 9 (Jan. 1964): 19.

130. The six: president, Dr. Neto; first vice-president, Matias Miguéis; war department, Manuel Lima; foreign affairs, Mário de Andrade; organization and cadres, Lúcio Lára; finance and economy, Desidério da Graça.

131. MPLA, *First National Conference*, p. 27.

132. According to Portuguese sources, as early as June 1959, Lára, then studying in Frankfurt, West Germany, organized a group of African

"communists" and "separatists" into the *Comitê de Libertação dos Territórios Africanos sob o Dominio Português*. A few months later he integrated this committee into the Paris-based *Movimento Anti-Colonialista* (MAC), within which MPLA militants such as Mário de Andrade played prominent roles. Amândio César, *Angola 1961* (Lisbon: Verbo, 1962, p. 101, and Marcum, *Angolan Revolution*, 1: 41.

133. For the text of Lára's address at the inauguration of the school, see *Vitória ou Morte*, Apr. 27, 1963, pp. 15–17. Sequentially, instruction was to cover the documents of the (Dec. 1962) national conference, including problems of guerrilla warfare; proceed with a study of guerrilla warfare, looking at the experience of other countries and movements, as well as at geographical, historical, and other specifics of the Angolan situation; and conclude with lectures and reading on broad political issues such as colonialism, neocolonialism, underdevelopment, and political and social systems. The full three-stage course was to last three months. Ibid.

134. From opening speech by Mário de Andrade at school inauguration. Ibid., Mar. 12, 1963, p. 14.

135. Ibid., Apr. 27, 1963, p. 17.

136. MPLA, *First National Conference*, p. 22.

137. See Marcum, *Angolan Revolution*, 1: 236–248.

138. These goals, set forth briefly in the "Convention" that created the FNLA (Mar. 27, 1962), were published in the FNLA's *Angola: Bulletin d'information* (Léopoldville) 1, no. 1 (Feb. 19, 1963): 17–18.

139. "Aperçu des organisations nationalistes angolaises," from the FNLA's European press service bulletin, *Uhuru*, no. 1 (Nov. 1962) as reprinted in GRAE, Ministère de l'Information, "Revue de presse," no. 22 (Léopoldville, Dec. 11, 1962, mimeo.). The conclusion that there was little difference between FNLA and MPLA platforms was seconded by some European journalists, for example, Mario Pasquale, *Tribune de Lausanne*, Jan. 17, 1963.

140. As the *União das Populações do Norte de Angola* (UPNA). See Marcum, *Angolan Revolution*, 1: 56–64.

141. Singular of Ovimbundu.

142. Ibid., pp. 93, 136–137; and FNLA, *Angola: Bulletin d'information* 1, no. 1 (Feb. 19, 1963): 8.

143. Marcum, *Angolan Revolution*, 1: 137, 174.

144. André Massaki continued in his (passive) role as PDA president until December 1964, but Kunzika, as vice-president, really led the party.

145. Marcum, *Angolan Revolution*, 1: 248. Dombele's limited ministerial functions did include some interaction with Congolese officials on behalf of Angolan refugee community interests. *Courrier d'Afrique*, Jan. 29, 1963.

146. Alphonse Morin N'Simba, president of the JDA, became head of a JFNLA executive council, while Manuel André Miranda of JUPA was selected to head a larger (but inactive) JFNLA National Council.

147. See Marcum, *Angolan Revolution*, 1: 294.

148. The letter, ref. no. 00130/63, informed the FNLA executive committee that Pedro Barreiro Lulendo and Alexandre Pemo had been authorized to discuss procedures for the LGTA's incorporation within the front.

149. Report by Carlos Kassel (Carlos Gacel Castro), "Origen y Desarrolio

del Sindicalismo Libre en las Colonias Portuguesas de Africa" (Léopoldville, 1963, typescript). Plans also called for the convening of a national congress, publication of a regular LGTA bulletin, and the creation of an LGTA section among Angolan Chokwe mine workers in Northern Rhodesia. Lack of funds forced an indefinite postponement of these plans.

150. *Courrier d'Afrique*, Feb. 23, 28, 1963.

151. Alexandre Pemo in LGTA, "Communiqué" (Léopoldville, Feb. 24, 1963, mimeo.).

152. No public statement was issued concerning the decision, thus allowing the LGTA to cloak its embarrassment.

153. Marcum, *Angolan Revolution*, 1:239, 241.

154. During February, Roberto and the LGTA were visited by officials from the ICFTU, UGTT, and AFL-CIO. FNLA, *Angola: Bulletin d'information* 1, no. 2 (Mar. 10, 1963). On Feb. 25, the LGTA executive bureau held a work session with Irving Brown (AFL-CIO) in quest of support for its organizational, propaganda, and educational programs. *Le progrès* (Léopoldville), Feb. 27, 1963.

155. The GRAE represented an effort to replicate an Algerian (GPRA) precedent. See Marcum, *Angolan Revolution*, 1: 247.

156. At the time it was created, the GRAE undertook as a "specific mission" to "solicit the early recognition of all governments." GRAE, "Declaration of Principles" (Léopoldville, Apr. 17, 1962, mimeo.). Early recognition was not forthcoming and when asked about this, the GRAE minister of information, Rosário Neto, replied: "It is not the GRAE's aim to be recognized. It is rather its labor which will favor it with a victory over its enemy in Angola." FNLA, *Angola: Bulletin d'information* 1, no. 2 (Feb. 19, 1963): 9.

157. Ibid., p. 4.

158. The initials PDA/UPA/FNLA/GRAE are used in this book in varying combinations selected to indicate the elements or functional levels *actually* or principally involved. Hence, for example, UPA/GRAE indicates a two-level formula that excludes the PDA; FNLA/GRAE represents activity at a coalition level.

159. See Marcum, *Angolan Revolution*, 1: 258–260.

160. *Le progrès*, Mar. 18, 19, 1963. Also attending these ceremonies were such Congolese personalities as General Joseph Mobutu, André Boboliko (*Union des Travailleurs Congolais*), and Emmanuel Bamba (minister of finance) and diplomatic representatives from Dahomey, Liberia, Mali, Sudan, Tunisia, and UAR. JUPA, *Juventude Revolucionária*, Apr. 30, 1963.

161. *Courrier d'Afrique*, Mar. 27, 1963. The *Courrier*'s reporter wrote of military exercises by thousands of "determined and disciplined" young soldiers "bearded in the style of the Algerian maquis."

162. FNLA, *Angola: Bulletin d'information* (Tunis), Jan. 1963, p. 7.

163. *Jeune Afrique*, Dec. 17–23, 1962, p. 19.

164. *Le monde*, Feb. 1, 1963.

165. Lima had been the principal coordinator of and an instructor in the military training program organized in Morocco under the Algerian FLN.

166. Interview with Manuel Lima by Rabat correspondent of *Atlas* (Algiers), May 10–16, 1963.

167. To counter common-front sentiment within his own officer corps,

Roberto warned ELNA commanders that a merger would elevate educationally advantaged mestiço officers into command positions over Africans. Roberto, interview with author, New York, Jan. 1, 1963.

168. MPLA, *Vitória ou Morte*, Feb. 4, 1963.

169. *A Província de Angola* (Luanda), Mar. 5, 1963.

170. Until November 1962, Viriato da Cruz was responsible for MPLA lectures on ideology, one of which, "Aspectos do Nacionalismo Angolano," given in mid-October, was cited by *Vitória ou Morte*, Oct. 17, 1962, p. 3, for its "clarity and substance." On November 15, 1962, however, da Cruz wrote an open letter criticizing the ideological assumptions of other MPLA leaders and thereby terminated his role as a political instructor. Gérard Chaliand, "Problèmes du nationalisme angolais," *Les temps modernes* (Paris) 21, no. 231 (Aug. 1965): 284.

171. Suami's press conference was held at Portuguese army headquarters in Luanda, Mar. 2, 1963, and was published in *A Província de Angola*, Mar. 5, 1963.

172. On Feb. 21, 1963, the MPLA issued a communiqué in Brazzaville (no. 5/63, doc. 32/63, AM/CS) reporting that Suami had been wounded and had fallen into enemy hands while leading a Jan. 30 (not Jan. 20) attack in the Mboma-Lubindo region of Cabinda. This was followed two weeks later by a communiqué (doc. 38/63) from the MPLA's Political Military Committee (Léopoldville) announcing the results of an inquiry into the incident: Suami had been delivered to the Portuguese by the *sanzala* (village) of Tshivovo and had made his press statement under an intense "psychological pressure" that violated the Geneva Conventions (1929 and 1949) on the treatment of prisoners of war.

173. See Marcum, *Angolan Revolution*, 1:130–135.

174. The need of an incumbent colonial authority to explain anticolonial revolution in terms of a "world wide communist conspiracy" is discussed by Eqbal Ahmad in "Revolutionary Warfare and Counterinsurgency," in Norman Miller and Roderick Aya, eds., *National Liberation: Revolution in the Third World* (New York: Free Press, 1971), pp. 181–184.

175. For example, René Pélissier describes the northern conflict as a "caricature" of a proper nationalist revolt that followed upon an invasion by "UPA commandos who included not only Angolans but a sizable number of troublemakers from the Léopoldville population." René Pélissier, "The Armed Revolt of 1961," in Douglas L. Wheeler and René Pélissier, *Angola* (New York: Praeger, 1971), pp. 177, 181.

176. *New York Times*, Mar. 25, May 12, 1961.

177. Marcum, *Angolan Revolution*, 1:210–219.

178. See ibid., pp. 178–180, 234.

179. A GRAE communiqué of June 18, 1962 (Léopoldville, mimeo.), describes an "inspection tour" by Pinock and "members of his cabinet" to such border centers as Soyo, Songololo, and Songa and a warm reception by both Congolese authorities and thousands of refugees "singing patriotic songs."

180. Reverend David Grenfell, "Political Notes" (Kibentele: Feb. 15, 1965, typescript).

181. Border crossings were never especially hazardous for UPA militants.

Initial March 1961 attacks on such Portuguese posts as Buela, Madimba, Luvaca, Cuimba, and Canda had not been necessary as René Pélissier, "Armed Revolt," p. 181 implies, "to give free passage to UPA commandos," though such attacks did help to circumscribe the range of Portuguese counteraction.

182. The first group was apprehended at Kimbuba (July 27), the second at Kipemba (July 29). Davezies, *La guerre d'Angola* (Bordeaux: Ducros, 1968), p. 60.

183. Marcum, *Angolan Revolution*, 1: 228–231.

184. UPA, "Joint Declaration of Messrs. Holden Roberto and João Batista" (Léopoldville [Dec. 1961?], mimeo.).

185. Marcum, *Angolan Revolution*, 1:135–136, 228–229, 236–239.

186. See Davezies, *La guerre d'Angola*, p. 84.

187. Ibid., pp. 21–34. Without differentiating between areas and groups under effective UPA jurisdiction and the possibly larger number that fell outside its control, most writers accepted the Portuguese view, that UPA forces were "often drugged" and massacred whites, mestiços, assimilados, and Ovimbundu contract workers. UPA forces thereby convinced non-Bakongo that a UPA victory would result in "the elimination of other Angolans," a massacre of "some eighty percent of the population." Pélissier, "Armed Revolt," pp. 178, 184. In making blanket claims of control over all fighting units, the UPA, of course, invited such conjecture.

188. Marcum, *Angolan Revolution*, 1: 237–239. According to an MPLA source, Batista launched his attack on Bembe in the hope of chasing the Portuguese from the town and establishing there the base for an internal revolution independent of external UPA control. Inacio Mendès in Davezies, *La guerre d'Angola*, p. 35.

189. Robert Davezies, *Les angolais* (Paris: Editions de Minuit, 1965), p. 81.

190. Marcum, *Angolan Revolution*, 1: 212–214.

191. According to Roberto in a New York interview, Jan. 1, 1963, twelve of Bomboko's followers were shot, and Bomboko, really an ex-UPA "turncoat" named Bombo, was taken to Fuesse and executed. Other reports indicate that Bomboko, though the target of repeated UPA efforts "to liquidate him," was still alive and active as of mid-1963. MPLA, "Memorandum à la conférence du comité de coordination de l'aide aux mouvements de libération nationale" (Dar es Salaam, June 25, 1963, mimeo.). According to MPLA reports, Bomboko died in 1964 from tuberculosis contracted in his damp forest redoubt near Colua. See Davezies, *Les angolais*, pp. 30, 41, and MPLA, Comité Directeur, "Communiqué," doc. 57 (Brazzaville, Dec. 21, 1964, mimeo.).

192. Davezies, *Les angolais*, p. 41, 79.

193. Davezies, *La guerre d'Angola*, p. 104.

194. MPLA, Comité Directeur, "Communiqué," doc. 61/63 (Léopoldville, May 14, 1963, mimeo.).

195. In its communiqué (May 16, 1963), the FNLA, "with vehemence and repugnance," refuted "the sordid allegations " of the MPLA and "formally denied the existence of any MPLA military units inside Angola." "If it did exist," such a unit "existed only in the imagination of those who would have it so."

196. MPLA, "Déclaration à la presse," doc. 65/1963 (Léopoldville, May 17, 1963, mimeo.).

197. *Courrier d'Afrique*, May 19–20, 1963. In March, the FNLA had denied earlier charges of fratricide and invited African states to create a military commission of inquiry to study the situation on the spot. *Angola: Bulletin d'information*, 1, no. 2 (Mar. 10, 1963), p. 2. See also *Courrier d'Afrique*, Apr. 20, 1963.

198. See *Révolution africaine*, Aug. 29, 1963. On July 4, 1964, Roberto told Jacques Vignes and Robert Davezies: "Unfortunately, in fact, there were several infiltrations. We wiped them out, this I acknowledge. They entered a war zone. They should have asked for a laissez-passer. This is a rule to which there are no exceptions." Asked whether such a laissez-passer would have been granted, he replied negatively: "In the absence of a prior agreement on strategy, nothing is possible in this domain." Davezies, *Les angolais*, p. 189.

199. Letter signed by Rev. Domingos da Silva, Anibal de Melo, Desidério da Graça, Henrique Carreira, and Lúcio Lára, MPLA, doc. 304/C/CD/1963, Léopoldville, May 17, 1963, mimeo.

200. According to an MPLA partisan, a group of 150 men, organized by villages, did move north from Mazumbo de Nambuangongo in February 1964, crossing the Congo frontier on March 1 at Songololo. From there "most" continued on to the ELNA base at Kinkuzu, while others joined the MPLA at nearby Lucala. Davezies, *Les angolais,* p. 82. In December 1964, MPLA sources in the Congo cited the "recent arrival" of Marcelino Mirando and others with letters of support and appeals for help from Angola as proof of the MPLA's political following in the Nambuangongo-Dembos area. MPLA, Comité Directeur, "Communiqué," doc. 57 (Brazzaville, Dec. 21, 1964, mimeo.).

201. For example, Jonas Savimbi in *Al Amal* (Tunis) as reproduced in FNLA, *Angola: Bulletin d'information* 1, no. 1 (Feb. 19, 1963): 11.

202. Predictably the MPLA saw Angolan disunity as slowing insurgent action ("Mario Andrade Speaks," *Spearhead* 2, no. 1 [Jan. 1963]: p. 25), whereas the UPA/GRAE insisted that total unity existed among Angolan insurgents, as distinct from exiles (FNLA, *Angola: Bulletin d'information* 1, no. 2 [Mar. 10, 1963]: p. 2).

203. Interview with author, New York, Jan. 1, 1963.

204. See, for example, Holden Roberto, "La vie en Angola" (Accra, Dec. 1958, typescript).

205. Agostinho Neto, "The Historical Evolution," *Toward Angolan Independence* (Brussels: World Assembly of Youth, 1963), p. 9. See also *Vitória ou Morte* (French ed.), (Feb. 1963) and Neto, "People in Revolution," in *Portuguese Colonies: Victory or Death* (Havana: Tricontinental, 1971), p. 15.

206. Thus Agostinho Neto viewed the UPA, as well as the PDA, as narrowly Bakongo (interview with the author, Philadelphia, Dec. 21, 1962), and Holden Roberto considered the MPLA to be under the influence of Mbundu "particularism" centered in a leadership group from Icolo e Bengo (Catete), headed by Agostinho Neto and Déolinda Rodrigues de Almeida (interview with the author, New York, Jan. 1, 1963).

207. MPLA, Comité Directeur, "Communiqué" (Léopoldville, Mar. 26, 1962, mimeo.).

208. To the MPLA, conflict between Portuguese Catholic and North American Protestant missions reflected a more basic competition between Portuguese colonialism and American imperialism. See *L'Angola* (Algiers: Information CONCP, 1969), p. 31.

209. See Lawrence W. Henderson, "Protestantism: A Tribal Religion," in Robert T. Parsons, ed., *Windows on Africa: A Symposium* (Leiden, Netherlands: E. J. Brill, 1971), pp. 61–80.

210. For a detailed study of the development of education in Angola, see Michael A. Samuels, *Education in Angola, 1878–1914. A History of Culture Transfer and Administration* (New York: Teachers College Press, 1970).

211. Despite their "initial Marxist ideas," had not Agostinho Neto, Mário de Andrade, and Viriato da Cruz "all achieved recognition as poets," not as revolutionaries? Seeking external parallels, the FNLA statement continued: although tactically Félix Houphouet-Boigny of the Ivory Coast affiliated himself with the French Communist party in 1946, his leadership subsequently reflected his (planter) class background. GRAE, "Revue de presse," Dec. 11, 1962.

212. The moral imperative for revolutionary petit bourgeois nationalists to commit "class suicide" and transform themselves into a genuinely progressive leadership closely associated and identified with overwhelmingly rural, black African masses was most cogently argued by the nationalist leader of Guinea-Bissau, Amilcar Cabral, in "The Struggle in Guinea," *International Socialist Journal* 1 (June 1963): 441–443 .

213. Mário de Andrade, "La crise du nationalisme angolais," *Révolution africaine*, June 27, 1964, p. 13.

214. See Emmanuel Kunzika, "Angolan Unity," *Toward Angolan Independence* (Brussels: WAY, 1963), p. 16, and "Allocution prononcée par M. Emmanuel Kunzika à l'occasion du deuxième anniversaire de la Révolution angolaise 16 Mars 1963" (Léopoldville, mimeo.), p. 3.

215. See Andrade, "La crise du nationalisme angolais."

216. Luis de Camoëns was Portugal's greatest (sixteenth century) poet.

217. Kunzika, "Angolan Unity," pp. 16–17.

218. Ibid., p. 17.

219. Ibid., p. 19.

220. Dr. Neto, *Sun* (Baltimore), Dec. 21, 1962.

221. Mário de Andrade, "Colonialism, Culture and Revolution," in *Portuguese Colonies*, p. 49.

222. Whereas Soviet sources emphasized the class role played by "illegal workers'" circles of Luanda "in the founding of the MPLA [*International Affairs* (Moscow) 9, no. 3 (Mar. 1963), p. 116], other observers stressed the "Europeanized" or "neo-bourgeois" cultural characteristics of the MPLA's leadership (such as Mario Pasquale in *Tribune de Lausanne*, Jan. 17, 1963). David Grenfell wrote of an encounter with acculturated MPLA officials (Lúcio Lára and Daniel Chipenda) in June 1963: "At times during our talk, I felt that I was talking to a Portuguese and consciously altered my wording when referring to the Portuguese." Grenfell, "Memorandum re Complaints from MPLA."

223. MPLA, *First National Conference*, p. 16.

224. *Le figaro*, Apr. 8, 1963.

225. In mid-1963, Portuguese police in Angola rounded up more than a

score of white liberals suspected of being in touch with the MPLA. *New York Times*, Oct. 10, 1963.

226. Portuguese "liberals" reminded Clos of those in the French left who had wagered on the Algerian provisional government (GPRA) of Ben Khedda in Tunis and "for whom all problems between France and Algeria were to be resolved as if by magic on the day of independence." *Le figaro*, Apr. 8, 1963. Andrade also saw Algerian parallels: " There is a Portuguese minority which is really African and which has shared imprisonment with nationalist militants. Our position in regard to them is the same as that of the [Algerian] FLN to the European minority in Algeria." *Révolution africaine* (Algiers), May 18, 1963, p. 13.

227. *Le figaro*, Apr. 6–7, 1963.

228. Radio Brazzaville in *Africa Research Bulletin* (PSC series) 5, no. 3 (Mar. 1968): 1022–23.

229. In the words of the FNLA, "[Agostinho] Neto speaks of 'class' and we very much agree, for the *mestiço-assimilado* group, in our humble opinion, constitutes the prototype of what will be an Angolan national bourgeoisie if the Revolution we want should fail." FNLA, *Uhuru-Angola*, no. 2 (Lausanne?) (March 1963): 7.

230. Published first in the Luanda press (1889–1901), these articles were reprinted in Lisbon. They constituted a response to "the racial attacks of a settler newspaper, *Gazeta de Loanda*," and "an angry attack on the very nature of Portuguese civilization" and the "character" of "newly-arrived settlers," and dared "to state that Angola was the land of the black man." Douglas Wheeler in Wheeler and Pélissier, *Angola*, p. 106.

231. Ibid., pp. 97–98. For a comprehensive study of white settlement and related racial attitudes and practices, see Gerald J. Bender, *Angola Under the Portuguese: The Myth and the Reality* (Berkeley: University of California Press, 1978).

232. Wheeler and Pélissier, *Angola,* p. 112.

233. See Norton de Matos, *Memórias e Trabalhos da Minha Vida* (Lisbon, 1945), 3: 24.

234. Ibid., pp. 148–149.

235. Wheeler in Wheeler and Pélissier, *Angola*, p. 251.

236. See, for example, René Pélissier, "Nationalismes en Angola," *Revue française de science politique* 19, no. 6 (Dec. 1969): 1199, and Pélissier, "Armed Revolt," p. 179. Writing for a British journal, Premier Salazar similarly blamed Angolan insurgents for sowing "the seed of racial antagonism which was [previously] non-existent." António de Oliveira Salazar, "Realities and Trends of Portugal's Policies," *International Affairs* (London) 39, no. 2 (April 1963): 183.

237. *New York Times*, Dec. 16, 1963.

238. See Reverend F. James Grenfell, "Some Causes of the Revolt in the North of Angola in 1961" (unpublished typescript, May–June 1961). See also UPA literature on European, quá racial, dominance, for example, "Assimilados e Indígenas, Segundo Conceito Português," *Juventude Revolucionária*, Apr. 30, 1963, pp. 10, 16, and "Quais Angolanos?" ibid., May 15, 1963, pp. 6–8.

239. See Davezies, *La guerre d'Angola*, pp. 23, 39.

240. GRAE, "Revue de presse," Dec. 11, 1962.

241. Centre angolais de recherches et de documentation, "Révolution angolais et lutte de classes," *Afrique en marche* (Kinshasa, 1968, mimeo.), pp. 7–17.

242. FNLA circles cited (what were to them compromising) family ties linking MPLA leaders with European-oriented opposition groups such as the *Frente de Unidade Angolana* (FUA) assertedly "led by" the brother (Ernesto Larafilho?) of the MPLA's Lúcio Lára. Ibid., p. 13.

243. See, for example, the "Déclaration de principes du GRAE," in FNLA, *Angola: Bulletin d'information* 1, no. 2 (Mar. 10, 1963): pp. 8–10.

244. See "Convention du Front de Libération National de l'Angola," ibid., 1, no. 1 (Feb. 19, 1963): 17. On land reform, see also Roberto's comments in *Courrier d'Afrique*, July 5, 1963.

245. UPA, Steering Committee, *The Struggle for the Independence of Angola* (1960).

246. Andrade, "La crise du nationalisme angolais." For an English translation of the MPLA program, see Thomas Okuma, *Angola in Ferment: The Background and Prospects of Angolan Nationalism* (Boston: Beacon Press, 1962), pp. 112–117.

247. MPLA, "Transcription de l'interview accordé par M. Mário de Andrade, chef du département des affaires extérieures du MPLA à M. Elio Rogati, Redacteur de l'édition africaine de l'Agenzia Giornalistica Italia" (Algiers, [May 1963], mimeo.).

248. Holden Roberto, "I Prefer Peaceful Solutions," *Continent 2000* (Kinshasa and Paris), no. 12 (Sept. 1970): 19. Equating "ideology" with an authoritarian socialist or communist system, Roberto consistently stressed his "non-ideological" position: "the longer a war continues, the more extremist people become. As far as GRAE is concerned, we are trying to prevent the struggle from becoming ideological. If tomorrow our people are caught up by an ideology it will not be our doing. We are fighting a war against oppression and we are opposed to all forms of oppression, ideological among others." Ibid., p. 20. Consistent in refusing "to impose an ideology on our people during the period of armed struggle," Roberto said that the people should be asked "what they want" after independence. See interview in *Révolution africaine*, Aug. 29, 1964. pp. 12–13.

249. As seen from Salazar's Lisbon, MPLA ideology derived directly from a "traditional communist program" whereas the UPA had no ideology, being simply a movement of "racist Negroes." J. Salazar Braga, "Political Make-up of the Terrorist Movement of Angola," *Ultramar* (Lisbon) 5, no. 15 (special issue, 1964), in Joint Publication Research Service 27, 295 (Nov. 9, 1964), p. 44.

250. António de Figueiredo, *Portugal and Its Empire: The Truth* (London: Victor Gollancz, 1961), p. 129. Depicting "the aims" of the UPA as "a little more ambiguous," Figueiredo alleged that UPA leadership, presumably motivated by a desire to promote racial cleavage, had actually planned "terrorism" to provoke Portuguese retaliation against "millions of defenseless Africans." Ibid., pp. 132–133.

251. Yves Bénot, *Idéologies des indépendances africaines* (Paris: François Maspero, 1969), p. 160.

252. MPLA, Délégation Permanente en Algerie, "Déclaration" by Mário de Andrade, Brussels, Apr. 27, 1963 (Algiers, Apr. 1963, mimeo.), and Andrade, "L'Angola et le problème de l'unité" (Algiers [Spring 1963], mimeo.).

253. Andrade, "La crise du nationalisme angolais."

254. See, for example, *Vitória ou Morte*, Apr. 27, 1963, p. 20; ibid. (French ed.), May 20, 1963, pp. 3, 12–13; and MPLA, *First National Conference*, pp. 13–14.

255. Andrade, "L'Angola et le problème de l'unité."

256. *Remarques congolaises* (Brussels) 5, no. 16, May 11, 1963, p. 162.

257. Groups such as *L'Action Catholique Ouvrière de l'Angola* (*Courrier d'Afrique*, Dec. 18, 1962); *Juventude da Igreja de Cristo em Angola* (a Protestant group in which the MPLA's Déolinda Rodrigues de Almeida served as head of community relations—*Le progrès*, Jan. 1, 1964); and the *Cercle Culturel Indépendant des Jeunes Angolais* (ibid., July 19, Oct. 12–13, 22, 1963).

258. Dr. Liahuca was one of several dissidents within UPA ranks to express the view that Roberto was cultivating an anti-MPLA obsession as a means of diverting attention from internal grievances and demands for more political accountability within the movement. Accordingly in 1962 Liahuca declined the post of GRAE minister of interior. Although he remained director of the less political SARA—and its only African (Ochimbundu) physician—his political influence within the UPA/GRAE fell sharply thereafter.

259. The MPLA's Department of Organization and Cadres announced that a competitive match had been held on March 9 in Léopoldville to help select a Free Angola team "open to all Angolans" (*Courrier d'Afrique*, Mar. 24/25, 1963); an FNLA Organizational Committee concurrently undertook to register "anyone interested" in joining its own Angola-in-exile football teams (Ibid., Mar. 21, 1963).

260. The "convention" of the FNLA stated that it would include all "truly representative" Angolan movements that accepted "the general policies of the Front. " Each candidacy for admission was to be subject to a "study in depth" by a special membership committee. FNLA, *Angola: Bulletin d'information* 1, no. 1 (Feb. 19, 1963): 8, 17, and ibid. 1, no. 2 (Mar. 10, 1963): 7, for statements by Roberto inviting MPLA membership application.

261. Andrade, "Déclaration," April 27, 1963 (see n. 252); also Andrade, "Angola, propositions de paix," *Jeune Afrique*, Nov. 26–Dec. 2, 1962, p. 16.

262. "The Front has said it is ready to cooperate with any party which accepts a debate within the Front. The MPLA, on the other hand, would feel belittled if it agreed to join a front which it did not help to form, and demands prior dissolution of the FNLA; on these terms it would be prepared to discuss with the UPA and the PDA [separately] on a party basis. But, for the FNLA, it would be sheer suicide to stand down, in view of the responsibility it has adopted toward the National Liberation Army of Angola. Consequently, there is no progress toward the unity of our three parties." Kunzika, "Angolan Unity," p. 18.

263. GRAE, "Revue de presse," Dec. 11, 1962.

264. Andrade, "L'Angola et le problème de l'unité."

265. For example, a well-publicized petition signed by 152 Angolan refugees in the Pointe Noire region of Congo-Brazzaville; MPLA, *Vitória ou Morte*, Apr. 27, 1963, pp. 1–3.

266. GRAE, "Revue de presse," Dec. 11, 1962.

267. "Within this front the MPLA will watch to the safekeeping of its political personality." MPLA, *First National Conference*, p. 12. An MPLA proposal circulated in 1962 failed to lay out a specific structure or indicate the authority that it would give to the "large national union" of political, religious, ethnic, social, military, and other forces that would constitute its projected common-front. MPLA, "Memorandum aux gouvernements africains sur la formation d'un prétendu gouvernement provisoire de la république de l'Angola" (Léopoldville, Apr. 15, 1962, mimeo.).

268. GRAE, "Revue de presse," Dec. 11, 1962; Pasquale, "Situation de la révolution angolaise."

Notes to Chapter 2

1. See John Marcum, *The Angolan Revolution: The Anatomy of an Explosion (1950–1962)* (Cambridge: The MIT Press, 1969), 1: 175, 255–256.

2. See *El Moudjahid* (Tunis), May 12, 1961, p. 6.

3. CONCP, *Bulletin d'information* (Rabat), no. 5 (Nov. 1962), and MPLA, *Vitória ou Morte* (Léopoldville), Nov. 17, 1962.

4. *Courrier d'Afrique* (Léopoldville), Nov. 9, 1962.

5. See United Nations, General Assembly, Fourth Committee, "Déclaration faite par M. Agostinho Neto, président du Mouvement Populaire de Libération de l'Angola (MPLA)," 1427 sess., New York, Dec. 17, 1962, mimeo., p. 5.

6. See Marcum, *Angolan Revolution*, 1: 67–68, 70, 135, 140, 222.

7. GRAE represented the Angolan counterpart of the *Gouvernement Provisoire de la République Algérien* (GPRA). Ibid., p. 247.

8. Simon Malley, "Holden ouvre la porte," *Jeune Afrique* (Paris), Jan. 28–Feb. 3, 1963, p. 11.

9. See *Le monde* (Paris), Jan. 18, 1963, and *New York Times*, Jan. 18, 1963.

10. Radio Algiers, Domestic Service, 2145 GMT, Dec. 6, 1962.

11. *Le monde*, Jan. 18, 1963.

12. *Al Chaab* (Algiers), Jan. 18, 1963, and *Courrier d'Afrique*, Jan. 20–21, 1963. Though these arms were placed at the disposition of the FNLA, the organization was left with the problem of transporting them to the Congo—where they would arrive only many months later.

13. See Arslan Humbaraci, *Algeria: A Revolution That Failed* (New York: Praeger, 1966), pp. 161–162. Ben Bella's decision to aid Roberto ran counter to the advice of such associates as Mohammed Harbi and to the personal relationship that Ben Bella had already established with Mário de Andrade. In the view of Robert A. Mortimer, it "promptly involved Algeria in the infighting of liberation movement politics." Mortimer, "The Algerian Revolution in Search of the African Revolution," *The Journal of Modern African Studies* (London) 8, no. 3 (Oct. 1970): 371.

14. Then president of the Commission on Foreign Affairs, Algerian National Assembly; in 1967, he became administrative head of Algeria's governing party, the *Front de Libération Nationale* (FLN).

15. For an account of the press conference, see FNLA, *Angola: Bulletin d'information* (Léopoldville) 1, no. 1 (Feb. 19, 1963): 2–3.

16. Where he met Fanon, Mohammed Boumendjel, and Dr. Mostefai.

17. FNLA, *Angola: Bulletin d'information* 1 (Feb. 19, 1963): 2–3.

18. Ibid.

19. See *Al Amal* (Tunis), Jan. 24, 1963.

20. In mid-January, the neighboring government of Morocco sent a representative from its foreign office (A. Lahrizi) to establish contact with the MPLA's new leadership in Léopoldville. MPLA, *Vitória ou Morte* (French ed.), Feb. 4, 1963, p. 2.

21. Ibid., pp. 3–6.

22. *Courrier d'Afrique*, Jan. 31, 1963; and FNLA, *Angola: Bulletin d'informa-tion*, 1, no. 1 (Feb. 19, 1963): 3–4.

23. MPLA, Délégation Permanente en Algérie, "Déclaration" by Mário de Andrade, Brussels, Apr. 27, 1963 (Algiers, Apr. 1963, mimeo.) (hereafter cited as "Déclaration" by Andrade). Andrade also restated the MPLA's readiness to accept Algerian "good offices" for the purpose of unity dis-cussions at any time.

24. Marcum, *Angolan Revolution*, 1: 264–266.

25. It would have been in character for Roberto, who was presumably briefed in Algiers on the purpose of the Slimane mission, to delay his return from Tunis to avoid a confrontation on the common-front issue. Back in Léopoldville some weeks later, he asserted publicly that "foreigners" had no right to force the issue of Angolan unity. *Courrier d'Afrique*, Apr. 20, 1963.

26. Humbaraci, *Algeria*, pp. 159–160.

27. FNLA, *Angola: Bulletin d'information*, 1, no. 1 (Feb. 19, 1963): 3–4.

28. For the text of dos Santos' speech at the opening, see *Vitória ou Morte* (French ed.), May 20, 1963.

29. *Année africaine 1963* (Paris: Editions A. Pedone, 1965), p. 162.

30. *Vitória ou Morte*, Mar. 12, 1963, pp. 4–5.

31. Held on Feb. 6, 1963, this ceremony was officiated by the Moroccan foreign minister and attended by members of the diplomatic corps. Ibid., Apr. 27, 1963, p. 5.

32. On the subject of volunteers, Roberto's silence contrasted with the MPLA's voluble enthusiasm. See Mário de Andrade, "The Struggle of the Angolan People," *Afro-Asian Bulletin* (Cairo) 5, nos. 1–4 (Jan.–Apr. 1963): 19–20.

33. In this regard, Arslan Humbaraci commented: "Both East and West were soon to learn that the handling of Algeria's grandiose and belligerent African policy was based on planning about as skillful and durable as that of a child building sandcastles." Referring to his own advice to Commander Slimane and Brahimi Lakdar: "I did try at least to disabuse them of some of their wilder ideas about raising battalions to march on Luanda—though not with much success." Humbaraci, *Algeria*, p. 159.

34. In its March 23, 1963, issue, *Révolution africaine* pointed to the continuing shipment of NATO equipment to Portugal and commented: "This foreign aid does not prevent the Salazarists from protesting against foreign intervention in the internal affairs of Overseas Portugal, and among other things, against the growing number of Algerian volunteers coming forth to fight alongside the Angolan people."

35. MPLA, refs. (Adoula) 127/F/PRES/63, and (Kasavubu) 128/F/PRES/ 63 (Léopoldville, Mar. 1963, mimeo.).

36. MPLA, "Reminder on the Angolan Question for the OAU Conference of Foreign Affairs Ministers" (Lagos, Feb. 24, 1964, mimeo.).

37. Open letter to presidents of the Chamber of Representatives and the Senate, ref. 162/F/PRES/63 (Léopoldville, Mar. 26, 1963, mimeo.).

38. Marcum, *Angolan Revolution*, 1: 207.

39. Ibid., pp. 65, 180, 259.

40. "Déclaration" by Andrade.

41. Marcum, *Angolan Revolution*, 1: 207, 305–306. Maneuvering within the labyrinth of Congolese politics, the MPLA also sought, unsuccessfully, to promote parliamentary debate on Congolese-Angolan relations. Andrade hoped to get Congolese deputies to demand a more "dynamic" approach to the problem of Angolan disunity, but the Congolese parliament proved to be an ephemeral and ineffectual political lever. "Déclaration" by Andrade.

42. See Crawford Young, "The Politics of Separation: Katanga, 1960–63," in Gwendolen M. Carter, ed., *Politics in Africa: Seven Cases* (New York: Harcourt, Brace and World, 1966), pp. 167–206.

43. Rosário Neto announced that the FNLA had decided to open an office in Elizabethville (FNLA, *Angola: Bulletin d'information* [Tunis], no. 1 [Jan. 1963]), and Mário de Andrade announced the MPLA's decision to send a mission to Katanga ("Déclaration" by Andrade).

44. He reported that he had been informed by a Katangese "cabinet source" that Portuguese officials in Angola had been giving "every assistance" in the fight against the U.N. *Washington Star*, Jan. 6, 1963. A Katanga public relations organ in the United States subsequently alleged that according to "American intelligence sources," U.N. forces were turning captured Katangese arms over to "communist guerrillas" in Angola by way of "communist agent Mário de Andrade." "It is reported," the organ continued, imaginatively, "that the Angolan terrorists headed by Andrade and Roberto Holden (reputed to be an agent of the East German secret police) plan to foment disorder in Angola and then have the U.N. intervene to 'restore order' and in the process drive out the Portuguese who have ruled this part of Africa for centuries, after first discovering it in 1482." *Journal du Katanga* (Cleveland, Ohio), Mar. 15, 1963.

45. For the text of Adoula's statement see FNLA, *Angola: Bulletin d'information* (Léopoldville) 1, no. 3 (Apr. 10, 1963). See also *Sunday Bulletin* (Philadelphia), Mar. 17, 1963. For details concerning the regroupment of select mercenary-gendarme forces inside Angola, see purportedly intercepted documents signed by Commander R. Denard (Feb. 13, 1963), Klébert (U.N. doc. A/C.4/625/add. 1), and "A.H." (U.N. doc. A/C.4/625/ add. 1) in Pierre A. Moser, *La révolution angolaise* (Tunis: Société l'Action d'Édition et de Presse, 1966), pp. 239–246.

46. *Yearbook of the United Nations, 1964* (New York: Columbia University Press, 1966), p. 92.

47. UPA recruiters had been active in Elizabethville and Jadotville for a brief period just prior to secession in July 1960.

48. According to interviews with UPA and PDA officials, Léopoldville, Aug. 1963.

49. See Chap. 1.

50. Interview with author, Léopoldville, Aug. 4, 1963.

51. Desirous of conveying an image of political continuity, Marcos Kassanga described the UNA as the re-creation of an earlier organization, the *União dos Naturais de Angola* (UNATA) of Sá da Bandeira (1948–1958). See Marcum, *Angolan Revolution*, 1: 113–114; and testimony by Marcos Kassanga before the Committee on Decolonization. United Nations, General Assembly, Doc. A/AC. 109/SR 387, Sept. 22, 1965, pp. 10–11.

52. Marcum, *Angolan Revolution*, 1: 236–242.

53. André Kassinda, "Curriculum Vitae" (Léopoldville, Apr. 10, 1965, mimeo.), and *Année africaine 1963*, p. 161.

54. See UNA-Zambia, memorandum signed by Paul Kassongo and John Victor (Lusaka, May 28, 1965, mimeo.).

55. Marcum, *Angolan Revolution*, 1: 106–108, 297–298.

56. Letter to the author, Dec. 31, 1966.

57. João Chisseva, "Ngau, ngau, ngau! O Sino da liberdade tocou" (Apr. 1966, unpublished typescript).

58. See Marcum, *Angolan Revolution*, 1: 117–118, 156, 298.

59. Chisseva, "Ngau, ngau, ngau!" and interview with Smart Chata, Lusaka, May 12, 1967.

60. Chokwe constituted only a minority of the Lualaba population, and ATCAR received but two out of eleven ministries in the Lualaba government formed in May 1963. Nonetheless UPA organizers in Kolwezi were reportedly arrested by that government on Muhunga's orders. Ibid., and interview with Jonas Savimbi, Léopoldville, Aug. 4, 1963.

61. Its program called for "immediate, unconditional, real and complete independence." "UNA Statutes, Program, and Memorandum to the OAU Summit Conference in Cairo" (Joint Publications Research Service 26,533, Sept. 24, 1964).

62. See Morocco, Ministry of Foreign Affairs, *African Conference of Casablanca* (January 1961), and Marcum, *Angolan Revolution*, 1: 208–209, for a discussion of the Casablanca-related Khatib Plan for the liberation of Portuguese Africa.

63. Nigeria, Federal Ministry of Information, *Proposed Charter of the Inter-African and Malagasy Organization* (Conference of Heads of African and Malagasy States, Jan. 25–30, 1962). The conference resolution, however, did include a general statement on Angola that urged Portugal to cease opposing African nationalism.

64. The Permanent Conciliation Commission of article 31 in the Lagos charter became the Commission of Mediation, Conciliation and Arbitration in article 19 of the OAU Charter. The Charter of Casablanca had made no provisos for the eventuality of intramural disputes.

65. "Charter of the Organization of African Unity," article 2, in Colin Legum, *Pan-Africanism: A Short Political Guide*, rev. ed. (New York: Praeger, 1965), p. 282.

66. Marcum, *Angolan Revolution*, 1: 312.

67. *Alger républicain*, May 11, 1963.

68. *New York Times*, May 13, 1963.

69. *Révolution africaine*, May 18, 1963, p. 13. In action against Portuguese forces, MPLA units, he claimed, had recently "liquidated" thirty soldiers and captured (then shot) two noncommissioned officers.

70. Interview with correspondent of *Le monde*, May 12, 1963, republished in *Vitória ou Morte* (French ed.), May 20, 1963. For a general restatement of MPLA foreign policy on the eve of the Addis Ababa meeting, see Mário de Andrade, "L'Angola et le problème de l'unité," *Partisans* (Paris), no. 10 (May–June, 1963): 90–98.

71. FNLA, "Memorandum adressé par le Front National de Libération de l'Angola (FNLA) à la conférence des chefs d'états indépendants d'Afrique tenue à Addis Abéba du 23 au 25 mai 1963" (mimeo.). In a separate presentation to the conference, Jonas Savimbi urged African governments to send a commission of inquiry to visit nationalist-held zones of Angola and to create a special fund to support Angolan nationalists through the intermediary of the Congolese government. FNLA, *Uhuru-Angola*, no. 4 (Lausanne?) (July 1963): 1–2.

72. Speech delivered at meeting of Central African Students Association (MAZAZI), International House, New York, Dec. 30, 1962. UNEA, *A Voz do Estudante Angolano* (Philadelphia), no. 2 (Dec. 1962–Jan. 1963). Text also published in *Newsletter* of the Organization of Arab Students in the USA, 9, no. 2 (Winter 1963).

73. Legum, *Pan Africanism*, p. 136.

74. *New York Times*, May 25, 1963.

75. *Washington Post*, May 24, 1963.

76. *West Africa* (London), Aug. 10, 1963, p. 887.

77. KwameNkrumah, *Africa Must Unite* (New York: Praeger, 1963).

78. As related by Russell W. Howe in *Washington Post*, May 25, 1963.

79. Marcum, *Angolan Revolution*, 1: 261–263.

80. Text of conference resolutions in Legum, *Pan-Africanism*, p. 295.

81. See n. 71.

82. See Roberto's Dec. 30, 1962, address to Central African students, *A Voz do Estudante Angolano*, no. 2 (Dec. 1962–Jan. 1963).

83. CONCP, *Bulletin d'information* (Rabat), May 10, 1962, p. 4; see also ibid., Sept. 5, 1962, p. 22.

84. Roberto made no effort to revive an abortive 1962 alliance between the UPA and a group of Dakar-based Guinea-Bissau nationalists. See Marcum, *Angolan Revolution*, 1: 309–310.

85. Congolese assistance was subsequently offered also to nationalists from Spanish African territories. Pursuant to an accord reached with party leader Antanasio Ndong (*Le progrès*, Nov. 6, 1963) a representative (Adolfo Obiang) of the *Movimento Nacional de Liberación de la Guinea Ecuatorial* (MONALIGE) arrived in Léopoldville in December 1963. This movement became the sixth to be represented in the Congolese capital at the invitation of Holden Roberto. GRAE, *Angola informations* (Algiers), Jan. 8, 1964, p. 9.

86. *Révolution africaine*, June 1, 1963, p. 12.

87. *Courrier d'Afrique*, May 12–13, 1963.

88. *La presse du Cameroun* (Douala), May 24, 1963.

89. *Time*, May 31, 1963, p. 29. The article (picked up in Algiers by *Révolution africaine*, June 8, 1963), compounded Roberto's embarrassment by adding: "This month, at a makeshift hospital in Léopoldville, three young, Algerian-trained MPLA fighters told a grim tale of an ambush at the Loge River, deep inside the Triangle [nationalist fighting zone], in which Roberto's men massacred the rest of their fourteen-man guerrilla unit.

90. "Maghreb Arabe Presse," Radio Rabat (Morocco), June 11, 1963, 1630 GMT, English.

91. Radio Algiers, Domestic Service, June 12, 1963, 2000 GMT, French.

92. *New York Times*, June 10, 1963.

93. Ibid., June 15, 1963.

94. *Révolution africaine*, June 1, 1963, p. 13, and ibid., June 8, 1963, p. 6.

95. Ibid., June 8, 1963, p. 6.

96. *L'Homme nouveau* (Brazzaville), June 16, 1963; see also *La semaine africaine* (Brazzaville), June 23, 1963. In a Lisbon press statement, Portuguese Foreign Minister Alberto Franco Nogueira had expressed readiness to open talks with states neighboring Angola with a view to collaboration in economic and technical fields. *New York Times*, June 13, 1963. In a declaration on June 10 (doc. 75/63, AM/CCS, Léopoldville), the MPLA Steering Committee warned African states against falling into this diplomatic "trap." Only the Angolan people through the agency of their political organizations, it said, were qualified to negotiate their future.

97. René Gauze, *The Politics of Congo-Brazzaville* (Stanford: Hoover Institution Press, 1973), pp. 125–134. For a report on Youlou's "triumphal" visit to Katanga in early 1961, see *L'Homme nouveau*, Feb. 19, 1961.

98. Congolese and UPA/GRAE authorities distrusted Youlou's close ties with Paris as well as his designs on Cabinda.

99. Translated from French text distributed by GRAE.

100. *New York Times*, June 7, 1963.

101. Statement by Moroccan minister for African affairs, Abdelkrim Khatib, Radio Prague, July 3, 1963, 0921 GMT, English; Radio Ghana, Domestic Service, July 6, 1963, 1800 GMT.

102. *Diário de Notícias* (Lisbon, July 2, 1963), looking for allies in any quarter, quoted approvingly from an MPLA communiqué that denounced Congolese recognition of Roberto's "puppet government."

103. *New York Times*, July 10, 1963.

104. According to some reports, the Portuguese retaliated for a time by withdrawing a fleet of dredgers with which they kept clear the navigational channels at the mouth of the Congo River. *East Africa and Rhodesia* (London) 39, no. 2025 (Aug. 1, 1963): 1036.

105. Estimate by Portuguese officials in Léopoldville, *New York Times*, June 25, 1963.

106. In a statement before the U.N. Security Council on July 24, 1963, Foreign Minister Franco Nogueira did denounce a "new conception of international law" under which: "When the Republic of the Congo (Léopoldville) officially establishes military training camps against Angola, it is a lawful act; but if we did the same in some Portuguese territories it would be an unlawful action. When people say that they are going to send volunteers against Angola, it is a lawful intention, and they are called volunteers; if we did the same, that would be unlawful, and the volunteers would be called mercenaries." By not pressing his case, however, the foreign minister tacitly acquiesced in the Congo's "unlawful" action. Portugal, Ministry of Foreign Affairs, *Portugal Replies in the United Nations* (Lisbon: Imprensa Nacional, 1970), p. 349.

107. MPLA, Comitê Director, "Comunicado" (Léopoldville, June 29, 1963, mimeo.). On June 13, Radio Léopoldville (1130 GMT, Domestic,

French) announced that Foreign Minister Mabika-Kalanda had had conversations with Dr. Neto concerning assistance that the Congolese government was expected to give to his movement.

108. The reasoning went like this: Washington viewed the UPA as pro-Western and the MPLA as neutralist at best. The fact that Ben Bella was willing to aid the UPA could only be explained by a desire to please Americans. *Le monde*, Feb. 1, 1963, and *France observateur*, Feb. 7, 1963.

109. António de Oliveira Salazar, *Declaration on Overseas Policy* (Lisbon: Secretariado Nacional de Informação, 1963), pp. 31–32.

110. See interview with Lára in Robert Davezies, *Les angolais* (Paris: Editions de Minuit, 1965), p. 205. See also *France observateur*, Aug. 8, 1963, p. 9, and Gérard Chaliand, "Problèmes du nationalisme angolais," *Les temps modernes* 21, no. 231 (Aug. 1965): 270.

111. *New York Times*, May 22, 1963.

112. Based on discussions with State Department and White House officials, Washington, D.C., Spring, 1963.

113. *New York Times*, Jan. 4, 1964. Asked in May 1963 if he thought that the United States was aiding both Portugal and the UPA (as a fallback position), Mário de Andrade replied cautiously: "I can neither confirm nor disprove it." MPLA, "Transcription de l'interview accordé . . . à Elio Rogati. . . ."(Algiers [May 1963], mimeo.).

114. G. Mennen Williams to author, Aug. 20, 1969. According to State Department sources, on Aug. 2, 1963, Dean Rusk told Portugal's Franco Nogueira that the United States had advised "in strong terms" against recognition.

115. Department of State, circular telegram to African and European posts, July 3, 1963.

116. The UPA/GRAE broadcasts included nationalist "news," hymns, and folklore and represented a resumption of a UPA/GRAE radio propaganda series cut off in late 1961 by Interior Minister Christophe Gbenye who had transferred broadcasting privilege to the MPLA. GRAE, "Communiqué," no. 17 (Léopoldville, July 10, 1963, mimeo.); *Courrier d'Afrique*, July 12, 1963.

117. Also on the MPLA delegation were Luis de Azevedo, Jr., Anibal de Melo, Noemia Tovira, and Daniel Chipenda.

118. *L'Homme nouveau*, July 7, 1963; see also MPLA, "Tradução em português do discurso do Presidente Youlou," doc. 88/63, AM/LF (Léopoldville, July 1, 1963, mimeo.).

119. *Année africaine 1963*, p. 164.

120. See chap. 3.

121. *Révolution africaine*, July 6, 1963, p. 10, and *L'Année africaine*, p. 164. According to a subsequent MPLA document, preliminary discussions for such an alliance had been initiated as early as January 1963. MPLA, "Reminder on the Angolan Question."

122. FDLA, "Conferência de Imprensa do Dr. Agostinho Neto, Presidente do FDLA" (Léopoldville, July 10, 1963, mimeo.). See also *L'Homme nouveau*, July 14, 1963, on Brazzaville roundtable origins of FDLA.

123. "Conferência de Imprensa do Dr. Agostinho Neto." See also *Courrier d'Afrique*, July 11, 1963.

124. "Conferência de Imprensa do Dr. Agostinho Neto."

125. MPLA, Comitê Director, "O MPLA e o Reformismo Colonial," "Comunicado" (Léopoldville, Apr. 18, 1963, mimeo.).

126. "Conferência de Imprensa do Dr. Agostinho Neto."

127. *Mouvement de la Jeunesse Ouvrière Angolaise* (MJOA). See *Révolution africaine*, Mar. 30, 1963, p. 10.

128. Marcum, *Angolan Revolution*, 1: 176.

129. Delegation headed by Emile M'Bidi Dongala. *Mizan Newsletter* (London) 6, no. 5 (May 1964): 6.

130. Marcum, *Angolan Revolution*, 1:291–293.

131. *Courrier d'Afrique*, Mar. 1, 1961. Later Mayembe served for a while as assistant secretary-general of the MDIA.

132. See statement by MNA Executive Committee, May 14, 1963, in United Nations, Committee on Decolonization, A/AC. 109/pet. 149, Aug. 8, 1963.

133. Marcum, *Angolan Revolution*, 1: 90–92, 164–168, 287–289, 339–342.

134. Those who joined the FDLA had become known as the *Aliança dos Conguenses de Expressão Portuguesa*, as distinguished from the larger, parent *Associação dos Conguenses de Expressão Portuguesa*. The latter claimed to have expelled the *Aliança* faction on Oct. 29, 1961. Statement by Ngwizako Central Committee, July 14, 1963. U.N., Committee on Decolonization, A/AC 109/pet. 58/add. 1, Oct. 22, 1963.

135. Garcia Faustino Malheiros, André Monteiro Kiangala, and Manuel Baptista N'Dimba.

136. For resolutions of the Ngwizako congress (June 29–July 1) and Central Committee statement of July 8, see U.N. Committee on Decolonization, A/AC 109/pet. 58/add. 1, Oct. 22, 1963. Out of frustration, Ngwizako exiles occasionally accused the Portuguese (along with the UPA) of exterminating the population of the Kongo kingdom and appealed to the United Nations and International Court of Justice for help. Letter to U.N. secretary-general, signed by Committee in Exile of Ngwizako and Ambassadors of the King of the Congo at Songololo [Garcia Faustino Malheiros. Monteiro André Kiangala, Martins Kialenuela, etc.], Mar. 21, 1963. Yet they also persisted in petitioning Portuguese authorities to permit them to install a new king in São Salvador. A Mar. 19, 1963, letter to the Portuguese ambassador in Brazzaville, contained a characteristic mix of appeals and accusations including: "The Communist that we know is he who has imposed laws on a country that does not belong to him; it is he that we have repudiated. We have seen from this that Portugal is Communist. For if this is not true, why has Portugal imposed laws above the Kingdom of the Kongo?" U.N. Committee on Decolonization. A/AC 109/pet. 164, Oct. 22, 1963.

137. See Ngwizako letters to the U.N. Trusteeship Council, Dec. 2, 1962, and president of the U.N. General Assembly, Nov. 27, 1962, in U.N. Committee on Decolonization, A/AC 109/pet. 58, Mar. 8, 1963.

138. "O MPLA e o Reformismo Colonial."

139. *Courrier d'Afrique*, Mar. 27, 1963; see also *Année africaine 1963*, pp. 162–163.

140. See Marcum, *Angolan Revolution*, 1: 169–170, 286–287.

141. United Nations, General Assembly, *Report of the Special Committee on Territories under Portuguese Administration*, 17th sess. (A/5160), Aug. 15, 1962, p. 96.

142. See MDIA, "Petition du Mouvement de Défense des Intérêts de l'Angola presentée à la commission de tutelle de la dix septième assemblée générale de l'Organisation des Nations Unies (ONU)" (New York, Nov. 28, 1962, mimeo.).

143. A journey allegedly approved unanimously at an MDIA directors' meeting (June 26–27, 1963) attended by Simon Diallo Mingiedi and others who less than two weeks later joined the FDLA. *Le progrès*, July 12, 1963.

144. Ibid., Aug. 19, 1963. This appeal for volunteers was repeated in October but with no indication as to what might have been done with any earlier volunteers. MDIA, *Le patriote angolais* (Léopoldville), Oct. 14, 1963.

145. Marcum, *Angolan Revolution*, 1: 234–235.

146. François Lélé to the chairman, Special Committee on Territories under Portuguese Administration, doc. A/AC 109/pet. 147, Aug. 8, 1963. For the text of an Oct. 22, 1963, letter to Premier Salazar demanding the release of Nto-Bako prisoners, see ibid. And for firsthand reports on the crackdown on Nto-Bako inside Angola, see Grenfell's *Notes* (Kibentele, 1963, mimeo.), *passim*.

147. In early 1963, following a red-carpeted junket in Angola, Otto Hapsburg wrote a book in which he described Alberto as a "courageous" man. He predicted that if Alberto would work with M'Bala of the MDIA, together the two could create "the foundations of the first valid Angolan democratic movement." Hapsburg, *Européens et africains: L'entente nécessaire* (Paris: Librairie Hachette, 1963), p. 238. In August 1963, Alberto was quoted as saying that he planned to stand for office in forthcoming Angolan legislative elections. But the open elections he anticipated did not take place, and the albeit modest notion of "internal independence" for a "multiracial" Angola within a "Portuguese Community" that he garrulously promoted proved to be too unorthodox for Portuguese authorities. They cut him off, leaving him with little more than an external public relations role. *La semaine africaine* (Brazzaville), Aug. 11, 1963.

148. United Nations, General Assembly, Fourth Committee, 1408 meeting, Dec. 4, 1962.

149. *L'Homme nouveau*, July 14, 1963.

150. *Le progrès*, Aug. 28, 1963.

151. The MPLA took no public notice of Lélé's overture. FDLA, "Mise au point du FDLA sur la déclaration faite à Luanda par M. Angelino Alberto" (Léopoldville, n.d., mimeo.). See also *Le progrès*, Aug. 3–4, 1963. The FNLA gave maximum publicity to Alberto's bid to join forces with Agostinho Neto, whom it now denounced in unprecedentedly acid language as a "traitor" and "renegade." Voice of Free Angola broadcast published in GRAE, "Revue de presse," no. 15 (Léopoldville, Aug. 2, 1963, mimeo.).

152. In a subsequent November about-face, Lélé publicly praised Roberto and hinted, again in vain, his readiness to join GRAE. *Le progrès*, Nov. 7, 1963.

153. FDLA, "Convention du Front Démocratique pour la Libération de l'Angola" (Léopoldville, July 8, 1963, mimeo.).

154. For a personal background, see Marcum, *Angolan Revolution*, 1: 207.

155. MPLA, "Communiqué," doc. 94/63/PA/CS (Léopoldville, July 9, 1963, mimeo.).

156. See Marcum, *Angolan Revolution*, 1: 299–300.

157. The other three suspended were Tomaz dos Santos, Manuel Custodio, and Luiz Miguel. MPLA, Steering Committee, "Comunicado," doc. 49/63 (Léopoldville, Mar. 12, 1963, mimeo.).

158. *Jen-min Jih-pao* (Peking), Apr. 28, 1963, p. 3.

159. MPLA/Viriato, "Proclamation aux membres du Mouvement Populaire de Libération de l'Angola" (Léopoldville, July 5, 1963, mimeo.); see also Agence congolaise de presse, "Journée du dimanche," in GRAE, Ministère du l'Information, "Revue de presse," no. 7 (Léopoldville, July 7, 1963, mimeo.), and *Courrier d'Afrique*, July 8, 1963.

160. *Courrier d'Afrique*, July 8, 1963; *New York Times*, July 9, 1963.

161. For the FUA background, see Marcum, *Angolan Revolution*, 1: 280–282. In February 1963, FUA circulated a clandestine newspaper, *Kovaso*, in which it called for a meeting with MPLA and other Angola nationalists for the purpose of creating a common front. José Júlio Gonçalves, "A Informação em Angola," in *Angola: curso de extensão universitária ano lectivo de 1963–1964* (Lisbon: Instituto Superior de Ciências Sociais e Política Ultramarina, 1964), p. 306.

162. *Courrier d'Afrique*, July 9, 1963.

163. According to FNLA, *Angola informations*, Sept. 16, 1963. See Manuel Vinhas, *Aspectos actuais de Angola* (Lisbon: author's edition, 1961), and Vinhas, *Para um diálogo sôbre Angola* (Lisbon: author's edition, 1962).

164. The statement was read before an assemblage of several hundred persons by José Bernardo Domingos (an Mbundu). Viriato da Cruz, sensitive to antimestiço sentiment, remained in the background as Miguéis and Domingos spoke. Then da Cruz arose to field all press questions—an indication of his underlying leadership role and his proficiency in French.

165. MPLA/Viriato, "Conférence de presse du comité directeur provisoire du MPLA" (Léopoldville, July 12, 1963, mimeo.).

166. da Cruz quoted from a self critical PCP document, *Perspectivas do Desenvolvimenta da Luta Nacional contra a Ditadura Fascista* (n.p., Jan. 1963).

167. da Cruz quoted Alvaro Cunhal, secretary-general of the PCP, as disavowing such leadership aspirations in a broadcast over Radio Free Portugal (Prague?), June 23, 1963.

168. Viriato da Cruz, "What Kind of Independence for Angola?" *Revolution* (Paris) 1, no. 9 (Jan. 1964): 16–17, also published as da Cruz, "Problems of the Angolan Revolution," *The Voice of Africa* (Accra) 4, nos. 9–10 (Sept.–Oct. 1964): 18–24. See also da Cruz, "O Futuro dos Brancos em Angola," in *Angola através dos textos* (São Paulo: Editora Felman-Rêgo, 1962), pp. 83–85.

169. Karl Marx, *The Eighteenth Brumaire of Louis Napoleon* (Moscow: Foreign Language Publishing House, n.d.), p. 13.

170. da Cruz, "What Kind of Independence?" p. 18. It was for such criticisms that da Cruz was accused by some of being an opportunist who, denying the inevitability of neocolonialism in the event of an FNLA victory, adoped the "racist" stance of the UPA. See Gérard Chaliand, "Problèmes du nationalisme angolais," *Les temps modernes* (Paris), 21, no. 231 (Aug. 1965): 284.

171. da Cruz, "What Kind of Independence?" p. 19.

172. MPLA/Viriato, "Conférence de presse."

173. da Cruz, "What Kind of Independence?" pp. 18, 22.

174. *Courrier d'Afrique*, July 9, 1963.

175. MPLA, Steering Committee, "Comunicado," doc. 90/63 (Léopold-ville, July 6, 1963, mimeo.).

176. MPLA, "Communiqué," doc. 94/63 (Léopoldville, July 9, 1963, mimeo.).

177. *Le progrès*, July 12, 1963.

178. MPLA, "Memorandum à la conférence du comité de coordination de l'aide aux mouvements de libération nationale" (Dar es Salaam, June 25, 1963, mimeo.). In Paris MPLA foreign secretary Mário de Andrade expressed the hope that the Dar es Salaam meeting would act "in such manner as to constrain" Angolan nationalists to unite. *Année africaine 1963*, p. 164.

179. Untitled FNLA memorandum signed by Holden Roberto to the "Bureau of Coordination for Assistance to Nationalist Movements, Dar es Salaam, Tanganyika" (Léopoldville, June 20, 1963, mimeo.) (hereafter cited as Roberto to "Bureau of Coordination").

180. *East African Standard* (Nairobi), July 2, 1963.

181. OAU, "General Report of the Goodwill Mission of the Coordinating Committee for the Liberation of Africa to the Angola Nationalists, Léopoldville, 13–18 July, 1963" (Léopoldville, mimeo.). See appendix 2 for the full text.

182. *New York Times*, July 8, 1963.

183. Ibid.

184. *Courrier d'Afrique*, July 5, 1963. See also interview with Roberto, Radio Geneva, July 3, 1963 in Moser, *La révolution angolaise*, pp. 216–219.

185. Roberto to "Bureau of Coordination."

186. GRAE, "Conférence de presse de Mr. Holden Roberto" (Léo-poldville, July 4, 1963, mimeo.).

187. *New York Times*, July 11, 1963.

188. In a Cairo statement made shortly after the OAU hearings, Andrade dissociated himself from the creation of the FDLA, "an association of movements lacking a common policy base," and declared himself "no longer linked to any political organization." See Pierre Pascal Rossi, *Pour une guerre oubliée* (Paris: Julliard, 1969), p. 78.

189. MPLA, "Memorandum: For the Attention of the Honorable Committee of Coordination for the Liberation of Africa," signed by Agostinho Neto, Dakar, Aug. 1963 (Léopoldville, mimeo.) (cited hereafter as MPLA, Dakar memorandum).

190. FNLA, "Memorandum présenté par le Front National de Libération de l'Angola (FNLA) à la commission de réconciliation des mouvements nationalistes angolais à Léopoldville" (Léopoldville, July 1963, mimeo.).

191. Ibid. For Roberto's testimony, see "Extrait du procès verbal des réunions du comité de conciliation des partis nationalistes angolais," *Remarques africaines* (Brussels), July 11, 1964, p. 335.

192. According to an Algerian account of the proceedings, the MPLA military numbered two hundred; some thirty had joined ELNA, ninety were with da Cruz, and the remaining eighty remained with Neto. *Révolution africaine*, Aug. 3, 1963, p. 7.

193. In late April, he was quoted as saying that thousands of Angolans had taken refuge in the countryside under horrible conditions and that after two

years of fighting "the situation [was] not brilliant." *Courrier d'Afrique*, Apr. 24, 1963.

194. *Révolution africaine*, Aug. 3, 1963, p. 7.

195. *Remarques africaines*, July 11, 1964, pp. 333–334.

196. "General Report of the Goodwill Mission."

197. Ibid.

198. *Courrier d'Afrique*, July 24, 1963; see also FDLA, "Comunicado" (Léopoldville, July 19, 1963, mimeo.).

199. MPLA, "Memorandum: For the Attention of the Honorable Committee of Coordination for the Liberation of Africa" (August 1963). For discussion of the Matumona allegation, see Chap. 1.

200. OAU, Council of Ministers, "Procès verbal" (Dakar, Aug., 1963, mimeo.), pp. 36–39.

201. *Jeune Afrique*, Sept. 9–15, 1963, p. 15.

202. "Angola: Ce que l'on croyait reglé!" *Révolution africaine*, Aug. 1, 1964, p. 15.

203. "L'Angola: la minute de verité," *Révolution africaine*, Aug. 3, 1963, pp. 6–9, and John Cooley, *East Wind over Africa* (New York: Walker and Co., 1965), p. 127.

204. Sylvain Goujon, "Angola: liquidation politique de la 'bourgeoisie nationale,'" *Le peuple—La sentinelle* (Geneva-Lausanne), Aug. 22, 1963; *Libertoire* (Paris), no. 96 (Dec. 1963): 6–7.

205. Mário de Andrade (who also cited such factors as opposition to the FDLA by "progressive elements" within the MPLA and propaganda excesses) in "La crise du nationalisme angolais," *Révolution africaine*, June 27, 1964, 13–14, and Lúcio Lára in Robert Davezies, *Les angolais* (Paris: Les Editions de Minuit, 1965), p. 204.

206. Silas Cerqueira (a Portuguese political exile) in *Année africaine 1963*, p. 155.

207. Davezies, *Les angolais*, pp. 203–204.

208. CONCP, Second Conference, "Discours du Dr. Agostinho Neto" (Dar es Salaam, Oct. 1965, mimeo.). See also MPLA, "Dez Anos de Existência, Dez Anos de Luta em Prol do Povo Angolano" (Dar es Salaam, Feb. 4, 1967, mimeo.), pp. 6–7. MPLA and CONCP statements and articles covering this period omit any reference to the FDLA.

209. A group of fifty MPLA militants arrived in Algeria for military training at the very time the OAU mission was at work in Léopoldville. *Le progrès*, July 16, 1963.

210. See *Révolution africaine*, Aug. 3, 1963, pp. 6–9. In an important unsigned article reportedly written by Patricia McGowan Pinheiro, the FLN organ laid out the reasons for Algerian abandonment of the MPLA and commented, "Cuba has already shown us that it is not always those parties with well structured revolutionary programs [for example, the MPLA] that make revolutions" (p. 9).

211. Basil Davidson, "Unity in Angola?" *West Africa* (London), Dec. 14, 1963, p. 1399.

212. Ibid. Among those impressed by the GRAE successes of June–July 1963 was this author who wrote an overly sanguine appraisal of GRAE achievements and prospects; John Marcum, "The Angola Rebellion: Status Report," *Africa Report* (Washington) 9, no. 2 (Feb. 1964): 3–7.

213. One of Washington's concerns about Adoula's June recognition of the GRAE was that it meant that Roberto would "find it essential to exploit his new legitimacy and increased stature by pursuing an aggressive role in Angola in order to establish himself as the one Angolan leader capable of carrying out effective operations [inside] Angola." Department of State, circular telegram, July 3, 1963.

Notes to Chapter 3

1. GRAE, *Angola informations* (Algiers), Aug. 24, 1963.

2. Ibid., Jan. 8, 1964.

3. This situation prevailed and even grew worse until the GRAE office in New York was finally closed down (or faded away) in 1969 or 1970.

4. Speech before an open meeting of UNEA students, International House, New York, Nov. 29, 1963, author's notes.

5. Cadre School statutes adopted Apr. 3, 1964.

6. On February 4, 1964, da Cruz appeared on Algerian radio/television with an FNLA spokesman, Nicolas Vieira. He emphasized that the FNLA would have "to transform" itself into a well-structured, peasant-based revolutionary organization if it were to realize its historical calling. *El Moudjahid* (Algiers), Feb. 15, 1964.

7. In March, Savimbi contacted the American embassy in Léopoldville, warned that da Cruz was dangerously pro-Chinese, and urged that the United States intercede to dissuade Roberto from admitting him into the FNLA.

8. GRAE, Ministère de l'Information, "Communiqué," no. 44 (Léopoldville, Apr. 21, 1964, mimeo.).

9. Roberto attributed this deliberate slowness to a need to carefully appraise da Cruz' qualifications. Robert Davezies, *Les angolais* (Paris: Les Editions de Minuit, 1965), p. 188.

10. According to interviews with GRAE officials, Léopoldville, May 1964.

11. In November, also, François Lélé, who had announced in August that his faction of Nto-Bako was joining the FDLA, switched with the tide, praised Holden Roberto and hinted of his group's willingness to join the GRAE. Lélé's offer received some press coverage but no taker. *Le progrès* (Léopoldville), Nov. 7, 1963.

12. Ibid., Dec. 6, 1963. A short time before, this same MDIA group had strongly criticized OAU recognition of the GRAE. MDIA, *Le patriote angolais* (Léopoldville), no. 3 (Nov. 15–30, 1963).

13. *Le progrès*, Dec. 9, 1963.

14. Notably first and second vice-presidents Dr. Diavita Garcia (from Damba) and António Jabes Josias (from São Salvador, former chairman of the MPLA's local Léopoldville committee).

15. The former president and party "elder," André Massaki, retained the title of honorary president and general councillor. Interview with Kunzika, Washington, D.C., Jan. 25, 1966.

16. Born May 29, 1937, at Lobito, Valentim was of Ovimbundu parents. He completed his secondary education at the liceu in Sá da Bandeira in 1958 and then began university studies at Coimbra, Portugal, under a Protestant scholarship. In July 1961, he fled with other African students to France. In

May 1963, by then a student at Temple University in Philadelphia, he was elected president by UNEA's second general assembly held in Switzerland. See "Rapport sur la reúnion de l'assemblée générale ordinaire de l'Union Nationale des Etudiants Angolais (UNEA) les 10, 11, 12 mai 1963 à Rügel (Suisse)" (Fribourg, Switzerland, May 17, 1963, mimeo.).

17. Some were published in the local press, for example, *Le progrès*, July 16, 20–21, 1963.

18. GRAE, *Angola informations*, Sept. 4, 1963.

19. *Angolan Student* (edited by Eduardo Webber), Oct. 15, 1963. See also ibid., Aug.–Sept. 1963.

20. Ibid., Nov. 15, 1963.

21. The PDA had its own women's organization, the *Mouvement de Femmes Democrates de Angola* (MFDA).

22. GRAE, *Angola informations,* Nov. 4, 1963; *Le progrès,* Nov. 5, 27, Dec. 12, 1963.

23. *Le progrès*, Dec. 14–15, 1963.

24. Ibid., Aug. 2, 1963.

25. In his *Notes* (no. 8, May 26, 1963), Grenfell related the visit to Kibentele (Lower Congo) of an LGTA organizer, Manuel Cunha, just returned from the Bembe region of Angola where he reported that he had registered a thousand new LGTA members. A year-end report by the LGTA claimed that committees had been organized inside the Cabinda enclave by the head of its Cabindan section, Alexandre Pemo. LGTA, "Trabajos realizados en 1963 por la Liga General de Trabajadores de Angola" (Léopoldville, Nov. 16, 1963, typescript).

26. ICFTU, Eighth World Congress, Amsterdam, July 7–16, 1965, *Draft Report on Activities and Financial Reports 1962–1964* (Brussels: ICFTU, 1965), p. 51.

27. Pedro Rana attended a seminar for labor leaders from developing countries organized by the Friedrich-Ebert Stiftung at Bad Godesberg, West Germany. *Le progrès*, Nov. 7, 1963. Pierre Naninthela represented the JLGTA at an ICFTU gathering of young labor leaders in Vienna. Ibid., July 30, 1963.

28. Ibid., Nov. 19, 1963. The AFL-CIO's African specialist, Irving Brown, had had preliminary talks with the LGTA executive committee in Léopoldville that September. Ibid., Sept. 5, 1963.

29. ICFTU, *Draft Report,* p. 50. In November 1963, the ICFTU released a special report on labor conditions in Portugal's African territories. The report decried the total absence of African trade unions and alleged that "certain forms of forced labor" persisted as revealed by "confidential instructions" that conflicted with "legal provisions" covering labor recruitment and by government tax policies that obliged Africans to work—at fixed low wages—"for the all but exclusive benefit of Portugal." ICFTU, "Memorandum to the XVIIIth Session of the General Assembly of the United Nations on the Situation of the Workers in Portuguese Colonies" (New York, Nov. 1963, mimeo.). These criticisms of Portuguese policy were considerably stronger than those of an earlier study mission of the International Labor Organization (ILO). ILO, *Official Bulletin*, supp. 2, vol. 45, no. 2 (Apr. 1962).

30. LGTA, "Trabajos realizados en 1963."

31. LGTA, "Plan de Actividades Previsto para 1964 Contando con la Asistencia Economica del Fondo Internacional de Solidaridad/CIOSL" (Léopoldville, Nov. 17, 1963, typescript). See also interview with Lulendo in *Le progrès*, June 13, 1964, and GRAE, *Angola informations*, Nov. 4, 1963.

32. Statement signed by regional UNA secretary for press and information, Bueti Chitandula, *Essor du Katanga* (Elizabethville), Aug. 12, 1963.

33. Arrested in October 1963 and transferred to a Léopoldville prison (Makala), where Roberto allegedly threatened to have him executed, Kassinda escaped to Brazzaville forty-five days later. André Kassinda, "Curriculum Vitae" (Léopoldville, Apr. 10, 1965, mimeo.).

34. For a denunciation of OAU-Congolese recognition of the UPA/GRAE by Victor, head of the UNA in Jadotville, see *Essor du Katanga*, Sept. 18, 1963; for a reply by Emmanuel Barbosa Tchiyuka (a Chokwe) on behalf of GRAE, see ibid., Oct. 2, 1963.

35. UNA-Zambia, memorandum, signed by John Victor, Speke Makina, and Paul Kassongo, Lusaka, July 14, 1965.

36. On a tour of East Africa in early 1965, John Victor announced that the UNA headquartered in Lusaka intended to open a branch office in Dar es Salaam where it could be in contact with the OAU's Liberation Committee. Agence France Presse, Nairobi, Feb. 5, 1965.

37. Interview with author, Sept. 3, 1968.

38. GRAE, *Angola informations*, Nov. 4, 1963, p. 12.

39. *Notre Afrique* (Elizabethville), Oct. 21–26, 1963.

40. See FNLA, *Angola: Bulletin d'information* (Léopoldville), no. 6 (Nov. 15, 1963): 3.

41. *Le progrès*, Sept. 27, 1963.

42. *Essor du Katanga*, Mar. 6, 1964.

43. Jorge Valentim, "Informations sur l'évolution de la lutte angolaise" (n.p., May 28, 1964, mimeo.).

44. *Le monde*, May 14, 1963.

45. Valentim to author, Feb. 13, 1964.

46. John Marcum, *The Angolan Revolution: The Anatomy of an Explosion (1950–1962)* (Cambridge: The MIT Press, 1969), 1: 298–299.

47. Elected committee chairman at the Chingola meeting, Moses Sanjilu soon came under fire for alleged involvement with the United Federal party of the European-dominated Central African Federation from which Northern Rhodesia was breaking away. Other officers elected with him included James Muwema (Luchazi leader), vice-chairman; James Mugombo, secretary; and Smart Chata, treasurer. Interview with Chata, Lusaka, May 12, 1967.

48. In addition to Chata, the committee included Solomon Njolomba (Lwena), vice-chairman, and Willis Ndumba (Lwena), secretary. Ibid.

49. Interviews with Smart Chata, Willis Ndumba, Holden Roberto, 1967.

50. Vice-chairman, Nelson Chicoma; secretary, Willis Ndumba; treasurer, Smart Chata. *Northern News* (Lusaka), Mar. 26, 1964.

51. Though he had had some association with Ambroise Muhunga, Chiringueno rejected Muhunga's ATCAR as "purely Congolese." Chiringueno to author (Présidence no. 8/PNA/66), Feb. 28, 1966. See also U.N., Committee on Decolonization, A/AC. 109/pet. 430, Jan. 3, 1966. PNA, "Statuts" (Tshikapa, Feb. 1, 1964, typescript), made no mention of Chokwe aspirations as such and declared that "armed struggle" was the "only means available to the Angolan people for obtaining independence" (article 6).

52. At his invitation, a group of seventeen Malange and Uige "chefs coutumiers" visited GRAE headquarters in April 1963. *Courrier d'Afrique*, Apr. 17, 1963.

53. For a Portuguese perception of Rosário Neto's role, see *Diário de Luanda*, Sept. 14, 1963.

54. For a report on one of Rosário Neto's visits to Kwango (between Popokabaka and Kizamba), see FNLA, *Angola* (Léopoldville), 1, no. 11 (June 1–15, 1964): 18, and no. 12 (June 15–30, 1964): 13–14. Portuguese forces reportedly bombed and then attacked the Kasongo-Lunda base in September 1964. Agence Tchadienne dePresse (Ft. Lamy, Chad), Sept. 29, 1964.

55. Subject to arrest for speaking out against mass arrests and executions, they included Fernando Falcão, a prominent Lobito engineer, Dr. António Ferronha, a teacher in the Nova Lisboa liceu, and Sebastião Coelho, director of Radio Club Huambo.

56. Luciano Kassoma, "The Outbreak of the Angolan Revolution in the South" (Lincoln University, 1965, typescript).

57. UNASA, "Acção Positiva," Comunicado no. 1/63 [refa. V/comunicado no. 15, MI GRAE] (Lobito, Aug. 20, 1963, typescript).

58. UNASA, Cabinete dos Serviços Secretos, "Relatório" (Lobito, Aug. 31, 1963, typescript). See also Marcum, *Angolan Revolution*, 1: 154–156. The racial symbolism of the "mestiço traitor" was unmistakable. The mestiços of central Angola were partially integrated into the ruling stratum (European) of colonial society on racial-cultural grounds; they were thus characteristically perceived by Africans as privileged and condescending, and they were deeply resented. Ibid., p. 106. The extent to which the Portuguese policy of dividing persons into sociological categories of "civilized" and "uncivilized" had fostered racial consciousness among blacks was attested to in the following comments by Dr. Ian Gilchrist, a Canadian physician, returned to Angola in mid-1961 after several years' absence. "I saw a tremendous number of small things . . . e.g., the separate toilets in the center of a Nova Lisboa park, marked 'Europeans' and 'Indigenas.' These things give the lie to the myth of Portuguese racial equality. This color bar was much more noticeable in 1961 than in 1951, when it had been more of a culture bar." Gilchrist, letter to the chairman, (U.N.) Special Committee on the Situation with Regard to . . . the Granting of Independence (Léopoldville, Apr. 1963, mimeo.).

59. For a description of the government's preventive terror of 1961, in which Africans in the Andulo region were allegedly "shot for simply being found with pencils and pens"—a sign that they were "potentially dangerous"—see ibid.

60. UNASA, "Relatório."

61. Kassoma, "Outbreak."

62. A Sele born Sept. 23, 1937, at Kapir-Gabela, Adão José Domingos Kapilango attended the liceu of Nova Lisboa and was one of the principal organizers of the CSRSA.

63. Born Oct. 20, 1938, at Cachimbuelengue (in the Luvemba-Bailundo area of Huambo district), Kassoma attended the Protestant school at Dondi (1954–1959) before entering the Escola Comercial at Lobito in 1960. Inducted into the army in Feb. 1961, he participated briefly in operations against UPA insurgents in the Nambuangongo region that spring. Kassoma later completed university studies in the United States in agriculture and soil science before returning to Angola in 1971 to join UNITA insurgents in the interior.

64. Luciano Kassoma, "My Visit to the Lion's Den in Angola" (1967, typescript).

65. In mid-1964, an Angolan student publication announced the arrival in Katanga of three additional "resistance leaders" from Lobito: Abreu Kayaya, Oseis Tshinguiluguili, and Castro Hosi. "Le periscope révolutionnaire angolais," no. 1 (Oegstgeest, Netherlands, Nov. 1964, mimeo.).

66. One of those Europeans who at personal cost had empathized with young African nationalists of central Angola, Ferronha was the author of two widely used Angolan textbooks: *Elementos de Filosofia: Introdução à Filosofia e Psicologia* (Novo Redondo, Angola: Profissional Misionária, 1960), and *Fundamentos de Filosofia, Lógica, Etica, Estética, Gnoseologia, Metafisica* (Luanda: Grafica Portugal, 1962).

67. Kassoma, "Outbreak."

68. *Courrier d'Afrique*, Aug. 6, 1963.

69. See ibid., Aug. 7, 1963; *Le progrès*, Dec. 26, 1963.

70. GRAE, *Angola informations*, Sept. 16, 1963, p. 9; Roberto UNEA speech, Nov. 29, 1963 (International House, New York); and "Briefing Memorandum" from G. Mennen Williams to Dean Rusk, Dec. 18, 1963.

71. *West Africa*, Aug. 10, 1963, p. 887.

72. Ibid.

73. Kenneth Kaunda's United National Independence Party (UNIP) of Northern Rhodesia, was allocated £50,000, and nationalists of Mozambique and South West Africa were each scheduled to get £20,000. OAU, Council of Ministers, "Procès verbal" (Dakar, Aug.1963, mimeo.), p. 33.

74. Portuguese sources assessed guerrilla units inside Angola at between 4,000 and 5,000 (*Christian Science Monitor*, Oct. 9, 1963), while FNLA officials claimed to have trained and fielded 7,500 to 10,000. (Roberto UNEA speech, Nov. 29, 1963; *New York Times*, Oct. 22, 1963).

75. *New York Times*, Oct. 22, 1963.

76. Ibid., Dec. 16, 1963.

77. Ibid.

78. Ibid., Oct. 8, 1963.

79. See J. Salazar Braga, "Political Make-up of the Terrorist Movement of Angola," *Ultramar* (Lisbon) 5, no. 15 (special issue, 1964) in Joint Publications Research Service, 27, 295 (Nov. 9, 1964), p. 47.

80. Grenfell of the Kibentele reception center estimated the refugee population (in the Congo) to have reached at least 300,000 by December 1963. *Le progrès*, Dec. 19, 1963.

81. On the role of Portuguese air power, see Edgar Pereira de Costa

Cardoso, *Presença de Força Aérea em Angola* (Lisbon: Edição da Secretaria de Estado de Aeronautica, 1963).

82. Because the Portuguese did not count as battle deaths those who subsequently died of wounds and omitted the victims of military accidents from their statistics, these figures were understated, perhaps by 50 percent. *Christian Science Monitor*, Oct. 9, 1963.

83. Roberto had announced as early (and probably prematurely) as April 1963 that South West Africans were training at Kinkuzu. *Courrier d'Afrique*, April 20, 1963.

84. *New York Times*, Dec. 16, 1963.

85. GRAE, *Angola informations*, Sept. 4, 1963, p. 8. The PAC's Machema had limited himself to a communiqué heralding "close collaboration" with GRAE. *Courrier d'Afrique*, Aug. 16, 1963.

86. See John A. Marcum, "The Exile Condition and Revolutionary Effectiveness: Southern African Liberation Movements," in Christian P. Potholm and Richard Dale, eds., *Southern Africa in Perspective: Essays in Regional Politics* (New York: Free Press, 1972), pp. 270–275.

87. See Oct. 2, 1964, press statement by Commander José Kalundungo in Davezies, *Les angolais*, pp. 211–213.

88. For this he was criticized by the Léopoldville press (*Présence congolaise*, July 20, 1964) as well as by the MPLA ("Communiqué de presse," Dec. 43/64 [Brazzaville, Aug. 13, 1964, mimeo.]).

89. *Yearbook of the United Nations, 1964* (New York: Office of Public Information, 1966), p. 93.

90. Kalundungo in Davezies, *Les angolais*, pp. 211–213. According to Kalundungo, he was one of only six non-Bakongo in the original ELNA officer trainee contingent of twenty-two sent to Algeria in 1961 (p. 212).

91. According to Russell Warren Howe, at the end of March the OAU voted $84,000 in military funds for the GRAE that Roberto was notified he would receive in April. *Washington Post*, Mar. 29, 1964.

92. See M. Crawford Young, "Rebellion and the Congo," in Robert I. Rotberg and Ali A. Mazrui, eds., *Protest and Power in Black Africa* (New York: Oxford University Press, 1970), pp. 969–1011.

93. Ambassador Abdelamid Adjali. FNLA, *Angola: Bulletin d'information* 1, no. 11 (June 1–15, 1964): 9.

94. R. W. Howe in *Washington Post*, Mar. 29, 1964.

95. *Le progrès*, June 16, 1964.

96. See appendix 2.

97. *Le progrès*, Nov. 6, 1963. In addition to its medical service for refugees staffed by eleven doctors (compared with two doctors working for the GRAE-related SARA), CVAAR ran a number of Angolan refugee schools—thirty-six according to the MPLA. See MPLA, "Quelques faits qui demontrent l'incapacité du 'GRAE' à conduire la lutte du peuple angolais et la conduite arbitraire du 'comité des neufs' dans la question angolaise" (Brazzaville [1964], mimeo.).

98. In response to the November orders to shut down MPLA/CVAAR facilities and operations, the head of the Kwango provincial government, P. Tabaka, wrote: "Before stopping this Movement's activities in the Kwango territory and in the Republic of Congo, it should be wise to replace its social

and relief organization. MPLA has accomplished a big task of relief among the Angolan refugees in the Kwango province. It has opened dispensaries, helped with clothes and food its countrymen who need them. Holden Roberto's organization has never done such work in spite of its constant presence in this province." MPLA, "MPLA Delegation Intervention at the Liberation Committee of the Organization of African Unity" (Dar es Salaam, June 3, 1964), p. 5. It was not until Mar. 28, 1964, that the Kwango government acted on the central government's orders. See letter to MPLA from Kwango government in MPLA, "MPLA and Positions from the Congolese Authorities of the Provinces Bordering Angola after 'Grae' Recognition" (Brazzaville, 1964, mimeo.) (hereafter cited as "MPLA and Authorities of the Provinces").

99. Permission granted to Luis de Azevedo, Jr., by Kongo Central minister of interior, André M'Pika, at Benseke-Futi, Oct. 21, 1963, doc. no. 05/590/4eme DMI, C1 AI. On Nov. 4, M'Pika wrote MPLA authorizing it to open offices "wherever [it] wants." Benseke-Futi, doc. 05/ 626/4eme, DMI, C728. "MPLA and Authorities of the Provinces."

100. "MPLA Delegation Intervention."

101. Daniel Chipenda and António Condesse were arrested in Nov. 1963. Ibid.

102. Pascal Luvualu and Bernard Dombele were arrested in Feb. 1964. Ibid., and *Le progrès*, Feb. 3, 1964. In Dec. 1963, two disillusioned MPLA militants, Mário Augusto da Silva (treasurer of CVAAR) and Moes Lourenço da Silva, obtained laissez-passers from the Portuguese embassy in Léopoldville and flew to Luanda. *Le progrès*, Dec. 17, 1963.

103. FDLA first vice-president, Emmanuel Loureiro (Ngwizako), opened an FDLA Brazzaville office on July 27, 1963. See FDLA, "Déclaration de l'ouverture du bureau du Front Démocratique pour la Libération de l'Angola (FDLA) à Brazzaville" (Brazzaville, July 27, 1963, mimeo.).

104. *Courrier d'Afrique,* July 19, 1963; *Le progrès,* July 20–21, 1963; FNLA, *Angola-Uhuru*, no. 4 (Lausanne?) (July 1963): 15.

105. *Révolution africaine*, June 27, 1964, p. 14. In his *Notes* (no. 20, Kibentele, Aug. 29, 1963), Reverend David Grenfell recounts a conversation of Aug. 23, 1963, at MPLA headquarters in Léopoldville with a former Kibokolo deacon who told him that "in a recent talk given by Agostinho Neto, they were told that the Portuguese would never come to terms with UPA because they hated Holden Roberto. On the other hand, many of the Portuguese were willing to talk with him [Neto], therefore the way to peace and independence was for the Angolans to rally behind him and leave UPA well alone.

106. *Révolution africaine*, Aug. 24, 1963, p. 2.

107. A UGEAN seminar on Angolan unity at Rabat, Morocco, in Sept. 1963 was the scene of just such heated debate among pro-Neto, pro-da Cruz, and pro-Andrade elements. For the evolution of student opinion on this and related matters, see *O Estudante Angolano* (Vienna), nos. 19–23 (Aug.–Dec. 1963).

108. Roberto met with Massamba-Debat in November (Radio Brazzaville, 1700 GMT, Nov. 6, 1963) and congratulated him upon his election as Brazzaville president in December. GRAE, "Communiqué" (Léopoldville,

Dec. 21, 1963, mimeo.). He even extended formal GRAE recognition to Massamba-Debat's new government. *Le progrès*, Jan. 25–26, 1964. But Roberto failed to gain Brazzaville support or recognition for the GRAE.

109. As early as Jan. 1964, MPLA-related publications began calling for close cooperation with such "progressive" forces as the *Conseil National de Libération* (CNL). Centro de estudos angolanos, *Boletim* (Algiers), Jan. 4, 1964, p. 10.

110. JMPLA, *Juventude e Revolução* (Brazzaville), Nov. 30, 1964, p. 7.

111. MPLA, *Vitória ou Morte* (English ed.). no. 1 (Brazzaville, Feb. 1964).

112. MPLA, "Conferência dos Quadros: Relatório Geral" (Brazzaville, Jan. 1964, mimeo.).

113. MPLA, *Programa* (Brazzaville: Edição do MPLA, 1966).

114. Radio Léopoldville, Domestic O63O GMT, Jan. 18, 1964.

115. Congo-Léopoldville, Tunisia, Algeria, Morocco, Dahomey, Mauritania, Senegal, Niger, U.A.R., Nigeria (de facto), Mali, Libya, Rwanda, Guinea, Liberia (de facto), Tanzania, Kenya, Togo. FNLA, *Angola* (Léopoldville) 1, no. 12 (June 15–30, 1964): 4. By Dec. 31, 1965, the figure had reached twenty-five states according to Pierre A. Moser, *La révolution angolaise* (Tunis: Société l'Action d'Edition et de Presse, 1966), p. 120.

116. *Le progrès*, Feb. 28, 1964. Iraqi recognition (Feb. 9, 1964) was expected by some observers to open the way for new sources of military aid. *World Outlook: Perspective Mondiale* (Paris), Feb. 28, 1964, p. 15.

117. For examples of these, see FNLA, *Angola: Bulletin d'information* 1, nos. 4–5 (Oct. 15–31, 1963): 4–6.

118. Expectations set forth in its response to de jure recognition by Mali. GRAE, "Communiqué," no. 3 (Léopoldville, Jan. 17, 1964, mimeo.).

119. Ibid., no. 5 (Jan. 21, 1964).

120. *New York Times*, June 7, 1963.

121. *L'Homme nouveau*, July 21, 1963.

122. *Le monde*, Aug. 3, 1963.

123. *Le progrès*, Aug. 8, 1963.

124. *La semaine africaine* (Brazzaville), Aug. 11, 1963. GRAE denounced Youlou's initiative as procolonialist. "Communiqué," no. 19 (Léopoldville, July 29, 1963, mimeo.).

125. *L'Homme nouveau*, Dec. 16, 1962.

126. Ibid., July 14, 1963.

127. CAUNC had to this point favored integrating Cabinda with Congo-Léopoldville. See Marcum, *Angolan Revolution*, 1: 295. Its president, Henriques Tiago Nzita, had lived for some time in Stanleyville (Kisangani). *L'Homme nouveau*, Dec. 9, 1962.

128. *Courrier d'Afrique*, Aug. 6, 1963.

129. FLEC, "Congrès des partis politiques cabindais tenu à Pointe-Noire (République du Congo-Brazzaville) du 2 au 4 août 1963" (Point Noire, Aug. 4, 1963, mimeo.). See also *L'Homme nouveau*, Aug. 11, 1963, and United Nations, General Assembly, doc. A/AC 109/pet. 166, Oct. 22, 1963.

130. The essence of this accord had already been hammered out at tripartite meetings on July 8 and 14. *Le progrès*, July 11, 1963, and FLEC, "Congrès des partis politiques cabindais."

131. Other officers included Henriques Tiago Nzita (CAUNC), vice-

president; António Eduardo Sozinho Zau (Alliama), foreign affairs; and Simon Luemba, secretary-general.

132. GRAE, *Angola informations,* Oct. 19, 1964.

133. FLEC was permitted to open an office on Brazzaville's Avenue de la France. *Le progrès,* Dec. 11, 1963.

134. FLEC, N/ref. no. EXT/AESZ/37/63, Sept. 6, 1963.

135. Voting in favor were Brazil, China, Ghana, Morocco, Norway, the Philippines, the USSR, and Venezuela.

136. United Nations, Security Council, Resolution S/5380, July 31, 1963.

137. United Nations, Security Council, S/PV. 1049, July 31, 1963. U.S. abstention was reportedly based on disapproval not of the requests made of Portugal but of the clause in the resolution declaring that "the situation in the Territories under Portuguese administration is seriously disturbing peace and security in Africa." The State Department felt that the resolution should have said only that it was "likely" to do so. *New York Times,* Aug. 1, 1963. Sierra Leone's foreign minister, John Karefa Smart, spoke for embittered Africans when he reacted to this American stance: "As long as it is only African villagers that are being killed or maimed, bombings by planes and shootings by soldiers do not constitute a breach of the peace and do not even threaten to do so. The framers of the Charter did not have such inconsequential matters in their minds." United Nations, Security Council, S/PV. 1046, July 29, 1963.

138. António de Oliveira Salazar, *Declaration on Overseas Policy* (Lisbon: Secretariado Nacional da Informação, 1963), p. 5.

139. *New York Times,* Aug. 13, 1963.

140. The *Times* asked editorially: "Moreover, with nearly all the other colonies of Africa getting sovereignty and independence, how is it even possible to argue that the people of Angola and Mozambique will not—or even should not—also demand sovereignty and independence?" Ibid., Aug. 15, 1963.

141. Salazar, *Declaration on Overseas Policy,* p. 31. Attribution of economic motives to American anticolonialism was, of course, also central to Marxist analysis. A report to the Fifth Congress of the Portuguese Communist party in October 1957 had warned that "American imperialists constituted serious competition for the old colonial powers." U.S. capital, it said, had already achieved "a remarkable, even predominant position" in several African colonies, including Angola and Mozambique. See Louis Odru, "Les événements d'Angola," *Cahiers du communisme* (Paris) 37, no. 5 (May 1961):1040.

142. *New York Times,* Aug. 17, 1963. Since July 1961, Salazar had been made aware that if he carried out reforms to achieve self-determination, the United States was prepared to provide "financial and technical assistance in the territories in cooperation with [Portugal]" and would "help seek other national and international sources of such assistance." Department of State to American Ambassador Eldrick in Lisbon, telegram, July 28, 1961. Pursuant to National Security Action Memorandum no. 60 (July 14, 1961), it had been decided that "if Salazar embark[ed] upon a more liberal colonial policy," the United States would "grant reasonable Portuguese requests for economic assistance in accordance with existing commitments." The State Department had consulted both the Export-Import Bank and the Interna-

tional Development Bank about possible assistance to Portugal "as a consequence of reform programs." Loans, not aid grants, were envisaged, because of Portugal's large gold and foreign exchange reserves. With the loss of privileged African markets, Portugal, it was believed, would also require help in reorienting its export industries. Department of State, "Memorandum for Mr. McGeorge Bundy, The White House," from Chairman of Task Force on Portuguese Territories in Africa, Aug. 2, 1961.

143. António de Oliveira Salazar, *Our Duty Is Also to Be Proud of the Living* (Lisbon: Secretariado Nacional da Informação, 1963), p. 7.

144. *Le monde*, Aug. 31, 1963.

145. The awkwardness of the American position was described in a July 18 speech by J. Wayne Fredericks, deputy assistant secretary for African affairs, who concluded that "in our relations with the rest of Africa, we may find ourselves having to acquiesce in more extreme action or face sharply reduced influence, to the detriment of other important objectives." *The Department of State Bulletin*, 49, no. 1260 (Aug. 19, 1963): 284.

146. Underlying Ball's approach was his stereotypical American view that "Africa remained the Dark Continent after most other parts of the globe had long had contacts with Western civilization . . . In the latter half of the nineteenth century, Africa, as the last remaining vast unexplored area of the world, suddenly worked its magnetic attraction on an intrepid band of French and English eccentrics and romantics who competed to discover its exotic mysteries." He continued, "Because of its late and limited contact with the West, Africa missed most of the great tides and forces that laid the foundations for the development in other lands." George W. Ball, *The Discipline of Power: Essentials of a Modern Structure* (Boston: Little, Brown, 1968), pp. 243–244.

147. Ibid., pp. 249–250.

148. Ibid., p. 251.

149. Ibid., p. 248.

150. *New York Times*, Sept. 17, 1963.

151. *Washington Post*, Oct. 31, 1963. As early as July 1961, Franco Nogueira, "bitter and accusatory," had told American Ambassador Eldrick in Lisbon that he believed Roberto had American support and that the "U.S. had ulterior economic designs on Angola and other African areas where U.S. interests were rapidly acquiring shares in industrial enterprises." Dispatch from American embassy, Lisbon, July 11, 1961.

152. *Le monde*, July 31, 1963.

153. Portuguese "military sources" were reported to have "unofficially confirmed" that they could, by sinking three ships at the mouth of the Congo River, block access to Léopoldville's only port, Matadi. *Le soir* (Brussels), Oct. 8, 1963.

154. *Le progrès*, Oct. 16, 1963.

155. Ghana, Guinea, Liberia, Malagasy, Morocco, Nigeria, Sierra Leone, Tanganyika, and Tunisia.

156. For statements by Franco Nogueira relating to his exchanges with the African states, see Portugal, Ministry of Foreign Affairs, *Portugal Replies in the United Nations* (Lisbon: Imprensa Nacional, 1970), pp. 365–387.

157. See U Thant's report on the discussions: United Nations, Security Council, doc. S/5448, Oct. 31, 1963.

158. Roberto was upset that he had not been kept informed or consulted by African participants during the course of the discussions. FNLA, *Angola: Bulletin d'information,* 1, no. 7 (Nov. 30, 1963): 14. In a letter of Nov. 5 to U Thant, he warned against seeking a solution "at the expense of the legitimate aspirations of the Angolan people" for independence. *Le progrès*, Nov. 7, 1963. He followed this up with a letter to the president of the Security Council in which he opposed the resumption of talks, which could only cause "delay" and "confusion." Ibid., Dec. 12, 1963.

159. *Le progrès*, Nov. 6, 1963.

160. Statement of Dec. 9, 1963, in Portugal, *Portugal Replies,* pp. 377–378. Franco Nogueira recounted the history of Portuguese efforts to engage the UN and African states in sustained dialogue. "Last year, when we wholeheartedly accepted the United States proposal for the appointment of two international rapporteurs with a view to finding out the actual situation in Portuguese overseas territories the African countries turned down the proposal. In replying . . . we made the following proposals: first, that meetings should be held between the Portuguese Government and the African Governments of contiguous territories; secondly, that matters of common interest should be discussed; thirdly, that non-aggression agreements should be negotiated with the necessary guarantees. . . . [It is] very peculiar that countries that claim to be the victims of alleged aggression should flatly refuse to negotiate a non-aggression pact. Then on 6 June 1963 my Government invited African Governments to send whatever qualified representatives or leaders they might name to see for themselves the conditions in the Portuguese overseas territories. On 12 July 1963 those invitations were reiterated and a frank and constructive dialogue with the interested African countries was suggested. . . . We received no response, we received no reaction. Then on 24 July 1963 we invited the Foreign Ministers of Tunisia, Liberia, Sierra Leone and Madagascar, in their capacities as representatives of the Addis Ababa conference, to visit Angola and Mozambique at their convenience. The invitation was contemptuously turned down" (p. 377).

161. United Nations, Security Council, Resolution S/5481, Dec. 11, 1963.

162. *Kenya Calling* (Nairobi), Dec. 21, 1963, pp. 4–5.

Notes to Chapter 4

1. *Le progrès*, Sept. 5, 1963.

2. Although the French embassy in Léopoldville explained that diplomat Jean-Pierre Gadou had been sitting on the platform behind Roberto in a "private" not an "official" capacity, the incident caused a stir. Roberto commented: "Obviously this is a new French policy—not recognition, but it means that France has taken a step toward us." *Washington Post*, Mar. 24, 1964.

3. *New York Times,* Jan. 4, 1964.

4. John Marcum, *The Angolan Revolution: The Anatomy of an Explosion (1950–1962)* (Cambridge: The MIT Press, 1969), 1: 61–62.

5. Ibid., p. 182.

6. Upon his arrival as Kennedy's ambassador to Lisbon in September 1963, Admiral George W. Anderson took charge of ongoing negotiations

for a new accord to cover continued American military use of the Azores. Anderson's public comment that the islands were of "vital importance" to Atlantic defense encouraged the Portuguese to press their demands for a quid pro quo in the form of American support for their African policy. *New York Times*, Sept. 26, 1963. In a memorandum to W. Averell Harriman, "Program for Portuguese Africa," May 2, 1963, Assistant Secretary of State for African Affairs G. Mennen Williams noted that Portuguese sensitivities had caused the U.S. to modify its anticolonial stance at the U.N. and to limit both contact with nationalists and assistance to refugees and students from Portuguese African territories.

7. Marcum, *Angolan Revolution*, 1: 268.

8. Roberto's letters were dated Nov. 27, 1962, and Dec. 19, 1962, respectively, and probably were transmitted via African diplomats to the U.S. mission at the United Nations in New York.

9. The Department of State recommended to the White House that no reply be made to the Dec. 19, 1962, letter. William H. Brubeck to Bromley Smith, memorandum, Jan. 31, 1963.

10. In Léopoldville, GRAE nationalists lauded Kennedy as a champion of racial equality and, like Abraham Lincoln, a victim of "negrophobia." FNLA, *Angola: Bulletin d'information* 1, no. 7 (Léopoldville, Nov. 30, 1963) 3, 17–18.

11. *Le progrès,* Dec. 14–15, 1963.

12. *New York Times,* Jan. 4, 1964.

13. Some saw Roberto's bid for communist support as a ploy to force the United States to be more forthcoming. See, for example, Suzanne Bonzon in *Année africaine 1964* (Paris: Editions A. Pedone, 1966), p. 105. Nonetheless, U.S. embassy officials in Léopoldville took seriously a warning by LGTA adviser Carlos Kassel that Roberto, in fact, was contemplating a basic reorientation of his external relations. Dispatch from U.S. embassy to Department of State, Dec. 30, 1963.

14. *New York Times*, Jan. 8, 1964. There were subsequent press reports from the Congo of U.S.-backed political moves to block the Angolans from receiving communist arms. Ibid., Jan. 25, 1964.

15. In Paris, the (Trotskyist) United Secretariat of the Fourth International welcomed this "encouraging sign" that help from "revolutionary Marxists" might begin to move the FNLA toward a socialist program and away from "American imperialism." *World Outlook* (Paris), Jan. 10, 1964.

16. For such criticism voiced by Roberto in interviews given in advance of his January policy shift, see *New York Times*, June 29, 1963, and *Christian Science Monitor*, Dec. 7, 1963.

17. V. Midstev in *Pravda*, Mar. 17, 1964. See also Y. Konovalov, "Problems of Liberation of the Last Colonies in Africa," *International Affairs* (Moscow) 10, no. 4 (April 1964): 39. In an interview with the Czechoslovak news agency, Ceteka, Roberto noted approvingly that a number of Angolans were studying in socialist countries and called for new initiatives to lay the basis for longterm cooperation with those states. FNLA, *Angola* 1, no. 14 (Léopoldville, July 15–31, 1964, mimeo.): 14–15, 18.

18. The last such communiqué promised departure of a delegation in July for Peking, Moscow, Prague, Belgrade, and London. GRAE, "Commu-

niqué," no. 73 (Léopoldville, July 3, 1964, mimeo.).

19. Roberto subsequently announced that when "circumstances" permitted, the trip to China would be rescheduled. Having themselves fought for their liberation, the Chinese, he said, would surely understand the delay. *Jeune Afrique,* Apr. 4, 1965, p. 15.

20. *Année africaine 1963* (Paris: Editions A. Pedone, 1965), p. 165.

21. *Tribune de Lausanne,* Jan. 24, 1964.

22. *Foreign Report* (London), March 26, 1964, pp. 3–4.

23. According to Savimbi's travel companion, Florentino Duarte, the East Europeans were most eager "to learn more of the [different] tendencies within the FNLA." See exchange of letters between Savimbi and Duarte (letters that bear on the evolution of the Roberto-Savimbi split) in FNLA, *Angola* 1, no. 14 (Léopoldville, July 15–31, 1964): 3–7. Duarte, born in 1942 at Luanda and schooled in Brazzaville, had studied in Tunis and Liège (Belgium) before taking up political science, as did Savimbi, at the University of Lausanne.

24. Interview with Mike Marshment in UNITA, *Kwacha-Angola* (special edition, London, 1972), p. 15.

25. Augusto Tadeu Pereira Bastos, a twenty-two year old, previously pro-MPLA mestiço from Benguela, who had been studying at American University, Washington, D.C. Bastos boasted to the press that GRAE had an army of twenty-five thousand (*Unita* [Rome], July 23, 1964), announced plans to visit India to arrange military training for GRAE partisans (*Agence France Presse,* Aug. 24, 1964), and then left GRAE just as abruptly as he had entered. Roberto fired him in October for embezzling GRAE funds.

26. MPLA, "MPLA Delegation Intervention at the Liberation Committee of the Organisation of African Unity" (Dar es Salaam, June 3, 1964, mimeo.).

27. See letters in FNLA, *Angola* 1, no. 14 (July 15–31, 1964). Savimbi's idea was to form his own party and then negotiate "a front with Neto" in Brazzaville.

28. *Le progres,* May 16–18, 1964. This anti-da Cruz stance was transmitted to André Massaki, president of the FNLA National Council, in an open letter (n.d.) signed by the president of the UNEA section in Switzerland, Jeronimo Wanga. The FNLA National Council rejected student objections to da Cruz's entry. FNLA, "Lettre adressée à Union Nationale des Etudiants Angolais (UNEA)-section suisse" (n.d., Léopoldville, mimeo.). The Swiss (largely Bakongo) section of UNEA later repudiated the Wisen query as representing only a small minority. GRAE, "Communiqué," no. 74 (Léopoldville, July 4, 1964, mimeo.).

Reflecting the general decline of GRAE prestige, however, an earlier (March–April 1964) gathering of fifty-two Angolan students of diverse political persuasion at a technical seminar in Geneva had called for the convening of a unity conference of all Angolan political movements and for the reopening of CVAAR (MPLA) medical/refugee services in the Congo. See Premier Seminaire Technique des Etudiants Angolais, "Communiqué final" (Geneva, Apr. 1, 1964, mimeo.); and *Remarques congolaises et africaines* (Brussels), July 11, 1964. In the United States, a key (Bakongo) UNEA leader, Paul Touba, deplored the "errors" and disunity of GRAE leadership, ridiculed the hyperbola of its military communiqués, and offered student mediation of leadership quarrels and student participation in a conference to reunite and reorganize revolutionary forces. Paul Touba, "Politico-Military Crisis in the Angolan Revolution" (New York, July 1964, mimeo.); Touba, "Angola, Mère Patrie: Qui te Sauvera?" *A Voz do Estudante Angolano* (New York), no. 13 (Aug. 1964); and Touba, "Angola: Time of Trouble," ibid., no. 14 (Sept. 1964).

29. See chap. 3.

30. See letters in FNLA, *Angola* 1, no. 14 (July 15–31, 1964).

31. Letter, Kunzika to Neto, Mar. 10, 1964, PDA, ref. DIR/1201/64.

32. Statement of Oct. 2, 1964, in Robert Davezies, *Les angolais* (Paris: Edition de Minuit, 1965), p. 212.

33. Savimbi now accepted charges that in 1961–1962 Roberto and his aides had ordered the "massacre of thousands of 'Southern Angolans'" as well as predominantly mestiço MPLA patrols. See letters in FNLA, *Angola* 1, no. 14 (July 15–31, 1964).

34. Jorge Valentim, "Information sur l'évolution de la lutte angolaise" (n.p., May 28, 1964, mimeo.).

35. The *Times* of London, July 26, 1964, cited diplomatic circles as believing that Tshombe would prove "ungrateful" to the Portuguese because of his domestic need to win left-wing support and to avoid alienating 250,000 Angolan refugees.

36. "Déclaration de Monsieur Jonas Savimbi Ministre des affaires étrangères du GRAE" (Cairo, July 16, 1964, mimeo.).

37. At that time, he had asserted that GRAE forces controlled "nearly all of the northern part" of Angola and that the war was "spreading" into the interior. Radio Moscow, 2:00 GMT, Apr. 7, 1964.

38. Savimbi's resignation produced a *New York Times* story, "Africans Hear Resistance in Angola Has Collapsed," July 19, 1964. His statement was reproduced and distributed by the MPLA (doc. 44/64, Brazzaville, Aug. 17, 1964, mimeo.) and published by *Remarques congolaises et africaines*, Sept. 12, 1964, pp. 374–375. See also *Le monde*, July 22, 1964.

39. This was the apparent thrust of Nkrumah's question put to the heads of state in Cairo: "What could be the result of entrusting the training of freedom fighters against imperialism into the hands of an imperialist agent?" Kwame Nkrumah, *Africa's Finest Hour* (speech delivered by President Nkrumah at the Conference of African Heads of State and Government in Cairo on July 19, 1964) (London: Ghana High Commission, 1964). See also MPLA, "Communiqué," doc. 43/64 (Brazzaville, Aug. 13, 1964, mimeo.).

40. See Jonas Savimbi, "Où en est la révolution angolaise?" *Remarques congolaise et africaines*, Nov. 25, 1964, pp. 489–495. In May 1964, Savimbi approached the American embassy and this author, who was in Léopoldville at the time working with a refugee education project, for an air ticket to Europe. Neither the embassy nor the author met his request. Savimbi chose to interpret the author's response not for what it was—an unwillingness to intervene in an internal political matter as well as a lack of funds—but instead as a sign that he was serving as a "political adviser" to Roberto. Savimbi subsequently wrote acknowledging that this had been a "misinterpretation." Letter to the author, Sept. 22, 1965.

41. D.D.D. [Djibril Demba Diop?], "Où en est la révolution angolaise?" ibid., Oct. 14, 1964, pp. 428–430, and open letter from Johnny Edouard to the editor of ibid., distributed by GRAE, Bureau d'Alger (Algiers, Dec. 15, 1964, mimeo.). In 1966, Savimbi told John de St. Jorre of the *Observer* (London) that one of his reasons for leaving GRAE was that Roberto refused to set up GRAE missions in Western countries in order to convince them that the rebellion was more than just a series of bandit raids. de St. Jorre, "UNITA" (Lusaka, July 26, 1966, unpublished typescript).

42. Described as a "pillar of reaction" in GRAE, "Communiqué," no. 81, July 21, Savimbi was dismissed from his post as foreign minister on July 28. GRAE, "Communiqué," no. 85, July 29.

43. Nkrumah, *Africa's Finest Hour* (London: Ghana High Commission, 1964). For a description of Nkrumah's advocacy of Union Government at Cairo, see W. Scott Thompson, *Ghana's Foreign Policy, 1957–1966* (Princeton, N.J.: Princeton University Press, 1969), pp. 350–356.

44. *Spark* (Accra), Aug. 9, 1963; see also ibid., Nov. 29, 1963.

45. Ibid.

46. Colin Legum, *Pan-Africanism: A Short Political Guide* (New York: Frederick A. Praeger, 1965), p. 141.

47. Julius K. Nyerere, *Mkutano wa Cairo* (speech by the President of the United Republic of Tanganyika and Zanzibar, Cairo, July 20, 1964) (Dar es Salaam: Unguja, 1964).

48. *Spark* had been consistently critical of the OAU's decision to recognize Roberto's government in exile. This had provoked GRAE protests against *Spark*'s "fulminations" and the failure of Ghana to contribute to the Angolan struggle. See open letter from Rosário Neto, minister of information, to Koffi Batsa, director of *Spark*, GRAE, doc. no. 84/20/21/INFOR./964 (Léopoldville, Feb. 7, 1964, mimeo.).

49. OAU, Assembly of Heads of State and Governments, "Verbatim and Summary Records," first sess., pt. IV, 8th meeting (Cairo, July 21, 1964, mimeo.), pp. 10–13.

50. Appeals made by Jonas Savimbi at the Lagos meeting of OAU foreign ministers in February (*Le progrès*, Feb. 25, 1964) and by Roberto at a May meeting of the ALC in Dar es Salaam. The latter is discussed in a paper on GRAE foreign policy written by Pedro Vaal Hendrik Neto, JUPA, "A Dar-es-Salam e ao Cairo" (Léopoldville, [1964], mimeo.).

51. OAU, "Verbatim and Summary Records," 7th meeting, pp. 2–8.

52. *Jeune Afrique* (Paris), July 27, 1964, p. 16. The same figure is given in D.D.D., "Où en est la révolution angolaise?" p. 430.

53. OAU, "Verbatim and Summary Records," 8th meeting, pp. 26–31.

54. Ibid., p. 35.

55. Roberto alleged that just three months earlier, Massamba-Debat had rejected his personal request that GRAE's refugee relief services (SARA) be permitted to function in Congo-Brazzaville (where the MPLA's service, CVAAR, already operated). Ibid., p. 38.

56. Twenty-eight had been so killed during the past six months. Ibid., p. 6.

57. Ibid., pp. 9–10.

58. With some exceptions: Sierra Leone would have had the OAU demand that Holden Roberto accept the MPLA en bloc into GRAE; Kenya was of the opinion that the OAU, which had already seated GRAE as a

regular, official delegation, would be going back on its own commitments if it did not simply ask the MPLA to dissolve itself; and Tanganyika suggested that Roberto might be asked to accept two or three leaders of the MPLA into GRAE to avoid the eventuality of Brazzaville's having to host adversary movements. Ibid., passim.

59. The ascendancy of the *Front de Libération Nationale* (FLN) over Messali Hadj's *Mouvement National Algérien* (MNA).

60. See Frantz Fanon, *The Wretched of the Earth* (New York: Grove Press, 1963).

61. OAU, "Verbatim and Summary Records," 8th meeting, pp. 32–34.

62. Ibid., pp. 36–37.

63. FNLA, *Angola informations*, Oct. 19, 1964.

64. *L'Etoile du Congo*, Aug. 13, 1964.

65. *Diário Popular* (Lisbon), Dec. 3, 1964.

66. *Alliance des Jeunes Angolais pour la Liberté*. See Marcum, *Angolan Revolution*, 1: 290–291.

67. *Le progrès*, Nov. 6, 1963.

68. Ibid., July 12, Aug. 10–11, 1963.

69. Matondo and Makumbi, respectively, assumed the status of president and secretary-general of the FPIKP, the same posts they held in the PPA.

70. Ibid., Oct. 18, 1965.

71. See FPIKP petition, Nov. 24, 1965, United Nations, Committee on Decolonization, doc. A/AC.109/pet.429, Jan. 31, 1966.

72. See *Courrier d'Afrique*, June 10, 1965; *Le progrès*, Oct. 23, 1965.

73. José Milton Putuilu of Ngwizako was named FPIKP director of foreign affairs.

74. Alphonse Matondo to author, Mar. 14, 1966, ref. no. 173/03/66/Pres. MAP. See also FPIKP, "Conférence de presse de Monsieur Matondo Alphonse Proença" (Léopoldville, Oct. 10, 1965, mimeo.).

75. See FPIKP petition.

76. David Grenfell, *Notes*, no. 30 (Kibentele), Nov. 19, 1965.

77. UPRONA, "Statuts constitutifs de l'Union Progressiste de Nso en [*sic*] Angola" (Léopoldville, Aug. 8, 1965, mimeo.), title VI, art. 23.

78. Carlos Vunzi, a former resident of Kibokolo, had spent over a year as a political prisoner in Angola before taking refuge in the Congo. Other UPRONA officers included vice-presidents Bernard Lungieki and Antoine Panda and secretary-general David Muanza.

79. UPRONA, "Communica" (Léopoldville, Mar. 21, 1966, mimeo.)

80. Letter, Mar. 7, 1966.

81. See Marcum, *Angolan Revolution*, 1, chap. 2.

82. Some of the former refugees persuaded to return to Angola by the Nto-Bako president, Angelino Alberto, were jailed when they did return. What was acceptable outside—talk of negotiated independence—was viewed as dangerous and unacceptable inside. Grenfell, *Notes*, no. 34 Dec. 17, 1965.

83. See letters from Nto-Bako/Lélé: to U.N. secretary-general, Nov. 26, 1963, United Nations, Committee on Decolonization, doc. A/AC. 109/pet. 235, Apr. 28, 1964; to Portuguese minister of justice, May 25, 1964, ibid., A/AC. 109/pet. 235/add. 1, Apr. 28, 1964; to Premier Salazar, Aug. 12,

1965, ibid., A/AC. 109/pet. 416/add. 1, Sept. 14, 1965, which listed the names of twenty-six Nto-Bako members allegedly incarcerated in Luanda; and Nto-Bako/Lélé petition to president of Trusteeship Council. Mar. 28, 1966 urging that pressure be brought to bear on Portugal to grant amnesty to prisoners and negotiate independence. Ibid., A/AC. 109/pet. 471, June 29, 1966.

84. Memorandum, Nov. 6, 1965, ibid., A/AC. 109/pet. 428, Jan. 31, 1966.

85. Ibid., A/AC. 109/pet. 427, Jan. 31, 1966.

86. These included Nto-Bako's principal leader inside Angola, Armando Manuel da Cruz. See letter, Dec. 14, 1970, to secretary-general, ibid., A/AC. 109/pet. 1167, Apr. 22, 1971.

87. *Diário de Notícias* (Lisbon), Aug. 21, 1965. In a Dec. 28, 1963, letter to Secretary-General U Thant, the MDIA had reported confidently that in July 1963 General Chairman M'Bala had been sent to Angola where he was bringing the movement's "noble work" to "fruition." United Nations, doc. A/AC. 109/pet. 237, Apr. 28, 1964.

88. Letter submitted to U.N by Nto-Bako, Dec. 14, 1970, doc. A/AC. 109/pet. 1167, Apr. 22, 1971.

89. See chap. 2.

90. UNA, "Memorandum to Their Excellencies, the Chiefs of State or of Government of Africa, 2nd 'Summit' Conference, Cairo," July 17, 1964 (Joint Publication Research Service 26,533, Sept. 24, 1964), p. 11.

91. Kassanga met with Tshombe on July 23, 1964. Interview with author, Sept. 2, 1968.

92. Kassinda returned without a visa to Léopoldville, where he was arrested in October 1964. By his own account, as a result of conniving by Holden Roberto, he spent eighteen days in Ndolo prison before being "liberated by the Authorities of the Central Congolese Government" (Tshombe). André Kassinda, "Curriculum Vitae" (Léopoldville, Apr. 10, 1965, mimeo.).

93. United Nations, Committee on Decolonization, doc. A/AC. 109/SR. 387, Sept. 22, 1965, p. 9.

94. The theme of their leaflets was failure, corruption, and the need for new leadership in the Angolan revolution. See "Apelo ao Povo Angolano" (Léopoldville, Jan. 24, 1965, mimeo.), and "Angolanas, Angolanos! Grande Povo" (n.p., n.d., mimeo.).

95. See manifesto presented Apr. 4, 1965, to rally (grandly estimated by Kassanga at thirty thousand persons) in Léopoldville's Bock Park. CPA, "Manifeste" (Léopoldville, Apr. 4, 1965, mimeo.), and CPA, "Plateforme" (Léopoldville, Apr. 1, 1965, mimeo.), art. 7.

96. *L'Etoile du Congo* (Léopoldville), Apr. 9, 1965.

97. At its outset, CUNA publicly endorsed the formation of an Angolan common front under the direction of Holden Roberto, *Le progrès*, July 11, 1963. Its pro-GRAE secretary-general designate, Artur Manuel da Costa [Kosi] resigned on Aug. 2, 1963. See letter, Oct. 15, 1963, in United Nations, Committee on Decolonization, doc. A/AC. 109/pet. 282, June 26, 1964. CUNA, ignored by Roberto, soon began denouncing the GRAE leader for "dictatorial behavior" and for engineering arrests of political opponents. *Le progrès*, Aug. 19, 1963. CUNA's activities henceforth were limited largely to

periodic calls for an Angolan "united front." See "Statement by Mr. Kita Alphonse, Secretary-General of CUNA to the Eighteenth Session of the United Nations General Assembly," Oct. 6, 1963, and letter to U.N. Committee on Decolonization, June 1, 1964, doc. A/AC. 109/pet. 284, June 26, 1964. For some months in 1964, CUNA seems to have been allied with the MPLA as a member of the Democratic Front (FDLA), MPLA, *Boletim do Militante MPLA*, no. 1 (Brazzaville, May 25, 1964, mimeo.).

98. CUNA leadership: Henrique Pierre, president; Alphonse Kita, secretary-general; and José Manuel, political director.

99. The MNA thus renewed in 1965 an earlier association (1962–1963) with Kassanga and Kassinda. See chap. 2.

100. PNA president José Paulo Chiringueno to author, Feb. 28, 1966 (Présidence no. 8/PNA/66). On Dec. 7, 1965, Chiringueno wrote Secretary-General U Thant asking for U.N. recognition of the PNA "as one of the Angolan parties fighting to gain the independence of Angola." U.N., Committee on Decolonization, doc. A/AC.109/pet. 430, Jan. 3, 1966. In Feb. 1966, Chiringueno, just returned from six months on a political organizing mission along the Angola-Kasai (Congo) border, charged that the Portuguese police (PIDE) were massacring Angolans. He reported seeing ten mutilated African bodies in the Luachino River. PNA, Comité National, "Communiqué," no. 4 (Léopoldville, Feb. 6, 1966, mimeo.).

101. See Marcum, *Angolan Revolution*, 1: 241. UGTA officers as of Dec. 1966 (according to information provided by UGTA to the African-American Labor Center in New York) were Paul Bing, president; Bernardo Domingos, vice-president; André Kassinda, secretary-general; Carlos Manuel Pacheco, assistant secretary-general; and Mauricio Luvualu, secretary for international affairs and information.

102. See chap. 3. To add to the appearance of multiorganizational complexity, Marcos Kassanga presented himself during this period as head of a UNA youth wing, or *Movimento de Juventude Nacional Angolana* (JUNA). In addition a CPA youth movement, *Afrika-Vanguardia*, sprang forth under the direction of a "commissar in chief," Manuel Kiala.

103. CPA, "Convention," doc. no. 3/CPA/965 (Léopoldville, Apr. 30, 1965, mimeo.), signed by Kassinda (UNA), Henrique Pierre (CUNA), Francisco Maiembe [Mayembe] (MNA), Chiringueno (PNA), Mauricio Luvualu (UGTA), and Pierre Nanenthela (LGTA).

104. CPA, "Conférence de presse donnée par Soma André M. Kassinda Leader nationaliste angolais et membre du Conseil du Peuple Angolais 'CPA'" (Léopoldville, May 7, 1965, mimeo.). See also *Courrier d'Afrique*, May 8–9, 1965.

105. Portuguese funding of the CPA was suspected. Indicative of his modus operandi, Kassinda wrote to George Houser of the American Committee on Africa and to the author (Jan. 27, 1965) asking for personal gifts of clothes (suits) and books. He was not accommodated.

106. At a meeting of the OAU Council of Ministers in Nairobi (Feb. 26–Mar. 9, 1965), Tshombe reportedly told questioners that "the policy of Adoula towards GRAE was his" and that only other pressing needs prevented him from offering the help he would like. In Nairobi, Tshombe met several times with Roberto and gave him $300 so that he might fly north to

confer with his political confidants in Tunis before returning to Léopoldville. See Grenfell, "Political Notes" (Kibentele, typescript, Mar. 15, 1965).

107. Roberto told President Kasavubu that unless he received more cooperation from the central government, he would consider moving his GRAE offices to Lusaka. Grenfell, "Notes," Jan. 22, 1965. As Interior Minister Godefroid Munongo saw it, Roberto had been invited by "our adversaries" to create "operational bases" in neighboring states from which to attack the Congo. *Courrier d'Afrique*, Feb. 9, 1965.

108. Reuters cited a Portuguese spokesman as indicating that Tshombe met with Premier Salazar during a Lisbon stopover of several hours following official visits to Paris and Madrid. *New York Times*, June 10, 1965. There were also reports that "the large and still prosperous Portuguese business community in Léopoldville" was then "active in discouraging Congolese support" of Angolan nationalists. *Foreign Report* (London), no. 908, May 6, 1965, p. 4.

109. Tshombe reportedly told Roberto that he personally did not believe stories of Roberto's association with the rebels. Grenfell, "Notes," March 15, 1965.

110. CNL foreign affairs spokesman Thomas Kanza, in an interview with the official organ of the Algerian army, spoke of Roberto-UPA involvement in the death of Lumumba, counterinsurgency operations in Kwilu, and even Tshombe's relations with the Portuguese. *El Djeich* (Algiers), no. 25 (May 1965): 17. The MPLA reproduced and circulated CNL allegations of such "criminal" activities. MPLA, *Etudes et documents* (Algiers), no. 7 (June 1965). See also "Déclaration du Conseil National de Libération [Jan. 13, 1965] in *Remarques congolaises et africaines* (Brussels), Feb. 17, 1965, p. 22.

111. Gaston Soumialot on Zanzibar-Tanzania Domestic Service (Swahili), 1830 GMT, Jan. 28, 1965. See also *New York Times*, Jan. 29, 1965. A rival faction of the CNL headed by Egide Bocheley-Davidson took a contrastingly pro-GRAE stance. *Le monde*, Mar. 31, 1965; *Remarques congolaises et africaines*, Apr. 14, 1965, pp. 14–15.

112. See Edouard's mimeographed bulletin, *Angola informations*, passim.

113. Open letter, Roberto to Tshombe, June 21, 1965. GRAE, Présidence, no. 1.074/GC/V/65 (mimeo.).

114. That is the gist of what Tshombe told Salazar at their June 8 meeting in Lisbon, according to pro-Mobutu Congolese aides who accompanied Tshombe on his mission to the Portuguese capital. Grenfell, "Notes," Sept. 15, 1965.

115. Namely Miguel Pedro Vita, chief of staff, and Norbert Sengele, assistant chief of staff. "Déclaration faite par Mr. Armindo Freitas, membre de l'état major et directeur du centre de formation et instruction générale de l'Armée de Libération Nationale de L'Angola 'ALNA'" (Léopoldville: May 11, 1965, mimeo.). See also *Courrier d'Afrique*, May 12, 1965.

116. In addition to Bento as secretary-general, the rebel executive committee included Pierre Naninthela (assistant secretary-general), Alexandre Pemo, Raymond Fernandes da Silva (Mbala), Garcia Fragoso, Emmanuel Nsungu, Afonso Toko, Thomas Nlamvu, M. Diamanama, and Antoine Dumbi. *L'Etoile du Congo*, June 9, 1965.

117. Ibid., June 21, 1965. According to subsequent reports from GRAE, Taty had been suspended from his ministerial post prior to the attempted coup. GRAE, *Angola informations*, Aug. 31, 1965, p. 12.

118. GRAE, "Rapport sur l'incident provoqué au Kongo Central par la confiscation d'un camion du GRAE" (Léopoldville, n.d., mimeo.).

119. According to GRAE sources, as early as 1963 Taty was seen entering a car belonging to the Portuguese embassy. He explained at the time that the driver was a cousin. Despite this and what was later portrayed as repeated misuse of organizational funds, Taty was kept on in his ministerial role by Roberto. Thus over a considerable time he was in a position to deliver (and allegedly did so) military plans and other information to the Portuguese. GRAE, *Angola informations*, Aug. 31, 1965, p. 12.

120. The agent, M. Campos, worked for Motema-Léo. The Cabindan, Afonso Toko, an LGTA dissident (see n. 116), later described in detail how PIDE officials manipulated importunate exiles. In a political mea culpa, Toko wrote that when he broached the issue of autonomy for Cabinda and Angola, a police official looked him "in the white of the eyes" and said: "That shirt you are wearing isn't in very good shape." The official sent out for a new shirt. Toko then told him that he "needed a new suit as well as a shirt"—but settled for 15,000 Congolese francs. See GRAE, "Déclaration de M. Afonso Toko" (Léopoldville, June 28, 1965, mimeo.).

121. Having been rebuffed by Roberto to whom he had offered his services as a "political adviser," Artho, the sometime Swiss patron of Jonas Savimbi, turned against the GRAE president. He concluded that Roberto was incapable of "making the liberation of Angola more than a family affair, had no concrete political ideas of his own, did not know the situation inside Angola, and was unable to understand the degree to which the [political] situation had changed in the Congo." To Artho the situations in both Angola and the Congo pointed to the "futility of armed struggle." He embraced the politics of Moïse Tshombe and threw himself (and apparently funds raised for the aborted GRAE cadre school) behind a new cause—that of Kassinda and the CPA. Letter, Artho to author, May 17, 1965.

122. On June 20, a group of SARA medics announced their adhesion to the CPA. *L'Etoile du Congo*, June 21, 1965.

123. Led by the JDA president, Alphonse Nsimba.

124. On June 25, *L'Etoile du Congo* gave front-page coverage to three stories variously attacking GRAE, endorsing nonviolence, and supporting Taty's junta—including a statement by collaborator Jean M'Bala (MDIA) who had been residing in Angola since mid-1963.

125. Events and plans leading up to this assault are detailed in a "confession" by the principal LGTA participant: "Déclaration de Mr. Francisco Manuel Bento, un des promoteurs de l'assaut du 25 juin 1965 dirigé contre le bureau du Gouvernement Révolutionnaire de l'Angola en Exil 'GRAE' et membre du soi-disant nouveau comité-executif de la Ligue Générale des Travailleurs de l'Angola 'LGTA'" (Léopoldville, July 29, 1965, mimeo.). For statements by SARA medics implicated in the assault, see "Copia Literal e Integral das Declarações dos Srs. José Manuel Pombal et Vicente Manuel Alexandre, Ex-Enfermeiros do SARA, Apos o Assalto as Instalações do GRAE" (Léopoldville, June 27, mimeo).

126. Roberto itemized GRAE losses in an open letter to the central Congolese government (Présidence, N/Réf.: 1.073/Dos. PA-V/65, Léopoldville, June 26, 1965, mimeo.), and Kassinda presented his own accounting in "Aide-memoire à l'intention de l'Organisation de l'Unité Africaine 'OAU'" (Léopoldville, July 14, 1965, mimeo.).

127. Six months later, wishing to return to Kinshasa but fearful of arrest, Artho wrote to Roberto from Steinhausen, Switzerland. Warning of damaging revelations to the press should any harm come to him upon return, Artho offered to cut Roberto and his aide, J. Peterson, in on a block of stock in a Kinshasa business venture (Congomagasin). Roberto released Artho's letter to the press, and the latter remained in Switzerland. Artho to Roberto, Jan. 29, 1966. See *Courrier d'Afrique*, June 26, 1966.

128. *Afrique nouvelle* (Dakar), July 8, 1965.

129. *Le progrès*, July 10–11, 1965.

130. Marcum, *Angolan Revolution*, 1: 60, 65.

131. Necaca cited pilferage of SARA clothes and medicine and personal use of SARA vehicles. Statement to the press quoted in MPLA, "Memorandum à l'intention du conseil des ministres de l'OUA," (Accra, Oct. 1965, mimeo.).

132. *Angola informations,* Aug. 31, 1965.

133. Appearing as a bimonthly, a mimeographed bulletin entitled *UPA: A Voz da Revolução.*

134. The FPIKP fantasized that such a congress would create an executive committee that, assisted by OAU jurists and U.N. experts, would go to Portugal and negotiate Angolan independence. *Courrier d'Afrique*, May 4, 1966.

135. Lamvu (born about 1937) attended Protestant schools in the Congo and was trained as a medical technician in Belgium. Together with António Ernesto, he created the CBOA in March 1965. See CBOA, "Raisons de la création du comité des Bons Offices Angolais," ref. L.E./L.NG/67 (Brazzaville, May 26, 1967, mimeo.), and *Africa Research Bulletin* (PSC series) (London) 2, no. 7 (July 1965): 338a. Joining as secretary-general was a veteran leader of Cabindan separatist movements, Henriques Tiago Nzita (see Marcum, *Angolan Revolution*, 1: 295). *Courrier d'Afrique*, Apr. 28, 1966.

136. *L'Etoile du Congo*, Apr. 22, 1966.

137. *Daily Times* (Lagos), Oct. 18, 1965.

138. Kassinda testified before the U.N. Committee on Decolonization. A/C.4/SR1574 (Dec. 7, 1965), pp. 2–6. In apparent expectation of international handouts, the CPA prepared a long list of needs ranging from antiaircraft guns to wristwatches. CPA, "Besoins urgents et prements [sic] pour l'exécution et développement de l'action révolutionnaire entreprise par le Conseil du Peuple Angolais dans la réorganisation de la lutte" (Kinshasa, Mar. 9, 1966, mimeo.).

139. *Centro de Assistência Sócio-Sanitária* (CASA), an on-paper copy of SARA (GRAE) and CVAAR (MPLA).

140. The *Fôrças Armadas de Libertação de Angola* (FALA), of at most a few hundred men, led by a defector from the MPLA military, Commander Sozinho da Costa, and trained at a *Centro Revolucionário d'Aplicação Militar* (CRAM) near Benseke-Futi a few miles south of Kinshasa.

141. CPA, "Communiqué," doc. no. 154/CNE/966 (Kinshasa, May 30, 1966, mimeo.).

142. Named to the CNE were: Kassinda (UNA), president; José Paulo Chiringueno (PNA), vice-president and interior; Domingos de Sousa (CUNA), secretary-general; Kassanga (UGTA), external relations; Domingos Bernardo (CUNA), finances; Mendonça Fuato Balombo (UNA), information, propaganda, and administration; Eduardo Tshimpy (MNA), education; and Garcia de Costa N'Simba (LGTA), social affairs. Ibid. See Kassanga's petition, "On Behalf of the Government of the Council of the People of Angola in Exile" submitted from Lincoln Univ., Pa., U.N., Committee on Decolonization, A/AC.109/pet.576 (Feb. 27, 1967).

143. *L'Etoile du Congo*, June 14, 1966. *Ghanaian Times* (Accra), June 15, 1966. Writing in the Paris journal *France-Eurafrique* 18, no. 176 (Aug.–Sept. 1966): 17, Yves-Marie Choupaut depicted the CPA as a dynamic movement that regrouped UPA and MPLA militants and threatened rapidly to isolate Roberto. Roberto called a press conference to ridicule the CNE as a traitorous "joke." *Courrier d'Afrique*, June 15, 1966.

144. Kassinda accused Taty and Armindo de Freitas of "selling revolutionary plans" to the Portuguese. CPA, "Communiqué," no. 154/CNE/966 (Kinshasa, May 30, 1966, mimeo.). In August 1966, Grenfell at Kibentele read JMAE leaflets promising food, clothes, and weapons to ELNA soldiers who joined Taty's force, which Grenfell estimated to number up to three hundred men. Pointing to Mobutu, the JMAE argued that the future belonged to "the military," not quarreling, corrupt politicians (viz. GRAE). Grenfell interview with author, Apr. 23, 1967.

145. Externally the weekly *Jeune Afrique*, June 26, 1966, labeled Kassinda and the CPA a "fifth column."

146. According to Eduardo Pinock, all members of the CBOA were arrested and held at Kinkuzu, as were fourteen MPLA soldiers arrested at Songololo. Grenfell, "Political Notes" (Kibentele, Aug. 30, 1966, typescript). *Révolution africaine* (Algiers), no. 214 (Mar. 20–26, 1967): 29 and ibid., no. 218 (Apr. 17–23, 1967): 4.

147. *L'Etoile du Congo*, July 28, 1966; *Courrier d'Afrique*, July 29, 1966.

148. Agence France Presse, *Bulletin d'Afrique* (Paris), Mar. 10, 1967. Within GRAE circles, it was later said that Kassinda had been taken inside Angola where he met his death "trying to escape." Grenfell, "Political Notes" (Mar. 20, 1967). In November, one of the founders of CUNA (CPA) reported that his movement too was "'dead' just as all the other small parties were." Grenfell, "Notes," no. 41 (Nov. 25, 1966).

149. Agence France Presse, *Bulletin d'Afrique*, Mar. 10, 1967. According to Roberto, Lamvu, who had faked illness and then run away from the Kinkuzu dispensary, was the only one to have escaped as of March 1967. Grenfell. "Political Notes" (Mar. 20, 1967).

150. See chap. 3.

151. Marcum, *Angolan Revolution*, 1: 88–89.

152. PDA, "Conférence de presse de Mr. Emmanuel Kounzika, vice-premier ministre du GRAE et président du PDA: La révolution angolaise et ses trames" (Léopoldville, July 30, 1965, mimeo.).

153. Excerpt of Dec. 31, 1964, report reproduced in Kunzika to Roberto, GRAE, CVP-PG/255/65, Dec. 16, 1965 (Kinshasa, typescript).

154. *Angola informations*, Apr. 24, 1965.

155. The PDA, in contrast to the UPA, functioned under a comprehensive and operative set of internal rules and orders. See PDA, "Statuts, fonctionnement des commissions, règlement d'ordre interieur du Parti Démocratique de l'Angola" (Léopoldville, 1965, mimeo.).

156. MPLA/Viriato: Matias Miguéis, Jorge Manteya Freitas, Alexandre António, José Kabuangata, André António Domingos, Manuel João Leite, Vicente Sebastião, António Amaro, Jorge Manzila, Vidal Bartolomeu, Domingos dos Santos, André Kukia, José Miguel, Graça da Silva Tavares (absent), Viriato da Cruz. PDA: André Massaki, Emmanuel Kounzika, Garcia Diavita, António Jabes Josias, Ferdinand Dombele, Sébastien Lubaki, André Mvila, Simon Diallo Mingiedi, Augustin Kaziluki, Samuel Teka, Martin Nsumbu, Norbert Kiatalwa (absent), Antoine Kidimbu, Sanda Martin, Domingos Vetokele.

157. Letter later circulated as part of a collection of documents in PDA, *Mondo: A Voz Democrática* (Léopoldville, Dec. 1965, mimeo.).

158. For Roberto's report on the Accra meeting, see *UPA: A Voz Revolução* (Léopoldville, Nov.–Dec. 1965, mimeo.).

159. Letter, Kunzika to Sebastian Chale (OAU Liberation Committee), Dec. 1, 1965, GRAE, CVP-PG/250/65.

160. Letter, Kunzika to Roberto, Dec. 16, 1965, GRAE, CVP-PG/255/65. Two examples of harassment: (1) concerned that the PDA might be linked with Savimbi, Roberto had PDA offices and the personal residences of Kunzika and PDA official Sanda Martin searched in mid-1964. Robert Davezies, *Les angolais* (Paris: Editions de Minuit, 1965), p. 215, (2) José M. Peterson's UPA sûreté broke up a Kunzika press conference on July 30, 1965, at the point when Kunzika spoke out in favor of convening a national conference of the FNLA.

161. Letter, Kunzika to Mobutu, Dec. 28, 1965, GRAE, CVP-PG/?/65.

162. PDA, "Monsieur António Josias: motif de votre démission du comité directeur du PDA," Dir. 1503/66 (Kinshasa, July 25, 1966, mimeo.).

163. Approximately eleven hundred in primary schools and one hundred in the fledgling secondary school. See Canadian Teachers' Federation, *Newsletter* (Ottawa) 22, no. 4 (Apr. 1966), and "Angolan Secondary Institute—Needs" (New York, Feb. 1966, mimeo.).

164. Leaders of the Casablanca group included two PDA Central Committee members, Sanda Martin and Samuel Silva, as well as former MDIA leaders Augustin Kaziluki and Simon Diallo Mingiedi.

165. PDA, "Clarification de la situation politique du PDA" (Léopoldville, Sept. 26, 1964, mimeo.).

166. Recently returned from studies in Belgium, the Bazombo journalist, former PDA vice-president, and long-time adversary of Holden Roberto, Antoine Matumona (see Marcum, *Angolan Revolution*, 1:250–251), helped orchestrate the anti-GRAE press campaign.

167. *Courrier d'Afrique*, Apr. 14, 1965. Mingiedi's article was translated and published as "The Angolan Revolution in Disarray" in Joint Publications Research Service, 35,324, May 4, 1966, p. 16.

168. Kunzika to the author, June 6, 1966.

169. *Courrier d'Afrique*, July 7, 1966.

170. PDA, "Communiqué à la presse" (Kinshasa, July 7, 1966, mimeo.).

171. See PDA, "Monsieur António Josias."

172. Ceremonies at which over five hundred primary and seventy-five secondary school students were promoted. For names of the students, copies of examinations taken, and speeches given, see GRAE, "Palmares de l'institut d'enseignment secondaire angolais 'IESA'" (Kinshasa, July 16, 1966, mimeo.).

173. For a discussion of intergenerational conflict and the propensity of African party youth wings to act as political dissidents grounded in an age-homogeneous subculture, see Aristide Zolberg, *Creating Political Order: The Party State of West Africa* (Chicago: Rand McNally Co., 1966), pp. 74–75.

174. Born in the Congo of Angolan Bazombo parents, Mingiedi attended a Salvation Army School and became a schoolteacher. His criticism of Roberto and advocacy of a congress of Angolan nationalists earned him his Aug. 2 arrest on charges of treason. Protests against the arrest by a host of Bazombo groups gave rise to adverse publicity for GRAE—but failed to influence Roberto. *Courrier d'Afrique*, Aug. 4, 8, 9, 11, 1966.

175. Ibid., Aug. 4, 1966. In fact Kunzika opposed Mingiedi's arrest.

176. Ibid., Aug. 7, 1966.

177. Committee headed by Alphonse N'simba, president; Pierre Sibu, first vice-president; Gabriel Kiala, second vice-president; André-Marie Konoko, secretary-general; Alphonse da Costa, assistant secretary-general (directly involved in arrest of Mingiedi); and André dos Santos, education. See PDA, "Bilan politique de la JDA—et révocation de son comité directeur," doc. 9/66 (Kinshasa, Aug. 25, 1966, mimeo.).

178. *Le progrès*, Aug. 2, 1966.

179. PDA, "PDA n'est pas dissout" (Kinshasa, Aug. 3, 1966, mimeo.).

180. *Jeune Afrique*, Feb. 13, 1966, p. 13. Edouard was replaced in Algiers by Nicolas Vieira.

181. Alphonse Videira (B.A. in economics); Sebastião Ramos Pinto (B.A. in political science). *Courrier d'Afrique*, Mar. 29, 1966.

182. Peterson was sometimes referred to as GRAE's "minister of interior." Ibid., May 7–8, 1966.

183. GRAE, "Plate-forme du Front National de Libération de l'Angola (FNLA)" (Kinshasa [1966], mimeo.).

184. For press reports dwelling on this condition, see *Courrier d'Afrique*, July 16–17, 18, 19, Aug. 1, 31, 1966.

185. da Cruz partisans were denounced as dishonest opportunists and tools of imperialism. MPLA, *Boletim do Militante MPLA*, no. 1 (Brazzaville, May 25, 1964, mimeo.).

186. *Angola informations*, Oct. 19, 1964.

187. *Le progrès*, Nov. 18, 1965; *Le monde*, Feb. 6–7, 1966. In efforts to save the two, Roberto appealed to President Massamba-Debat (*Angola informations*, Dec. 1965) and to the OAU (*Courrier d'Afrique*, Dec. 8, 1965) urging them to intercede. Kunzika appealed to Neto (PDA, doc. D.8/65, Kinshasa, Dec. 1, 1965, mimeo.), and the MPLA/Viriato sent telegrams, letters, and memorandums to Brazzaville and beyond (JMPLA, "Onde esta a Honra Nacional?" *Angola 66* (Oegstgeest, Netherlands, 1966), pp. 7–9. According to some reports, Lúcio Lára presided over a "ten minute" trial that condemned Miguéis and Miguel to death. *Notícias* (Lourenço Marques), May

14, 1966. Other accounts cited Azevedo as blaming the Congolese army for the incident. *World Outlook: Perspective Mondiale* (Paris), Feb. 24, 1967, p. 209.

188. *Angola 66* (Oegstgeest, Netherlands, 1966), pp. 7–9.

189. JMPLA/Viriato, "Circular," no. 2/A/66 (Kinshasa, Nov. 15, 1966, mimeo.); MPLA/Viriato, Comitê Director Provisório, "Commemoration de la deuxième anniversaire de la mort de deux patriotes assassinés à Brazzaville en novembre 1965" (Kinshasa, Nov. 12, 1967, mimeo.).

190. In 1964, da Cruz told author Richard Gibson that he would prefer devoting himself to literature but felt obliged by "a number of good comrades" to continue a political leadership role. da Cruz was a man of unquestioned moral and political integrity. But there was a real question in Gibson's mind as to whether he was "ruthless or fanatical enough to make a successful leader in the maelstrom of African liberation." Gibson to the author, Feb. 20, 1970.

191. The exiled Mozambican writer, Virgilio de Lemos, saw in da Cruz the man who might be able to rally the dispersed and intrigue-ridden forces of Angolan nationalism into an effective revolutionary movement. See *L'Afrique actuelle* (Paris), no. 4 (Jan. 1966): 41.

192. In the words of Daniel Chipenda: "This is when our difficulties with the Chinese comrades began." *Daniel Chipenda*, interview, Lusaka, Zambia, Aug. 28, 1969 (Seattle: Liberation Support Movement, 1969), p. 15.

193. See, for example, Hsinhua, *Daily Bulletin* (London), June 21, 30, 1966. da Cruz traveled as part of an Afro-Asian Writers' Delegation to Tanzania, Zambia, and Somalia in late 1966. Ibid., Jan. 27, 1967.

194. *West Africa*, Aug. 6, 1973, p. 1096. da Cruz reportedly had been at odds with Chinese officials for some time before his death. Alfredo Margarido, "Angola: La mort de Viriato da Cruz," *Revue française d'études politiques africaines* (Paris), no. 92 (Aug. 1973): 14–16.

195. Founded at Songololo (Kongo Central) and headed by Manuel Francisco Bento (ex-LGTA) with Bernard Dombele (ex-UNTA). A USRA office was established in Kinshasa in Apr. 1966. *Le progrès*, Jan. 12, 1966; *Courrier d'Afrique*, Apr. 18, 1966.

196. Raymond Fernandes da Silva (Mbala), a major participant in the June 6, 1965, attempt to create a new LGTA executive committee headed by Manuel Francisco Bento, quickly dissociated himself from that abortive effort. da Silva, "Mise au Point" (Léopoldville, June 10, 1965, mimeo.). In September, however, he wrote a scathing report that accused LGTA leaders of nepotism, tribalism, corruption, and improper diversion of union funds to UPA/GRAE. He then used that report in seeking assistance from private sources in the United States where he was by that time studying on an American government scholarship. da Silva, "Rapport sur la Ligue Générale des Travailleurs de l'Angola 'LGTA'" (New York, Sept. 22, 1965, holograph). Carlos Kassel, the LGTA's principal organizer and link with the ICFTU (Marcum, *Angolan Revolution*, 1:176–177), had by this time given up on the LGTA/GRAE and left for Paris.

197. *Le progrès*, June 12, 1964.

198. In February 1964, Secretary-General Pascal Luvualu and Foreign Secretary Bernard Dombele were arrested after a UNTA congress in

Léopoldville called for a front uniting competing nationalist organizations. MPLA, "MPLA Delegation Intervention at the Liberation Committee of the Organisation of African Unity" (Dar es Salaam, June 3, 1964, mimeo.).

199. For example, a statement denouncing Kassinda and the CPA for exploiting anti-Roberto sentiment in order to destroy the revolution. UNTA, "Le travailleur de l'Angola," nos. 4–5 (Léopoldville, Apr.–May 1965, mimeo.).

200. In 1965, the UNTA's foreign secretary, Bernard Dombele, spoke at the annual Algerian trade union congress and a representative of UNTA's youth wing (*Mouvement de la Jeunesse Ouvrière Angolaise*) attended an international conference of teachers in Algiers. Ibid. UNTA maintained relations with the All-China Federation of Trade Unions and its secretary for social affairs, Moise Sébastien, visited Peking in June 1966. Hsinhua, *Daily Bulletin*, June 11, 1966.

201. See statement on common front by Ndongala Mbidi of UNTA to the U.N. Committee on Decolonization, doc. A/6700/add. 3 (Oct. 11, 1967), pp. 256–259.

202. Letter, FNTA to AFL-CIO, SN/ND.D/0025/64, Sept. 8, 1964.

203. A list of material needs was presented to the AFL-CIO by FNTA Secretary-General S. David N'Dombasie. Letter, SG/ND.D.-/00194/66, Jan. 18, 1966. Other FNTA officers were Albert D. Loukau, president; Antoine Manzambi, first vice-president; Adolphe Lundoloki, second vice-president; and Antoine R. Domingos, secretary for foreign affairs. FNTA list (Léopoldville, Sept. 2, 1965, mimeo.). The French spelling of first names suggests the émigré character of the movement. See also FNTA, "La FNTA et le problème angolais" (Léopoldville, Feb. 16, 1966, mimeo.).

204. *Le progrès*, Oct. 26, Nov. 5, 1965, Jan. 12, 1966.

205. The CSLA (see Marcum, *Angolan Revolution*, 1: 294) cooperated with MDIA and Nto-Bako–organized campaigns to persuade Angolan refugees to return home. It boasted that in 1964 over four thousand CSLA members moved back across the border to work "within the framework of the CSLA" inside Angola. CSLA, "Rapport des activités de la Confédération des Syndicats Libres Angolais (CSLA) depuis sa création en septembre 1962 jusqu'au 1er juin 1968" (Kinshasa, July 12, 1968, mimeo.). The CSLA opposed armed insurgency and argued for change through dialogue with the Portuguese. See CSLA, "A la veille du cinquième anniversaire de la révolution armée de l'Angola la . . . CSLA lance un appel pathétique aux instances internationales et africaines" (Léopoldville, March 1966, mimeo.). The CSLA was led by Gracia Kiala, president; J. Sukama, general vice-president; A. Lukombo, first vice-president; and André Kiazindika, secretary-general.

206. *Portugal Democrático* (São Paulo) 9, no. 86 (Sept. 1964): 7.

207. CSLA, "Communiqué" (Kinshasa, July 31, 1966).

208. *Courrier d'Afrique*, Jan. 27, 1965.

209. "Communiqué Conjoint" signed by S. David Dombasie (FNTA), Davidson Ditutala (UGTA), and H. Simon Ladeira (CGTA) in CGTA. *A Esperança*, no. 2 (Léopoldville, Mar.–Apr. 1965, mimeo.).

210. Marcum, *Angolan Revolution*, 1: 293–294.

211. On Feb. 15, 1964, Simon Ladeira-Lumona assumed the CGTA presidency. *Courrier d'Afrique*, Nov. 8–9, Nov. 10–11, 1969.

212. For a statement of the CGTA's philosophy of "syndicalist pluralism," see *A Esperança*, no. 1 (Jan.–Feb. 1965).

213. For example, in 1966 the CGTA secretary-general, Pedro Makumbi-Marquès, and the administrative secretary, Pedro Hilário Antonio, attended a course for trade unionists in France, while President Ladeira-Lumona participated in an education seminar in Switzerland, and others participated in programs organized by the *Union des Travailleurs Congolais* (UTC). Ibid., no. 6 (2d trimester, 1966).

214. The CGTA's most ambitious project called for the creation of a comprehensive rural development program based on agricultural cooperatives. CGTA, "Centre Temo" (Kinshasa, n.d., mimeo.). CGTA officials also sought access to UNESCO literary and teacher-training programs. See statement by CGTA President Ladeira-Lumona to the U.N. Committee on Decolonization, doc. A/6700/add. 3 (Oct. 11, 1967), pp. 246–249.

215. From Malcolm X Savimbi "learned much about the revolution taking place in America, much about the significance and profound values of that revolution and the links—for a long time camouflaged by the enemy—that are bound to exist between the struggle of Blacks in America and Blacks in Africa. Malcolm X was assassinated a few months later. But his message has marked Savimbi forever." "Who Is Jonas Savimbi? A Short Political Biography," *Kwacha-Angola* (London), Mar. 12, 1974.

216. "From then on," Savimbi later told English journalist Mike Marshment, "I decided that one could not move about lobbying African countries for support but must try to be in the homeland; also to understand the problems as they exist at home. This is why from the very beginnings of our Party, the aim, the goal, the line that we set forth was to RETURN HOME." Ibid., special edition (1972): p. 15.

217. "Who Is Jonas Savimbi?"

218. He would later confirm: "To tell the truth I never intended to belong to that movement." *Notícia* (Luanda), Aug. 24, 1974. (Joint Publication Research Service, 63,155, Oct. 8, 1974), p. 18.

219. Putting at only three thousand the total number of guerrillas trained at Kinkuzu, Kalundungo alleged that in addition to sixty-five ELNA soldiers held (or killed) in Léopoldville, Roberto held another 325 disaffected recruits from Katanga prisoner at Kunkuzu where they had been forcibly returned by Adoula's army after trying to escape. Under Tshombe Congolese troops had intervened during a new mutiny and carried off seven ELNA officers, including specialists in weaponry and communications. See Davezies, *Les angolais*, pp. 211–213. These "revelations" by Kalundungo stood in sharp contrast with what he as ELNA commander had been saying up to that time. In early 1964 Kalundungo boasted that ELNA units had extended the range of their military action from Nambuangongo to Andulo 240 kilometers south of Luanda. *Portugal Democrático* 8, no. 81 (Mar. 1964): 7; see also Ghana News Agency (Accra), Jan. 22, 1964.

220. Liahuca publicly reproached Roberto for "tribalism," that is, preventing SARA from extending its refugee services beyond Kongo Central to extra-Bakongo communities in Kwango, Kasai, and Lualaba. Ibid., pp. 214–215.

221. Amangola, "Manifesto" (Brazzaville, Dec. 11, 1964) in *Basta* (Oegstgeest, Netherlands [Dec. 1965], mimeo.), pp. 9–14. Signers included

Savimbi, Kalundungo, and Liahuca. See also Jorge Alicerces Valentim, *Qui Libere l'Angola* (Brussels: Michèle Coppens, 1969), pp. 40–42.

222. Amangola open letter, July 14, 1965.

223. MPLA, Comitê Director, "Comunicação aos Militantes do MPLA," doc. 86 (Brazzaville, July 1, 1965, mimeo.).

224. MPLA militants beat up Amangola partisan Alexandre Magno Pedro in July 1965, prompting an open letter of protest (July 14, 1965) from Pedro, Liahuca, their wives, Rev. Marcelino Nyani, and Miguel Casimiro. Other signers of the Amangola manifesto, including Kalundungo, may be assumed to have departed Brazzaville (some for China) before this time.

225. Jonas M. Savimbi, "Porque Posso Escolher a Morte pela Libertação de Angola se Outro Caminho não Houver" (Dar es Salaam, Aug. 1965) in *Basta*, pp. 23–27. Savimbi accused the MPLA of maneuvering through the OAU's Liberation Committee in an effort to block his return to Zambia.

226. Letters, Valentim to the author, Sept. 14, 1964, Nov. 6, 1964.

227. In September 1964, the U.S. section of UNEA elected a "nonpartisan" slate of officers (José Belo Chipenda, president) and began publishing a bulletin, *Unidade Angolana*, that eschewed political polemics. In Vienna Fidelino Loy de Figueiredo resigned his post as GRAE representative, and during 1964 and 1965, many other students withdrew from all party affiliations. *Sous le drapeau du socialisme* (Paris), no. 10 (Oct. 1964).

228. *Le periscope révolutionnaire angolais* (1964–1965); *Basta* (1965–1966); *Angola 66* (1966)—all published in the Netherlands.

229. "Confidential Memorandum about the Angolan Situation Presented by Jorge Alicerces Valentim" (Lusaka, Dec. 21, 1964, typescript).

230. See *Révolution africaine*, Apr. 18, 1964, pp. 21–22.

231. UGEAN accused COSEC of promoting UNEA and fomenting division among Angolan students. UGEAN, "Circular as Secções," CE/10/64 (Algiers, June 15, 1964, mimeo.).

232. "Compte rendu de l'assemblée extraordinaire de l'Union Nationale des Étudiants Angolais" (Utrecht, 1965, mimeo.). Other members of the executive committee were André Mankenda, vice-president; João Macondecua, deputy vice-president; Léopoldo Trovoada, secretary-general; Nicolau Mabeka, deputy secretary-general; Job de Carvalho, information; Domingos de Carvalho, deputy of information; Jacob Pereira, social affairs; Afonso Aniceto, deputy of social affairs; Carlos Nensala, finance; and Jackson Munzila, treasurer. For a report on the assembly and preparations leading to it, see Carlos Nensala, "Estudantes Angolanos, Secção de UNEA nos Estados Unidos da América" (New York, Oct. 12, 1965, mimeo.). See also *Angola 66* (Oegstgeest, Jan. 1966, mimeo.).

233. An active minority in the U.S. section of UNEA refused to recognize the legality of the Utrecht meeting and wrote COSEC protesting its involvement. Letter to International Student Conference, Sept. 10, 1965; signers included Paul Touba, Francisco Lubota, and Raymond Fernandes da Silva (Mbala).

234. *Basta*, pp. 15–16.

235. Letter, Savimbi to Valentim, Lusaka, Jan. 30, 1966. See also article by Savimbi under the pseudonym Evimbi Molowini, "E Agora Que os Que Morrem Tem de Ultrapassar a Morte," *Angola 66* (Oegstgeest, Feb. 1966,

mimeo.), pp. 15–16. In the second issue of *Basta* (Feb. 1966), Valentim published a long letter criticizing the CPA as counterrevolutionary and declared for Amangola.

236. The CPAD immediately denied that there was any link between itself and the CPA. A December 1965 visit to Lusaka by Kassinda did not dispel doubts about his revolutionary commitment, and Valentim was asked to make an unequivocal choice between the two. CPAD, "Carta Circular aos Angolanos" (Lusaka, Jan. 26, 1966, mimeo.). Valentim responded in a letter (Mar. 8, 1966) pledging solid support to the CPAD.

237. CPAD leadership: Savimbi (ex-UPA), president; Smart Chata (ex-UPA), vice-president; Lufuino Moses Muliata (Kaniumbu), secretary. Political bureau: Rui Teixeira (ex-UPA, ex-SARA), Kayaya Kanjundo, Royal Kangenda, Solomon Njolomba (ex-UPA).

238. FNLA, *Angola* (Léopoldville), Nov. 15, 1964.

239. Ibid., Nov. 30, 1964.

240. According to Willis Ndumba, Nyerere gave the office £1,500 more than it had ever received from Roberto (interview with author, Aug. 1966).

241. Sept.–Nov. 1964: organizer made contacts at Cazombo, Lutembo, Luso; Oct. 1964: team held discussions with chiefs and formed UPA branches at Lutembo (Chief Zezengomba's area) and Lukuse; Dec. 1964: organizer (D.K. Mapulanga) still inside at time memorandum was written. UPA, "Confidential Memorandum to the Honourable Members of the African Liberation Committee of Nine on the Angolan Struggle" (Lusaka, Jan. 13, 1965, mimeo.). Signed by R. Domingos Gil, chief representative; Willis C. Ndumba, secretary-general; J. M. Khamalata, refugee secretary; and Solomon K. Njolomba, education secretary. Copies were sent to Roberto and the Zambian minister of home affairs.

242. Kunzika to Chale, Dec. 1, 1965, GRAE, CVP-PG/250/65.

243. UPA, "Confidential Memorandum."

244. Ibid.

245. See chap. 3.

246. See summary of 346th meeting, May 28, 1965 (Lusaka), U.N., Committee on Decolonization, A/AC.109/SR.346 (July 16, 1965), A/AC.109/pet.398 (June 21, 1965), and pet.398/add.1 (July 7, 1965).

247. Summary of the 346th meeting and A/AC.109/pet.397 (June 21, 1965), signed by S. K. Njolomba, D. K. Mapulanga, S. G. Chata, and W. G. Ndumba, all ex-UPA.

248. The travails of Angolan refugees in Katanga were set forth in a letter to Jorge Valentim from an exile *Comité des Angolais au Katanga*, Elizabethville, Feb. 26, 1966.

249. "To the Missionaries of the United Church Board for World Ministries, New York," Sept. 21, 1965.

250. ". . . It is necessary that a new formula which includes all Angolan forces should be realized. The struggle for the liberation of Angola is not an ideological struggle. It is a democratic national struggle of a popular nature. This struggle has to incorporate everyone from the sincere chief who dislikes the odious Portuguese colonial system up to the most enlightened revolutionary; from the worker in the plantations to the popular catechist who brings with him the masses in the villages; from the workman who lives

on a starvation salary to the Catholic Priest who has nothing to do with the feudal and colonial regime; from the primary or secondary student to the Government or the private teacher who only receives colonial regime scorn and humiliation; from the isolated peasant in the valleys and the mountains who only gets from his work poverty to the contract laborer who does not even know the warmth of home. This irresistible and invincible force can only be directed by people who have come out from African masses which suffer most from colonial domination. Those who are directly or indirectly linked to the feudal and colonialist regime cannot inspire confidence in the Angolan masses. This struggle is not ideological because it cannot exclude anybody. It has to unite all. Political and economic theories which are supported in atheistic attitudes do not fall in line with the feelings of African belief. The African believes in a higher Being whatever his name may be, or whatever the place where he is worshipped. There is an ancestral force which transcends man. All alienation from this feeling which is profoundly popular will tend to divide the forces which could openly show themselves against colonial domination" [which sounded very much like excluding the MPLA defined by Savimbi as ideological and atheist]. Ibid.

251. Ibid. Savimbi expressed the hope that such exiles as Dr. Liahuca, Alexander Magno, and Rev. Marcelino Nyani in Brazzaville, and Jeronomo Wanga, Ruben Sanjovo, Victor Afonso, and Jorge Valentim (students) in Europe would join the struggle inside Angola.

252. Report on UNITA by John de St. Jorre of the *Observer* (typescript, July 26, 1966); and UNITA, Central Committee, "Declaration of UNITA on Unity of Angolan Liberatory Movements" (Lusaka, June 22, 1966, mimeo.).

253. The conference was organized by Isaya Masumba, who had been inside Angola since August. Preconference political work had extended from Lunda south to Cuando Cubango districts and involved nationalists of diverse ethnic backgrounds. The conference was chaired by Muliata L. Kaniumbu. UNITA, *Kwacha-Angola* (Orgão de Informação e Propaganda da UNITA), no. 1 (Lusaka, 1966, mimeo.).

254. "Constitution of UNITA," art. 2. The constitution set forth three principles to govern UNITA decision making: "Collective Direction, Democratic Centralism and Criticism and Self-Criticism." (art. 7, para. 5).

255. Central Committee members were Smart G. Chata, Muliata L. Kaniumbu, Solomon K. Njolomba, Daniel M. Kapozo, Isaac Mbunda, Mutaipi M. Mkumbi, Alexandre Magno Pedro, Evimbi Molowini (Savimbi), José Kalundungo, Kapesi Fundanga, Jacob Hosi, Franco Mateos, Isaya Masumba, Dunduma Chiuka, and Samuel Chivala.

256. *Kwacha-Angola*, no. 1 (1966).

257. Along such eastern streams as the Mukanda, Lungué-Bungu, Luia, Luanginga, Lukonia, Luvusi, Luondze, Lumai, Luziyi, and Mitete. See UNITA, "What Is the UNITA and Its Efforts to the Liberation of Angola" (Lusaka, Spring 1966, mimeo.).

258. In Kinshasa, Roberto brandished a telegram from Savimbi that read: "Roberto Holden, people asked me call on your patriotism understand critical period our struggle. Genuine African forces have to [be] united." *Courrier d'Afrique*, June 24, 1966.

259. Other civilian members were Kaposo Muliata (finance), Musole M. Mutaipi (social affairs), David Musonga (labor). *Kwacha-Angola*, no. 4 (Sept.–Oct. 1966). A number of positions on the Central Committee were left open to be filled by new leadership to emerge during the course of the struggle as well as by Angolan students who joined that struggle. See open letter to Angolan students from Jorge Valentim, Sept. 1966 (Oegstgeest).

260. Other military of Central Committee rank were Isaya Musumba, political commissar for armed forces, and Samuel Chiwale, head of military coordination.

261. Landlocked Zambia faced inherently hostile governments across four borders: Angola and Mozambique (Portugal), Rhodesia, and Caprivi (South Africa). For Zambian strictures laid down to liberation movements, see Zambia, letter from the Office of the President to the Chief Representative, Union of Populations of Angola, ref. S/OP/119/06, Nov. 4, 1965 (text in appendix 2).

262. "Constitution of UNITA," art. 2, para. 4, and *Kwacha-Angola*, no. 2 (June 1966).

263. Ibid., no. 3 ([Aug.] 1966).

264. *Zambia News* (Lusaka), July 31, 1966. "Soldiers and weapons infiltrated from outside without the conscious and clear support of the people inside the country are meaningless and therefore cannot decide the battle against Portuguese colonialism." *Kwacha-Angola*, no. 3 ([Aug.] 1966).

265. *Kwacha-Angola*, no. 3 ([Aug.] 1966).

266. *Zambia News*, July 31, 1966.

267. UNITA military reports often gave accounts of rifles and other weapons captured. See *Kwacha-Angola*, no. 4 (Sept.–Oct. 1966). Savimbi had read works of the Greek Cypriot Colonel George Grivas whom he considered an inspiring example of how to lead a rebellion without external aid. *O'Comércio* (Luanda), Sept. 30, 1974.

268. Martin Meredith (*Zambia News*, July 31, 1966) was especially impressed by what he considered Savimbi's realistic appraisal of Portuguese military strength and his openness to nonviolent (civil disobedience) as well as violent action.

269. Ibid., June 19, 24, 1966. In July, Zambia accused the Portuguese of destroying a border village (Chipatela) in its Northwest province with 3.5-inch rockets from U.S.- and British-made bazookas. Ibid., July 21, 1966.

270. Letter from Savimbi to the Missionaries of the United Church, Sept. 21, 1965.

271. MPLA, *Boletim do Militante MPLA*, no. 1 (Brazzaville, May 25, 1964): 7.

272. The MDIA defected to join the PDA/FNLA in Nov. 1963. FDLA members as of May 1964 were MPLA, UNTA, Ngwizako, MNA, and CUNA (which subsequently joined the CPA in April 1965).

273. For example, GRAE, "Communiqué," no. 54 (Algiers, Apr. 15, 1965, mimeo.).

274. *Angola informations*, Jan. 9, 1965.

275. The FDLA is not mentioned in official MPLA histories such as "Dez Anos de Existência, Dez Anos de Luta em Prol do Povo Angolano" (Dar es Salaam, Feb. 4, 1967, mimeo.).

276. MPLA, "Communiqué de presse" (Brazzaville, Aug. 31, 1964, mimeo.).

277. Andrade was one of the principal organizers of the second CONCP conference at Dar es Salaam in October 1965. See his "Document de Base" in *La lutte de libération nationale dans les colonies portugaises: La conférence de Dar es Salaam* (Algiers: Information CONCP, 1967), pp. 20–42; see also Andrade, "Le mouvement de libération dans les colonies portugaises," *Partisans*, nos. 29–30 (May–June 1966): 102–104. In June 1966, Andrade testified on behalf of the CONCP before the U.N. Committee on Decolonization. U.N. General Assembly, *Official Records,* Annexes 23d sess., doc. A/6300 rev. 1 (New York, 1966, pp. 351–353. In this testimony, the article in *Partisans* and subsequent statements, he argued that Portugal was able to field and maintain a colonial army of some 120,000 only because of support from NATO and "international capitalism." *Le monde,* Dec. 11–12, 1966, and *Jeune Afrique,* Jan. 8, 1967, p. 25.

278. See JMPLA, *Juventude e Revolução,* no. 2 (Brazzaville, Nov. 30, 1964): 5–9.

279. Letter dated Feb. 29, 1964: MPLA, *Vitória ou Morte* (English ed.), (Brazzaville, Feb. 1964). See also Luis de Azevedo, Jr., "Memorandum. Situation actuelle de la révolution angolaise" (Algiers, Feb. 23, 1964, mimeo.).

280. *Vitória ou Morte* (Feb. 1964) and MPLA, "Reminder on the Angolan Question for the OAU Conference of Foreign Affairs Ministers (Lagos, Feb. 24, 1964, mimeo.).

281. *East African Standard* (Nairobi), May 30, 1964.

282. MPLA, Steering Committee, "Statement" (Brazzaville, May 14, 1964, mimeo.).

283. The memorandum charged that UPA men were not only terrorizing Congolese villages but were kidnapping Cabindans on night raids, imprisoning them near Luali, and exacting $35 each for their release; they were murdered in the bush if they couldn't pay. MPLA, "MPLA Delegation Intervention at the Liberation Committee of the Organisation of African Unity" (Dar es Salaam, June 3, 1964, mimeo.). The OAU Liberation Committee chairman, Oscar Kambona, reaffirmed the OAU's recognition of GRAE and rejected the MPLA petition on the grounds that the committee could not recognize two governments. *East African Standard,* June 11, 1964.

284. MPLA, "Memorandum à la conférence des chefs d'états et du gouvernement" (Cairo, July 17, 1964, mimeo.).

285. A measure of credit for MPLA success at Cairo was ascribed to the lobbying of the MPLA delegation, Luis de Azevedo, Jr., Eduardo Santos, Miguel Baya, and Luís de Almeida. MPLA, "Le MPLA à la conférence du Caire" (Brazzaville, Aug. 1, 1964, mimeo.).

286. See, for example, Algier's *Révolution africaine,* Aug. 1, 1964, p. 15, and Radio Lagos (Oct. 22, 1964), in *Africa Research Bulletin* (PSC series), 1, no. 10 (Oct. 1964): 172C–173A.

287. MPLA, "Report of the Conciliating Committee Between the Angolan Revolutionary Government (GRAE) and the People's Liberation Movement of Angola (MPLA)" (n.p., [1964], mimeo.). See also *Révolution africaine,* Dec. 5, 1964.

288. MPLA, "Resolution of the Committee of Nine on the Report of the Tripartite Committee (Congo-Brazzaville, Ghana, U.A.R.) on the Reconciliation of the Political Parties in Angola" (Dar es Salaam, Nov. 25, 1964, mimeo.).

289. GRAE, Johnny Edouard, "Conférence de presse" (Algiers, Nov. 27, 1964, mimeo.).

290. *Angola informations*, Mar. 15, 1965.

291. MPLA, "Memorandum sur la question angolaise à l'intention de la conférence de l'OUA au niveau des ministres des affaires étrangères" (Nairobi, Feb. 26, 1965, mimeo.).

292. GRAE, "Communiqué," no. 49 (Algiers, Mar. 10, 1965, mimeo.); Agence France Presse, Apr. 10, 1965. The MPLA, however, represented the council's action as "recognition" and approval of assistance for it. MPLA, "Communiqué" (Brazzaville, Mar. 14, 1965, mimeo.).

293. Journalist Joseph Lelyveld noted that observers in the Congo were skeptical of Roberto's optimism because his movement "was going nowhere fast before Mr. Tshombe became Premier." *New York Times*, Oct. 20, 1965.

294. Alfredo Margarido, "L'OUA et les territoires sous domination portugaise," *Le mois en Afrique* (Paris), no. 22 (Oct. 1967): 96.

295. In a letter to the Conciliation Committee, Johnny Edouard asked for ten days' advance notice of any meeting and for assurances that all minutes would be subject to the approval of all discussants at the end of each session. He said that GRAE would not consider participating until these conditions were met. Letter MAE/I.013/0/66 from Algiers, Jan. 6, 1966.

296. See interview with Agostinho Neto in *Horoya* (Conakry), Nov. 24, 1965.

297. A rising young Ochimbundu politician, Daniel Chipenda, who headed the MPLA's youth wing (JMPLA), spent a month in the U.S.S.R. in early 1964. *Komsomol'skaya Pravda* (Moscow), May 22, 1964.

298. *Pravda*, Dec. 16, 1964, reproduced in MPLA, *Etudes et documents*, no. 5 (Algiers, Dec. 1964, mimeo.). Radio Moscow, GMT 1630, Dec. 18, 1964. See also Y. S. Oganisyan, "Motive Forces of the National Revolution in Angola" (in Russian), *Narodni Azii I Afriki* (Moscow), no. 1 (1965).

299. For example, M. Domogatskikh (*Pravda*, June 16, 1965) reported visiting a school for the political indoctrination of MPLA "freedom fighters" inside the Cabinda enclave.

300. Ibid., Mar. 8, 11, 16, 25, Apr. 22, 1965. See also *Izvestia* (Moscow), June 11, 1966.

301. A Cabindan known as "Veneno" allegedly led a group of UPA defectors to the MPLA. *Pravda*, Mar. 16, 1965.

302. *Angola informations*, Jan. 9, Mar. 15, 1965. *Africa Research Bulletin* (PSC series) 1, no. 12 (Dec. 1964): p. 209c.

303. Message from MPLA foreign secretary Luis de Azevedo, Jr., *Pravda*, Aug. 11, 1965; see also *Le monde*, Aug. 12, 1965.

304. Tass (International Service, English, 2128 GMT, Moscow, Aug. 3, 1966) carried additional expressions of gratitude by Neto for "the exceptionally great material help and moral support rendered and being rendered by the Soviet Union and other socialist countries to our difficult struggle against Portuguese colonialism."

305. *Pravda*, Apr. 22, 1965.

306. For a favorable Czechoslovak report on the Cabinda front and the need for Angolan unity, see *Dokumentacni prehled* (Prague), no. 6 (Jan. 28, 1966). Writing in the Austrian Communist party organ, *Volksstimme* (Vienna, Apr. 2, 1966), H. de Schrijver reported that the MPLA had converted Cabinda into a "virtual training school for guerrillas."

307. In Algiers, Roberto's aide, Johnny Edouard, systematically denounced Soviet and Portuguese Communist party "revisionists" and praised China and Maoist Portuguese opposition groups such as the *Frente de Acção Popular* (FAP). *Angola informations*, no. 7 (Dec. 1965). See also "Conférence de presse de M. Rezende Alvaro, directeur du service d'information au Gouvernement Angolais en Exile faite à Bruxelles le 4 février 1965" published in GRAE, "Communiqué," no. 45 (Algiers, n.d.).

308. In January 1965, Luis de Azevedo, Jr., applauded the "courageous decision" of Indonesia's pro-Chinese Sukarno government to withdraw from the United Nations. New China News Agency, Jan. 14, 1965. That April, Lucila Neto led a four-member MPLA women's delegation to China. Ibid., Apr. 25, 1966. In February 1966, an MPLA youth delegation visited Peking. Hsinhua, *Daily Bulletin*, Feb. 9, 1966. In August 1966, Lucila Neto traveled to Albania and signed a joint statement with the Albanian women's movement. Radio Tirana (French), 1700 GMT, Aug. 15, 1966.

309. In June 1966, a Chinese correspondent visited Brazzaville, interviewed "Angolan Freedom Fighters," lauded their determination to fight despite the hardships of their campaign in Cabinda's Mayumbe forests, and reported their "warm affection and admiration for Chairman Mao Tsetung's thought"—but never once identified the MPLA by name. Hsinhua, *Daily Bulletin*, June 21, 1966.

310. *Foreign Report* (London), no. 908 (May 6, 1965).

311. *New York Times*, Oct. 23, 1966. See also "Brazzaville—Cuba's New Base?" *African Review* (London), (Aug. 1966): 10–11.

312. For the text of Roberto's speech, see *Review of International Affairs* (Belgrade), 15, no. 350 (Nov. 5, 1964), pp. 76–77. The MPLA also petitioned the conference for support. See MPLA, "Message à leurs excellences les chefs d'états et de gouvernements participant à la IIème conférence des pays non-alignés" (Brazzaville, Oct. 5, 1964, mimeo.).

313. Disbarment applauded by the MPLA (*Remarques africaines*, July 7, 1965) and the Soviet Union (Tass, International Service [English], 1013 GMT, May 11, 1965) and denounced as a Soviet "maneuver" by GRAE (*Angola informations*, Aug. 31, 1965). For the text of Agostinho Neto's speech at the Winneba conference, see MPLA, "Neto à Winneba," doc. 82 (Brazzaville, Aug. 1, 1965).

314. Luis de Azevedo, Jr., of the MPLA spoke on behalf of all the CONCP parties at the First Solidarity Conference of Asia, Africa, and Latin America, Havana, Jan. 3–15, 1966. The MPLA was the sole Angolan participant at an Afro-Asian economic seminar in Algiers (Mar. 22–27, 1965). *Information Bulletin, World Marxist Review* (Toronto), May 13, 1965, pp. 55–56. And the JMPLA was the sole Angolan delegation at a seminar of the World Federation of Democratic Youth held at Accra, Apr. 20–22, 1965. At meetings such as a solidarity seminar for Vietnam held in Algiers in July 1965, the MPLA was again the exclusive representative of Angola. See "Déclaration de

solidarité des mouvements de libération africaine avec le peuple du Vietnam a l'occasion de la semaine de solidarité avec le peuple du Vietnam" (Algiers, July 19, 1965, mimeo.), signed for MPLA by Luis de Almeida.

315. Robert Davezies, *La guerre d'Angola* (Bordeaux: Editions Ducros, 1968), pp. 65–66. Includes names of many of those arrested.

316. Ronald H. Chilcote, "Salazar's Portugal: Anniversary on Thin Ice," *The Nation* (New York), May 30, 1966, p. 640.

317. Given a Portuguese passport in return for "secret information," on March 1, 1965, Ferreira reportedly flew to Luanda. The MPLA condemned him to death in absentia. MPLA, Comitê Director, "Comunicado," doc. 67 (Brazzaville, Mar. 2, 1965, mimeo.). See also *Le monde*, Mar. 31, 1965. MPLA defections tended to nourish racial cleavage. Johnny Edouard responded to Ferreira's flight "with a valid Portuguese passport" by alleging that "relatives" (read European and mestiço relatives) of MPLA leaders "shuttled back and forth between Luanda and the two Congos." Shuttlers included "a cousin" of MPLA organizational secretary Lúcio Lára and the sister of Luis de Almeida said to have flown from Lisbon to visit her brother in Algiers. *Angola informations,* Apr. 24, 1965, and GRAE, Mission d'Algérie, "Les mensonges ont courte vie," doc. 10/22/66 (Algiers, Jan. 1966, mimeo.).

318. Before resigning from the MPLA Steering Committee in April 1965, dos Santos criticized Neto's alleged readiness to accept a settlement based on "internal autonomy" for Angola and declared his sympathy for MPLA dissidents da Cruz and Miguéis. GRAE, "Les mensonges ont courte vie," and *Angola 66* (Feb. 1966).

319. A product of MPLA military training in Ghana and Morocco (1961–1963), da Fonseca had been in charge of MPLA military supplies in Brazzaville. He claimed that large quantities of materiel from the Soviet Union were being unused while the party issued fictitious communiqués about supposed military exploits in Cabinda. da Fonseca's first attempt at escape (from military jail at Dolisie) failed when he, seven Cape Verdeans (allegedly arrested by Daniel Chipenda and later executed), and two other Angolans (David Nlau and António Domingos Niala) were recaptured and, according to da Fonseca, tortured on orders of MPLA officials. On his second try, da Fonseca managed to escape alone across the Congo River to Léopoldville. Ibid.

320. *A Província de Angola*, June 2, 1966.

321. MPLA, "Appel au gouvernement du Congo-Léopoldville et à l'Organisation de l'Unité Africaine" (Brazzaville, Aug. 4, 1964, mimeo.).

322. *Boletim do Militante MPLA*, May 25, 1964, p. 15. Arrested in March 1964 at the behest of Holden Roberto, António dos Santos Ambrosia died in October that same year. MPLA, Comité Directeur, "Communiqué de presse" (Brazzaville, Oct. 14, 1964, mimeo.). See also Radio Havana, 2010 GMT, Oct. 20, 1964.

323. Telegram to Congolese (Léopoldville) Minister of Interior, MPLA, doc. 106 (Brazzaville, Dec. 9, 1965, mimeo.). *Le progrès*, Dec. 14, 1965.

324. *Le progrès*, Nov. 18, 1965.

325. See petition by FLEC president Luis Ranque Franque to U.N. Committee on Decolonization, doc. A/AC.109/pet. 337, Apr. 9, 1965.

326. MPLA, Steering Committee, note to Foreign Ministers of OAU, doc. 61 (Brazzaville, Jan. 26, 1965, mimeo.).

327. UNTA, *Le travailleur de l'Angola*, Nos. 4–5 (Léopoldville, Apr.–May 1965).

328. Intelligence gathering was reputedly led by Alberto Makaia, Alfredo Futi, and Manuel Magahaës e Pedro of FLEC. MPLA, Comitê Director, "Comunicado," doc. 67 (Brazzaville, March 2, 1965, mimeo.).

329. In June 1964, ELNA claimed to have overrun two Cabindan villages and captured a cache of Portuguese arms in an operation that took the life of the commander who led it, Clemente Mamata. FNLA, *Angola: Bulletin d'information* 1, no. 11 (Léopoldville, June 1–15, 1964, mimeo.).

330. David Grenfell, *Notes,* no. 20 (Kibentele, June 10, 1966, mimeo.).

331. Ibid., no. 28 (Aug. 19, 1966). By late 1966, some of JMAE's up to three hundred members were reported to be dissatisfied with their treatment by Portuguese superiors. Ibid., no. 40 (Nov. 18, 1966). On Taty's efforts to undermine the MPLA, see MPLA, *Vitória ou Morte* (Brazzaville, Mar.–Apr. 1966).

332. The first class of sixty soldiers, known as the "Ferraz Bomboko Class," graduated from the *Centro de Instrucção Revolucionária* on March 4, 1965. Instruction was directed by a five-man team: Fernando Brica, Gilberto Teixeira da Silva, Francisco Rangel, Carlos Rocha, and Benigno Vieira Lopes. Davezies, *La guerre d'Angola*, pp. 64–65.

333. Portuguese forces were under five thousand. See article by Mohamed Aissaoui in *Révolution africaine*, July 25, 1964, pp. 12–15. See also Benoit Keita, "Enclave de Cabinda," *Remarques africaines*, Feb. 3, 1965, pp. 18–19; and Luis de Azevedo, Jr., "Liberation Struggle in Angola," *Review of International Affairs* (Belgrade), 17, no. 381 (Feb. 20, 1966), pp. 17–18.

334. MPLA Algiers representative Paulo Jorge in *Révolution africaine*, Feb. 8–14, 1968, p. 31.

335. Mário de Andrade, "Le mouvement de liberation nationale dans les colonies portugaises," *Partisans*, nos. 29–30 (May–June 1966): 100.

336. *Boletim do Militante MPLA*, May 25, 1964, p. 14.

337. Also known as Maiombe or Bayumbe.

338. Basil Davidson, *In the Eye of the Storm: Angola's People* (Garden City, N.Y.: Doubleday and Co., 1972), p. 234. On Cabindan regionalism, see Marcum, *Angolan Revolution*, 1:173–174.

339. See the critical analysis of MPLA Cabinda operations by a sympathetic Mozambican writer, Virgilio de Lemos, in *L'Afrique actuelle* (Paris), no. 4 (Jan. 1966): 41; no. 5 (Feb. 1966): 34; and no. 10 (Aug.–Sept. 1966): 50. On-the-spot observation during the summer of 1966 led Canadian Baptist Rev. Charles Harvey to conclude that most MPLA claims to military activity in Cabinda could be discounted. Grenfell, *Notes,* no. 40 (Nov. 18, 1966).

340. *Courrier d'Afrique*, Apr. 21, 1966. The paper judged GRAE with equal harshness, describing its leadership as ineffectual, self-enriching, and corrupt.

341. See article by Paula de Serra in *Jornal do Congo* (Carmona, Angola), Aug. 21, 1966.

342. See chap. 1.

343. According to MPLA sources, by mid-June 1964, UPA gangs had massacred over 150 MPLA partisans (forty of whom had at least some

secondary education). JMPLA, Steering Committee, open letter (Brazzaville, June 15, 1964, mimeo.).

344. *Revista de Angola* (Luanda) 6, no. 122 (June 16–30, 1966).

345. See chap. 1. Born Apr. 4, 1941, at Píri, Dembos, Caetano, who assumed the nom de guerre of "Monstro Imortal," received military training at Brno, Czechoslovakia. He commanded the MPLA's northern operational zone from 1966 to 1970, when he was sent for further military training to Yugoslavia. He later served in Cabinda and in 1974 became a member of the MPLA Political Bureau and chief of staff for MPLA army operations. *O'Comércio* (Luanda), Jan. 31, 1975.

346. A November 15, 1965, meeting of the MPLA "action committee" for Nambuangongo had selected Domingos Luis António to go to Brazzaville in quest of help. He succeeded in getting through to Brazzaville where he waited six months while the Cienfuegos Column was made ready. Davezies, *La guerre d'Angola*, pp. 85–86. See also Basil Davidson, "The MPLA Wins Out," *West Africa*, July 18, 1977, p. 1472.

347. UPA forces south of the Loge River led by Protestant pastors, António Panzo da Gloria (Mbundu of Kinguengo-Kabari) and António Fernandes de Brito (Bakongo of Kimbumbe-Zala), had enjoyed an advantage over MPLA partisans farther south given UPA control of exit routes to the north. With the arrival of the well-armed Cienfuegos Column, however, the balance of power changed, and the UPA leaders quickly released local MPLA prisoners (including local MPLA committeeman Almeida João Pereira, also a Protestant pastor, and José João de Castro) from the UPA village of Kinguengo-Kabari. Ibid., pp. 107–108.

348. Conclave held at MPLA center known as Ngalama. Ibid., pp. 86–88.

349. Ibid., p. 88; Davidson, "The MPLA Wins Out." According to Portuguese journalist Fernando Farinha (*Notícia* [Luanda], Sept. 28, 1968), UPA forces ambushed and inflicted heavy casualties on the Cami Column both north and south of the M'Bridge River. The president (Lourenço Casimiro) of a new MPLA student organization, *União dos Estudantes Angolanos* (UEA), went in with the Cami group.

350. José João de Castro cited four Kimbundu-speaking *senzalas* that were aligned with the UPA: Kinguengo-Kabari, Kibalo, Mucondo, and Zombo-Makandu. "There are no Kikongo-speakers who belong to the MPLA. All who speak Kikongo belong to the UPA. All those who speak Kikongo—Ambriz, Zala, Bembe, Nova Caipemba, all of them belong to the UPA." Ibid., pp. 111–112.

351. David Grenfell, *Notes*, no. 34 (Sept. 30, 1966).

352. *New York Times*, Sept. 17, 1964; MPLA, "Communiqué," doc. 46 (Brazzaville, Sept. 26, 1964, mimeo.).

353. See Marcum, *Angolan Revolution,* 1:87, 162–163, 216, 300.

354. See letter from Savimbi to the missionaries of the United Church, Sept. 21, 1965.

355. Davidson, *In the Eye of the Storm*, p. 242.

356. See *Etumba* (Brazzaville), Aug. 18, 1966, and MPLA, *Vitória ou Morte*, no. 6 (Aug.–Sept. 1966).

357. *Le monde*, Sept. 15, 1966. See also "The MPLA Announces the Opening of the Eastern Front" in MPLA, *Angola in Arms* 1, no. 1 (Dar es Salaam, Jan. 1967).

Notes to Introduction to Part II

1. See Edgar O'Ballance, "The War Potential of Portugal," *Military Review* (Ft. Leavenworth, Kan.) 44, no. 8 (Aug. 1964): 84–90, and *The Military Balance, 1971–72* (London: The Institute for Strategic Studies, 1971), p. 21.

2. Stockholm International Peace Research Institute, *The Arms Trade with the Third World* (New York: Humanities Press, 1971), p. 668, and Elizabeth Morris, "Portugal's Year in Africa," in Colin Legum, ed., *Africa Contemporary Record, 1970–71* (London: Rex Collings, 1971), p. A93. According to official Portuguese sources, between 1960 and 1970 the proportion of Portugal's GNP devoted to defense rose from 4 to 7 percent (and from 1 to 4 percent in Angola and from 1 to 3 percent in Mozambique). Less than 1.5 percent of Portugal's GNP went to education. "Between Africa and Europe: A Survey of Portugal," *The Economist* (spec. suppl.), Feb. 26, 1972, p. 21. The exiled opposition leader, Mário Soares, asserted that over 50 percent of Portugal's government budget was going to defense and security. Mário Soares, "The Legacy of Salazar," *The Nation*, Apr. 17, 1972, p. 491.

3. FPLN-Delgado, "Communiqué" (Algiers, Dec. 5, 1964, mimeo.).

4. *Révolution africaine* (Algiers), Nov. 21, 1964. Like Delgado, FAP activists were impatient for dramatic action; they were thus organizing among Portuguese workers in France and West Germany.

5. FPLN, "Portugal Livre: Boletim da Frente Patriótica de Libertação Nacional" (Algiers, 1964?, mimeo.). The sixth congress of the Portuguese Communist party in September 1965 rejected the notion that a military coup by a handful of officers (Delgado's approach) or the actions of pro-Chinese "chauvinists" could produce a socialist revolution in Portugal. See Milorad M. Drachkovitch, *Yearbook on International Communist Affairs, 1966* (Stanford: Hoover Institution, 1967), p. 141.

6. FPLN-Delgado, "Communiqué" (Quelque part à la frontière, Oct. 1964, mimeo.).

7. FPLN-Delgado, "Communiqué" (Algiers, Dec. 5, 1964, mimeo.), and "Memorandum" presented by Delgado to President Ben Bella of Algiers, FNLA-Delgado, doc. no. P/301 (Algiers, Dec. 15, 1964, mimeo.).

8. *New York Times*, Mar. 5, 1965.

9. Ibid., Apr. 28, 1965.

10. The FPLN published tributes to its alienated, then deceased, ex-leader. For example, a letter from Luis de Almeida of the MPLA in FPLN, "Pour un Portugal libre et démocratique: Bulletin d'information" (Algiers, May 1965, mimeo.).

11. A monthly, *Liberdade*; occasional *Cahiers anti-imperialistes*; and frequent communiqués from its Algiers office.

12. *Courrier d'Afrique*, Aug. 11, 1966.

13. See Norman R. F. Maier, *Frustration: The Study of Behavior Without a Goal* (Ann Arbor: University of Michigan Press, 1949).

14. Dr. F. A. S. Jensen, "Psychological Aspects of the Isolation of Refugees," MHCR/304/63, GE 63-17135 (paper presented to the Conference on Socially Handicapped Families, Paris, UNESCO, Feb. 10–12, 1964); Dr.

H. Strotzka, "Psychological Aspects of Integration," MHCR/120/60 (Geneva: UNHCR, 1960); and U.N. General Assembly, Dr. H. Strotzka, Report on the Mental Health of Refugees and in Particular of Special Cases in Austria, Germany, Greece and Italy, A/AC. 96/84 (Sept. 9, 1960).

15. For a detailed analysis of these factors as they affected African liberation movements, see John Marcum, "The Exile Condition and Revolutionary Effectiveness: Southern African Liberation Movements," in Christian P. Potholm and Richard Dale, eds., *Southern Africa in Perspective* (New York: Free Press, 1972), pp. 262–275, 380–388.

16. Interview with Agostinho Neto by Hans-Dieter Bräuer, "This Is Victory," *World Student News* (Prague), 23, nos. 3–4 (1969): 25.

17. Exile politics in general has received "little attention from political scientists," constituting a research subject that "tends to make one appreciative of the conditional, tenuous nature of 'facts.' " Paul H. Lewis, *The Politics of Exile: Paraguay's Febrerista Party* (Durham, N.C.: University of North Carolina Press, 1968), p. xii. In *The Anatomy of Revolution* (New York: Vintage Books, 1952), p. 230, Crane Brinton observes that although what happens to émigrés "remains one of the most obscure parts of the sociology of revolution," the harshness of exile generally embitters, rigidifies, and narrows those who experience it.

18. In "A Hard Look at Africa's Liberation Movements—or a Study in Disunity," *Race Today* (London) 1, no. 4 (Aug. 1969): 111, Richard Gibson argued that "contradictions" within the liberation struggle could "only be resolved through their airing in debate in the forums of Africa and the world, except where the lives of men engaged in military operations are concerned."

19. Agostinho Neto, "Quem é o Inimigo, Qual é o Nosso Objectivo," lecture at the University of Dar es Salaam (Feb. 7, 1974, mimeo.). See appendix 4.

20. See, for example, UNITA Central Committee, *Angola: Seventh Year* (London, 1968), and *Peking Review*, Feb. 13, 1970, pp. 21–22.

21. *Zambia News* (Lusaka), Mar. 5, 1967; *Times of Zambia* (Ndola), Feb. 25, 1969; *Africa and the World* (London) 5, no. 50 (Aug. 1969): 16–17.

22. A regional headquarters was established inside eastern Angola, but despite Neto's claim that the MPLA's central headquarters had been transferred inside (*Nationalist* [Dar es Salaam], May 20, 1968), its principal political leaders continued to operate out of Lusaka, Dar es Salaam, and Brazzaville.

Notes to Chapter 5

1. PDA, *Informations mensuelles* (Kinshasa), Dec. 5, 1969. Born Dec. 27, 1938 at Banza Mayanga in northern Angola, Gadimpovi was schooled in Kinshasa and later studied mass education at the Heimvolkshochscule, Göhrde, West Germany (1964–1965).

2. Born about 1942 at Novo Redondo, Umbundu-speaking, Miranda had lived in Benguela before attending Catholic seminary in Cabinda. He served previously as a UPA Youth leader and head of the stillborn National Council of *Jeunesse*-FNLA.

3. The accord called for an end to all hostile propaganda between the two movements and the freeing of any members of one held by the other. *Le monde*, Oct. 18, 1966.

4. *Jeune Afrique*, Oct. 30, 1966, p. 31; *L'Etoile du Congo* (Kinshasa), Oct. 24, 1966.

5. See chap. 2.

6. A Kinshasa court sentenced the former head of Zaire's security services, M. Akafomo, to six months in prison for accepting a bribe of $120,000 for the escape of the Portuguese prisoners who had been provided with documents showing them to be Italian technicians. *Africa Contemporary Record, 1972–73* (London: Rex Collings, 1973), p. 2761. Peterson's fate at the hands of the FNLA is rumored to have been that befitting a "traitor" who had, it seems, been collaborating with the Portuguese for some years.

7. Tuba, who as a student had been critical of Roberto's leadership (see chap. 4, n. 28), turned the New York office over to another French-speaking Bakongo, Raymond Fernandes Mbala, who had earlier participated in an attempt by anti-Roberto elements to take over the LGTA trade union (see chap. 4, n. 116, n. 196).

8. Neto set up UPA committees among an estimated eighty thousand Angolans resident in Kwango (Grenfell, *Notes* (Kibentele),) no. 13, Apr. 15, 1966) at points along the Angolan border: Kasongo-Lunda, Mukumbi, Swa-Kibula, Kizamba, Panzi, and Kahemba. UPA, *A Voz da Revolução* (Léopoldville), no. 1 (1966).

9. Notably the governor, Pierre Masikita, and Senator André Mwaku of Kasongo-Lunda. *Courrier d'Afrique* (Léopoldville), Jan. 29–30, 1966.

10. In March 1966, Rosário Neto officiated at Kinkuzu ceremonies marking the fifth anniversary of the March 15 uprising in northern Angola. *Le progrès* (Léopoldville), Mar. 25, 1966; for the text of his speech, see *A Voz da Revolução*, no. 1 (1966). In 1968, Rosário Neto spoke before the U.N. Commission on Human Rights on behalf of GRAE. For the text, see FNLA, *Liberté et terre* (Kinshasa) no. 2 (Aug. 1968): 10–12.

11. Rosário Neto, to (name withheld), Mar. 16, 1971.

12. Arrested on Nov. 17, 1969, Rosário Neto was held prisoner without trial until his release in broken health in mid-1972. A Jan. 17, 1971, appeal by his wife, Maria da Conceição, former head of the UPA's women's organization, asking President Mobutu to intercede, went unacknowledged.

13. Rosário Neto, to (name withheld) Mar. 16, 1971.

14. David Grenfell, *Notes,* no. 31, Sept. 9, 1966.

15. Ibid.

16. The PDA in contrast to the UPA continued to undertake such informational missions in the years that followed. See for example, PDA, *Informations mensuelles* (Kinshasa) (Oct. 24, 1969).

17. Agence France Presse, June 18, 1971; *Financial Times* (London), June 23, 1971. The OAU continued to recognize the FNLA as a movement.

18. Account based in part on interviews with Roberto, Paulo Tuba, and others by George M. Houser, Kinshasa, June 1973. Commander Matumona, the officer who reportedly gave the order to shoot Roberto, was one of three former MPLA officers who, after defecting to the FNLA,

had risen during two years at Kinkuzu to command posts in police and training operations. *La libre belgique* (Brussels), June 12, 1972.

19. Agence France Presse, Mar. 19, 1972; *Diário de Notícias* (Lisbon), Mar. 20, 1972; and *New York Times*, Mar. 20, 1972.

20. Figure given by Roberto to George Houser.

21. In addition to former MPLA officers said by Roberto to have "infiltrated" from Brazzaville to instigate trouble at Kinkuzu (*La libre belgique*, June 12, 1972), those executed were said by FNLA sources in Kinshasa to have included officers trained in India, Tunisia, and Turkey.

22. In a speech on March 19, 1972, at the FNLA medical center in Franquetti (now Kingantoko), Roberto invoked the need for vigilance against those who would commit "treason" against the revolution; he then collapsed from fatigue. Agence France Presse, Mar. 19, 1972.

23. See GRAE, Département des relations extérieures, *Notre lutte se poursuit et se poursuivra jusqu'à l'indépendance totale* (Kinshasa [?], 1972), p. 5.

24. A new PDA executive committee installed in April 1972 was headed by Samuel Nteka, president; Pedro Gadimpovi, vice-president; and Sébastien Lubaki Ntemo, secretary-general. LGTA, *Angola Operária*, no. 4 (Kinshasa, 1972). André Massaki continued to hold the honorary titles of general councillor of the PDA and president of the National Council of the FNLA.

25. The Institut d'Enseignement Secondaire Angolais (IESA). For Kunzika's address on the occasion of IESA's graduation ceremonies, July 5, 1970, see PDA, *A Voz Democrática* (Kinshasa, July 1970).

26. Pursuing his own education, he completed a degree in political science at the National University of Zaire for which he submitted a prudently bland thesis on Angolan nationalism. Emmanuel Mayala Kunzika, "La formation de la nation angolaise par la lutte de libération" (Université Nationale du Zaire, 1974).

27. Paulo Tuba in interview with George Houser, Kinshasa, June 1973.

28. Billed as a UPA conference and held at Kingantoko near Kinshasa. GRAE, *Notícias Breves*, Kinshasa, June 1, 1972.

29. Born Feb. 14, 1943, and educated through secondary school in Luanda, Kabangu left Angola in 1962 and went to Yugoslavia the next year where he studied electronics on a scholarship arranged through the UPA in Kinshasa. Returned to Kinshasa in 1969, he assumed various responsibilities in the FNLA and reportedly married a sister of Holden Roberto. Kabangu claimed fluency in Portuguese, Kimbundu, Kikongo, French, English, Serbo-Croat, Spanish, and Italian.

30. Born Nov. 27, 1939, in Luanda, Mateus Neto completed his secondary education in Lisbon (Oeiras National Liceu). While studying political science and public administration at the University of Vienna, he also took courses at an agricultural school where his training included work on irrigation in Israel and water utilization in the Netherlands. In 1966, he joined the FNLA, which sent him to Sweden to represent it while he pursued his studies in economics.

31. Born Sept. 28, 1934, at Quessua, Malange, Abrigada studied theology at the Presbyterian Seminary at Carcavelos, Portugal (1957–1959), and Richmond College, University of London (1959–1960). He then pursued liceu studies in Portugal until 1961 when he fled to England and then West

Germany where he studied medicine and (1970–1972) represented the FNLA until he was called to Kinshasa (May 1972). See Abrigada interview in *Vorwaerts* (Bonn), Nov. 23, 1972, and statement to International Labor Organization in Conférence International du Travail, *Compte rendu provisoire*, no. 29 (58th sess., 27 meeting, June 23, 1973), pp. 28–30.

32. Roberto's principal foreign affairs spokesman since the departure of Jonas Savimbi in 1964, Johnny Eduardo (no longer Edouard) born around 1942 at São Salvador, attended grade school in Matadi, where his father, Eduardo Pinock, was station master: Marcum, *Angolan Revolution*, 1:56–61. He subsequently studied at the Institute of Political Studies, Kinshasa, enrolled in a law course by correspondence (University of Paris), and, as an émigré, taught himself Portuguese. Appointed deputy head of foreign affairs was Pedro Vaal Hendrik Neto, an Mbundu born Nov. 25, 1944, at Gabela, South Cuanza, who studied at the Luanda liceu before joining the FNLA in 1962 at Léopoldville, where he also studied at the Zaire Institute of Information Sciences.

33. See ibid., p. 297.

34. For a report on the first meeting of the new Council of Ministers published in a new GRAE weekly "internal information" bulletin, see *Notícias Breves*, June 1, 1972. Included in the council deliberations were two secretaries of state—Angelo Messamessa of information, plan and economics and João Baptista Nguvulu of education.

35. Speaking over Radio Kinshasa on the occasion of the eleventh anniversary of the uprising in northern Angola, Roberto said that the three-year plan would focus on the development of cooperatives for small family farms and the harnessing of the physical and financial resources of Angolans in exile. GRAE, *Nouvelles breves* (Kinshasa), June 25, 1972. Background papers setting forth needs had already been prepared for education by Pedro Vaal Hendrik Neto, rural settlement and agricultural cooperatives by the LGTA secretariat, and public health by Carlos G. Kambandu (Kinshasa, Feb. 21, 1972, mimeo.).

36. Among the more ambitious was FNLA, "12 anos de Revoluçâo" (Kinshasa, Dec. 31, 1972, mimeo.).

37. Organizational work directed by Ngola Kabangu and a new representative in Lubumbashi (Elizabethville), Simão Chivinga. See GRAE, *Nouvelles breves*, June 25, 1972; *Notícias Breves*, Aug. 11, Oct. 30, 1972.

38. *Nouvelles breves*, June 25, 1972. The conference never took place.

39. Payable to the GRAE Department of Finance. Ibid.

40. Roberto maintained that the FNLA was conducting a "national liberation," not an internationally linked "ideological" struggle. See interview with Germain M'Ba in *Le progrès*, Apr. 2, 1967. He warned against "infiltration" of Angola's "national revolution" by foreign ideologies. *Notícias Breves*, June 1, 1972.

41. "We are not Marxists," Paulo Tuba told *24 heures, feuille d'avis de Lausanne* (Switzerland), Apr. 1, 1974, but they intended to renegotiate contracts with foreign investors and expected to establish a one-party state. Roberto made well known his rejection of "scientific socialism"—for example, to the *Times* (London), Dec. 27, 1972—and drew praise as a fellow anticommunist from the likeminded. Fernando Luis Cascudo, "Holden

Roberto," *Manchette* (Rio de Janeiro), Apr. 25, 1975, pp. 106–107 (Joint Publications Research Service 64, 866, May 29, 1975, pp. 1–2).

42. The FNLA portrayed itself as a "revolutionary party" rooted in the land and negritude and dedicated to agrarian reform, educational development and social justice. GRAE, "Plate-Forme du Front National de Libération de l'Angola (FNLA)" (Kinshasa, [1966], mimeo.).

43. *Dossier de l'Afrique australe* (Gonesse, France), no. 1 (Jan.–Feb. 1971): 17.

44. See speech by Zaire's Foreign Minister Mario Cardoso at Kinshasa ceremonies commemorating the tenth anniversary of the Angolan war, *GRAE Actualités* (Kinshasa), no. 3 (1971).

45. In 1972, the *Associação das Mulheres de Angola* was revived with a push from Ngola Kabangu. *Notícias Breves,* June 1, 1972. For a discourse on "The Role of Women in the Revolution" by AMA president Liliana Miguel, see ibid., July 29, 1972.

46. The *União Nacional dos Estudantes Angolanos* in Kinshasa continued to function in association with the FNLA. In the United States, UNEA was split between pro-FNLA students who in 1966 formed their own section (see "Compte rendu du meeting tenu à New York City au 25 du 26 novembre 1966," mimeo.) and published an occasional bulletin, *Angolais militant* (New York, 1967), on the one hand, and a dominant group of "neutralists" who expressed their diverse views in *Unidade Angolana* (New York, 1965–1966), *Angolan Student's Voice in the USA* (Philadelphia, 1968), and *Angola Flash* (New York, 1971). In Europe, there was no longer a functioning, FNLA-related UNEA section.

47. In November 1972, the GRAE Department of Education claimed a primary school enrollment of over thirty-two hundred in Zaire and nine thousand in "liberated areas" of Angola taught by 70 and 230 instructors, respectively. Secondary and technical school enrollment was said to be over 600 with 27 instructors. GRAE, "Rapport sur les activités militaires et sociales couvrant la période allant de juillet à octobre 1972" (Kinshasa, mimeo.).

48. In 1972, SARA, which counted 3 doctors (including Roberto's brother), 43 qualified nurses, and 150 nurses aides, a fifty-bed hospital at Kingantoko, and several dispensaries along the Angolan border, reportedly mounted an anticholera campaign in the Dembos region of northern Angola, as well as among Angolans in Zaire. See ILO statement of Dr. Abrigada, FNLA, *Actuality*, no. 5 (Sept. 1973): 27.

49. Figure given by LGTA official Pedro Rana in April 27, 1967, interview with author, Kinshasa, in which he also said that the International Confederation of Free Trade Unions (ICFTU) was cutting back on its assistance.

50. LGTA, *Angola Operária*, no. 2 (1967), no. 3 (1967), and [no. ?], June 15, 1973.

51. Of the groups discussed in chap. 4, the FNTA and USRA had ceased to exist. The UGTA, founded by the ill-fated André Kassinda, continued to exist, but its secretary-general, Maurice (Mauricio) Luvualu, was turned over to Portuguese authorities by the Kinshasa government in 1971. The CSLA (linked with the Bazombo, pacifist MDIA) claimed in 1968 to have 57,926 members, but, in fact, it led a shadowy, impecunious existence. See

its imaginative "Rapport activités de la Confédération des Syndicats Libres Angolais (CSLA) depuis sa création en septembre 1962 jusqu'au ler juin 1968" (Kinshasa, July 12, 1968, mimeo.).

52. AALC, "Report on the Angolan Trade Unions in Exile" (Kinshasa, Nov. 1, 1967, typescript). By October 1971, some 115 Angolans had participated in such seminars and courses. *AALC Reporter* (New York) 6, no. 9 (Oct. 1971).

53. *Elima* (Kinshasa), July 31, 1973.

54. Other principals were Garcia Makitumbu, assistant secretary-general; Pedro Ngumbi, external relations; Jackson Lukoki, assistant for external relations; Pedro Bomono, coordination; Daniel Sadidos, information; Pedro Rana, cadre training. *Labor in Perspective* (Kinshasa) 4, no. 12 (Dec. 1973), and *AALC Reporter* 8, no. 11 (Dec. 1973).

55. See Lamvu's April 22, 1967, letter to the secretary-general of the OAU and his October 20, 1967, communication to the U.N. Committee on Decolonizaton, A/AC.109/pet.688, add. 1, Dec. 27, 1967; *La dépêche* (Lubumbashi), July 14, 1967; and yet another appeal for external support of his efforts to overcome the "factional rivalries and fratricidal quarrels" that had led Angolans to "despair" and "confronted them with the alternative of either submitting to the movement which holds sway in their locality or being the victims of persecution and extortion" in letter of April 25, 1968 from Brazzaville, to U.N., Committee on Decolonization, A/AC.109/pet.1002, July 22, 1968.

56. The CNA, also known as *Tulengala*, was said to include the previously existing Nto-Bako, MDIA, Ngwizako, RCCKP, CBOA, and UGTA, as well as the newly formed *Union Révolutionnaire des Etudiants Angolais* (UREA), and the *Union Générale des Etudiants Angolais* (UGEA). U.N., Committee on Decolonization, A/6700/add.3, Oct. 11, 1967, pp. 250–252. CNA leaders Gracia Kiala (CSLA) and Jacob-Jacques Zimeni (Nto-Bako/Angelino Alberto faction) petitioned the UN for "moral and financial support." Ibid., A/AC.109/pet.993. June 13, 1968.

57. See ibid., A/AC.109/pet.914, Apr. 17, 1968, pet.914/add.1, May 28, 1968, and pet.914/add.2, July 22, 1968.

58. See Marcum, *Angolan Revolution*, 1:89–92, 164–169, 287–289.

59. U.N., Committee on Decolonization, Ngwizako to Prime Minister Salazar, Sept. 21, 1965, in A/AC.109/pet.425, Oct. 29, 1965, and Ngwizako to Salazar and President Thomaz, Dec. 12, 1967 in A/AC.109/pet.915, Apr. 17, 1968.

60. Ngwizako to Spanish ambassador, Kinshasa, Mar. 4, 1971, ibid., A/AC.109/pet.1173, May 12, 1971.

61. Ibid.

62. For names and particulars on arrests and disappearances, see letter of Apr. 4, 1970, to President Mobutu from Ngwizani a Kongo (Ngwizako) signed, as were all previous mentioned communications, by Garcia Faústino Malheiros and André Montciro Kiangala.

63. See Jorge Sangumba, "Concrete Efforts Toward Unity" in *Kwacha-Angola* (London), special ed. (Dec. 1972): 49. See also "The Student Interview: Dr. Jonas Savimbi," *The Student* (Leiden, Neth.) 12, no. 1 (Sept.–Oct. 1967); 13. The Savimbi–de Melo talks were held in the presence of a

Zambian official, Jonas Kachivanga. They failed, in Savimbi's view, because the MPLA was intent on getting UNITA expelled from Zambia. UNITA Office, London, "African Journalist in the Angola Liberated Area," interview with Savimbi taped by Japhet Kachoto of the *Times of Zambia* (Angola) (July–Aug. 1972): p. 4."

64. "Student Interview."

65. Sangumba, "Concrete Efforts Toward Unity."

66. The following account of the Lusaka discussions was given by Roberto to Reverend David Grenfell and Reverend Theodore Tucker in June 1967. After an initial session with Kaunda, in which the Zambian leader told Savimbi, "You do not help matters if you leave a party because you cannot have your own way," Roberto and Savimbi talked privately. The principal matter at issue was Roberto's stipulation that UNITA should be dissolved. "Kaunda was strong on this point—that he would not allow another Angolan nationalist party to function on Zambian territory. Savimbi reported back that [UNITA] would need more time to reach a decision. The second man in UNITA was an Angolan who had been many years in Zambia and had been politically active in Zambian politics with a trade union group opposed to Kaunda. He was quite willing for Savimbi to join GRAE but only as president of UNITA. Holden then reported the situation to Kaunda. His reply was that the party must then be banned and that Savimbi would have to leave Zambia. Holden pleaded that Savimbi be allowed to stay and the party allowed to continue but without any recognition. This was because of the presence of MPLA in Zambia, and Holden reasoned that while UNITA was there it would counteract MPLA efforts. To this Kaunda agreed. He told Holden that he did not like having MPLA in Zambia but circumstances forced this on him. Zambia gets much support from African states that are sympathetic to MPLA and Zambia needs all the support she can get." Grenfell, "Political Notes" (Kibentele, June 17, 1967, typescript).

67. Ibid. (Jan. 10, 1966) and ibid. (Mar. 20, 1967). Pro-UNITA refugees arriving in Lubumbashi were subject to arrest at the instance of Sikunda. Jeremias Chitunda to the author, Aug. 15, 1967.

68. "Student Interview."

69. *Le monde*, Dec. 28, 1966; *A Província de Angola* (Luanda), Dec. 30, 1966.

70. Many were reportedly former members of the *Association des Tshokwe du Congo de l'Angola et de la Rhodésie* (ATCAR). *Le figaro* (Paris), Apr. 6, 1967.

71. John de St. Jorre, (London) *Observer* Foreign News Service, Lusaka, Feb. 27, 1966. The Portuguese admitted to six civilian casualties only, but the raid had a strong psychological impact.

72. Press conference of Feb. 24, 1967, in *Kwacha-Angola* (Lusaka) (Jan.–Feb. 1967). According to Savimbi, UNITA raided civilian households to whom the government had distributed weapons because it was "easier to get arms from the settlers than the soldiers." *Zambia News* (Lusaka), Mar. 5, 1967.

73. John Edlin in *Zambia News*, Mar. 5, 1967.

74. Participating were Presidents Boumedienne (Algeria), Nyerere (Tanzania), and Ould Daddah (Mauretania) and a representative from Guinea. See Shirley Graham Du Bois, "The Little African Summit," *Africa and the World* (London) 3, no. 31 (May 1967): 9–11. In Lusaka, Smart Chata

396 NOTES TO PAGE 192

assumed the role of acting president of UNITA in which capacity he presented a petition (A/AC.109/pet.679) to the U.N. Committee on Decolonization meeting at Kitwe, Zambia, in June 1967.

75. Sangumba, "Concrete Efforts Toward Unity."

76. *Kwacha-Angola* (Lusaka), no. 5 (1967). On March 20, 1967, Roberto confided to David Grenfell that he would leave in five days for Lusaka and hoped to bring Savimbi back to Kinshasa. The Portuguese, he said, were pressing the Zambian government to hand Savimbi over to them, and the Zambians would be "relieved if Savimbi would come to Kinshasa." A month later, Roberto told Grenfell that he had cancelled his trip because Savimbi had gone to Cairo. Finally in June, Roberto reported that the Egyptian chargé d'affaires in Kinshasa had informed him that Savimbi was "no longer interested in joining GRAE." See Grenfell, "Political Notes," Mar. 20, Apr. 25, June 17, 1967.

77. M. J. Marshment in "UNITA" (London, 1970, typescript) gives the following account of the incident based on an interview with Savimbi: "He sent a message to his commanders instructing them to leave the line alone but it is a month's march to the line, and before the message arrived the line was cut again. When the message did arrive it did not reach all the commanders at the same time and the line was cut yet again. All this caused the Zambian government considerable embarrassment."

78. The MPLA said that it had "deliberately desisted" from cutting the railroad in deference to Zambian interests. "MPLA Information and Combat," doc. N. 1/S/67 (Lusaka, Apr. 4, 1967, mimeo.). Mobutu confronted Roberto with Portuguese assertions that FNLA forces had been involved. Roberto, who had undertaken not to disrupt the line over which much of Katanga's mineral exports traveled, called his own Katanga regional commander to Kinshasa for questioning. He then reassured Mobutu that the FNLA had not been involved and said the Portuguese were trying to drive a wedge between himself and the Zairian leader. Grenfell, "Political Notes," June 17, 1967.

79. "Who Is Jonas Savimbi? A Short Political Biography," *Kwacha-Angola* (London), no. 12 (Mar. 12, 1974). According to Savimbi, he was given an audience by the Zambian minister of presidential affairs, Mainza Chona, but no explanation as to why he was being deported. "African Journalist in the Angola Liberated Area," pp. 12–13.

80. Martin Meredith in *Zambia News*, July 31, 1966.

81. Savimbi alleged that Tanganyika Concessions was giving money to the MPLA in the mistaken belief that the MPLA controlled territory through which it ran. "African Journalist in the Angola Liberated Area," p. 3.

82. Though it professed not to know the "concrete causes" involved, the MPLA hailed the expulsion of Savimbi, whom it compared with the Cabindan collaborator, Alexandre Taty. MPLA, *Angola in Arms* (Dar es Salaam) 1, no. 5 (July–Sept. 1967). In an interview with Viktor Leontyev over Radio Moscow on January 7, 1968 (GMT 1900, Portuguese), however, Agostinho Neto said that the Zambians had discovered that Savimbi was just an "agent of foreigners," mainly Americans. "The MPLA," he added, "discovered that some Zambians, due to tribal and political quarrels, had joined the Portuguese for military training to learn sabotage methods, and therefore to

fight against the Zambian Government. Jonas Savimbi was connected with this opposition movement to the Zambian Government." As a result, Neto said, "that group," which called itself UNITA, "does not now exist."

83. Among the friends was Zambian Vice-President Simon Kapwepwe who broke with Kaunda in 1970–1971. According to Basil Davidson, Savimbi had persisted in organizing among Angolan refugees in Zambia against government wishes and had aroused Zambian suspicions that he was linked to the American Central Intelligence Agency. Basil Davidson, "Dans la brousse de l'Angola avec les guérilleros du MPLA," *Le monde diplomatique* (Paris), no. 198 (Sept. 1970): 19.

84. As a student in Switzerland, Savimbi had always lived well. One on-the-spot African observer wrote this author in Dec. 1969: "Savimbi collected some sacks of money from the people inside Angola around 1967 and left with these saying he was going out to buy arms. When I got to Zambia in 1968 I met a number of South African ladies with nice big radios and other things and the name Savimbi was on everyone of their lips—the presents he lavished about, what a good dancer and entertainer he was, etc.—and finally he had taken off with one of them (who was married) to Cairo. I am inclined to think that his being thrown out of Zambia may have been more connected with his behaviour than his operations as he wanted to make everyone think or understand."

85. *Zambia News*, Aug. 13, 1967.

86. Ibid.

87. Statement issued in Lusaka, Aug. 14, 1967.

88. Ethnic and regional affinity helped to explain close ties between UNITA and SWAPO. When in Dar es Salaam, Savimbi used SWAPO's post office box as his mailing address.

89. *Times of Zambia* (Ndola), Oct. 10, 1968, Feb. 25, 1969.

90. Ibid., Jan. 14, 1970. "Let him do it and see where it gets him," was the response of the *Times of Zambia* (Jan. 15, 1970) to what it rejected as blackmail.

91. "African Journalist in the Angola Liberated Area," p. 2. Lusaka's persisting distrust of Savimbi was based partly on UNITA cooperation with the secession prone Lozi of Zambia's western border region of Barotseland. Charles K. Ebinger, "External Intervention in Internal War: The Politics and Diplomacy of the Angolan Civil War" *Orbis*, 20, no. 3 (Fall 1976): 688.

92. *Kwacha-Angola* (London), no. 4 (June 1970).

93. Unwilling "to come home" and face the Portuguese and unable to control his own exile forces at Kinkuzu except through the intervention of "foreign" troops, Roberto ought to leave Angola to those prepared to fight and die inside the country. A "farce" as leader of a liberation movement. Roberto ought simply to join the government of Zaire. Savimbi, interviewed in "African Journalist in the Angola Liberated Areas," pp. 6–7.

94. Study by António Vakulukuta (known also as António Nicolau) from Pereira de Eça done as part of work for licence, University of Grenoble, France, 1971, excerpted in "UNITA: Structure, Politics, Perspectives," *Kwacha-Angola* (London), special ed. (Dec. 1972): 77–78. After receiving his degree in 1971, Vakulukuta returned clandestinely to Angola where he became a member of the UNITA Central Committee. For his subsequent

report on conditions inside, see "Reflexions d'un Maquisard," ibid. (Jan.–Apr. 1973); also interview in *A Província de Angola*, June 10, 1974.

95. *Kwacha-Angola* (Lusaka), no. 5 (1967).

96. Dennis M. Chipoya to MPLA Zambia Representative, Lusaka, Jan. 12, 1967.

97. Doubts shared by British author Basil Davidson who suggested that Savimbi was living clandestinely in Zambia, enjoying the protection of Zambian friends who shared "his openly anti-white, anti-*mestiço* attitudes." Davidson, "Dans la brousse de l'Angola" See also MPLA, "Documents Issued by the MPLA Representation in Sweden," no. 1 (Stockholm, 1971, mimeo.).

98. See M. J. Marshment's "UNITA" (1970) and his letter to *Africa Report* 16, no. 3 (Mar. 1971); reports by Fritz Sitte in *Zambia Daily Mail* (Lusaka), Aug. 7, 1971, and *Observer* (London), Apr. 9, 1972; interview with Savimbi by Japhet Kachoto of the *Times of Zambia*, "African Journalist in the Angola Liberated Area" (July–Aug. 1972), *Times of Zambia*, Sept. 26, 1972; Malik Chaka in *Zambia Daily Mail*, Oct. 30, 1973, and *Sunday Times of Zambia* (Ndola), Dec. 2, 1973; series of articles by Leon Dash, *Washington Post*, Dec. 23, 24, 25, 26, 1973; and Bernard Rivers, "Angola: Massacre and Oppression," *Africa Today* 21, no. 1 (Winter 1974): 41–45.

99. Born around 1939, the son of Barão Puna in Cabinda, Miguel N'Zau Puna studied for six years at a Christian seminary in Malange and then worked for the port administration at Noqui (Bas Zaire) before going to Tunisia where he spent five years studying agronomy. According to UNITA, the UPA "for years" tried to entice Puna into its ranks but failed "because GRAE was not correct in its revolutionary approach." Jorge Sangumba to author, Oct. 30, 1968.

100. "Politburo": Jonas Malheiro Savimbi, president and supreme commander; Miguel N'Zau Puna, secretary-general and general political commissar; Tuta Kafula, organizing secretary; Samuel Chitunda, chief of staff and secretary for coordination; José Samuel Chiwale, chief field commander; João Vicente Viemba, secretary for social affairs and popular education; Moises Kayombo, operational commander; Jorge Isaac Sangumba, secretary for foreign affairs; Fwamini DaCosta Fernandes, secretary for pan-African affairs and national patrimony; David "Samwimbila" Chingunji, secretary for military planning and training (killed July 18, 1970, in encounter with Portuguese forces at Kavimbi); Gaio Francisco Cacoma, secretary for cadres; and Antunes Kahal, secretary for finance and administration. "II Congress of UNITA," Central Base, Freeland of Angola, Aug. 24–30, 1969 (London, 1969, mimeo.).

101. Born around 1944 in Huambo, Chiwale went to China in 1965 and emerged in the early 1970s as UNITA's top multilingual and popular military leader. See *Notícia* (Luanda), Aug. 24, 1974, *Wall Street Journal*, Jan. 22, 1976.

102. "Samuel Chitunda" was a nom de guerre for Samuel Piedoso Chingunji. Born about 1938 in Bié, he completed a seven-year liceu cycle at Nova Lisboa and Silva Porto and was an officer in the Portuguese army. Chitunda died of "cerebral malaria" in January 1974.

103. Born about 1942 at Teixeira da Silva (Bailundo), Sangumba studied

at the Luanda seminary, completed a liceu cycle at Nova Lisboa, graduated from Manhattan College, New York (B.A. in political science), and studied international relations at Institute of World Affairs, University of London. See Jorge Sangumba, "UNITA and Angola's Struggle for Independence," *The New African* (London) 8, no. 1 (1969): 6–8, and interview in *Jornal do Brasil* (Rio de Janeiro), Nov. 9, 1975.

104. For several years, UNITA's secretary for pan-African affairs, Fwamini "Tony" DaCosta Fernandes, maintained a UNITA office at Cairo's Zamalek center for African liberation movements. Born around 1941 in Cabinda, Fernandes graduated from Luanda's seminary and later studied economics at the University of Fribourg, Switzerland.

105. Jorge Sangumba depicted the return of Angolan students from Europe as part of UNITA's plan to implement the dictum that "true liberation will come only from inside Angola." Letter to the author, Apr. 14, 1971.

106. See chap. 3.

107. After studying agricultural engineering in Florida, Kassoma earned the M.S. degree in soil sciences at Michigan State University. In February 1971, after six years in exile, he returned to Angola via Zambia. For a description of his journey inside, the nature of life in UNITA territory (farms, political perceptions, health and military activity), and Portuguese use of herbicides against nationalist crops, see his open letter of April 5, 1971, "Report from Angola by a Militant Who Has Just Arrived at UNITA Central Base," *Kwacha-Angola* (London), no. 7 (June 1971): 11–15. Kassoma was killed in a Portuguese bombing raid on UNITA territory in mid-1972, as was another American-educated student returnee, César Martins (a Luandan).

108. John de St. Jorre of the *Observer* had so described him (Lusaka, July 26, 1966, unpublished typescript).

109. See, for example: "Open Letter Addressed to Protestant Missionaries Who Served in Angola" (Central Base, Freeland of Angola, Oct. 1969); "Letter from Angola" addressed to "Our Friends Who Have Served the Church of Christ in Angola" (Central Base, 2d Region, Freeland of Angola, Oct. 24, 1970); "We Have Our Own Philosophy," from speech at 1969 UNITA congress in *Kwacha-Angola* (London), special ed. (Dec. 1972): 25–26; "Discurso de Orientação Política e Ideologica da UNITA," a 1970 speech inside Angola (London, June–July 1972, mimeo.); interview with Yvette Jarrico, Aug. 1970, in UNITA, "Angola, Portugal and Allies (NATO) Facing Defeat," document 1 (London, June 1971, mimeo.); "Mensagem do Finn do Ano 1970: Para Todos os Membros, Militantes, Activistas da UNITA" (Freeland of Angola, Dec. 1970, mimeo.); and "Mensagem do Presidente da UNITA, Jonas Savimbi, aos Quadros et Militantes da UNITA no Exterior" (Central Base, 2d Region, Freeland of Angola, May 1971, mimeo.).

110. *Kwacha-Angola* (London), no. 6 (Jan. 1971, and "Discurso de Orientação Política e Ideologica de UNITA." Alluding to the Soviet Union, Jorge Sangumba wrote in 1968, "some of the socialist countries are now a thoroughly treacherous and reactionary force in the world, objectively aligned with the imperialist countries against the world revolution not only

in Africa but also in Asia and Latin America. . . . they speak in the name of a cause they long ago betrayed." Sangumba to the author, Oct. 30, 1968.

111. A UNITA communiqué of 1971 quoted Mao to the effect that the enemy should be "the principal source" of guerrilla arms. *Kwacha-Angola* (Stockholm, Sweden), no. 2 (June 1971). Self-reliance was a constantly iterated theme as, for example, in Savimbi's speech to UNITA's third congress in August 1973. *UNITA-Bulletin* (Jamaica, N.Y.), no. 1 (1974): 7.

112. *24 heures, feuille d'avis de Lausanne*, Aug. 4, 1972.

113. "African Journalist in the Angola Liberated Area," p. 10.

114. "Option idéo-pratique de l'UNITA," in *L'UNITA dans la lutte pour l'indépendance nationale* (London, Mar. 1972), p. 11; *Kwacha-Angola* (Lusaka), no. 3 (Aug. 1966); Hsinhua, *Daily Bulletin* (London), July 4, 1968.

115. "Discurso de Orientação Política e Ideologica da UNITA," pp. 1–2.

116. Jorge Sangumba, "Open Letter to OSPAAAL" (Organization of Solidarity of the Peoples of Africa, Asia, and Latin America—Tricontinental) (London, Apr. 6, 1970, mimeo.). In 1972, an unidentified UNITA spokesman told Swiss journalist Guido Olivieri that his movement sought to develop the "national conscience" of Angolans and to create a new man who was "better" because he was "free." As for "communism" and "doctrines," they were dismissed as "slogans." *24 heures, feuille d'avis de Lausanne*, Aug. 4, 1972.

117. "Discurso de Orientação Política e Ideologica da UNITA," p. 5.

118. A UNITA spokesman was quoted as saying that it was obliged to study the techniques by which the Portuguese army was sometimes successful in developing good relations with the local population. UNITA "never" killed civilians and sought to gain local support as a constructive, protective force. *24 heures, feuille d'avis de Lausanne*, Aug. 4, 1972.

119. *Kwacha-Angola* (London), no. 4 (June 1970).

120. "Student Interview," p. 12.

121. Interview with Yvette Jarrico.

122. See *Kwacha-Angola* (London), no. 4 (June 1970).

123. Fritz Sitte, "Angola's Guerrilla Republic," p. 39, and Sitte, *Flammenherd Angola* (Vienna: Verlag Kremayr and Scheriau, 1972). Sitte had traveled in FNLA territory in early 1970: "47 Tage mit den 'ROHOS' im Dschungel Angolas," *Schweizerische Allgemeine Volkszeitung* (Zöfingen, Switzerland), no. 23, June 6, 1970, pp. 5–7, and no. 24, June 13, 1970, pp. 5–7.

124. An afternoon session of the congress devoted to a discussion of how to promote cooperation between UNITA and Afro-Americans was addressed by K. Akpan of the ALSC and Charles Simmons, an Afro-American correspondent covering the UN in New York, both of whom pledged support. *Zambia Daily News*, Oct. 30, 1973.

125. For congress coverage and resolutions, see Fernandes Neves, *Negritude e Revolução em Angola* (Paris: Edições "Etc.," 1974), pp. 114–124; see also *UNITA-Bulletin* (Jamaica, N.Y.), no. 1 (1974).

126. Among the Bakongo who assumed functions within UNITA were American-educated Joaquim Ernesto Mulato and Alexandre Francisco. In Europe Jorge Valentim (Free University of Brussels) organized a pro-UNITA meeting of (ex-UNEA) students ("Seminar of Angolan Students" [Switzerland, Aug. 31–Sept. 2, 1968, mimeo.]), which called for a "United

Front of all Angolan forces." As a fervent but erratic UNITA supporter, Valentim continued to act as a pro- (but unofficial) UNITA publicist. See, for example, "Conversação com Jorge Valentim ("Africa," Aug. 2, 1968, mimeo.), and *Qui Libere l'Angola* (Brussels: Michele Coppens, 1969).

127. UNITA, "Résolutions du premier seminaire des militants de l'UNITA en Europe" (Zöfingen, Switzerland, Jan. 9–10, 1971, mimeo.); see also *Aargauer Tagblatt* (Aarau, Switzerland), Jan. 11, 1971. UNITA's external ranks proved susceptible to the "anarchy" and "indiscipline" of exile politics, occasioning a sharp reprimand and call to discipline by Sangumba in 1972. UNITA, "Circular No. 1: A Todos os Militantes e Sympathizantes da UNITA no Exterior de Angola" (London, Nov. 1972, mimeo.).

128. Commander Samuel Chiwale told the U.N. Committee on Decolonization meeting in Zambia, May 1971, that nearly eight thousand children were attending rudimentary bush schools in UNITA-held areas as of 1969–1970. *Kwacha-Angola* (London), no. 7 (June 1971).

129. See chap. 4.

130. Also signed by Mm. Mwandumba. Agence France Presse, *Bulletin d'Afrique*, Dec. 31, 1966.

131. Basil Davidson, "Walking 300 Miles with Guerillas Through the Bush of Eastern Angola," *Munger Africana Library Notes* (Pasadena, Calif.), no. 6 (Apr. 1971): 9.

132. Paulo Jorge, MPLA director of information and propaganda, discusses the "huge problem" and need for time to train illiterate easterners for middle cadre roles in *Interviews in Depth, MPLA-Angola*, no. 4 (Richmond, B.C., Canada: Liberation Support Movement, 1973), p. 12. For interviews with locally recruited military cadres, see Basil Davidson, *In the Eye of the Storm: Angola's People* (Garden City, N.Y.: Doubleday, 1972), pp. 257–260.

133. For example: "Our Heritage: Portrait of a Great Angolan Queen," *Angola in Arms* 1, no. 1 (Jan. 1967): 5; Agostinho Neto, "People in Revolution," in *Portuguese Colonies: Victory or Death* (Havana: Tricontinental, 1971), p. 15; and dedication of the Rainha Nzinga Library in Luanda in December 1974 by the MPLA, *O'Século* (Lisbon), Dec. 23, 1974. See also poem "Jinga Mbandi, Primeira Guerrilheira" by Anesia Miranda in *Angola, Cultura e Revolução*, Caderno no. 3 (Algiers: Centro de Estudos Angolanos, 1966), pp. 25–26.

134. According to Portuguese sources, quarrels over the mestiço issue led to a wave of leadership resignations from the MPLA in 1966. *Diário* (Lourenço Marques), Sept. 29, 1970.

135. From Catete near Luanda, Déolinda Rodrigues was related to Agostinho Neto. See Marcum, *Angolan Revolution*, 1:300–301. Arrested with her were Irene Cohen, Lucrecia Paim, Engracia dos Santos, and Teresa Alfonso. *Courrier d'Afrique*, Mar. 4–5, 1967.

136. Eugenia Neto, "Poems from a Death Cell," *Angola in Arms* 2, no. 4 (July 1971), and MPLA, Comité Directeur, "Un bilan odieux" (Brazzaville, Mar. 18, 1967), which details the history of "arrests and assassinations" of MPLA militants by "Holden's bands."

137. See Marcum, *Angolan Revolution*, 1:215–217. Others arrested included MPLA officials Simão Nelumba and Fernando Miranda. *Bulletin d'Afrique*, Dec. 10, 1966.

138. "Conférence de presse du Dr. Agostinho Neto, président du MPLA" (Brazzaville, Jan. 3, 1968, typescript).

139. MPLA appeals to President Mobutu to end the systematic molesting and persecution of MPLA supporters went unanswered. See *Courrier d'Afrique*, Mar. 6, Apr. 26, 1967. Arrests extended to students, for example, Carlos Lengema, belonging to the MPLA-related *União dos Estudantes Angolanos* (UEA). *Bulletin d'Afrique*, Mar. 22, 1967.

140. Born José Mendes de Carvalho around 1942 at Dalatando (Salazar), Major Henda (nom de guerre) was a nephew of Agostinho Neto. He commanded the Cabinda front (1964–1966) before becoming general coordinator of the MPLA's Military Commission. *MPLA informations* (Algiers, Mar. 1969, mimeo.).

141. Born Nov. 20, 1923, in Luanda and one of the first blacks to graduate from the Luanda Liceu, Boavida obtained his medical degree from the University of Porto (1952) and undertook subsequent medical training in Barcelona and Prague. He joined the MPLA in 1960, headed the CVAAR (predecessor to SAM) medical-refugee service in Kinshasa, and was one of the first MPLA officials to join the guerrillas inside on the eastern front where he was known as "Ngola Kimbanda." Ibid. He was replaced at the head of SAM by Dr. Eduardo Santos. See also Marcum, *Angolan Revolution*, 1:206.

142. For a description of the raid by a visiting survivor, see Don Barnett, *With the Guerrillas in Angola* (Richmond, B.C., Canada: Liberation Support Movement, 1970). The Liberation Support Movement published a posthumous English translation of Boavida's *Angola: Five Centuries of Portuguese Exploitation* in 1972, and an interview with Boavida accompanying a *Memorandum of Activities of Medical Assistance Services* (SAM) in 1970.

143. Notably that of "Major Ingo" (Benigno Vieira Lopes), former commander of the Cami Column and political commissar of the first (Dembos-Nambuangongo) region, who denounced the MPLA as corrupt and communist. *O'Século* (Lisbon), Sept. 25, 1972; *Notícias* (lourenço Marques), Oct. 18, 1972. An MPLA defector, Madelena Meneses, described living conditions in MPLA-held areas as deplorable. *O'Seculo*, Aug. 16, 1972. Other defectors "confessed" to a lack of discipline and to fratricide within the MPLA military. *Jornal do Congo* (Carmona), Apr. 8, 1971. Francisco Barros, the MPLA representative in Cairo defected to the FNLA (July 1970). FNLA, *Liberté* (Cairo, Aug. 1970), and *24 heures, feuille d'avis de Lausanne*, July 16, 1970. And in Lusaka, the MPLA's representative, Anibal de Melo, was lost to the MPLA not by defection but by a crippling auto accident.

144. *Bulletin d'Afrique*, May 16, 1970.

145. *Etumba* (Brazzaville), Apr. 19, 1969.

146. *Africasia* (Paris), no. 11 (Mar. 16–29, 1970).

147. Paulo Jorge, *Interviews in Depth*, p. 4.

148. For the rationale behind the creation of the CCPM, see Kapiassa Husseini, "An Interview with Dr. Agostinho Neto," *Motive* (Nashville, Tenn.) 31, no. 4 (Feb. 1971): 58.

149. A Luandan mestiço born February 6, 1933, a cousin of Mário de Andrade, he represented MPLA in Morocco (1962) and then became an officer in the MPLA guerrilla army. Interviewed in the *Standard* (Dar es

Salaam), Apr. 23, 1971, and by Aquino de Bragança in *Africasia*, no. 38 (Apr. 12–25, 1971): 19–21.

150. Born in May 1931, the son of a Protestant pastor and first general secretary of the Church Council of Central Angola (1966–68), Rev. Jesse Chipenda. The father, arrested in 1968 and tortured in a Luanda prison, died at the São Nicolau political prison camp in 1969. Marie Crosby, "The Life History of Jesse Chipenda" (New York, Mar. 20, 1970, typescript). Daniel Chipenda, a former professional soccer player, moved between Dar es Salaam, Lusaka, and eastern Angola, where he developed a considerable personal political following. Interviewed in *Daniel Chipenda* (Seattle: Liberation Support Movement [1969]).

151. Born Lúcio Rodrigo Leite Barreto de Lára (April 9, 1929), the son of a wealthy mestiço sugar plantation owner. In 1968 he underwent treatment in the Soviet Union for a heart ailment. Interviewed in *Etumba*, June 27, 1970, and *Africasia*, no. 58 (Jan. 24–Feb. 6, 1972): 17–18.

152. Born around 1942 in the Zaire district of northern Angola, Monimambu received military training in Ghana, Morocco, the Soviet Union, and Algeria and succeeded Major Henda as head of the MPLA Military Commission in 1968. Interviewed in *Spartacus Monimambu* (Seattle: Liberation Support Movement, 1970).

153. See *Programa* ([Brazzaville?]: Edição do Movimento Popular de Libertação de Angola, 1966).

154. "Relatório das Decisãos" of MPLA conference, Feb. 22–26, 1968 (Dolisie), in Davidson, *Eye of the Storm*, p. 285.

155. Lúcio Lára in *Africasia*, no. 58 (Jan. 24–Feb. 6, 1972): 18. For a description of the MPLA's Center for Revolutionary Instruction (CIR), see *Report of the MPLA to the U.N. Committee on Decolonization* (Seattle: Liberation Support Movement, 1969), pp. 44–48.

156. Paulo Jorge, *Interviews in Depth*, p. 29.

157. *Spartacus Monimambu*, p. 21.

158. Basil Davidson, "Dans la brousse de l'Angola avec les guerilleros du MPLA," *Le monde diplomatique* (Paris), no. 198 (Sept. 1970): 19. See also *História de Angola: Apontamentos*, Caderno no. 2 (Algiers: Centro de Estudos Angolanos, 1965), and statement by Agostinho Neto in *Révolution africaine*, Feb. 7–13, 1970, pp. 21–22.

159. For Dr. Neto's most comprehensive statement of political philosophy, his lecture of February 1974 at the University of Dar es Salaam, see appendix 4.

160. Paulo Jorge, *Interviews in Depth*, p. 11.

161. *MPLA 1970* (Seattle: Liberation Support Movement, 1970), p. 8.

162. See speech by Agostinho Neto over Radio Tanzania, June 6, 1968, in *Messages to Companions in the Struggle* (Richmond, B.C.: Liberation Support Movement, 1972), pp. 11–12.

163. See "Blueprint to Consolidate the Position of the MPLA in Eastern Angola," *Angola in Arms* 1, no. 5 (July–Sept. 1967): 3–6, 12; *Angola in Arms*, special issue (Feb. 1968): 4.

164. "Conférence de presse du Dr. Agostinho Neto." That May, Neto declared to the press that the transfer had been completed. *Nationalist* (Dar es Salaam), May 20, 1968.

165. *MPLA informations* (Algiers, Mar. 1969, mimeo.). The assembly of

August 23–25 was also attended by a Zambian journalist, Tommy Chibaye (*Zambia Daily Mail*, Sept. 6, 1968) and representatives of the North American-based Liberation Support Movement. The assembly voted to accept whites as "sympathizer members" of the MPLA. See Roy Harvey, *People's War in Angola: Report on the First Eastern Regional Conference of the MPLA* (Seattle: Liberation Support Movement, 1970), p. 24.

166. See comments of MPLA director of information and propaganda in Paulo Jorge, *Interviews in Depth*, pp. 4–5.

167. *LSM News* (Richmond, B.C.) 1, no. 2 (Aug. 1974).

168. *Standard* (Dar es Salaam), Dec. 20, 1971; Agence France Presse, Feb. 3, 1972.

169. Agostinho Neto presided over the meeting (Sept. 27–Oct. 3, 1971) in eastern Angola, which was attended by some three hundred militants and focused largely on the need to prepare for such a congress. *Africasia*, no. 56 (Dec. 27, 1971): 29. See also *Angola in Arms* 2, no. 6 (Sept.–Oct., 1971). Since its last meeting in 1968, six central committee members had lost their lives: Commanders Hoji Ia Henda, Benedito, Janguinda, Kimakienda, and Cuidado, and Political Commissar Levsky. *Road to Liberation: MPLA Documents on the Founding of the People's Republic of Angola* (Richmond, B.C.: Liberation Support Movement, 1976), p. 28.

170. Davidson, *Eye of the Storm*, p. 265.

171. *Daily News* (Dar es Salaam), Aug. 10, 1972, June 16, 1973, and *Daily Telegraph* (London), Mar. 5, 1973.

172. See Gaetano Pagano, "Visit to MPLA and Their Liberated Areas, May–September 1974" (International University Exchange Fund, 1975). This was the same offensive that in mid-1972 took the lives of Luciano Kassoma and other UNITA militants.

173. *Diário de Notícias*, May 20, 1973. In July 1973, the Portuguese high command in Luanda reported a marked decline in the numbers and activities of Angolan nationalists who were, it added, "faced with a crisis of ideas and fatigue." *Notícias* (Lourenço Marques), July 3, 1973, p. 2.

174. Davidson, *Eye of the Storm*, p. 287.

175. Ibid., p. 242.

176. Colin Legum, "A Study of Foreign Intervention in Angola," in Colin Legum and Tony Hodges, eds., *After Angola: The War over Southern Africa* (London: Rex Collings, 1976), p. 11. See also Ebinger, "External Intervention," p. 688.

177. Legum, "A Study of Foreign Intervention," p. 11. Neto followed up a January 1973 visit to Moscow (see interview, Radio Moscow, 1630 GMT, Jan. 27, 1973) with February visits to Hungary, Rumania, Bulgaria and Yugoslavia. MPLA, *Vitória ou Morte*, Apr. 14, 1973.

178. "Note to the Zambian Government Regarding the Counter-Revolutionary Currents within the Movement," signed by Agostinho Neto, Lusaka, June 3, 1973. Minor spelling and punctuation changes by the author.

179. Reference to the assassinations of Eduardo Mondlane (FRELIMO) and Amilcar Cabral (PAIGC) in 1969 and 1973, respectively.

180. Presumably a reference to the unity pact entered into with the FNLA in December 1972.

181. For earlier conversations with Commander Paganini (an Ochimbundu) on the eastern front see Davidson, *Eye of the Storm*, chap. 1.

182. In September 1973, the MPLA Steering Committee declared that it possessed "firm proof that during the period in which Daniel Chipenda was responsible for the logistics of MPLA, UNITA received arms which belonged to us by means of a subversive tribal network organized by Chipenda himself." *Road to Liberation*, p. 35.

183. A commander on the eastern front since 1968, Manuel António Muti deserted in Zambia and then denounced Neto and the MPLA in an interview with the *Diário de Notícias*, May 20, 1973.

184. "Open Letter to the Militants," signed by Daniel Chipenda, Lusaka, July 1973. See also *Notícia* (Luanda), Sept. 14, 1974, pp. 35–42, and *Remarques africaines* (Brussels), Jan. 1, 1975, pp. 37–38.

185. In August 1973, Neto issued a statement calling on "all the militants, all the bodies of the Movement, from the base to the top, to take maximum precautions with the deserters of the army and controlled areas of the enemy, as well as with new applicants to the membership of the Organization, in order to prevent new infiltrations of enemy agents into our ranks." MPLA, "Note on Deserters and Applicants to Membership of MPLA" (Lusaka, Aug. 10, 1973, mimeo.). And in late August, Lúcio Lára announced publicly that Portuguese intelligence had mounted a plot to assassinate Dr. Neto. *Sunday Times of Zambia* (Ndola), Aug. 26, 1973.

186. The Dec. 13, 1972 agreement creating the *Conselho Supremo da Libertação de Angola*.

187. "Open Letter to the Militants."

188. "Note on Deserters."

189. *Le monde*, May 31, 1974.

190. UNTA, "Déclaration et programme de l'Union Nationale des Travailleurs Angolais (UNTA)" (Kinshasa, Jan. 2, 1968, mimeo.); see also *L'Etoile du Congo* (Kinshasa), May 16, 1968.

191. An assignment that was the result of an accord between Dr. Neto and UNTA General Secretary Pascal Luvualu. Ibid. and Paulo Jorge, *Interviews in Depth*, p. 17.

192. See, for example, UNTA's occasional Kinshasa information bulletin, *Le travailleur de l'Angola*.

193. The UEA (successor to the transterritorial UGEAN—see chap. 1) was founded in Brazzaville, Sept. 1966. *Année africaine 1966* (Paris: Editions A. Pedone, 1968), p. 144.

194. *El Moudjahid* (Algiers), Feb. 6, 1969.

195. For a discussion of the work of the *Serviço de Assistência Médica do MPLA* (SAM) and the women's *Organização das Mulheres de Angola* (OMA), see Paulo Jorge, *Interviews in Depth*, pp. 16, 20. On MPLA schools see "Concept of Revolutionary Education," *Angola in Arms* 3, no. 1 (Jan.–Feb. 1972).

196. Portuguese observers saw in Brazzaville policy a long-range desire to "absorb" Cabinda and thereby expand the Congo Republic's ocean frontage. See, for example, H. Felgas, *Os Movimentos Terroristas de Angola, Guiné, Moçambique: Influencia Externa* (Lisbon: 1966). But pro-Cabindan sympathies of Brazzaville political and administrative leadership of Cabindan

extraction may also have been an important factor. It is noteworthy, for example, that Alfred Raoul, who had been premier and a cabinet minister (1968–1971), later assumed a leadership role in the Cabindan Liberation Front (FLEC). *Le monde*, May 17, 1975.

197. See petition of August 31, 1966, by Luis Ranque Franque, president, and António Eduardo Sozinho Zau, foreign secretary, on behalf of the *Frente para Libertação do Enclave de Cabinda* (FLEC), U.N., Committee on Decolonization, doc. A/AC. 109/pet. 567, Dec. 8, 1966.

198. See ibid., pet 643, May 25, 1967, addressed to UN "Liberation Committee," May 2, 1967, signed by Henriques Tiago Nzita, secretary-general, and Henri Charles Tembo, deputy secretary-general.

199. *Bulletin d'Afrique*, Feb. 1, 1967.

200. MPLA sources alleged that Nzita was linked with the "well known traitor" Alexandre Taty. Ibid. See also ibid., May 28–29, 1967.

201. U.N., Committee on Decolonization, Doc. A/AC.109/Pet.641, May 25, 1967.

202. Ibid., pet. 641, May 25, 1967. Members of the GPRFE cabinet were prime minister and foreign affairs, Pedro Simba Macosso; health and social affairs, Alberto Macaia; interior, Joel Zepherino Guimbi; finance, Demas Guta Macosso; information and propaganda, Marcos Alexandre; youth and sports, Linga Casimir.

203. *Financial Times* (London), Aug. 8, 1967, and Aquino Ray, "Le pétrole angolais au service de la contre-révolution," *Révolution africaine*, Oct. 9–15, 1967, p. 34.

204. See chap. 1.

205. "Declaração de Compromismo" signed at Tunis, Jan. 31, 1960, and promptly sidestepped by Roberto.

206. See, for example, *Jornal do Congo*, June 22, 1967.

207. Whether one accepts the authenticity of documents detailing alleged UNITA-Portuguese collaboration against the MPLA (*Afrique-Asie*, July 8, 1974), it seems obvious that it was to the perceived advantage of the Portuguese to ensure that UNITA survived as a third force able to help check MPLA power in eastern Angola. At the very least, this meant that Portuguese forces would not press for a knockout blow against UNITA.

208. *Bulletin d'Afrique*, Nov. 29, 1966.

209. *Togo Presse* (Lomé), June 25, 1968.

210. *Ethiopian Herald* (Addis Ababa), June 29, 1968.

211. *El Moudjahid*, July 17–18, 1968.

212. *Bulletin d'Afrique*, Mar. 3, 1970.

213. Excerpt from Savimbi's letter of May 30, 1969, to Justin Bomboko made public on August 20, 1969, at the Seventh Assembly of the World Assembly of Youth (WAY), Liège, Belgium, by Emmanuel Kunzika. PDA, *Informations mensuelles*, Oct. 24, 1969.

214. See Jonas Savimbi, "La paix au Congo et la libération de l'Angola," *Remarques congolaises et africaines*, Feb. 17, 1965, pp. 20–21.

215. Savimbi to Raoul, June 10, 1970. *UNITA: The Armed Struggle in Angola* (Boston: Black Survival Press, 1973).

216. For example: *Times of Zambia*, Dec. 15, 1969, Dec. 19, 1970; *Zambia Daily News*, May 25, 1972; and frequent memorandums to the OAU, for

example, "Statement Addressed to the African Liberation Committee of the Organization of African Unity," *Kwacha-Angola* (London), no. 1 (Jan. 1969).

217. Jacob Khamalata in *Times of Zambia*, Dec. 19, 1970.

218. On September 25, 1965, Neto told Belgrade's TANYUG news agency (International Service, 1127 GMT) that OAU mediation was improving chances for MPLA cooperation with "Angola's other leading anti-colonialist organization," the FNLA.

219. On August 29, Radio Cairo announced prematurely that the UPA and MPLA had amalgamated within a common front. Cairo Domestic Service (Arabic), 1900 GMT, Aug. 29, 1966.

220. Composed then of Congo-Brazzaville, Egypt, and Ghana.

221. Agreement signed by Luis de Azevedo, Jr., Daniel Chipenda, Paulo Jorge, and Francisco Barros for MPLA and Nicolas Vieira and Manuel André Miranda for FNLA. For text, see MPLA, "Déclaration" (Dar es Salaam, Nov. 11, 1966, mimeo.).

222. Portuguese oppositionists welcomed it as a step toward a truly effective struggle against Salazar (*Portugal Democrático* [São Paulo] 11, no. 12 [Nov. 1966]), and Algeria's *Révolution africaine*, Oct. 22–29, 1966, saw it as a personal victory for Egypt's Dr. Fayek.

223. Roberto denied that the FNLA delegation had been authorized to sign the accord, which, he said, would require approval by the FNLA's National Council (an action he appeared less than eager to recommend). *Jeune Afrique*, Oct. 30, 1966, p. 31, and *L'Etoile du Congo*, Oct. 24, 1966.

224. Agostinho Neto in *Bulletin d'Afrique*, Dec. 6, 1966, and Lúcio Lára in *Izvestia* (Moscow), Feb. 5, 1967. See also MPLA, "Déclaration." Roberto's repudiation of the Cairo agreement was seen as "discrediting" the FNLA and confirming the MPLA as the "dominant" Angolan movement by Jašo Babić, "The Struggle for Liberation in the 'White Triangle' of Africa," *Review of International Affairs* (Belgrade) 19, no. 430 (May 3, 1968): 18–20.

225. *Horoya* (Conakry), Nov. 24, 1965. Shortly before the signing of the abortive Cairo accord of October 1966, MPLA Vice-President Domingos da Silva stated that OAU pressure for a common front served Roberto's interests because the FNLA was in need of a reprieve. Reinforced by members of the Katanga-based *União Nacional Angolana* (UNA) who had just merged with it, the MPLA, he said, was in a position to assume full leadership of the Angolan struggle. And, he conjectured incorrectly, President Mobutu was likely to lift the ban on MPLA operations imposed by the Adoula and Tshombe governments. Interview with O. Ignatiev, *Pravda* (Moscow), Sept. 2, 1966.

226. OAU, African Heads of Government, 8th meeting, June 1971, doc. 57.

227. Participating in the Brazzaville discussions, May 31 and June 4–6, 1972, were FNLA—Holden Roberto, Johnny Eduardo, Ngola Kabangu, Mateus Neto, Carlos Kambandu, Sébastien Lubaki Ntemo, and André Massaki; MPLA—Agostinho Neto, Jacob Caetano, Inacio Baptista, and Lúcio Lára. GRAE, *Notícias Breves*, no. 2 (1972).

228. See Aquino de Bragança, "Vers l'unité?" *Afrique-Asie*, July 10, 1972, pp. 34–35.

229. An official statement announcing the agreement in principle was

issued jointly by Presidents Mobutu and Ngouabi. "La rencontre de Brazzaville" (Brazzaville, June 8, 1972, mimeo.).

230. OAU, African Heads of Government, 9th meeting, June 1972, doc. 80.

231. November 6–13. See George M. Houser, "Memorandum on MPLA-FNLA Unity" (New York, American Committee on Africa, Jan. 19, 1973). The FNLA sought an accord that would give the four sponsoring powers (Congo-Brazzaville, Tanzania, Zaire and Zambia) and their military technicians an important role in its implementation. "La position du GRAE face à la question du mouvement angolais de libération nationale," in GRAE, *Dossiers* (Kinshasa, June–Aug. 1972, mimeo.).

232. For the text, see Paulo Jorge, *Interviews in Depth*, pp. 32–36.

233. The GRAE, until then still-recognized by Zaire, formally ceased to exist.

234. *Daily News* (Dar es Salaam), Dec. 15, 1972.

235. Agence France Presse, Feb. 27, 1973. According to British journalist Simon Scott Plummer, Roberto insisted on an evaluation of FNLA and MPLA military forces by a commission consisting of representatives of Congo-Brazzaville, Tanzania, Zaire, and Zambia and international journalists. The MPLA rejected this, Roberto told Plummer, because it would reveal MPLA weakness in manpower "and give the lie to [its] widespread, communist-backed propaganda." *Times* (London), Dec. 27, 1972. This insistence upon military evaluation in which it expected to best its rivals conformed to an FNLA strategy dating back to 1967. *Bulletin d'Afrique*, Jan. 29–30, 1967.

236. *Révolution africaine*, June 14, 1973, pp. 24–26.

237. MPLA representative in Europe, Saydi Mingas, interviewed in Norway (*Friketen* [Oslo], Feb. 25–Mar. 2, 1974) said that the MPLA continued to seek its implementation because "if we cut out the FNLA, Africa will cut out the MPLA."

238. See *Le communiste* (Paris), Sept.–Oct. 1972, and *Afrique-Asie*, Aug. 20, 1973, reproduced in *Facts and Reports* (Amsterdam), Sept. 1, 1973, pp. 17–18.

239. *Afrique-Asie*, Nov. 11, 1973, in *Facts and Reports,* Nov. 24, 1973, p. 12.

240. UNITA, Central Committee, "Special Communiqué on Unification Conference Held in Kinshasa on 13th December 1972" (Freeland of Angola, Jan. 5, 1973, mimeo.).

241. *Kwacha-Angola* (London), no. 12, Mar. 12, 1974.

242. *Le monde*, Jan. 6, 1972.

243. The base was named after the Czechoslovak city where some MPLA soldiers were trained. According to Luanda journalist Fernando Farinha, an MPLA deserter led Portuguese troops to the Brno base near Combe de Zombo. *Notícia* (Luanda), Sept. 28, 1968. See also *Jornal do Congo*, May 16, 1968.

244. According to Portuguese army sources as reported in *De Groene Amsterdammer* (Amsterdam, Netherlands), July 11, 1973.

245. Fernando Farinha in *Notícia*, Feb. 21, 1970.

246. Al Venter, *The Terror Fighters* (Cape Town: Purnell, 1969), p. 31.

247. "Circular Confidencial" signed for MPLA Comitê director by Coor-

dinator Finseky, Third Region, Moxico, June 12, 1970.

248. *Kwacha-Angola* (London), no. 2 (June 1969), no. 4 (June 1970), no. 9 (July–Sept. 1972).

249. *Epoca* (Lisbon), June 19, 1972. (Joint Publication Research Service, no. 56, 914, Aug. 29, 1972, p. 2.).

250. UNITA guerrillas were "helpless" against the MPLA's automatic weapons, mortars, bazookas, and grenades. Fernando Farinha and Moutinho Pereira writing on ten years of war in *Notícia*, Oct. 10, 1970. In mid-1970, Portuguese officials disseminated a statement attributed to a former UNITA militant, Tiago Sachilombo, which called upon the populace to join Portuguese forces in fighting against the MPLA, which, it alleged, had been killing UNITA supporters since 1966. *Diário de Notícias* (Lisbon), June 24, 1970.

251. *Times of Zambia*, Mar. 23, 1972.

252. *Neue Zürcher Zeitung* (Zürich), Mar. 12, 1972.

253. UNITA, "Especial Communiqué" (Central Base, Angola, Feb. 4, 1970, mimeo.).

254. Interview with author, May 3, 1967. For 1968, the MPLA announced that its guerrillas had killed 2,760 and wounded 2,160 enemy soldiers at a cost of 80 MPLA killed and wounded. *El Moudjahid*, Feb. 6, 1969.

255. *Times of Zambia*, Apr. 27, 1968.

256. *Star* (Johannesburg), July 31, Aug. 1, 1968. *Rhodesia Herald* (Salisbury), July 30, 1968.

257. *Rhodesia Herald*, July 29, 1968; *Notícia*, June 1, 1968.

258. Wilf Nussey in *Star*, Aug. 5, 1968. On MPLA eastern insurgency, see also Daniel Limukonda in *Zambia Daily Mail*, Mar. 8, 1968; Tommy Chibaye in *Standard* (Dar es Salaam), Dec. 13, 1968; and Don Barnett, *With the Guerrillas in Angola* (Seattle: Liberation Support Movement, 1970).

259. *Star*, Aug. 5, 1968.

260. An estimated sixty Alouettes were in service in Angola by 1971. *Gazette de Lausanne*, Apr. 15, 1971. See S. J. Bosgra and Chr. van Krimpen, *Portugal and NATO*, 3d ed. (Amsterdam, Angola Comité, 1972), pp. 26–28.

261. *Road to Liberation*, p. 24.

262. MPLA units, which had to carry military supplies hundreds of miles overland from Zambia, lacked such weaponry as heavy mortars, recoilless cannons, and ground-to-ground missiles, which by then were being employed by the PAIGC insurgents in Guinea-Bissau. Davidson, "Walking 300 Miles," p. 20. See also Davidson, "Angola in the Tenth Year: A Report and an Analysis, May–July 1970," *African Affairs* 70, no. 278 (Jan. 1971): 37–49, and report on travel with MPLA inside Angola by Winter Lemba, *Times of Zambia*, Jan. 2, 3, 6, 7, 8, 1970.

263. Substances reported used included cacodylic acid (with arsenic) and picloram (produced commercially as Tordon by Dow Chemical). *Angola in Arms* 2, no. 1 (Feb. 1971). According to the American Committee on Africa in New York, "U.S. exports of herbicides to Portugal quadrupled between 1969 and 1970, the year Portugal began to use them in Angola." See "The Status of the Liberation Struggle in Africa" (New York, June 1, 1971).

264. Rui de Pinto, *The Making of a Middle Cadre* (Richmond, B.C.: Liberation Support Movement, 1973), p. 105.

265. *De Groene Amsterdammer*, July 11, 1973. In October 1970, the MPLA lost one of its top military commanders, Justino Frederico (Leão Veneno), an Ochimbundu from Andulo, in action against the Portuguese in the Bié district. *Tricontinental Bulletin* (Havana), no. 63 (July 1971): 45.

266. *Jeune Afrique*, Feb. 12, 1972. For reports on the eastern front by outside observers in 1971 and 1972, see Soviet journalist Pavel Mikhailov in *Junge Welt* (East Berlin), July 7, 8, 1971; Finnish National Student Union team, Mikka Lohikoski and Börje J. Mattsson, *Report of a Visit to the Liberated Areas of Angola* (Helsinki, Kunnallispaino, 1971); and Rolf-Henning Hintz, *Frankfurter Rundschau*, July 1, 1972.

267. See annual U.N. secretariat report on Angola, Committee on Decolonization, doc. A/AC. 109/L.842, Feb. 28, 1973, p. 12. See also *Daily News* (Dar es Salaam), Aug. 10, 1972.

268. *De Groene Amsterdammer*, July 11, 1973.

269. *Africasia*, no. 6 (Jan. 5–18, 1970): 15–16.

270. *Daily Telegraph* (London), Mar. 5, 1973.

271. *Daily News*, June 16, 1973.

272. Anthony R. Wilkinson, "Angola and Mozambique: the Implications of Local Power," *Survival* (International Institute for Strategic Studies, Sept.–Oct. 1974), p. 218. In his New Year's message of 1974, Neto warned: "By military means, by the infiltration of PIDE/DGS agents [Portuguese secret police] into our ranks, by exploiting tribal, racial, class, cultural and other differences, and even trying to influence border countries, the imperialists are, at this moment, making enormous efforts to weaken and even destroy MPLA, the only organized force in Angola which consistently opposes colonialism." MPLA, *Angola in Arms* (LSM, Jan.–Apr. 1974).

273. MwanaNgola and an initial contingent of 144 UNITA soldiers were welcomed with fanfare by the FNLA, *Liberté et terre* (Kinshasa), no. 3 (Jan. 1969), and denounced as "tribalist tools of imperialism" by UNITA, *Kwacha-Angola* (London), no. 2 (June 1969).

274. Area cited in retrospective interview with Savimbi, *A Província de Angola*, Aug. 13, 1974. In September 1970 official American estimates put Savimbi's forces at two hundred armed personnel and perhaps two thousand sympathizers. Department of State, "Angola: An Assessment of the Insurgency," Sept. 16, 1970.

275. U.N. doc. A/AC.109/L.842, Feb. 28, 1973, p. 7.

276. Wilkinson, "Angola and Mozambique."

277. See Steve Valentine in *Times of Zambia*, Sept. 11, 12, 1969; M. J. Marshment, "UNITA" (London, unpublished typescript), and Marshment's letter to *Africa Report*, 16, no. 3 (Mar. 1971): 42; Fritz Sitte in *Times of Zambia*, Aug. 7, 1971, and *Zambia Daily Mail*, Aug. 7, 1971; also Sitte, "Angola's Guerrilla Republic," *Observer* (London), Apr. 9, 1972, and Sitte in *Vorwaerts* (Bonn), June 28, 1972; Japhet Kachoto in *Times of Zambia*, Sept. 26, 1972; Malik Chaka in *Zambia Daily Mail*, Oct. 30, 1973, and *Sunday Times of Zambia*, Dec. 2, 1973; Leon Dash in *Washington Post*, Dec. 23, 24, 25, 26, 1973; and Bernard Rivers, "Angola: Massacre and Oppression," *Africa* (London), no. 31 (Mar. 1974): 31.

278. *De Groene Amsterdammer*, July 11, 1973.

279. Born June 23, 1947, at Nova Sintra (Bié), Samuimbila began political

organization work in Mexico in 1965 and was a member of the UNITA political bureau at the time of his death, July 18, 1970, during an attack on the Portuguese post of Kavimbi on the Benguela Railroad. "Samuimbila" translated means "the man who unites the people by singing revolutionary songs." *Kwacha-Angola* (London), no. 6 (Jan. 1971), and *Times of Zambia*, Dec. 14, 1970.

280. In early 1972, UNITA claimed to have extended its military activity to both Bié and Huila districts and as far south as the Cunene-Namibia (South West Africa) border. UNITA, "Special Communiqué of the Armed Forces" (Jan. 31, 1972, mimeo.).

281. Fernando Farinha and Moutinho Pereira writing in Luanda's *Notícia*, Oct. 10, 1970, described UNITA as the only Angolan movement that, "although in a state of deterioration," had "won the sympathy of the masses it [had] indoctrinated."

282. John Edlin in *Zambia News*, Mar. 5, 1967.

283. "The Angolan People Forge Ahead Along Road of Armed Struggle," *Peking Review*, Feb. 13, 1970, pp. 21–22.

284. Interview with an "authorized" UNITA spokesman by Guido Olivieri, *24 heures, feuille d'avis de Lausanne*, Aug. 4, 1972.

285. See "La longue trahison de l'UNITA," *Afrique-Asie*, July 8, 1974. See also, *Times of Zambia*, June 13, 1974. UNITA denounced the "letters" as forgeries and *Afrique-Asie* for an "unprincipled" effort to discredit it by publishing them even though the journal acknowledged never having seen the originals. UNITA, *Angola* (London, June–Aug. 1974, mimeo.). On alleged UNITA collaboration, see also *Expresso* (Lisbon), Nov. 12, 1975.

286. *Diário de Notícias*, June 27, 1974. Jack Bourderie writing in *Afrique-Asie*, July 8, 1964, saw this comment as part of a conspiracy to build up UNITA's prestige.

287. Wilkinson, "Angola and Mozambique."

288. For a description of this area as visited by a three-man team of Swiss observers in 1968, see GRAE, "Press Conference Held in Kinshasa on September 3, 1968 by Pierre-Pascal Rossi" (Kinshasa, Sept. 3, 1968, mimeo.), and Pierre-Pascal Rossi, *Pour une guerre oubliée* (Paris: Juilliard, 1969); see also Rossi, "Fifty Days with the Angolan Guerrillas," *Continent 2000* (Kinshasa), no. 12 (Sept. 1970): 5–16, and earlier report from Portuguese side by Jean-François Chauvel, *Le figaro* (Paris), Apr. 5, 1967.

289. The "cruel tactic" of mining "jungle tracks" became the FNLA's most effective military activity. Gilbert Comte, *Le monde*, Jan. 5, 1972.

290. *L'Etoile du Congo*, Dec. 13, 1966; Angola Office, New York, *Free Angola* (July 29, 1967); *Le progrès* (Kinshasa), June 1, 1970; FNLA, *Liberté* (Cairo, Aug. 1970, mimeo.). In 1970, the FNLA invited the Red Cross to visit six Portuguese prisoners of war held at Kinshasa, handed over to the organization two young Portuguese girls who had survived a nationalist raid inside Angola, and proposed a prisoner exchange with Portugal. *Le GRAE et le sort des prisonniers de guerre* (Kinshasa: GRAE Department of Foreign Relations, 1970). See also GRAE, "Communiqué" (Geneva, Switzerland, Mar. 12, 1971), and GRAE, *Actualité*, no. 4 (May 1973): 14–15.

291. From an account by Swedish journalist Olle Wästberg who visited COA during a thirty-nine day journey into FNLA territory in mid-1969.

Wästberg, "We Caught Rats with our Bare Hands to Get a Little Meat"
(Stockholm, Swedish Features, 1969, mimeo.), p. 8. See also Wästberg,
Angola (Stockholm: Bokforlaget PAN/Norstedts, 1970).

292. The FNLA claimed to control about one-sixth of Angola, "not a
coherent area, but numerous dispersed zones, villages lying in isolated
jungles." Wästberg, "We Have Fought for Nine Years and We're Going to
Be Free—If It Takes Another Ten" (Stockholm, Swedish Features, 1969,
mimeo.), p. 3. In its requests for OAU support, the FNLA stressed the need
for antiaircraft weaponry, which "we never cease" to ask for and "that has
always been promised us" by the Liberation Committee. Portuguese bombs
inflicted heavy civilian casualties, and the absence of antiaircraft materiel
represented a "great handicap." FNLA, "National Liberation Front of
Angola's (FNLA's) Report to the OAU Liberation Committee, January–
June 1968 Period" (Kinshasa, 1968, mimeo.).

293. For example, in retaliation for May–June 1969 attacks on road
transport in the Quibaxi-Dange region, attacks deemed to have benefited
from local African informants, the Portuguese army allegedly arrested all
the men of one small village, laid them bound up on a road, and drove
caterpillar road machinery over them. In other villages, the army "cut off
people's toes and split up their noses." Wästberg, "We Have Fought for Nine
Years."

294. James Grenfell, *Notes* (Lukala), no. 1 (July 3, 1970). For reports on a
mid-1970 journey into the FNLA's northern zone by an Austrian journalist,
see Fritz Sitte, "47 Tage mit den 'Rohos' im Dschungel Angolas,"
Schweizerische Allgemeine Volkszeitung (Zöfingen, Switzerland), June 6, 13,
1970; Sitte, "Die Heimliche Republik," *Alle Welt* (Vienna), no. 26 (Nov.–Dec.
1970): 14–17; and Sitte, "Bevrijde Angolese Republiek," *Bijeen* (Deurne,
Netherlands), 4, no. 2 (Feb. 1971): 38–45.

295. Itinerant Portuguese traders who crossed back and forth over the
Kwango River frontier reportedly served colonial authorities as informants
on guerrilla and refugee activities. *L'Etoile du Congo*, July 18, 1968.

296. ELNA, "Eastern Angola: Situation in General" (Lunda, May 31,
1970, typescript).

297. Ibid.

298. Ibid. For an analysis of Portuguese counterinsurgency, including
massive resettlement in protected villages (*aldeamentos*, as the Portuguese
called them), see Gerald J. Bender, "The Limits of Counterinsurgency: An
African Case," *Comparative Politics* 4, no. 3 (Apr. 1972): 331–360.

299. ELNA, "Eastern Angola."

300. According to a German observer, Gerd Janssen, insurgency leveled
off at a lower constant figure of incidents: (1,845 in 1971 versus 2,548 in
1970), and the Portuguese casualty rate declined (85 soldiers and 201
civilians in 1971 versus 117 and 238, respectively, in 1970). *Handelsblatt*
(Duesseldorf), Mar. 3–4, 1972, p. 22. In 1971, the Stockholm International
Peace Research Institute (SIPRI) estimated the contesting Angolan forces as
Portuguese, 75,000 to 80,000; MPLA, 3,000 to 3,500 (400–500 to 1,500
inside); FNLA, 3,000 to 3,500 (250–350 to 1,000 inside); UNITA, 500 (all
inside). SIPRI, *The Arms Trade with the Third World* (New York: Humanities
Press, 1971), p. 669.

301. In a dramatic speech that invoked Frantz Fanon and a Zairian version of manifest destiny, Mobutu proclaimed to the United Nations General Assembly on Oct. 4, 1973, that "henceforward, all of Zaire is mobilized to confront the racists and colonialists of southern Africa."

302. According to Colin Legum, the FNLA conscripted five thousand Angolans in Zaire. *Africa Contemporary Record, 1973–74* (London: Rex Collings, 1973), p. B519; Wilkinson, "Angola and Mozambique." FNLA, *Actuality* (Kinshasa), no. 5 (Sept. 1973). In April 1973, a Zaire foreign ministry spokesman told an international forum in Oslo, Norway, that his government was continuing to provide "military assistance" to the FNLA in the form of "training camps" and "proper equipment." Statement by Ngandu Mualaba, Apr. 12, 1973, in Olav Stokke and Carl Widstrand, eds., *Southern Africa. The UN–OAU Conference, Oslo 9–14 April 1973*, Vol. 1 (Uppsala, Sweden: Scandinavian Institute of African Studies, 1973), p. 99. Simon Scott Plummer visited Kinkuzu in late 1962 aboard a Zairian Puma helicopter and reported morale and discipline to be high. *Times*, Dec. 27, 1972. *A Província de Angola*, May 29, 1972.

303. *Salongo* (Kinshasa), Mar. 21, 1974.

304. Ibid.

305. Ibid., Mar. 20, 1974.

306. FNLA, *Actualités* (Kinshasa), no. 6 (Mar. 1974).

307. *Salongo*, Dec. 26, 1973, Jan. 26, Mar. 22, 1974.

308. According to U.S. government sources, Louis concluded that MPLA insurgency had stagnated. Officials, Department of State, Dec. 1975, interviews with author.

309. Marcum, "Exile Condition."

310. In August 1972, Savimbi claimed that although "not a single country" had given it a "single bullet," UNITA had come into possession of modern weapons—machine guns, mortars, bazookas. These weapons had been "captured not only from the Portuguese soldiers, but, and I can't hide it, also from the MPLA in defensive operations." "African Journalist in the Angola Liberated Area," p. 5.

311. *O'Comércio*, Sept. 30, 1974.

312. For a general discussion of transnational relations among revolutionary organizations, see J. Bowyer Bell, "Contemporary Revolutionary Organizations," *International Organization* 25, no. 3 (Summer 1971): 503–518.

313. The public proceedings of the conference were published in *La lutte de libération nationale dans les colonies portugaises* (Algiers: Information CONCP, 1967).

314. The fourth movement was the Committee for the Liberation of São Tomé and Principe (CLSTP).

315. The FNLA/GRAE complained that it was the "principal target" and "exclusive victim" of "violent" CONCP accusations. GRAE, "Le GRAE et la CONCP: Conférence des organisations nationalistes des colonies portugaises" (Léopoldville, Apr. 17, 1965, mimeo.).

316. *Standard*, Oct. 4, 1965.

317. Mário de Andrade, "Le mouvement de libération nationale dans les colonies portugaises," *Documents CONCP* (Rabat, Morocco, 1966, mimeo.).

318. Luis de Azevedo, Jr., of the MPLA spoke for all CONCP movements

at the Tricontinental Conference in Havana in January 1966. "Discours du représentant des peuples des colonies portugaises (CONCP)" (Havana, Jan. 8, 1966, mimeo.).

319. Decision taken at an Aug. 1966 meeting in Brazzaville. *Etumba*, Sept. 15, 1966.

320. Its propaganda work included publication of a 140–page booklet, *L'Angola* (Algiers: Information CONCP, 1969).

321. Formed in 1965, COREMO was a successor to UDENAMO. See Richard Gibson, *African Liberation Movements: Contemporary Struggles Against White Minority Rule* (New York: Oxford University Press, 1972), pp. 287–290.

322. *L'Action* (Tunis), Apr. 17, 1968. See also FLING, *Bombolom* (Dakar) 1, nos. 8–9 (1968). FLING was a fractious grouping of Guinean exiles, resentful of the prominent role of Cape Verdians in the PAIGC, without a military force, and eager to strike a bargain with the Portuguese.

323. See Basil Davidson, *The Liberation of Guiné* (Baltimore: Penguin Books, 1969); Lars Rudebeck, *Guinea-Bissau: A Study of Political Mobilization* (Uppsala, Sweden: Scandinavian Institute of African Studies, 1974); and Africa Research Group, *Race to Power: The Struggle for Southern Africa* (Garden City, N.Y.: Doubleday-Anchor Press, 1974), pp. 235–288.

324. See Ronald H. Chilcote, "Mozambique: The African Nationalist Response to Portuguese Imperialism and Underdevelopment," in Christian P. Potholm and Richard Dale, eds., *Southern Africa in Perspective* (New York: Free Press, 1972), pp. 183–195; Brendan F. Jundanian, *The Mozambique Liberation Front* (Geneva: Institut Universitaire de Hautes Etudes Internationales, 1970); Eduardo Mondlane, *The Struggle for Mozambique* (Baltimore: Penguin Books, 1969); Walter Opello, "Internal War in Mozambique: A Social-Psychological Analysis of a Nationalist Revolution" (Ph.D. diss., University of Colorado, 1973); George Houser and Herb Shore, *Mozambique: Dream the Size of Freedom* (New York: Africa Fund, 1975); and Tony Hodges, "Mozambique: The Politics of Liberation," in Gwendolen M. Carter and Patrick O'Meara, eds. *Southern Africa in Crisis* (Bloomington: Indiana University Press, 1977), pp. 48–88.

325. See chap. 2. See also Robert Davezies, *Les angolais* (Paris: Editions de Minuit, 1965), p. 258, and N'dab'ezitha, "South Africa's Stake in Angola," *Mayibuye* (ANC, Dar es Salaam), Sept. 13, 1968, p. 8.

326. For reports of MPLA-SWAPO cooperation in southeastern Angola, see "Communist-Backed Southern African Terrorist Onslaught," *Africa Institute Bulletin* (Pretoria) 6, no. 5 (June 1968): 130–148.

327. See report on and declarations of Khartoum Conference (Jan. 18–20, 1969) in *African Communist* (London), no. 37 (second quarter, 1969): pp. 13–24. See also ANC, *Sechaba* (Dar es Salaam) 3, no. 3 (Mar. 1969), and 3, no. 4 (Apr. 1969).

328. *African Communist*, p. 21. The OAU Liberation Committee stayed away from what was viewed by some as a Soviet initiative to undermine the committee's authority and assume leadership of the Southern African liberation struggle. Alan Hutchinson, *China's African Revolution* (London: Hutchinson and Co., 1975), p. 238.

329. According to *Pravda*, Jan. 21, 1969, Peking sent a large group of

correspondents to the Khartoum Conference in an effort to subvert it and "undermine Africa's trust in the USSR." China's Hsinhua published denunciations of the Khartoum meeting by excluded liberation movements (UNITA, COREMO, Zimbabwe African National Union [ZANU], Pan-Africanist Congress [PAC]) and such organizations as the Afro-Asian Journalists' Association in Peking, who portrayed it as a power play by Soviet "revisionists." Hsinhua, *Daily Bulletin* (London), Jan. 23, Mar. 21, 1969.

330. The committee was composed of representatives of the six movements plus AAPSO and World Council of Peace. *Afro-Asian Peoples* (Cairo) 11, no. 4 (Aug.–Sept. 1969): 53–55.

331. "Statement of the MPLA on the Khartoum Conference," *MPLA informations* (Algiers) (Mar. 1969).

332. Potlako Leballo (president) and T. T. Letlaka, representing PAC; Paulo Gumane COREMO; M. K. H. Hamadziripi ZANU. *Le progrès*, Apr. 2, 1967.

333. A representative of the ANC was also present. *Kwacha-Angola* (Lusaka) (Jan.–Feb. 1967).

334. According to UNITA sources, SWAPO "made extensive use of UNITA" in crossing from Zambia through Angola to Namibia, although the fact that SWAPO received "substantial aid from the Soviet Union" confronted this "operative alliance" with a "particularly sensitive issue." *UNITA: The Armed Struggle in Angola* (Boston: Black Survival Press, 1973). See also Gibson, *African Liberation Movements*, p. 138.

335. *Armed Struggle in Angola*. The PAC and ZANU sent written statements of support to UNITA's third congress held inside Angola in August 1973. *UNITA Bulletin* (Jamaica, N.Y.), no. 1 (1974): 10.

336. For example, the statement by eight movements, including COREMO, PAC, ZANU, and an unidentified "group from Angola" (presumably FNLA), denouncing a Soviet-sponsored seminar in Cairo. Hsinhua, *Daily Bulletin*, Nov. 15, 1966.

337. David Kimche, "Black Africa and the Afro-Asian People's Solidarity Movement," *Asian and African Studies* (Jerusalem) 4 (1968): 115.

338. Interview with Paulo Jorge, *Tricontinental* (July–Aug. 1968): Joint Publications Research Service, No. 46, 465, pp. 67–70. MPLA membership in OSPAAAL resulted in, among other things, publication of *Portuguese Colonies: Victory or Death* (Havana: Tricontinental, 1971), including articles by Agostinho Neto and Mário de Andrade.

339. For example, Radio Havana, 2045 GMT (Africa service), Feb. 24, 1967, 2040 GMT, Feb. 15, 1967, 2145 GMT (domestic service), Sept. 17, 1968.

340. See *Granma* (Havana), Oct. 13, 1971.

341. Rui de Pinto, *The Making of a Middle Cadre*, p. 74.

342. UNITA, "Open Letter to OSPAAAL" (London, Apr. 6, 1970, mimeo.).

343. For the text of his address, see MPLA, *Angola in Arms* 1, no. 3 (Aug.–Sept. 1970). A UNITA delegation led by Jorge Sangumba also attended the Lusaka conference. See UNITA, "Memorandum to the Summit Conference of the Non-Aligned Countries to Be Held in Lusaka, Zambia" (Freeland, Angola, Aug. 19, 1970, mimeo.), signed by Savimbi;

and UNITA "Statement" signed by Jorge Sangumba (Lusaka, Sept. 2, 1970, mimeo.).

344. See Radio Belgrade, domestic service, 1830 GMT, Jan. 19, 1968; Agence France Presse, Feb. 23, 1973.

345. *Notícias de Portugal*, May 19, 1973.

346. "A Oposição Portuguesa e o Movimento de Libertação Nacional" (document de base, 2d CONCP Conférence, Dar es Salaam, Sept. 1965), a CONCP analysis of Portuguese opposition movements. See also *Pravda*, Apr. 7, 1966. For the FPLN statement on its "antiimperialist" cooperation with CONCP movements, see *El Moudjahid*, July 22, 1968. In July 1967, the Central Committee of the PCP confirmed its "active solidarity" with the cause of African independence. *Information Bulletin* (World Marxist Review, Toronto), Oct. 2, 1967, p. 7.

347. "Bulletin d'information du Front Patriotique de Libération Nationale" (Algiers [1966?], mimeo.). FPLN publications carried material on and by CONCP movements, for example, the FPLN monthly, *Liberdade* (Algiers). See also Robert Davezies, *La guerre d'Angola* (Bordeaux: Ducros, 1968), p. 129.

348. In Algiers the FPLN published a series of autobiographical statements by Portuguese army deserters that detailed brutalities committed against Africans, FPLN, "Déclarations des déserteurs de l'armée colonialiste portugaise" (Algiers, mimeo. series).

349. The FPLN depicted Portugal itself as a colony to be liberated from the oppressive exploitation of German, American, English, and other Western capital. *Révolution africaine*, Nov. 13–20, 1965.

350. FNLA, *Angola informations* (Algiers), no. 17 (Dec. 1965).

351. In 1970, the FNLA offered to exchange a PIDE officer that it held prisoner for release of an FPL leader, Eduardo Cruzeiro, incarcerated in Spain. GRAE, "Communiqué" (Cairo, Jan. 30, 1970, mimeo.).

352. FPL, "Communiqué à la presse" (Paris, Oct. 19, 1972, mimeo.).

353. See *Remarques africaines*, Jan. 1–15, 1973, p. 7.

354. In a face-to-face encounter in Kinshasa, Telli told Roberto that OAU assistance was contingent on his achieving "unity of action" with the MPLA, and Roberto responded by blaming the OAU for promoting disunity by abandoning its 1963 decision to accord exclusive recognition to the FNLA. *Bulletin d'Afrique*, Nov. 29, 1966. Diallo Telli was especially critical of the FNLA and Kinshasa government for blocking MPLA access to northern Angola. *Ethiopian Herald*, June 28, 1968.

355. In 1970, Chris Roberts of the *San Diego Union*, Apr. 26, 1970, estimated that a total of $150,000 in OAU funds had been allocated to Angolan nationalists for that year. Most observers adjudged Soviet aid to be quantitatively "vastly more important" than OAU aid. See Russell Warren Howe, *Sun* (Baltimore), Mar. 19, 1969, and *Christian Science Monitor*, Mar. 8, 1969.

356. *Bulletin d'Afrique*, Nov. 29, 1966, Feb. 3, 1967.

357. GRAE, "Rapport sur les activités militaires et sociales couvrant la période allant de juillet à octobre 1972" (Kinshasa, Oct. 1972, mimeo.). From 1964 to 1967, according to Roberto, the FNLA received a total of £26,500 from the Liberation Committee. For text of his statement see PDA, *Mondo* (Kinshasa), no. 1 (Feb. 1967). In 1968, Roberto complained to the

heads of African governments that even the 1967 arms shipment (400 rifles, 125 revolvers, 200 machine guns, 400 grenades, 27 rocket launchers, 10 mortars, funds for one jeep) compared unfavorably with OAU action in equipping an MPLA contingent of 1,500 troops with uniforms, blankets, shoes, bayonets, rucksacks, machetes, mackintoshes, medicine, 2 lorries, 2 jeeps, and 10 rubber boats. "Memorandum from the Revolutionary Government of Angola in Exile (GRAE) to Chiefs of African States" (Kinshasa, 1968, mimeo.).

358. *Dossier de l'Afrique australe* (Gonesse, France), no. 1 (Jan. 1971): 13.

359. *Financial Times* (London), June 23, 1971. The MPLA had long lobbied for derecognition, which it hailed as a political victory. MPLA, *Angola in Arms* 2, no. 4 (July 1971).

360. According to the State Department, "Angola: An Assessment of the Insurgency" (Sept. 16, 1970).

361. The term used in the Zaire press to describe the three-power relationship. *Salongo*, Mar. 21, 1974.

362. At Lubumbashi Roberto also met the U.N. Undersecretary General Tan Ming Chao of China. FNLA, *Actuality*, no. 5 (Sept. 1973): 17.

363. *Daily News* (Dar es Salaam), July 29, 1973.

364. Colonel Mbita and Major Sidki, Aug. 4–11, 1973. *Actuality*, no. 5 (Sept. 1973), p. 29.

365. Ibid., p. 17. Strongly supportive of President Massamba Debat (it allowed its soldiers to serve in his bodyguard), the MPLA saw its influence in Brazzaville decline after Captain Ngouabi's successful coup d'etat in 1968. See Ebinger, "External Intervention," pp. 680–681.

366. MPLA, *Angola in Arms*, special issue (Feb. 1968): 5.

367. *A Província de Angola*, July 1, 1974. In a 1968 petition to the OAU Liberation Committee, UNITA suggested that it might have achieved "much more" if it had received help from African states. UNITA urged the OAU to send a commission of inquiry inside Angola to see "*who* is doing *what*." The OAU ignored this and all subsequent UNITA petitions. *Kwacha-Angola* (London), no. 1 (Jan. 1969): 7–9.

368. Notably annual "working papers" covering political and economic events, for example, the Committee on Decolonization, "Angola," doc. A/AC.109/L.918, Feb. 4, 1974.

369. The proceedings, including discussion and reports of U.N. actions, were published in two volumes by the Scandinavian Institute of African Studies at Uppsala. Olav Stokke and Carl Widstrand, eds., *Southern Africa* (U.N.-OAU Conference, Oslo, 9–14 April 1973).

370. Davidson, "Walking 300 Miles with Guerrillas," p. 8. The Stockholm International Peace Research Institute estimated that the Soviets provided 35 to 40 percent of the total military resources of all the nationalist movements of the Portuguese territories. *The Arms Trade with the Third World* (New York: Humanities Press, 1971), p. 666.

371. Figure given in interview with author, Dec. 1, 1975. On the basis of Western intelligence estimates, British Brigadier W. F. K. Thompson put the figure of Soviet aid during 1960–1974 at £27 million. *Daily Telegraph*, Apr. 11, 1975. The Soviets also allowed the MPLA to channel messages through their African embassies.

372. The figure for such trainees was put at "several thousand" in "Angola

after Independence: The Struggle for Supremacy," *Conflict Studies* (London), no. 64 (Nov. 1975): 5.

373. See, for example: "Speech by Comrade Agostinho Neto" (Commemorating the 50th anniversary of the October Revolution), *Information Bulletin, World Marxist Review* (Prague) (Nov. 1967): pp. 166–167; "Discours d'Agostinho Neto" (commemorating the 100th birthday of Lenin), *Les idées de Lenin transforment le monde* (Moscow: Editions de l'Agence de Presse Novosti, 1971), pp.·277–279. See also interviews: *Otechestven Front* (Sofia), Jan. 31, 1968; interview in Hanoi by Romolo Caccavale, *L'Unita* (Rome), Aug. 25, 1971; and *Weg und Ziel* (theoretical organ of the Austrian Communist Party, Vienna), May 1973, pp. 190–192. (Joint Publications Research Service, Aug. 3, 1971, no. 53748, pp. 4–9).

374. Following through on a decision of the Khartoum Conference of 1969. *Afro-Asian Peoples* 11, no. 4 (Aug.–Sept. 1969): 54. The Soviet delegation presented a paper ("Portugal's War on Africa") in which it criticized Western-NATO support of Portugal and pledged the Soviet Union to remain "loyal to its policy of rendering consistent and firm support" to those fighting for their independence.

375. See preconference background article in *L'Unita*, Feb. 4, 1970; conference speeches, resolutions, and documents in *Sechaba* (London) 4, no. 9 (Sept. 1970); and R. Zehnder, "Conférence d'appui aux peuples des colonies portugaises" (Geneva, June 1970, mimeo.) for analysis of conference work, including that of its judicial commission's study of the problem of gaining recognition for liberation movements under international law.

Denied participation, the FNLA and UNITA both denounced the conference as an instrument of Soviet manipulation. FNLA statement in *Actualités*, no. 1 (June 1970), FNLA, "Lettre ouverte à tous les democrates" (Dec. 15, 1970, mimeo.), and FNLA, "Comunicato" (Rome, June 29, 1970, mimeo.). UNITA, "Press Statement on the Rome Conference, June 27–29, 1970" (London, June 30, 1970, mimeo.). For critical coverage by the Italian organ of the Fourth International, see *Bandiera Rossa* (Rome), June 15–July 15, 1970.

376. *Le monde*, July 6, 1970.

377. An assessment accepted by the U.S. Department of State. See U.S., Senate, *Angola: Hearings before the Subcommittee on African Affairs of the Committee on Foreign Relations*, 94th Cong., 2d sess., 1976, p. 185. Since 1964, according to William E. Schaufele, Jr., assistant secretary for African affairs, Soviet assistance had been funneled through leaders of the Portuguese Communist party. Ibid., p. 174.

378. According to Per Wästberg, Neto's perception was shared by the Portuguese socialist leader, Mário Soares. *Dagens Nyheter* (Stockholm), Mar. 11, 1975.

379. See the analysis by Bruce D. Larkin, *China and Africa, 1949–1950* (Berkeley: University of California Press, 1971), pp. 190–191.

380. Marshment, "UNITA," p. 2.

381. For example, Hsinhua, *Daily Bulletin*, July 4, 1968; and *Peking Review*, Feb. 13, 1970, pp. 21–22. Previously in 1967, Chinese news reports from Cairo occasionally quoted statements by the local FNLA representative, Nicolas Vieira, without identifying his political affiliation. Vieira's en-

thusiastic praise of Mao Tse-tung and his condemnation of Soviet "revisionists" presumably earned him some recompense. Hsinhua, *Daily Bulletin,* June 21, July 12, Aug. 16, 30, 1967.

382. Two UNITA representatives attended a July 1971 women's conference in Tirana, the capital of China's diminutive Albanian ally. *Kwacha-Angola* (Stockholm), no. 2 (July 1971). UNITA's Second Congress praised the Cultural Revolution for transforming China into a "center of World Revolution" and condemned the Soviet Union's "naked invasion" of Czechoslovakia. "II Congress of UNITA" (Aug. 1969). A January 1971 gathering of UNITA militants in Europe saluted the "struggle of the People's Republic of China and Albania against imperialism and its accomplices." "Résolutions du premier seminaire des militants de l'UNITA en Europe."

383. *UNITA Bulletin* (Jamaica, N.Y.), no. 1 (1974): 10. Subsequently, however, Savimbi told South Africa's *Financial Mail* (Johannesburg), May 9, 1975: "The Chinese promised to support us in the struggle. They did not."

384. Hsinhua, *Daily Bulletin,* Feb. 4, 1971, and Radio Peking, international service, English, 1752 GMT, Feb. 11, 1971.

385. Colin Legum, "National Liberation in Southern Africa," *Problems of Communism* 24 (Jan.–Feb. 1975): 7.

386. Other members of the MPLA delegation were Lúcio Lára, Alberto Neto (MPLA representative in Scandinavia), José António (commander of the south regional zone), and Ananias Escorcio (commander of the north regional zone). *Daily Bulletin,* Aug. 4, 1971.

387. See, for example, the modest coverage of MPLA activity in *Peking Review,* Apr. 20, 1973, p. 29.

388. Other members of the FNLA delegation were Johnny Eduardo Pinock, Samuel Abrigada, Mateus Neto, Pedro Gadimpovi, and two military commanders (Marques Barroso and Landa-Mwono). *Salongo,* Dec. 5, 1973, and FNLA, *Actualités,* no. 6 (Mar. 1974).

389. Describing the Chinese as "very gracious, decent, hardworking and happy," Roberto said that because most FNLA leaders were the sons of peasants, the FNLA delegation "focused much of [its] attention on agricultural matters." *Salongo,* Dec. 29–30, 1973.

390. For texts of speeches and reportage on the trip, see *Actualités,* no. 6 (Mar. 1974).

391. For texts of speeches, articles, and interviews related to the journey, see ibid.; *Salongo,* Jan. 26, 1974; and FNLA, "Amitié roumano-angolaise" (Kinshasa, Jan. 23, 1974, mimeo.). Members of the FNLA delegation were Johnny Eduardo Pinock, Pedro Gadimpovi, Hendrik Vaal Neto, Mme. Mateus Neto, Ngola Kabangu, Paulo Tuba, Commander Garcia Samson Salva, and Mme. Monteiro Bedi. See also *Scînteia* (Bucharest), Jan. 22, 1974.

392. *Salongo,* Mar. 22, 1974.

393. Ten cases presented by Ambassador Siddhartharry. *Courrier d'Afrique,* Feb. 23, 1967.

394. *African Diary* (New Delhi) 7, no. 30 (July 23–29, 1967): 3489.

395. *Africa Quarterly* (New Delhi) 7, no. 2 (July–Sept. 1967): 195.

396. According to FNLA sources interviewed by George Houser in Kinshasa, August 1973.

397. *Navhind Times* (Goa), Sept. 30, 1972.

398. A detailed accounting of Western arms sales and economic help to Portugal was published in successively updated versions of *Portugal and NATO* (Amsterdam, Angola Comité, 1972 [3d ed.]). See also Basil Davidson, "Arms and the Portuguese," *Africa Report* 15, no. 5 (May 1970): 10–11, and *Washington Post*, Apr. 4, 1971.

399. *Bulletin d'Afrique*, July 10, 1970.

400. Stokke and Widstrand, *Southern Africa*, 1: 216.

401. Ibid., 2: 306, 313.

402. Ibid., p. 318.

403. FNLA, *Actuality*, no. 5 (Sept. 1973): p. 16.

404. See letter to *Le monde diplomatique* (unpublished) by Jonas Savimbi in UNITA, "Angola: Portugal and Allies (NATO) Facing Defeat," doc. I (London, June 1971, mimeo.), p. 21.

405. See Sietse Bosgra, "Territories Under Portuguese Domination: Proposals for Action," in Stokke and Widstrand, *Southern Africa*, 2: 79–88, and ibid., 1: 245–246.

406. Notably the Dutch monthly, *Angola: Nieuwsblad over het Portuguese Kolonialisme*; the English-language press clippings of *Facts and Reports*; a Dutch translation of Don Barnett and Roy Harvey's MPLA interviews, *De Bevrijding Van Angola; Portugal en de Nato; Angolese Verhalen;* and numerous other booklets, press releases, calendars, and posters.

407. Angola Comité, Press communication, Dec. 12, 1972. See also *Le Monde*, Mar. 21, 1972.

408. See Neto's speech to the UN-OAU Oslo conference (Apr. 10, 1973) in Stokke and Widstrand, *Southern Africa*, 1:90.

409. The London committee published a CONCP-oriented bulletin, *Guerrilheiro*.

410. Letter, *Angola Comité* to liberation support committees, Mar. 18, 1971.

411. "Rapport sur la création d'un réseau de soutien à l'UPA" (Nov. 1962, typescript).

412. *Jeune Afrique*, Mar. 3, 1970, p. 13.

413. Goujon occasionally wrote under the name Mario Pasquale; for example, in *Le peuple* (Lausanne), Jan. 17, 1963; he helped get pro-FNLA articles into publications of the Fourth International—such as *Quatrième internationale* (Paris), no. 21 (Feb.–Mar. 1964), no. 24 (Mar. 1965), and no. 27 (Feb. 1966)—and of the anarchist press—for example, *Libertaire* (Paris), no. 96 (Dec. 1963). He also published a number of articles under his own name, among them, "Une civilisation tropicale," *Le point* (Brussels), no. 8 (Feb. 1967): pp. 14–16, and "Révolution angolaise," *Le point*, n.s., no. 1 (Feb. 1969): 22–25.

414. "Gouvernement révolutionnaire de l'Angola en exil refuse le 'don' du comité executif du COE" (Geneva, Sept. 20, 1971, mimeo.), and *Journal de Genève*, Sept. 21, 1971. Goujon protested in visits and letters to the council against its action, which was defended by Rev. Eugene C. Blake as reflecting the conclusions of a careful study by council staff that showed the MPLA to be the most effective and important Angolan movement. *La suisse* (Geneva), Sept. 25, 1971. Baldwin Sjollema, executive secretary of the Program to

Combat Racism, defended council action in "Concerne: document du GRAE: informations aux églises du 14/12/71" (Geneva, Dec. 16, 1971, mimeo.); and GRAE attacked it in GRAE, "Mise au point" (Kinshasa, Jan. 24, 1972, mimeo.).

415. *Richard Gibson Reports* (London), Sept. 1971.

416. Stokke and Widstrand, *Southern Africa*, 2: 25–32, 337.

417. *Kwacha-Angola* (London), spec. ed. (1972), pp. 54–54d.

418. *Observer*, Apr. 9, 1972.

419. For example, the Sangumba interview in *Cooperazione* (Basel, Switzerland), Sept. 19, 1970.

420. Williams advocated "clandestine" U.S. assistance to African nationalists who would follow a moderate strategy of building a nonviolent political underground and resort to strikes and demonstrations to win independence. G. Mennen Williams, "Portuguese African Territories: Action Memorandum" to Secretary Dean Rusk, Apr. 29, 1964.

421. Dispatch from Anderson, U.S. embassy, Lisbon, Mar. 25, 1966.

422. In 1965, Dr. Grainha do Valle, chief of the Atlantic Pact section of the Portuguese foreign ministry, expressed "disillusionment" with NATO. Noting that some nonmembers had less trouble obtaining arms from NATO countries than did Portugal, he indicated that Lisbon was weighing whether to support the French move. Dispatch from U.S. embassy, Lisbon, Nov. 9, 1965. The Portuguese government angrily rejected "repeated high-level efforts by U.S. officials" to obtain the return of seven B-26 bombers purchased illegally in the United States through a Swiss firm in 1965. The discovery of their delivery had led to charges of CIA involvement, an inconclusive trial, and adverse publicity. At U.S. "insistence," however, the aircraft were not "moved from the metropole" and were thus of no use to Portugal in Africa. See statement by Colgate S. Prentice, acting assistant secretary for congressional relations, in reply to an inquiry from Senator Clifford P. Case, *Congressional Record* 116, pt. 30, 91st Cong., 2d sess., Dec. 8, 1970, p. 40345. See also *New York Times*, Sept. 21, 22, 23, Oct. 8, 12, 15, 1966. The Portuguese stalled on American requests to install long-range aid to navigation facilities (LORAN-C) on Portuguese territory until the project was abandoned in 1966 as technically bypassed. See also criticism of NATO by Premier Salazar, ibid., Mar. 24, 1966.

423. Dispatch from U.S. embassy, Lisbon, May 20, 1967.

424. For example, interview with Brigadier General Robert N. Ginsburgh, USAF, Nov. 26, 1968. Rather than the socialization of the NATO Defense College in Rome where Portuguese officers joined peers from more democratically governed Atlantic countries for five-and-a-half month study courses, it was the socialization of the colonial wars and the ideas of African nationalists that would impact upon reform-minded officers—all of which was contrary to the expectations of American military observers.

425. See, for example, David M. Abshire, then executive director of the Center for Strategic and International Studies, Georgetown Univ., in "Strategic Implications," David M. Abshire and Michael A. Samuels, eds., *Portuguese Africa: A Handbook* (New York: Praeger, 1969), p. 444.

426. In January 1969, Lisbon submitted a written request for the opening of negotiations at an unspecified date. Washington replied that it was

"ready" to consider its proposals at any time, but discussions were limited to informal exchanges through mid-1970. U.S., Senate, "United States Security Agreements and Commitments Abroad," *Hearings before the Subcommittee on United States Security Agreements and Commitments Abroad of the Committee on Foreign Relations*, vol. II, pts. 5–11, 91st Cong., July 15, 1970, p. 2405.

427. See Testimony of Roger Morris, Senate Foreign Relations Committee, Subcommittee on Africa, Sept. 16, 1976.

428. For an account of the genesis and implementation of the "tar baby" option by a Washington bureaucracy preoccupied with the war in Vietnam, see Anthony Lake, *The "Tar Baby" Option: American Policy Toward Southern Rhodesia* (New York: Columbia University Press, 1976), pp. 123–157.

429. For the text of the "Study in Response to National Security Study Memorandum 39: Southern Africa," Aug. 15, 1969 and background analysis, see Mohamed A. El-Khawas and Baring Cohen, eds., *The Kissinger Study of Southern Africa* (Westport, Conn.: Lawrence Hill and Co., 1976).

430. Henry A. Kissinger, *The Troubled Partnership: A Reappraisal of the Atlantic Alliance* (New York: McGraw-Hill, 1965), p. 205.

431. See testimony of Undersecretary of State U. Alexis Johnson in U.S., Senate, "Executive Agreements with Portugal and Bahrain," *Hearings before the Committee on Foreign Relations*, 92d Cong., 2d sess., Feb. 1–3, 1972, p. 49.

432. The accord of December 9, 1971, also included free loan of a hydrographic ship, the USNS *Kellar*; a grant of $1 million for educational reform, the funds to come from the U.S. Department of Defense; and a two-year waiver of Portugal's annual support payments ($175,000) for the U.S. Military Assistance Advisory Group stationed in Lisbon. See texts of notes constituting the agreement in *Department of State Bulletin* 66, no. 1697 (Jan. 3, 1972): 7–9. As it turned out, the Portuguese government made little use of its eligibility for Export-Import Bank financing.

433. Gone were what Caetano called "internal difficulties in North American politics" (meaning anticolonialism) that had blocked an earlier accord and obliged the United States to use Azores facilities on an ad hoc basis. *Notícias de Portugal* (Lisbon), Dec. 18, 1971. The Department of State acknowledged in an unpublished "Background Paper" (Dec. 9, 1971) that renewal of the Azores contract had been impossible in 1962 because of "Portuguese dissatisfaction with U.S. policies toward Portuguese Africa," policies that, though it did not so state, had obviously softened. For a chronicle of U.S.-Portuguese relations on the Azores, see Tad Szulc, "Letter from the Azores," *The New Yorker*, Jan. 1, 1972, pp. 54–55. See also John A. Marcum, *The Politics of Indifference: Portugal and Africa, A Case Study in American Foreign Policy* (Eastern African Studies, Syracuse University, N.Y., 1972).

434. The agreement was to expire February 4, 1974. Citing the "short period" covered by the accord and predicting that the enormously wealthy United States would soon return to economic health ("times of the fat cow" [*vacas gordas*]), Caetano looked with optimism toward the "opportunity" for "new cooperative arrangements" ahead. *Notícias de Portugal*, Dec. 18, 1971. He was prone to underestimate the economic drain of Vietnam on the United States just as he underestimated the attrition of African wars on Portugal.

435. *Hearings before the Committee on Foreign Relations*, pp. 51–54, 101.

436. *Department of State Bulletin* 70, no. 1803 (Jan. 14, 1974): 25–26.

437. Gerald J. Bender, "Kissinger and Angola: Anatomy of Failure" (unpublished typescript, 1976), p. 6; see also *Notícias de Portugal*, Dec. 29, 1973.

438. Tad Szulc, "Lisbon and Washington: Behind the Portuguese Revolution," *Foreign Policy*, no. 21 (Winter 1975–76): p. 21.

439. Over twenty-seven hundred Portuguese military personnel trained in the United States through 1970. See Robert A. Diamond and David Fouquet, "Portugal and the United States," *Africa Report* 15, no. 5 (May 1970): p. 17.

440. *International Herald Tribune* (Paris), Jan. 6, 1971; *Star* (Johannesburg, weekly ed.), June 26, 1971. Boeing 727s and 707s were sold previously to Portuguese airlines, which, in turn, chartered them to the Portuguese government to transport troops, without provoking protests from the United States. In 1972, a research unit of the United Nations Secretariat noted that "the increased use of aircraft for transport of troops is reported to have gone a long way toward solving one of Portugal's major military problems." U.N. General Assembly, Committee on Decolonization, doc. A/AC. 109/L 756, Mar. 24, 1972, p. 23.

441. "As you are aware, since 1961 the United States has prohibited the export of arms for use in Africa by any of the parties to the disputes in Portuguese Guinea, Angola, and Mozambique. There has been no change in this policy: any press reports suggesting otherwise are in error." David D. Newsom, Assistant Secretary for African Affairs, to the author, Oct. 8, 1971. See also Newsom, "United States Policy Toward Africa," *Department of State Bulletin* 62, no. 1615 (June 8, 1970): 718.

442. See John Marcum, "The United States and Portuguese Africa: A Perspective on American Foreign Policy," *Africa Today* 18, no. 4 (Oct. 1971): 30–32.

443. Newsom to the author, Oct. 8, 1971. Despite allegations by the American Committee on Africa (ACOA) that "U.S. exports of herbicides to Portugal quadrupled between 1969 and 1970, the year Portugal began to use them in Angola," the American government felt no need to verify and control such exports. See "The Status of the Liberation Struggle in Africa" (New York, ACOA, June 1, 1971, mimeo.).

444. António de Oliveira Salazar, *Declaration on Overseas Policy* (Lisbon: Secretariado Nacional da Informação, 1963), pp. 30–31.

445. *New York Times*, Jan. 1, 1966.

446. In 1972, Gulf paid $18 million in royalties, $43 million in income tax, and $90,000 to a mining fund. Gulf executive William R. Cox to Edward A. Hawley, Apr. 4, 1973. Gulf management argued that its development of oil resources widely considered to be "transforming [the] economic outlook in Angola" (*New York Times*, July 7, 1968) constituted a "politically neutral" act. "Gulf Statement to Trustees, Ohio Conference, The United Church of Christ," Columbus, Ohio, Sept. 10, 1970.

447. American imports from Portugal, Angola, and Mozambique totaled $396 million in 1973. *Statistical Abstract of the United States, 1975*, 96th ed. (Washington, D.C.: U.S. Government Printing Office, 1975), pp. 815–817,

and *Africa Contemporary Record, 1972–73* (London: Rex Collings, 1973), p. C49.

448. *Washington Post*, July 17, 1975.

449. See U.N., Committee on Decolonization, doc. A/9623, Part V, Oct. 8, 1974, pp. 3–48.

450. *New York Times*, Sept. 25, Dec. 19, 1975.

451. House of Representatives, Committee on Foreign Affairs, *Policy Toward Africa for the Seventies*, 91st Cong., 2d sess., 1970, p. 124.

452. Working with Downs and Roosevelt Inc. of New York, the Overseas Companies of Portugal mounted a development-oriented promotional campaign. They published the monthly *Intelligence Report* (Lisbon) on "political, social and economic developments" in Angola and Mozambique and such brochures as *The Cunene Development Plan* (Lisbon, 1973).

453. *Angola: Some Views of Development Prospects*, vol. 1: *Socio-Political Aspects*, and vol. 2: *Industrial and Technical Approaches* (Croton-on-Hudson, N.Y.: Hudson Institute, 1969).

454. At the peak of its operations in 1964, the American Committee on Africa's (ACOA) Emergency Relief for Angola (ERA) expended approximately $7,680 out of a total ACOA budget for 1964 of just over $145,000. Figures supplied by ACOA executive director, George Houser, Dec. 21, 1966.

455. Meeting in Washington in September 1964, some one hundred ANLCA delegates passed resolutions calling upon the American government to seek alternatives to the Azores bases, tighten up the arms embargo on Portuguese Africa, assist refugee students from those territories, and urge Portugal to embark upon a major educational and economic development effort with U.N., Brazilian, or other external help. ANLCA, "Resolutions" (Washington, D.C., Sept. 23, 1964). See also conference background paper, John A. Marcum, "American Policy and the Portuguese Colonies" (Sept. 1964, mimeo.). ANLCA held its third conference in Washington in January 1967. It called on the American news media to use more black reporters to improve the accuracy of information coming from Portuguese Africa. ANLCA, "Resolutions" (Washington, D.C., Jan. 28, 1967). Following this assembly, the ANLCA faded away.

456. An offshoot of the Iowa Socialist League, the group first met secretly as the International Liberation Front and entertained such "lofty, even romantic goals" as the creation of a "University in Exile" to serve as a "recruitment center and front for political and military training." Eventually it hoped "to recruit and train defectors and draft dodgers for high-level military activities directed against NATO bases and installations in Africa and elsewhere, perhaps setting up bases within liberated zones in Angola, Mozambique, etc." Don Barnett, "LSM: Problems in Theory, Strategy and Practice," *LSM News* (Richmond, B.C.) 1, no. 2 (Aug. 1974): 11.

457. On the margins of the conference, the LSM activists discussed with their hosts how to realize a "mutually critical and political rather than patronizing and philanthropic" LSM-MPLA relationship. Their discussions at a forest hideout were interrupted "when a hand grenade fell from a guerrilla's shirt pocket as he leaned over to stir a nearby fire. Two MPLA comrades were killed, including the Zone 'B' commander, whose *nom de*

guerre ironically was Cuidado, meaning 'caution.' " But they proceeded to lay out plans for active collaboration. Ibid., p. 12.

458. Ibid., p. 13. LSM publications are cited passim in this volume.

459. See part 2 of Barnett, "LSM: Problems in Theory, Strategy and Practice," *LSM News* 1, no. 3 (Dec. 1974): p. 18.

460. *LSM News* 2, no. 2 (Summer 1975): 29.

461. For example, the Toronto Committee for the Liberation of Portugal's African Colonies and the Boston-based Africa Research Group; see Africa Research Group, *Race to Power: The Struggle for Southern Africa* (Garden City, N.Y.: Doubleday, 1974), pp. 183–234.

462. The Association of African and Afro-American Students at Harvard-Radcliffe produced the UNITA-focused pamphlet, *The Armed Struggle in Angola* (Boston: Black Survival Press, 1973).

463. These groups were dismissed by the LSM as "cultural nationalist and opportunist" organizations susceptible of being wooed by an "all-Black" UNITA. Barnett, "LSM: Problems" (pt. 2), p. 20.

464. Meeting at Greensboro, North Carolina, on April 28, 1973, the national executive of the ALSC voted to support the PAIGC, FRELIMO, ZANU-ZAPU, and UNITA. ALSC minutes, Apr. 28–29, 1973, p. 4.

465. Akpan was accompanied by three other Afro-Americans: Malik Chaka, a journalist working with Pan-African Skills, Dar es Salaam; Leon Dash of the *Washington Post*; and Charles Simmons, a freelance reporter at the United Nations. On the Afro-American role at the congress, see Chaka in the *Zambia Daily Mail*, Oct. 30, 1973.

466. *UNITA Bulletin*, no. 1 (1974): p. 9.

467. See "U.S. Dollars Kill Black Nationalists," *AFAR Newsletter* (New York), no. 3 (June 1970).

Notes to Chapter 6

1. *Guardian* (London), Jan. 14, 1972.

2. Elizabeth Morris, "Portugal's Year in Africa," in Colin Legum and John Drysdale, eds., *Africa: Contemporary Record, 1968–69* (London: Africa Research Ltd., 1969), p. 51.

3. See immediate postcoup account by Henry Giniger, *New York Times*, Apr. 26, 1974. For earlier signs that army defections were becoming serious, see *Noticias e Factos* (New York), Sept. 29, 1970, and *Financial Times* (London), Jan. 8, 1971.

4. With 600,000 Portuguese émigrés, Paris became the "second largest Portuguese city." "Between Africa and Europe: A Survey of Portugal," *Economist* (London), supplement, Feb. 26, 1972.

5. See Elizabeth Morris, "Portugal's Year in Africa," in Colin Legum, ed., *Africa: Contemporary Record, 1972–73* (London: Rex Collings, 1973) p. C49.

6. See Gerald J. Bender, "Portugal and Her Colonies Join the Twentieth Century: Causes and Initial Implications of the Military Coup," *Ufahamu* (Los Angeles) 4, no. 3 (Winter 1974): 124.

7. Armed Revolutionary Action (ARA) destroyed seventeen military aircraft at Tancos Airbase in one operation, bombed ships, attacked trains, blew up ammunition dumps, damaged NATO facilities, and disrupted

communications, all with skill and drama. See U.N., Committee on Decolonization, doc. A/AC.109/L765, Mar. 24, 1972, p. 27. *Financial Times,* Jan.
14, 1972; *Le monde,* Nov. 10, 14–15, 1971. Other groups ranging from
Maoist to anarchist included the League for Union and Revolutionary
Action (LUAR) led by Herminio de Palma Inacio; Revolutionary Brigades
of the Algiers-based Patriotic Front (FPLN); and Communist Revolutionary
Action (ARCO).

8. *Times* (London), Nov. 17, 1971.

9. U.N., doc. A/AC.109/L765, pp. 27–28.

10. Ibid., p. 27.

11. Western Europe provided some 58 percent of Portugal's imports and
bought about 54 percent of its exports. The comparable figures for Portugal's trade with its African provinces were 14 percent and 25 percent.
"Between Africa and Europe," *Economist,* p. 14. See also *Portugal and EEC*
(Amsterdam: Angola Comité, 1973).

12. Such notables as President Américo Thomaz, former foreign minister
Alberto Franco Nogueira, and General Kaúlza de Arriaga.

13. Between 1967 and 1971, the percentage of defense costs borne by the
overseas territories rose from 25.2 percent to 32.3 percent. In 1971,
Portuguese Secretary of State for the Treasury Costa André predicted that
it would be possible "to organize the defense of the overseas provinces more
and more within the internal ambit of each province." U.N., Committee on
Decolonization, doc. A/AC.109/L765, p. 22.

14. According to Portuguese sources, as of October 1971, 50 percent of
the troops fighting in Mozambique were Africans. Ibid., p. 23. By offering
literacy and technical training along with entry into special-status commando and paratroop units, the government converted the armed forces
into the best avenue of upward socioeconomic mobility for thousands of
young Africans.

15. Ibid., p. 15. In Guinea-Bissau, which lacked a large European community and where African insurgents held a sizable portion of the territory,
the colonial administration under General António de Spínola simply
abandoned the colonial raison d'être of assimilation. In a display of pragmatic heresy, it issued a directive in 1971 that called for revising Portugal's
"civilizing" work to adjust it to "pluricultural" African societies whose
people were now said to have the legitimate right to wish to progress within
their own culture. U.N., Committee on Decolonization, doc. A/AC.109/
L766, Mar. 21, 1972, pp. 4–5. Nothing like this recognition of a right to
retain an African identity and culture, however, was proclaimed for the
Africans of Angola and Mozambique prior to the April 1974 coup.

16. See, for example, Marcel Niedergang, *Le monde,* Apr. 1, 1972.

17. António de Spínola, *Portugal e o Futuro* (Lisbon: Arcadia, 1974).

18. See Kenneth Maxwell, "Portugal e o Futuro: Analise Conjuntura,"
New York Review of Books, June 13, 1974, pp. 16–21.

19. U.S., Senate, *Hearings Before the Subcommittee on African Affairs of the
Committee on Foreign Relations,* 94th Cong., 2d sess., 1976, pp. 16–17.

20. See Gerald J. Bender and Stanley P. Yoder, "Whites on the Eve of
Independence: The Politics of Numbers," *Africa Today* 21, no. 4 (Fall 1974):
23–37. Franz-Wilhelm Heimer puts the figure a bit lower, at 320,000.

Heimer, "The Decolonization Conflict in Angola, 1974–1976," Arnold Bergstraesser-Institut, Freiburg, 1977.

21. A referendum, argued Agostinho Neto, would only be "used by the Portuguese to prolong their presence in our country." *El Moudjahid* (Algiers), May 27, 1974.

22. For the text of Spínola's statement of July 27, 1974, see Colin Legum, ed., *Africa: Contemporary Record, 1974–75* (London: Rex Collings, 1975), p. C38. Black troops of the Portuguese army successfully pressed for army intervention to halt the violence, which was abetted by local white police. *O Angolense* (Luanda), Oct. 11, 1974.

23. Ibid., p. C40.

24. The FNLA warned that locally born Portuguese who considered themselves Angolan should desist from forming "racist"political parties and either join existing liberation movements or create a single, overall political formation to represent white interests within the framework of majority rule. FNLA, *Indépendance totale* (Kinshasa), Aug. 29, 1974. For MPLA rejection of Portuguese proposals, see *Zambia Daily Mail* (Lusaka), Aug. 16, 1974.

25. The PCDA fired its implicated secretary-general, Dr. António Ferronha. *Província de Angola,* Oct. 3, 1974, PCDA leaders António Navarro and ex-paratroop Colonel Costa Campos were arrested while the ex-director of the daily *A Província de Angola*, Correia de Freitas, and Lt. Colonel Gilberto Santos e Castro, who reportedly tried to persuade Portuguese military units to stage a countercoup, escaped. Ibid., Oct. 27, 1974. Two leading businessmen, Dr. Fernandes Vieira and Corte Real, were arrested in November on charges of "economic sabotage." Among the alarmed, diehard settler movements that formed during this period, the *Frente de Resistência Angolana* (FRA) modelled itself after the illfated Secret Army Organization (OAS) that had tried to block independence for (French) Algeria in the last stages of its war for independence. *Africa Contemporary Record, 1974–75*, p. B535; and two underground groups incorporated "secret army" in their names, the *Exército Secreto de Intervenção Nacional de Angola* (ESINA) and *Exército Secreto de Angola* (ESA). Other white extremists organized within a *Frente Radical para uma Angola Portuguesa* (FRAP).

26. Among them, resuscitated Bakongo movements, for example, *Movimento de Defesa dos Interesses de Angola* (MDIA) and *Partido Democrático Nto-Bako de Angola. A Província de Angola,* Sept. 6, 1974; Radio Luanda, 1200 GMT, Oct. 17, 1974.

27. See the analysis by Gilbert Comte, *Le monde,* May 14, 1975.

28. See John Marcum, *The Angolan Revolution,* 1: 280–282.

29. *Le figaro,* May 19, 1974.

30. *A Província de Angola,* Sept. 11, 22, 1974; *New York Times,* Oct. 4, 1974. See also Franz-Wilhelm Heimer, "Decolonisation et legitimité politique en Angola," *Revue française d'études politiques africaines,* June 1976, pp. 53–55.

31. *O'Comércio* (Luanda), Dec. 2, 18, 1974; *O'Século* (Lisbon), Jan. 14, 1975.

32. See letter to the Hoover Institution, Stanford University, for a description of conditions at the São Nicolau Recuperation Camp as presented by João Paulo and João Bolwele (MDIA-*Resistente*), Luanda, Aug. 12,

1974. See also protests against conditions at São Nicolau forwarded to the U.N. by Vice-President L. Kiala and other Nto-Bako officials, Kinshasa, Dec. 14, 1970.

33. Alberto, whose hatred for Holden Roberto occasionally prompted him to make positive statements about the MPLA (*O'Comércio*, Oct. 16, 1974), created the new *União Nacionalista Angolano* (UNA): Garcia, an ex-Matadi bookkeeper, headed up the *Partido de Reunificação do Povo Angolano* (PRPA); and Lélé became president of the Carmóna-based *Partido Democrático Nto-Bako de Angola* (*A Província de Angola* [Luanda], June 4, 1974). See also *Notícia* (Luanda), June 22, 1974. The FNLA denounced all such political returnees as traitorous collaborators whom would-be Portuguese architects of neocolonial order wished to foist upon Angola. FNLA, *Indépendance totale*, Aug. 29, 1974.

34. Another faction known as the *MDIA-Resistente* was led by João Paulo (president) and João Bolwele (first counsellor). *A Província de Angola*, June 7, 1974.

35. Ibid., May 10, 1974.

36. As the secretary-general of the old *Union Générale des Travailleurs de l'Angola* (UGTA) and president of a new People's Progressive Front of Angola, *O'Século*, June 28, 1974.

37. Mauricio Luvualu had reportedly received a year of trade union training in Moscow (1964–1965). Upon release from forced labor by the Portuguese in 1974, he (and some friends imprisoned with him) received financial compensation, money that he used to create the CNTA. A representative of the African-American Labor Center (AALC) visiting Luanda in Oct. 1974, however, concluded that Luvualu did not know "how to organize" or "run" a union. Peter Loebarth, AALC memorandum, Kinshasa, Oct. 10, 1974.

38. See *Star* (Johannesburg), weekly ed. June 22, 1974. Mauricio Luvualu, a UNITA sympathizer, was unchallenged for labor leadership until the MPLA took over, implacing its own *União Nacional dos Trabalhadores Angolanos* (UNTA).

39. *O'Século*, Sept. 3, 1974; Marcum, *Angolan Revolution*, 1: 76–82.

40. Members of the relatively important *Frente Socialista Democrática de Angola* (FRESDA), the *Movimento Democrático de Angola* (MDA), and the *Movimento Democrático do Huambo* joined the MPLA. Others grouped within the Nova Lisboa (Huambo)-based *Movimento Popular de Unidade Angolana* (MOPUA) rallied around Jonas Savimbi of UNITA.

41. *International Herald Tribune* (Paris), June 3, 1974.

42. *Neue Zürcher Zeitung* (Zürich), Aug. 9, 1974; Radio Lisbon, 2300 GMT, Sept. 10, 1974; see also Christopher Stevens, "The Soviet Union and Angola," *African Affairs* (London) 75, no. 299 (Apr. 1976): 141.

43. FNLA, *Indépendence totale*, Aug. 29, 1974. To reinforce its ties with Rumania, the FNLA sent two delegations to Bucharest during the summer of 1974—one led by Samuel Abrigada to attend celebrations marking the thirtieth anniversary of the liberation of Rumania from Germany, the other led by Manuel Miranda to attend the United Nations Conference on Population. Ibid., Sept. 7, 1974. A March 1974 visit to Bucharest by Agostinho Neto had failed to block the FNLA-Rumanian Association. *Romania Libre* (Bucharest), Mar. 5, 1974.

44. *O'Século*, Aug. 4, 1974.

45. Legum, *Africa: Contemporary Record, 1974–75*, p. B530. *New York Times*, Aug. 25, 1974.

46. *Daily News* (Dar es Salaam), Sept. 27, 1974. On Oct. 1, the FNLA's observer at the United Nations, Paulo Tuba, stated that the front had recently "stepped up" its "offensive in northern Angola" and taken a number of important centers in the area of Uige-Carmona. *New York Times*, Oct. 6, 1974. See also *A Província de Angola*, Sept. 25, 1974.

47. *O'Século*, Oct. 1, 1974; May 19, 1975; *A Província de Angola*, Oct. 7, 1974.

48. See *Marchés tropicaux* (Paris), Oct. 25, 1974, p. 2996.

49. *Le monde*, May 15, 1975.

50. The efforts of some Bakongo schoolteachers to create local MPLA committees in the Uige-Negage area were reportedly blocked by FNLA threats of violence. Franz-Wilhelm Heimer, "Décolonisation et légitimité politique en Angola," *Revue française d'études politiques africaines*, June 1976, p. 58n.

51. Hsinhua, *Daily Bulletin* (London), July 4, 1968.

52. According to UNITA, there were over fifteen hundred of these former militants who "had been languishing in the prisons of São Nicolau, Tarrafal and the Cape Verde Islands from as far back as 1968." UNITA, Political Bureau, "Communiqué," June 24, 1974.

53. *O'Século*, June 18, 1974.

54. *A Província de Angola*, July 1, 1974.

55. Notably members of MOPUA (see n. 40). *Star*, weekly ed., July 6, 1974.

56. Annual Conference of UNITA (July 16–19, 1974), "Final Communiqué," July 20, 1974.

57. *A Província de Angola*, Aug. 13, 1974.

58. "Under the old regime," Comte wrote, "the great majority of Angolans sympathized with the nationalists, listened to their radio broadcasts, but did not participate in their struggle." Most concerned themselves with "improving their lot" within the existing order. Now many saw in Savimbi hope for a peaceful transition to a new order. *Le monde*, May 15, 1975.

59. In a June 28, 1974, interview with executive editor Hoyt W. Fuller of *Black World* (Oct. 1974, pp. 56–79) in Lusaka, Sangumba and Tony Fernandes described UNITA as a "socialist" movement "within Marxism/Leninism lines." They said UNITA was eager to unite with its rivals but unwilling to accept MPLA "multiracialism" because it would mean domination by mulattoes and assimilados. Whites would be "accepted as visitors—nevermore as leaders." In August 1974 a Washington D.C.-based group, The Friends of Angola (Florence Tate, coordinator) formed to support Angolan liberation by "providing political and financial assistance to UNITA."

60. Statement by Fernando Wilson (Santos), an Ochimbundu born around 1950 at Benguela who studied law in Portugal, then Switzerland. *Star*, weekly ed., Nov. 16, 1974.

61. *Africa Research Bulletin* (PSC series) 11, no. 5 (July 11, 1974), p. 3273.

62. Letters published by the pro-MPLA journal, *Afrique-Asie*, no. 61 (July 8, 1974) and pronounced forgeries by UNITA, which called for an interna-

tional commission of inquiry. *O'Século*, Aug. 9, 1974.

63. Agostinho Neto interviewed in *Révolution africaine*, Nov. 15–21, 1974.

64. Bilateral agreements that called for an end to all hostile acts, physical and verbal, and for cooperation in pushing for full independence. The UNITA-FNLA accord (Nov. 25, 1974) signed in Kinshasa cited a need to protect Angola from "extremism from any quarter." *Africa Research Bulletin* (PSC series) 11, no. 11 (Dec. 15, 1974), p. 3438. The UNITA-MPLA accord signed at Luso (Dec. 18, 1974) in the presence of Portugal's pro-MPLA Admiral Coutinho pledged not to allow the injustices of the colonial system to be carried over into independence. Ibid. 11, no. 12 (Jan. 15, 1975), p. 3465.

65. The postcoup May 13 decision taken at the ALC's twenty-third session at Yaoundé, Cameroon, preceded an ad hoc committee study, which led to Kampala in October (*Daily News*, Oct. 12, 1974).
OAU reportedly granted UNITA about $32,000 (*Zambia Daily Mail*, Oct. 19, 1974), and General Amin gave Savimbi another $42,000 when he visited the call for OAU recognition. Ibid. 11, no. 11 (Dec. 15, 1974), p. 3419. The

66. The conference (Oct. 26–29) reportedly was attended by 650 delegates somewhere in UNITA's eastern base area. It expanded the Political Bureau from ten to fifteen and the Central Committee from twenty-four to forty members. Legum, *Africa: Contemporary Record*, 1974–75, p. C56.

67. In mid-November, Jorge Valentim, the UNITA representative in Lobito, boasted that Angolans were joining UNITA's army at the rate of three hundred a day. See political survey, *O'Século*, Nov. 13–15, 1974.

68. *LSM News* (Richmond, B.C.) 1, no. 3 (Dec. 1974): 18–19.

69. The initial manifesto signed by nineteen was followed by another signed by seventy (including students in Europe). *Revolta Activa* leadership included Mário de Andrade, who after a brief and apparently unsuccessful venture into guerrilla life via Zambia (*Le monde*, June 4, 1974), had resumed life in exile where, with Marc Ollivier, he coauthored a structural analysis of contemporary Angola, *La guerre en Angola: Etude socio-économique* (Paris: François Maspero, 1971); Gentil Viana, a former associate of Viriato da Cruz who had spent nine years in China translating Mao's works into Portuguese; Floribert "Spartacus" Monimambu, former eastern zone commander who rejected an MPLA command assignment in the north; Reverend Domingos da Silva, aging MPLA vice-president; and veteran MPLA physician/leaders, Dr. Hugo de Menezes, Dr. João Vieira Lopes, and Dr. Eduardo dos Santos.

70. See *Le monde*, May 31, June 7, 1974; *O'Século*, July 31, 1974; *Afrique-Asie*, June 10, 1974, reprinted in *Facts and Reports* (Amsterdam), June 22, 1974, p. 15.

71. See Marcum, *Angolan Revolution*, 1: 137n., 300, 334. Most recently reincarcerated in 1971, Pinto de Andrade smuggled out a letter to the court judge, which was published in France as "Pourquoi j'ai été jeté six fois en prison," *Informations catholiques internationales* (Paris), Mar. 15, 1971, pp. 23–25. See also MPLA, *Angola in Arms* (Dar es Salaam) 1, no. 3 (Mar.–Apr. 1967): 4–5.

72. Brazzaville authorities joined Father Andrade in mediating between the two factions. See Andrade's account of his efforts on behalf of MPLA unity, Radio Brazzaville, 1800 GMT, July 9, 1974.

73. For the text of the accord, see *Afrique-Asie*, June 24, 1974, in *Facts and Reports*, Aug. 3, 1974, p. 14.

74. Ibid., June 10, 1974, in *Facts and Reports*, June 22, 1974, p. 15. João Hailonda, the MPLA/Neto representative in Lusaka, alleged that Chipenda had also proposed a merger with UNITA to form a new *Partido Revolucionário Campones de Angola* (PRCA)—of which Chipenda would be president. *A Província de Angola*, June 10, 1974.

75. Interview with Bridget Bloom, *Financial Times* (London), Sept. 25, 1974.

76. Represented at Bukavu (July 27–28) by Holden Roberto (FNLA) and Agostinho Neto, Daniel Chipenda, and Gentil Viana (MPLA).

77. For the text of the Bukavu communiqué, see *Facts and Reports*, Aug. 31, 1974, p. 21.

78. *Times of Zambia* (Ndola), Aug. 8, 1974.

79. A formula that was, according to Agostinho Neto, imposed by the four African presidents and OAU. Bruno Crimi, "Trois monologues," *Jeune Afrique*, Sept. 14, 1974, pp. 61–63.

80. MPLA/Chipenda, "Press Release" (Lusaka, Aug. 29, 1974, mimeo.).

81. The Netoists argued that they had conceded an undeserved congress majority to the "revolt" factions in a "spirit of conciliation." They therefore proposed that a two-thirds majority be required for "fundamental decisions"; however, the "revolt" groups insisted upon "imposing" their will by simple majority. Neto also alleged that fifteen FNLA militants had infiltrated the Chipenda delegation. MPLA/Neto, "Statement of the MPLA Leadership and Delegates to the Congress" (Lusaka, Aug. 22, 1974, mimeo.); *Road to Liberation: MPLA Documents on the Founding of the People's Republic of Angola* (Richmond, B.C.: Liberation Support Movement, 1976), pp. 39–40; *Daily News*, Aug. 26, 1974. Representatives of the Congo, Somalia, Tanzania, Zaire, Zambia, FRELIMO, the PAIGC, and OAU attended the congress.

82. MPLA/Chipenda, "Press Release."

83. MPLA, "Communiqué" (Brazzaville, Sept. 3, 1974, mimeo.) signed by Agostinho Neto, Daniel Chipenda, and Joaquim Pinto de Andrade.

84. Also reported present at the Sal talks were Hendrik Vaal Neto and Ngola Kabangu, FNLA; Luis de Azevedo, Jr., and Vitor Kambuta, MPLA/Chipenda. *Diário de Lisboa*, Oct. 12, 1974; see also *Salongo* (Kinshasa), Sept. 16, 1974.

85. *Sunday Times* (London), Oct. 20, 1974. On Sept. 27, Spínola met with twenty-three representatives from Angolan ethnic and white groups in Lisbon and promised independence by Oct. 1976.

86. *O'Século*, Oct. 15, 1974. For a time, Chipenda had maintained that he, as vice-president, was waiting for Agostinho Neto to come to Kinshasa to work out his difficulties with Holden Roberto. *New York Times*, Oct. 6, 1974.

87. Crimi, "Trois monologues" (see n. 79 above), p. 62.

88. MPLA/Chipenda, "Press Release."

89. MPLA/Chipenda, "Conférence de presse" (Kinshasa, Oct. 23, 1974, mimeo.); MPLA/Chipenda, "Conferência de Imprensa" (Kinshasa, Oct. 29, 1974); and Chipenda interview, Dec. 12, 1974, in Charles K. Ebinger, "External Intervention in Internal War: The Politics and Diplomacy of the

Angolan Civil War," *Orbis*, 20, no. 3 (Fall 1976): 686.

90. *Facts and Reports*, Jan. 25, 1975, p. 16.

91. *O'Século*, Jan. 8, 1975.

92. Crimi, "Trois monologues," p. 61.

93. Legum, *Africa: Contemporary Record, 1974–75*, p. A25.

94. *Road to Liberation*, p. 37.

95. Born Lopo Fortunato Ferreira do Nascimento on July 10, 1942, in Luanda and Kimbundu-speaking, he was schooled in Luanda where he completed a course of studies at the Vicente Ferreira Commercial School. Arrested in 1959 and again in 1963, he worked as a labor organizer after his second release (1968), becoming chairman of the Syndical Commission of Brewery Workers. *O'Comércio* (Luanda), Jan. 31, 1975.

96. One of the MPLA's leading mestiço intellectuals, Rocha, born about 1940, directed the regional Center for Revolutionary Instruction set up in eastern Bié in 1969. An MPLA militant since the late 1950s, he became editor of the movement's Luanda journal, *Vitória Certa*. See interviews with Rocha in Ole Gjerstad, *The People in Power* (Richmond, B.C.: Liberation Support Movement, 1976), pp. 84–102.

97. Born in the early 1940s, José Eduardo studied in Moscow, married a Russian, and served as MPLA representative in Yugoslavia before assuming the Brazzaville post.

98. Other Central Committee members were Henrique de Carvalho Santos ("Onambwe"), Saydi Mingas, Evarista Domingos ("Kimba"), Pascal Luvualu (head of UNTA), António dos Santos França ("Ndalu"), Eugénio Verissimo da Costa ("Nzaji"), João Luis Neto ("Xietu"), Paulo Silva Mungungu ("Dangereux"), Ambroise Lukoki, Manuel Francisco Tuta ("Batalha"), Sapilinya, Tchizainga, Bonifacio Kinda ("Kantiga"), Gilberto Teixeira da Silva ("Jika"), killed in combat in Cabinda, January 1975, Herminio João Excórcio, Nito Alves, César Agusto ("Kiluanje"), Aristides Van-Dúnem, José Van-Dúnem, Manuel Pedro Pacavira, Eduardo Evaristo ("Bakalof"), Bernardo Ventura, Lopes Maria, Jamba-Ya-Mina, Armado Campos. *Road to Liberation*, pp. 41–42.

99. *El Moudjahid*, Dec. 17, 1974.

100. Secretary Kissinger in written reply to Senator Dick Clark, U.S., Senate, *Hearings Before the Subcommittee on African Affairs*, p. 52.

101. According to the American Department of State, the Soviets at that time "began delivering the first consignment of a $6 million shipment of military supplies to African liberation movements through Dar es Salaam. There is no evidence that a significant amount of military equipment later reached the Rhodesian or South African liberation movements, the only [ones] other than the MPLA for which the equipment could have been intended. Moreover, Dar es Salaam had previously served—and continued to serve—as an important transit point for the shipment of Soviet and bloc equipment to the MPLA." Ibid., p. 184.

102. Ibid.

103. In Cabinda's coastal society, several aristocratic families enjoyed special status and influence, among them, the Franque, Mingas, Puna, Monteiro, and Zau families. See *A Província de Angola*, Aug. 1, 1974.

104. *La semaine* (Brazzaville), July 7, Oct. 6, 1974; *Epanza* (Kinshasa), Oct. 26, 1974.

105. The Portuguese spelling of his name is Augusto Tchiovu.

106. *Elima* (Brazzaville), Dec. 21, 1974. Nzita enjoyed the support of a number of returned São Nicolau internees.

107. *Marchés tropicaux,* Sept. 27, 1974, p. 2741.

108. Legum, *Africa: Contemporary Record, 1974–75*, p. B536; *Le monde*, May 16, 1975.

109. *Le monde*, May 17, 1975.

110. Ibid.; Agence France Presse, Sept. 3, 1974; *Frankfurter Allgemeine Zeitung*, Sept. 17, 1974.

111. *La semaine*, Nov. 17, 1974.

112. *Le monde*, May 31, 1974.

113. *La semaine*, Nov. 17, 1974.

114. *Le monde*, May 17, 1975.

115. *Expresso* (Lisbon), Jan. 25, 1975.

116. For the text of the declaration (which acknowledged responsibility to carry out U.N. General Assembly, res. 1514 [XV], 1960), see Legum, *Africa: Contemporary Record,* 1974–75, pp. C38–C39.

117. Also at Mombasa, the FNLA and MPLA signed a bilateral accord in which they undertook to "end all types of hostilities and propaganda that could impede frank and sincere collaboration" between the two movements. Legum, *Africa: Contemporary Record, 1974–75*, p. B538.

118. Text published as *Angola: The Independence Agreement* (Lisbon: Ministry of Mass Communication, 1975).

119. Angelino Alberto, Francisco Lélé, and João Niege, representing a *Frente Nacional dos Pacifistas Angolanos*, lobbied in vain at Alvor to secure a place for themselves in the new order. *O'Século*, Jan. 15, 1975.

120. A ten-member National Defense Commission headed by the High Commissioner in Angola was appointed to oversee the integration of eight thousand soldiers from each liberation movement and twenty-four thousand Portuguese soldiers into a national army. The African movements were represented on the commission by Commander Pedró Timótio Barreiro Kiakanwa (born 1949, Saõ Salvador, Bakongo, trained in Tunisia) for ELNA-FNLA, Commander Jacob João Caetano (born 1941, Píri, Mbundu, trained in Czechoslovakia) for FAPLA-MPLA, and Captain Sabino Sandele (born 1941, Andulo, Ochimbundu, trained in eastern Angola) for FALA-UNITA. See *Angola: Rumo à Independência o Governo de Transição* (documentos e personalidades) (Luanda: Livrangol, 1975).

121. For texts of the Alvor and preceding agreements among the liberation movements, speeches at the inauguration of the transition government, and biographic data on government members, see ibid.

122. José de Assunção Alberto N'Dele, born Aug. 13, 1940, in Cabinda. studied at Luanda seminary and taught school for a short time in Cabinda before joining the UPA at Léopoldville in 1961. N'Dele went to Switzerland (University of Fribourg) in 1962 to study social science. Active in UNEA, he represented UNITA in Switzerland from 1966 on and participated in UNITA's third congress inside Angola (1973) at which he was elected general treasurer.

123. Monteiro: Born Nov. 7, 1941, in Huambo, a mestiço graduate of Coimbra Law School, poet, editor, activist in Coimbra cultural group. He was arrested in 1973 for suspected MPLA activity. In December 1974,

Monteiro was appointed director of information of the junta government in Luanda. Mingas: Born Feb. 13, 1942, in Cabinda, he studied at industrial school in Luanda and then in Lisbon where he excelled in athletics. After joining MPLA in the mid-1960s, he went to Cuba where in 1970 he completed a course in agriculture, livestock, and economic planning, which he then followed up with a period of military training. He directed CIR cadre training in eastern Angola from 1971 to late 1972, when he became the MPLA representative in Sweden; Boavida: A Kimbundu-speaking mestiço born June 23, 1928, in Luanda, graduated from Coimbra Law School, served as defense lawyer in 1960 at the "trial of 50," was arrested on Feb. 4, 1961, and worked for sixteen years as an attorney for the National Union of Employees in Commerce and Industry. See *O'Comércio*, Jan. 31, 1975.

124. See chap. 5. Representing the FNLA as secretary of state for commerce and tourism was a former associate of Viriato da Cruz and ex-MPLA official (Marcum, *Angolan Revolution*, 1: 254, 299), Graça da Silva Tavares. Schooled in Malange and Lisbon, with a *licence* from the University of Fribourg, Switzerland, Tavares was an anathema to the MPLA, which said it had expelled him (Dec. 1962) for misappropriating funds. *Diário de Notícias*, May 19, 1975. According to the FNLA, he and members of his family were later singled out for persecution by MPLA authorities. FNLA, "Communiqué on MPLA Criminal Actions" (Kinshasa, [1975], mimeo.).

125. Dembo: An Mbundu born at Hungo, Nambuangongo (Aug. 25, 1944), he attended mission primary school at Canacassala, fought with FNLA guerrillas (1961–1964), attended secondary and technical school in Algeria (1965–1969), and then went to a Tunisian military academy (1969–1970). Abandoning the FNLA, in 1970 he went to France where he completed a course in electrical engineering and joined UNITA (1971). After the coup, he served with the UNITA office in Luanda and then in Carmona. Wanga: An Ochimbundu, he was born around 1934 at Chissamba, Bié, attended the Protestant school at Dondi, the liceu at Nova Lisboa and Sá da Bandeira, and began university studies in Lisbon in 1961. He completed his studies in mathematics at the University of Lausanne, where he was active in UNEA; he then taught and administered at a lycée in Gabon. Chitunda: Born at Chimbuelengue, Bié, Feb. 20, 1941, Jeremias Kalandula Chitunda studied at mission schools (Dondi, Bela Vista) and secondary schools in Nova Lisboa. After escaping from Angola in 1964, he went to the United States, where he completed a B.S. degree in mining engineering at the University of Arizona and later became head of the industrial engineering department of Hecla Mining Co., Casa Grande, Arizona. He returned to Angola in Jan. 1975. *O'Comércio*, Jan. 31, 1975; Chitunda to author, Sept. 11, 1976.

126. The American choice, Holden Roberto, publicly asserted that Angolans as Christians "actively" rejected communism. Agence France Presse, Feb. 18, 1975. He was eulogized as an anticommunist who would seek Brazil's help. Fernando Luis Cascudo, "Holden Roberto," *Manchette* (Rio de Janeiro), Apr. 25, 1975.

127. See Seymour M. Hersh in *New York Times*, Dec. 19, 1975, and Roger Morris, "The Proxy War in Angola: Pathology of a Blunder," *The New Republic*, Jan. 31, 1976, p. 21.

128. Colonel Martins y Silva broke these figures down as follows: FNLA—7,500 northern Angola, 250 Lunda-Moxico, 1,000 Shaba frontier, 5,000 Zaire training camps (Kizamba, Tukaka, Tshikapa, Kinkuzu); MPLA—1,000 southern Dembos, 1,000 Lunda-Moxico, 1,500 Maiombe-Cabinda, 2,000 eastern frontier; MPLA/Chipenda—2,000 Zambia, 750 eastern Angola; UNITA—3,000 Moxico and west of Luso. *Remarques africaines* (Brussels), Jan. 31, 1975, p. 4.

129. James Dingeman, "Portuguese and African Liberation Movement Force Levels in Angola, 1961–1976" (New York, 1976, unpublished manuscript). Based upon an exhaustive perusal of published reports, the Dingeman figures break down as follows: FNLA—9,000 Angola, 12,000 Zaire training camps; MPLA—2,300 in field, 5,700 in training, 2,000 Chipenda, plus prospect of recruiting 4,000 Katangese gendarmes; UNITA—4,000 in field, 4,000 in training. Portuguese forces totaled some 30,000. The *Economist Intelligence Unit* (London), 1st qtr., 1975, set the figures at 15,000 FNLA, 6,000 MPLA, and 1,000 UNITA.

130. With the caveat that its estimates were "complicated by the lack of first-hand information and the natural tendency of movement leaders to exaggerate the size of their forces," the Department of State responded to questions by Senator Dick Clark with the following figures for January 1975: FNLA—5,000–6,000 trained, 5,000 training in Zaire; MPLA—5,000–7,000 trained and armed (excluding Chipenda troops), "several thousand" in training, "several thousand" armed but untrained followers in Luanda; UNITA—2,000 in field and "beginning a campaign" to mobilize a "larger military force." U.S., Senate, *Hearings Before the Subcommittee on African Affairs*, p. 191.

131. Testimony of Assistant Secretary for African Affairs, William E. Schaufele, Jr., ibid., p. 192.

132. Kenneth L. Adelman, "Report from Angola," *Foreign Affairs* 53, no. 3 (Apr. 1975): 568.

133. See n. 25. *O'Século*, Mar. 24, 28, 1975.

134. According to Gerald J. Bender, "Kissinger and Angola: Anatomy of Failure" (typescript, 1976), n. 16.

135. *New Times* (Moscow), Feb. 14, 1968, pp. 22–23.

136. Morris, "Proxy War."

137. *Guardian* (London), Feb. 15, 1975.

138. Reports from Ninda near the Zambian border, where Chipenda's group held a conference in late January (*Diário de Notícias* [Lisbon], Jan. 25, 1975), indicated that some 130 of his men went over to the MPLA and UNITA around early February (*Zambia Daily Mail*, Feb. 3, 1975), and eight military commanders rejoined the MPLA (*Sunday Times of Zambia* [Ndola], Feb. 23, 1975).

139. *New York Times*, Feb. 24, 1975. A five-member UNITA delegation met with MPLA/Chipenda representatives at Ninda in mid-February. But Chipenda preferred to cast his lot with the FNLA, which assured him of Zaire's support. It also reflected the fact that Chipenda and Savimbi were rivals for support within the large Ovimbundu population. Alluding to charges that Savimbi had collaborated with the Portuguese army, Chipenda suggested to the Kinshasa press that "his childhood friend still had some explaining to do." *Zaire*, Feb. 21, 1975.

140. *Dagens Nyheter* (Stockholm), Feb. 21, 1975.

141. An observation of George Houser, who, during a March 15–25 visit to Angola, recorded general agreement there on two things: difficult though it was, a coalition was necessary since "no party had the following and the power to be able to govern Angola alone," and "there was a real possibility of civil war." Houser, "A Report on Guinea-Bissau, Cape Verde and Angola: Part III, Angola" (American Committee on Africa, New York, May 26, 1975, mimeo.).

142. *Sunday Times* (London), Mar. 30, 1975; *Financial Times*, Mar. 29, 1975.

143. *Frankfurter Allgemeine Zeitung*, Mar. 29, 1975; *Washington Post*, Mar. 27, 1975.

144. *Financial Times*, Mar. 29, 1975. Also *Star*, weekly ed., Mar. 29, 1975. A few survivors of Caxito gave accounts of the massacre. FNLA support in Luanda plummeted. *Observer* (London), Apr. 20, 1975.

145. For a careful reconstruction of these events, see Tony Hodges, "How the MPLA Won in Angola," in Legum and Hodges, eds., *After Angola: The War over Southern Africa* (London: Rex Collings, 1976), pp. 49–51. According to Johnny Eduardo, the FNLA leadership in Luanda recommended all-out war against the MPLA, but Roberto imposed a delay, saying that "when the time came the war must be between two armies without the civilian population in the middle." *Star*, weekly ed., Apr. 5, 1975.

146. *Le monde*, May 15, 1975.

147. *Expresso*, May 17, 1975.

148. *New York Times*, Sept. 25, 1975.

149. See testimony of Schaufele, p. 175.

150. For a while, Portuguese officials tried to intercept the inflow of arms. The Yugoslav ship *Postoyna* was sent out of Luanda harbor after it was discovered unloading military equipment. But this only detoured the materiel through Pointe Noire.

151. According to Gerald Bender, American officials estimated the value of Soviet arms arriving from March to July as between $5 million and $10 million. "Kissinger and Angola," p. 17. The FNLA cataloged alleged Soviet air and sea deliveries in "A Statement on Soviet Intervention in Angola" (Sept. 1975, mimeo.), in which it also said that "the Soviet Union supplemented its donations of military equipment with a cash allocation of U.S. $150,000 per year." This information may have come from the CIA, which was feeding intelligence into the FNLA and UNITA from its Luanda station (according to information presented to the House Select Committee on Intelligence, Oct. 29, 1975).

152. Hodges, "How the MPLA Won," p. 50. UNTA charged that the FNLA minister of interior, Ngola Kabangu, winked at the hoodlums hurling grenades and rockets at its headquarters. *O'Século*, June 4, 1975.

153. Led by General Nataniel Bumba, these forces shared the MPLA's antipathy toward the Mobutu government. Colin Legum, "Foreign Intervention in Angola," in *After Angola*, p. 14, and testimony of Schaufele, p. 183.

154. Colin Legum in *Observer*, May 18, 1975.

155. *O'Século*, May 9, 1975. Up to this point, the FNLA seems to have been

the aggressor most often, but "at the end of May and in early June, the MPLA launched a counteroffensive." Christopher Stevens, "The Soviet Union and Angola," *African Affairs* 75, no. 299 (Apr. 1976): 140.

156. *Diário de Notícias*, May 1, 1975.

157. *Washington Post*, Jan. 6, 1976.

158. *Diário de Notícias*, May 16, 1975.

159. *Star*, weekly ed., Apr. 5, 1975.

160. Legum, "Foreign Intervention in Angola," p. 13. During a tripartite meeting in Kinshasa in early April, Kaunda was joined by Julius Nyerere in persuading a "hesitant" Mobutu Sésé Séko that Savimbi represented the "best hope" for a peaceful transfer of power in Angola. *Star*, weekly ed., Apr. 19, 1975.

161. He considered civil war unlikely given that "anyone who starts a war will force the unity of the other two movements against themselves." *Financial Mail* (Johannesburg), May 9, 1975; see also *El Moudjahid* (Algiers), Apr. 16, 1975.

162. See Jonas Savimbi, *Communicação ao Povo Angolano* (Luanda: UNITA Department of Information and Propaganda, 1975).

163. *Expresso*, Feb. 15, 1975. "At the UNITA offices in Luanda and Lobito" observed George Houser in March, "it was particularly noticeable that a good minority of Portuguese were on hand going through the procedure of taking out membership." Houser, "A Report." See also *Star*, weekly ed., May 3, 1975. Among the African converts to UNITA was Marcos Kassanga, who announced his adhesion in a press conference at Nova Lisboa (now Huambo). *A Província de Angola*, Mar. 19, 1975.

164. In April, Charles Mohr reported from Luanda that "informed observers" thought that UNITA would win 45 percent, the MPLA 30–35 percent, and the FNLA the remainder if an election were held at that time. *New York Times*, Apr. 24, 1975. An earlier poll conducted by a Luanda newspaper put relative popular support for the three at UNITA 45 percent, MPLA 25 percent, FNLA 20 percent. *Africa* (London) Mar. 1975, p. 40. Believing that their inferiority in political cadres would put them at a disadvantage, the FNLA and UNITA had rejected an MPLA proposal that the three work out a common program and a single list of candidates for the planned legislative election *A Província de Angola*, Feb. 15, 1975.

165. *O'Século*, Feb. 22, 1975.

166. *Le monde*, May 14, 1975.

167. Hodges, "How the MPLA Won," p. 51.

168. For text of Nakuru Agreement see *After Angola*, pp. 69–75.

169. *New York Times*, July 18, 1975.

170. *Notícias* (Lourenço Marques), July 29, 1975.

171. Hodges, "How the MPLA Won," p. 53.

172. *Le monde*, May 17, 1975.

173. On April 29, Congolese Premier Henri Lopez affirmed: "There is a case for Cabinda. Cabinda is historically and geographically different from Angola." Cabindans ought to be allowed to decide for themselves whether they wish to be part of Angola. *O'Século*, May 1, 1975.

174. On May 7, President Mobutu called for a referendum to determine Cabinda's future. *Le monde*, May 10, 1975.

175. *Expresso*, May 31, 1975.

176. Also in the FLEC "government" were Defense Minister Jean da Costa and Foreign Affairs Minister Charles Sumba Pena. *Notícias* (Lourenço Marques), Aug. 14, 1975. See also Marcum, *Angolan Revolution*, 1: 173n.

177. *Jornal de Angola* (Luanda), Aug. 8, 1975. Apparently hoping that FLEC might use the time to revitalize itself, Ngouabi reportedly slowed the transshipment of Soviet arms to Angola, thus occasioning an urgent visit by Neto to Brazzaville in early July. Interviews with U.S. State Department officials by Charles Ebinger, "External Intervention," p. 689.

178. For text of the OUA resolution see *After Angola*, p. 67.

179. In July, Amin announced his support for Cabindan independence (the position of his close ally President Mobutu). *Diário de Notícias*, July 4, 1975.

180. Algeria, Burundi, Ghana, Kenya, Lesotho, Morocco, Niger, Somalia, Upper Volta, and Uganda.

181. See Legum, "Foreign Intervention in Angola," p. 29.

182. Ibid., pp. 28–29.

183. Testimony of Henry A. Kissinger, Feb. 6, 1976, *Hearings Before the Subcommittee on African Affairs*, p. 9.

184. Although the CIA had proposed assistance to UNITA in January and again in June, and Jorge Sangumba had been accorded an audience with State Department officials as far back as early 1973, this was apparently the first substantial U.S. help UNITA received.

185. Jon Blair, "Unscrambling America's Role in the Angolan Fiasco," *Times*, June 23, 1976.

186. *New York Times*, Dec. 14, 1975. For an insightful, comprehensive analysis of the background to and rationale for the July decision, see Bender, "Kissinger and Angola," see also Gerald J. Bender, "La diplomatie de M. Kissinger et l'Angola," *Revue française d'études politiques africaines*, June 1976, pp. 73–95.

187. Testifying on June 16, the author recommended that the United States "seize the opportunity to exert its diplomatic influence on behalf of a political as over against a military solution to Angola's political crisis. In doing so, it should limit itself to modest and constructive support of efforts by Lisbon and the Organization for African Unity to further the cause of a unified state. It should set a big-power example and desist from any overt or covert intervention thus putting it in a credible position to discourage such intervention on the part of others, except for possible peacekeeping action by the OAU. . . . During the months immediately ahead, the United States should unobtrusively but wholeheartedly encourage efforts by Lisbon or the OAU to promote Angolan unity and discourage civil war. It should also be openly and convincingly prepared to establish respectful relations with those who end up governing Angola, whoever they may be." U.S., Senate, *Hearings Before the Subcommittee on African Affairs*, 94th Cong., 1st sess., June 11–29, 1975, pp. 93–94.

188. Jon Blair, *Times* (London), June 23, 1976, estimated that between July 17 and the end of October, about $14 million in automatic rifles, mortars, antitank weapons, and other equipment left over from Vietnam was funneled to UNITA and the FNLA.

189. The staff of the House Select Committee on Intelligence cited CIA costing procedures and the use of surplus equipment to arrive at this doubling estimate. See leaked version of committee report, "Pike Papers," *Village Voice*, Feb. 20, 1976. *Los Angeles Times* (Dec. 21, 1975) put the figure at close to $100 million.

190. British and French aid to UNITA reportedly included Lonhro pilots and a jet plane for Savimbi and soldiers hired by French intelligence (SDECE). *Sunday Telegraph* (London), Feb. 6, 1977; *New York Times*, Mar. 10, 1976; *Washington Post*, Jan. 6, 1976.

191. Bender, "Kissinger and Angola," p. 23. See also *New York Times*, Mar. 10, 1976. One of the most dubious provisions in the July outlay was half a million dollars for propaganda activity to build up the images of the FNLA and UNITA. Such a buildup, which could be calculated to increase the political appeal of the two movements within the United States, seemed to do violence to the principle that the CIA should not become a domestic lobbyist for foreign causes.

192. Immanuel Wallerstein, "Luanda Is Madrid," *Nation*, Jan. 10, 1976, pp. 12–17.

193. Such radical, Third World–oriented publications as *Afrique-Asie* pounded at China's perceived folly in issue after issue.

194. Agence France Presse, Mar. 21, 1975.

195. *El Moudjahid*, June 5, 1975.

196. *Le monde*, July 18, 1975.

197. *Financial Mail* (Johannesburg), May 9, 1975.

198. *Afrique-Asie*, July 14, 1975, p. 17. In Lisbon on his return from China, Lára said that he thought it was "still possible" to achieve a three-way understanding provided that *all* interference by foreign interests "voraciously converging" on Angola could be removed. Radio Lisbon, 2230 GMT, June 9, 1975.

199. According to Bender, "Kissinger and Angola," p. 43, American intelligence sources learned that "China was giving up on the FNLA" as of early June. "Apparently, the Chinese were very disappointed in the performance of the FNLA troops, a view which was shared by almost all American observers"—although this did not deter the Ford administration from intensifying its relationship with the FNLA.

200. For example, *Washington Post*, July 28, 1975.

201. Interviews with Zaire embassy officials, July–Aug. 1975 by Ebinger, "External Intervention," p. 689.

202. FRELIMO had long short-circuited Savimbi's efforts to establish direct links to Tanzania. Jonas Savimbi, "Discurso de Orientação Política e Ideologica da UNITA" (London, UNITA Office, June–July 1972), p. 12.

203. Episodic discussions between UNITA and MPLA took place from mid-June until late August when talks between Lopo do Nascimento and José N'Dele held under Portuguese auspices in Lisbon failed to produce an MPLA-UNITA coalition. *A Província de Angola*, June 15, 17, 1975; *De Volkskrant* (Amsterdam), Aug. 27, 1975; and Hodges, "How the MPLA Won," p. 54.

204. UNITA, "The River Cuanza Manifesto" (New York, June 17, 1976, mimeo.). According to Savimbi, Nyerere reneged on the agreement he had

made with the Chinese and UN1TA. Legum, "Foreign Intervention in Angola," p. 12. British journalist Robert Moss asserts that the Chinese supplied UNITA with seven tons of arms during the first half of 1975. *Sunday Telegraph*, Feb. 6, 1977.

205. *Sunday Times of Zambia*, Sept. 28, 1975.

206. Radio Kinshasa, 1610 GMT, Oct. 27, 1975. In a broadcast from its northern "capital" at Carmona, the FNLA said that Chinese advisers were being sent home because they showed more interest in ideology than in military tactics. *Los Angeles Times*, Nov. 27, 1975.

207. Agostinho Neto announced after a visit to Bucharest in March 1974, during which he met President Ceausescu, that Rumania was aiding the MPLA. *Daily News* (Dar es Salaam), Mar. 16, 1974.

208. *O'Século*, Apr. 3, 1975.

209. *Times* (London), Oct. 30, 1975.

210. *San Diego Union*, Apr. 27, 1970; *The Economist*, June 29, 1968, p. xiv.

211. Department of State analysis, "Angola: An Assessment of the Insurgency" (Washington, D.C., Sept. 16, 1970).

212. In 1969, the South African Foreign Trade Association docked a freighter with fifty separate commercial exhibits at Luanda in the belief that impending Angolan industrial development offered a prime market for South Africa. *RSA World* (Pretoria) 5, no. 3 (1969): 46.

213. J. M. de Wet, commissioner general for indigenous peoples, South West Africa, *Star*, weekly ed., Apr. 5, 1975.

214. See John A. Marcum, "Southern Africa after the Collapse of Portugal," in Helen Kitchen, ed., *Africa: From Mystery to Maze* (Lexington, Mass.: D.C. Heath, 1976), pp. 77–133.

215. François Campredon, Agence France Presse, June 10, 1975.

216. A report in Lisbon's by then left-wing *Diário de Notícias* (Aug. 14, 1975) suggested that the South Africans acted in collusion with UNITA. See also *Le monde*, Aug. 16, 1975. By the terms of an agreement for the construction of a series of dams along the Cunene, the South Africans had been previously permitted by the Portuguese to station a small security force at the site of the first ($63 million) project at Caluque. *Star*, weekly ed., Dec. 20, 1975.

217. *Daily Mail* (London), Sept. 5, 1975. This South African incursion produced banner headlines in the African press, for example, "S. African Troops in Angola," *Standard* (Nairobi), Sept. 1, 1975.

218. *Guardian* (London), Sept. 4, 1975.

219. *Windhoek Advertiser*, May 30, 1975.

220. *Star*, weekly ed., May 3, 1975. According to Robert Moss, Savimbi met with a South African intelligence officer in Europe in March. At a second meeting in Lusaka on April 14, he requested South African arms but was refused because of his unwillingness at that time to form an alliance with the FNLA. *Sunday Telegraph*, Feb. 6, 1977.

221. *Windhoek Advertiser*, June 12, 1975.

222. *Washington Post*, Aug. 8, 1975.

223. U.S. intelligence credited Savimbi's forces with three thousand weapons (Bender, "Kissinger and Angola," p. 15); David Martin put the figure at seven thousand (*Standard* [Nairobi], Jan. 3, 1976). UNITA was

reportedly given some arms by Portuguese units (*O'Século*, Apr. 3, 1975) and Zambia (*Expresso*, Oct. 11, 1975).

224. As of August, Portuguese estimates put UNITA forces as high as twenty-two thousand with the FNLA at thirty thousand and the MPLA seventeen thousand. *Observer*, Aug. 24, 1975.

225. Roberto reportedly met with the South Africans in Kinshasa in July 1975. On the strength of his undertaking to join forces with Savimbi, the South Africans delivered second-hand light machine guns, rifles and mortars to the FNLA in August. *Sunday Telegraph*, Feb. 6, 1977.

226. Views expressed by UNITA spokesman Jorge Sangumba in *Jornal do Brasil* (Rio de Janeiro), Nov. 9, 1975.

227. Radio Johannesburg (International Service), 1600 GMT, Feb. 3, 1977.

228. According to Robert Moss, the Zaire soldiers spent most of their time "preying on the local girls." *Sunday Telegraph*, Feb. 6, 1977. Field research by staff assistants to Senator John Tunney (*Times*, June 23, 1976) put Zaire's contribution at eleven armored cars and sixty soldiers.

229. Writing from Angola in mid-October, René Lefort described South Africa as having assumed a "very discreet" but "determinant" role in the training and arming of UNITA troops. *Le monde*, Oct. 22, 1975. According to David Martin, in late September Savimbi told Zambia's Kenneth Kaunda "that he had virtually ceded an 80-kilometre strip of southern Angola" stretching from the Atlantic to the Zambian border, to South Africa. He was warned that this could become a springboard for further South African encroachment." *Standard* (Nairobi), Jan. 3, 1976.

230. Members of the *Exército de Libertação Portuguesa* (ELP) led by Captain Aparicio ("Garibaldi"). They accompanied the South Africans as far as Sá da Bandeira.

231. For a detailed report by Robert Moss on the exploits of Operation Zulu see *Sunday Telegraph*, Feb. 6, 1977.

232. Dail Torgerson of the *Los Angeles Times*, Nov. 27, 1975, reported that at least four South African 130mm howitzers were deployed in the FNLA Oct.–Nov. drive on Luanda. He saw two of the huge guns along with a dozen members of a South African artillery battery in Ambriz where they were flown from Caxito by South African C130 transports in mid-November to avoid capture by MPLA troops as they threw back the FNLA offensive. On South African intervention see also Sean Gervasi, "Continuing Escalation in the Angola Crisis" (American Committee on Africa, New York, Dec. 19, 1975); Legum, "Foreign Intervention in Angola," pp. 15–16, 36–37, and *Le monde*, Nov. 16–17, 1975.

233. *Washington Post*, Apr. 26, 1976. South Africa thus succeeded in breaking up what it knew to be a longstanding UNITA-SWAPO alliance. *Die Transvaler* (Johannesburg), May 23, 1975.

234. "Statement of Mr. Edward W. Mulcahy, Deputy Assistant Secretary for African Affairs before the Subcommittee on African Affairs, Senate Foreign Relations Committee" Washington, D.C., Oct. 24, 1975, mimeo.).

235. "We have seen press reports alleging South African activities in support of the non-MPLA forces in Angola, but we have not initiated any discussions or consultations with the South African Government on Angola

and we have no plans to do so. We continue to believe that the Angolan people should be left free to resolve their own differences without outside interference." Department of State, "Press Briefing Paper," Dec. 1, 1975.

236. Morris, "Proxy War in Angola," p. 21.

237. Responses by Kissinger and Deputy Assistant Secretary Mulcahy to questions put by Senator Dick Clark, *Hearings Before the Subcommittee on African Affairs*, pp. 53, 187. See also Tad Szulc, "Why Are We in Johannesburg?" *Esquire*, Oct. 1974, p. 48.

238. *Hearings*, p. 13.

239. *New York Times*, Feb. 7, 1976; *Sunday Telegraph*, Feb. 7, 1977.

240. *Newsweek*, May 17, 1976, p. 53. Asked whether he approved of South African involvement, Assistant Secretary Schaufele responded: "It was not approval, so much, as that we could understand South Africa's perception of its role." *To the Point* (Johannesburg) 3, no. 3 (Feb. 20, 1976): 15.

241. See the independence day speech of Agostinho Neto in *Road to Liberation*, pp. 1–8.

242. President Samora Machel of already independent Mozambique, along with leaders of Guinea-Bissau, the Cape Verde Islands, and São Tomé, joined Neto in condemning "the imperialist aggression" of South Africa and called on all "democratic forces of the world" to recognize the state and government that the MPLA was preparing. Text of resolutions as broadcast on Radio Lourenço Marques, 0500 GMT, Nov. 10, 1975, in *Facts and Reports*, Nov. 29, 1975, p. 13.

243. Neto did not believe in continental African unity as a "desirable goal." He preferred a "non-aligned, internationalist" stance and opposed OAU intervention in the Angolan war. See interview in *Afriscope* (Lagos), Aug. 1975, pp. 6–14. Savimbi contrastingly identified with a pan-Africanist perspective (*Financial Mail,* May 9, 1975) and sought OAU involvement.

244. *El Moudjahid*, Nov. 15, 1975. While most were black and spoke Kimbundu, no less than six were perceived by a UNITA spokesman, Jeremias Chitunda, to be mestiço. Chitunda to author, Oct. 1976.

245. Born in São Tomé around 1940 of an Mbundu father, Machado was schooled in Luanda and spent thirteen years in Portuguese jails and internment camps for his political activity.

246. An Mbundu born around 1945 at Píri, North Cuanza, Alves led MPLA guerrillas in the vicinity of Luanda and emerged in 1975 as an ambitious spokesman for black as against mestiço power and was regarded by some as second only to Neto in influence within the MPLA. See interview in *Afriscope*, Dec. 1975, pp. 59–61. See also interview in Gjerstad, *The People in Power*, pp. 103–107.

247. In addition to CONCP allies, Algeria, Congo-Brazzaville, Guinea-Conakry, Madagascar, Mali, and Somalia recognized the PRA.

248. On Dec. 9, Jonas Savimbi told a press conference in Lusaka that South Africa was not helping UNITA, which remained dedicated to the liberation of Namibia. Radio Lusaka, GMT 1800, Dec. 9, 1975.

249. Radio Lagos, Nov. 8, 1975, cited by Legum, "Foreign Intervention in Angola," p. 29.

250. *New York Times*, Nov. 28, 1975.

251. Under the banner headline "Savimbi Admits Betrayal," Tanzania's

Daily News (Nov. 16, 1975) quoted UNITA's leader as telling a group of foreign correspondents in Lobito: "I need people to fight with armoured cars that we cannot operate ourselves. They are South African or Rhodesian, but there are more French." The foreign troops, including mercenaries who had fought in Biafra, were being supplied by C130 transport planes flying from bases in South West Africa to Silva Porto and Benguela. Tanzania recognized the PRA on Dec. 5. Ibid., Dec. 6, 1975.

252. *New York Times*, Jan. 4, 1976.

253. *Facts and Reports*, Jan. 14, 1976, p. 13.

254. *New York Times*, Nov. 20, 1975. Robert Moss put the figure at four thousand. *Sunday Telegraph*, Jan. 30, 1977. The South African Defense Force later stated that the troops it led had held back from taking all of Angola in deference to Jonas Savimbi, who believed that he could reach a political agreement with the MPLA if he just held on to his own ethnic home territory. Savimbi, it said, sought to spare Angola further destruction and bloodshed. Radio Johannasburg, International Service, 1600 GMT, Feb. 3, 1977.

255. See the analysis by Don Oberdorfer, *Washington Post*, Feb. 18, 1976. Cuban sources fix the time of the creation of training centers at Dalatando (Salazar), Benguela, Henrique de Carvalho (Saurimo) and Cabinda as early October. Ibid., Jan. 12, 1977.

256. The U.S. government first noticed "indications" of Cuban personnel (still presumably of an advisory/technical nature) on July 25. *Hearings Before the Subcommittee on African Affairs*, p. 83.

257. Robert Moss gives the following details. On July 16 in Havana, Premier Castro asked visiting AFM leader Otelo Saraiva de Carvalho to arrange for Portuguese permission for Cuban military to enter Angola. In August, the MPLA sent "Iko" Carreira to Moscow to ask for help, only to have the Soviets suggest that he try the Cubans. Shortly thereafter Commander Raul Diaz Arguelles (later killed in an encounter with South African troops) led a Cuban delegation to Luanda where he arranged for the increase in Cuban assistance. *Sunday Telegraph*, Jan. 30, 1977. Much of this is confirmed by Cuban sources. *Washington Post*, Jan. 12, 1977.

258. *Washington Post*, Apr. 10, 1977.

259. *Times*, Oct. 24, 1975, June 23, 1976.

260. See account by Colombian author Gabriel Garcia Marquez, *Washington Post*, Jan. 10, 1977.

261. In May 1976, Defense Minister Pieter Botha said that South African troops could easily have gone into Luanda in early November but were pulled back because "the United States had pleaded" against such a move. *Daily Telegraph*, May 7, 1976.

262. The Cubans were widely credited with organizing the successful defense of the city. See Caryle Murphy in *Washington Post*, Jan. 16, 1976. Writing in *Jeune Afrique* (June 10, 1977, p. 15), N'Zamba K. Afri-Ku-Nyeng would later credit Katangan gendarmes with having played a major role in the defense of Luanda.

263. A force of two thousand Cabindans, mercenaries, and Zairians failed to break into Cabinda in three days of desultory fighting. This was a humiliating defeat for Zaire. *Washington Post*, Nov. 10, 1975; *New York Times*, Feb. 2, 1976.

264. Observation of Philippe Pons with FNLA troops in the north. *Le monde*, Sept. 10, 1975.

265. David B. Ottaway in a perceptive analysis of the FNLA's collapse, *Washington Post*, Feb. 19, 1976.

266. According to some reports, North Korean instructors attached to the Zaire army stepped in to replace the Chinese when they left in mid-1975. *Daily Telegraph*, Nov. 28, 1975.

267. *New York Times*, Jan. 30, 1976.

268. Fidel Castro, *Angola: African Girón* (speech commemorating the 15th Anniversary of victory at Playa Girón) (Havana: Editorial de Ciencias Sociales del Instituto Cubano del Libro, 1976), pp. 14–20.

269. See interview with Mateos Neto, *Afrique-Asie*, Oct. 20, 1975, pp. 15–17; *Bulletin d'Afrique*, Aug. 29, 1975.

270. *Washington Post*, Feb. 19, 1976.

271. *Diário de Notícias*, Aug. 25, 1975; *O'Século*, Aug. 25, 1975.

272. Roberto ascribed his defeat to material deficiencies. "Not so long ago I was about 20 kilometers away from Luanda. . . . But I was not equipped to bear up against the heavy weapons, tanks, missiles, helicopters, Migs and other sophisticated arms of the Soviet-Cuban expeditionary corps. We fell back." *Washington Post*, Feb. 15, 1976.

273. Johnny Eduardo Pinock and José N'Dele alternated as premier in a government that included many who had served in the defunct transitional government. For the full roster of ministers, see Hodges, "How the MPLA Won in Angola," p. 57.

274. *Washington Post*, Feb. 19, 1976. As early as the beginning of October there were press reports of tension and skirmishes between the FNLA/ Chipenda and UNITA. *Expresso*, Oct. 4, 1975.

275. *Financial Times*, Dec. 30, 1975, Jan. 2, 14, 1976.

276. The predominance of African names in UNITA leadership contrasted with the MPLA where Portuguese names remained at least as prevalent as in the past.

277. As late as Sept. 26, 1975, the MPLA reported that it confronted hostile SWAPO soldiers in southern Angola. *Financial Times*, Sept. 27, 1975.

278. *Star*, weekly ed., Mar. 13, 1976.

279. UNITA, "South Africa Gains in MPLA-Pretoria Pact" (New York, Mar. 31, 1976, mimeo.).

280. *Sunday Telegraph*, Feb. 13, 1977; and report of aides to Senator John Tunney, *Hearings Before the Subcommittee on African Affairs*, p. 165. *Times*, June 23, 1976.

281. In a battle at Bridge 14 (Dec. 9–12) north of Santa Comba, the one major encounter between the two expeditionary forces, the South Africans claimed to have killed some 200 Cubans at a cost of four South African lives. At the time of the January withdrawal, Pretoria put its losses at thirty-three South Africans killed as against an estimated more than two thousand Cubans. *Sunday Telegraph*, Feb. 13, 1977.

282. See report by Tom Lambert describing UNITA's two-week training course at Kapolo camp near Silva Porto. *Los Angeles Times*, Jan. 18, 1976.

283. René Lefort visited a mass grave of 235 MPLA victims at Huambo. *Le monde*, Feb. 18, 1976. UNITA would subsequently issue communiqués

detailing allegations of atrocities and mass killing by Cuban troops. UNITA, "Fidel Castro's Troops Continue to Kill and Maim the People in Angola" (New York, Oct. 18, 1976, mimeo.).

284. For example, A. Vakulukuta (Ovambo) took leadership of elements of SWAPO that joined with UNITA in the Cunene bush, and veteran Chokwe leader Smart Chata held a military command in the east; Puna, Chiwale, and others resumed their underground life.

285. Jonas Savimbi, "Open Letter to All Peoples of the World," Sept. 25, 1976 (New York, Dec. 8, 1976, mimeo.).

286. *Hearings Before the Subcommittee on African Affairs*, p. 10; *New York Times*, Dec. 25, 1975.

287. *Diário de Notícias*, July 28, 1975; *Le monde*, Sept. 25, 1975; *Jornal Novo* (Lisbon), Oct. 2, 1975; *Star*, weekly, Oct. 11, 1975.

288. A torrent of newspaper and television coverage, even a rash of college teach-ins, warned of a "new Vietnam." The author appeared on NBC's "Meet the Press" and recommended an end to American intervention. *Meet the Press*, 20, no. 1, Jan. 4, 1976.

289. *New York Times*, Dec. 20, 1975. The House of Representatives followed with a 323 to 99 rejection of what Dr. Kissinger had termed the "trivial sums," the "tens of millions of dollars" with which he proposed to stave off an MPLA military victory. In February, however, the director of the CIA, George Bush, declined to rule out the possibility that American intelligence agencies were continuing financial or other support to anti-MPLA forces in Angola. Ibid., Feb. 16, 1976.

290. South African Minister of Defense Pieter W. Botha. Ibid., Jan. 26, 1976.

291. *Izvestia*, Oct. 10, 1976.

292. Interview with Lára, *Afrique-Asie*, Nov. 15, 1976, pp. xii–xv.

293. See David B. Ottaway, "Angola's Offbeat Leader," *Washington Post*, June 13, 1976.

294. Lára in *Afrique-Asie*.

295. Several government and military leaders, including Minister of Finance Saydi Mingas, were killed in the abortive May 27, 1977 coup led by Nito Alves (principal organizer of the Luanda *poder popular* structure) and José Van Dúnem with the alleged complicity of other prominent figures, notably Jacob Caetano and David Aires Machado. Significantly, Basil Davidson described Alves and another former maquis commander and coup organizer, Eduardo Evaristo ("Bakalof"), as Dembos "regionalists." *West Africa*, July 18, 1977. See also *Le monde*, May 29, 1977; *Jeune Afrique*, June 10, 1977, pp. 20–21; *Afrique-Asie*, July 25, 1977, pp. 25–30.

296. For a description of UNITA insurgency and strategy by a black American journalist who traveled for seven months in UNITA territory and attended a (March 1977) UNITA congress near Huambo, see Leon Dash, *Washington Post*, Aug. 7–13, 1977. See also reportage by R. Bruce McColm and David Smith, *Christian Science Monitor*, Dec. 21, 1976; a critical assessment of UNITA "banditry" as seen from Bié (Silva Porto) by Basil Davidson, "Bandits and Invaders," *West Africa*, July 25, 1977, pp. 1518–1521; and interview with Jorge Sangumba, *Volksrant*, July 7, 1977.

297. In May 1977, Agostinho Neto suggested that the Gulf Oil Corpora-

tion might be citing alleged threats by impotent Cabindan separatists as means of extracting better advantage from contract negotiations then underway. *Afrique-Asie*, May 3, 1977, p. 25. FLEC was still plagued by exile divisions, one wing led by Francisco Lubota, another by Henrique Tiago Nzita and a third group Mouvement de Libération de Cabinda [MOLICA]) by Jean da Costa. *Diário de Notícias,* Apr. 15, 1976; June 21, 1977.

NAME INDEX

Abrigada, Samuel Francisco da Costa, 188, 256, 391n31, 419n388, 428n43
Acone, Antonio, 101
Adjali, Abdelamid, 356n93
Adoula, Cyrille, 36, 39, 42, 66–68, 70, 73–74, 77–80, 105, 107, 121, 123, 129, 132–133, 145, 147, 303, 351n213, 368n106
Afonso, David, 69
Afonso, Victor, 380n251
Ahmed, Kaid. *See* Slimane, Commander
Akpan, Kwando, 239, 400n124, 425n465
Alberto, Angelino, 85, 89, 144–145, 245, 347nn147, 151, 366n82, 428n33, 433n119
Alexandre, António, 87–88
Almeida, Déolinda Rodrigues de, 88, 198, 334n206, 338n257, 401n135
Almeida, Luis de (also d'Almeida), 93, 382n285, 385nn314, 317, 388n10
Almeida, Vasco Vieira de, 256
Alves, Lopes, 254
Alves, Nito, 259–261, 272, 279, 281, 432n98, 442n246, 445n295
Amachree, Godfrey, 128
Amaro, António, 373n156
Amin, Idi, 221, 262, 430n65, 438n179
Anderson, George, 79, 234, 237–238, 361n6
Andrade, Aristides, 322n16
Andrade, Joaquim Pinto de, 249–251, 279, 430nn 71, 72
Andrade, Mário de, 10–18 *passim*, 25, 28, 56–66 *passim*, 71, 86, 94–96, 122, 169, 204, 248, 322n16, 323n31, 324n37, 328n99, 329nn109, 124, 130, 330n132, 335n211, 339n13, 341nn43, 44, 345n113, 349nn178, 188, 350n205, 382n277, 430n69
"Angola Livre." *See* Muti, Manuel
Aniceto, Afonso, 378n232
António, Alexandre, 373n156
António, José, 419n386

Araujo, Gomes de, 178
Arguelles, Raul Diaz, 443n257
Arriaga, Kaúlza de, 426n12
Artho, Walter, 101–102, 148–149, 370n121, 371n127
Azevedo, Luis de, Jr., 157, 170, 251, 345n117, 357n99, 375n187, 382n285, 383n303, 384nn308, 314, 407n221, 413n318, 431n84

Ball, George W., 127–128, 360n146
Balombo, Mendonça Fuato, 372n142
Bamba, Emmanuel, 331n160
Baptista, Inacio, 407n227
Barata, Temudo, 254
Barnett, Don, 238–239
Barros, Francisco, 402n143, 407n221
Bartolomeu, Vidal, 373n156
Bastos, Augusto Tadeu Pereira, 363n25
Batista, João, 43–44, 333n188
Baya, Miguel, 382n285
Becu, Omer, 105
Bedi, Mme. Monteiro, 419n391
Ben Bella, Ahmed, 17, 62–65, 71–72, 76, 79, 93, 141–142, 160, 339n13, 345n108
Bender, Gerald J., 263, 436n151
Benedito, João Gonçalves, 151, 198, 211, 404n169
Bennett, William T., 234
Bento, Francisco Manuel, 148, 369n116, 375nn195, 196
Bergerol, Jane, 258
Bing, Paul, 368n101
Biyoudi, Jean, 124
Blake, Eugene C., 420n414
Boavida, Américo ("Ngola Kimbanda"), 198, 200, 402n141
Boavida, Diógenes, 256, 272, 434n123
Boboliko, André, 331n160
Bocheley-Davidson, Egide, 369n111
Bolwele, Joáo, 427n32, 428n34
Bomboko, Ferraz (Bombo), 44–45, 211, 333n191, 386n332

447

Nkrumah, Kwame, 17, 72–73, 125,
    137–140, 364n39, 365n43
Nlamvu, Thomas, 369n116
Nolo, Daniel, 89
N'Simba, Alphonse Morin (also Nsimba),
    330n146, 370n123, 374n177
N'Simba, Garcia de Costa, 372n142
Nsumbu, Martin, 373n156
Nsungu, Emmanuel, 369n116
Nteka, Samuel, 391n24
Ntemo, Sébastien Lubaki, 189, 391n24,
    407n227
Nujoma, Sam, 74
Nyani, Marcelino, 378n224, 380n251
Nyerere, Julius, 139–140, 164, 177, 209,
    227–228, 249–250, 265, 379n240,
    395n74, 437n160, 439n204
Nzinga, Mbande "Queen Jinga," 48, 197
Nzita, Henriques Tiago, 124, 205, 253,
    261, 358nn127, 131, 371n135,
    406n200, 433n106, 446n297

Obiang, Adolfo, 343n85
Obote, Milton, 72
Oliveira, António de Aranjo, 247
Oliveira, Manuel Resende de, 256

Pacheco, Manuel, 368n101
Paganini, 202, 405n181
Palme, Olaf, 232
Panda, Antoine, 366n78
Paulo, Amadeu João, 176
Paulo, João (MDIA), 427n32, 428n34
Pedro, Alexandre Magno. See Magno
Pélissier, René, 332n175
Pembele, Ferdinand, 88
Pemo, Alexandre, 330n148, 352n25,
    369n116
Pena, Charles Sumba, 438n176
Pereira, Almeida João, 176, 387n347
Pereira, Jacob, 378n232
Peterson, José Manuel, 35, 36, 43,
    68–69, 106, 108–109, 151, 156, 164,
    186, 371n127, 390n6
Pierre, Henrique, 368nn98, 103
Pinheiro, Patricia McGowan, 350n210
Pinock, Eduardo, 19, 42, 52, 68,
    332n179, 372n146, 392n32
Pinock, Johnny Eduardo. See Edouard,
    Johnny
Pintado, V. Xavier, 22
Pinto, Sebastião Ramos, 374n181
Pinto-Bull, Benjamin, 223
Plummer, Simon Scott, 408n235,
    413n302

Porter, Adrian, 67
Puna, Miguel N'Zau, 194, 398nn99, 100,
    445n284
Putuilu, José Milton, 88, 366n73

Qaddafi, Muammar el, 246
Quadros, Jânio, 24

Rana, Pedro, 352n27, 393n49, 394n54
Rangel, Francisco, 386n332
Raoul, Alfred, 208, 254, 406n196
Rio, Manuel, 226
Roberto, Holden, 9 et passim
    anticommunist, 17, 237, 240, 276,
        324n41, 434n126
    leadership, 15–18, 32–37, 68, 99, 101–
        103, 113, 116–120, 134–140, 146–154,
        167, 172, 183, 185–191, 197–198, 227–
        228, 246, 261, 274, 276–277, 305–306,
        324n40, 325n50, 331n167, 337n248,
        370n121, 397n93, 407n223, 416n225,
        444n272
Rocha, Carlos [Dilolwa], 252, 272,
    386n332, 432n96
Rodrigues, Déolinda. See Almeida,
    Déolinda Rodrigues de
"Rommel," 269
Roosevelt, Franklin D., 293
Roquete, 202
Rusk, Dean, 126, 345n114

Sahnoun, Mohamed, 187
St. Jorre, John de, 212, 365n41
Salazar, António, 1, 5, 12, 13, 20, 23,
    53–54, 58, 79, 124–128, 144, 147,
    179–180, 197, 234, 237, 283, 298, 300,
    323n27, 336n236, 359n142, 369n108
Salva, Garcia Samson, 419n391
Samuimbila. See Chingunji, David
Sandele, Sabino, 433n120
Sangumba, Jorge Isaac, 163, 194, 196,
    225, 233, 247, 398n100, 103,
    399nn105, 110, 401n127, 415n343,
    429n59, 438n184
Sanjilu, Moses, 353n47
Sanjovo, Reuben, 380n251
Santos, André dos, 374n177
Santos, Domingos dos, 373n156
Santos, Eduardo dos, 63, 65, 76, 173,
    382n285, 385n318, 402n141, 430n69
Santos, Henrique de Carvalho
    [Onambwe], 432n98
Santos, Marcelino dos, 74, 229
Santos, Tomaz dos, 348n157
Santos e Castro, Gilberto, 261, 427n25

SUBJECT INDEX